MW00636363

REVOLUTIONARY POLITICS
&
LOCKE'S *TWO TREATISES OF GOVERNMENT*

Revolutionary Politics & Locke's *Two Treatises of Government*

RICHARD
ASHCRAFT

Princeton University Press • Princeton, New Jersey

Published by Princeton University Press, 41 William Street,
Princeton, New Jersey 08540
In the United Kingdom: Princeton University Press,
Guildford, Surrey

Library of Congress Cataloging in Publication Data will
be found on the last printed page of this book

ISBN 0-691-07703-7 (cloth) 02248-8 (pbk)

This book has been composed in Linotron Aldus

Clothbound editions of Princeton University Press books
are printed on acid-free paper, and binding materials
are chosen for strength and durability. Paperbacks, although
satisfactory for personal collections, are not usually
suitable for library rebinding

Printed in the United States of America by Princeton
University Press, Princeton, New Jersey

For David

CONTENTS

PREFACE

IN writing this book, I have sought to realize three interrelated objectives. First, I want to establish the basis, both in terms of the author's intentions and in relation to an intellectual and political context, for an interpretation of John Locke's political thought that gives primary importance to the radical political meaning of his ideas. I have placed Locke within a world of political and religious dissidents in Restoration England and have asked, What kinds of social conventions of meaning did the inhabitants of this world draw upon in order to make sense out of their own actions and the place of those actions within the social life of seventeenth-century England? And how does our understanding of that world, as seen from the perspective of these dissidents, contribute to our appreciation of the meaning of the arguments and problems that constitute the core of Locke's political thought?

My second aim has been to provide a case study of a political movement—its organization, ideology, social composition, its internal debate over tactics to be employed, and so forth. It happens that this movement arose in late-seventeenth-century England, but in terms of a sociological analysis of certain kinds of organizational problems faced by a political movement, its historical location does not obviate the ability of such a study to contribute something toward our understanding of political movements, viewed as sociological phenomena. Although the religious and political dissidents who are the focus of this aspect of my study were merely a vocal minority in their society, they were an organized minority. Through their organization, these radical critics were able to put pressure on the government. This pressure manifested itself in diverse ways. It might assume the form of an ideological critique through the writings—sermons, tracts, newspapers—they produced, or it could be expressed through petitions, demonstrations, electoral campaigns, and ultimately, through a reliance upon armed resistance. Of course, these various manifestations of political pressure met with varying degrees of success, viewed in terms of the realization of the political aims of the radicals. Successful revolutions have never lacked for interpreters of their meaning among later generations of historians, but failed attempts at political revolution are the tide pools of historical investigation. Yet, for that very reason, they may be worth our attention, or at least, so I have assumed in attempting to carry out the second objective of this book.

Before indicating my third purpose in writing this book, something more needs to be said concerning the ways in which the first two aims are interrelated, for I have not supposed them as distinctly separable as this analytical and rather schematic rendering of my objectives has made them appear to be. I said above that I placed Locke in the context of a radical political movement, but the fact is that he placed himself within that movement. To establish Locke as a participant in the political movement of the 1670s and 1680s may be a fact of some biographical importance with respect to the historical John Locke, but that is not the point of my undertaking, although naturally it is an evidential foundation for the argument I do want to make. What is essential is that the meaning of the act of theorizing about politics as a form of communication between the theorist and his prospective audience presupposes some understanding of what the theorist believes he is doing through undertaking such an action, and also of what others—both those who are presumptively members of the theorist's intended audience and those who are not—believe is significant with respect to that action.

I have elaborated upon my reasons for adopting this approach to political theory in the Introduction. What I have to say about this point here can perhaps best be phrased in negative terminology, as a preliminary warning to the reader of this book of what he or she ought not to expect in terms of my intentions in writing it. That is, I have not attempted to write a new intellectual or political biography of John Locke, however valuable such an endeavor might be from the standpoint of historical scholarship. As I happen to believe that such a work is very much needed, I can certainly appreciate the temptation others might feel to view this study within a biographical framework. That, however, is not the perspective I have adopted. In order to understand the relationship of Locke's ideas to those of other participants in the radical political movement, it is important in reconstructing the intellectual and political context of that movement not to sever the connection between Locke's ideas and the historical individual Locke, simply in the interest of providing the larger picture. In other words, the biographical dimensions of the argument are necessary elements of a theory of meaning and interpretation in which authorial intentions are accorded a significant role. Moreover, the meaning one assigns to those intentions and the ideas to be interpreted depends, in part, upon the kinds of specific actions executed by the historical subject: Locke. Locke's participation in a radical political movement gives an existential dimensionality to the meaning of his political thought that cannot be grasped in any way other than on the basis of biographical evidence.

From the other side, my effort to provide an account of a particular political movement, though obviously dependent upon a familiarity with the historical characteristics of Restoration England, is not meant to serve as a new history of that period. Indeed, I am very much aware of the inappropriateness of viewing this study, even in the narrowest sense, as a political history of England from 1670 to 1690. But since I have not attempted to write such a work, I hope the reader will not object if I demur at the outset from accepting such an attribution with respect to this book. What I have tried to do is to gain some appreciation of how the political life of late seventeenth-century England was perceived from one specific perspective; that is, from the standpoint of the political and religious dissidents who comprised the radical political movement of the 1680s. Quite obviously, there were and are other viewpoints in terms of which the political events of this period might be interpreted, not to mention the so-called objective and omniscient approach frequently employed by historians through the form of a chronological narrative. Though I, too, have proceeded more or less chronologically in my discussion of the radical movement, beginning in 1670 and ending with the Glorious Revolution, I have concentrated my attention upon the organizational dimensions of this political movement. As might be expected, one encounters peaks and valleys in attempting to describe the organization of a movement, and this sometimes translates into a more cursory treatment of a particular historical moment when, in terms of either their writings or their political actions, the radicals were relatively ineffective from the organizational standpoint. It also means that I have felt free to neglect (relatively speaking) a consideration of those political events which, from another perspective, might be assumed to have great historical significance but which, for one reason or another, were far less important to the radicals themselves. Naturally, this last statement has to be tempered with a certain amount of common sense, since, as I argue in the Introduction, there are sometimes good reasons for the interpreter to focus upon particular historical factors that lie outside of or are inadequately accounted for in terms of the phenomenological consciousness of the historical actors themselves—in this case, the participants in the radical political movement.

What I have attempted, therefore, is a marriage of Locke's ideas with the actions and objectives of a political movement in which Locke was a participant and for which his ideas served as an articulate expression of the meaning of those actions and goals. This merger of intentional objectives presents certain problems with respect to the style of presentation of the argument I wish to make, in that one chapter may be focused almost entirely upon Locke, while another chapter may be devoted to a discussion of the political movement, in which Locke makes an appearance perhaps only fleetingly. Moreover, some chapters may concentrate on reconstructing the ideological dimensions of the political conflict, while others detail the specific actions taken by members of the political movement. I can see no means by which this shifting of levels of the argument, or the bracketing of one part of it while another part of it is being discussed, can be avoided, and I must plead for a certain amount of patience on the part of the reader in his or her confrontation with the technical realization of the intellectual goals I have described above.

My third objective in this study is to provide an argument by exemplar of how political theory ought to be studied and interpreted. Apart from a few remarks in the Introduction, there is no general discussion of methodology or of various conceptions of political theory in the pages that follow. Yet, I dare to hope that this work is an illustrative contribution to a longstanding debate concerning the methodology appropriate to the social sciences, and to the interpretation of the meaning of social action. For many years, I have felt dissatisfied with the artificial compartmentalization that characterizes the study of politics. Texts in political theory are assigned to the province of philosophical analysis or the use of literary techniques; historical information relating to traditions of thought or of political organization to the historian; sociological data that provide the larger framework for politics to the political sociologist; and actual policy decisions made by political actors to the political scientist. I do not find the reasons for this compartmentalization intellectually convincing, and in that sense, this work is, in its entirety, an argument against such methodological divisions and disciplinary boundaries.

My own presuppositions about political theory, along with a few methodological assumptions I have employed in this study, are discussed in the Introduction, which also enumerates a few of the problems that are specific to a consideration of the political life of Restoration England or of the political ideas of Locke. The Introduction is meant to serve as a practical reference for the reader as to the guidelines according to which I have navigated my way through the material presented in succeeding chapters.

However, as there is no concluding summary of the substantive arguments advanced in this book, perhaps it will be useful to offer a very brief sketch here of what is contained in those chapters. Chapter 1 identifies a few fundamental problems rooted in the political life of Restoration England that supplied the focuses for political discussion in the 1670s and 1680s. The second chapter outlines the intellectual dimensions of a particular controversy generated by a concerted and sweeping attack upon religious Dissenters launched by the Anglican church, with some assistance provided by the state. Although this political debate involved contributions from some very important figures in the intellectual life of

Restoration England—including John Owen, Richard Baxter, and Andrew Marvell—it has never been examined, nor has its significance been recognized. I argue that because of the nature and scope of the controversy sparked by Samuel Parker's *Discourse of Ecclesiastical Polity*, which lasted for virtually the whole decade of the 1670s, the Dissenters were forced in their replies to produce, in effect, a defense of every aspect of the intellectual framework that supplied the meaning for religious dissent in seventeenth-century England. Chapter 2 thus tries to establish the basic parameters of the political consciousness of the leading critics of Church and State in the 1670s. It is within this broad framework, I argue, that the radical political theory of the 1680s developed.

Chapter 3 provides an account of Locke's intellectual and political development during the first two decades of the Restoration. Both aspects of that development are traceable to one overriding political problem: the toleration of religious dissent, and the attitudes and ideas that supported one's practical response to that issue. As Locke changed his position on the question of toleration, I argue, he moved from a rather perfunctory intellectual acceptance of the established boundaries of Restoration political life toward a standpoint with which the critics of those institutions were identified. Locke's association with the first Earl of Shaftesbury placed him, politically speaking, within the orbit of political and religious dissent. During the 1670s, Locke began to explore the intellectual dimensions of a defense of toleration; that is, one that could draw upon epistemological, moral, religious, economic, and political arguments. This undertaking, I suggest, owes much not only to Locke's political activities on behalf of Shaftesbury, but also to the stimulation provided by the Parker controversy. It is no mere coincidence, I maintain, that the discussions that launched the *Essay Concerning Human Understanding* occurred during the height of the debate generated by Parker's *Discourse of Ecclesiastical Polity*, or that most of the central themes of that controversy found their way into Locke's work.

Chapter 4 describes the socioeconomic status of the constituency that formed the heart of the radical political movement in the 1680s. Particular emphasis is placed upon the rather surprisingly widespread practice of voting on the part of members of the class of artisans, tradesmen, laborers, and even those on public relief during the three elections held between 1679 and 1681. The evidence relating to this subject, I argue, necessitates, on the one hand, some reassessment of the meaning that the political ideas of the Levellers could have had for their contemporaries, and on the other, a greater appreciation of the extent to which these ideas and the meaning attached to them survived the demise of the Leveller movement and were carried forward as a subterranean element of Restoration political life. On the first point, I side with a number of Professor Macpherson's recent critics in maintaining, against his reading of the Putney debates, that the Levellers were advocates of manhood suffrage, and that, based on the data alluded to above, they were much further removed from being the kind of wild-eyed or naive radicals than they have sometimes been made out to be by later historians. I also contend, against the grain of some recent scholarship, that the style of argument, terminology, and basic presuppositions of the Levellers' political theory made a distinctive and lasting impression upon the political consciousness of individuals living in seventeenth-century England, and that it ought not to be viewed as having dissipated into some amorphous, widely accepted, or easily tolerated appeal to a natural rights/natural law theory during the 1680s and 1690s. Indeed, as I show in later chapters, when this language reappeared in the political writings of the radicals during those decades, contemporaries showed no hesitancy in linking it with the Levellers, and with the socioeconomic constituency with which such political ideas had been associated in the Leveller movement.

Chapters 5 and 6 provide a detailed exploration of the ideological debate that developed during the exclusion crisis (1679–1681), and of the relationship between that debate and the arguments contained in Locke's *Two Treatises of Government.* Chapter 5 considers the interconnections among various types of arguments and evidence deployed on behalf of the Whig political position in the course of this political conflict. Chapter 6 focuses upon the appeal of particular arguments advanced in exclusion tracts to specific socioeconomic groups in the context of the electoral campaign waged by the Whigs. A considerable portion of this chapter is devoted to an interpretation of the chapter on property in the *Second Treatise,* seen from the vantage point of the kinds of political objectives that guided the Whig political movement in 1680–1681. Much has been written about Locke's theory of property, but in my view, the extent to which it incorporates a radical political viewpoint has not been adequately appreciated.

Chapter 7 discusses the theoretical and practical aspects of a reliance upon armed resistance against the government, since, following the dissolution of the Oxford Parliament in 1681, the radical Whigs under Shaftesbury's leadership began to give serious consideration to this issue. Chapter 8 identifies the individuals, including Locke, who were prepared to translate the ideas of resistance into action. I demonstrate the links that existed among the language used by the radicals, their political theory justifying armed resistance, and the means by which both these aspects of their ideology were instrumentally employed to create a revolutionary political organization.

Chapter 9 attempts, on the one hand, to provide an account of the radicals in exile in Holland, where most of them (including Locke) fled following the discovery in 1683 of their plans for an insurrection, and on the other, to supply evidence supporting the allegation of Locke's participation in the planning of and financial contribution to Monmouth's Rebellion in 1685. Except for one article published many years ago, and a very recent work on the rebels who fought with Monmouth, scholars have paid little attention to the political activities of these radical exiles. This is all the more surprising, given the fact that six years of Locke's life were spent living in exile in Holland as a member of this radical community. Based upon the evidence supplied by manuscripts in the British Library, I have tried to reconstruct, though very sketchily, the activities, organization, ideas, and social relationships of the members of this community, and to situate Locke in that political context.

Following the defeat of Monmouth, it could be argued that the truly radical character of the political movement organized by Shaftesbury in the 1680s came to an end. Yet, resistance to popery and the Stuart tyranny did not end with the defeat of Monmouth and the ascension of James II to the throne. Chapter 10 discusses the problems and internal divisions created among the radical exiles in Holland by both these events, and especially by James' policy of toleration extended to the Dissenters through his suspension of the penal laws directed against them. This chapter provides an interpretation of Locke's *Letter Concerning Toleration* in the context of the international controversy on that subject generated by James II's political policies, and as with the earlier treatment of Locke's theory of property, I show what meaning his arguments in this work had for those who retained the radical political commitments that were forged during the political struggles led by Shaftesbury.

Chapter 11 offers an assessment of the role played by the radicals in the planning, execution, and defense of the Glorious Revolution. Contrary to the assertion of a number of scholars, I show that there was a distinctively radical perspective from which that event was viewed, as expressed in a comparatively small though not insignificant number of political works published between 1688 and 1690. Locke's *Two Treatises of Government* was one of these works, and this chapter presents a reading of the *Second Treatise* in relation to the arguments being advanced by the radicals in this period. I offer some detailed evidence in the form of responses by critics of the radical political position to support the recent findings by other scholars that Locke's work was not welcomed as an ideological defense of the Glorious Revolution by those Whig and Tory magnates who managed that affair. This chapter brings to a close the discussion of Locke's intentional activity of thinking through and writing down the political theory expressed in the *Two Treatises of Government*, but the Postscript takes up the specific question of what Locke's purposes were in publishing that work. Curiously, this question has never really been seriously considered, but as I try to show, there was a particular political meaning associated with this action, in the context of an ideological critique mounted by the radicals on the left of the course taken by the Glorious Revolution following the establishment of William and Mary on the throne.

Notwithstanding the length of this journey, some individuals have urged that I pursue the story further. Even if reasons of space did not argue against such an undertaking, I must decline the suggestion simply in terms of the objectives I have attached to this study. I set out to show the connection between Locke's political ideas and a particular political movement, and in my opinion, that political movement came to an end with the Glorious Revolution. Naturally, I do not mean to suggest that religious or political dissidents suddenly disappeared from the scene, as Mark Goldie, in a very fine article, has shown that they did not. Nevertheless, within a year or two of the Glorious Revolution, the overwhelming majority of radicals who had been associated with Locke and Shaftesbury were dead, had turned Jacobite, or had accepted positions within the government with which they generally identified themselves. Other radicals, of course, would arise to fight other battles, drawing upon their predecessors' language and arguments, including those contained in the *Two Treatises*, but that is another, and a different, story.

It might also be reasonably argued that Locke's political radicalism came to an end with the publication of the *Two Treatises*, and that, for the remaining fourteen years of his life, he lived within the confines of the political orthodoxies of established Whiggism. In my view, this is a subject worth further exploration, and I do not believe that the existing biographical information on Locke is adequate to support the kind of detailed and contextual response that this question deserves. Still, that is a matter for Locke's biographers to consider, and, for reasons I have already given, that is not a pathway I have chosen to follow in this work insofar as it diverges from an understanding of the conditions under which the arguments and political theory of the *Two Treatises of Government* were produced.

Finally, in anticipation of the objection that might be raised against my usage throughout this study of the term *radical* to characterize Locke and the participants in the political movement, I recognize, as I think my critics will concede, that there is no simple or easy solution to the methodological problems inherent in the decision to employ or not to employ such an ideologically laden term. One could, of course, formulate some ideal type of a radical, drawn either from the interpreter's own conception of what radicalism means or from some consensually accepted historical usage of the term, as applied, for example, to the English Civil War radicals. From either standpoint, the individuals discussed in this book might be adjudged not to be radicals, or at least, not true radicals. I am frankly not persuaded of the helpfulness of such a position in gaining insight into the historically rooted meaning of the activities of those who constituted the political movement of the 1680s, and I have, therefore, adopted a more historicist approach to the subject, by allowing the political actions taken by and against these individuals to provide the basic meaning for my usage of *radical*; that is, as a description of their location at the far left end of the political spectrum as it existed during the period of their activities. The dimensions of radicalism do not lie wholly on the plane of ideas, and, insofar as the mobilization of individuals to engage in revolutionary action constitutes an important part of any definition of political radicalism, I believe that label can appropriately be applied to the subjects of this study.

I have received much help and encouragement in this undertaking, for which I am extremely grateful. I am most fortunate in having had the advice of three of the most knowledgeable and perceptive readers imaginable, and I have benefited greatly from their comments on the manuscript. Even if he had not been one of those readers, Professor K. H. D. Haley would deserve an acknowledgment for the debt that I, and others, owe to him for his biography of the first Earl of Shaftesbury. It stands head and shoulders above any other biography of a Restoration figure, and my reliance upon this scholarly work is obvious. James Tully's detailed notations on my manuscript were, almost without exception, incorporated into the final version of this book. To the third reader, J. G. A. Pocock, however, I owe the greatest debt. He kindly sent me a lengthy set of comments and notations on the manuscript, in addition to those contained in his reader's report. I have not always agreed with his remarks, but I have invariably found them stimulating, and I am deeply appreciative of his generosity in the effort he contributed to making this a better work. I am also indebted to my friend and colleague, E. Victor Wolfenstein, not only for the suggestions he offered on this manuscript, but also for our many years of conversations about political theory. Though he was not a reader of this manuscript, I should like to acknowledge the influence the scholarly work of Quentin Skinner has had upon my thinking about political theory, an influence strengthened through the correspondence I have had with him over the years.

I want to express my thanks to the following libraries and institutions for granting me access to the manuscripts and other materials in their custody: the Keeper of Manuscripts at the Inner Temple; the Public Record Office; All Souls College, Oxford; the Henry E. Huntington Library in San Marino; the Nottingham University Library; the Bodleian Library, Oxford; Dr. William's Library, London; and the British Library, especially the staff of the Manuscript Room. To the staff of the William Andrews Clark Library (UCLA), I owe a special thanks for their always helpful and friendly assistance over many years.

I want to thank Sage Publications for granting me permission to reprint material from my article, "Revolutionary Politics and Locke's *Two Treatises of Government*," *Political Theory* 8, no. 4 (November 1980): 429–486. I also want to thank the William Andrews Clark Library for allowing me to use material that originally appeared in my seminar paper, "Locke's *Two Treatises of Government* and the Exclusion Crisis: The Problem of Lockean Political Theory as Bourgeois Ideology," which was published as part of a monograph, *John Locke*, by the Library. I have rewritten and incorporated material from these two articles into several chapters, especially chapters 5–7.

I am grateful to the American Council of Learned Societies for granting me a fellowship that allowed me to write the first draft of this work. I also want to thank the chairman of my Department, Professor Richard Sisson, for his encouragement and assistance in the completion of this project. My research assistants, Cindy Lumpkin and Sandi Goldstein, were tireless in their efforts to locate the materials I needed, and were superbly successful in finding answers to the questions I put to them. The political theory students at UCLA, graduate and undergraduate, have been a constant source of stimulation in my effort to think through the problems discussed in this book, and I owe them a great deal. A special acknowledgment of thanks must go to my friend, Jack Miles, for the time and interest he devoted to this work. Working with Sandy Thatcher of the Princeton University Press has been a true pleasure, and I very much appreciate his support and help in getting this project into print.

NOTE ON THE TEXT

In general, I have modernized the highly erratic spelling and punctuation found in seventeenth-century documents. I have begun the new year on January 1, but I have tried to preserve the local (English or Continental) date in any narrative of events.

A full reference is provided the first time a work is cited in each chapter, and a shortened reference is given thereafter. Only twentieth-century publishers are given in the references.

Much of the evidential support for my argument must necessarily be assigned to the footnotes, and both the need to supply the historical information pertaining to the subjects of this study and the controversial character of the general argument of the book have contributed to their size and number.

ABBREVIATIONS

Works by Locke

Correspondence	*The Correspondence of John Locke*, ed. E. S. De Beer, 8 vols., Oxford: Clarendon Press, 1976
Early Draft	*An Early Draft of Locke's Essay*, ed. R. I. Aaron and Jocelyn Gibb, Oxford: Clarendon Press, 1936
ECHU	*An Essay Concerning Human Understanding*, ed. Peter H. Nidditch, Oxford: Clarendon Press, 1975
ELN	*Essays on the Law of Nature*, ed. W. von Leyden, Oxford: Clarendon Press, 1954
FTG, STG	*Two Tracts on Government*, ed. Philip Abrams, Cambridge: Cambridge University Press, 1967 (*First* or *Second Tract on Government*)
Laslett	Introduction or notes to *Two Treatises*
LL #	*The Library of John Locke*, ed. John Harrison and Peter Laslett, Oxford: Oxford University Press, 1965 (# of entry)
MS	Locke MS, Bodleian Library, Oxford University
STCE	*Some Thoughts Concerning Education*, in *The Educational Writings of John Locke*, ed. James L. Axtell, Cambridge: Cambridge University Press, 1968
Toleration	*A Letter on Toleration*, ed. Raymond Klibansky and J. W. Gough, Oxford: Clarendon Press, 1968
TT; FT; ST	*Two Treatises of Government*, 2d ed., ed. Peter Laslett, Cambridge: Cambridge University Press, 1967 (*First* or *Second Treatise*)
Works	*The Works of John Locke*, 12th ed., 9 vols., 1824

Works by Others

Add. MS	Additional Manuscripts, British Library, London
Burnet	Gilbert Burnet, *History of My Own Time*, ed. Osmund Airy, 2 vols., Oxford, 1897
Cobbett	William Cobbett, ed., *The Parliamentary History of England*, 36 vols., 1806–1820
Cranston	Maurice Cranston, *John Locke*, London: Longmans, Green, 1957
CSPD	*Calendar of State Papers, Domestic*
Dalrymple	John Dalrymple, *Memoirs of Great Britain and Ireland*, 3 vols., 1790
Ferguson	James Ferguson, *Robert Ferguson the Plotter*, Edinburgh, 1887

Filmer	Robert Filmer, *Patriarcha and Other Political Works*, ed. Peter Laslett, Oxford: Basil Blackwell, 1949
Fox-Bourne,	H. R. Fox-Bourne, *The Life of John Locke*, 2 vols., 1876
Grey	Anchitell Grey, *Debates of the House of Commons*, 10 vols., 1763
Haley	K. H. D. Haley, *The First Earl of Shaftesbury*, Oxford: Clarendon Press, 1968
HMC	Reports of the Historical Manuscripts Commission
Jones	J. R. Jones, *The First Whigs: The Politics of the Exclusion Crisis, 1678–1683*, London: Oxford University Press, 1961
King	Peter King, *The Life of John Locke*, 2 vols., 1830
Lacey	Douglas R. Lacey, *Dissent and Parliamentary Politics in England, 1661–1689*, New Brunswick, N.J.: Rutgers University Press, 1969
Macaulay	Thomas Babington Macaulay, *The History of England from the Accession of James II*, 5 vols., New York: Thomas Nelson and Sons, n.d.
Morrice	Roger Morrice MSS, "The Entering Book, Being an Historical Register of Occurrences from April 1677 to April 1691," 2 vols., Dr. Williams's Library, London
MS PWV or PWA	Portland Manuscripts, University of Nottingham Library
Ogg	David Ogg, *England in the Reign of Charles II*, 2d ed., 2 vols., Oxford: Clarendon Press, 1956
PRO 30/24/	Papers of the Earl of Shaftesbury, Public Records Office, London
Secret History	Ford, Lord Grey, *The Secret History of the Rye House Plot*, 2d ed., 1754
Sprat	Thomas Sprat, *A True Account and Declaration of the Horrid Conspiracy against the Late King*, 1685

REVOLUTIONARY POLITICS
&
LOCKE'S *TWO TREATISES OF GOVERNMENT*

INTRODUCTION

The Secretary of State listened with intense interest as the man across from him confessed his involvement in a plot to assassinate the king and spoke of the activities of many others who planned to raise a general insurrection in England. Within hours of this confession, John Locke hastily departed from London, taking with him the unfinished manuscript of the *Two Treatises of Government*. Ahead lay six years of hiding and life as a political exile in Holland for the author of one of the classic works of Western political literature. In this book, I propose to say something about how these events are interrelated and what significance that relationship has for our understanding of Locke's political theory, and of the *Two Treatises of Government*, in particular.

The reader will decide whether this endeavor is successfully carried out in the succeeding pages, but it may be wondered why the connection of the *Two Treatises* with the revolutionary activities of a comparatively small number of individuals in the 1680s should be made. And even assuming such a connection can be made, aside from imparting such information as might satisfy one's historical curiosity, what could possibly be learned about Locke's political theory from the historical uncovering of its genesis? Based upon the education and training I received in political theory, and my subsequent reading of the secondary literature in the field, these questions are likely to be asked, and it is to these interrogatories that this Introduction is addressed.

For many years, political theory has been conceived as a subcategory of philosophy. And as a subsidiary, it has been subject to the governing rules of its parent discipline. As a consequence, the epistemological and methodological practices of philosophy have assumed a dominant importance in the interpretive literature on political theory. Hence, interpreters are inclined to search for systematic logical relationships among the concepts contained in a work of political theory, or to extract from the latter universally valid or timeless principles, analogous to the axioms of geometry or the laws of physics, or to employ certain propositions advanced by the theorist as empirically verifiable or falsifiable hypotheses, or to take the text as a kind of private language, whose meaning is revealed by unraveling the internal connections between certain statements by the author. In other words, a particular work of political theory is assumed to make sense insofar as it can be explained or reconstructed using one or more of these philosophical approaches, although interpreters differ among themselves as to which approach best describes the enterprise of philosophy itself.[1]

Whatever the specific philosophical premise adopted by the interpreter, hundreds of monographs, articles, and textbooks on political theory have been written within the parameters of a general framework that allows the author to "assume that political theory is a body of philosophical and scientific knowledge . . . regardless of when and where it was originally written . . . On this assumption, a whole range of writers from Plato to Mill will be studied without attention to the particular conditions which surrounded them at the time they wrote."[2] Even when this operative assumption is not so starkly stated, the fact is that the practice of political theory, including the way in which courses on political theory are taught within universities, embodies and reinforces this conception of what political theory is and how it is to be understood. It is true, the merits of possessing a knowledge of the social and political conditions under which political theories were formulated are sometimes admitted, for example by John Plamenatz in his major study of political theory, although it is not the axis from which he approaches the subject.[3] In other words, the

[1] Political theorists should be "guided by the modern trend of general philosophical work, which is to give attention to meanings and careful definition of terms" (J. Roland Pennock, "Political Science and Political Philosophy," *American Political Science Review* 45 [December 1951]:1082). See also, George Sabine, "What Is a Political Theory?" *Journal of Politics* 1 (February 1939):1-16; Anthony Quinton, ed., *Political Philosophy*, Oxford: Oxford University Press, 1967, pp. 1–3; Leo Strauss, *What Is Political Philosophy?* Glencoe, Ill.: Free Press, 1959; H. J. McCloskey, "The Nature of Political Philosophy," *Ratio* 6 (June 1964):50–62; John Plamenatz, *Man and Society*, 2 vols., New York: McGraw-Hill, 1963; Dante Germino, *Modern Western Political Thought*, Chicago: Rand McNally, 1972; James A. Gould and Vincent V. Thursby, eds., *Contemporary Political Thought*, New York: Holt, Rinehart and Winston, 1969, pp. 2–3; D. D. Raphael, *Problems of Political Philosophy*, New York: Praeger, 1970. We read political theory for the "universal ideas contained in the classic theories" (William T. Bluhm, *Theories of the Political System*, Englewood Cliffs, N.J.: Prentice-Hall, 1965, p. 13). Dante Germino, "The Revival of Political Theory," *Journal of Politics* 25 (August 1963):441–444; David Thomson, ed., *Political Ideas*, New York: Basic Books, 1966, pp. 9ff.; Leo Strauss and Joseph Cropsey, eds., *History of Political Philosophy*, Chicago: Rand McNally, 1963, preface; Dante Germino, *Beyond Ideology: The Revival of Political Theory*, New York: Harper and Row, 1967, p. 9.

[2] Andrew Hacker, *Political Theory: Philosophy, Ideology, Science*, New York: Macmillan, 1961, p. 12; Plamenatz, *Man and Society*, vol. 1, introduction; Germino, *Western Political Thought*, p. viii.

[3] Thus, while a knowledge of the circumstances under which a political theory was written "may contribute" something to our understanding of that political theory, "we can learn more about [political theorists'] arguments by weighing them over and over again than by extending our knowledge of the circumstances in which they wrote" (Plamenatz, *Man and Society*, 1:ix–x).

point about the practice of political theory is important because, while certain intellectual concessions are made to a historically grounded approach to political theory by most contemporary political theorists, these concessions do not reflect the dominant beliefs or practices of those theorists. Or, to put it another way, from their standpoint, there may be a contingent but there is no essential relationship between the meaning of a political theory and its historical genesis. Thus, historical investigation can play no significant role in shaping or reshaping one's conception of political theory or in the interpretation of a specific text within the pantheon of the great works of political theory.

I have undertaken this study on the basis of a different set of assumptions. In my view, a political theory is a set of structured meanings that are understandable only in reference to a specified context, wherein the concepts, terminology, and even the internal structure of the theory itself are viewed in relation to a comprehensive ordering of the elements of social life. The purposive vagueness of this reference to social life derives not only from the fact that the primary axis of meaning of a political theory may be associated with the contextual world either of the theorist or of the interpreter, but also from the fact that political ideas can be related to the social life-world in two different, though not wholly separable, ways. A political theory is both a form of social consciousness that, as Hegel put it, allows individuals to feel at home in the world they have created, and at the same time, it supplies the criteria according to which the social actions appropriate for changing that world are rendered meaningful.

In the first instance, political ideas, along with ideas drawn from religion, philosophy, economics, literature, and so on, are constitutive elements of the social consciousness of individuals within a particular culture. Some political ideas are thus incorporated into this cultural consciousness in such a manner as to act as constraints upon the kinds of beliefs and practices that a member of that society can engage in or define as political actions. In this respect, political theories represent a particular configuration of beliefs and actions that appear meaningful to members of a specific society because they can be related to a set of socially constituted practices shared by an audience to whom the theorist has addressed himself. As a form of communicative action, political theory is not simply the product of an individual mind, however great that political theorist might be. As Karl Mannheim observed,

> Strictly speaking it is incorrect to say that the single individual thinks. Rather it is more correct to insist that he participates in thinking further what other men have thought before him. He finds

> himself in an inherited situation with patterns of thought which are appropriate to this situation and attempts to elaborate further the inherited modes of response or to substitute others for them in order to deal more adequately with the new challenges which have arisen out of the shifts and changes in his situation.[4]

From this standpoint, it is always relevant to raise questions concerning the meaning of a particular political theory that are referrable to the actor's social life-world, the nature of the intended audience, and the purposes for which the political theory was formulated. Political theory in this sense takes on a comprehensive character, extending into seemingly remote areas of intellectual life, as part of the effort to refashion the cultural dimensions of meaning from the standpoint of the political actors. If we accept that the meanings that make up our world are a continuously developing structure, then the emergence of a political theory represents an attempt to articulate one of the possible "patterns of thought" within the range of structured meanings that comprise the social consciousness of members of a particular society. In viewing Locke's political theory as a particular expression of social consciousness for individuals living in seventeenth-century England, therefore, I have tried to show how patterns of thought developed that drew together certain philosophical, religious, economic, and sociological assumptions held by seventeenth-century Englishmen in order to provide a supporting structure for a set of concretely stated political objectives associated with Locke's political theory and with the actions of the audience to whom it was addressed.

One of the corollaries attached to an approach that views political theory as an admixture of concepts and metaphors drawn from various disciplinary areas of thought is that the meaning of these political ideas is expressed through several levels of thinking. Political theory, that is, is no more confined to a few great books than it is the conceptual property of a few extraordinary individuals. Rather, a more descriptively diverse characterization of political theory is needed precisely in order to appreciate its breadth and scope as a cultural phenomenon. The sociological dimensions of political consciousness cannot be captured by the definition of political theory prevalent in the secondary literature on political theory. Although I believe these general methodological propositions are applicable to any attempt to arrive at an understanding of the cultural consciousness of one or more groups within a particular society at any time, certainly they take on an increased practical importance during periods of intense social conflict. For, in seeking to mobilize individuals from different races, classes, age groups, and geographical areas, political parties or

[4] Karl Mannheim, *Ideology and Utopia*, New York: Harcourt, Brace, 1936, p. 3.

movements express themselves not only through the highly formalized medium of books, but also through newspapers, pamphlets, sermons, broadsides, and various literary forms (plays, novels, poetry). Political theory as a social language flows through all these media.[5]

These sources have generally been ignored as part of the interpretive framework for a discussion of political theory, because whatever political comments they may contain are regarded as being too pedestrian to merit consideration in the literature on political theory. This neglect simply reinforces the propensity to identify political theory with philosophy—or, rather, with a few works written by philosophers—through the exclusion of other documentary evidence that might have a bearing on the social meaning of a particular political theory. The intellectual rationale for this myopic conceptualization is usually stated in terms of a dichotomy between philosophy and ideology, with all levels of thought—save the highest—being relegated to the latter category of consciousness. I have discussed elsewhere some of the difficulties of maintaining such a distinction.[6] Suffice it to say here that, viewed from the sociological standpoint that considers political theory in relation to a socially defined audience whose members seek to obtain certain practical advantages through social action, ideology is not by definition a low level of philosophy; on the contrary, a philosophical argument is merely one form of ideological response to those obstacles within the social life-world which inhibit the realization of these objectives. The point, therefore, is not to replace "lower" levels of thought with the "higher" level of philosophy, but to demonstrate the interrelationships that obtain among all the levels of the political consciousness of the group or collectivity.

A second corollary that follows from this approach to political theory is that it democratizes the notion of political theory. It is implicit in the remarks above that political theory is produced by thousands of individuals, and not merely by a few philosophers or academicians. Nor is it only an enlargement of the intelligentsia that I have in mind. As the army debates at Putney and the coffeehouse discussions in the seventeenth century demonstrate, rank-and-file soldiers and tradesmen were capable of expressing their political theories with an impressive cogency and intensity of feeling. This discovery would be far less surprising were it not for the emphasis we have heretofore placed upon the systematic logical properties of a political theory. If, on the other hand, the emphasis shifted toward the substantive core of a political theory, the way in which it is di-

[5] For reasons of space, I have not attempted to incorporate literary sources into my discussion of political theory in this study.

[6] Richard Ashcraft, "Political Theory and the Problem of Ideology," *Journal of Politics* 42 (August 1980):687-705.

rected toward the resolution of a set of practical social problems and the means by which it assimilates the justificatory arguments necessary to resolve those problems, we might well be prepared to accept that such a political theory is available to a very extensive constituency, certainly one that reaches down to the lowest socioeconomic levels of society.[7]

This recognition leads to the second crucial dimension of political theory: the fact that it is focused upon a set of specific social actions that are designed to achieve practical benefits for the holders of a particular political perspective (though not necessarily benefits that are exclusive to them). Toleration for religious beliefs, extension of the franchise, civil rights, and equal treatment under the law are illustrations of what I have in mind. To achieve these objectives almost always involves a redistribution of political, economic, or social power. The willingness of the holders of power to accede to these demands for redistribution has a definite bearing upon the degree and type of mobilization undertaken by those making the demands.[8] Hence, the most indeterminate aspect of political theory, in my view, is not the relatively stable patterns of thought in which it is rooted, despite the fact that these patterns are continuously being reformulated from time to time, nor is it the contingently defined practical issues that are perceived as problems to be resolved through political action; rather, it is the form of organization through which these ideas and practical demands find expression.

To some extent, the institutionalization of political parties has rendered the question of political organization less problematic, but even where such highly developed institutions predominate, large-scale spontaneous social movements have arisen outside these parameters (for example, in France in May 1968; the anti–Vietnam war movement in the

[7] "Underlying even the profound insights of the genius are the collective historical experiences of a group" that shape the expectations, purposes, and activity of the theorist and his audience (Mannheim, *Ideology and Utopia*, p. 269). Moreover, political theories have their "roots basically in a group situation in which hundreds and thousands of persons, each in his own way, participate in the overthrow of the existing society" or in its maintenance (p. 27).

[8] Though I approach the problem from a different perspective, I have benefited from Erik Allardt's stimulating discussion of the "culture-building" features of a revolutionary movement and its revolutionary ideology which, however, does not necessarily alter the existing power relations between groups. The need to devise a methodology capable of giving due weight to both "culture" and "structure" (his terms) in relation to the changes brought about by revolutionary ideologies is especially important in those cases in which a political movement failed to achieve significant structural changes in the distribution of political power, but nevertheless did effect a lasting cultural change through the triumph of its political language. This, it seems to me, is the situation of the political radicals who are the focus of this study (Erik Allardt, "Culture, Structure and Revolutionary Ideologies," *International Journal of Comparative Sociology* 12, no. 1 [March 1971]:24-40).

United States). In the context of seventeenth-century political life, I have thought it appropriate to refer to the collection of Dissenters, Whigs, and radicals as a political movement. This terminology is compatible with that employed by contemporary social scientists, for whom "a social movement represents an effort by a large number of people to solve collectively a problem that they feel they have in common."[9] In this case, we can designate a core problem—religious toleration—around which other related problems developed.

The linkage between history and political theory in this study is therefore expressed through the concrete organizational form of a political movement. Locke's political theory, I shall argue, arose within the context of a political movement in which he was a participant, along with thousands of others. The *Two Treatises of Government* was, in effect, the political manifesto of this movement. Much of the meaning of Locke's political theory is thus rooted not only in a particular perception of social reality he shared with others in seventeenth-century England, but it is also tied in rather concrete terms to the specific political objectives around which large numbers of individuals organized themselves in the 1670s and 1680s under the leadership of the Earl of Shaftesbury.

The problems of drawing out the connections between a political theory and its historical context do not all lie on the plane of determining what conceptual apparatus is best suited to carrying out this endeavor. There are, in addition, certain specific difficulties attached to the effort of supplying the historical dimensions of the context for John Locke's political theory. The 1680s in England was a decade marked by a pervasive fear of Catholicism, a widespread belief that a conspiracy existed to reestablish that religion in England, and the practice of severe repression directed against political and religious dissidents. The lies, suspicion, deceit, and treachery that infiltrated the political arena during this period present serious problems with respect to the integrity of the evidence upon which the historian generally relies. Historical investigation becomes a difficult undertaking when the boundaries of collective paranoia or official dissimulation cannot be easily determined, or when secrecy and deception have become socially widespread practices.[10]

[9] Hans Toch, *The Social Psychology of Social Movements*, New York: Bobbs-Merrill, 1965, p. 5.

[10] As J. R. Jones remarks, the Restoration period is "devoid of honesty and consistency," and is "pervaded by cynicism" (J. R. Jones, *Country and Court: England, 1658-1714*, Cambridge: Harvard University Press, 1978, p. 8). "The history of this period," according to Trevelyan, "is essentially one of intrigue" and what he calls "the reigns of terror" of the Stuarts (G. M. Trevelyan, *England under the Stuarts*, London: Methuen, 1965, pp. 324-325, 368).

The very thing that makes historical investigation difficult, however (namely, the secret and conspiratorial character of political life), is, as it happens, the most important point to be understood with respect to the political actions and arguments of Locke and those who were his political associates in the 1680s. For, much of the meaning of the latter's theoretical perspective is derived from their perception of social reality in these terms. Hence, for anyone who wishes to integrate political theorizing with the historical events of the 1670s and 1680s, there is no choice but to come to grips with the historical material, however problematic it may be, viewed against the normal evidential standards relied upon by historians. In making my way through manuscripts, newspapers, correspondence, and hundreds of tracts and sermons, I have attempted to reconstruct how this social reality was perceived, primarily by the members of a radical political movement, but sometimes, by their opponents as well.

To speak of the practical organization of interests and the importance of policy objectives to a social movement is to recite a banal and basic presupposition with which virtually all sociologists, anthropologists, and political scientists begin their investigations. Nevertheless, interpreters of political theory have generally traveled through history unencumbered by this piece of intellectual baggage. But, apart from reemphasizing the importance of the practical dimensions of political theory, there is also a need to break down the rather firm dichotomy between interests and ideas that obtains among a sizable body of practical-minded social scientists. On the one hand, political slogans, symbols, and party manifestoes, precisely because they constitute part of the process of organizing and implementing the political thinking of large masses of people, are extremely important expressions of ideas. Indeed, these exclamatory ideas provide the basic organizational context for any systematic intellectual framework that has been elevated to a place of prominence in the history of political theory. The significance of attempting to take into account the organizing role of ideas is that it makes the practical objectives of a political theory a major axis for the interpretation of the meaning of the concepts employed by the theorist. At the same time, however, the meaning of a political theory cannot be simply deduced or derived from a catalog of empirically defined interests associated with a particular group of individuals. However concretely one conceives of the practical interests and motivations of a set of political actors, there are patterns of thought, socially established conventions, and constraints upon the practice of political communication that must be rendered meaningful through a reference to the self-understood forms of thought in the consciousness of the historical actors themselves. In this study, I have tried to identify the social composition of the audience for Locke's political theory both with respect to their socioeconomic interests and in terms of the social language they employed. These two factors were linked organizationally in the form of a political movement that sought to realize certain specific practical objectives through social action.

Thus, insofar as political theory draws its social significance from the meanings it incorporates from inherited patterns of thought, attention needs to be paid to the usage of a social language that has a particular salience for identifiable social groups, the appeal to respected cultural authorities and important historical events, and the manner in which presuppositions drawn from other, nonpolitical, areas of social life are deployed on behalf of the political theory. Insofar as political theory functions as part of a process of mass mobilization of individuals to engage in certain social actions, the interpreter requires a detailed knowledge of how different social groups perceive the political problems in their society, what practices they believe will lead to a solution of these problems, and what consequences follow from both the perceptions of the problems and the actions proposed or taken to resolve them with respect to the structure of social relationships in that society. According to the conception of political theory I have employed in this study, therefore, the conjunction of history and political theory is possible only on the presupposition that the latter is itself a sociological phenomenon to be investigated.

To end the discussion there would be misleading. It is not sufficient to emphasize the importance of sociologically defined factors to one's conception of political theory; it is also necessary to preserve the connection between the historical individual and the particular way in which political ideas are systematically organized in a specific work. As Alfred Schutz phrased the point,

> If the social sciences aim indeed at explaining social reality, then . . . [they] must include a reference to the subjective meaning an action has for the actor.[11]

Since I regard the writing of a work of political theory (the *Two Treatises of Government*) as a social action, this means that the actor's intentions, as well as the social conventions of meaning applicable to that type of social action, need to be taken into account if the political theory produced through this action and concretized in a discrete object (book, sermon, tract) is to have a meaning that preserves the existential identity of its

[11] Alfred Schutz, "Concept and Theory Formation in the Social Sciences," in Dorothy Emmet and Alasdair MacIntyre, eds., *Sociological Theory and Philosophical Analysis*, London: Macmillan, 1970, p. 15.

author. Thus, in addition to delineating the larger dimensions of the political theory associated with the participants in the radical political movement of the 1680s, I have tried to provide a framework for understanding the subjectively intended meaning of Locke's action in writing the *Two Treatises of Government.*[12]

It is easy to posit, on the general level of the methodological debate that has raged within the social sciences since the nineteenth century, that there is an incompatibility between the methods appropriate for understanding social structures, historically unique problems, and the subjectively intended meaning of individual action. Moreover, since I view political theory as ideology, and have therefore considered Locke as an ideologist of a political movement, it is also easy to become trapped under the weight of such polemically charged labels as "bourgeois" or "liberal." As Mannheim noted, in an observation that I believe is relevant to both points,

> Nothing is simpler than to maintain that a certain type of thinking is feudal, bourgeois or proletarian, liberal, socialistic, or conservative, as long as there is no analytical method for demonstrating it and no criteria have been adduced which will provide a control over the demonstration. Hence the chief task in the present state of research is to elaborate and concretize the hypotheses involved in such a way that they can be made the basis of inductive studies.[13]

In other words, while I recognize that, in sketching the basic outlines of my approach to political theory in this Introduction I have raised issues

[12] Since I believe, as an empirical generalization, that most human actions are referrable to a framework of multiple intentions, and that this is especially the case in the undertaking of a highly complicated action such as writing a work of political theory, I am not advancing the claim that this study has successfully recovered *the* subjectively intended meaning of Locke in writing the *Two Treatises of Government.* I have, however, emphasized throughout what I believe were Locke's political objectives in writing that work, and I am prepared to argue that, from his viewpoint, these were the most important, though not the only, elements that comprise the subjectively intended meaning of that action. For a useful discussion of the methodological issues relating to this point, see the following articles by Quentin Skinner: "Meaning and Understanding in the History of Ideas," *History and Theory* 8, no. 1 (1969):3-53; "Conventions and the Understanding of Speech Acts," *Philosophical Quarterly* 21, no. 79 (April 1970):113-138; "'Social Meaning' and the Explanation of Social Action," in *Philosophy, Politics and Society*, 4th ser., ed. Peter Laslett and W. G. Runciman, Oxford: Basil Blackwell, 1972, pp. 136-157; "Some Problems in the Analysis of Political Thought and Action," *Political Theory* 2, no. 3 (August 1974):277-303. Also, see Charles Taylor, "Interpretation and the Sciences of Man," *Review of Metaphysics* (September 1971), pp. 3-51; Alasdair MacIntyre, "Ideology, Social Science, and Revolution," *Comparative Politics* 5, no. 3 (April 1973):321-342; J. G. A. Pocock, *Politics, Language and Time*, New York: Atheneum, 1971.

[13] Mannheim, *Ideology and Utopia*, p. 50.

that are deeply enmeshed in the most important theoretical controversies within the social sciences, I have tried in this study to follow Mannheim's admonition to concretize those issues. That is, I have sought to interpret Locke's political theory from the standpoint of the importance of the subjectively intended meaning he wished to convey through the action of writing the *Two Treatises of Government*. At the same time, I have viewed this action as part of a larger network of social actions engaged in by Locke, and perforce by others. These actions represent a collective endeavor to restructure the relations of power in seventeenth-century England. They can, therefore, be studied using the methods one would employ in order to understand the phenomena of social movements, ideologies, and revolutions. If, in endeavoring to integrate these interpretive objectives, I have sublimated the discussion of the methodological problems they raise to the effort to provide a historical reconstruction of Lockean political theory, this is largely due to the fact that I can see no other means by which to effect a theoretical synthesis.

Thus far, the discussion has focused upon the social consciousness of political actors and the manner in which political theory reflects and reshapes that social consciousness. Some mention must also be made, however, of those causal relationships which are not adequately accounted for by a theoretical perspective defined exclusively in terms of the phenomenological consciousness of historical subjects, but which are nevertheless important to the interpretation of the beliefs and actions of these subjects. Thus, class divisions, long-term economic tendencies, and other structural factors must be included as part of any explanation of the production of political theory as a distinctly sociological phenomenon.[14] In relating these causal relationships to the structures of meaning prevalent in seventeenth-century England, the self-reflective dimensions of an interpretation assume a primary importance. By that I mean that assertions of causal relationships in the past are themselves meaningful within the framework of the social language of the present. Whatever one may say regarding the historical accuracy of specific statements in the works of Marx or Weber with respect to the origins of capitalism, the question of what relationship exists between causal forces and belief systems within the domain of social action is decidedly an issue the resolution of which is, for us, an essential determinant of the meaning of "social science."[15]

[14] For a clear and helpful statement of these issues, see Brian Fay, *Social Theory and Political Practice*, London: Allen and Unwin, 1975.

[15] I have discussed elsewhere this question as it relates to the social theories of Marx and Weber, and as it structures the contemporary debate within social science (Richard Ashcraft, "Marx and Weber on Liberalism as Bourgeois Ideology," *Comparative Studies in Society and History* [March 1972]:130-168; idem, "Class and Class Conflict in Contemporary Capitalist Societies," *Comparative Politics* [January 1979]:225-245).

Viewed from the perspective of the individual, numerous causal relationships external to his consciousness that nevertheless determine his actions can always be identified. From the standpoint of a social collectivity, a class or a social movement, however (especially when its social consciousness is seen in relation not only to internally generated ideas and arguments, but also in the context of what its opponents were saying), the number of causal relationships that are external to the social consciousness of the political actors, and that need to be incorporated into the interpreter's account of that social consciousness, are much fewer than many social scientists believe. On the other hand, it is fair to say that though they may be few in number, such relationships are invariably of great explanatory significance.

This, too, is a thorny and complicated methodological issue whose exploration would require much more space than I can devote to it here. But perhaps it will prove helpful to offer a concrete illustration of what I mean. The Whigs as a political party identified themselves as ideological opponents of monarchical absolutism, and as defenders of commercial expansion and the trading interests of England. What they did not see, and what was therefore not a part of their political consciousness, was the causal relationship that existed between the growth of commercial trade and the increasing absolutism of Charles II. The customs revenue that accrued to the king increased as England's trade prospered, and this growth in revenue tended to free the king from his dependency upon parliamentary grants of money. Yet, not until James II's precipitous grab of this source of income immediately after his brother's death did the connection between absolutism and customs revenue begin to enter into the political consciousness of the Whigs. From our standpoint, however, this causal relationship is both meaningful and important, not only as a historical fact to be added to our knowledge of Restoration England or the place of England in the international economy of the seventeenth century, but also because it serves as a kind of negative dimension of our understanding of certain ideological arguments advanced by the political actors of the period. Indeed, one might even say that causal factors often have an ironical relationship to the social consciousness of historical subjects, viewed from our standpoint.

In this case, the Whigs perceived a growing tendency on the part of Charles to dispense with Parliament, and they explained this tendency in terms of what they suspected were secret financial dealings with Louis XIV. In this they were not wrong; but as we now know, the amounts of money given to Charles II by the French king were wholly inadequate to free him from a dependency upon Parliament. If, therefore, one were determined to explain the basis of Charles' absolutism—and this, of course, is an essentially contestable proposition from the standpoint of an interpretation of the historical events of the period—the explanation offered by the Whigs, however necessary it might be to an understanding of *their* ideology and political actions, would not be adequate for our understanding of those beliefs and actions. Other instances (the effects of long-term economic tendencies that increased the size and the politically radical composition of the seventeenth-century electorate, for example) are discussed below.

And, from the other side, one could approach the interpretation of seventeenth-century political theory through the use of a model of capitalism in which certain causal relationships are postulated that are supposed by the interpreter to lie just outside the boundaries of the consciousness of seventeenth-century individuals.[16] It is sometimes said that capitalism developed behind the backs of those who brought it into existence, and if one adopts a sufficiently long-term view of historical development, there is a recognizable kernel of truth in this remark. In the short-term, however, such assertions tend to sacrifice too much of what is essential for establishing the empirical dimensions of the context to the imputation to the historical actors of ideas and intentions that are derived from the interpreter's model in order to make them responsible for formulating their ideas or for acting in accordance with the prerequisites of that model.

Since I am not making a blanket condemnation either of the use of ideal types or of a reliance upon presuppositions that the interpreter must, willy-nilly, impose upon his treatment of the historical actors, we are obviously discussing matters of degree and judgment. Moreover, my purposes in this Introduction are limited to clarifying for the reader some of the methodological assumptions I have adopted, and in that regard, I will only say that I have not found general references to capitalism or to the rise of the bourgeoisie to be particularly useful in this study. And yet, it could be reasonably contended that the entire undertaking is shaped by my own convictions that such terms are relevant to an understanding of seventeenth-century England. In other words, *capitalism* has a tremendously important practical-theoretical significance, especially as perceived through the eyes of Marx, for my understanding of history, social relations, and political theory. Nevertheless, in emphasizing the importance of class divisions, or economic factors, even when they appear as part of causal explanations, I have tried to consider these phenomena, as in the example cited above, simply as particular instances lying outside the social consciousness of the actors. *We* may choose to see them as ex-

[16] C. B. Macpherson, *The Political Theory of Possessive Individualism*, Oxford: Oxford University Press, 1962.

amples of false consciousness or as part of the historical development of capitalism; indeed, I would be prepared to argue that there are good reasons in support of the assertion that we should see them in this way. But that is no warrant, in my judgment, for attributing either the concepts or intentions defined in relation to those concepts to the historical subjects themselves.

Nearly ten years ago, I wrote:

> What makes [Locke's] theory political is not the philosophical cogency of his definition of political power; nor is it the textual consistency of his use of terminology; nor, finally, is it the empirical accuracy of his account of the origins of political power or the institution of property. It is, simply, the relevance of Locke's argument about the exercise of political power to an existent political movement within his society. A theory is political, in other words, only in relation to the maintenance or furtherance of the social, political, and economic objectives of a specifically identifiable group within society.[17]

At the time I wrote these words, I did not have this study in any of its particular dimensions in mind; rather, I was simply attempting to make a point about the nature of political theory in the context of a debate over the methodological presuppositions subscribed to by contemporary political theorists. Yet, as I have suggested above, general arguments about these matters have a limited utility, and there comes a point when the discussion can be advanced, if it can be advanced at all, only through shifting the controversy onto a terrain where the empirically grounded propositions that structure that controversy can take on a concrete expression. From the standpoint of the safety of an enclosed theoretical position in which all possible outcomes of the debate with an opposing perspective are known in advance, the shift in terrain can sometimes be treacherous. It is always problematic, since the importance of contingent elements to the theoretical framework is necessarily given increased emphasis. Still, from another vantage point, the very ability to marshal contingent empirical phenomena in a comprehensive and systematic manner is what defines the intellectual quality of a theoretical framework, just as the ability to mobilize millions of separate individuals into an organized political collectivity describes an important feature of political life. Both qualities are essential to political theory as I have defined it. I have written this book with the intention of illustrating that point.

[17] Richard Ashcraft, "On the Problem of Methodology and the Nature of Political Theory," *Political Theory* 3, no. 1 (February 1975):20.

1
THE FRAMEWORK OF POLITICAL DISCUSSION

In 1670, on a bleak December day, a small group of men affixed their signatures to a document that launched England on a perilous course. They had concluded a treaty of alliance between England and France, and yet everything was not as it appeared. Beneath the façade of serious purpose, a courtly charade was being staged by Charles II. For most of the dignitaries present, this was the second treaty-signing ceremony they had attended in the last nine months. The first Treaty of Dover had been a highly secretive affair, and for good reason. That document contained clauses in which Charles II promised to declare his adherence to the Roman Catholic religion. Payment of £200,000 and assignment of 6,000 French troops by Louis XIV were to assist the English king in the execution of this grand conversion. Although Charles professed his confidence that his subjects would not "fail in their due obedience to their sovereign," nevertheless, since "there are always unquiet spirits" who threaten the peace of the kingdom, the timing of this fateful pronouncement was to be left to the English king's judicious discretion.[1]

Now, in this return engagement, two of the leading champions of the rights and relief of the Protestant Dissenters, Lord Ashley and the Duke of Buckingham, were among the ministerial signatories for England.[2] Despite the genuine affection Charles felt toward the latter, his boyhood friend, it could hardly be denied that Buckingham and Shaftesbury were two of the most "unquiet spirits" in the kingdom. Accordingly, in this version of the Treaty of Dover, no mention was made of Charles' espousal of Catholicism in return for French subsidies or troops. The drama had shifted from one of the mysteries of religious and political intrigue to a more prosaic portrayal of the commercial and military preparations necessary for a joint war against the Dutch. The Royal African and East India companies, as well as other segments of the mercantile class, which exercised considerable influence both at Court and in Parliament, had long

[1] The first Treaty of Dover was signed in May 1670; the second, on December 21, 1670 (Ogg, 1:348). The complete text of the secret Treaty of Dover is printed as an appendix in G. M. D. Howat, *Stuart and Cromwellian Foreign Policy*, New York: St. Martin's Press, 1974, pp. 166-171.

[2] From 1661 to 1672, Anthony Ashley Cooper was known as Lord Ashley, and thereafter as the first Earl of Shaftesbury. I have referred to him throughout according to this title, by which he is best known as a historical figure.

pressed for a war against the Dutch as a means of undermining the latter's dominance in colonial trade. "What we want," the Duke of Albemarle declared, "is more of the trade the Dutch now have."[3] Thus, despite popular misgivings about "the French interest," this treaty could be viewed as a nationalistic reassertion of English mercantile interests. As one of the king's deceived subjects later reflected, "we knew not what snake lay in the grass." We believed the Treaty of Dover was signed "for the benefit of our trade and navigation."[4] This is, in fact, the way in which it was presented to the nation by Charles II—as the instrument whereby Britain could extend her empire beyond the sea and once again become supreme as a commercial power.[5]

The double-sided character of the Treaty of Dover expresses the symbiotic relationship that existed throughout the last half of Charles II's reign between the development of English commercial superiority and the efforts of Charles and others to refashion the English monarchy according to the model of French absolutism. Charles was convinced that his cousin, Louis XIV, knew how to rule; the latter was the very image of a king who demanded, and received, absolute obedience from his subjects. Some part of his success in this endeavor certainly appeared to be due to the assistance he received from the doctrines and practices of Catholicism.[6] From an early age, individuals were socialized by their teachers and priests into the habits of submission to the authority of an absolutist monarch. Yet, Charles was acutely aware of the fact that neither Catholicism nor an unquestioning acceptance of civil authority had taken firm root in England.

In addition to England's commitment to Protestantism, there was also the irritating problem of money, which constituted a check upon the

[3] Albemarle summarized "the zeal with which a vociferous section of the merchant community clamoured for a Dutch war" (Charles Wilson, *England's Apprenticeship, 1603–1763*, London: Longman, 1965, p. 165; idem, *Profit and Power: A Study of England and the Dutch Wars*, London: Longmans, Green, 1957, p. 93). For the complaints against the Dutch from merchants, see Ethel Bruce Sainsbury, *A Calendar of the Court Minutes of the East India Company, 1668–1670*, Oxford: Clarendon Press, 1929, pp. 13, 81, 108, 126–127; William R. Scott, *The Constitution and Finance of English, Scottish and Irish Joint-Stock Companies to 1720*, 3 vols., Cambridge: Cambridge University Press, 1912, 1:282.

[4] *A Complete History of the Late Revolution*, 1691, p. 4.

[5] Maurice Ashley, *Charles II*, London: Panther Books, 1973, p. 175; C. Wilson, *Profit*, p. 157; J. R. Jones, *Country and Court: England, 1658–1714*, Cambridge: Harvard University Press, 1978, p. 106.

[6] "The essence of [Charles II's] foreign policy had been to identify himself with the cause of absolutism: for this reason he had gravitated towards France . . . That policy was related to the pursuit of Catholic interests. There was an identity between Catholicism and absolutism which all princes in the seventeenth century recognized" (Howat, *Stuart Foreign Policy*, pp. 140–141; Ashley, *Charles II*, p. 164; Dalrymple, 1:90).

king's authority. The constant need for the king to present himself as a supplicant before Parliament to request that they grant him sufficient revenue to finance his administrative obligations and personal indulgences did not accord well with the image of French absolutism, at least as it was perceived by some members of Charles II's court. Was there some means by which he could escape from these Lilliputian constraints upon the exercise of his kingly power?

If Charles II had attempted, by a straightforward declaration of belief to carry out the religious clauses of the secret Treaty of Dover, he would certainly have faced far more serious opposition from Parliament than that inspired by a cautious reluctance on their part either to grant the king too much revenue or to forgo their claim to supervise and inspect its expenditure. At the same time, however, the ostensible commercial and military objectives of the treaty actually provided the basis upon which Charles II was able to raise a structure of monarchic absolutism. From 1660 to 1700, there was a remarkable growth in the tonnage of shipping, reflecting the considerable expansion in England's trade during this period, and both of these were, in turn, accompanied by a dramatic increase in customs and excise revenue.[7] Thus, insofar as the treaty (and its consequential outcome, the Third Dutch War) proved to be a catalyst in the expansion of the English shipbuilding industry and in the promotion of trade, the resulting increase of customs revenue, which accrued to the king, enabled Charles to draw closer to his objective of freeing himself from a dependency upon parliamentary grants of revenue.[8]

The political paradox attached to the pursuit of this policy of absolutism was pointed out by a contemporary who, writing in the 1680s, lamented that Charles II "should fall to so abject a state as to become a French pensioner." This arrangement, he declared, was "more than

[7] C. Wilson, *Apprenticeship*, pp. xii, 211; Ogg, 2:421; E. Lipson, *The Economic History of England*, 6th ed., 3 vols., London: Adam and Charles Black, 1961, 2:190. For the recognition of this point by contemporaries after 1690, see Lipson, *Economic History*, 3:91; Roger North, *Examen*, 1740, p. 487.

[8] "The astonishing increase" in shipbuilding "that resulted from Charles II's policy" in the Third Dutch War is noted by R. W. K. Hinton, *The Eastland Trade and the Common Weal in the Seventeenth Century*, Cambridge: Cambridge University Press, 1959, p. 153; cf. ibid., pp. 108–110; Ralph Davis, *The Rise of the English Shipping Industry*, London: Macmillan, 1962, pp. 14–15. Moreover, shipping was one of the largest employers of labor, accounting for approximately 20 percent of all nonagricultural workers (C. Wilson, *Apprenticeship*, p. 171). "In 1660 no one could have foreseen that, with the development of English industry and commerce, the revenue from customs and excise would eventually reach such a figure as to make Charles and his successor independent of parliament" (Ogg, 1:158). For the figures on the excise and customs revenue and confirmation of the fact that these financial sources provided the basis for Stuart absolutism, see C. D. Chandaman, *The English Public Revenue, 1660–1688*, Oxford: Clarendon Press, 1975, pp. 31, 35, 61.

enough eternally to blast the memory of an English Monarch."[9] It is true that, against this somewhat exaggerated assessment, the historical reputation of Charles II seems to have survived his concealed financial subservience to Louis XIV rather better than the author of *The Secret History of Whitehall* imagined. Nevertheless, the considerable risks posed by the Treaty of Dover to the political stability of the Restoration Settlement should not be underestimated.[10] Whatever the specific dangers posed by Charles' endorsement of Catholicism, they were undoubtedly compounded by his decision to practice a deliberate deception upon some of his own ministers and upon his Protestant subjects in the form of this second spurious but public treaty.

Writing to his sister, Henrietta, who carried the terms of the secret treaty to Dover, and who acted as an agent on behalf of France and Louis XIV, Charles cautioned, "I must again conjure you that the whole matter must be an absolute secret, otherwise we shall never compass the end we aim at." Later, when Buckingham began to grow suspicious, Charles advised his sister that "it will be good that you write sometimes to [Buckingham] in general terms that he may not expect that there is [*sic*] further negotiations than what he knows . . . he may suspect that there is something of [the Catholic] interest in the case, which is a matter he must not be acquainted with, therefore you must have a care not to say the least thing that may make him suspect anything of it."[11]

Nevertheless, almost from its signing, suspicions as to the treaty's content and purposes began to seep into the political arena. Rumors of a secret treaty with France involving subsidies to Charles that freed him from a dependency upon Parliament, and even allegations concerning the "Catholicity" of the treaty were widespread in the 1670s. In an influential tract published in 1673, the author wrote that the English have tried

[9] David Jones, *The Secret History of Whitehall*, 1697, p. 79 (pagination disordered).

[10] "The importance of the Treaty of Dover can scarcely be overrated . . . this dissociation of the King from his people was responsible for the miseries to which, for more than a generation" the English people were subjected (Osmund Airy, *Charles II*, London: Goupil, 1901, p. 163). In 1697, the author of *A Free Discourse wherein the Doctrines Which Make for Tyranny Are Displayed* made the same point (p. 17).

[11] Cyril Hughes Hartmann, *Charles II and Madame*, London: William Heinemann, 1934, pp. 230, 245. The first letter is dated January 20, 1669, and the second April 25, 1669. On January 25, 1669, a secret meeting was held in the Duke of York's lodgings, with Arlington, Clifford, and Lord Arundel present, at which Charles disclosed his intentions to espouse Catholicism, and to enlist the aid of France in support of this declaration. The king said he had called them together "to have their advice about the ways and methods fittest to be taken for the settling of the Catholic religion in his kingdoms and to consider the time most proper to declare himself" (p. 233). For evidence indicating the seriousness of Charles' intentions to explore the *possibility* of making such a declaration, see Cyril Hughes Hartmann, *Clifford of the Cabal*, London: William Heinemann, 1937, pp. 153–162.

to persuade themselves that the French alliance and the Dutch War were merely instruments "for the advancement of trade," but the suspicions that something more sinister lay behind this foreign policy are too great. He challenged the king's advisers to "tell us plainly whether they are *paid* for making the French King the Universal Monarch; and whether . . . England must at least be made tributary to the French."[12] This challenge was echoed when the treaty was presented to Parliament. If these are the public articles, one member asked, what are the secret articles of this treaty?[13] The extent to which the Treaty of Dover fostered suspicions of Charles' intentions and undermined public confidence in his political leadership can hardly be overestimated. As more than one historian has noted, "secrecy, popery, and despotism" became the watchwords of the decade. Gradually, "the happy Restoration" receded into the distance of memory, and, increasingly, the remainder of Charles II's reign after 1670 was marked by "fears and jealousies," and the growth of anxieties aroused by real and imagined plots and conspiracies to disturb the public order. The language of political discourse developed, by degrees, a tone of bitterness and despair. From the signing of the Treaty of Dover, it was only a matter of time—a few years for some, a decade for many others—until Charles II was accused of conspiring to subvert the constituted religious and political order.

Andrew Marvell was one of the first to fire a warning shot across the bow of Charles II's administration, declaring that "there has now for divers years a design been carried on to change the lawful government of England into an absolute tyranny, and to convert the established Protestant religion into downright popery." Both aims, Marvell argued, would destroy the constitutional structure of English politics.[14] The precise historical origins of this "design" might be supposed by some to extend back into the previous century, but for Marvell, the dangers of this drift toward tyranny could be more easily perceived in the policies and actions pursued by Charles II and his advisers. The Treaty of Dover, which Marvell called "a work of darkness," proved to be a Pandora's box; and by 1677, when his *An Account of the Growth of Popery and Arbitrary Gov-*

[12] Pierre Du Moulin, *England's Appeal from the Private Cabal at Whitehall to the Great Council of the Nation the Lords and Commons in Parliament Assembled*, 1673, pp. 35, 39–40. Also, see the reports of the Danish envoy to England, Waldemar Westergaard, *The First Triple Alliance*, New Haven: Yale University Press, 1947, p. 468.

[13] G. N. Clark, *The Later Stuarts*, Oxford: Oxford University Press, 1940, p. 76. The actual document presented to Parliament was a modified version of the second Treaty of Dover.

[14] Andrew Marvell, *The Complete Works*, 4 vols., 1872, 4:248.

ernment appeared, the spirits of controversy, conspiracy, and chaos had already been loosed upon the land.[15]

The debate among historians as to Charles II's intentions in negotiating a secret treaty with France still rages inconclusively with respect to the degree of relative importance one ought to attribute to the economic or the religious objectives of Charles' policies in order to account for his actions, but in a significant sense, this debate misses the crucial point to be made about the treaty—namely, that once its existence and some of its details became part of the political consciousness of those in opposition to the Court in the 1670s and 1680s, the treaty provided a bedrock of evidential support for the suspicions of a conspiracy on the part of the king and his advisers to subvert the Constitution.[16] For, it was this conviction, that they were *opposing* a conspiracy and *defending* the ancient constitution against its secret enemies at home and abroad, which supplied much of the justification for the political policies and practices of the radicals in the decade prior to the Glorious Revolution. The context of revolutionary politics was thus shaped by the belief that "the King as well as the Duke [of York] were in the conspiracy to alter the Constitution and overturn our religion."[17] From this standpoint, the pervasive atmosphere of suspicion, distrust, and conspiracy that prevailed in England in the 1670s and 1680s constitutes an extremely important element of the contextual meaning of the political arguments and political theories formulated during this period.

More immediately discernible than Charles II's disguised intentions was the campaign of political repression of the Dissenters supporters of the Anglican church launched in 1669–1670. Despite Charles II's promise at Breda to grant "a liberty to tender consciences" as part of the Restoration Settlement, the reestablished Anglican church had, from the outset, opposed such a move. Instead, church leaders sought to enforce a strict religious conformity. The early 1660s witnessed the ejection of thousands of ministers from their livings, the discouragement of many others—including Locke—who chose not to pursue a career in the Church, and the harrassment and imprisonment of Dissenters according to several parliamentary measures that together comprised the Clarendon Code.[18] If these repressive efforts were temporarily abated by the

[15] Marvell, *Works*, 4:266.

[16] For a summary of various historians' opinions of Charles' intentions in signing the Treaty of Dover, see Howat, *Stuart Foreign Policy*, pp. 130–131.

[17] *An Impartial Enquiry into the Administration of Affairs in England*, [1684], p. 23. For a discussion of the importance of this tract and a suggestion as to its author, see below, Chapter 7, note 207.

[18] Modern historians have generally absolved Clarendon of the chief responsibility for

Lord Chancellor's impeachment and fall from power and by the dislocations caused by outbursts of plague and the Great Fire of London in 1666–1667, the embers of persecution were certainly fanned by the vitriolic and defamatory language of Samuel Parker's *Discourse of Ecclesiastical Polity*, published in 1669.[19] Parker, at this time one of Archbishop Sheldon's chaplains, but later elevated to the Bishopric of Oxford, conceded the "vehemence and severity" of his style of writing. He defended that approach, however, on the grounds that Dissenters were "like the savage Americans," and one could not expect to "argue rude and boistrous zealots out of their folly merely by the strength of calm and sober reason."[20] Rather, against such misguided zeal what was needed was an even greater zeal on the part of the established church.[21] Parker's purpose in writing the *Discourse*, he admitted, was not to persuade Dissenters to the virtues of Anglican beliefs; rather, his real aim was "to awaken authority," both civil and spiritual, to the threat posed by the existence of Dissenters, who were the "worst and most dangerous enemies" of all forms of authority. Parker's work was therefore quite explicitly intended to encourage the strict enforcement of the penal laws against Nonconformists, "a wild and fanatic rabble," as he viewed them.[22] The *Discourse on Ecclesiastical Polity* was, to put it simply, a declaration of war upon all religious dissidents. As might be imagined, Parker's *Discourse* provoked numerous replies and responses, some of them from the best minds of the Restoration period. The particular issues and the general structure of that debate, in which the parameters of the ideological conflict of the 1680s were laid out, will

---

the harshest measures and enforcement of the Clarendon Code, in favor of Gilbert Sheldon (Keith Feiling, *A History of the Tory Party, 1640–1714*, Oxford: Clarendon Press, 1924, pp. 104–105; Victor D. Sutch, *Gilbert Sheldon: Architect of Anglican Survival, 1640–1675*, The Hague: Martinus Nijhoff, 1973, p. 95). Excerpts from the Clarendon Code Acts are printed in J. P. Kenyon, ed., *The Stuart Constitution, 1603–1688*, Cambridge: Cambridge University Press, 1966, pp. 371–382, and at greater length in W. C. Costin and J. Steven Watson, eds., *The Law and Working of the Constitution: Documents, 1660–1914*, 2 vols., London: Adam and Charles Black, 1952, 1:5-36.

[19] Samuel Parker, *Discourse of Ecclesiastical Polity*, [1669]. Parker's *Discourse* was part of a general ideological campaign directed against the Dissenters launched by Sheldon, to which several of his other chaplains also contributed books (Sutch, *Sheldon*, p. 109; C. E. Whiting, *Studies in English Puritanism from the Restoration to the Revolution, 1660–1688*, London: Society for Promoting Christian Knowledge, 1931, p. 502).

[20] Parker, *Discourse*, pp. i, vi, ix.

[21] Parker, *Discourse*, pp. ix-x. Parker had been raised as a Puritan and had been part of small group of ascetic Puritans at Oxford during the Commonwealth. After the Restoration, he reversed himself, becoming one of the most violent defenders of the Anglican church. He became a chaplain to Archbishop Sheldon in 1667 (John Stoughton, *History of Religion in England*, 6 vols., London: Hodder and Stoughton, n.d., 3:433–434).

[22] Parker, *Discourse*, p. x; cf. ibid., p. ii.

be discussed in Chapter 2. My concern here is simply to draw attention to the political consequences that attended those policies which were, or which came to be perceived as, expressing the government's position.

This is an issue for which it is difficult to find the precise terminology, partly because the government was not then—nor is it now—a monolithic organization with a single purpose guiding its actions, and partly because the perception of purposes underlying particular policies by citizens neither is necessarily accurate in relation to the intentions of the actors exercising power, nor does such a viewpoint generally emerge all at once among the members of some specific social group directly affected by such policies—in this case, the Dissenters. Nevertheless, when these allowances have been made, the fact remains that in 1669–1670 there was a sharp and perceptible turn toward the political repression of religious dissent that helped to crystallize and intensify an active opposition to Church and Court.[23]

There is no reason to doubt the sincerity of the belief held by religious leaders such as Archbishop Sheldon, or his successor, William Sancroft, that Anglican doctrines needed to be defended against the errors represented by nonconformity, but one is struck by the systematic, comprehensive, and businesslike tone of the instructions sent out by Sheldon to all his bishops, deans, and chancellors as part of this renewed counteroffensive by the established church. In his letter, Sheldon orders his bishops to "make speedy inquiry" within their dioceses as to "what and how many conventicles, or unlawful assemblies or church meetings are held" in the various parishes, how many people usually attend them, "and of what condition or sort of people they consist, who are their ministers . . . what authority they pretend for their meetings, and from whom, and upon what hopes they look for impunity." This request for information was to be passed downward to the lower levels of administrative authority within the church, along with an admonition to such officials "requiring them to make their inquiries diligently and with all speed." Writing to the Bishops of London and Norwich, Sheldon made a special point of emphasizing that the impression that the king favors the conventicles of the Nonconformists was a mistaken one, and he recounts the substance of a conversation he had with the king in which the latter promised his sup-

[23] There is abundant evidence "that in 1670 there was a great revival of persecuting activity" (G. Lyon Turner, *Original Records of Early Nonconformity under Persecution and Indulgence*, 3 vols., London: T. Fisher Unwin, 1911, 3:56; Sutch, *Sheldon*, p. 115). One correspondent wrote to the Secretary of State that "it must rejoice every loyal and honest person to see the [Conventicle] Act so vigorously executed" (*CSPD*, 10:261). Also, see the reports in Westergaard, *Triple Alliance*, pp. 259–289.

port for any bishops who undertook to supress such meetings.[24] Indeed, in his letter to William Fuller, Bishop of Lincoln, Sheldon reminded Fuller that he was present when the king disavowed his support for Dissenters. In that conversation, Charles had placed some of the blame for such unlawful meetings upon the laxity of the church hierarchy in maintaining religious discipline, and he promised the bishops the wholehearted assistance of civil magistrates in the suppression of the Dissenters. Those magistrates who failed to enforce the law and its penalties were to be reported by the bishops directly to the king, who would deal with them.[25]

In July 1669, Charles II issued a proclamation against the Dissenters, threatening them with a stricter enforcement of the legal penalties for nonconformity.[26] A few months later, the Privy Council, acting on a complaint from Archbishop Sheldon, ordered the removal of two dissenting ministers from the East India Company.[27] There was, in other words, some degree of coordination and effective support within the executive branch of the government for the policy Sheldon had enunciated in his letter to the bishops.

However, for reasons to be discussed below, the king's policy toward religious suppression was far more complicated than the one of unequivocal support that he had apparently conveyed to Archbishop Sheldon. One month after issuing his declaration against the Dissenters, Charles not only pardoned the fines levied against three men arrested for refusing to attend church, he also issued orders that the remunerative penalties attached to the statute under which the men had been prosecuted would henceforth not be enforced.[28] Nevertheless, putting aside for the moment the king's ambivalent attitude toward the Dissenters, there was in 1669 a regrouping of conservatives, mostly comprising officials within the church, but also including some individuals who were, or would soon become, government ministers or influential propagandists. These men—

[24] Add. MS 19399, fol. 107. Sheldon had made an earlier attempt (in 1665) to obtain this information, but the effort in 1669 appears to have been a more comprehensive one. The first set of questions, however, did include a query as to whether the Dissenters were "well affected towards the government" (Frank Bate, *The Declaration of Indulgence, 1672*, London: Archibald Constable, 1908, p. 49).

[25] Add. MS 34769, fol. 70.

[26] Stoughton, *History of Religion*, 3:384. In the Sancroft papers, there is a document drawn up by John Brydall in July 1669, in response to an order issued by the Privy Council, which presents the legal case, largely derived from Elizabethan statutes, for the suppression of conventicles (Tanner MS 44, fol. 120).

[27] Tanner MS 44, fol. 162. Sheldon was not only a staunch Royalist, but "as a member of the Privy Council, he was an active politician" (Feiling, *Tory Party*, p. 127).

[28] Arthur Bryant, *Charles II*, London: Longmans, Green, 1931, p. 204n.

Sheldon, William Sancroft, Leoline Jenkins, John Nalson, Samuel Parker, Roger L'Estrange, Edmund Bohun, Laurence Hyde, and several others—fashioned something like a party policy designed to oppose any alteration in what they took to be the basic principles of Church and State. They maintained an informal, but discernible, defensive alliance, exercising a custodial concern for the highflying Cavalier beliefs.[29] Later, in the 1680s, these beliefs and the actions of these individuals were to supply the core of what emerged as the Tory party.[30]

Sheldon followed up his earlier requests for information with additional letters in 1670 to his bishops reiterating the importance of suppressing conventicles, and reminding them to "address themselves to the civil magistrates" for assistance in this campaign of repression. For, with "the assistance of the civil power," these "seditious" people will be brought back into "the unity of the Church and uniformity in God."[31] Early in 1670, Parliament came to the aid of the church, enacting a Second Conventicle Bill, which was designed to stiffen the penalties against Nonconformists and to encourage their enforcement. In its original draft form, the bill would simply have equated any conventicle with the definition of a "riot," thus merging completely the notion of religious dissent with political sedition and disorder—precisely the identification Parker had insisted upon at length in his *Discourse*. As finally passed, however, the law did not go this far. It empowered a single justice of the peace (in place of the two justices mandated by the original Conventicle Act of 1664) to take punitive action against Dissenters. The mere recording of the offense of nonconformity by the justice of the peace would be "taken and adjudged a full and perfect conviction" of the accused. Moreover, by providing that those who gave information leading to the conviction of Dissenters were entitled to receive one-third of the fines levied, the act supplied a public legitimization of the practice of the professional informer.[32] In addition to strengthening the penalties against religious dissent, therefore, the Conventicle Act of 1670 further heightened an atmosphere already charged with suspicion, conspiracy, and hostility. As

[29] Feiling describes the individuals at this meeting as "the Church and Cavalier Party." They were resolved to defend the present Church government and "the Cavalier interest" (*Tory Party*, p. 136; D. T. Witcombe, *Charles II and the Cavalier House of Commons, 1663–1674*, New York: Barnes and Noble, 1966, p. 92).

[30] Feiling, *Tory Party*, pp. 180–197.

[31] Add. MS 19399, fols. 113–114.

[32] For the discussion in this and the following paragraph, I am indebted to Lacey, pp. 57ff. Excerpts from the 1670 Conventicle Act are in Kenyon, *Stuart Constitution*, pp. 383–386; Costin and Watson, *Documents*, 1:36–39.

one member of Parliament commented on the bill, "here is a general distrust of the whole nation, in effect."[33]

The Conventicle Bill was attacked for the arbitrary and absolute power it placed in the hands of a single magistrate, against whose judgment the defendant could claim no judicial remedy. Such a grant of power, it was argued, which exceeded that of all other judges and juries in the kingdom in its allowance for the confiscation of an individual's property by the magistrate, was "directly against our fundamental laws." Indeed, some critics ventured so far as to issue a warning that the bill might place individuals in a situation where they would feel themselves "obliged to disobey the law" in order to uphold the principles established by the Magna Charta. In Marvell's view, this act quite simply expressed "the quintessence of arbitrary malice."[34] Despite these attacks, the law went into effect a week before Charles' signing of the secret Treaty of Dover.

Charles II's administration in 1670 was thus embarked on two courses, which were sometimes reinforcing, sometimes contradictory in their directional thrusts; acting through the Anglican church hierarchy, Parliament, and sometimes through the executive bureaucracy, the seditious conspiracy of nonconformity was to be vigorously prosecuted; while, acting through the king, the Duke of York, and some members of the Court, greater political and religious influence was to be accorded to Catholicism. The latter policy, however, could not be openly pursued, given the extreme antipathy most English subjects felt toward "the popish superstition." Charles II, therefore, was faced with the problem of undermining the first policy in order to achieve the objectives of the second; that is, by fostering the spread of Catholicism under the general cover of a toleration for Nonconformists. This political dilemma, and the ultimate consequences of Charles' moves toward toleration, were readily apparent to anyone who harbored the slightest suspicion that the Court, the Church, or both, displayed tendencies that favored the restoration of Catholicism to England. And by the 1670s, as has already been intimated, that suspicion was rather widely held by individuals of various classes and ranks in society, within and outside of the government.

Yet, if reliance can be placed on the accuracy of a document purporting to present the substance of a discussion between Charles II and his sister, Henrietta, which occurred during the week the secret Treaty of Dover was signed, then Charles' policy was a bit more complicated in its design than that encompassed by the dilemma just described. According to these

[33] Cobbett, 4:445.

[34] Lacey, pp. 60–62. William Penn also argued that the act struck "at the very foundation of our English laws and government" (Edward Beatty, *William Penn as Social Philosopher*, New York: Columbia University Press, 1939, p. 123).

notes, Charles' overall strategy was to secure a foundation for monarchical absolutism in England. The first step was to gain the Anglican church's support for the absoluteness of the king's authority through the prosecution of Nonconformists, and then, once this had been achieved, he could win the Dissenters' support for the king's supremacy in religious matters through the exercise of his prerogative to grant them toleration.[35] The two aspects of this policy would be mutually reinforcing if the persecution of Dissenters were sufficiently vigorous to make them that much more grateful and indebted to the king's indulgence when it was granted. In the summer of 1670, an intensive campaign of harassment was mounted against conventicles, which included the use of the militia in London to break up the meetings of the Nonconformists.[36] Charles confided to the French ambassador that he hoped that a strenuous enforcement of the Conventicle Act would provoke sufficient resistance by the Dissenters that it would provide him with an excuse to call up the troops to restore public order, and incidentally, thereby supply him with a standing army.[37] If the objectives of this strategy could be realized, then it might indeed be possible for Charles to achieve his political goal with respect to the monarchy. He might also be in a position, with a standing army at his disposal, to announce his commitment to Catholicism.[38]

[35] Tanner MS 44, fol. 202. In Clifford's notes and memoranda made at the time of the secret Treaty of Dover, there is support for this strategy. According to them, the king is advised to make some declaration that would "quiet the minds of the church of England . . . [and] by all means you must endeavor to keep them your friends." But, once the Anglican church has been reassured, the king could "also give assurance of liberty of conscience," which might be achieved through the use of the royal prerogative (Hartmann, *Clifford*, pp. 153–155). Thus, Charles must first gain control as the head of the established church, and, once his absolute authority in ecclesiastical matters had been granted, there would remain no grounds upon which Anglicans could register their objections to his use of that authority to grant toleration. When the second Conventicle Bill was under consideration in the House of Lords in late 1669, the king's supporters (possibly prompted by Charles himself, who was present at these debates) did in fact attempt to insert a clause into the bill that reaffirmed the absoluteness of the king's "supremacy in ecclesiastical affairs."

[36] Ogg, 1:207; Bate, *Indulgence*, pp. 68–69; *CSPD*, 10:236–237.

[37] Dalrymple, 1:44, 106. For a detailed description of the brutal tactics employed in this "strenuous enforcement" against John Hicks, later a participant in Monmouth's Rebellion, see G. L. Turner, *Original Records*, 3:586–590. For a more general discussion, see Charles F. Mullett, "Toleration and Persecution in England, 1660-1689," *Church History* 28, no. 1 (March 1949):18–43.

[38] In making preparations for the declaration of Charles' Catholicism, Clifford's notes give the highest priority to "making new fortifications and repairing the old" ones; also, the guards must be reformed and constituted of men the king can trust; existing garrisons should be strengthened, and some regiments abroad should be brought home. "There must also be an alteration of the Lord Lieutenants and deputy Lieutenants." Once these preparations had been completed, the king could turn to the religious strategy, described above

This proposed domestic triumph, according to this document, was part of a larger global policy, designed to undermine the political and economical power of the Dutch. So long as Holland was the refuge for regicides, rebels, and Republican plotters, it was argued, it would serve as "the perpetual source of rebellion in England." Thus, the destruction of the Dutch republic would have the salubrious effect of diminishing the influence and activity of "the Commonwealth faction in England." Economically, England would benefit by displacing Holland as a colonial trading power in various parts of the New World. The subsequent increase in commerce and shipping accruing to England would, in turn, attract foreign merchants, bankers, and tradesmen to her shores in order that they might invest and increase their wealth in the new trading center of the world market, and the whole process would feed upon itself, increasing the wealth and riches of England and, by that means, the power of the English sovereign.

According to his sister, when Charles heard these policies laid out for his approval, they made such a sensible impression upon him that he was transported into a kind of ecstasy.[39] Generally, Charles II's transportation into states of ecstasy was provided by less esoteric pleasures than those associated with the contemplation of global political policies. Nevertheless, there is sufficient evidence to accept this account of his strategy as a plausible explanation of the actions he actually did take. In any case, I am less concerned with attempting to determine precisely what Charles' intentions may have been than with sketching the dimensions of the political policies as those inside and outside the government perceived them in 1670. And, with respect to that question, it must be conceded that, even admitting the accuracy of this sketch of Charles' foreign and domestic policy, few of his contemporaries could have pieced together its fragmentary elements into a single unified whole, although as we shall see, it is just possible that sometime around 1675 Shaftesbury was in a position to perceive all the basic aspects of this grand design.

One feature of the turn toward an intensification of political repression that did accord with Charles II's anti-Dutch foreign policy was a Repub-

(Hartmann, *Clifford*, pp. 153–155). During the period of negotiations of the secret treaty, Charles wrote to his sister: "I am securing all the principal ports of this country, not only by fortifying them as they ought to be, but likewise, the keeping them in such hands as I am sure will be faithful to me upon all occasions" (Hartmann, *Charles and Madame*, p. 254). It was also suggested that the Dutch War would give Charles "a pretext for keeping up troops outside your kingdom" and the existence of these troops under the king's command would keep Parliament in check and render it "more amenable" than it has been (pp. 279–280).

[39] Tanner MS 44, fol. 203.

lican scare in 1669–1670; that is, an increased fear of the real or imagined activities of the Commonwealthmen in England. Rumors suddenly circulated that General Ludlow had returned to England, that London was full of old Cromwellian soldiers, and that there was "some great and evil design on foot." In late November 1669, even Andrew Marvell reported the general belief that "Commonwealthmen flock about the town," holding "dangerous meetings."[40] Archbishop Sheldon demanded a "speedy" report from his bishops on the activities of the Dissenters because he "presumed" that they were as "alarmed with continued reports of the frequency of open conventicles and unlawful meetings" as he was. In the draft of his letter, Sheldon referred to the "great disorders and disturbances" caused by the Nonconformists "and others disaffected to the government of the Church."[41] These fears and rumors stemmed from the presence in London at the end of 1669 of nearly twenty thousand Cromwellian soldiers, many of whom were unemployed, and who were therefore thought to be ready to take up arms against the government.[42] Yet, neither Sidney nor Ludlow were in England, and a number of formerly militant officers were still in prison. No one has uncovered evidence indicating that any rising was being planned. Nevertheless, Charles issued a proclamation on June 10, 1670, ordering all cashiered soldiers to depart from London by June 16, and not to return before mid-December.[43]

Throughout the 1660s, efforts were made by government and Church authorities to link Dissenters with republicanism as part of a campaign to suppress dissent.[44] An abortive Fifth Monarchist uprising led by Thomas Venner in 1661, and another planned rising in 1663, provided the pretext for the politically repressive statutes of the Clarendon Code.[45] The cries against Republicans engaged in "disorders" in 1669 thus appear to have

[40] Marvell, *Works*, 2:290–292; Bate, *Indulgence*, p. 65; Maurice Lee, Jr., *The Cabal*, Urbana: University of Illinois Press, 1965, p. 179.

[41] Add. MS 34769, fol. 70; MS Add. c.308, fol. 142, Bodleian Library. In 1670, a band of marauders calling themselves Levellers terrorized the countryside in Worcestershire and attracted considerable attention (Max Beloff, *Public Order and Popular Disturbances, 1660-1714*, London: Oxford University Press, 1938, p. 23).

[42] Dalrymple, 1:91–92.

[43] *CSPD*, 10:267. On the enforcement of the proclamation, see Westergaard, *Triple Alliance*, p. 259.

[44] Stoughton, *History of Religion*, 3:321, 461; G. L. Turner, *Original Records*, 3:42; James Walker, "Dissent and Republicanism after the Restoration," *Baptist Quarterly* 8, no. 5 (January 1937):263–280.

[45] Bate, *Indulgence*, pp. 16, 44–45; Ogg, 1:208–209; Henry Gee, "The Derwentdale Plot, 1663," *Transactions of the Royal Historical Society*, 3d ser. 11 (1917):125–142. More than 4,000 Quakers were imprisoned in the wake of Venner's uprising (Clark, *Later Stuarts*, p. 20). Venner's son and some of those involved in the Derwentdale plot later participated in Monmouth's Rebellion.

signaled the renewed efforts of the Church and State to persecute Dissenters. In this specific case and in general, the charges were without substance, but there was a self-fulfilling quality to them, so that by the 1680s, it was true that a very large proportion of those who comprised the radical political movement were Dissenters in their religious beliefs. This is not to minimize the fact that, throughout the Restoration period, there were indeed individuals inside and outside of England who were engaged in plotting against the government, nor can the latter's less subtle responses to these individuals be ignored.[46] Nevertheless, the fact remains that, for their own political purposes, Church and State authorities helped to create a political atmosphere of conspiracy, suspicion, and rebellion which, in the following decade, not only became the pervasive framework of political discussion, but also assumed a degree of reality that not even the government had anticipated.

In 1669, Charles II's administration was deeply in debt. Both the debt and a general awareness of its existence had been growing for several years. A new Treasury commission had been appointed in 1667 to look into the government's disastrous financial condition following the Second Dutch War. One estimation placed the level of indebtness at £2,500,000. Various schemes of retrenchment in expenditure or to provide greater efficiency in the collection of revenues were offered, and in some instances were adopted.[47] At best, these measures could stabilize expenditures; they would never, in the foreseeable future, remove the government's existing indebtedness. By late 1669, precisely at the moment the secret negotiations for the Treaty of Dover were going forward, it had become clear to Charles that only a very considerable expansion in trade could improve the government's revenues to the point where it might escape from its Sisyphean fate of borrowing and indebtedness.[48]

[46] Several assassination attempts were made upon Ludlow and Sidney in the 1660s, and, in 1664, John Lisle, one of Ludlow's associates, was murdered in Switzerland (Edmund Ludlow, *Memoirs*, 2 vols., Oxford: Clarendon Press, 1894, 1:xliv–xlv; W. C. Abbott, "English Conspiracy and Dissent, 1660–1674, II," *American Historical Review* [July 1909], pp. 696–722). In August 1670, Sir William Temple, the English ambassador to Holland, personally supervised an unsuccessful attempt to seize Cornet Joyce in Rotterdam (William Temple, *Works*, 4 vols., 1814, 2:144–152).

[47] Lee, *Cabal*, pp. 130–132, 146. Although there were several concurring and obvious reasons that economizing measures had to be taken by the government, it has been suggested that Charles ordered a comprehensive review of government expenditure in order to determine precisely to what degree he was financially dependent upon parliamentary support (Ogg, 1:340).

[48] Lee, *Cabal*, p. 136; Lacey, p. 59. Referring to the Third Dutch War, J. R. Jones observes that "the real aim of the war was to free Charles from dependence on parliament and his subjects" (*Country and Court*, p. 106).

When the king greeted Parliament in February 1670, he told them:

> When we last met I asked you for a supply, and I ask it now again with greater instance. The uneasiness and straightness of my affairs cannot continue without very ill effects to the whole kingdom. Consider this seriously and speedily. It is yours and the kingdom's interest as well as mine, and the ill consequences of a want of an effectual supply must not lie at my door. And that no misapprehensions or mistakes touching the expenses of the late war remain with you, I . . . do affirm to you that no part of those moneys that you gave to me for that war have been diverted to other uses, but on the contrary, besides all those supplies a very great sum hath been raised out of my standing revenue and credit, and a very great debt contracted, and all for the war.[49]

In response to this plea, some funds (£400,000) were voted by Parliament, but the amount was insufficient even to mobilize the naval fleet that England was pledged to raise for the war against the Dutch. In the end, the king was forced to resort to two short-term expedients in order to raise the revenue the government required. Knowing the fierce hostility toward France that many members of Parliament had voiced during the debates on the supply bill, Charles warned the Commons that if they did not vote him sufficient funds to carry on the war, the French would proceed against the Dutch without England's assistance, and Parliament would then be faced with an even more powerful and fearful monarch, upon whose generous feelings toward its partner in the alliance they could hardly hope to pledge the safety of the country. In short, it was essential that, given the Treaty of Dover, England uphold its share of the war effort, as much to achieve its objective against the Dutch as to protect its rear flanks from the French.[50] And for this, more money would have to be granted by Parliament. This argument carried some weight, but it hardly improved any long-term prospects for cementing an alliance with France that Charles might have entertained. English feeling toward the Dutch might blow hot and cold, but throughout the 1670s and 1680s, fear and hostility toward France were fairly constant and important elements of English political life. Charles II's appeal for funds, though partially

[49] Cobbett, 4:442. Charles had, in fact, spent some of his household revenue on the war. But in his memorandum, Clifford had suggested that £100,000 could be "reserved . . . without suspicion" from the funds appropriated for the navy, to be used by Charles in carrying out "the grand design" of a conversion to Catholicism (Hartmann, *Clifford*, p. 153).

[50] Lee, *Cabal*, p. 144.

successful, did little to assuage, let alone reverse, this Francophobic attitude.

The long-term consequences of the second expedient are much more difficult to gauge. The government's debt was primarily owed to a handful of financiers and bankers who had lent it money—often at high rates of interest—and who were repaid out of future incoming revenues from the customs, excise, hearth, or other taxes. Because these sources of revenue had been pledged for the repayment of past debts so far into the future—eighteen months, according to one estimate—Charles II's administration had, in effect, no current cash funds at its disposal, other than what it could obtain from further borrowing from the bankers or from special appropriations granted by Parliament. By the end of 1671, it was obvious that Parliament's reluctance to vote the kind of supply requested by the king made it impossible to depend upon that body for any solution to the government's serious financial problems. Despite opposition from most members of his Privy Council, Charles decided in January 1672 to suspend the repayment of the government's debt, thus freeing the incoming revenue for current expenditures for war supplies. Once this step was taken, there was of course sufficient money available to prosecute the war. And given the economic constraints upon Charles II's administration, the gamble upon an early military victory over the Dutch and the financial rewards such a victory carried with it was not entirely farfetched, viewed purely in economic terms.

It is interesting, therefore, that Shaftesbury, who was Lord Chancellor, and among the king's ministers the most vociferous opponent of this Stop of the Exchequer, generally conceded the short-term economic benefits of the move, but he argued on constitutional grounds that it would do the goverment irreparable harm. It was, he asserted, a form of confiscation of private property effected through arbitrary action, and as such it violated the basic principles of law and justice upon which a constitutional government was founded. The king's action would, therefore, seriously undermine the confidence that merchants, tradesmen, and bankers would in future place in the government, and, especially in the king's commitments to them. The credit of the government, Shaftesbury argued, ought not to be bargained away for short-term economic gain, for if businessmen once lost their confidence in the government, it might not be recovered for years.[51] In short, it was a policy fraught with peril insofar as it opened a wedge of mistrust between an important sector of the community and the government.

Confidence in "the King's own word" was badly shaken by the Stop of

[51] Haley, pp. 295–296, 307n.

the Exchequer, and as one contemporary writer put it, "the common faith of a nation [was] violated."[52] Even as late as 1693, Lord Halifax could reflect that the damaging consequences following "the breach of the Exchequer credit by King Charles" had made "men very shy of parting with their money" with respect to the underwriting of government projects.[53] Shaftesbury's general prediction, therefore, was certainly true in the sense that during the 1670s many merchants and financiers developed an increasing sense of alienation from the political policies they associated with Charles II and the Court.[54] How much of this drift away from the government owed its origins to Charles' action in stopping repayment of the debt (or more generally, to the 1670 alliance with France) and how much of it was due to other factors is hard to say. The charge levelled by some contemporaries that all bankers and merchants were Commonwealthmen was absurd, although viewed with hindsight, it, too, is not without its self-fulfilling prophetic features with respect to the development of a radical political movement in the 1680s, to which members of this social group made a significant contribution.

The House of Lords committee, which had been appointed in the fall of 1669 to consider "the fall of rents and decay of trade within the kingdom," recommended in its report that "some ease and relaxation in ecclesiastical matters will be a means of improving the trade of this kingdom."[55] This belief that Protestantism and commercial expansion were mutually compatible and that religious toleration was an important encouragement to the advancement of trade formed a crucial element in the political consciousness of Restoration England. Even so, Parliament was not inclined to translate this widely held belief into legislation. Charles II, however, in 1672 exercised his royal prerogative to grant an indulgence to Nonconformists, suspending the enforcement of the penal laws against both Dissenters and Catholics.

For reasons already alluded to, this action by the king set the cat among the pigeons so far as the Dissenters were concerned. Some of them were

[52] Lipson, *Economic History*, 3: 236. Evelyn recorded in his diary that the king's action "lost the hearts of his subjects" and seriously damaged the credit of the government. And, the latter's credit "being thus broken did exceedingly discontent the people" (John Evelyn, *The Diary of John Evelyn*, ed. E. S. De Beer, 6 vols., Oxford: Clarendon Press, 1955, 3:607). Five of the largest bankers shortly thereafter suffered bankruptcy (C. Wilson, *Apprenticeship*, p. 215).

[53] Lipson, *Economic History*, 3:240.

[54] Chandaman, *Public Revenue*, p. 18; Margaret Priestley, "London Merchants and Opposition Politics in Charles II's Reign," *Bulletin of the Institute of Historical Research* 29, no. 80 (November 1956):205–219.

[55] Haley, pp. 256–257. Shaftesbury was appointed a member of this committee on October 25, 1669.

reluctant to concede that the king *had* the constitutional power to suspend the law through an act of his arbitrary will, even when the consequences of such an action carried obvious political benefits for themselves. Others who might have been willing to support the king in the exercise of his prerogative were extremely suspicious of the fact that Catholics would benefit from this policy of toleration, and that, in itself, was sufficient reason for them to attack the indulgence. Still other Dissenters suspected that the latter was merely a temporary political stratagem designed to stifle their opposition to the Dutch War. Indeed, this much was conceded by one of Charles II's ministers, though of course not publicly. The purpose of "the late Declaration His Majesty hath made in favor of the nonconformists," Arlington wrote, "was that we might keep all quiet at home whilst we are busiest abroad."[56] Nevertheless, while they certainly were not ignorant of these aspects of the king's policy, most Dissenters were willing to accept the relief from persecution the law offered them on straightforward pragmatic grounds. As one of them put it: We have faced fines, imprisonment, seizure of our property, banishment, and even death; the indulgence "defends us" from these actions. Why should we not accept it?[57] The Presbyterians, for example, came in a body to express their gratitude to the king for the Act of Indulgence. John Owen, on behalf of the Independents, also presented an address thanking Charles for establishing toleration. Other Dissenters wrote tracts in defense of the lawfulness of the king's power in ecclesiastical affairs, or persuading Dissenters that there was nothing in their religious or political beliefs that prevented them from "receiving the fruit and benefit of the King's . . . favor and indulgence."[58]

Simmering just beneath the surface of the political debate over trade, Catholicism, toleration, and the alliance with France, was the inveterate issue of a standing army. One of the first parliamentary acts of the Restoration had placed the control of the militia in the king's hands.[59] At the time, no serious objections were voiced against this action, perhaps because everyone was conscious of the fact that divisiveness over this issue had been a precipitant cause of the Civil War. However, as the chasm be-

[56] Ashley, *Charles II*, p. 187. The declaration of war was issued two days after the Declaration of Indulgence.

[57] Lacey, pp. 65–66; Bate, *Indulgence*, pp. 88ff.

[58] Stoughton, *History of Religion*, 3:398–399. It is estimated that 3,500 licenses were granted to Nonconformists in the space of ten months. A list of those receiving licenses is printed as appendix 7 to Bate, *Indulgence*.

[59] Costin and Watson, *Documents*, 1:17–20. For a discussion of the importance of this issue during the seventeenth century, see Lois G. Schwoerer, *No Standing Armies: The Antiarmy Ideology in Seventeenth-Century England*, Baltimore: Johns Hopkins University Press, 1974, especially chap. 6.

tween king and Parliament widened toward the end of the first decade of Charles II's reign, the existence of and control over the armed forces became an increasingly contentious issue. Looking back in 1679 on how matters had developed to that point, Roger Morrice recorded in his journal that, in passing the Second Militia Act, Parliament had "violated the fundamental laws of the kingdom and had assisted arbitrary power . . . by declaring the militia to be in the power of the king solely which never Parliament before had done."[60]

When Parliament assembled on February 14, 1670, Charles II was attended to the House of Lords with full military honors. Whether the king's appearance was intended "to accustom the people to the idea of a standing army," some members of Parliament subsequently came to view Charles' actions within that context during the 1680s.[61] While he was engaged in the negotiations of the secret Treaty of Dover, Charles had quietly placed the control of various forts and arsenals in the hands of officers he felt he could trust absolutely, a tactic he later employed with great effect during the exclusion crisis.[62] In fact, through the Militia Act passed by the Scottish Parliament, Charles II had already acquired twenty-two thousand troops who, at his disposal, were committed "to oppose invasions, to suppress insurrections, or for any other cause in which his authority, power, or greatness was concerned."[63] In 1673, the Duke of Lauderdale, the king's minister in Scotland, had reportedly been so indiscreet as to suggest that these Scottish troops might be used to silence the parliamentary opposition. Such statements only fueled the already widely held belief that the very existence of this army under the king's command represented an attempt to alter the English Constitution. In any case, Lauderdale's suggestion was used as the basis for the impeachment proceedings against him organized by the parliamentary opposition.[64] The Commons simultaneously drew up a petition against a standing army, which they presented to the king. And, by the time Morrice made his journal notation, Parliament had attempted through legislation to remove the militia from Charles' control.[65]

In the decade beginning in 1670, therefore, there was a cluster of prob-

[60] Lacey, p. 34.

[61] Airy, *Charles II*, p. 167.

[62] Bryant, *Charles II*, p. 206; Hartmann, *Charles and Madame*, p. 254.

[63] Lee, *Cabal*, p. 39.

[64] Ashley, *Charles II*, pp. 198, 200; Haley, pp. 340-341; Schwoerer, *No Standing Armies*, p. 105.

[65] At the end of November 1678, Parliament passed a bill that placed the militia under its control, which prompted Charles to use his veto for the first time (Bryant, *Charles II*, p. 278).

lems to which a significant proportion of the participants in political life directed their attention. The question of an alliance with France, the spread of or return to Catholicism, religious toleration, advancement of trade, the prospects of a standing army—these were not issues that could be viewed as lying within the normal day-to-day sphere of administrative decisions.[66] It is true that these problems and their solutions were sometimes viewed by Charles as matters lying wholly within the province of the king's personal authority, at least as an ultimate goal with respect to his conception of the monarchy, but even he knew, as a matter of political reality, that there was widespread opposition to this political perspective among his subjects. Each of these problems was embedded in a network of interlocking issues with potentially far-reaching implications. They were, in other words, matters of constitutional importance, relating to fundamental questions concerning the nature of government, political obligation, and the use of violence to achieve political objectives.

I am not suggesting that a rigid dichotomy ought to be drawn between policy and constitutional issues. On the contrary, it is essential to insist upon the point that these problems must be seen as having arisen out of the ordinary policy-making process of political life in seventeenth-century England. Nevertheless, these particular topics possessed a special significance insofar as they indicate the parameters of the political consciousness of England in the 1670s, as I have tried to sketch it briefly in this chapter. At the same time, it is also important to show that the constitutional significance of these problems is not merely a post facto reconstruction of the historian. The political actors themselves recognized and articulated the deep-seated implications of these problems with respect to the stability of the social order. Of course, not all social groups were equally sensitive to all issues, and many individuals experienced shifts and reversals in their attitude toward one or more of these problems during the 1670s. Not until the end of that decade did a definite convergence and alignment begin to take shape in the form of an organizational effort to unite those elements of society whose political perspective placed them in opposition to the actions of the king and Court with respect to the issues discussed above. As we shall see in the next chapter, the ideological basis for this organizational unity was already available in the form of the arguments, concepts, and language of the political debate of the 1670s that focused upon the issue of religious toleration.

Charles II had concluded a secret treaty with France in which he promised to espouse Catholicism, which as a religious/political doctrine would provide the ideological foundations for the English monarchy as an ab-

[66] Ogg, 1:379–380.

solutist institution. He had decided upon a war against the Dutch in order to improve the prospects for English colonial trade, and through an exercise of the royal prerogative, he enforced a Stop of the Exchequer in order to acquire the funds necessary to prosecute this war. Charles sought the means to free himself from financial dependence upon Parliament as a matter of general policy. He extended indulgence to Nonconformists, including Catholics, through the use of his prerogative. And he took special care to preserve and extend his control over the militia and the armed forces. All of these actions could be, and eventually were, viewed as forming a pattern or tendency that propelled England along a course toward absolutism and arbitrary rule, thus threatening the continued existence of constitutional government. How such a political perspective came to express the political thinking of those thousands of individuals who participated in a revolutionary political movement in the 1680s is a question to which we shall address ourselves in the chapters that follow.

2
IDEOLOGICAL DIMENSIONS OF DISSENT

By 1670, the major points of controversy in the debate over the toleration of different religious beliefs were well known. The arguments and issues had been formulated during the English Civil War thirty years previously, and some of them, of course, could claim an even more ancient heritage. In this sense, a renewed political demand for toleration or an increased effort to suppress religious dissent simply released developed patterns of response and counterresponse. Participants in the theoretical conflict, like experienced chess players, drew upon an inherited stock of moves and gambits to defeat their opponents. Yet, as in a chess match, there remained an essential indeterminacy, not only as regards the outcome, but also with respect to the particular style and character of each new confrontation.

It is important to grasp the interplay of forces that constitutes this determined indeterminacy of political debate. There is, on the one hand, a cultural dimension to ideology, in which assumptions, concepts, and arguments appear to be effortlessly carried forward through time. Ideas are borrowed from earlier thinkers, the same principles are cited and defended through an appeal to familiar authorities, and so on. In short, a tradition of thought—or rather (viewing the debate as a whole), several traditions of thought—emerge, and these traditions come to be associated with a certain set of problems. This situation is likely to persist at least until these problems have been solved.[1]

[1] As indicated in the Introduction, I regard this statement about the relationship between political theory and political problems as a historical generalization. Some political theorists have insisted that there are perennial or timeless issues at the center of political life and thought. Not only does this position remove all historicity from the problems (and the concepts that deal with them), but it does so without providing any standards for discriminating among an infinite number of timeless issues that could conceivably characterize the structure of political theory. It is hardly surprising, therefore, that none of the adherents of this viewpoint feels compelled to explain on the basis of what evidence he has assigned timeless values to some political concepts (e.g., "liberty" or "private property") and not to others (e.g., "divine right of kings," "slavery," or "class conflict"). On the other hand, practical solutions to political problems do not invariably assume the form of theoretical resolutions, nor do they always provoke an extended theoretical debate. Moreover, it sometimes happens that, as the consequence of the political triumph of one group or party over others, the theoretical formulation of the problem will disappear. And, in a broader sense, this might also be the consequence of the internal disintegration or disappearance of the social group

How these problems are solved is, in the context of the contending possibilities that shape the political struggle among existing social groups, indeterminate; certainly, at least, from the standpoint of the theoretical claims associated with any particular tradition of thought. What is crucial for understanding this dimension of ideology is a mass of specific information, intricately bound up with the organizational relationships that obtain among the various social groups. It is this organizational or political dimension of ideology that is too often overlooked for the sake of preserving the cogency of a historical narrative in which the outcome of this political struggle is already known. This sense of organizational contingency is especially difficult to recapture when one is writing about revolutionary movements that failed to achieve their objectives.[2] The temptation for the historian to evaluate such movements as having been lost causes from the outset is a formidable barrier to the kind of detailed examination of the movement's internal organization, in relation to its external opposing forces, which is a necessary precondition for restoring some sense of the indeterminacy actually experienced by the historical actors themselves. It is true that in a political atmosphere marked by the tendency to see a conspiracy or an uprising everywhere, those endeavors which embody genuine organizational possibilities are not always easily distinguishable from those conspiracies which are merely the expression of the paranoid fears of particular individuals or groups. For this reason, careful attention paid to the problems of organization helps to provide a firm ground from which to assess the hopes and fears of contemporaries concerning the likelihood of revolutionary change in their society.

Depending upon how one views the phenomenon, therefore, a particular political debate, such as the one concerning toleration in the 1670s, might appear to be structured entirely by theories and ideas that were already there, in the sense of being available to the historical participants. Alternatively, one might attach a special importance to this specific debate, less because what was said was necessarily original, than because, as a matter of fact, it provided the impetus for those organizational activities which are, in themselves, of historical significance. It should be obvious

---

that supplied the existential support for a specific set of arguments. In short, although it can be maintained as an empirical generalization that political theory is always tied to and emerges out of set of concrete political problems, any postulated relationship between a theoretical debate and a practical solution to those political problems must be assessed on the basis of a specific historical investigation.

[2] I apologize for the use of an inelegant phrase like "organizational contingency," but this is due in part to the fact that I regard the effort to organize large numbers of people to engage in political action (marches, demonstrations, revolutions) as a generic sociological phenomenon for which there is no suitable metaphor; and, in part, I wish to emphasize that it is just this action, whether people are organized or not, that is indeterminate.

that one need not be faced with an either/or choice as rigid as this analytical distinction might appear to suggest, but it does need to be stressed that there is a shift in emphasis as one moves from one perspective to the other.

As the Introduction suggested, I will attempt to give due emphasis to both aspects of ideology as they relate to the development of Locke's political theory. This means, on the one hand, indicating what stock of ideas and assumptions were available to Locke upon which he could draw in order to formulate a theoretical response to a certain set of problems; and on the other, it involves a consideration of those beliefs and arguments insofar as they are specifically necessary features of an explanatory account as to why such individuals as Locke engaged in particular forms of organizational activity that they believed would produce a solution to those problems.

In this chapter, therefore, I will sketch the outlines of a political debate in the 1670s that focused upon the problem of the toleration of religious dissent, but that in its totality actually encompassed a much broader range of contested issues than the notion of toleration might suggest at first glance. Both the intensity with which the arguments were advanced and the wide-ranging quality of the arguments themselves were, I shall argue, significant stimulants to the development of a political consciousness which, by the 1680s, had become increasingly distrustful of efforts to mediate through practical compromises the differences between those holding opposing theoretical positions. I am not suggesting that subsequent attempts to make a revolution ought to be viewed as the inevitable outcome of this debate, but I am saying that it did call forth both the specific arguments and the general intellectual framework constitutive of a political perspective in which revolution is viewed in the context of self-defense, and also, that it heightened the necessity for threatened groups (initially the Dissenters, but later other groups as well) to develop some practical organizational means of defending themselves.

In Chapter 3, I will consider the importance of the issues raised in this political debate with specific reference to Locke's political thinking and activity during the 1670s. In addition, however, the latter must be viewed in conjunction with Locke's role as a personal friend and trusted adviser to the leading opposition politician during this period, Lord Shaftesbury. A discussion of that relationship will, in turn, lead to a more general assessment of the nature of the political forces that Shaftesbury forged into a powerful weapon to be wielded against the established authorities of Church and State.

Although, in retrospect, Samuel Parker's *Discourse of Ecclesiastical Polity* is so provocative in its use of abusive language that it can hardly appear surprising that it provoked numerous replies, it is highly unlikely that it formed part of Parker's intention to offer the *Discourse* as a contribution to an intellectual debate about the merits of toleration. The fundamental assumption underlying the "vehemence and severity" of Parker's language was that opponents of the absolute authority of the king in matters of Church and State were, quite simply, not rational beings. The object, therefore, was to "silence them," not to reason with them.[3] Such persons were "wild and savage," and what was worse, they were "unalterably resolved never to be convinced" of the "truths" Parker was defending. Hence, he had no illusions concerning his own ability "to pierce their thick and inveterate prejudices," nor did he expect their conversion to his viewpoint. What they required, he insisted, was a zealous dose of punishment.[4]

We must "root up" the principles propagated by the Dissenters, Parker argued, "and brand and punish all persons that publicly profess them."[5] Since he believed the multitude to be "wild and unreasonable," and in general incapable of thinking, it was not necessary to punish them for merely imbibing the mistakes of their ministers.[6] However, severe punishment directed against "a few ringleaders" would do much to calm the masses; it "will quickly scare them into better obedience."[7]

Though Parker did offer an argument of sorts against the Dissenters' position, he was convinced that the latter did not really possess any substance. Thus, in the last analysis, dissent from authority was essentially an expression of "willfulness"; that is, a manifestation of willful disobedience.[8] Since he was defending the absoluteness of the will of the Sovereign, for Parker, there was clearly no room whatsoever for the tolerance of dissent. However starkly or softly the point was phrased, the only alternatives to complete obedience were silence and imprisonment.

John Owen, leader of the Independents, tried to persuade Richard Baxter to write a reply to Parker's *Discourse*. Failing in this, Owen himself undertook the task of stating the Dissenters' case in *Truth and Innocency*

[3] Samuel Parker, *Discourse of Ecclesiastical Polity*, [1669], p. ix. Other critics pursued this theme, declaring that Dissenters were incapable of conducting or understanding a rational argument. See C. E. Whiting, *Studies in English Puritanism from the Restoration to the Revolution, 1660-1688*, London: Society for Promoting Christian Knowledge, 1931, p. 512.

[4] Parker, *Discourse*, pp. x, xii. The state ought to "punish them with the severest inflictions" (p. 18).

[5] Samuel Parker, *A Defence and Continuation of the Ecclesiastical Polity*, 1671, p. 541.

[6] Parker, *Discourse*, p. xlii; cf. ibid., pp. ii, 7, 13, 15, 21-23.

[7] Parker, *Defence*, p. 117.

[8] Parker, *Discourse*, pp. xii, 105.

Vindicated.[9] He deplored Parker's "new way" of arguing, in which "a direct and particular debate of the matters specially in difference" between the Nonconformists and the Anglican church was rejected in favor of an "unparalleled heap" of "invectives" and abuse directed against the former.[10] Moreover, this tactic was adopted, Owen charged, for the sole purpose of trying to make it appear that "mere dissent itself" is, ipso facto, politically subversive.[11] Parker's "purpose was to expose [the Dissenters] to persecutions, or to the severity of penal laws from the magistrate, and, if possible . . . to popular rage and fury."[12]

Other Dissenters echoed Owen's amazement at the ferocity of Parker's attack.[13] In *The Authority of the Magistrate about Religion Discussed,* John Humfrey labeled the *Discourse* a barbarous work, "breaking the hedge of what is Sacred, laying open the enclosures of all morality and civility in making the worthy common and level with the infamous." It was, he suggested, an "affront" to "the whole nation" that such a book should be published. If, Humfrey wrote, it is a basic principle of justice that every man " is bound to defend his neighbor from injury (so far as he can) as well as do him none," then all of us have an obligation to condemn Parker's violation of this precept of natural justice.[14] Humfrey's metaphorical response is interesting because it reveals what he and others took to be the exceptional nature of this new attempt to suppress religious dissent. Disagreements, like occasional violations of property rights, are bound to arise in civil society, but so long as there is a basic respect for the principle of private property or for the rationality of individuals, such conflicts can be peacefully resolved. Parker, however, had clearly gone beyond these normal boundaries of civility in his *Discourse*, and by "break-

[9] William Orme, *Memoirs of the Life, Writings, and Religious Connections of John Owen*, 1820, p. 339. Baxter thought Owen did a good job of answering Parker, and that the former's esteem among the Nonconformists was greatly enhanced because of his reply (*Life of Richard Baxter*, ed. Matthew Sylvester, 1696, pt. 3, p. 42; but see note 25 below).

[10] John Owen, *Truth and Innocency Vindicated: In a Survey of a Discourse Concerning Ecclesiastical Polity*, 1669, pp. 2–3, 11. The *Discourse*, Owen charged, was both a "novel and uncouth" work (p. 4). To Baxter, Parker's writings were a "most voluminous torrent of . . . malicious rhetoric" (R. Baxter, *Life*, pt. 3, p. 42).

[11] Owen, *Truth*, pp. 153, 401.

[12] Owen, *Truth*, p. 61; R. Baxter, *Life*, pt. 3, p. 142.

[13] Parker's *Discourse*, Baxter observed, was written more scornfully and virulently against the Nonconformists than any other book he had ever known (R. Baxter, *Life*, pt. 3, p. 41). See also Burnet, 1:467.

[14] John Humfrey, *The Authority of the Magistrate about Religion Discussed*, 1672, pp. 6–7. Slingsby Bethel, in *The Present Interest of England Stated*, 1671, commented that Parker's "railing principles" were such a departure from the normal boundaries of discourse that his book was an embarrassment to the defenders of the Anglican church (p. 35).

ing the hedge" of a rational debate over principles, he had placed himself in a state of war with his opponents.

Despite Parker's subsequent rejoinder that he was "neither fierce nor abusive" in his temperament, there can be little doubt that the Dissenters read his intentions correctly.[15] He had, after all, referred to them as "enemies and outlaws to human society," suggesting that the nation's welfare might be best preserved "by cutting off such persons as are pests and enemies to it."[16] Moreover, the fact that the *Discourse* obviously had the approval of Archbishop Sheldon, coupled with the propensity of some magistrates to respond enthusiastically to this authoritative endorsement of persecution, meant that the state of war in which Dissenters had been placed in 1670 necessitated a practical response on their part that went beyond the publication of tracts refuting the arguments advanced by their Anglican critics. Parker's *Discourse of Ecclesiastical Polity*, as Owen observed, represented "a new way" of confronting the issue of toleration, one in which appeals to the truth of some of the Dissenters' beliefs might turn out to be wholly ineffectual against "dogmatical assertions" backed by the force of political power.[17] Indeed, Parker actually went so far as to license a book in which it was claimed that an individual had been murdered by Anabaptists in New England as part of his campaign to stir up public feeling against the Nonconformists. Both the incident and much else in the book were spurious. Upon complaint to the king by William Kiffin, the leader of the Anabaptists in London, Parker was forced to confess the truth.[18]

If Parker's intentions were plain, the substantive theoretical proposition he defended in the *Discourse* was also deceptively simple: The Sovereign's will is absolute with respect to all actions of individuals within civil society. It is a deceptively simple thesis because, while it receives nothing like the depth of intellectual support accorded to it by Hobbes in *Leviathan*, it is polemically employed by Parker as the axis from which he launched a broad-gauge assault upon virtually all of the elements that comprised the intellectual framework of the Dissenters' perspective. Thus, he challenges their view of the origins of government, their definition of "conscience," their belief in "reason," their assumptions about morality, revelation, natural law, their epistemological distinction between faith and knowledge, their philosophical arguments concerning "will" and "understanding," and so on. Parker repeatedly heaps abuse upon the merchants, tradesmen, and "arrogant mechanics" who provide

15 Parker, *Defence*, preface.

16 Parker, *Discourse*, pp. vi, 221.

17 Owen, *Truth*, pp. 2, 9.

18 R. Baxter, *Life*, pt. 3, p. 106.

the social support for religious dissent. The *Discourse*, in other words, makes up for what it lacks in the way of a detailed reasoned defense of its own presuppositions through a comprehensive attack upon the existential and theoretical dimensions of dissent.

Owen tried to be equally comprehensive in his reply, but his work was merely one of many critiques of the *Discourse*. Other writers fastened upon some particular aspect of Parker's argument, such as the nature of reason or morality, the limits of knowledge, or the Sovereign's authority, in order to discuss these issues in greater detail than Owen had done in *Truth and Innocency*. Many of these tracts were, in turn, answered by others, thus giving birth to several subsidiary debates focused around a specific topic. Parker's book, therefore, unleashed a flood of pamphlets, many of which explored the various tangents of the central argument of the *Discourse*. In this respect, as well as for the severity of its language, it was an epochal work viewed in terms of the development of a radical political consciousness during the last third of the seventeenth century.[19]

For Parker, either one accepted "the Divine Institution of government," or one held that all political power is reducible to the exercise of force.[20] The nature of this "divine appointment" is left suitably vague. Although he subscribes to a theory of paternal authority with respect to the origins of government, Parker never asserts, in so many words or with scriptural citations, that either divine appointment or patriarchal authority is necessarily part of man's inheritance from Adam. Instead, he presents divine appointment as part of "the constitution of human nature" as created by God.[21] This proposition elides into one affirming that God created individuals in a state of subjection to parents.[22] Thus, "the first governments in the world were established purely upon the natural right of paternal authority, which afterward grew up to a kingly power by the increase of posterity." The civil magistrate began as the father of a family, but as families multiplied, he became the ruler of a city.

> And hence it came to pass that in the first ages of the world, monarchy was its only government, necessarily arising out of the Con-

[19] Nearly twenty years later, Ferguson was still berating Parker's *Discourse*, singling it out as the work that, more than any other, was responsible for the troubles and persecutions of the Dissenters (Robert Ferguson, *A Representation of the Threatening Dangers*, 1688, p. 37 [*LL* #2467]). This was also the view of William Denton in *Some Remarks Recommended unto Ecclesiastics of All Persuasions*, p. 16. This tract was published in 1689 and was included with Denton's *Jus Regiminis: Being a Justification of Defensive Arms in General*.

[20] Parker, *Discourse*, p. xxxv.

[21] Parker, *Discourse*, p. 122.

[22] Parker, *Discourse*, p. 124.

stitution of human nature; it being so natural for families to enlarge themselves into cities by uniting into a body.[23]

The reader will search in vain through the hundreds of pages of the *Discourse of Ecclesiastical Polity*, or through those of its *Defence and Continuation*, for any elaboration or a more sophisticated version of this account of the origins of government. Indeed, the *Discourse* is a rather remarkable work for its ability to avoid touching upon *any* of the intricacies or subtleties attached to either the divine appointment or the patriarchal explanations of the origin of legitimate authority. Parker asserted a political orthodoxy in its barest essentials, and proposed either to ignore or to beat down anyone who crossed over that line under the pretense of having a better political theory. The justification of a policy of political repression had no need for such gratuitously complicated, and more important, unreliable weapons. It was clear to him that either one was a supporter of monarchy, in which case one acknowledged that the king was "vested with an absolute and uncontrollable power," or one was a "zealous Commonwealthman" and part of a "republican faction."[24]

John Owen was hardly in the best position to refute this charge, having been a prominent Commonwealthman.[25] Instead, he took the higher ground in his reply, leaving the precise form—and even the origins—of government indeterminate, but insisting that there were obligations imposed upon individuals by the Law of Nature that no civil magistrate could set aside by an act of his will.[26] "We say," Owen declared, "that

[23] Parker, *Discourse*, pp. 29, 31.

[24] Parker, *Defence*, pp. 255, 635–636; *Discourse*, p. xxxiv.

[25] In addition to his having been Oliver Cromwell's chaplain, and his having preached a notorious sermon, "Human Power Defeated," before Parliament in 1649, celebrating Cromwell's triumph over the Levellers at Burford, Owen had been involved with Desborough and Fleetwood in the "Wallingford House conspiracy," organized in 1659 to depose Richard Cromwell in favor of the "good old cause" of republicanism (Orme, *Memoirs*, p. 115; James Moffat, *The Life of John Owen*, London: Congregational Union of England and Wales, 1911, pp. 49–50). Parker, of course, reminds his readers of Owen's political past. In the *Defence*, he referred to Owen as the great "bellwether" of the seditious sectarians, and charged that he had never really renounced his old principles of rebellion. Owen and his followers, Parker asserted, manifested "an undaunted adherence to their old principles and their old cause . . . The *Good Old Cause* sticks as close to them as Original Sin" (*Defence*, pp. 629–632, 636). Baxter believed that Owen's political past had allowed Parker to score a propaganda victory against the Dissenters in his reply to Owen. Hence, the latter's "unfitness" to act as the chief spokesman and defender of the Nonconformists, Baxter concluded, resulted in "a general injury to the nonconformists" (R. Baxter, *Life*, pt. 3, p. 42). This was hardly a charitable judgment on Baxter's part, considering his refusal of Owen's request that he assume the role of spokesman for the Dissenters.

[26] Owen simply affirms the right of the magistrate to decide controversies in matters of "human concerns," according to the original grant of his authority (*Truth*, p. 112). In

antecedent to the considerations of the power of the magistrate, and all the influence that it hath upon men or their consciences, there is a superior determination of what is true, what false in religion, what right and what wrong in the worship of God."[27] Without this "antecedent obligation binding to obey the just law and constitutions of the Commonwealth," Robert Ferguson added, civil laws and contracts would signify nothing.[28]

To Parker, all this was beside the point. He, too, believed in natural law, and he accepted the proposition that there were "obligations antecedent to those of human laws."[29] But whether the existence of such obligations provided the warrant for any individual to challenge the will of the Sovereign was the real issue; and on this point, Parker was prepared to reject the epistemological claims of any individual to have a knowledge of natural law sufficient to justify such an action.

Owen's reticence to specify a preference for a particular form of government (though there could be little room for doubt in his case as to what that preference was) was not shared by all of Parker's critics. Humfrey maintained that the fundamental maxim of government was *salus rei publicae suprema lex*. The king, like any other individual, was therefore bound to act for the public good and was liable to subvert the constitution of government if he did not so act.[30] The government of England, he observed, was a mixed government, and "the supreme legislative power in this nation lies in the King and his two houses *jointly*." This was suspect, but not unfamiliar doctrine. Humfrey, however, pressed the point further. Postulating a hypothetical situation, that a decade later was to assume a reality and greater practical significance than he could have foreseen, Humfrey argued that if the two houses of Parliament were divided over an issue— presumably, a fundamental issue—then "the constitution is broken, that being broken, the government is dissolved, and

another place, he asserts that "all political government in the world consists in the exercise of principles of natural right, and their just application to times, ages, people, occasions and occurrences," but Owen never spells out how, precisely, this precept comes to be embodied in particular political institutions (p. 335).

[27] Owen, *Truth*, pp. 100, 243–244; Richard Baxter, *The Second Part of the Nonconformists Plea for Peace*, 1680, pp. 12, 15, 36–38. Although this tract was not published until 1680, it was, according to Baxter, "mostly written many years past," during the period of the Parker controversy, and prior to and in conjunction with the joint work, *The Judgment of Non-Conformists of the Interest of Reason in Matters of Religion*, 1676, of which Baxter was one of the coauthors.

[28] Robert Ferguson, *A Sober Enquiry into the Nature, Measure, and Principle of Moral Virtue*, 1673, p. 72.

[29] Parker, *Discourse*, pp. 113–114, 132, 174.

[30] Humfrey, *Authority*, p. 17.

the power returned at that season to the people." The people were then at liberty to constitute for themselves whatever government they pleased, since this was their original condition prior to the establishment of civil society.[31] That is, Humfrey declared himself squarely in favor of that form of social contract theory which sanctioned "the mutual agreement of the people themselves in choosing their governor and kind of government, as they judge best for their general advantage."[32] This was clearly a radical view, only slightly mitigated by Humfrey's refusal to sanction any form of resistance to the magistrate, and it was the political position to which Parker claimed all Dissenters, secretly or openly, subscribed.

The political catechism of dissent was presented, and criticized, in *Toleration Discussed in Two Dialogues*, by Roger L'Estrange, who entered the debate on Parker's side.[33] According to L'Estrange, it consisted of the following propositions: Power is originally in the people; they establish government through a social contract; the legislative power of society is chiefly in Parliament; the king is an executive holding office as a trustee and a servant of the people; if he breaks the social contract, he may be resisted as a tyrant; government is then dissolved and power returns to the people.[34] Each of these propositions was to receive extensive and detailed consideration in the political pamphlets of the 1680s, but suprisingly, they merited only cursory treatment by the participants in the 1670s debate. The really interesting feature of the latter, so far as political theory is concerned, is the villainous role assigned to Hobbes' political theory, from which both sides in the dispute were anxious to disassociate themselves.

Virtually all the Dissenters charged Parker with being a Hobbesian.[35] For them, Hobbes' philosophy meant "an opposition to all natural laws" or to any standard of justice "antecedent to social constitutions." From

[31] Humfrey, *Authority*, p. 29. Twenty years later, in the radical tract, *Good Advice Before it be Too Late*, 1689, Humfrey reaffirmed this position. For a discussion of Humfrey's views, see chapters 10 and 11 below.

[32] Humfrey, *Authority*, p.75. This argument also served, of course, to legitimize retrospectively the actions of the Rump Parliament during the Interregnum. I am grateful to Professor Pocock for calling this point to my attention.

[33] Roger L'Estrange, *Toleration Discussed in Two Dialogues*, 1670. L'Estrange had published a tract in 1663 entitled *Toleration Discussed*, but while some of the arguments from this pamphlet are incorporated into the 1670 work, the latter is much longer and considerably revised; hence, it represents L'Estrange's decision to intervene in the Parker controversy.

[34] L'Estrange, *Toleration Discussed* (1670), pp. 60–71.

[35] Robert Ferguson, *The Interest of Reason in Religion*, 1675, p. 433; Humfrey, *Authority*, p. 67; Charles Wolseley, *The Reasonableness of Scripture-Belief*, 1672, epistle dedicatory. For Richard Baxter's attack on Hobbes, see *Second Part*, pp. 123–132.

this standpoint, it was then possible to argue for acceptance of the will of the Sovereign as the necessary standard according to which all human actions are judged. It was this attempt to persuade kings "to invade or usurp the throne of God," as Owen put it, that linked Parker and Hobbes in the minds of the Dissenters.[36] The two men also shared the belief, Humfrey wrote, that individuals lacked competence as rational agents to decide for themselves between right and wrong, good and evil.[37] If this were so, Owen argued, then the notion that God created individuals as rational beings capable of living in peace and gaining their salvation through the exercise of their private judgment would have to be dismissed, as he believed that it was by Hobbes' "new atheism."[38] In short, "the whole fabric" of Protestantism, as the Dissenters viewed it, was overthrown by this denial of human rationality.

On these two points, there were indeed plausible grounds for asserting that Parker was Hobbesian. He certainly had nothing whatsoever to say on behalf of the rationality of individuals, who almost always appeared to him in the form of a nightmarish collectivity: "the giddy multitude."[39] As for Parker's resolution of all standards of morality into the will of the civil magistrate, here one must distinguish between belief in a principle and a matter of practice. Parker insisted, as we have seen, upon his belief in natural law and divine morality—as, indeed, Hobbes had maintained on his own behalf in *Leviathan*. In practice, however, final judgments regarding human actions remained with the Sovereign. Parker's critics, for reasons that will be discussed below, viewed this as an effective denial of natural law morality, masked by its rhetorical affirmation. It might be argued that the Dissenters misunderstood Hobbes' argument in *Leviathan*, but, given their interpretation, they had reason to suspect that the author of the *Discourse of Ecclesiastical Polity* had "fallen in with Mr. Hobbes."[40]

In fact, Parker's relationship to Hobbes is a complicated and rather devious one. In the preface to the *Discourse*, Parker includes the younger generation of Dissenters among those who have "swallowed" the principles of Hobbes' philosophy.[41] Later in the work, he refers to "a late wild hypothesis concerning the nature and original of government"—namely, Hobbes' concept of the state of nature—which, he asserts, "as odd as it is,

[36] Owen, *Truth*, p. 383; Ferguson, *Sober Enquiry*, p. 51.

[37] Humfrey, *Authority*, pp. 68–69.

[38] Owen, *Truth*, pp. 256, 372–373; R. Baxter, *Second Part*, p. 132.

[39] Parker, *Discourse*, pp. 21–22, 152. "The minds of the multitude are . . . wild . . . mad and raving . . . their crazy heads . . . unruly and seditious temper" (pp. 13, 15).

[40] Humfrey, *Authority*, p. 67.

[41] Parker, *Discourse*, p. xxv.

is become the standard of our modern politics."[42] Parker's aim, it would appear, was to exclude from his discussion any version of the social contract theory except the one offered by Hobbes, and to identify that version with the antimonarchical views of the Dissenters. Parker's reading of Hobbes—and even more, his assessment of the influence of Hobbes' political thought among the Dissenters—is, to say the least, questionable.

At the same time, Parker struggled hard to divorce his own position from that of Hobbes. He denounced the "false and imaginary state of the world" portrayed in *Leviathan* as a "fable," to which he contrasted his own view of "the *real state* of things"; that is, "a serious view of the true and real posture of the nature of things."[43] Hobbes' notion of the state of nature is rejected by Parker as a denial of God's goodness because it supposes that He placed the individuals He created in a miserable "natural condition"; it is rejected for being "inconsistent" with the familial origins of civil society as a natural extension of political authority; it is rejected for undermining the moral status of the Laws of Nature by making "mere self-interest" the basis of an individual's obligations; and it is rejected for allowing no distinction to be made between lawful princes and usurpers, with the consequence that "all government will be founded upon force and violence."[44]

Parker devotes thirty pages of the *Discourse* to a detailed critique of Hobbes' thought along these lines, which certainly lends some credence to his disclaimer of being a Hobbesian. Nevertheless, whenever he considers the slightest deviation from a strict adherence to the Church and State as presently constituted, the resulting "anarchy" described by Parker matches exactly Hobbes' portrayal of the state of nature.[45] It is especially in his argument against a reliance upon the "private judgment" of individuals, which "would naturally" lead to "a state of war," that Parker employs Hobbesian language against the Dissenters. Thus, to avoid this condition, "it was necessary there should be one supreme and public judgment to whose determination the private judgment of every single person should be obliged to submit himself."[46] Throughout the *Discourse*, other linguistic expressions and arguments borrowed from Hobbes are utilized by Parker. Hence, while his formal critique of *Leviathan* cannot be simply dismissed, neither does it suffice as a means of freeing Parker from the influence that work clearly had upon his own political thought.

[42] Parker, *Discourse*, pp. 116–118.
[43] Parker, *Discourse*, pp. 119–121.
[44] Parker, *Discourse*, pp. 112–141.
[45] Parker, *Discourse*, pp. 7, 156, 158, 214, 301, 309, 312–313, 318.
[46] Parker, *Discourse*, pp. 28–29, 262–265.

Even if Hobbes had been less of a sinister figure than he was for the participants in the debate, and even if "Hobbesian" had been less frequently hurled as an epithet designed to close off further discussion of an issue, it is unlikely that the basic categories of political theory would have received more extensive treatment than they did. Political theory, in its narrower definition, was a secondary concern in this debate; for, despite Parker's accusations as to their seditious intentions, the Dissenters were generally content with political institutions as they existed, provided religious toleration was granted them.[47] Their arguments, therefore, were chiefly focused upon topics other than politics. And yet, Parker was not wholly mistaken in attributing political significance to the issues of individual autonomy, liberty of the will, the relationship of reason to Christian doctrine, and so on. Viewed in the broadest sense, these precepts did constitute a theory of political and social behavior.

It was easy for Parker to join his critique of Hobbes' reduction of morality to self-interest with his attack upon the Dissenters' appeal to "conscience," since for him, the two notions were identical. What else, he asked, could the so-called conscience of every private man be but his own self-interest? "Everything any man has a mind to is his conscience; and murder, treason, rebellion plead its authority." To make conscience, which is only "every private man's own judgment and persuasion of things," to be the ground of all morality, Parker argued, cannot be regarded as a step toward progress in ethical theory in relation to Hobbes' doctrine.[48] The fact is that most men are ignorant, and their minds are governed by absurd principles, "so that were they entirely left to their own conduct, in what mischiefs and confusions must they involve all societies?"[49] In short, conscience reduced to self-interest would return us to a Hobbesian state of war.

To counter this simplistic but not ineffective critique, the Dissenters had to defend a highly structured argument, building upon several interconnected presuppositions. They had to assume that individuals were autonomous rational agents with a liberty of will, which, however, was not always conformable to reason; and the latter could not be simply equated with the empirical use of their individual faculties, but had an objective (divine) status independent of those faculties, though it could not be supposed to embody precepts that were in some fundamental way irreconcilable with the employment of those faculties. Even in this cursory state-

[47] James Walker, "Dissent and Republicanism after the Restoration," *Baptist Quarterly* 8, no. 5 (January 1937):279.

[48] Parker, *Discourse*, p. 6.

[49] Parker, *Discourse*, p. 7; cf. *Indulgence to Dissenters in Religion . . . Is Destructive Both to Church and State*, 1673, p. 9.

ment, it is obvious that there are several curves and turns in the argument that are not easily negotiable, and the appreciation of its scenic beauty requires a great deal more sympathetic patience than Parker was willing to concede.

"Conscience," Ferguson explained, "is properly nothing else but the soul reflecting upon itself and actions, and judging of both according to law."[50] The law, of course, was natural law. Hence, the argument presupposed the juncture of these assumptions: that individuals exercised autonomous private judgments; that they were rational beings capable of rational judgments; and that there was an objective determination of right and wrong discoverable through the use of reason.

> Every man must have a judgment of private discretion to compare the matters which are enjoined him with the rule, in respect to his own actions; or else he acts as a brute . . . Conscience lies in this very point.[51]

The very concept of human beings as "reasonable agents," Humfrey argued, was at stake in the dispute with Hobbes and Parker.[52] "Every rational creature under heaven," Baxter declared, is endowed with and must rely upon private judgment in order to "know and guide their duties to God and man. And to deny them this is to make them brutes, and kings to be but governors of cattle."[53] To assert that one could not trust "private men" in their judgments, Owen wrote, is to turn men into hogs. What is the point, he asked, of their having reason, understanding, and judgment at all, if it is not to be relied upon as a guide to their actions?[54] Since, for the Dissenters, natural law was grounded upon "the rational faculty" of man, not to accept that individuals could determine their moral and religious duties through the exercise of individual reason "is in effect to deny a man to be rational."[55]

Parker's response to this point was a straightforward denial that most individuals were rational agents. "If all men were as wise and honest as Socrates," he declared, then they might very well be "left entirely to their own liberty."[56] Perhaps this was Parker's attempt to inject a piece of dark humor into the debate—considering the fate of Socrates for having fol-

[50] Ferguson, *Sober Enquiry*, p. 65.

[51] Humfrey, *Authority*, p. 72; R. Baxter, *Second Part*, p. 45; Wolseley, *Scripture-Belief*, pp. 30–33.

[52] Humfrey, *Authority*, p. 69.

[53] R. Baxter, *Second Part*, p. 45.

[54] Owen, *Truth*, pp. 372–373.

[55] Wolseley, *Scripture-Belief*, pp. 32–33.

[56] Parker, *Discourse*, p. 162.

lowed his conscience—but he was serious enough in his loathing for "the rabble," a term that stops just short of being synonymous with "mankind." Nor was Parker alone in holding such views, for those who joined the debate on his side were also inclined to lay great emphasis upon "the corruption of human nature" as a bedrock principle of their argument for persecution.[57]

For Owen, Ferguson, and the Dissenters, the defense of the individual as a rational agent was inseparable from a view of the universe as an ordered system of divinely established laws. There was, they maintained, an unbroken chain of reason, a network of purposive motion, within which man must discover his place, and in the very process of doing so, confirm the rationality of the order of which he was a part. "Exempt conscience from an absolute, immediate, entire, universal dependence on the Authority, Will, and Judgment of God, according to what conceptions it hath of them," Owen warned, "and you disturb the whole harmony of divine Providence in the government of the world; and break the first link of that great chain wherein all religion and government in the world do depend."[58] The problem for the Dissenters, therefore, was to find some means of bridging the subjective and the objective dimensions of reason. Since they were convinced that God had created an ordered world comprising both, they never doubted that this task could, with some effort, be accomplished. To posit a reliance upon the authority of the civil magistrate as a substitute for the individual's use of his reason in the performance of his moral obligations was not only a lazy and impious solution to this problem, it signified a failure to recognize the problem from a truly Protestant perspective; that is, one emphasizing the *individual's* relationship to God. Thus, when Parker thought of conscience as "the soul reflecting on itself and actions," what he saw was an image of monstrous corruption, degeneracy, and weakness, in dire need of authority; what the Dissenters saw in that reflection was the light of reason and "a radical disposition in us for grace."[59]

Much of the debate initiated by the *Discourse* was therefore preoccupied with defining the nature of reason, and in particular with determining its role in relation to religious belief. Parker's characterization of humanity as virtually devoid of reason, and his portrayal of Dissenters as willful fanatics, whose religion flowed from and preyed upon the lusts, passions, and ignorance of individuals, were used repeatedly throughout the *Discourse* in support of the charge that religious dissidents were all

57 *Indulgence to Dissenters*, p. 9.

58 Owen, *Truth*, p. 70.

59 Ferguson, *Sober Enquiry*, p. 282.

"enthusiasts," people guided by "inspiration," and by mysterious, superstitious beliefs.[60] Fifth Monarchists, Quakers, Muggletonians, the Family of Love, Baptists, Independents, and Presbyterians were all lumped together with any charlatan who claimed to have seen a vision or a miracle. In Parker's mind, these "mysteries of fanaticism," as he called them, were the natural manifestations of religious dissent.[61] There was no point in trying to distinguish between them, since they all sprang from a wild imagination. If reason had no place in religion, and imagination was to be stamped out, that left only will—or authority—as the supreme arbiter of religious doctrine.

Thus, it was crucial for the Dissenters in their replies to defend themselves from the charge of being enthusiasts. In the process of constructing this defense, they undertook a systematic consideration of the question, What is the role of reason with respect to religious belief and, specifically, Christian doctrine? The titles of the pamphlets they wrote testify to their concern: *A Seasonable Recommendation and Defense of Reason in the Affairs of Religion*; *The Judgment of Non-Conformists of the Interest of Reason in Matters of Religion* (signed by ten Nonconformist ministers, including Richard Baxter); *The Reasonableness of Scripture-Belief*; and Robert Ferguson's two important works, *A Sober Enquiry into the Nature, Measure, and Principle of Moral Virtue*, and *The Interest of Reason in Religion*. As the authors of *The Judgment* declared, how far man's reason has to do with matters of religion has become one of the "Church-troubling controversies of these times" and the locus of "deep accusations" levelled against Nonconformists.[62] Nothing less than "the very foundations of the Christian faith," had been called into question by Parker's *Discourse*.[63] As one of the Dissenters framed the challenge, "the most eminent truths" of Christianity had to be rescued from the "weak impotent defense" provided for them by those who relied upon either "the great ills of idolatry and superstitition," or the wild claims advanced by "all sorts of enthusiasts." The Dissenters proposed to distinguish themselves by employing the standard of reason as the measure of their Christian beliefs, and by wielding it as a critical weapon against the ritualistic practices of Catholicism or the Anglican church or the imaginative delusions of the sectarians. The objective, Wolseley stated, was to demonstrate that Christianity "must upon rational grounds necessarily be es-

[60] Parker, *Discourse*, pp. 74–76; *Defence*, pp. 308, 688.

[61] Parker, *Discourse*, p. 76; cf. ibid., p. 23.

[62] R. Baxter et al., *Judgment of Reason*, p. 1.

[63] *A Seasonable Recommendation and Defense of Reason in the Affairs of Religion*, 1670, p. 1.

tablished."[64] Or, as Andrew Marvell put it, what they envisioned was "reason religionated and christianized."[65]

My task, Ferguson advised the reader of *The Interest of Reason*, is "to vindicate the non-conformists from the aspersions lately cast upon them; as if they were defamers of reason, disclaiming it from all concerns in religion."[66] Ferguson's argument, in fact, merits detailed consideration, not only for the intelligence and sophistication with which it is formulated, but also because Ferguson's religious views were in close proximity to those of Owen, and his political views, as we shall see, were virtually identical with those of Locke.[67]

In *A Sober Enquiry*, Ferguson sets out to defend the proposition that religion must depend upon "a rational choice" exercised by the individual.[68] Since religion consists of two parts—natural religion (or morality) and supernatural religion (or Christianity as revealed in the Scriptures)—this means (1) that morality can be defined as "whatever is required of us by the Law of Nature in the light of reason,"[69] and (2) that the general proposition entails an argument on behalf of "the reasonableness of Scripture-belief."[70] The general covering assumption for both of these convictions is that "God [in] creating man a rational creature, endowed

[64] Wolseley, *Scripture-Belief*, epistle dedicatory; cf. *ECHU*, 1:3, 24, 26. Wolseley's point that the attack upon the use of reason in religion was a political strategy of Catholicism was a commonly shared belief among Dissenters, and it helps to explain the tremendous emphasis they placed upon reason in their conception of Protestantism. See, for example, *Seasonable Recommendation*, p. 32; Ferguson, *Interest*, pp. 165–166.

[65] Andrew Marvell, *The Complete Works*, 4 vols., 1872, 4:126. Addressing himself directly to Parker, Marvell stated the point in more sober language. "Human reason guided by the Scripture in order to salvation," he wrote, "I take . . . to be as serious a thing as you would make it ridiculous" (3:387).

[66] Ferguson, *Interest*, p. 62.

[67] In the 1670s, Ferguson was serving as John Owen's assistant, and the two men remained close friends (Peter Toon, *God's Statesman: The Life and Work of John Owen*, Exeter: Paternoster Press, 1971, p. 156; cf. *CSPD*, 28:443). Owen and his brother, Colonel Henry Owen, often provided Ferguson with a hiding place during the 1680s when the government periodically issued warrants for the latter's arrest. It is not clear when Ferguson became part of Shaftesbury's circle, and thus intimately acquainted with Locke, but his *Interest of Reason* was dedicated to Thomas Papillon, who was one of Shaftesbury's friends and business associates.

[68] Ferguson, *Sober Enquiry*, epistle dedicatory. This was also Wolseley's objective in *Scripture-Belief*. epistle dedicatory. Ferguson's work is dedicated to Wolseley.

[69] Ferguson, *Sober Enquiry*, p. 28; Wolseley, *Scripture-Belief*, p. 32; Richard Baxter, *The Judgment of Non-Conformists about the Difference between Grace and Morality*, 1676, p. 7.

[70] Ferguson, *Sober Enquiry*, epistle dedicatory. The subtitle of Wolseley's work is *A Discourse Giving Some Account of Those Rational Grounds upon Which the Bible Is Received as the Word of God.*

him with faculties and powers capable of knowing what was congruous to the Nature of God and his dependence on him, and what was not."[71]

Ferguson is no less forthright in his defense of the importance of choice to a definition of religion. Although "no action can be moral that is not free, yet its morality doth not lie formally in its freedom." Nevertheless, "freedom intrinsically belongs to every action, as it is a human action."[72] Freedom and rationality are thus constitutive elements of human nature because, Ferguson argued, God desires from us "a rational subjection" to His authority.[73] In the longstanding theological dispute regarding the nature of the Deity, Ferguson is on the side of those who stress God's goodness and rationality. Hence, when "we acknowledge the Divine will the measure of what is good and evil, we do not understand it with respect to its sovereignty and arbitrariness, but with respect to its sanctity and holiness. Whatever he wills is good not because his will is arbitrary and unlimited; but because he can will nothing unbecoming his purity."[74]

This does not mean, however, that man's obligation to obey God's will is simply a function of the latter's rationality. Rather, "all those duties either to God or man" which are imposed upon us by religion, "we are obliged to by the rule of *creation*." The obligations we lie under belong to us, in other words, because God has created us to be the kind of beings we are, and we are obliged "to love, reverence, and worship God" because we owe Him an unrepayable debt for everything that we are.[75] Ferguson's defense of creationism is especially interesting in light of Locke's similar resolution of the problem of man's obligation to God in the *Essay Concerning Human Understanding*, and also in the *Two Treatises of Government*.[76] Creationism allows Ferguson (and Locke) to argue that while the individual's obligation to God is objective and an inescapable consequence of the fact of his creation, the fulfillment of this obligation is likewise

[71] Ferguson, *Sober Enquiry*, p. 57.

[72] Ferguson, *Sober Enquiry*, pp. 48–49; Wolseley, *Scripture-Belief*, p. 68; R. Baxter, *Judgment of Grace*, p. 7; idem, *Judgment of Reason*, p. 14.

[73] Ferguson, *Sober Enquiry*, p. 51.

[74] Ferguson, *Sober Enquiry*, pp. 56–57.

[75] Ferguson, *Sober Enquiry*, pp. 29, 51, 99. This is also Baxter's position (*Life*, p. 22).

[76] The obligation we owe to God, Locke argues, "seems to derive partly from the divine wisdom of the lawmaker, and partly from the right which the Creator has over His creation." Thus, "since God is supreme over everything and . . . since we owe our body, soul, and life . . . to Him alone, it is proper that we should live according to the precept of His will. God has created us out of nothing and, if He pleases, will reduce us again to nothing: we are, therefore, subject to Him in perfect justice and by utmost necessity" (*ELN*, pp. 183, 187, 199; *ECHU*, 2:28, 8; 4:3, 18; *ST*, par. 6). For a discussion of the importance of creationism to Locke's thought, see James Tully, *A Discourse on Property: John Locke and His Adversaries*, Cambridge: Cambridge University Press, 1980, pp. 4-50.

made possible from the constitution of his nature as a rational being, provided that man makes use of his reason.

This emphasis upon the active use of reason ruled out any support for the doctrine of innate ideas.[77] In *A Sober Enquiry*, but especially in *The Interest of Reason*, Ferguson dismisses the Platonic or Cartesian assumptions of innate knowledge.[78] "I know no ideas formally innate; what we commonly call so, are the results of the exercise of our reason."[79] Thus, "we are furnished with such faculties, which if we exert and exercise in comparing such acts and their objects," then, Ferguson maintains, it is "impossible" that we should not recognize which actions are conformable to and which actions are in violation of the laws of morality.[80] Moreover, like Locke, he insists that "there are as well indubitable maxims of reason, relating to moral practice, as there are relating to science." So that "the foundations of mathematics as well as of ethics" are grounded in the exercise of our reason.[81]

This argument, however, presents Ferguson with some of the same difficulties faced by Locke in the *Essay Concerning Human Understanding*, with respect to the question, How are we to distinguish "self-evident truths"—which both men believe includes principles of morality as well as those of logic and mathematics—from those same propositions viewed as part of man's innate knowledge? Ferguson's answer is that self-evident truths are *natural* truths, being founded in the nature of God or man, such that "we cannot without doing violence to our rational nature, but pay them assent."[82] Clearly, the question arises at this point as to how we can arrive at a knowledge of the Law of Nature, and whether that knowledge is self-evident. In reviewing the various responses to this question, Ferguson observes that some thinkers, such as Cicero, have taken "the consent and harmony of mankind" to be "the best medium of arriving at a sure knowledge of the law of nature." Such an epistemological standard

[77] This statement is misleading if it is taken to apply to the views of all the leading Dissenter thinkers. Many of them, including Owen, certainly included phrases in their writings that appear to support some version of a theory of innate ideas. Ferguson, therefore, is more likely to have been an exception in this respect than a representative of the Dissenters' viewpoint. It is true that, in general, they all shared a belief in the active use of reason, but the specific reference in the text to a denial of innate knowledge refers to Ferguson's argument in particular.

[78] Ferguson's position appears to have hardened between 1673 (*Sober Enquiry*) and the publication of *The Interest of Reason* in 1675. The latter work is more definite in its rejection of the argument for innate knowledge.

[79] Ferguson, *Interest*, p. 41; idem, *Sober Enquiry*, pp. 57–58.

[80] Ferguson, *Sober Enquiry*, p. 58.

[81] Ferguson, *Sober Enquiry*, pp. 58–59; *ECHU*, 3:11, 16; 4:3, 18.

[82] Ferguson, *Interest*, pp. 22-23; idem, *Sober Enquiry*, p. 60

is too uncertain, Ferguson argues, due to the great diversity of customs and cultures among nations.[83] Other thinkers, including Saint Paul, have identified natural law with "the dictates of right reason," but this definition is not acceptable because "right reason is rather the instrument of discovering the Law of Nature, than the Law of Nature itself."[84] In the final analysis, Ferguson concludes, "the Law of Nature is not so much a Law which our nature prescribes unto us, as a law prescribed into our nature."[85] This naturalistic response—that a particular quality attributable to individuals, or the necessity of assenting to self-evident truths, or the basic character of natural law as something that is "wrought into the essential composition of our nature"—forms the bedrock of Ferguson's argument.[86] It reveals, at the same time, why some readers might have suspected that this was merely an updated version of the theory of innate knowledge.

Still, the Dissenters' stress on activity was an essential point, and, in their minds at least, it distinguished their position from one that subscribed to the givenness of innate ideas. It may be that both "science and faith" presuppose a few self-evident truths, Ferguson observes, but most of the principles we hold to be true "are discovered by a chain of ratiocination."[87] These precepts are no less true or valuable if they are rightly formulated "by regular trains of argumentation" and are systematically presented to others. In fact, at one point, Ferguson presents something like a communicative theory of truth, holding that even if an individual had received a direct inspiration from God concerning some matter, he could have no way of convincing other individuals of its truth except "by producing the grounds" of his conviction through an appeal to reason and evidence, that is, "by rational evidence satisfying our understandings."[88] Thus, as Wolseley observed, most of our knowledge consists of propositions that "are discovered by a chain of *induction*, and our assent to them

[83] Ferguson, *Sober Enquiry*, p. 79; cf. ibid., pp. 61, 70.

[84] Ferguson, *Sober Enquiry*, p. 80; cf. ibid., pp. 62, 168. Wolseley identified the Law of Nature with "the dictates of right reason" (*Scripture-Belief*, p. 32).

[85] Ferguson, *Sober Enquiry*, p. 81.

[86] Ferguson, *Sober Enquiry*, p. 60; idem, *Interest*, pp.22–23. This is also the position defended by Locke in his lectures on natural law. "Since man has been made such as he is . . . there necessarily result from his inborn constitution some definite duties for him, which cannot be other than they are." Thus, natural law "is a fixed and permanent rule of morals . . . so firmly rooted in the soil of human nature" that "human nature must needs be changed before this law can be either altered or annulled" (*ELN*, p. 199).

[87] Ferguson, *Interest*, p. 24.

[88] Ferguson, *Interest*, pp. 57-58. "No man inspired by God, can by any revelation communicate to others any new simple ideas which they had not before from sensation or reflection" (*ECHU*, 4:18, 3).

proceeds from an *industrious exercise of reason*."[89] The labor and active use of reason was therefore vital to man's status as a rational being; in a sense, the *process* of reasoning was more important than the specific truth arrived at. Since Ferguson believed in a set of determinate natural laws, this is an exaggerated statement of his position, but, given the need of these Dissenters to differentiate between their perspective and that of those who relied upon innate knowledge, or "pretended inspiration" in order to support the same natural law precepts, perhaps the exaggeration is necessary in order to appreciate the force of the argument in its polemical context.[90]

The emphasis upon the importance of reason to religion could be carried too far, with the consequence that one might be charged with being a Socinian.[91] In order to avert this danger, it was necessary to reaffirm the centrality of revelation to religion, though in such a manner as to avoid equating the revealed truths of Christianity with the "mysterious" or "the irrational."[92] Reason, the Dissenters held, could lead one to a knowledge of natural law obligations, to a knowledge of the world of objects, and to a knowledge of the existence of God (according to the argument from design). Reason could, in other words, endow one with the status of being a moral philosopher; it could not, on its own, lead one to the truths of Christianity. Reason was therefore an insufficient means for securing one's salvation.[93]

"The religion of nature, and precepts of moral goodness," Ferguson declared, "are unfolded with more perspicuity and plenitude in the Scriptures, than in any, or all of the writings of the philosophers. Moral virtues were never so established by the Light of Reason, as they are by the

[89] Wolseley, *Scripture-Belief*, p. 73.

[90] Ferguson, *Interest*, p. 57. Given their rejection of the "idolatry and superstition" associated with a reliance upon ritualistic authority on the one hand, and their rejection of the religious claims made by "all sorts of enthusiasts on the other," it was virtually impossible for the Dissenters to avoid this emphasis upon the activity of reason (Wolseley, *Scripture-Belief*, epistle dedicatory; see note 64 above). When Locke confronts this issue in his early draft of the *Essay Concerning Human Understanding*, he, too, cites the Catholics on the one hand and the Quakers on the other as examples of religion defined by "reasoning from received principles" or as compounds of "the grossest absurdities and improbabilities." Both reject the rationally grounded defense of religion for which Locke is attempting to lay the foundations (*Early Draft*, p. 64; cf. *ECHU*, 4:20, 10).

[91] However, both Owen and Ferguson had written works against Socinianism. One of Owen's two books against the Socinians—a reply to John Biddle's *Scripture Catechism*—was commissioned by Cromwell's Council of State in 1655 (H. John McLachlan, *Socinianism in Seventeenth-Century England*, Oxford: Oxford University Press, 1951, pp. 128–129, 279–280). For Ferguson's discussion of Socinianism, see *Interest*, pp. 584–585.

[92] Ferguson, *Sober Enquiry*, pp. 171, 294–295.

[93] Ferguson, *Interest*, pp. 45–50; Wolseley, *Scripture-Belief*, pp. 46ff.

Laws of the Gospel . . . In a word, it is only the Bible that gives us a complete system of the Laws of Nature."[94] Revelation not only "builds upon the Law of Nature," but, according to Ferguson, "the only sure, universal, perfect system of natural law" is to be found in the Scriptures.[95] However perfect man's reason might have been prior to the Fall, "much of that homage and practical obedience which we pay to God" necessarily "results from truths depending on mere revelations."[96]

Ferguson does not rest content with this defense of revelation. He feels compelled, as did Locke in the *Essay*, and later, in *The Reasonableness of Christianity*, to attack philosophy, and the claims of philosophers.[97] In the epistle dedicatory of *The Interest of Reason*, Ferguson concedes the usefulness of philosophy, especially "against the rude assaults of petulant adversaries" of religion. Nevertheless, philosophy "hath often proved a very great nuisance" for having introduced absurd dogmas and insignificant terms into theological discussions.[98] In fact, he insists, "whoever will trace the errors which have invaded divinity to their source, must resolve them into absurd maxims of philosophy as their chief seminary."[99] Again, the implications underlying this critique could be extended too far. Not only Locke's *Essay Concerning Human Understanding*, but also Ferguson's *Sober Enquiry* and *The Interest of Reason* are highly sophisticated philosophical works; they are not intended to be crude appeals for the jettisoning of philosophy as part of human experience.[100] And yet, there is in these writings a radical dissatisfaction being expressed with the claims made by philosophers, past and present, as to what individuals can know and also as to what kind of knowledge they must be presumed to possess. There are some things in Aristotle's *Ethics* and in the writings of

[94] Ferguson, *Sober Enquiry*, pp. 266–267; cf. ibid., p. 35; R. Baxter, *Judgment of Grace*, p. 16. For Locke's statement of this point, see *Works*, 6:140–141.

[95] Ferguson, *Sober Enquiry*, p. 82; *Works*, 6:143, 147.

[96] Ferguson, *Sober Enquiry*, p. 172; *ECHU*, 4:7, 11; *Works*, 6:140.

[97] Ferguson, *Sober Enquiry*, pp. 35, 266–267; Wolseley, *Scripture-Belief*, p. 56; Owen, *Truth*, p. 192. "It is plain that the teaching of philosophy was no part of the design of divine revelation" (*Works*, vol. 7, preface). For a more extended discussion of Locke's critical attitude toward the claims of philosophy relative to those of religion, see Richard Ashcraft, "Faith and Knowledge in Locke's Philosophy," in *John Locke: Problems and Perspectives*, ed. John W. Yolton, Cambridge: Cambridge University Press, 1969, pp. 194–223, esp. pp. 218–223.

[98] Ferguson, *Interest*, epistle dedicatory.

[99] Ferguson, *Interest*, pp. 28, 246ff.

[100] Macaulay, who obviously never read them, refers disparagingly to Ferguson's "theological treatises . . . in the dusty recesses of a few old libraries" (1:479). I trust I have made it clear to the reader that not only is Macaulay mistaken in his conception of the intrinsic philosophical value of these works, but also that anyone interested in Locke's *Essay Concerning Human Understanding* would be well advised to consult Ferguson's books.

some other philosophers which are "of great worth and use to Christians," Baxter wrote, "but they are all poor [and] defective . . . in comparison of the Gospel of Christ."[101] This qualitative difference between the texts of philosophy and those of religion expresses a sociological conviction that places the faith of an "honest ploughman" above the claims of those who possess an "academical education."[102] If Christianity is "reasonable," therefore, it is so, in part, because it is simple and easily understood by the majority of mankind in a way in which philosophy is not and never has been.[103]

The necessity of revelation and "Scripture-light" to religion forces Ferguson to take up the problem of establishing the boundaries between knowledge arrived at through the use of reason and faith as a vital ingredient of Christian doctrine.[104] At times, the dichotomy between reason and faith seems to be phrased in absolute terms. The Gospel, and hence, the faith necessary for its acceptance, Ferguson writes, "lies in a higher region than human reason in its most daring flight can mount to."[105] Nevertheless, much of Ferguson's argument attempts to draw faith back within the gravitational pull of reason. "There can be no act of faith," he asserts, "without a previous exercise of our intellects about the things to be believed." Faith may be "an unwavering assent to some doctrine on account of a divine testimony," but "our reason must be antecedently persuaded that the testimony is divine before it can assent to the doctrine."[106] It is on the basis of this premise that Ferguson and other Dissenters are able to justify "the use and serviceableness of reason in proving the divinity of the Scripture."[107]

[101] R. Baxter, *Judgment of Grace*, p. 16.

[102] R. Baxter, *Second Part*, p. 188. In a work written in 1673, William Penn also attacked the philosophy taught in "our modern universities, to the corrupting of Christian doctrine." The Quakers, he argued, were not opposed to reason, but merely to "unnecessary studies . . . intricate disputations, obscurity of language" and other encrustations of modern philosophy and "academic education" (William Penn, *The Select Works of William Penn*, 4th ed., 3 vols., 1825, 2:262).

[103] This is the central thesis of Locke's *Reasonableness of Christianity* (Ashcraft, "Faith and Knowledge," pp. 218–223).

[104] "We may come to lay down the measures and *boundaries between faith and reason*: the want whereof may possibly have been the cause, if not of great disorders, yet at least of great disputes, and perhaps mistakes in the world. For till it be resolved how far we are to be guided by reason, and how far by faith, we shall in vain dispute, and endeavor to convince one another in matters of religion." (*ECHU*, 4:18, 1). I have argued elsewhere (Ashcraft, "Faith and Knowledge") that this sentence states the fundamental problem of the *Essay Concerning Human Understanding*.

[105] Ferguson, *Sober Enquiry*, p. 137.

[106] Ferguson, *Interest*, p. 21; idem, *Sober Enquiry*, p. 171.

[107] Ferguson, *Interest*, p. 56; Wolseley, *Scripture-Belief*, pp. 78–81.

At the same time, Ferguson maintains that "there neither is nor can be anything in Divine Revelation that overthrows the rational faculty or crosses it in its regular and due exercise."[108] He admits in discussing the question of miracles that they are an exception insofar as they do transcend the ordinary course of Nature. But, Ferguson argues, miracles must be viewed within the context within which they occur: as part of God's effort to instruct us in the truth.[109] Miracles, in other words, ought to be seen not so much as objective phenomena, but rather as a medium of communication; and, the Dissenters insisted, all communication with human beings presupposes a rational standard. Thus, "all Revelation is to instruct us in a reasonable, though supernatural way, and, therefore . . . in all things it must be consistent with our reason."[110] It is only Satan who uses his power to dazzle or to blind men to the truth. For Ferguson and for other Dissenters, reason and revelation are mutually confirmatory aspects of man's relationship to God. If one must give way to the other, it is clear what the Christian's choice must be. Ferguson concludes *The Interest of Reason* with the statement that reason is not obliged to resolve every problem in nature or religion so that the answer may be "comprehended by our narrow and shallow intellects . . . 'Tis enough that we can by rational proofs demonstrate the Bible to be the word of . . . God."[111] Viewing the debate as a whole, the general premise underlying the Dissenters' reply to Parker was "the more the understanding of a Christian discerneth the evidences, and true reasons of all things in religion," the more steadfastly will he adhere to it and support it. That is, "as a rational free agent, whose will must be guided by the light of his understanding."[112]

But is "the will" guided by "the understanding" in human action? What kind of "rational evidence" could be appealed to in answering that question? To the controversies concerning the nature of politics, moral-

[108] Ferguson, *Interest*, p. 20.

[109] Ferguson, *Interest*, pp. 101–103. God performs miracles "for the confirmation of truths," not to enforce doctrines that are not conformable to reason (*MS* f.5, fols. 37-38).

[110] Ferguson, *Interest*, p. 234. Wolseley dissents from this position that God only uses miracles to "instruct" us. At the same time, however, he holds that "all supernatural religion is discoursed unto men" according to those basic principles of rationality "such as are general and common to all mankind" (*Scripture-Belief*, pp. 78–81, 241ff).

[111] Ferguson, *Interest*, pp. 654–655.

[112] R. Baxter et al., *Judgment of Reason*, p. 14; R. Baxter, *Judgment of Grace*, p. 7. It is especially those who adhere to religion on the basis of custom and traditional authority, Wolseley argues, who have provided a "weak impotent defense of the most eminent truths," i.e., Christianity (*Scripture-Belief*, epistle dedicatory). For the argument that Locke's subscription to this viewpoint provided the intentional objective for writing the *Essay Concerning Human Understanding*, see Ashcraft, "Faith and Knowledge," pp. 198–199.

ity, and religion, therefore, must be added a philosophical debate, some aspects of which have already been touched upon. It is neither possible nor necessary to recapitulate here all the issues raised in this area of the general debate with Parker, but one central point of controversy does deserve some consideration. In the *Discourse,* Parker had adopted Hobbes' rigid dichotomy between mere belief or "opinion" and "action." "As long as our thoughts are secret, and locked up within our breasts," Parker declared, "they are out of the reach of all human power." But when these opinions "come forth into outward action," they become subject to the magistrate's authority. Thus, "all human authority and jurisdiction extends no farther than men's outward actions . . . Whereas liberty of conscience is internal and invisible, and confined to the minds and judgments of men."[113] A man's "understanding" was his "inward judgment of things" to which no one else could claim to have access. Everything else, in Parker's view, was a manifestation of "will," and as a perceptible phenomenon, it fell under the domain of the magistrate's authority.[114] Whether, in fact, the magistrate was actually concerned with any specific human action depended upon his judgment as to whether it was an action "capable of having any influence upon the public good or ill of mankind."[115] In practice, of course, no sovereign could possibly be concerned with all human actions, but that was hardly the point. Liberty, for the Dissenters, was not merely a practical concession consequent upon the limits of the magistrate's expenditure of energy. Rather, its defense was a matter of principle, and the issue thus had to be fought out on philosophical grounds. Indeed, from the Dissenters' standpoint, that was part of the problem—Parker had insufficiently thought through the philosophical implications of his own position. True, the dichotomy he offered secured the practical objectives of his argument by placing all power (theoretically) in the hands of the magistrate. But at what philosophical price was this political goal realized? It required nothing less than the absolute divorcement of the "will" from the "understanding." But if this was so, then what precisely was distinctive about human action, since even the behavior of animals had to be seen as a manifestation of their will? "Whatever men do as men," Ferguson insisted, "it is upon arguments and reasons that prevail with them. Those actions are not human, and so not moral which fall not under the conduct of the understanding."[116] "Man having vitality, intellection and free-will, and being a sociable crea-

[113] Parker, *Discourse,* pp. 90–91, 95.

[114] Parker, *Discourse,* pp. 317–318.

[115] Parker, *Discourse,* p. 93.

[116] Ferguson, *Sober Enquiry,* pp. 272–273. In his major contribution to this political debate (*The Great Case of Liberty of Conscience,* 1670), William Penn endorsed this view of the relationship between the will and the understanding (*Works,* 2:141).

ture . . . disposed to converse" with others, Baxter wrote, he "is a creature made to be governed according to his reason."[117] Thus, Wolseley declared, "all the actions of men proceed from the free choice and determinations of their own breasts. Every man's own will being the true cause of his own doings." To suggest otherwise was to imagine a state of existence "inconsistent with the freedom of a rational agent."[118] If reason and free will were not conjoined, therefore, the Dissenters argued that the concept of "human understanding" was rendered meaningless. Against Parker, they pressed home the point that rationality necessarily implied deliberation, discussion, arguments, and persuasion. To sacrifice these aspects of the human understanding to the magistrate's will was, in effect, an appeal to force. However difficult it might be to provide a philosophical reconciliation between objectified reason and the individual's free will, the Dissenters' conception of human nature required that they defend both propositions. Their defense of practical reason as a model of discussion and as the pathway for the individual's fulfillment of his moral obligations depended upon such a philosophical perspective.

Parker and his allies responded to these arguments in one of three ways. One might reply, as did the author of *Indulgence to Dissenters in Religion . . . Is Destructive Both to Church and State*, that, as a matter of fact, "the greatest part of the nation are miserably wanting in their duty; living in a known disobedience to the laws both of God and man."[119] From the standpoint of such realism, the Dissenters' appeal to human reason might be dismissed as being utopian in relation to the sociological knowledge possessed by the educated constituency of the debate over Parker's *Discourse*. But while this response supplied a basis for attacking the "mechanics" and "ploughmen" who sometimes served as preachers among the sectarians, it could hardly undermine the claims for reason of such sophisticated Dissenters as Owen or Baxter. The second tactic, adopted by the author of *A Representation of the State of Christianity in England*, maintained that "for men to be religiously frantick . . . renders [them] incapable of rational arguings and instructions."[120] Dissenters were, ipso facto, irrational, and therefore they were fit objects for the application of

[117] R. Baxter, *Second Part*, p. 10.

[118] Wolseley, *Scripture-Belief*, p. 68. "We have a power to begin, continue . . . or suspend" our actions, "so that the power of determining our faculties . . . to act or not to act . . . is that I think which we call the will" (MS f. 1, fols. 317–318). Later, Locke incorporated this notion of the will into the *Essay* as part of his definition of liberty (*ECHU*, 2:21, 10, 48, 51, 73).

[119] *Indulgence to Dissenters*, p. 9.

[120] *A Representation of the State of Christianity in England, and of Its Decay and Danger from Sectaries as well as Papists*, 1675, p. 19.

force. These were polemical replies, neither of which met the Dissenters' arguments on the philosophical ground that attempted to delineate the dimensions of the human understanding. Parker, of course, employs both critiques of the Dissenters in the *Discourse*, but his denial that human beings were rational agents required a more philosophical treatment of the issue.

Yet, did Parker really mean to defend a situation in which no amount of evidence or reasoning, no appeal to the understanding could redirect a person's will? On the other hand, if debate and reasoned arguments could have such an effect, why should people give absolute power to one individual in the first place, rather than lodge authority somewhere (in Parliament) where it would necessarily be subject to the give and take of rational debate? The metaphorical characterization of the argument is deliberate, for the political implications of the philosophical conflict between the absoluteness of the will versus the considered judgment of the understanding could hardly have escaped the attention of a seventeenth-century reader, especially viewed in the context of the controversy generated by the *Discourse of Ecclesiastical Polity*.

While the Dissenters were prepared to argue that the absolute dichotomy between will and understanding was philosophically absurd, their real interest lay in defending a particular conception of faith, one that presupposed an inseparable link between opinion and action. Owen formulated this philosophical argument in religious language in his reply to Parker.

> If conscience to God be confined to thoughts and opinions and speculations about the general notions . . . [of] true and false . . . the whole nature and being of conscience, and that to the reason, sense, and experience of every man is utterly overthrown.[121]

This, Owen explained, is because "liberty is no proper affection of the mind, or understanding . . . It is the will that is the proper seat of liberty; and what some suppose to be the ultimate determination of the practical understanding, is indeed an act of the will."[122] In maintaining this, Owen

[121] Owen, *Truth*, p. 256. The notion that moral principles "terminate only in speculation" is a "very strange and unreasonable" belief (*ECHU*, 1:2, 2).

[122] Owen, *Truth*, pp. 251–252; R. Baxter, *Judgment of Grace*, p. 9. By placing most of the statements about religion in the realm of probability, Locke is able to argue that dissent in the case of believing probable statements is a "voluntary action" dependent upon the individual's will. The same reasoning is applied to his defense of faith. Hence, with Owen and the Dissenters, Locke is able to justify dissent in matters of religious belief and to link that dissent with the "practical understanding" of probabilities dependent upon the exercise of the individual's will (*Early Draft*, pp. 66–67; cf. *ECHU*, 4:14, 1, 2; 4:15, 4).

carried the argument onto Parker's ground, since it is evident that liberty of the will thus defined would indeed provide a justification for the individual's willful dissent from the Sovereign's authority. This incursion was absolutely necessary, however, because Owen wanted to defend the concept of "the practical understanding," which effectively united reason and will. Even more, he was concerned to link conscience with "practical judgment," so that an individual's faith would *necessarily* be expressed through action.[123]

If an individual had, according to his understanding and conscience, determined from his study of Christianity "that such and such a thing is a duty, whose performance is required of him," Owen asked, "I desire to know, whether any obligation be upon him from thence to act accordingly?" If not, because the magistrate commands him otherwise, Owen declared, then *all* moral actions and obligations might be suspended on the same grounds. The issue for us, he wrote, is that conscience "obligeth men to act, or forbear accordingly."[124] As Ferguson put it, "our faith is not only at the root of our actions but has a *practical* status because it directs them."[125] That was the crux of the matter. Unless faith could be expressed, unless it exercised a practical influence over the lives of Christians, religion would stagnate and die. Christianity would be reduced to a set of rituals, external to the individual, possessing no living meaning for his existence. Therefore, there had to be an inseparable link between belief and action, will and understanding; the Dissenters' conception of faith, and ultimately their entire Protestant *Weltanschauung*, rested upon this foundation. In view of this, it is hardly surprising that Owen's *Truth and Innocency* is filled with references to worlds collapsing, orders being overthrown, and fabrics being rent asunder, in the face of Parker's challenge.[126]

The Dissenters' replies to the *Discourse of Ecclesiastical Polity* presented a picture of rational individuals having been created in a state of equality and freedom. For, as they repeatedly stressed, they were arguing on behalf of "what is common to all men." No one, therefore, was subject

[123] Owen, *Truth*, p. 253. "So that *liberty is not an idea belonging to volition*, or preferring; but to the person having the power of doing, or forbearing to do" (*ECHU*, 2:21, 10). By liberty of conscience, "we understand not only a mere liberty of the mind, in believing or disbelieving this or that principle or doctrine; but the exercise of ourselves in a visible way of worship" as a necessary expression of our beliefs, which, if we were to neglect, we would "sin, and incur divine wrath" (Penn, *Works*, 2:134).

[124] Owen, *Truth*, pp. 253, 257; cf. ibid., p. 146.

[125] Ferguson, *Sober Enquiry*, p. 170.

[126] Owen, *Truth*, pp. 70, 107, 256. Even Marvell wrote that Parker's *Discourse* "overturns the whole fabric of Christianity" (Marvell, *Works*, 3:85).

to the absolute will of any other person.[127] These individuals constituted a natural moral community, since they existed under an established framework of moral obligations owed to each other and to God. Through the use of their reason, they were capable of discovering these obligations embodied in the Law of Nature. This law not only imposed duties, but it also confirmed the rights of individuals, among which, the Dissenters claimed, was the right to follow the dictates of one's conscience. "Liberty of conscience," Owen declared, "is of natural right." It is a right "equally common unto all mankind."[128] Reliance upon their ability to reason assured these individuals that, for the most part, they were capable of living in peace together, and that disputes among themselves could be resolved by appeals to evidence, argument, and discussion. Though prone to weakness and corruption, they fought a never-ending battle against "the tyranny of lust and passion" that threatened their freedom and rationality.[129] These qualities they exercised in the form of a rational choice in providing for their own welfare.

Whatever one might say regarding the cogency and persuasiveness of the particular arguments employed to defend this perspective, it is not a politically innocent viewpoint. On the contrary, it describes a way of life, a set of social expectations about human relationships that the institutions established by individuals must seek to realize in practice. However esoteric discussions concerning the will or the understanding and the nature of reason and faith might appear to us, their political ramifications were not lost upon the audience to whom such discussions were addressed. In a more obvious sense, a certain view of authority was being attacked, and an alternative theory was being proposed in its place. We reject, the authors of *The Judgment* declared, "that inhumane, atheistical assertion, that in religion, inferiors must believe all that their superiors assert, and do all that they shall command . . . without using their own reason to discern . . . whether it be agreeable or contrary to the Laws of God."[130] It was a "great cause" of the spread of "superficial religion" that such a view should be promulgated by the Anglican church. Too many people, the Dissenters complained, were "taking the essentials of their religion too much on the *trust* of those that educate them." The consequence, they argued, was that this authoritative framework provided "an ill-laid foundation" for the maintenance of their faith.[131] The anonymous

[127] Owen, *Truth*, p. 313; cf. ibid., pp. 259–260; Ferguson, *Sober Enquiry*, pp. 61, 65; idem, *Interest*, pp. 23, 61; Wolseley, *Scripture-Belief*, pp. 71, 78.

[128] Owen, *Truth*, pp. 259–260.

[129] Ferguson, *Sober Enquiry*, pp. 286, 294.

[130] R. Baxter et al., *Judgment of Reason*, p. 18.

[131] R. Baxter et al., *Judgment of Reason*, p. 14; Wolseley, *Scripture-Belief*, epistle

author of *Non-Conformists No Schismaticks, No Rebels* stated the point in general terms. He offers a citation from Hooker's *Laws of the Ecclesiastical Polity* to the effect that "for men to be tied and led by authority, as it were with a kind of captivity of judgment . . . this is brutish." Hence, he concludes, to resign ourselves to the command of superiors simply on the basis of their appeal to authority, "is to say, that God would have us lay aside our reason, which he has given us for a guide."[132]

This appeal to Hooker as an authority cited in defense of man's use of reason was doubly ironic. For throughout the *Discourse* and its *Defence*, Parker had frequently claimed Hooker as an authority in support of his position. His "incomparable book of Ecclesiastical Polity," he wrote, is "so highly prized, and insisted upon by the regular and obedient sons of the Church, that they have in a manner cast the issue of the whole cause upon his performance."[133] *The Laws of Ecclesiastical Polity*, Parker argued, contained a "full and demonstrative" refutation of Puritanism and all the subsidiary forms of dissent flowing from it. It has never been answered by the Dissenters—Parker repeatedly challenges them to make the effort—because "it is unanswerable" as "a confutation of their cause."[134] Even the contrasting grounds on which Hooker is injected into the debate highlights the substantive issue in dispute between Parker and his critics. Parker cites Hooker because "the regular and obedient sons of the Church" have designated him as an acceptable authority; the Dissenters cite Hooker because he supports the view that God intended individuals to rely upon the use of their own reason.

Parker subscribed to a theory of professional competence; that is, he believed that those in authority in Church and State were "more competent judges" of laws and policies than anyone else. This, he asserted, "is the most common principle of human life."[135] The Dissenters, on the other hand, were committed to an equality of reason as a "common principle of human life." That a few leaders of the Church of England "should monopolize to themselves the name of rational divines," Ferguson wrote, is simply an expression of their overblown pride.[136]

However much he extolled the virtues of Hooker as a giant among pygmies, whose arguments against nonconformity had never been answered, Parker could not deny that the Dissenters had, in fact, been successful in

dedicatory. "*Nothing* can be *so dangerous, as principles* thus *taken up without questioning* or examination; especially if they be such as concern morality" (*ECHU*, 4:12, 4).

132 *Non-Conformists No Schismaticks, No Rebels*, 1670, p. 14.

133 Parker, *Discourse*, p. 199.

134 Parker, *Discourse*, p. 200; idem, *Defence*, pp. 546–551.

135 Parker, *Discourse*, p. 280.

136 Ferguson, *Interest*, p. 273.

attracting a significant following. Much of this success he attributed to their use of "a few gaudy metaphors and allegories" to deceive the credulous multitude.[137] The sectarians, he argued, had invented a new language, while misusing commonly accepted words, and in general, the Dissenters had undermined or subverted the genuine meanings of the terms employed in religious discourse. By contrast, according to Parker, the clergy of the Anglican church spoke "in plain and intelligible terms."[138] This point about meaning and language was important to Parker's argument in the *Discourse* because he predicated the uniformity of religious worship (which he was advocating) upon "certainty in the signification of words."[139] The misuse of words was simply a concrete instance of the Dissenters' general abandonment of rational discourse. Naturally, some of Parker's critics took up this issue in their replies. In *The Interest of Reason*, for example, Ferguson devotes more than a hundred pages to a discussion of the signification of words and to the uses of language.[140]

There was almost no area of cultural life, in fact, to which the conflict between Parker and his critics did not extend. In view of his initial broad-gauge assault upon the Dissenters in the *Discourse*, this is hardly surprising, but it reinforces the point that the furthest perimeters of the discussion were inescapably linked to the central challenge posed by Parker, which focused upon a theory of the nature and limits of political authority. In a sense, this was the most formidable aspect of his argument, and the one that his Dissenter critics found the most difficult to answer.

Parker simply insisted, over and over again, that whatever claims the Dissenters advanced concerning religion, philosophy, morality, or anything else, their true aims were essentially political. He was determined, therefore, to unmask their worldview, piece by piece, if necessary, in order to expose this political objective, which for him lay at the root of the problem. Liberty of conscience, he argued, was a misnomer; what the Dissenters actually wanted was "a liberty of practice."[141]

> So that when men will be the absolute masters of their own actions, it is not the freedom of conscience, but its power and sovereignty for which they contend.[142]

[137] Parker, *Discourse*, p. 74; idem, *Defence*, pp. 89–90, 308.

[138] Parker, *Discourse*, p. 75.

[139] Parker, *Discourse*, pp. 108–110.

[140] Ferguson, *Interest*, pp. 275–420. The relevant comparison here is, of course, book 3 of Locke's *Essay*.

[141] Parker, *Discourse*, p. 92; L'Estrange, *Toleration Discussed*, pp. 2–3.

[142] Parker, *Discourse*, p. 318.

This point had been stated by L'Estrange in *Toleration Discussed*, and he pursued it with his customary relentless vigor. Not only were the views of the Dissenters fundamentally political, L'Estrange declared, but "it can be nothing else but a confederacy" that so many people adhere to their views.[143] The Nonconformists, in short, "are in a direct conspiracy" against the established government. They are not merely a collection of individuals pleading indulgence on the grounds of conscience; rather, they are an organized faction, and as such, they constitute a danger to the political order.[144] "When people separate and rendezvous themselves into distinct sects and parties," Parker observed, they become "destructive of the common peace and amity of mankind" and "enemies and outlaws to human society."[145] What was at stake was really the right of people to organize themselves collectively in order to engage in a political struggle with those in authority. Not only to men such as Parker, but also to a much wider seventeenth-century audience, stated in these plain terms, such a "right" did not exist. And as a social fact, any such group, as a matter of presumption, was supposed, ipso facto, to constitute a "riot" or to be engaged in treasonable activities.

Understandably, the Dissenters found this a difficult charge to answer. That they were organized was obvious, but that they constituted a threat to the political order they strenuously denied. Yet, everyone knew from his reading of ancient history that political factions were dangerous from the standpoint of preserving social stability. The Dissenters were thus caught in the dilemma of having to choose between two tactics: Either they could deny that they were a political faction or, admitting that they were, they could argue against the maxim that such factions were necessarily subversive of the social peace.

In *Truth and Innocency Vindicated*, Owen attempted to pursue both arguments simultaneously. On the one hand, he tried to maintain that since politics dealt with "men's ease and profit" and matters of "convenience or advantage," the Dissenters were clearly not political in the sense of being concerned with such questions. They were interested in eternal principles and the higher concernments of religion.[146] Their only objective, Owen said, was to bring the "Christian religion into some nearer conformity to the primitive times and pattern," thereby restoring it "to its ancient beauty and glory."[147] To someone like Parker, this answer was wholly inadequate, not only because he was inclined to regard such

143 L'Estrange, *Toleration Discussed*, pp. 107–109, 113.

144 L'Estrange, *Toleration Discussed*, pp. 127–128; *Indulgence to Dissenters*, pp. 3, 9.

145 Parker, *Discourse*, p. vi.

146 Owen, *Truth*, pp. 335–336; cf. ibid., p. 245.

147 Owen, *Truth*, pp. 392–394.

professions of higher principle as rhetorical masks for more immediate practical objectives, but also because, even granting the sincerity of his opponents' beliefs, Parker refused to accept this as a mitigating excuse for the consequential damage to the public order caused by the Dissenters. "For, of all villains, the well-meaning zealot is the most dangerous."[148]

Owen's second response to the charge that religious dissent was, on its face, politically subversive, involved admittting that the Dissenters might cause some "inconvenience" to the body politic, but, he argued, such inconveniences had finite limitations and could not possibly produce the kind of evils of anarchy that Parker envisioned. No one denies, Owen wrote, that the existence of religious sects, and their toleration, causes "some inconveniences" to the commonwealth. Doubtless, it would be preferable "that we should be all of one mind" in matters of religion, "but seeing *de facto* this is not so, nor is it in the power of men" to make it so, the question is, "What is the best which in our present condition we can attain unto"?[149] Referring to the various divisions in religious opinion, Baxter admitted that it was regrettable "that we must call them parties."[150] Nevertheless, it was simply "frivolous" of Parker to imagine that "every non-observance of a penal statute invalidates the government of a nation," especially when "it contains no invasion upon, or intrusion into the rights of others."[151] Besides, what security could exist in Parkers's society where an individual was forced to live with "a continual contradiction between his faith and his practice?"[152] Such "a restless state of contradiction," Owen warned, would hardly provide the kind of guarantee of political stability for which Parker was contending. It was much more advantageous to the security of the commonwealth, therefore, if its members were allowed a "full satisfaction of mind," even if this resulted in some minor "civil disturbances."[153] And, in any case, the latter cer-

[148] Parker, *Discourse*, p. xliii.

[149] Owen, *Truth*, p. 293. It would "become all men to maintain *peace*, and the common offices of humanity, *and friendship, in the diversity of opinions*, since we cannot reasonably expect, that any one should readily, and obsequiously quit his own opinion, and embrace ours with a blind resignation to an authority, which the understanding of man acknowledges not." Indeed, this is the crux of the Dissenters' reply to Parker. For, as Locke explains, if "you would bring over to your sentiments" someone who disagrees with you, you must supply convincing arguments, based upon reason. You cannot expect anyone to "blindly submit to the will and dictates of another." And if an opponent does not "think our arguments of weight enough to engage him" in the process of reexamination, then we can hardly be blamed if "we should take it amiss" that he "should prescribe to us what points we should study" (*ECHU*, 4:16, 4).

[150] R. Baxter, *Judgment of Grace*, p. 17.

[151] Owen, *Truth*, pp. 124, 376–377.

[152] Owen, *Truth*, p. 118.

[153] Owen, *Truth*, pp. 121–122, 401.

tainly could not be equated with "savage anarchy," roaming herds of wild beasts, "the utter dissolution of government," or the rest of Parker's parade of horribles. Limited anarchy, or civil disobedience, however, is not (and certainly was not then) an easily defensible concept. The standard reply offered by established authority is a version of the domino theory: If compliance with one law is set aside for one social group, then other groups will advance similar claims for exemption against those statutes affecting their interests, and so on. In a word, if one law falls, they all fall. Stripped of all the colorful metaphors that surrounded it, this was, in fact, the gist of Parker's argument.

Parker had one more weapon in his arsenal, but it, too, was a powerful one. In the *Discourse,* he proposes to set aside the claim that toleration fosters the growth of trade on the grounds that even if this claim were true, it would not matter if its consequence were also the subversion of the peace of society, since no argument for toleration could possibly weigh in the balance against that result.[154] Still, Parker is "amused" by the fact that some "wonderfully grave and solemn statesmen" are so preoccupied with commerce that they "erect and encourage trading combinations," which "is only to build so many nests of faction and sedition . . . For 'tis notorious that there is not any sort of people so inclinable to seditious practices as the trading part of a nation." Hence, in Parker's view, the growth of trade meant quite simply the growth of sedition. If one reflects on the causes of the late Civil War, Parker wrote, it is "easy to observe how the quarrel was chiefly hatched in the shops of tradesmen."[155] If, as was generally believed, there was a connection between commerce and sectarian Protestantism, it was certainly one that Parker hoped to see broken. To put wealth into the hands of Dissenters "only puts weapons into the hands of madmen," and "there is no creature so ungovernable as a wealthy fanatic."[156]

Parker's awareness of and attack upon the social origins of dissent recurs as a leitmotif throughout the *Discourse*. Support for "the fanatic party," he observes, lies in the cities where their "visibility" in the form of demonstrations and riots overshadows their real strength measured in numbers. Their following "in country towns and villages . . . is inconsiderable." For Parker, there is a clear contrast to be drawn between the "quiet and composed people" who live in the country and the riotous fa-

[154] Parker, *Discourse*, p. xxxvii; idem, *Defence*, p. 43; L'Estrange, *Toleration Discussed*, p. 143. Bethel explicitly replies to Parker on the issue of trade and toleration in *Present Interest*, pp. 13, 35.

[155] Parker, *Discourse*, pp. xxxviii–xxxix.

[156] Parker, *Discourse*, pp. xl–xli.

natics who populate the cities and urban areas.[157] His disparagements of individual rationality and of the "wild and unreasonable" multitude are often merely generalized formulations of the more specific belief that the Dissenters, in practice, are willing to trust so many important matters to the judgment of "every arrogant mechanic."[158] From Parker's standpoint, this reflected a preposterously subversive view of the social structure of seventeenth-century England.

Owen replied to Parker's attack on the social status and economic activities of the Dissenters, but in a manner that left unchallenged the empirical assertions regarding the relationships among dissent, toleration, trade, wealth, and the demographic location of Dissenters. Instead, he sought to supply an alternative interpretation of the political importance of these relationships. "To preserve industrious men in a peaceable way of improving their own interests," he wrote, has generally been thought to be "the most rational" means of inducing people to live peaceably and quietly.[159]

> For as the wealth of men increaseth, so do their desires and endeavors after all things and ways whereby it may be secured . . . So men have thought to be far less dangerous, or to be suspected in government, who are well clothed with their own wealth and concerns, than such as have nothing but themselves to lose.[160]

Owen's position presupposed that if individuals were not otherwise interfered with, their preoccupation with "improving their own interests" would render them peaceful. Liberty, in other words, was an essential precondition for peace.

Moreover, Owen was not unwilling to offer a general defense of the pursuit of commerce in refutation of Parker's critique. Citing the authority of Solomon in support of the proposition that "the profit of the Earth is for all," he argued that "we may truly in England say the same of trade; all men know what respect unto it there is in the revenues of the Crown, and how much they are concerned in its growth and promotion." Owen then worked his way down from the king through the various levels of the social order in his justification of trade. "The rents of all from the highest to the lowest that have an interest in the soil," he wrote, "are regulated" by the rise and fall of trade. Without the latter, the "ancient and present splendor" of the aristocracy and gentry could never be maintained. Even more obvious was the fact that the corporations and guilds,

157 Parker, *Discourse*, p. xl; idem, *Defence*, p. 49.
158 Parker, *Discourse*, pp. 263, 283; cf. ibid., p. 164.
159 Owen, *Truth*, p. 77.
160 Owen, *Truth*, p. 78.

as "bodies of the common people," were dependent upon commercial expansion. In short, Owen concluded, "the interest of all the several parts of the Commonwealth do depend on the trade" of England. To discourage the growth of trade, as the *Discourse of Ecclesiastical Polity* did, was to "discourage all honest industry in the world."[161] If Dissenters were prominent in their support for the advancement of trade, therefore, far from this being an objection to be raised against them, Owen insisted, it was rather evidence in support of their claim to be concerned for the common good of the commonwealth.

Parker's declaration of war upon dissent in the *Discourse* was thus formulated as a comprehensive challenge, not only to the Dissenters' beliefs about virtually every aspect of cultural life, but also to their political, economic, and social existence. In meeting that challenge, the Dissenters were forced to think through and to articulate an equally comprehensive ideological defense of their position. There is in their writings no serious consideration given to the question of armed resistance to the magistrate.[162] But, if the attack on their fundamental beliefs were to be backed by the concentrated force at the government's disposal, or if their entire *Weltanschauung* faced the serious prospect of political extinction, would the defense of their faith assume "a practical status," because, as Ferguson had said, it directs their actions? In other words, would an ideological counterattack be transformed into a revolutionary political movement?

[161] Owen, *Truth*, pp. 79–80. It is relevant to note that the overwhelming majority of Owen's London congregation were tradesmen or merchants (Moffat, *Life of Owen*, p. 64).

[162] Humfrey takes up the issue of resistance to the magistrate, but explicitly rejects the doctrine in favor of nonresistance (*Authority*, pp. 53, 73). Richard Baxter also discusses the issue of resistance briefly, but directly, in the *Second Part* (pp. 57ff.), but he, too, argues that the problem should be put aside in this debate. One reason that this work was not published in the 1670s, Baxter tells us, is that he was persuaded by his dissenting colleagues that it was too sharply political.

3

THE DEVELOPMENT OF LOCKE'S POLITICAL THOUGHT

THE discovery of a large collection of Locke manuscripts within the last forty years has made the task of a modern interpreter of Locke's political thought both easier and, at the same time, more difficult.[1] It is easier to appreciate Locke's political perspective in its totality because these notebooks, journals, and correspondence provide the contemporary scholar with an access to the workings of Locke's mind that was not previously available. We can actually gain an insight into what Locke was thinking during a particular period of his life when he recorded his thoughts. Because these manuscripts enable us to view the developmental process of Locke's political thinking, an interpreter of his political thought is freed from the necessity of framing that interpretation solely in terms of an analysis that begins with the end result of that development: the *Two Treatises of Government*.[2] It is just this fact, however, that presents us with a difficulty. For, it is now clear that Locke's political theory, in the form with which we have become familiar, assumed that form only gradually over a period of twenty years.

That Locke's political theory developed over time is hardly a surprising phenomenon and would not, in itself, constitute a serious problem for the interpreter, were it not for the fact that this developmental process includes a rather sharp and definite break between the political writings of the early Locke and the much better known political works of his later life. Included in these manuscripts are two previously unpublished tracts on toleration, written in 1661–1662, and a series of lectures on the Law of Nature that Locke delivered at Oxford in 1663–1664. These manuscripts make it clear that a considerable number of what we would recognize as core elements of Locke's political thought are absent from any of his political writings prior to 1667. Locke, in the early 1660s, that is, was willing to grant the civil magistrate absolute and arbitrary power

[1] For a discussion of these manuscripts belonging to the Earl of Lovelace, purchased by the Bodleian Library, Oxford, in 1947, see the introduction by von Leyden to Locke, *Essays on the Law of Nature*, pp. 1–10; P. Long, *A Summary Catalogue of the Lovelace Collection of the Papers of John Locke in the Bodleian Library*, Oxford: Oxford University Press, 1959. Within the last twenty years, additional Locke manuscripts have been purchased by Paul Mellon and others and given to the Bodleian Library (Laslett, p. xiii).

[2] For example, Martin Seliger, *The Liberal Politics of John Locke*, London: George Allen and Unwin, 1968.

over all actions of individuals within society; he did not subscribe to a theory of natural rights; he was opposed to the toleration of religious dissent; he did not believe in parliamentary supremacy as an embodiment of the legislative power of society; there is no theory of property or of its importance to the origins of civil society in these writings; and he opposes the view that the people have a right to resist their rulers. Now, whatever one may say about traces of Locke's later political thought scattered here and there in these early writings, these are rather large holes in the fabric of Lockean political theory that we have been taught to salute as the banner of liberalism.[3]

The problem confronting the modern interpreter, therefore, is that of offering some explanation that could account for a radical shift in Locke's political thinking that occurred between 1660 and 1681, when he was at work on the *Two Treatises*. On the basis of a careful reading of all the manuscripts now available to us, however, an honest response must be that no obvious answer to this problem is contained in the documents themselves. Of course, several interpretations can be offered, with varying degrees of evidential support, but nowhere in the more than forty volumes of manuscripts does *Locke* tell us why he changed his mind about this or that issue, let alone why he reversed himself on the whole set of political propositions mentioned above. In the absence of such direct intentional statements to guide us, any interpretation must necessarily place a heavy reliance upon contextual evidence in its portrayal of the development of Locke's political thought.

The situation is even less satisfactory for one concerned with providing an account of Locke's religious perspective. For on the basis of what we know regarding the nature of intellectual life in seventeenth-century England, as well as from the specific evidence supplied by the previous chapter's discussion of the 1670s debate on toleration, it is extremely implausible to suppose that an individual's views on political and religious issues ran in entirely separable channels. If we had reliable information about Locke's religious convictions and practices between 1660 and 1680, therefore, that information might offer us a clue as to the reasons for the shifts in his political thought. The fact is, however, that we know even less about Locke's religious life during this period than we do about his political beliefs.[4]

Many journals and diaries kept by Locke's contemporaries record the

[3] I have discussed this point at greater length in "Natural Rights, Liberalism, and Toleration," paper presented to the conference on liberalism, at the Conference for the Study of Political Thought, New York, April 3–5, 1970.

[4] Cranston offers no evidence for his statement that Locke was a member of Benjamin Whichcote's London congregation in 1668 (Cranston, p. 124).

frequency of their authors' church attendance, which specific churches they attended, who their regular minister was, whose sermons they made a special effort to hear, and sometimes these manuscripts include comments on the particular sermon preached. Virtually none of this kind of information appears in the Locke manuscripts.[5] Now and then a revelatory detail has survived the arid indifference to such matters that pervades these writings, but it is highly unlikely that anything remotely approaching a picture of Locke's daily religious life can be reconstructed from them.

Certain general facts about Locke's religious position are, of course, well known. He was brought up in a family—perhaps even in a tradition, if one includes his grandparents—with Puritan sympathies. Locke's father sided with Parliament in the Civil War, and fought for Cromwell under his patron, Colonel Alexander Popham.[6] Locke spent four years as a student of Christ Church, Oxford (1656–1660), under the influence of John Owen, then Dean of the college, although neither the extent nor the lasting effects of that influence upon Locke's thinking can be easily determined.[7] Locke's particular tutor at Christ Church was Thomas Cole, who later became an important dissenting minister, with a large following in London, where he preached in the 1680s.[8]

Most of Locke's fellow university students, upon graduation, became members of the clergy. Although Locke appears to have considered this possibility as a career for himself at one point in his life, this considera-

[5] But see below (pp. 92–94) for a discussion of one manuscript, MS c.27.

[6] Cranston, pp. 2–17.

[7] John Owen served as Vice-Chancellor of Oxford until 1657. He was dismissed as Dean of Christ Church in 1660. For the next several years, Owen held religious meetings in his home that were attended by a number of Christ Church students, including William Penn (*The Correspondence of John Owen*, ed. Peter Toon, London: James Clarke, 1970, p. 125). There is a letter from Locke to J. O. written in the late summer of 1660. De Beer suggests that the correspondent is an obscure individual not even known to be a friend of Locke. The text and tone of the letter, however, written to someone for whom Locke has great respect and who he has known for some time, with references to their mutual friend, Robert Boyle, allusions to medical and scientific books, and particularly to the political atmosphere at Oxford, about which Locke is rather apologetic, all make it much more likely that John Owen was the recipient of the letter (*Correspondence*, 1:150–152).

[8] Cranston is mistaken in his characterization of Cole as being "not otherwise distinguished" (p. 32) than as Locke's tutor at Oxford. Both the Earl of Anglesey—who made a special effort to hear him preach—and Lord Wharton maintained a very high opinion of his abilities. So did John Owen, who was Cole's friend and mentor. Cole became a popular Independent preacher in London in the 1670s, and was associated with Owen in several lectureships. Later, he became head of a dissenting academy, counting among his pupils Samuel Wesley, father of the Methodist minister (Walter Wilson, *The History and Antiquities of Dissenting Churches*, 4 vols., 1808–1814, 3:79–80).

tion was short-lived and was never again revived.[9] Except for this fleeting theological temptation, Locke seems to have pursued a course of studies at Oxford that was steadfastly designed to provide him with an indulgence from having to take holy orders.[10]

Even on the basis of these sketchy details, it is reasonable to conclude that Locke was the kind of person who, in terms of his religious background and beliefs, might very well be drawn into the orbit of religious dissent between 1660 and 1680, as indeed he was. What we have, then, is the portrait of an intellectual whose religious and political views became increasingly radical as he grew older. The meaning of this development to Locke, in the form of an internal dialogue, however, is not part of the record. The reasons for the radicalization of Locke's political and religious thought *may* be embedded in some uniquely personal life experience of which we know nothing, though this seems unlikely. Yet, Locke was not the only individual to traverse the same religious/political spectrum during the Restoration. Thousands of his fellow countrymen—individuals who, like Locke, had joyously welcomed Charles II as their king in 1660—ended their lives in the 1680s by opposing him and his government. While it would be a mistake to assume that they all chose this course of action for exactly the same reasons, it can hardly be denied that an understanding of this process of radicalization, viewed as a social phenomenon, may prove helpful as part of an explanation for the similar development of Locke's religious and political thought.

Some support for this approach to the problem may be derived from the fact that the shifts in Locke's thinking occurred sometime after he left Oxford in 1665. Locke's rethinking of his position on certain religious and political questions, in other words, did not take place within the context of academic discussions, nor were they an outgrowth of the fulfillment of his tutorial obligations at Oxford.[11] On the contrary, the radicalization of Locke's political and religious thought occurred within the

[9] Cranston, p. 77; *Correspondence*, 1:214–216. A month after this letter from Strachey, Locke was elected Censor of Moral Philosophy at Christ Church for 1663–1664. Locke received another offer of a clerical position in late 1666, but by then (November 14, 1666) he had already received a dispensation that allowed him to retain his studentship "without being compelled to take holy orders" (*Correspondence*, 1:303–304; *CSPD*, 6:259).

[10] Cranston, pp. 88, 97. There is a draft proposal drawn up by Locke in 1690, presumably as a suggested piece of legislation, which would exempt fellows and scholars from the obligation of taking holy orders without having to seek a special dispensation to do so (MS c.25, fol. 45).

[11] "I have often heard him say, in reference to his first years spent in the University," Lady Masham wrote, "that he had so small satisfaction there from his studies (as finding very little light brought thereby to his understanding) that he became discontented with his manner of life" at the university (cited in Cranston, p. 38).

context of his active involvement in the world of public affairs. Despite the scholarly efforts by Peter Laslett, Maurice Cranston, and others, the importance of this point still has not gained the recognition it deserves in the secondary literature on Locke.[12] It is true that he is the author of one of the great classics of philosophy, the *Essay Concerning Human Understanding*, and that he spent ten years of his early life at Oxford. These two facts have sometimes been run together in order to create a picture of Locke as an Oxford don, a philosopher who also happened to write about politics, economics, education, and religion. This picture is historically false. The twenty-five years between Locke's leaving Oxford and the publication of the *Essay* are filled with the drama, intrigues, and dangers of political life. Some of those years were spent in holding public office, but mostly, they were years of living in political opposition to the existing government, of secret meetings, of false names and identities, of hiding, exile, conspiracy, and revolution. Locke's writings did not emerge from the environment of the detached philosopher, and certainly not from the sterile atmosphere of academic life at Oxford.[13] Rather, what we have come to recognize as the impressive intellectual contribution made by Locke to our cultural heritage arose out of the political turmoil that surrounded him as the trusted adviser to the most important opposition politician in Restoration England.

If Shaftesbury's name retains for us any positive resonance, it does so despite the calumny heaped upon it by a very powerful group of literary opponents. Neither Hume nor Macaulay in their histories of the Restoration made any attempt to conceal their antipathy toward Shaftesbury. But even their considerable influence pales by comparison with that of Burnet and Dryden, each of whom bequeathed to posterity an intense dislike for their contemporary.[14] The portrait of Shaftesbury as "wicked

[12] Laslett, pp. 25–37; Cranston, pp. 105–115.

[13] I am referring especially to the dominant views on politics and theology. The author of a recent study of Oxford in this period, although he overemphasizes the university's commitment to the progressive developments in science, he admits that Christ Church was among the most regressive colleges with respect to politics and theology (W. N. Hargreaves-Mawdsley, *Oxford in the Age of Locke*, Norman: University of Oklahoma Press, 1973, p. 37). On the conservative character of education at Christ Church, and Locke's role as a tutor there, see Hugh Kearney, *Scholars and Gentlemen: Universities and Society in Pre-Industrial Britain, 1500–1700*, Ithaca: Cornell University Press, 1970, pp. 123–125, 146.

[14] The few references to Shaftesbury in Macaulay speak of his "treacheries" and betrayal, his "manifold perfidy," and his lack of principles (Macaulay, 1:199, 248). Hume is less agitated, characterizing Shaftesbury as a man of boundless ambition and abandoned principles (David Hume, *History of England*, 8 vols., 1822, 8:92, 178). To Burnet, Shaftesbury "had no sort of virtue, for he was both a lewd and corrupt man and had no regard either to truth or justice" (Burnet, 1:173). Dalrymple thought Shaftesbury was devoid of all honor or feel-

Achitophel," an unscrupulous power-hungry politician, devious and double-dealing in his relationships with others, has become a generally accepted piece of one's knowledge of this historical period. This was not, however, Locke's view of Shaftesbury. Nor was it the view of thousands of other seventeenth-century Englishmen, for whom Shaftesbury was, in Locke's words, "a vigorous and indefatigable champion of civil and ecclesiastical liberty."[15]

Doubtless, it is too late at this remove to present Shaftesbury as a lovable figure, which may not, in any case, correspond to the historical reality. Nevertheless, the common view of him as an unprincipled politician is, I believe, quite mistaken. On this point, Locke is much closer to the truth than Macaulay and Dryden. Much of the difference in their viewpoints is explainable in terms of the fact that the latter did not share many of Shaftesbury's beliefs and principles, whereas Locke did. It is true that Shaftesbury shifted his position, more than once, in the course of his lifetime. Consistency, however, was not the most popular word in the seventeenth-century Englishman's vocabulary, and few individuals passed through the turbulent years from 1640 to 1690 without changing either their political or their religious beliefs, or both. Shaftesbury is no exception to this generalization, but neither are Locke, Dryden, or Burnet, all of whom found themselves faced with the task of having to repudiate views they had once advocated.[16]

While it is true that Shaftesbury's personality is to us, as it was to his contemporaries, somewhat enigmatic, there is no reason for us to be less informed as to his political perspective than they were. Shaftesbury maintained a deep-seated hatred for all forms of clerical authority and for attempts to enforce religious and political conformity.[17] On the one hand, this attitude underlined his support for religious toleration, his advocacy of which was rooted in his own Civil War experience. On the other hand, it made him a fierce opponent of popery, which he and many others regarded as the extreme expression of clerical authority and conformity. Since Shaftesbury could hardly conceive of popery apart from its association with political absolutism and the exercise of arbitrary power, his

---

ing, and even David Ogg called him "the Jekyll and Hyde of English politics" (Dalrymple, 1:172; Ogg, 1:330). For a response to the remarks of Dryden, Hume, Macaulay, and other historians' views of Shaftesbury, see W. D. Christie, *A Life of Anthony Ashley Cooper, First Earl of Shaftesbury*, 2 vols., 1871, 1:xiv; 2:472–482.

[15] This is Locke's epitaph for Shaftesbury (Haley, p. 739; cf. ibid., p. 734).

[16] Shaftesbury fought with the Royalists in the Civil War until 1643, when he joined the parliamentary side. Later, he served as a member of Cromwell's Council of State. Bishop Burnet reversed himself on the issue of nonresistance after 1687, and around the same time, Dryden converted to Catholicism.

[17] Haley, p. 28.

views on religious authority were embedded in a distinct political perspective. He was, as an opponent described him in 1674, "the most zealous defender of the Protestant religion" against its Catholic enemies at home and abroad.[18] Locke's friend, Jean Le Clerc, wrote of Shaftesbury that he "had so great an aversion to popery, tyranny, and arbitrary power, that though he was in other things very moderate, there was no moving of him in these respects."[19]

Shaftesbury was also a strong defender of parliamentary authority. His opponents thought this support extended as far as republicanism, and they frequently accused him of being a Commonwealthman, which of course he had once been, having served as a member of Cromwell's Council of State. Shaftesbury claimed that his efforts in helping to restore the monarchy and Charles II were sufficient proof that he was not opposed to a mixed form of government consisting of king and Parliament. This truth, however, stands alongside the fact that Shaftesbury was certainly supportive of those tendencies and social forces which accorded a central importance to representative institutions in English political life. In one of his pre-Restoration parliamentary speeches, he had defended "the people's legislative power, and . . . the supremacy and omnipotency of their representatives" in Parliament, and some of this populist belief and rhetoric retained an important place in Shaftesbury's political thought throughout his life.[20] For virtually the length of his entire career in politics, he appears to have held as fundamental precepts the necessity of annual parliaments, the right of subjects to petition for a redress of their grievances, and the obligation of Parliament to address itself to a redress of popularly expressed grievances.

These are, of course, very broad strokes, but they portray Shaftesbury as a person opposed to religious persecution in general and to popery in particular, and as an advocate of the rights of Dissenters and of Parliament, which is how his contemporaries perceived him. The precise manner in which these fundamental convictions were translated into practice can only be answered with reference to the specific political circumstances of the period, but it is obvious that any attempt to enforce Catholicism, an absolute monarchy, a theory of the divine right of kingship, or a policy of religious oppression upon the English people would push someone like Shaftesbury to the limits of his political identity.

As to Shaftesbury's socioeconomic attitudes and activities, there has

[18] This was the assessment of Edward Coleman, the Duke of York's secretary, cited in Martin Haile, *Queen Mary of Modena*, London: J.M. Dent, 1905, p. 50.

[19] Jean Le Clerc, *An Account of the Life and Writings of John Locke*, 3d ed., 1714, p. 10.

[20] This speech (March 28, 1659) is printed in Christie, *Shaftesbury*, 1:lxiii–lxxiii. It was reprinted in 1680, and subsequently in the *Somers Tracts* and *Harleian Miscellany*.

never been much controversy. He "was more keenly interested in matters of trade and overseas expansion than any other important politician of his day."[21] Shaftesbury's most recent biographer refers to "his capitalistic instincts," his extensive stockholding and commercial interests, and his explicit appeals to "the industrious part of the nation" for support of his political policies. He was, in short, "a representative of the rising new capitalistic forces in society."[22] Locke's biographer is equally forthright in his characterization. Shaftesbury, Cranston writes, "was the complete progressive capitalist in politics; he might almost have been invented by Marx."[23] In somewhat more modest terms, what is clear is that Shaftesbury was a politician attuned to the socioeconomic interests of merchants, tradesmen, and those who aligned themselves with the advancement of trade, to the religious interests of the Dissenters, and to the political interests of those who opposed any further extension of the king's power at the expense of Parliament or the people. If these interests were to be organized into a political movement, Shaftesbury would certainly become an obvious candidate for its leadership.

Moreover, from what we do know about his personality, Shaftesbury apparently lacked the pretentiousness and class-conscious contempt for social "inferiors" so often expressed by members of the seventeenth-century aristocracy, an attitude that effectively isolated them from social contact with the lower classes. Lady Masham wrote that Shaftesbury was "a great enemy to constraint and formality, having, above all men, the art of living familiarly without lessening anything at all of his dignity. Everything in him was natural, and had a noble air of freedom" about it.[24] These qualities allowed Shaftesbury to move freely in his association with individuals from all social classes, a fact that solidified his personal leadership of the Whig political movement in the 1680s.

Certainly, there was a warmth, freedom of access, and equality of re-

[21] Haley, p. 227. Shaftesbury was an opponent of monopolies, and among his papers are many letters from merchants expressing their gratitude to him for his support of trade (Benjamin Martyn and Dr. A. Kippis, *The Life of the First Earl of Shaftesbury*, 2 vols., 1836, 1:291–292). A later biographer discusses how carefully Shaftesbury went over the documents on trade that passed through his hands (Louise Fargo Brown, *The First Earl of Shaftesbury*, New York: D. Appleton-Century, 1933, pp. 130–149).

[22] Haley, pp. 234, 312; cf. ibid., p. 227. Shaftesbury owned stock in the Whalebone Company, a company for the buying and selling of raw silk, the Hudson Bay Company, the Royal Africa Company, and shares in the Mines Royal, in addition to a trading company designed to develop his financial interests in the Carolinas (pp. 227–233).

[23] Cranston, p. 107. "Shaftesbury was one of the first English statesmen whose approach to politics was entirely that of a 'capitalist'" (idem, "The Politics of John Locke," *History Today* 2 [September 1952]: 621).

[24] Haley, p. 218.

spect expressed in Shaftesbury's friendship with Locke. It may be an exaggeration to say that "with the exception of Locke," Shaftesbury "had no intimate friends"; what is true is that Locke was Shaftesbury's most intimate friend. For fifteen years, the two men maintained an "inviolable friendship." Locke "was with my Lord Ashley as a man at home, and lived in the family much esteemed."[25] For his part, Locke was at times effusive in his praise for Shaftesbury's keen judgment and intellectual abilities.[26] Locke was also steadfastly loyal to his patron, and at no time, not even in the twenty years after Shaftesbury's death, did Locke once criticize the Earl for any policy, belief, or personal action whatsoever.[27] Since Locke was regarded by contemporaries as a member of Shaftesbury's "family," this degree of commitment and cooperation is perhaps not surprising. Yet, the full importance of this fact cannot be appreciated unless it is recalled that Shaftesbury was the most controversial—hated and loved—political leader of the Restoration period. One has only to read the accounts of Locke's friends (such as Jean Le Clerc, Lady Masham, the third Earl of Shaftesbury, and Pierre Coste) to see that Locke's references to his relationship with Shaftesbury come well within the range of adulation and a profound sense of respect and loyalty matched, perhaps, only by Engels' references to Marx, with which this political friendship can very appropriately be compared.

Mention of this comparison also reminds us that we are speaking of two individuals who not only displayed a personal affection for one another but, as Ranke observed, they also shared "a community of ideas." "Locke's principles," he wrote, "are those of Shaftesbury."[28] Indeed, in a literal sense, this statement supplies the crucial axis for any account of the development of Locke's political ideas from the 1660s to the 1680s. Soon after Locke joined his "family," Shaftesbury

> advised him to . . . apply himself to the study of ecclesiastical and political affairs, which might have some relation to the business of a

[25] *Dictionary of National Biography*, s.v. "Anthony Ashley Cooper"; Le Clerc, *Life of Locke*, p. 8; Haley, p. 218; Cranston, p. 104.

[26] Pierre Coste writes of Locke's "constant esteem" for Shaftesbury: "I wish I could . . . give you a full notion of the idea, which Mr. Locke had of that nobleman's merit. He lost no opportunity of speaking of it; and that in a manner, which sufficiently showed he spoke from his heart" (Coste's "Character of Mr. Locke" is in Locke, *Works*, 9:161–174; cf. ibid., p. 167).

[27] The single possible exception to this statement is contained in Locke's letter to the Earl of Pembroke, November 28, 1684. For a discussion of the trustworthiness of Locke's statements in this letter, and the conditions surrounding its composition, see Chapter 9, pp. 430–441, below.

[28] Leopold von Ranke, *The History of England*, 6 vols., 1875, 4:166.

> minister of state. And Mr. Locke succeeded so well in these studies, that his Lordship began to consult him on all occasions of that nature. He not only took him into his library and closet, but brought him into the company of the Duke of Buckingham, my Lord Halifax, and other noblemen of the greatest wit and learning, who were pleased as much with his conversation as my Lord Ashley.[29]

Moreover, Shaftesbury entrusted Locke with "all the secretest affairs then in agitation and by my Lord's frequent discourse of state affairs, religion, toleration, and trade, Mr. Locke came to have a wonderful knowledge of these things."[30]

"I have searched in vain," Maurice Cranston admitted,

> for evidence of Locke's holding liberal views before his introduction to Lord Shaftesbury in 1666. There is much to show that Locke held such views soon afterwards; and I cannot help wondering if he learned them from Shaftesbury. For it is certainly not the case . . . that Shaftesbury learned his liberalism from Locke.

With respect to Locke's economic views, Cranston wrote:

> Locke learned from Shaftesbury to identify the interests of the nation with those of its investing and trading class . . . Locke might therefore be considered a member of the investing class whose interests his economic writings signally upheld.[31]

Without stretching the evidence further than its imprecision will allow, what is clear is that the development of what we have come to recognize as a Lockean political perspective occurred in the context of Locke's close association with Shaftesbury. This "firm and lasting friendship" was the most important personal and political event in Locke's life between the 1660s and the 1680s, and it seems reasonable to assume that much, if not the whole, of any explanation for the various shifts in Locke's political thought during this period must be rooted in this association.[32]

Locke, however, was more than simply Shaftesbury's friend or a member of his family. He was also Shaftesbury's political secretary and adviser; indeed, it was in terms of this role that most contemporaries knew of Locke, if they knew of him at all. Shaftesbury's grandson, who was

[29] Le Clerc, *Life of Locke*, p. 8.

[30] Laslett, p. 26.

[31] Cranston, "Politics of John Locke," pp. 620–621. Locke held a much broader view of mercantile and trading interests than a narrow interpretation of "the investing class" might imply.

[32] "Without Shaftesbury, Locke would not have been Locke at all" (Laslett, p. 27).

Locke's pupil, wrote that his grandfather entrusted Locke "with his secretest negotiations and made use of his assistant pen in matters that greatly concerned the State and was fit to be made public to raise that spirit in the nation which was necessary against the prevailing Popish Party."[33] Le Clerc also noted that Locke "gave his assistance to some pieces which his Lordship published."[34] There is a good deal of evidence to support these statements. Almost immediately after joining Shaftesbury's household in 1667, Locke drafted several versions of a proposal recommending toleration for Dissenters, a policy of which Shaftesbury had become a leading spokesman.[35] In 1668, Locke wrote a draft manuscript on the rate of interest "at the direction" of Shaftesbury, then Chancellor of the Exchequer. The following year, he drafted with Shaftesbury the *Fundamental Constitutions of Carolina*, for the colony of which the latter was an original proprietor.[36] When Shaftesbury became President of the Council of Trade, Locke was appointed the Council's secretary.[37] When Shaftesbury, as Lord Chancellor, was entitled to dispense a number of livings to the clergy, it was Locke who vetted the petitions from candidates and kept a record of such appointments.[38] On several occasions, Locke conducted research to discover legal and parliamentary precedents in support of Shaftesbury's political policies.[39] He made notes for, and very likely had a hand in writing, some of Shaftesbury's speeches.[40] Locke carried political messages from Shaftesbury to various Whig party leaders, and he helped with the distribution of Whig political pamphlets.[41] Locke kept a political journal for Shaftesbury dealing with bills pending in Parliament, an account of the speeches made, and notes on the debates.[42] He was involved in preparing witnesses, ar-

[33] Cranston, p. 159.

[34] Le Clerc, *Life of Locke*, p. 10.

[35] Cranston, pp. 111–112. Referring to these essays on toleration, Laslett notes that the evidence suggests "a close relationship in composition between Locke and Shaftesbury" (Laslett, p. 29n.).

[36] Laslett, pp. 29–30; Haley, p. 257.

[37] A new Council for Trade and Foreign Plantations was established on September 27, 1672, with Shaftesbury as President. Locke was sworn in as secretary on October 15, 1673. The council was abolished on December 21, 1674 (*Correspondence*, 1:354).

[38] PRO 30/24/4/pt.3/236; PRO 30/24/43/63.

[39] PRO 30/24/47/8; Haley, p. 297.

[40] PRO 30/24/47/30. There are notes in Locke's handwriting for Shaftesbury's speech as Lord Chancellor, February 18, 1673. Several of Shaftesbury's speeches are included in Locke's library (LL #2733–2735).

[41] During the height of the exclusion crisis, for example, Locke went to wait on Lord Russell to deliver a message from Shaftesbury, and was buying political pamphlets to be sent to Dr. Thomas in the country (*Correspondence*, 2:227, 323, 337, 376-377).

[42] PRO 30/24/5/pt.2/276. This journal covers the period from 1672 to 1674.

ranging for counsel, and other tasks during the popish plot.[43] Although very few letters between Locke and Shaftesbury have survived, some of those that have are filled with intelligence reports on political actions about to be taken by the government or on the execution of Whig party policies.[44] Locke accompanied Shaftesbury to many important political strategy meetings of Whig party leaders, including some where plans for mounting an insurrection were discussed.[45] In other words, Locke was deeply involved in Shaftesbury's political affairs; his duties as adviser and assistant pen were carried out with seriousness and, we may assume, with considerable efficiency.

The extent of Locke's political commitment to and activities for Shaftesbury has not received the prominence it deserves in the literature on Locke, largely owing to the Victorian attitudes of some of his biographers who created a myth of Locke's political innocence in order to safeguard their image of him as a detached philosopher.[46] But, as Cranston observes, this traditional view "is not on the face of it easily credible."[47]

[43] In the miscellaneous collection of papers and notes dealing with the popish plot in the Shaftesbury papers, some are in Locke's handwriting, and Locke records a note that he is to consult with Shaftesbury about the use of various lawyers (PRO 30/24/43/63).

[44] *Correspondence*, 1:417–420; 2:225–227.

[45] In July 1680, Shaftesbury and Monmouth retired to St. Giles to discuss political strategy, and Locke accompanied them (Cranston, p. 195). In August 1682, Shaftesbury was holding meetings to plan an insurrection, and "Locke spent the whole of the summer of 1682 with Shaftesbury while these consultations proceeded." On September 15, 1682, Locke accompanied Shaftesbury to the Earl of Essex's estate, where the Whig leaders worked on the details of the planned rebellion (Laslett, p. 32).

[46] Fox-Bourne was the chief propagator of this myth that Locke "had nothing to do with" the radical political activities of Shaftesbury or those around Monmouth (Fox-Bourne, 1:469–470, 478; 2:17). Ironically, he presented a substantial amount of evidence in the footnotes to refute this proposition. At the same time, he insisted that Locke was deeply involved in planning William's invasion of England "and had much to say respecting the arrangements for the projected revolution," though, in this case, he was unable to produce a single shred of evidence to support his conviction (2:57). Clearly, Locke as a Whig had to be remembered within the framework of Whig historiography, which similarly tended to exclude Shaftesbury from its story. Macaulay played a major role in this endeavor, not only by censuring Shaftesbury, but also by protecting Locke, who, as "a philosopher," could not be supposed to have been involved in any political intrigues (Macaulay, 1:490–491). This myth has been perpetuated into the twentieth century, among historians such as David Ogg, who wrote that Locke was the friend of "Shaftesbury the idealist, not Shaftesbury the plotter" (Ogg, 2:747). And, most regrettably, by De Beer, who, more than anyone else, has been responsible for maintaining the myth of Locke's noninvolvement in revolutionary political activities. Unfortunately, this attitude accounts for a number of specific mistakes in his edition of Locke's correspondence.

[47] The accumulated evidence relating to Locke's political activities between 1679 and 1689, as Cranston has observed, "all told against the myth of Locke's political innocence" (Maurice Cranston, "The Politics of a Philosopher," *Listener* [January 5, 1961], p. 18).

Once Locke's personal and political association with Shaftesbury is accorded its proper importance, however, the problem of explaining Locke's relationship to Shaftesbury's attempt to organize a revolution can no longer be swept aside by those faced with the task of interpreting Locke's political thought. For according to all accounts, "Shaftesbury was the most vehement supporter of the idea of a rebellion," and "it can scarcely be doubted that Locke shared his patron's general political outlook."[48] Yet, four years after the publication of his own biography of Locke, even Cranston conceded that "what has been obscured is Locke's connection with Shaftesbury's revolutionary activities."[49] In seeking to clarify the nature of that connection, we shall consider not only Locke's intellectual justification for the revolution that Shaftesbury planned, as expressed in the *Two Treatises of Government*, but also Locke's own participation as a political actor in the revolutionary movement.

As was indicated in Chapter 1, there were certain political problems that occupied the attention of those who participated in political life during the 1670s. These problems were, on the one hand, of immediate practical interest to thousands of people, and on the other, they raised challenging intellectual questions to which a number of writers attempted to provide answers. Simply as an intellectual and an individual member of English society, it is possible that Locke might have found himself drawn into a discussion of the issues raised by these political problems. As a political participant at the side of Shaftesbury, however, such concern was an almost inescapable consequence of his political activity. This does not mean that Locke wrote the *Essay Concerning Human Understanding* for Shaftesbury, in the same sense in which he wrote the *Essay on Toleration* or the *Two Treatises of Government* for Shaftesbury. And yet, just because the issues discussed in the *Essay Concerning Human Understanding* were, as we shall see, deeply relevant to a political perspective very closely aligned with that of Shaftesbury, neither can Locke's intellectual concerns be sharply divorced from the development of his political thought, which, I have argued, must be viewed in the context of his association with Shaftesbury. The fact is, what Locke wished to say through his writings is neither reducible to nor separable from Shaftesbury's political perspective. In the remainder of this chapter, I shall try to elucidate the dimensions of this historical conjuncture, giving due weight to Locke's intellectual confrontation with the problems raised by the political debate over toleration, without, at the same time, neglecting the im-

[48] Haley, pp. 722-723, 738-739; Jones, p. 209.

[49] Cranston, "Politics of a Philosopher," p. 18.

portance of the contribution that he and Shaftesbury made as political actors to the efforts to find some practical solutions to those problems.

The first hard evidence we have of Locke's abandonment of a political conviction that he had held in the early 1660s is to be found in an *Essay on Toleration*, which he wrote in 1667, shortly after joining Shaftesbury's household.[50] The *Essay* is a defense of religious toleration against arguments Locke himself had employed in his two unpublished tracts on toleration written while he was at Oxford. Since the arguments contained in these early tracts bear a striking resemblance to those used by Parker in his *Discourse of Ecclesiastical Polity*, it is worthwhile devoting some attention to this shift in Locke's political thought.[51] For as we have seen, a number of corollary issues were attached to the debate on toleration, such that a reformulation of one's position on the central problem could hardly fail to produce repercussions in one's thinking about several other questions.

The viewpoint adopted by Locke in his early writings on toleration can be briefly summarized: "All indifferent actions, of whatever sort they may be," Locke wrote, "lie under the power of him to whose discretion

[50] There are four drafts of this essay, of which the last appears to be the one in the Lovelace Collection at the Bodleian (Cranston, p. 111). The draft included among the Shaftesbury papers at the Public Record Office was published by Fox-Bourne (1:174–194). A collation of the differences between these two drafts is printed as an appendix to John Gough, *John Locke's Political Philosophy*, Oxford: Clarendon Press, 1956, pp. 197-200.

[51] Attention to these early tracts is made necessary, in part, by the propensity of various interpreters to deny that any significant development really took place in Locke's thinking about toleration. The editor of the tracts correctly notes that "they are in every sense profoundly conservative works" (p. 4), but then he finds only a "short distance" between Locke's early and late writings on toleration, due mostly to a modification of his epistemological perspective (p. 105). For Gough, Locke's "basic principles, on political power, the nature of a church, and toleration, were substantially unchanged throughout his life" (*Toleration*, introduction, p. 11; cf. ibid., p. 7). This nondevelopment thesis, initially advanced by King and Fox-Bourne, was originally intended to preserve Locke's status as a liberal from his earliest to his latest writings. It has now come full circle in an article that argues that Locke was always an absolutist and that liberalism and absolutism were not incompatible positions with respect to toleration. Thus, "absolutism and toleration are the same in principle despite their great difference in practice" (Robert P. Kraynak, "John Locke: From Absolutism to Toleration," *American Political Science Review* 74 [March 1980]:53–69). The absurdity of such a position rests with its failure to recognize what the political debate over toleration in seventeenth-century England was all about. To say that between John Owen and Samuel Parker there was merely a slight difference of epistemology, or substantially no difference at all, or that "in principle" they shared the same position, simply reflects an appalling degree of ignorance of the actual political conflict in which these individuals were engaged. That Locke began his writings on toleration on the side of Parker and the established church and ended on the side of Owen and the Dissenters should make us more, not less, sensitive to the *political* aspects of his development on this issue.

are delivered the liberty, fortunes, and the life itself of every subject."[52] Hence, the magistrate "has an absolute command over all the actions of men" in society, even to the extent that individuals must carry out their obligations "to obey those laws which it may be sinful for the magistrate to enact."[53] The magistrate "is the sole judge" according "to the free determination of his will" as to what will be "enjoined or forbidden" by law, and "we can take no rise to question the equity of his injunctions."[54] Moreover, the magistrate does not have to "make known the reasons of his edicts, 'tis enough if he himself be satisfied of them."[55] So that, Locke concludes, "it suffices for the legality and obligation of a law," if, regarding all actions, the magistrate "establishes whatever appears to him . . . to be in some way conducive to public peace and the welfare of the people."[56]

Once this defense of absolutism has been established, all possible objections framed from the standpoint of individual claims to conscience, right, or liberty are easily dismissed by Locke. Conscience, he argues, is "nothing but an opinion of the truth," which might indeed be tolerated if it is remembered that such opinions or beliefs remain within one's mind and are not expressed as outward actions.[57] With respect to the most important "opinions of the truth" (the principles of religion), Locke maintains that these require only our inward assent. "The great business of Christian religion lies in the heart," not in our external behavior, over which the magistrate exercises absolute authority. Thus, "true religion, i.e., the internal acts of faith" on the part of the individual "cannot be seen and therefore cannot be an example to others," or, more to the point, these "internal acts of faith" cannot be linked to action at all, and so cannot constitute a justification for any disturbance of the public order.[58] Since this "inner worship of the heart," which is "the essence and soul of religion," is "wholly silent and secret . . . completely hidden from the eyes and observation of men," there can be no grounds for appeals to individual conscience against the commands of the magistrate.[59]

There is even less reason for anyone to invoke the general category of private judgment, since "if private men's judgments were to be the moulds wherein laws were to be cast, it is a question whether we should

[52] *STG*, pp. 230–231.
[53] *FTG*, p. 152.
[54] *FTG*, pp. 126, 152; cf. ibid., pp. 118–119.
[55] *FTG*, p. 152.
[56] *STG*, p. 237; cf. *FTG*, p. 126; *STG*, pp. 218–220.
[57] *FTG*, p. 138; cf. ibid., p. 129.
[58] *FTG*, p. 173; cf. ibid., pp. 146, 167.
[59] *STG*, p. 214; cf. *FTG*, pp. 133–134, 164.

have any at all."[60] Such judgments are really nothing but "our own wills or fancies."[61] As Parker and L'Estrange later maintained, what proponents of toleration really desire, Locke argues, is a "liberty of actions" disguised under a plea for liberty of conscience. Yet, "the whole liberty of the conscience" is confined to the freedom of one's "understanding," and has nothing to do with action.[62] In these tracts, Locke even appears to argue against the doctrine of free will. In matters of religion, at least, God has "not so much as entrusted man with a liberty at pleasure to believe or reject" what He has commanded. Rather, God exercises "an immediate dominion" over men's minds, through which they "are brought to an assent" to His will.[63] From this standpoint, there is not even a practical need for a "liberty of conscience." Needless to say, it would be extremely difficult to make out a case for the importance of individuals exercising their reason in matters of religion, or for religion itself being viewed as the outcome of "a rational choice" on the part of individuals, starting from this Lockean presupposition. The practical consequence of the general argument Locke is making, however, is a simple denial that any distinction can be drawn between "dissent" from the magistrate's will and "rebellion."[64]

Even if God had not in some obscure sense obviated the necessity of a reliance upon private judgment and individual reason in matters of religion, Locke is horrified by the social consequences of such an assertion. "Grant the people once free and unlimited in the exercise of their religion and where will they stop?" he asks. The result would be "contention . . . persecution and . . . the tyranny of a religious rage" exercised by the mob. For, "the multitude . . . are as impatient of restraint as the sea . . . always craving, never satisfied," and nothing can be "set over them which they will not always be reaching out and endeavoring to pull down."[65]

[60] *FTG*, p. 137.

[61] *FTG*, p. 148.

[62] *FTG*, pp. 122, 126–127; *STG*, p. 238.

[63] *FTG*, pp. 127, 129.

[64] *FTG*, p. 136.

[65] *FTG*, pp. 158–159; cf. ibid., p. 120. Some commentators have suggested that Locke's opposition to toleration in the *Two Tracts* is merely a response to the impracticality of toleration in 1661. This argument has been most recently developed by James Tully in his introduction to *A Letter Concerning Toleration*, Indianapolis: Hackett Publishing Company, 1983. I do not think the evidence will support such an interpretation, and I agree with Abrams that "there is nothing in the Locke papers earlier than 1667 which suggests any sort of support for the practice of religious toleration" (*Two Tracts*, introduction, p.9). Moreover, as I have tried to show, there is simply no intellectual foundation for an argument in favor of toleration in these early writings, nor does Locke believe that there is any practical *need* for toleration, quite apart from the question of whether such a policy might work. In other words, Locke's opposition to toleration is not merely circumstantial, but goes to the substantive core of the debate over toleration. Finally, there is no one among Locke's con-

Private judgment, in other words, cannot be viewed as the determination of a single sober individual; it must be considered in its collective expression as the "ignorant multitude" or "the untamed beast," liable to engage in wanton and destructive acts.[66] For, like Parker, Locke declares the "greatest part of men" to have "the worst" sort of character.[67] Liberty placed in their hands would only lead to anarchy; what they require is discipline, order, and authority. "Men generally when . . . a free exercise of their religion [is] allowed," Locke observes, "are apt to grow wanton and know not how to set bounds to their restless spirits if persecution hang not over their heads."[68]

Still, as Parker was to argue, it is not really the ignorant masses who are to blame, but the "crafty men" and the "zealous partisans" who mislead the people; they are the real villains. "The overheated zeal of those who know how to arm the rash folly of the ignorant and passionate multitude with the authority of conscience" is at the root of all those revolutions which have "worn the vizor of religion." Under the pretense of instituting a reformation of "the errors of religion," these cunning and malicious men have been responsible for subverting the political order.[69] The magistrate, Locke argues, ought not to "indulge the distempers of some few dissatisfied" individuals who threaten the peace of the community.[70] "Punishments" are "the great instruments and remedies of disorders" and ought to be applied by the magistrate against dissidents in order to suppress this "willful" disobedience on their part.[71] Indeed, "the severer applications of authority" may be necessary in order to bring stubborn offenders into line. "Penalties and force," Locke insists, will "bend the dissenter to a submission and compliance."[72] One reason that Locke has so little hesitancy in recommending this repressive policy is that he regards publicly expressed religious claims merely as rhetorical masks that permit individuals to "grow into dangerous factions" and to cause "tumults" and sedition in civil society.[73] Toleration, in short, is simply another name for rebellion and anarchy.

If religious rights cannot be appealed to in order to legitimize dissent, neither are there any other allowable grounds for such claims by individ-

---

temporaries so far as I have been able to discover who, holding the same views as Locke espouses in the *Two Tracts*, is an advocate of toleration on any grounds whatsoever.

66 *FTG*, p. 158; *STG*, p. 211. "the ignorant minds of the crowd" (*STG*, p. 235).

67 *FTG*, p. 166.

68 *FTG*, p. 169.

69 *FTG*, pp. 120, 160–162, 170; *STG*, p. 211.

70 *FTG*, pp. 140, 145, 162.

71 *FTG*, p. 128.

72 *FTG*, p. 173; cf. ibid., pp. 127–128.

73 *FTG*, p. 150.

uals. In fact, there is in these writings no action imaginable by the magistrate, no condition of tyranny however odious, which can be invoked in order to set aside Locke's advocacy of absolute obedience by subjects.[74] Had these early writings by Locke been published in 1670, they would surely have been embraced by Parker and L'Estrange as a pithy summarization of their own case against the Dissenters. By then, however, Locke had changed his mind on virtually all of the important issues in contention.

Locke left England in November 1665, having accepted a position as secretary to Sir Walter Vane, an emissary sent by Charles II on a special diplomatic mission to the Elector of Brandenburg. During the few months Locke resided in Cleves, he was apparently impressed by the practice of religious toleration in that city. In a letter to Robert Boyle, he noted that Calvinists and Lutherans—even Catholics—were allowed to worship freely.

> They quietly permit one another to choose their way to heaven; and I cannot observe any quarrels or animosities amongst them on account of religion . . . [They] entertain different opinions without any secret hatred or rancor.[75]

It may be that this experience and firsthand observation caused Locke to change his mind about toleration, but the evidence for this supposition is very sketchy.

There are, however, some notes preserved in Locke's manuscripts that he made shortly afterward that possibly have a bearing on the change in his views toward toleration. They appear to be notes on a sermon, which Locke may have attended, preached by an unidentified Nonconformist minister.[76] The question addressed in the sermon is, "How faith comes to

[74] "The subject is bound to a passive obedience under any decree of the magistrate whatever, whether just or unjust, nor, on any grounds whatsoever may a private citizen oppose the magistrate's decrees by force of arms." It does not matter whether the magistrate is "indulging his own cruelty or greed or vanity," whether he "introduces a law only to enrich himself, to abuse his subjects," or for any other reason. Regardless of the magistrate's intention or the law's effects, the subject is bound "even to an active obedience" to the ruler's command (*STG*, p. 220). In the toleration debate, *there simply is no position to the right of or more conservative than this one.* If Parker represents, as he does, the extreme establishmentarian viewpoint, then it is an inescapable conclusion that Locke, as the author of the *Two Tracts on Government*, must stand alongside him, being in agreement with Parker on every major issue in this debate. (An exception might be made for the choice between paternal authority and consent relative to the origins of government, but Locke himself dismisses this point as being unimportant to the debate.)

[75] *Correspondence*, 1:228 (December 22, 1665).

[76] MS c.27, fols. 13–28. These notes are not listed in Long's *Catalogue;* they are dated January 20, 1666. If the year is 1666, Locke was in Cleves on that date. It is more likely,

be effectual . . . wherein lies the causality or the powerful influence of it?" In order to answer this question, it is necessary to consider "the nature of faith and the nature of man together, the powers and faculties he is endowed with, and the dependency one has upon another." In these notes, Locke argues that "man is an active and rational creature endowed with a faculty of apprehending good and evil, and according to his apprehension, choosing and coveting the one, but refusing and turning from the other." Hence, "what our understandings conceive and present us as good" is what we pursue as rational beings. Moreover, being convinced of the goodness of the object, "we can be content to endure trouble . . . contest with many difficulties, and overcome much opposition" in order to achieve it.[77]

There is an extended discussion, in answer to the original question, of the fact that "*faith worketh by love*." Two points raised by this discussion seem especially relevant for our consideration. First, it is stressed that faith must express itself through good works; it is not, *pace* Locke in his earlier works, merely an "inward assent" of the mind. On the contrary, faith "brings forth actions of piety and charity."[78] If it were merely a matter of belief, it would be an idle, empty faith.

> For there is no such thing properly as an idle faith. Faith is in its own nature an active and busy thing . . . its life consists in motion . . . Faith without works is dead.

In other words, faith "is not merely an inclination to believe," but as Owen and the Dissenters argued, it is necessarily expressed through action. Therefore, when an individual is demonstrating his faith, he must have that liberty of action which allows him to express his belief through

however, that the year is actually 1667. January 20 in that year was a Sunday, and Locke generally retained the Old Style in his dating of letters until March of the new year. It is more difficult to say where Locke was on January 20, 1667. There is a gap in the correspondence between mid-December and mid-February, and Cranston provides no information that would help to locate Locke in mid-January. It is extremely unlikely that he could have heard such a sermon preached at Oxford. A letter to Locke from a friend in Oxford written around the middle of February was sent to London (*Correspondence*, 1:306–307). The most plausible assumption, therefore, is that Locke had been in London for a few weeks, and was there on January 20, 1667. If so, he could certainly have heard this sermon preached by any one of that city's numerous Nonconformist ministers. Apart from the substance of the sermon, the language used, with references to "brothers" and "sisters," and "saints," is distinctly sectarian and Nonconformist. The Biblical text for the sermon is St. Paul's Epistle to the Galatians, specifically, Gal. 5:6.

[77] MS c.27, fols. 14–15.

[78] MS c.27, fols. 13, 16, 21.

"outward" manifestations of his worship of God. Without such freedom, it is argued, his faith will die, and "a dead faith is none" at all.[79]

Second, the proposition that faith works through love means that it must find expression through "affection and general goodwill for men." These sentiments are "not confined to those of our opinion or party," but need to be extended to all individuals. Faith in this sense "makes every man a neighbor, and a neighbor a brother."[80] Yet, there is prevalent among us another kind of false religious faith that is uncharitable "to those who are not of our way, our sect, or party." Because some individuals "forget their fallible and imperfect nature," they "express enmity" and exercise "a furious zeal" against others who do not share their views. Such men profess their faith "under a pretence of zealous contending fury," which produces only the "evil works" of "bitterness of spirit [and] contention."[81]

Now, these views are certainly closer to those of Owen—they might even be his views—than they are to anything Locke wrote in his two tracts on toleration. What it is not possible to determine from the Locke manuscripts, however, is whether Locke is simply recording an observation—the fact of toleration at Cleves, or what a particular minister said in his sermon on faith—or whether he himself has adopted these views, and such observations thus reflect his own position. It may be that as a consequence either of a changed conception of faith or of a more informed opinion as to the practical benefits of toleration, Locke rethought his earlier position on the problem. The only arguments proving that he did so, however, are those set forth in the 1667 *Essay on Toleration*.

In a sense, Locke's rethinking has to be assessed not only in terms of what is said, but also in terms of what is not said in this essay. That is, apart from the specific statements that signal the shift in his position on toleration, there is a more elusive general attitudinal change in his view of political life. It is elusive partly because the supporting arguments that would elucidate its specific texture are not elaborated in the *Essay*, and also because so much depends upon the emphasis given to a particular sentence or argument and how these are read in the context of a political perspective viewed as a whole. For example, Locke begins by laying down "a foundation, which I think will not be questioned or denied, viz., that the whole trust, power, and authority of the magistrate is vested in him

[79] MS c.27, fol. 23. The argument is specifically directed against the identification of faith with "an inclination to believe" or a "persuasion" of the mind as the realm within which one's freedom of religious action must be confined, as Locke had argued in the *Two Tracts*, and as Parker subsequently argued in the *Discourse*.

[80] MS c.27, fols. 16–17.

[81] MS c.27, fol. 26.

for no other purpose but to be made use of for the good, preservation and peace of men in that society over which he is set." This seems an innocuous enough premise, unlikely, as Locke said, to be questioned, but much depends upon whether it is read within a context of setting limits to the magistrate's power, or whether it is taken to be a declarative recognition of his unlimited powers to act for the common good, however that shall appear to him. "This being premised," Locke continues, "the magistrate ought to do or meddle with nothing but barely in order to secure the civil peace and property of his subjects."[82] The tone of the argument has taken a decidedly negative turning with respect to the magistrate's exercise of power, although we still do not know whether this represents merely a prudential warning that it would be well for the magistrate to heed, or whether a whole structured juridical argument based upon natural law, claims of natural rights, and determinations of the people as an organized moral community is about to be invoked to give force to this admonition. This question is in fact never satisfactorily answered in the *Essay*; or rather, Locke offers partial answers that point in both directions.

Locke divides opinions and actions into three categories: speculative, indifferent, and moral. Not only are these headings in themselves misleading, but in terms of what the debate over toleration was all about, Locke's sleight of hand occurs in the very fact of his positing a *list*. For, the real controversy was fought over a division *between* opinions and actions, not over various types of opinions and actions.[83] In any case, "purely speculative opinions and divine worship" turn out to involve beliefs and practices regarding the Trinity; Purgatory; Christ's personal reign on earth; the place, time, and manner of worshiping God, and so forth, or in other words, most of the opinions that distinguished a stodgy Anglican clergyman from a raving Fifth Monarchy man. The magistrate, Locke argues, cannot interfere with such beliefs; they have "an absolute and universal right to toleration."

This absolute right is moored in certain religious, political, and epistemological premises, none of which is really developed by Locke in the *Essay*. The religious presupposition seems to point to a heightened individualist—and therefore more radical—interpretation of Protestantism. The speculative opinions alluded to by Locke, he insists, concern matters "wholly between God and me." The magistrate has no juridical authority because it is not in the *nature* of religion, from this standpoint, that he

[82] Fox-Bourne, 1:174–175.

[83] Invariably, commentators on Locke and the toleration debate have focused their attention upon Locke's threefold division, and have thereby missed the point that the controversy was not over the types of opinions expressed, but rather, whether one was entitled to *act* publicly upon one's opinions.

should have any authority. The logical extension of this viewpoint, of course, led to the beliefs of the Anabaptists and other extreme sectarians who simply refused to recognize the magistrate's existence. Also, the individual's juridical claim to an absolute right is based upon the inherent limitations in the grant of power given to the magistrate by individuals. "Nor can it be thought," Locke writes, "that men should give the magistrate a power to choose for them their way to salvation, which is too great to give away, if not impossible to part with." Here, at least, we have the political form of a natural rights argument as later developed by Locke—the assertion that individuals are endowed (by God) with certain qualities and obligations that they *cannot* renounce to any political authority, even if they should choose to do so. Finally, Locke argues that the magistrate "ought not to prescribe me the way, or require my diligence" with respect to my religious salvation, for the reason of his "having no more certain or more infallible knowledge of the way to attain it than I myself" have. Magisterial interference is in this instance an indication that he has forgotten his fallible and imperfect nature. The equality of ignorance is, or ought to be, a powerfully limiting factor upon the social relationships between individuals in civil society.

It is on the basic opinion/action issue, however, that Locke's epistemological shift is most evident. It is pointless for the magistrate to interfere with the beliefs and practices of religious worship, Locke argues, "since, whatever the magistrate enjoined in the worship of God, men must in this necessarily follow what they themselves thought best," because once an individual "was fully persuaded" that his religious faith dictated a certain course of action, he would necessarily have to pursue it.[84] To the objection (which Locke himself had raised in the early tracts) that one must draw a sharp distinction between religious *opinions* and indifferent *actions*, Locke now replies:

> I answer that in religious worship nothing is indifferent, for it being the using of those habits, gestures, etc., and no other, which I think acceptable to God in my worshipping of him, however they may be in their own nature perfectly indifferent, yet when I am worshipping my God in a way I think he has prescribed and will approve of, I cannot alter, omit or add any circumstance in that which I think the true way of worship.[85]

Later in the *Essay*, he speaks of "actions flowing from . . . these opinions."[86]

[84] Fox-Bourne, 1:176–177.

[85] Gough, *Locke's Political Philosophy*, p. 197.

[86] Fox-Bourne, 1:180.

It is clear that Locke has abandoned the philosophical dichotomy between opinions and actions drawn by Hobbes and subsequently reaffirmed by Parker, the very dichotomy on which so much of the absolutist language in his own two tracts on toleration rested for its support. It is equally obvious, from this passage especially, that the entire problem of toleration needs to be viewed from a distinctly subjectivist standpoint to a far greater extent than Locke was previously willing to concede. Finally, the dominant concept in the *Essay* is that of "persuasion," a concept that had no place at all in Locke's early writings, since it was irrelevant both to the individual's religious convictions and to the relationship between the magistrate and his subjects.

The *Essay on Toleration* does not break any new theoretical ground in its defense of toleration. Locke's contemporaries had heard far bolder and more elaborate arguments on the subject. What would have taken aback some of the *Essay*'s readers if it had been published, however, are some of the practical assertions to which Locke was willing to commit himself in that work. The basic political message of the *Essay* is clearly articulated. Included in Locke's list of "speculative" actions are "kneeling or sitting in the sacrament," "wearing a cope or surplice," adult baptism, and various other manifestations of divine worship, all of which are entitled to an absolute right of toleration.[87] However innocuous such actions may appear to us, they are precisely those actions which statutes such as the Act of Uniformity or the Conventicle Act either proscribed or attempted to regulate. The *Essay*, therefore, represents a political attack upon the Clarendon Code.[88] Since much of this legislation was enacted in the wake of revolutionary uprisings, the question of how the public peace can be preserved if religious dissent is allowed could not be ignored. There was no point in arguing against the magistrate's unlimited authority, still less in advocating the repeal of existing laws, if the result was likely to encourage sedition and disorder. The weight accorded to this point by Parker in the *Discourse* at the expense of more sophisticated issues indicates just how powerful an obstacle this practical objection to the adoption of any policy of toleration was in the seventeenth century.
Locke confronts this problem head on in the *Essay*.

> The objection usually made against toleration, that the magistrate's great business being to preserve peace and quiet of the government, he is obliged not to tolerate different religions in his country since they being distinctions wherein men unite and incorporate into bodies separate from the public, they may occasion disorder, conspira-

[87] Fox-Bourne, 1:177.
[88] Haley, p. 225.

> cies and seditions in the commonwealth and endanger the government.

It is certainly a cogent rendering of the point Locke himself made in the two tracts, and which was hammered home relentlessly by L'Estrange and Parker in the 1670s debate. What could one do with such an assertion, apart from offering a straightforward denial of its conclusion? Even Owen shied away from any argument that raised the ugly threat of "factions" and attached that word to individuals united in defense of their religious beliefs. Locke, however, is willing to venture further into the uncharted waters of social conflict. "I answer," he writes,

> if all things that may occasion disorder or conspiracy in a commonwealth must not be endured in it, all discontented and active men must be removed . . . And if all numbers of men joined in a union and corporation distinct from the public be not suffered, all charters of towns, especially great ones, are presently to be taken away.

Prophetic words, these! True, recall of the city charters was not being contemplated in the late 1660s, but the goal of removing "all discontented and active men" was not so distant a prospect in some men's minds as Locke hoped. Moreover, as Parker's *Discourse* was to demonstrate, appeals to economic or urban analogies might prove of no avail as a defense of religious "corporations" if one's intent in opening the floodgates of persecution was to sweep them all away together.

In Locke's view, "men united in religion have as little and perhaps less interest against the government than those united in the privileges of a corporation. This I am sure, they are less dangerous as being more scattered."[89] Locke does not mean by this that they are disorganized; he concedes, in fact, that they are "a party of men," that is, a faction.[90] Rather, the point he hopes will prove convincing is his assertion that these religious sects "are apt to divide and subdivide into so many little bodies, and always with the greatest enmity to those they last parted from or stand nearest to, that they are a guard upon one another, and the public can have no apprehensions of them as long as they have their equal share of common justice and protection."[91] One might label this policy Peace through Sectarianism. It was not likely to prove a compelling argument to Locke's contemporaries. Nor was his not-so-veiled threat of revolution likely to be well received. "Let divines preach duty as long as they will," Locke remarks, " 'twas never known that men lay down quietly under

[89] Gough, *Locke's Political Philosophy*, p. 199.

[90] Fox-Bourne, 1:184–185.

[91] Gough, *Locke's Political Philosophy*, p. 199.

the oppression and submitted their backs to the blows of others, when they thought they had strength enough to defend themselves."[92] Quite apart from sectarianism, the very existence of which was abhorrent to many seventeenth-century Englishmen, Locke's cool acceptance of the Dissenters' enmity toward one another, his extolment of the public benefits of factional conflict, and his challenge to the magistrate that even if he employed "force and compulsion," he would not be able "to break a party of men that unite in the profession" of religious beliefs—these were not the messages his contemporaries wished to hear.

Nor is Locke reluctant to cite the example of Rome, "where so many different opinions, gods, and ways of worship were promiscuously tolerated." Against the view that it was precisely this factional conflict that eventually undermined the Roman social order, Locke argues that it was the "ill intentions" of the government and the latter's persecution of religious dissidents that caused the disorder. He repeats this point as a general presupposition, maintaining that so long as "persecution and force does not drive [the Dissenters] together," society need not fear that dissent will lead to "disorder, conspiracies and seditions."[93]

But, even if one could extrapolate a principle suitable to the requirements of Protestant sectarianism from the example of heathen practices in Rome, the principle could not be stretched to include Catholics. Their beliefs and practices were, prima facie, "absolutely destructive of all governments except the Pope's."[94] Considering the later importance of this issue, commentators on the *Essay* have passed over rather too lightly Locke's attitude toward Catholics in this work. There is no reason to believe that, in the whole of his life, Locke ever doubted that Catholicism was a theologically ridiculous, morally pernicious, and politically seditious doctrine. Each of these characteristics is commented upon in the *Essay*.[95] Yet none of these assumptions is considered within a framework in

[92] Fox-Bourne, 1:190.

[93] Gough, *Locke's Political Philosophy*, p. 199. For a discussion of the importance of this argument to John Humfrey and other advocates of toleration in the works they published in 1667, see J. A. W. Gunn, *Politics and the Public Interest in the Seventeenth Century*, London: Routledge and Kegan Paul, 1969, pp. 164-168.

[94] Fox-Bourne, 1:187.

[95] That papists are "irreconcilable enemies" to the government, of whose fidelity and promises there is no security, since they "can, upon occasion, dispense with all their oaths, promises, and the obligations they have to their prince" is an overriding consideration for not granting them toleration. In addition to this moral incapacitation to act as good citizens, Locke speaks derisively of their "blind obedience to an infallible pope, who has the keys of their consciences tied to his girdle." Besides, "the principles and doctrines of that religion" appeal primarily to less "inquisitive heads and unstable minds" (Fox-Bourne, 1:188). In the 1670s, Locke drafted a memorandum that phrases these beliefs in terms of questions to be

which it is necessary to advance intellectually convincing arguments on their behalf; they are simply taken for granted. And while this could also be said about a number of propositions that form part of Locke's position in the *Essay*, at least one can find elsewhere in the corpus of his writings a more elaborate treatment of them. This is not the case with respect to his view of Catholicism, which sometimes reappears in his later writings in the form of polemical characterizations, but which is never accorded anything like a systematic intellectual consideration by Locke.

Locke's perception of Catholicism—popery—was decidedly within the mainstream of his contemporaries' opinions on the subject, which reflected a deep-seated hatred and fear of the doctrine and its advocates. The intensity with which he and Shaftesbury abhorred the prospect of Catholicism's taking root in England and shaping its social, religious, economic, and political institutions is a point that must be insisted upon if one is to appreciate the considerable lengths to which they were willing to go in the 1680s in an effort to prevent just such a catastrophe from occurring.

In the *Essay on Toleration*, Locke characterized the Dissenters as individuals following the "sincere persuasions of their own conscience." And despite his passing allusion to resistance, he offers the general and reassuring observation that such individuals can be expected "quietly to submit" to the laws and its penalties.[96] For Locke, there is no question of employing force in order to bring about a change in the Dissenters' religious views. On the contrary, he emphasizes the point that we may "persuade them" to "become friends to the state, though they are not sons of the church." The matter was quite otherwise so far as Catholics were concerned. It was useless to rely upon "persuasion" with them, nor could one expect from Catholics the quiet display of passive obedience with which he credited the Dissenters. Locke was prepared to argue not only that force employed against Catholics was a justifiable political policy—no more "than what the cruelty of their own principles and practices are known to deserve"—but also, and inconsistently with the presuppositions of his own general argument, he maintained that the application of force even carried with it the prospects that Catholics would abandon their religious beliefs and join the ranks of Protestantism.[97] That a thinker such as Locke would tolerate such a glaring intellectual inconsistency can only be explained in terms of an attitude so deeply held that no reasoned argument against it—certainly none ever encountered by Locke

put to Catholic priests with the object of forcing them to renounce these principles (MS c.27, fols. 30a, 32).

[96] Fox-Bourne, 1:180.

[97] Fox-Bourne, 1:188–189.

in his lifetime—could overrule its explanatory status as an axiom of political life in seventeenth-century England.

Another such axiom, though less widely accepted than those associated with anti-Catholicism, was that toleration fosters the advancement of trade. This maxim is also defended by Locke in the *Essay*. At the end of that work, he promises to consider at greater length in another essay the "influence toleration is like to have upon the number and industry of your people, on which depends the power and riches of the kingdom."[98] Locke never wrote that essay, but he did write, shortly afterward, a manuscript discussing the lowering of the rate of interest and its effects upon the advancement of trade.[99]

In 1667–1668, Shaftesbury was very active in his efforts to improve England's trading position, which had suffered considerably in the wake of the Second Dutch War. He was a member of the special committee of the Privy Council charged with the responsibility of overseeing trade. Shaftesbury also appears to have played a role in securing, in 1668, the establishment of a separate Council of Trade, of which he was made a member. And, in the following year, he was appointed to a House of Lords committee created to consider the causes of "the fall of rents and decay of trade within the kingdom." Sir Josiah Child, a prominent merchant with the East India Company, argued before this committee in favor of a lowering of the rate of interest from 6 to 4 percent. The committee endorsed this recommendation in their report, but the House of Lords instructed them to reconsider the matter. To this end, it asked Shaftesbury and several other Lords to choose "three or four of a side of the ablest persons they knew to speak for it and against it, before the said committee."[100] It seems reasonable to suppose that Locke was one of the "ablest" persons Shaftesbury knew, for his manuscript *Some Considerations of the Lowering of Interest and Raising the Value of Money* addresses itself directly to Child's proposal. Locke takes the opposite view from Child, holding that "the price of the hire of money" should be de-

[98] Fox-Bourne, 1:194; cf. ibid., p. 187. The reference to "your people," and another to "the doctors of your several churches," seem to indicate that these draft essays on toleration were intended to be policy recommendations to Charles II, passed to him, of course, by Shaftesbury.

[99] This manuscript, MS e.8, written during 1668, was later revised and published in 1692 as *Some Considerations of the Lowering of Interest and Raising the Value of Money* (*Works*, 4:1–116). A transcript of MS e.8 was published by William Letwin, *The Origins of Scientific Economics*, London: Methuen, 1963, pp. 273–300. The basic argument is unchanged, though it is a little more clearly stated in the later work. In general, I have cited from Locke's *Works*, except where this would distort the meaning of the argument in the 1668 manuscript.

[100] Haley, pp. 255–256.

termined by the play of market forces and should not be regulated by legislation.[101] Though it represents a slight digression, this controversy is worth pursuing because it illustrates two important aspects of Locke's political thought that will reemerge later in our consideration of his position in relation to the political debate of the 1680s.

Child argued that "if interest of money were with us reduced to the same rate as it is with [the Dutch], it would in a short time render us as rich and considerable in trade as they now are."[102] Since Dutch merchants pay a lower rate of interest on the money they borrow to finance commercial ventures, they are able to undercut their competition from English merchants by lowering the prices of their goods, while still retaining the same profit margin. High interest rates, therefore, were an obstacle to commercial expansion. Moreover, Child observed that historically the great increase in wealth accruing to England had followed the lowering of the interest rate, from 10 to 8 percent and from 8 to 6 percent. Child was too shrewd a thinker to assert a simple causal relationship between the lowering of the interest rate and the expansion of trade, but that was certainly a plausible conclusion to be drawn from the way in which he stated his position. His opponents, including Locke, thus argued for the other side of this causal relationship: that the expansion of trade and the accumulation of wealth would naturally bring down the rate of interest. No legislative interference was necessary because the natural workings of the economy would achieve the result desired by Child.[103]

Locke's general position is clear enough, but his reasoning in arriving at this conclusion is not always clear or easy to follow because some of his basic assumptions are not elaborated. The socioeconomic ground of his argument is that it is "plenty of people and money in proportion to . . . land, which makes money cheap," and not the artifically instituted rate of interest. In Aristotelian terms, laws follow and are shaped by the socioeconomic structure of society. Lowering the rate of interest "will hinder trade," Locke argues, because "there being a certain proportion of money necessary for driving such a proportion of trade, so much of this money as lies still lessens so much of the trade."[104] Locke maintains that "the several wheels of trade" are driven by the quantity of money in circula-

[101] *Works*, 4:4–5. For a discussion of this point that relates Locke's argument to his general dislike of monopolies, see Karen Ivarsen Vaughn, *John Locke: Economist and Social Scientist*, Chicago: University of Chicago Press, 1982, pp. 59ff.

[102] Letwin, *Origins*, p. 11.

[103] G. S. L. Tucker, *Progress and Profits in British Economic Thought, 1650–1850*, Cambridge: Cambridge University Press, 1960, pp. 10, 14–19.

[104] Letwin, *Origins*, p. 274. William Petty advanced a similar argument (E. Lipson, *The Economic History of England*, 6th ed., 3 vols., London: Adam and Charles Black, 1961, 3:68).

tion and the speed with which it circulates in the economy; if either the quantity or the rapidity of the circulation of money declines, the "wheels of trade" will grind to a halt. The questions arise, therefore, What is it that puts money into circulation in the economy? And secondarily, How does that money continue to flow through the channels of commercial expansion?

If one assumed a simple relationship between bankers and merchants, it would seem that as the rate of interest declined, the latter would be encouraged to expand their commercial operations through borrowing money. To a successful merchant like Child, this was both an obvious maxim of practical experience and the limits of his theoretical argument. Locke, however, maintains that the rate of interest is largely a function of the quantity of money in circulation; hence, anything that affects or determines that quantity will raise or lower the rate of interest, regardless of the statutory rate. The chief factor adversely affecting rates of interest, Locke argues, are the London bankers. This is because they have "so large a proportion of the cash of the nation in their hands." They are, in effect, a monopoly in the money market. The result is, as in the case of engrossers of corn, that they are able to charge a higher price (interest rate) for their commodity than the natural workings of the market (or the legally set rate of interest) would allow.[105]

A legally lowered rate of interest will not resolve this problem, since not only will it not effect a redistribution of money out of the bankers' hands, but it will also induce other people to hoard their money rather than lend it out at low rates, thus withdrawing even more cash from circulation and trade.[106] This would inevitably force interest rates up despite the law, Locke argues, because the holders of great quantities of cash (bankers) will be able to set the price of money. Those who desperately need the money—artisans, tradesmen, and merchants—will be forced to pay whatever interest rate they can get from bankers. What is needed, Locke argues, is a more equitable distribution of money, so that individuals do not simply "carry it to London, to put it into the bankers' hands." Rather, the money should be lent out in the country in a more decentralized fashion, "where it is convenient for trade."[107]

Throughout the essay, Locke repeatedly defends the interests of the

105 *Works*, 4:8–9. This was certainly Shaftesbury's view. He wrote to Locke in 1674, complaining that the bankers managed to get "all the ready money of the kingdom into their hands so that no gentleman farmer or merchant" could obtain any money except "at almost double the rates the law allowed to be taken" (*Correspondence*, 1:420). In 1670, a member of Parliament complained that it was the high rate of interest that "rakes all the money of England into the bankers' hands" (Grey, 1:272).

106 *Works*, 4:12, 14.

107 *Works*, 4:9.

"industrious and thriving men" involved in trade against the "engrossing" bankers. Thus, "all encouragement should be given to artifacers," and "manufacture deserves to be encouraged"; yet, artisans, manufacturers, and tradesmen, Locke argues, will suffer the losses if the legal rate of interest is lowered.[108] The economy, in other words, was not structured around a simple relationship between bankers and merchants; one had to adopt a much wider view in assessing the growth of trade and riches. Both Child and Locke were arguing in favor of commercial expansion, but the latter was engaged in a polemic against bankers and, at the same time, offering what he believed was a more complicated picture of socioeconomic life than the one advanced by Child. This willingness on the part of Locke (and Shaftesbury) to think of trade in terms that included *all* the groups that could be placed under the category of industrious labor forms an important part of the radical Whig political perspective.

Secondly, the presumption that socioeconomic relations are determinant in structuring political systems is a fundamental characteristic of the Aristotelian-Harringtonian Whig political argument in general, and of Locke's argument regarding the state of nature and the institution of political society in the *Two Treatises* in particular.

The same Lords Committee that heard these and other arguments during the course of its consideration of the "decay of trade within the kingdom," recommended in its report "that some ease and relaxation in ecclesiastical matters will be a means of improving the trade of this kingdom."[109] Whether Locke was one of those who spoke for a policy of toleration before the Lords Committee, we do not know, but he certainly agreed with their recommendation. In a manuscript on trade, he noted that "arbitrary power," "arrests," and "imprisonment" are all "hindrances of trade," while "freedom of religion" is one of the "promoters of trade."[110] But the Lords Committee report was sent to the House in the late fall of 1669, and the House of Commons was of a different mind. It passed the Second Conventicle Bill, thus launching a campaign of political

[108] *Works*, 4:8–9, 15, 20, 28–29, 39. The polemical aspect of this argument against bankers is much more clearly stated in the revised version, but the basic argument concerning the unequal distribution of money in the hands of the bankers and its effect upon trade is essentially unchanged.

[109] Haley, pp. 256–257. Thomas Papillon, an active member of the Council for Trade, was one of those who testified before the Lords Committee that religious persecution was "a great . . . impediment to trade." However, he sided with Child, a fellow director of the East India Company, on the issue of interest rates (Letwin, *Origins*, pp. 38, 41; A. F. W. Papillon, *Memoirs of Thomas Papillon*, 1887, pp. 60, 71, 74).

[110] MS c.30, fol. 18.

repression against the Dissenters, egged on, of course, by the publication of Parker's *Discourse of Ecclesiastical Polity*.

With what degree of self-critical examination Locke read Parker we may only guess. Many of the arguments in the *Discourse* must have appeared to him as echoes from his own writings of the not-too-distant past. Yet, the manuscript notes Locke made on Parker's *Discourse* reveal no awareness of the reversal in his own thinking; they are merely terse and petulant in their rejection of Parker's arguments.[111] These notes provide us with an indication of the conclusions to which Locke now subscribed, but they say nothing at all about the process of thinking and the chain of reasoning by which Locke had come to those conclusions.

Locke begins by citing Parker's declaration that "the civil magistrate must have under his power all that may concern the end of government, i.e., peace." This statement was of course endorsed by Locke himself in his *Essay on Toleration*, but read within the context of Parker's argument, Locke interprets it as meaning that the magistrate ought to have power over men's consciences in matters of religion, a proposition that he rejects. Parker argued in support of his contention that since individuals were most likely to cause a disturbance of the public peace when issues of religious belief and conscience were the focus of controversy, it was especially with regard to such matters that a defense of the magistrate's absolute power was necessary. To which Locke appends the comment that Parker advocates the magistrate's employment of extreme "severity and strictness" against religious dissidents "because ordinary severity will not do."[112] Yet, since this *was* Parker's position—and Locke's position in the two tracts on toleration—it hardly qualifies as a response. Parker maintained that conscience was an extreme-case problem. For, "if conscience be ever able to break down the restraints of government, and all men have license to follow their own persuasions, the mischief is infinite . . . insomuch as there was never yet any Commonwealth that gave a real liberty to men's imaginations, that was not suddenly overrun with numberless divisions and subdivisions of sects."[113] At this point, Locke interjects, in the form of a question, the proposition for which he had formulated an argument in the *Essay on Toleration*: "Whether subdivision of opinions into small sects be of such danger to the government?"

To this implicit argument, he adds another drawn from the *Essay*. Admitting the magistrate's duty to preserve the public peace (which is allowed "by every sober man"), Locke asks "whether uniformity estab-

[111] MS c.39. The notes are dated 1670. A major portion of the notes was printed by Cranston, pp. 131–133.

[112] MS c.39, fol. 5.

[113] Samuel Parker, *Discourse of Ecclesiastical Polity* [1670], p. 21.

lished by law be (as is here supposed) a necessary means to it, i.e., whether it be at all dangerous to the magistrate he believing free will some of his subjects shall believe predestination, or whether it be more necessary for his government to make laws for wearing surplices than it is for wearing vests?" Locke had decided, by 1667, that these opinions and actions merited toleration, but an opponent like Parker was willing to pursue the controversy even to the distant reaches of free will versus predestination. Since no quarter was to be given in the hunt for political subversives, neither philosophy nor theology could offer them any sanctuary.

Locke's most effective critique is an epistemological attack upon Parker's assumption that the magistrate is in a privileged position to know more than any of his subjects what is essential to the fulfillment of an individual's religious obligations. Does Parker mean to assert, he asks, "that whether the magistrate's opinion be right or wrong he has power to force the subject to renounce his own opinions . . . and consent to those of the magistrate?" If so, then all claims for truth must rest upon the magistrate's "knowledge." Yet, if the fate of Christianity thus depends upon the magistrate's opinion, then why did Christ and the Apostles not address their "discourses and . . . miracles to the princes and magistrates of the world to persuade them" of its truth? Instead, Locke remarks, "by preaching to and converting the people they, according to this doctrine," laid the foundations by which individuals are forced to live "under a necessity of being either seditious or martyrs."[114]

It is not reading too much into Locke's comments on Parker's *Discourse*, I believe, to see in them the seeds of a two-pronged epistemological attack upon the claims of political authority with respect to matters of religion, an attack that was eventually to bear fruition in the *Essay Concerning Human Understanding* and *The Reasonableness of Christianity*. Against the knowledge claims of a single individual (the magistrate), Locke was prepared to assert the equality of reason, while against the interpretive claims of religious clerical authority, Locke argued for a populist and simplified version of Christianity that the majority of mankind could accept through self-instruction. I am not suggesting that Locke had necessarily arrived at these conclusions by 1670, only that Parker's *Discourse of Ecclesiastical Polity* gave him a considerable impetus to pursue these issues in some depth. Certainly, they clearly emerged in the writings of others published during the course of the debate generated by Parker's *Discourse* in the 1670s.

In addition to the epistemological defense of toleration, another set of issues about which Locke may have begun to think more deeply were

[114] MS c.39, fol. 7.

those pertaining to the origins of government. In his two tracts on toleration, Locke treated this subject as a hypothetical and largely irrelevant question. He noted that there were two "commonly" accepted theories as to the origins of government: paternal right and consent.[115] He was willing, for the sake of argument (since his opponent began from the latter presupposition) to accept the supposition that political authority was derived from the consent of the people, although he makes it plain that he does not wish to "meddle" with this problem.[116] For the purposes of resolving the controversy over toleration, Locke argues, it is not necessary "to review the forms of government or prescribe the number of the governors."[117] Since Locke treated all indifferent actions as being under the magistrate's authority, however constituted, the problem of the origins of that authority was indeed an irrelevant consideration.[118] Or, to put it another way, Locke recognized that a debate over the origins of government could only be meaningful in the context of an argument in which the limits of the magistrate's authority required a precise determination. To his opponent, Locke addressed the challenge, "I wish our author would do us the courtesy to show us the bounds of [indifferent actions] and tell us where civil things end and spiritual [things] begin."[119] If limits were to be placed upon the magistrate's power over indifferent religious actions, these limits would have to be rooted, in some fashion, in the original grant of power to the magistrate.[120] And, Locke reflected in his second tract, in order to gain a clear idea of what kind of limits ought to be placed on the magistrate's power over indifferent actions, "the subject must be examined a little more profoundly. The sources of civil power must be investigated and the very foundations of authority uncovered."[121] There is little evidence that Locke had, in fact, undertaken such an investigation by the time he wrote the *Essay on Toleration*, despite the fact that its argument does depend upon drawing a distinction between civil and religious indifferent actions. It is true, he seems more disposed to accept the theory of consent as the basis for political authority, but the origins of the latter is not a central issue in the *Essay*.[122]

[115] *STG*, p. 230. There "may perhaps" be a third viewpoint, which holds that all authority comes from God, "but the nomination and appointment of the person bearing that power is thought to be made by the people" (p. 231).

[116] *FTG*, p. 122.

[117] *STG*, p. 213.

[118] "Indifferent things of civil as well as religious concernment being of the same nature" (*FTG*, p. 153; cf. ibid., pp. 136, 138, 148).

[119] *FTG*, p. 139.

[120] *STG*, p. 240.

[121] *STG*, p. 229.

[122] Locke definitely rejects the applicability of a divine right theory of absolute monarchy to the English system of government. He is inclined to accept popular consent as the source

Parker's *Discourse*, however, forced the problem into the foreground of the discussion of toleration, precisely because he proposed to offer his opponents no means of escape from a commitment to the theory of consent, which even in its Hobbesian version, according to Parker, led toward republicanism, and hence sedition. Parker, therefore, placed his argument firmly on the foundations of patriarchal authority. "Fathers," he wrote, "have an absolute power over their children . . . And the first governments in the world were established purely upon the natural rights of paternal authority which afterward grew up to a kingly power by the increase of posterity."[123] Locke's response to this defense of the paternal right of government, "which is asserted not proved," might be termed one of cautious skepticism. If Parker means "that paternal monarchy descended upon [the] death of the father . . . wholly to the eldest son," then, Locke concludes, "monarchy is certainly *jure naturali*, but there can be but one rightful monarch over the whole world, i.e., the right heir of Adam." Locke, we may suppose, doubted that this proposition could be proved, or that anyone would seriously undertake to do so—Filmer's *Patriarcha* had not yet been published. If this argument from "natural right" cannot be established, however, then, Locke argues, "all government, whether monarchical or other, is only from the consent of the people."[124] That government instituted through consent is a theory acceptable by default, as it were, can hardly qualify as evidence of Locke's having investigated or "examined a little more profoundly" the "very foundations of authority," as he had proposed to himself in his second tract on toleration.

Like several other critics of Parker, Locke accuses him of following "Mr. Hobbs's doctrine" in his discussion of the civil magistrate's power. And in reply to Parker's declamations against "fanaticism" and the "fanatic spirit" in religion, he, too, hurls the charge back at Parker. What spirit is it, Locke asks, "which sets him so zealously to stir up the magistrate to persecute all those who dissent from him in [their] opinions and ways of worship"?[125] The general tone of these manuscript notes is one of polemical impatience. They are not especially informative as to Locke's substantive position, but they do reflect a certain stage in the development of his political thought. Some of the points he makes are carried forward from his 1667 *Essay on Toleration*, while others are identical to those advanced by Parker's Dissenter critics. Although the *Essay* is not

for political authority, but he is not prepared to defend that theory in the *Essay on Toleration* (Fox-Bourne, 1:180).

123 Parker, *Discourse*, p. 29.

124 MS c.39, fol. 7.

125 MS c.39, fol. 9.

without its merits as an example of Locke's intellectual abilities, it seems fair to say, in view of the evidence available to us, that by 1670, Locke had moved within the political orbit of the Dissenters on the primary issue of toleration and that he had done so without having worked out for himself the kind of intellectual defense of this political perspective that could be, and was, supplied by John Owen, Robert Ferguson, John Humfrey, Andrew Marvell, and others in their replies to Parker. This fact, I believe, became clear to Locke himself as he read the works generated by the controversy over the *Discourse of Ecclesiastical Polity*, and he set about to shore up the intellectual foundations of his political position.

In the Epistle to the Reader of the *Essay Concerning Human Understanding*, Locke writes:

> Were it fit to trouble thee with the history of this *Essay*, I should tell thee that five or six friends, meeting in my chamber and discoursing on a subject very remote from this, found themselves quickly at a stand by the difficulties that arose on every side. After we had awhile puzzled ourselves, without coming any nearer a resolution of those doubts which perplexed us, it came into my thoughts that we took a wrong course; and that before we set ourselves upon enquiries of that nature it was necessary to examine our own abilities, and see what objects our understandings were or were not fitted to deal with. This I proposed to the company, who all readily assented; and thereupon it was agreed that this should be our first enquiry. Some hasty and undigested thoughts, on a subject I had never before considered, which I set down against our next meeting gave the first entrance into the discourse; which having been thus begun by chance was continued by entreaty, written by incoherent parcels, and after long intervals of neglect, resumed again, as my humor or occasions permitted; and at last, in a retirement where an attendance of my health gave me leisure, it was brought into that order thou now seest it.[126]

From a manuscript note in his copy of the *Essay*, we know that James Tyrrell was one of the "five or six friends" who met for these discussions. Tyrrell also records that the question of the nature of the human understanding arose out of a discussion about "the principles of morality and revealed religion" and their relationship.[127] These issues, as we have seen, were, from the Dissenters' standpoint, at the heart of the controversy over Parker's *Discourse*. As the anonymous Nonconformist min-

126 *ECHU*, Epistle to the Reader, p. 7.

127 James Tyrrell's copy of the *Essay Concerning Human Understanding* is in the British Museum.

ister had maintained in his sermon, if one hoped to gain a clear insight into the nature of faith, it was essential to consider "the nature of faith and the nature of man together, the powers and faculties he is endowed with, and the dependency one has upon another." This is certainly the central problem addressed in the *Essay Concerning Human Understanding*.[128]

The discussions that gave rise to the *Essay* were held during the winter of 1670–1671, at the height of the pamphlet war provoked by Parker's book. By the following July, Locke had written a first draft.[129] If numerous troublesome questions remained unanswered, nevertheless, the general strategy underlying the draft is relatively clear. "Most of those propositions we think, argue, reason, discourse, nay, act upon," Locke observes, "are not evident and certain," nor can we "have undoubted knowledge of their truth." Such propositions have no more than a "probable" status, "and our assent to them" must be counted as "faith, not knowledge." In all cases of probability, someone may present "arguments . . . to persuade us to receive it [the proposition] as true," but claims for certainty are generally spurious.[130] Not only are most of our opinions only "highly probable," but Locke stresses the degree to which our religious beliefs fall into this category. For the most part, we imbibe these beliefs from parents or nurses, and they are maintained through custom. Hence, under the label of religion, we "swallow down opinions" given to us by the church, and "the grossest absurdities and improbabilities . . . go down glibly and are easily digested." These "received principles" are held even against "the clear evidence" of an individual's senses.[131] Locke defends the "voluntary action" of dissent in the case of probable statements. Such dissent is the act of the individual's will and is defensible not only as a response to probability statements, but it is also a necessary aspect of the individual's expression of faith. Thus, in all cases, including religious opinions, our ideas and actions must be guided not by any "received principles," but "by our faculty of reasoning."[132]

Locke was stung by Parker's *Discourse* into recording some tart responses to his political and theological assertions, but the early draft of

[128] Richard Ashcraft, "Faith and Knowledge in Locke's Philosophy," in *John Locke: Problems and Perspectives*, ed. John W. Yolton, Cambridge: Cambridge University Press, 1969.

[129] Tyrrell gave 1673 as the date of these discussions, but that is a mistake. The *Early Draft* and its successor (Draft B) were both written in 1671, and any paper presented by Locke at these discussions is certainly earlier than these drafts (Cranston, pp. 140–141; *Early Draft*, p. xiii). Fox-Bourne records Lady Masham's confirmation of the winter of 1670–1671 as the correct date (1:249).

[130] *Early Draft*, pp. 55–56.

[131] *Early Draft*, pp. 61–64.

[132] *Early Draft*, pp. 66–69.

the *Essay* represents, I believe, an attempt to outflank Parker by destroying the epistemological basis for his position. This line of attack is already evident in the writings of Ferguson and others, but no one pursued it to the lengths that Locke did during the next twenty years. In light of Locke's refusal to be more specific as to the nature of the "remote" subject of his original discourse, I can see no way of improving upon the status of this hypothesis than by suggesting that a reading of the *Essay Concerning Human Understanding* in the context of the tracts published during the 1670s debate with Parker throws a great deal of light upon the political significance of some of the philosophical issues discussed in that work as well as upon the internal structure of the *Essay* itself—that is, why certain points are discussed at all.

Meanwhile, the practical problem of toleration confronted Charles II's government on the eve of the Third Dutch War. The king asked Shaftesbury to provide him with an opinion as to whether he could declare an Act of Indulgence—or in more strictly legalistic terms, whether he could suspend the execution of penalties attached to existing statutes against Nonconformists—through the exercise of his royal prerogative. Shaftesbury delegated the responsibility for the answer to this question to Locke, who researched the precedents and supplied Shaftesbury with the necessary information to support the recommendation that the king did possess such power.[133] This conclusion was not surprising in view of Shaftesbury's own conviction that the king had this authority, but it has led some interpreters of Locke's thought to cite the recommendation as an instance of Locke's concession to authoritarianism. In fact, it was nothing of the sort.

What is true, as was noted previously, is that some Dissenters did harbor doubts as to whether the use of the king's prerogative was the proper political instrument for achieving religious toleration. But the majority of them accepted the Indulgence de facto, and some of them, including radicals like John Humfrey, even offered a theoretical defense of the king's prerogative.[134] The primary question for those who supported the

[133] There are two documents in Locke's hand in the Shaftesbury papers that deal with the king's jurisdiction over ecclesiastical matters (PRO 30/24/6B/429–430; Haley, p. 297).

[134] Lacey, pp. 64–65, 290–291; Frank Bate, *The Declaration of Indulgence, 1672*, London: Archibald Constable, 1908, pp. 88ff. Weston and Greenberg are mistaken in their assertion that "to espouse the rival community-centered view of government . . . was to deny the dispensing power as traditionally conceived," that is, in terms of the king's power to use his prerogative for the common good. Thus, "there was no place" in the radicals' view of government "for the royal dispensing power" (Corinne Comstock Weston and Janelle Renfrow Greenberg, *Subjects and Sovereigns: The Grand Controversy over Legal Sovereignty in Stuart England*, Cambridge: Cambridge University Press, 1981, pp. 22, 33). This is not true. Throughout the last half of the seventeenth century, numerous radicals, including

Indulgence was whether it secured the common good and not whether it enhanced the king's power. Generally speaking, Dissenters were inclined to accept the view that Parliament was more likely than the king to be in touch with the common good of society, but there were always exceptions to this rule, and with respect to the policy of toleration, Parliament had just registered its clear opposition to its adoption. To those who saw toleration as a "common good," therefore, use of the king's prerogative to achieve this end was precisely a case in point where the common good was not likely to be secured by any other political means. This was certainly Shaftesbury's view of the matter.[135]

Aside from his overt political support for toleration, some mention needs to be made of the personal, social, and business associations between Shaftesbury and the Dissenters. Or more accurately, a network of social interaction appears to have developed in the 1670s that brought several lords, and the members of their entourages, into relatively frequent contact with one another. The Duke of Buckingham and Shaftesbury, for example, began to cooperate more closely on political issues, and also to entertain each other socially more often. Buckingham was an important patron for John Owen and several other Dissenters. Shaftesbury, Owen, and other Nonconformists were holding meetings in the mid-1670s. At the same time, Buckingham, Shaftesbury, and Holles were holding frequent meetings.[136] Major Wildman, the Leveller, was Buckingham's chief steward and legal adviser, and as we shall see, he eventually moved into Shaftesbury's political camp.[137] The latter also maintained good relations with the Earl of Anglesey, a not-too-reformed old Puritan with close ties to the Dissenters. In his diary, Anglesey records social, and very likely political visits and dinners with Shaftesbury and Buckingham throughout 1671–1672. Anglesey seems to have been impressed with Locke's former tutor, Thomas Cole, and he made a special

Humfrey, Shaftesbury, and Locke, had no difficulty whatsoever in reconciling a defense of the king's dispensing power with their community-centered view of government.

135 Haley, pp. 297–298. Shaftesbury's view on the king's use of the prerogative is defended in *A Letter from a Person of Quality to His Friend in the Country*.

136 Add. MS 40860 (Earl of Anglesey's Diary, 1667–1675), fols. 7, 12; Haley, pp. 270–271; *CSPD*, 8:238; *Dictionary of National Biography*, s.v. "Anthony Ashley Cooper." Buckingham was one of those "much taken with" Locke's abilities (Cranston, p. 114).

137 On Wildman and Buckingham, see *CSPD*, 8:89; Maurice Ashley, *John Wildman: Postmaster and Plotter*, London: Jonathan Cape, 1947, pp. 11, 14, 185, 212. For Wildman and Shaftesbury, see Ashley, *Wildman*, pp. 218, 222. Wildman also appears to be one of those assisting Shaftesbury in the prosecution of the popish plot after he moved away from Buckingham (Haley, p. 475; PRO 30/24/43/63). Besides Wildman, other servants of Buckingham gravitated toward Shaftesbury—notably Colonel John Scott, who is discussed in Chapter 4.

effort to attend his sermons. He was also very close to Owen, another frequent visitor to his home. So was Sir Charles Wolseley, another patron of the Dissenters.[138] Thomas Wharton, who had strong ties with the Dissenters, also began to drift into closer cooperation with Shaftesbury during this period. Like Anglesey, Wharton was one of Thomas Cole's supporters.[139]

Robert Ferguson was at this time an assistant to John Owen. His *Sober Enquiry into Moral Virtue* was dedicated to Charles Wolseley, and his *Interest of Reason in Religion* to Thomas Papillon, a merchant and longtime friend of Shaftesbury. Sometime during the 1670s Ferguson became closely associated with Shaftesbury, acting as his chaplain, and with Locke, as his assistant pen.[140] During the period of the Indulgence, numerous friends and associates of Locke and Shaftesbury obtained licenses as Nonconformists. These included Locke's friend, Robert Pawling, and his tenant and friend, William Stratton.[141] Locke's former pupil, Edward West, was particularly active as an intermediary in obtaining licenses for

[138] Add. MS 40860, fols. 7, 9, 12, 23, 28, 31, 59, 77; Add. MS 18730 (Anglesey's diary, 1675–1684), fols. 85ff.; Lacey, pp. 103, 448, 460. Anglesey's wife and daughter were members of Owen's congregation. Shaftesbury and Wolseley had served together on the Council of State during the Interregnum (Haley, p. 75).

[139] Haley, pp. 410, 413ff., 425 (Wharton and Shaftesbury). See Cole's letter (1673) to Wharton, indicating that he had found a tutor for his son (MS Rawlinson Letters 51, fol. 18). Wharton also maintained a close friendship with Owen (Lacey, pp. 103, 473). Cole, along with Ferguson, was one of those assisting Owen in the 1670s (W. Wilson, *Dissenting Churches*, 3:79–80; *Owen Correspondence*, [ed. Toon], p. 161). In addition to Owen, John Howe was a close friend of Wharton; some of Howe's works are dedicated to Wharton's wife. When Wharton left England for Holland in 1685, Howe accompanied him, remaining in exile there, where, incidentally, he renewed his friendship with Locke (Lacey, p. 473; W. Wilson, *Dissenting Churches*, 3:19–37; C. E. Whiting, *Studies in English Puritanism from the Restoration to the Revolution 1660–1688*, London: Society for Promoting Christian Knowledge, 1931, p. 415.

[140] William Orme, *Memoirs of the Life, Writings, and Religious Connections of John Owen*, 1820, p. 393. Ferguson received a small legacy in Owen's will. (*Owen Correspondence* [ed. Toon], p. 184; Haley, pp. 654, 709–733).

[141] A license was granted to Robert Pawling to be a Presbyterian teacher on December 9, 1672 (G. Lyon Turner, *Original Records of Early Nonconformity under Persecution and Indulgence*, 3 vols., London: T. Fisher Unwin, 1911, 1:579). For Pawling's fanatic and extreme Whig views, see Edward M. Thompson, ed., *Letters of Humphrey Prideaux to John Ellis*, 1875, pp. 80, 84; Anthony Wood, *The Life and Times of Anthony Wood*, 5 vols., Oxford: Clarendon Press, 1892, 2:463, 496). His friendship with Locke is discussed in Chapter 7. John Hicks, with whom Locke may have resided occasionally and whose house he used as a mailing address, received a license as a Presbyterian (*CSPD*, 14:309; G. L. Turner, *Original Records*, 1:196, 424, 581). William Stratton, a relation of Locke's by marriage, and the manager of his property in Somerset, appears to be the individual granted a Nonconformist's license, but this is less certain (Bate, *Indulgence*, p. lxxi).

other Nonconformists.[142] So was Robert Blaney, one of Shaftesbury's assistants and a member of his household.[143] A number of Shaftesbury's associates were both Nonconformists and merchants such as William Kiffin and Thomas Firmin.[144]

It is difficult to impose any strict order on these and a myriad of other items of specific information of a similar nature, and yet some account needs to be taken of the fact that there was an extended circle of politicians, writers, clergy, and merchants, who were sympathetic to and leaders of the community of Dissenters who maintained close communication and a network of social interaction with one another. Shaftesbury, and those around him (including Locke), constituted one important nucleus of this extended circle. As early as 1672, Richard Baxter recognized Shaftesbury as the chief political defender of the Protestant cause. Shaftesbury had become, Baxter wrote, "the head of the party that were zealous for the Protestant cause, and [he] awakened the nation greatly by his activity."[145] The existence of these social and political relationships is also worth noting for the bearing it has on the fact that many of these individuals later became active leaders of the radical movement in the 1680s. And, finally, it is not of least importance that these individuals were clearly well known to Locke, and he to them, as a consequence of these associations and interaction in the 1670s.

From 1672, when Shaftesbury became Lord Chancellor, his importance as a political figure steadily increased. Concomitantly, Locke's political activities on Shaftesbury's behalf also increased. He was now conducting research, writing speeches, screening clerical appointments, maintaining a parliamentary journal, and fulfilling other specific demands, in addition to his secretarial duties in connection with Shaftesbury's trading and colonial interests.[146] At the beginning of 1673, Shaftesbury delivered his famous *delenda est Carthago* speech to Parliament, designed to enlist their support for the Third Dutch War. Despite the hostility conveyed by its most famous phrase, the speech as a whole was a reasoned attempt to

[142] Edward West received his B.A. from Christ Church, Oxford, in 1655. Both Locke and Thomas Cole served as his tutors. He was ejected as a Nonconformist minister in 1662. He built a special meeting place for conventicles in London (G. L. Turner, *Original Records*, 1:87, 206, 260, 421; 3:209, 211).

[143] Haley, p. 440 (Blaney and Shaftesbury); G. L. Turner, *Original Records*, 1:297–298; 3:462, 478. A license was granted to Samuel Wilson, a Presbyterian, who may have been the same individual who was Shaftesbury's secretary (G. L. Turner, *Original Records*, 1:554, 565).

[144] Cranston, p. 127 (Firmin, Locke, and Shaftesbury); Haley, pp. 228, 232; MS c.1, fols. 14, 53–55 (Locke and Shaftesbury's financial dealings with Kiffin).

[145] *Life of Richard Baxter*, ed. Matthew Sylvester, 1696, pp. 106, 109.

[146] PRO 30/24/42/59; 30/24/5/Pt. 2/276; Haley, p. 311; Fox-Bourne, 1:286–289.

justify the war on straightforward economic grounds. All the world knows, Shaftesbury declared, that the chief and only interest of Holland lies in its trade; "therefore whoever rivals their trade must be irreconcilable to them." Since England was its chief trading rival, it followed that she must be viewed by the Dutch as their "eternal enemy both by interest and inclination." In essence, Shaftesbury told Parliament, this war was a "contest . . . for the trade of the whole world."[147] This was of course the line Charles II had attempted to sell Parliament. Nevertheless, the war for trade also independently corresponded to the complaints of many merchants, passed on to Shaftesbury, that the Dutch were capturing a larger share of the colonial trade at the expense of England.

It was around this time or shortly thereafter, it is said, that Shaftesbury became aware of the secret Catholic clauses of the Treaty of Dover. Possibly he discovered this intelligence through certain agents sent to England by the Dutch in 1673, or perhaps he learned of these clauses from one of his fellow ministers who had signed the secret treaty.[148] Certainly

[147] Earl of Shaftesbury, *Speech*, February 5, 1673 in the second collection of *Somers Tracts*, 4 vols., 1750, 3:214; Haley, p. 283.

[148] The French ambassador, Colbert de Croissy, wrote to Louis XIV that Arlington had told Shaftesbury about the secret clauses of the Treaty of Dover, for which, he claimed, "I have only too much evidence" (Cyril Hughes Hartmann, *Clifford of the Cabal*, London: William Heinemann, 1937, p. 265). Ogg accepted the evidence that Shaftesbury learned of the secret from Arlington in the spring of 1673, but some historians remain skeptical (Ogg, 1:367). The tradition within the Shaftesbury household, however, as recorded by his steward, Sir Thomas Stringer, maintains that the earl learned the secret from Buckingham (Christie, *Shaftesbury*, 2:86–87). This was also asserted by the author of *The Life of Mr. Locke*, 1705 (p. 9), published shortly after Locke's death, for which, however, Stringer was almost certainly not the source. In addition, there was a rather active spy ring of agents working for Holland, including William Carr, William (later Lord) Howard, Peter Du Moulin, John Trenchard, John Ayloffe, and Richard Goodenough (K. H. D. Haley, *William of Orange and the English Opposition, 1672–4*, Oxford: Clarendon Press, 1953, pp. 56–59). Carr was a close friend of Locke from their student days at Oxford; he later maintained that Howard had been in close touch with Shaftesbury during this period (Add. MS 37981, fol. 57). Du Moulin, besides being the author of the tract *England's Appeal from the Cabal* (LL #1046), which broadly hinted at the secret treaty, had served as secretary to the Council of Trade, and knew Shaftesbury well. He sent several agents from Holland to England with a letter to Shaftesbury requesting a private interview for the purpose of passing along some secret, but his agents and the letter were intercepted (*CSPD*, 14:325–326, 480, 484). Nevertheless, Haley remains skeptical that Shaftesbury learned of the secret clauses of the Treaty of Dover from any of these possible sources (Haley, pp. 304, 313–314, 324). He insists that if Shaftesbury had known the secret, he would have published or made use of the information in his political campaign against Charles II. This seems a rather unrealistic reading of the political situation. In the first place, Shaftesbury might very well have been told of the treaty's clauses without having in his possession any hard evidence to back up any public accusation against the king. Secondly, even if he had such evidence, the press in England in the 1680s was not *so* free as to tolerate its publication, nor did Shaftesbury have enough

it is true that from 1673 onward, Shaftesbury became an increasingly outspoken critic of the growth of Catholic influence in the government. He also became, more generally, a focal point of the opposition to a whole range of policies pursued by the king. Between 1673 and 1679, Shaftesbury's overall political strategy can best be understood in terms of his efforts to secure a dissolution of Parliament and the election of a new one.

In April 1675, the king referred in his speech opening the session of Parliament to "the pernicious designs of ill men" who were trying to compel him to dissolve Parliament. A few days later, he launched a counterattack against these "ill men" by sending a bill to the House of Lords whose object was "to prevent the dangers which may arise from persons disaffected to the government." Beneath this suspicion-ridden phraseology lay a requirement that all members of Parliament were to take an oath declaring that taking up arms against the king was not lawful upon any pretense whatsoever, and they were also to pledge that they would not under any circumstances endeavor to alter the existing government of the Church or State. This legislative attempt to remove from office individuals who were suspected of holding dangerous and subversive principles provoked a famous debate in the House of Lords, with Shaftesbury leading the opposition to the bill.

Various lines of attack were put forward. It was argued that the bill represented "the highest invasion of the liberties and privileges of the peerage that possibly may be." The legislation was condemned as an infringement on the exercise of free speech and debate in Parliament. More ominiously, it was observed that "it necessarily brings in the debate in every man's mind, how there can be a distinction then left between absolute and bounded monarchies, if monarchs have . . . no fear of human resistance to restrain them."[149] These and other arguments were advanced not only in the parliamentary debates, but also in a series of pamphlets setting forth the opposition's position on a number of issues that widened the scope of the political debate.

In *Two Seasonable Discourses Concerning the Present Parliament*, the author declared that "it is according to the Constitution of the Government, the ancient laws and statutes of this realm, that there should be frequent and new Parliaments." The Cavalier Parliament, elected in 1660, had sat for fifteen years; it was time to elect a new one, for, without fre-

---

power at his disposal to insure his own or anyone else's protection if it were published. In my view, Haley underestimates Shaftesbury's sources of intelligence, which were excellent. That Shaftesbury learned of the secret Catholic clauses of the Treaty of Dover sometime in 1673 is, I believe, nearly certain; from whom he learned that secret is much more difficult to determine.

[149] Haley, pp. 373–377.

quent parliamentary elections, the very principle of government based upon the consent of the people is jeopardized. Granted, the author wrote, that it is "the King's undisputed prerogative to call and end Parliaments when he please[s]." Nevertheless, he warned, even "the greatest prince cannot avoid being limited by the nature of things." There comes a time, he argued, "when it is morally demonstrable that men cease to be representatives" of the people, both because the people have had no opportunity to determine through elections where to place their trust, and because the interests in the country at large and within the legislature itself change over time, as factions, parties, and cabals arise, thus significantly altering the original electoral relationship between the people and their representatives. A standing Parliament is almost as great an evil as a standing army. Yet, the author warned, there is "an inveterate party" of men who want to establish "an absolute, military government."[150] These were the views of Shaftesbury, Buckingham, and other members of the growing opposition to Charles II's administration.

Similarly, in *A Letter from a Parliamentarian to His Friend*, the author describes a threat to our ancient English liberties posed by the king's "encroaching prerogative." It is especially the Anglican church hierarchy who are "creatures to prerogative" and the chief promoters of its extension. The *Letter from a Parliamentarian* explicitly appeals to the country gentry to recognize the dangers inherent in the designs of the Court party. It asks the gentry to withdraw their support from the church prelacy because this support has the effect of "buoying up the Bishops in their harsh and irreconcilable spirit." Like *Two Seasonable Discourses*, the *Letter from a Parliamentarian* inveighs against the creation of a standing army, and it demands the reinstitution of "our old known rights of annual parliaments."[151]

Several other pamphlets appeared in 1675 that restated and developed these themes, but one of them is of special interest. *A Letter from a Person of Quality to His Friend in the Country* was not only the most important tract in this propaganda war waged against the government by Shaftesbury (and others), it is also the work that most clearly summarizes and defends his political position. This is hardly surprising, for, if Shaftesbury himself did not write the *Letter*, then someone very close to him did.

Although the *Letter* is primarily an account of the debate on the Test Bill in the House of Lords, the author begins with a review of "a project

[150] *Two Seasonable Discourses Concerning This Present Parliament*, 1675, in *State Tracts*, 1689, pp. 65, 68.

[151] *A Letter from a Parliamentarian to His Friend*, 1675, in *State Tracts*, pp. 70–71. Locke owned one of the other notable tracts published as part of this campaign (LL #2209).

of several years standing" to establish an absolute monarchy in England. Behind this conspiracy to undermine the constitutional government are "the great churchmen" and some recently created ministers of state. These two groups have endeavored

> to make a distinct party from the rest of the nation of the high episcopal men and the old cavaliers . . . Next, they design to have the government of the church sworn to as unalterable: and so tacitly owned to be of divine right . . . [then] they declare the government absolute and arbitrary; and allow monarchy, as well as episcopacy, to be jure divino, and not to be bounded or limited by any human laws. And to secure all this, they resolve to take away the power and opportunity of parliaments to alter any thing in church or state; only leave them as an instrument to raise money, and to pass such laws as the court and church shall have a mind to . . . And as the top-stone of the whole fabric . . . to increase and keep up a standing army.

For the first time, the breathtaking scope of a conspiracy many had long suspected existed was laid out for the reader in plain terms. In support of this allegation, the author of the *Letter* presents an interpretation of the legislation enacted during Charles II's reign that sees in these statutes a tendency or underlying development toward political absolutism. The Corporation Act of 1661, he argues, gave the central government control over local governments and the appointment of magistrates. The Militia Act of the same year gave the king control over the militia and a standing army, and it thus "swears us into a military government." The Act of Uniformity of 1662, which forced "a very great number of worthy, learned, pious and orthodox divines" to give up their livings and to leave the Anglican church, effectively silenced the opposition within the church to a hard-line defense of absolute monarchy. Thus, the government took its first steps to control the towns, the church, and the army as possible sources of opposition to its objectives.[152]

The *Letter* then recounts the arguments (made to the author) for the king's Act of Indulgence as put by Lord Clifford, a Catholic, and by Lord Shaftesbury, in order to illustrate the differences between "the aims of their parties" with respect to the question of the king's authority. Lord Clifford maintained, simply, that "the king . . . might settle what religion he pleased and carry the government to what height he would." For Clifford, the king's inherent power was sufficient justification for an Act of Indulgence, or for any other act, provided that he was prudent enough

[152] *Works*, 9:201–202.

to take control of the forts and the stocks of ammunition, as in fact, Charles II did. Shaftesbury argued for Indulgence on the grounds that legal precedents existed that supported the king's suspension of the execution of a law, and more generally, because "without a standing, supreme executive power, fully enabled to mitigate, or wholly to suspend, the execution of any penal law, in the intervals of the legislative power," the people would be left without any means of having their grievances redressed in the absence of a sitting Parliament. The only alternative to this remedial exercise of the prerogative would be to require that the legislature should always be in session, which, Shaftesbury argued, "when considered [is] no other than a perfect tyranny."[153] Shaftesbury's justification for the prerogative is thus placed within the context of a temporary expedient exercised for the common good between legislative sessions and subject to the legislature's ratification when it does meet.[154] In the particular case of the Induglence, it was also important that "a vast number of people not be made desperate at home, while the king was engaged with so potent an enemy abroad." Hence, the Induglence was a means of insuring that the Dissenters "might be at rest" during the war with the Dutch.[155]

Shaftesbury's argument, however, extends into the hypothetical future. He was convinced that "the protestant religion in England" could only be preserved if it rested on a foundation of religious toleration. For, "he begged me to consider," the author writes, "if the church of England should attain to a rigid, blind, and undisputed conformity, and that power of our church should come into the hands of a popish prince; which was not a thing so impossible, or remote, as not to be apprehended," then, Shaftesbury argued, all the power of church and state could be directed against Protestantism. If, on the other hand, toleration were "an established law," then Protestantism, even under a popish prince, "would still be kept up amongst the cities, towns, and trading places, and the worthiest and soberest (if not the greatest) part of the nobility, and gentry, and people."[156] Toleration, besides being in itself a morally justifiable policy, was also for Shaftesbury an important barrier to the absolute political power at the disposal of a future popish prince. Shaftesbury concluded his argument to the author of the *Letter* by asking him to consider "whether liberty and property were likely to be maintained long, in a country like ours, where trade is so absolutely necessary to [its] very being" and where religion was "the only accessible way to our civil rights," without

[153] *Works*, 9:205–206.
[154] Haley, p. 298.
[155] *Works*, 9:204.
[156] *Works*, 9:207–208.

toleration. The latter was thus both a socially necessary element of England's material well-being and, under certain imaginable practical circumstances, it could become the only axis for the individual Englishman's claim to his civil rights. In other words, as a defense against popery, arbitrary power, and tyranny, and as the means for insuring the advancement of trade and the protection of civil liberties, toleration was the keystone of Shaftesbury's political policy.

The *Letter* concludes by repeating several earlier warnings about the attempts of "the new party" to establish a French-style absolute monarchy in England, the clergy's willingness to justify this absolutism with a theory of the divine right of kings, the danger of a popish successor to the crown, and the prospect that a standing army may be created, or is already in existence—all of these actions "are directly contrary to Magna Charta, our properties, and the established law and government of the nation."[157]

The publication of the *Letter* caused a sensation. Within two or three days of its appearance on the streets of London, a House of Lords Committee had been appointed to discover and punish its author. The pamphlet itself was publicly burned by the hangman outside the Houses of Parliament.[158] The author was never found, but several well-placed sources maintained that Locke was its author. The *Letter from a Person of Quality to His Friend in the Country* was printed by P. Desmaizeaux in his *A Collection of Several Pieces of Mr. John Locke*, published in 1720. The *Letter* was subsequently included in later editions of Locke's *Works*, and it was generally accepted as his work by Locke's biographers. In the preface to his *Collection*, Desmaizeaux described the various pieces or manuscripts that had come into his possession, and he provided some information concerning their composition. Of the *Letter* he wrote that it was Shaftesbury's decision to publish an account of the parliamentary debates on the Test Bill, but "he desired Mr. Locke to draw up this relation; which he did under his lordship's inspection, and only committed to writing what my Lord Shaftesbury did in a manner dictate to him." As Desmaizeaux notes, the *Letter* contains "a great many strokes, which could proceed from nobody but my lord Shaftesbury himself," especially, "the characters and eulogisms" of the other Lords who are mentioned in the tract.[159]

Desmaizeaux did more than simply print the *Letter* as it was given to him by Locke's cousin, Peter King. He compared the text of the *Letter*

[157] *Works*, 9:226.

[158] Haley, p. 392.

[159] Desmaizeaux's introduction is reprinted in *Works*, 9:149-158; cf. ibid., p. 152.

with other writings by Locke; he read the pamphlets published in response to the *Letter* in 1675–1676 and drew up a short account of that debate; and, obviously from the circumstantial account he provides of its composition, he conversed with individuals who had known Locke intimately.[160] Quite a few of these individuals—Anthony Collins, Peter King, Jean Le Clerc, Pierre Coste, and Lady Masham—were still alive when the *Letter* was published as Locke's work. None of them demurred from this attribution or suggested that someone other than Locke was its author. On the contrary, the third Earl of Shaftesbury indicated that he also believed that Locke had written the *Letter*.[161] And, if we recall Le Clerc's testimony that Locke gave "his assistance" to some pieces that Shaftesbury "published," it seems likely that this is also a reference to the composition of the *Letter*.[162]

Against this attribution by Locke's friends stands a letter from Locke to Lord Pembroke, which he wrote from Holland in December 1684. In this letter, Locke declared, "I here solemnly protest in the presence of god, that I am not the author, not only of any libel, but not of any pamphlet or treatise whatsoever in print good bad or indifferent." These are strong words. Locke's letter to Pembroke is a lengthy one, and its context and significance will be considered more fully below, but the letter contains so many prevarications and outright lies that, simply as a document, it merits a unique classification as the most untrustworthy and one of the most puzzling items Locke ever wrote.[163] Without entering into the many difficulties raised by this letter, and giving Locke the benefit of the doubt in this particular instance, what he may have meant is that he was not *singly* the author of any tract then in print. Technically, this state-

[160] These efforts are recorded in the Desmaizeaux papers in the British Library (Add. MS 4222, fols. 229–252).

[161] Cranston, p. 159.

[162] The phraseology used by Le Clerc is interesting. He says Locke "gave his assistance to some pieces which his Lordship published, to stir up the English nation to have a watchful eye over the conduct of the Roman Catholics, and to oppose the designs of that party." This is almost a precis of the *Letter*, and the remarks are made in the course of Le Clerc's discussion of the period just before Locke went to France in 1675—and presumably they are meant to be applicable to that period (Le Clerc, *Life of Locke*, p. 10). One of the shrewdest critics of the *Letter* also drew a distinction between the individual "who wrote it and . . . he who prepared the materials, and then supplied the pen-man with them" (Marchemont Needham, *A Pacquet of Advices and Animadversions Sent from London to the Men of Shaftesbury*, 1676, p. 50).

[163] *Correspondence*, 2:661–666. It is solely on the basis of this letter that *A Letter from a Person of Quality* was removed from the canon of Locke's *Works*. It was first printed by Christie in his biography of Shaftesbury in 1871 (1:261). Five years later, Fox-Bourne cited Christie as his source for rejecting Locke's authorship of the *Letter* (1:336). For a discussion of this letter, see Chapter 9, pp. 430–441, below.

ment is true, given that he could view any previous writings, whatever his share in their authorship, as having been written "under the direction of" Shaftesbury, in the manner described by Desmaizeaux. In the last analysis, therefore, these writings could be viewed as lying within the responsibility of his patron.

I believe this is what Locke did mean, and that Desmaizeaux's description of the *Letter*'s composition is an accurate one. The work was obviously written under Shaftesbury's supervision, employing the language he used in his speeches. Apart from Shaftesbury himself, no one besides Locke was in a position to write the *Letter*, nor so far as I am aware, has any other individual ever been suggested as its author.[164] Shaftesbury may have been the source of the eulogisms of the other Lords, but did he write of himself:

> The earl of Shaftesbury, a man of great abilities and knowledge in affairs, and one that, in all this variety of changes of this last age, was never known to be either bought or frighted out of his public principles.[165]

Perhaps, for purposes of literary disguise, he did write these lines, but they certainly express the view of Shaftesbury held by Locke.

On November 8, 1675, the *Letter* was ordered by the Lords "to be burned by the common hangman."[166] The next day, a contemporary ob-

[164] There has never been much difficulty in accepting Locke's role in the authorship of the *Fundamental Constitutions of Carolina*, though, of course, Locke did not, strictly speaking, "write" them. In speaking of this work, De Beer says that "it was written probably in association with Shaftesbury . . . Though some of the language, and even some of the matter, may have been supplied by Locke, Shaftesbury is to be regarded as the author and Locke as his assistant" (*Correspondence*, 1:395). This is a sensible interpretation of their joint authorship, one that I believe should be applied to the *Letter* as well. This appears to be the view of Cranston (p. 158) and Haley (p. 393). It should be noted that parliamentary speeches, unless published separately, were not a matter of public knowledge nor was this material available to any writer. Given the sharp political tone of the *Letter*, if Shaftesbury himself did not write the *Letter*, and if, as we may presume, he did not want the authorship of the tract known, there was, at this time, no one, save Locke, to whom he could have entrusted this task.

[165] *Works*, 9:213.

[166] The *Letter* appears to have been published the first week of November, and created an immediate uproar. Marvell reported the discussion in the House of Lords "to inquire out the printer and author" of the *Letter*, as well as the decision to have the pamphlet burned (Andrew Marvell, *The Complete Works*, 4 vols., 1872, 2:482). It was just at this time Locke hastily decided to go to France (Fox-Bourne, 1:336). He did not have time to go to Oxford to obtain permission for his absence from the chapter of the college, as courtesy dictated. Someone else in Oxford packed up his belongings and books for him. Someone made an inventory of goods he had left behind at Shaftesbury's residence. Locke did not even wait to receive his half-yearly rents that his uncle had collected for him (*Correspondence*,

served, "the Lords have been again very angry about the book [the *Letter*] which they yesterday condemned to be burned, and quarrelled with the Lord Privy Seal, [Anglesey] who was the Chairman to the Committee appointed to examine it, for not being severe enough upon it."[167] On November 10, the *Letter* was publicly burned at two different locations in London. That was enough for Locke. On that day, or the one following, he hastily packed his bags and left London.[168]

For the next three and a half years, Locke traveled in France. This was one of those periods in his life when he attempted to think through the problems associated with the *Essay Concerning Human Understanding*. In the notes preserved in his journals and commonplace books, there are many recorded between 1675 and 1679 that are reproduced in the text of the *Essay*. These notes show that Locke continued to be concerned with the issues raised by the 1670s debate on Parker's *Discourse*. Shortly after he arrived in France, Locke made a long note in his journal discussing the obligation of laws with reference to religion. After having posited that "there are virtues and vices antecedent to and abstract from society," and that "the rule and obligations" pertaining to these moral precepts "is antecedent to human laws," he argues that "no human law can lay any new obligation on the conscience." That is, there is a natural system of morality in terms of which "all human laws" must be regarded as "penal laws." A human law merely attaches pain to our already existing natural law obligations as a means of enforcement.[169] This raises the question, however, as to whether our religious obligations can be fulfilled if we are forced to carry them out under the threat or the application of pain. A hint of Locke's answer is contained in his observation that even God attaches penalties and pain to His laws, but are we thereby forced into salvation by God? No direct answer is given to this question, but if, as we may assume, Locke intends a negative reply as part of his general justification for free will, then much depends upon clarifying the boundaries that distinguish our natural actions and obligations from those which are the product of rational consent. This problem, however, is not taken up; instead, the note moves on to other territory, defining "indifferent" things, commenting upon the extent of the civil magistrate's power, drawing out the relationship between religious or scripturally com-

1:433). Everything, in other words, points to a very hasty departure on Locke's part, simultaneous with the appearance in print of the *Letter*.

[167] Alfred Morrison, *Catalogue of the Collection of Autograph Letters and Historical Documents*, 2d ser. (The Bulstrode Papers, 1667–1675, vol. 1), 1897, p. 323.

[168] Locke left England on November 12, 1675 (MS f.1, fol. 1).

[169] MS f.1, fol. 123 (February 25, 1676); King, 1:114.

manded duties and the various forms of government, and remarking upon the practice of passive obedience by the Dissenters.[170]

In the summer of 1676, Locke recorded his thoughts in a series of notes that extended for a period of six weeks. He began with a definition of the will. "We have," he asserted, "a power to begin, continue, vary, stop, or suspend as we think fit . . . So that the power of determining our faculties . . . to act or not to act, to act this way or that way in all cases when they are capable of obedience is that I think which we call the will."[171] Two days later, he entered a note on "idolatry," which discusses the nature of religious worship and the manner in which we acknowledge God's "power and sovereignty and our dependence" upon Him, as well as the relationship between "faith and obedience" with respect to outward actions.[172] From here, Locke moves to a discussion of pleasure and pain and a characterization of human passions. God, he writes, "has framed the constitution of our minds and bodies" so as to be responsive to pleasure and pain "for ends suitable to His goodness and wisdom."[173] Shortly thereafter he concludes that morality and religion presuppose a belief in God and that "anyone who would pass for a rational creature" must subscribe to such a belief.[174]

Locke then returns to a discussion of toleration and the enforcement of penal laws. "Penal laws made about matters of religion in a country where there is already a diversity of opinions," he argues, "can hardly avoid that common injustice which is condemned in all laws whatsoever." This point, however, exposes an epistemological problem: "the great dispute in all this diversity of opinions is where truth is," a question to which Locke does not have—or, at least, does not record—the answer.[175] Instead, he sets this epistemological issue aside in order to distinguish between the respective "provinces" of religion and government.[176] But after a brief consideration of this topic, he is led back to a discussion of the boundaries between faith and reason. "In matters of religion," Locke observes, "it might be well if anyone would tell how far we are to be guided

[170] Locke discusses God's attachment of penalties to the civil laws he gave to the Jews (MS f.1, fols. 125–126; King, 1:117).

[171] MS f.1, fols. 317–318; *Early Draft*, p. 80.

[172] MS f.1, fol. 321; *ELN*, p. 261.

[173] MS f.1, fol. 326; *ELN*, p. 265.

[174] MS f.1, fols. 369–370 (July 29, 1676); *Early Draft*, p. 82.

[175] MS f.1, fols. 412–413; *ELN*, p. 274.

[176] MS f.1, fol. 414. These "provinces [are] to be kept well distinct" (*ELN*, p. 275). In 1673–1674, Locke had drawn up a paper "On the Difference between Civil and Ecclesiastical Power," in which he argued that penalties attached to civil laws were not "the proper means to procure obedience" in matters of religion (King, 2:108–119).

by reason and how far by faith. Want of this is one of the causes that keeps up in the world so many different opinions and religious sects."

In other words, the problem of enforcing the penal laws against Dissenters leads, in one sense, back to a consideration of natural law, the nature of God, and the structure of morality and religion and their relationship to pleasure and pain—matters that are antecedent to the origins and function of human laws—but it also leads to a practical recognition of the existence of a diversity of opinions, a phenomenon that arises because it is so difficult for individuals to determine where truth is, and this question, in turn, cannot be answered with respect to matters of religion unless we first establish how far we are to be guided by reason and how far by faith in our religious beliefs and practices. Thus, Locke declares, the "setting down a strict boundary between faith and reason . . . ought to be the first point established in all disputes of religion."[177] Locke then attempts to demarcate these boundaries, but he immediately runs into "great difficulties about free will which reason cannot resolve." This obviously poses a serious dilemma as to how to determine "where to appeal to faith and quit reason" if we cannot be certain of what "powers" we actually have, or of the nature of their operations regarding any sort of knowledge whatsoever. Most of these difficulties are, for the moment at least, resolved by a confidence on Locke's part that God has created us as free agents and as rational beings and that He would not, therefore, have endowed us with these qualities if the consequence of their employment was such as to lead individuals into a state of hopeless and irreconcilable contradiction. Hence, faith, as attached to revelations from God, for example, "can never convince us of anything that contradicts our knowledge."[178] Locke takes up the problem of miracles, but he insists, as Ferguson and others had, that miracles are only employed by God in order to confirm our faith, and not to undermine our knowledge.[179] The truth of a revelation cannot be "greater than our own knowledge," since its "certainty depends upon our knowledge that God revealed it," and He would not require us to believe anything that would "overturn all our principles and foundations of knowledge, render all our faculties useless

[177] MS f.1, fol. 415; *ELN*, p. 275. I believe Locke's phrasing of the issue here is, in fact, a restatement of the purpose and topic of discussion of the "meetings" that first gave rise to the *Essay Concerning Human Understanding*. That is, the group met to consider "how far we are to be guided by reason and how far by faith" in matters of religion, but came to realize that the answer to this question depended upon first "setting down a strict boundary between faith and reason," and this, in turn, necessitated establishing the limits of our knowledge gained through reason.

[178] MS f.1, fols. 417–419; *ELN*, p. 276.

[179] MS f.1, fol. 424; *ELN*, p. 278.

and wholly destroy the most excellent part of his workmanship or understanding and put man in a condition wherein he will have less light, less conduct than the beasts that perish."[180]

Not only does faith "not take away the landmarks of knowledge" or subvert "the foundations of reason," but if, on the other side, we cannot set out "the distinct provinces of faith and reason," then, Locke warns, some men will be able to assert that there is "no use, no room for reason at all" in matters of religion. This assertion can then be used to sanction an infinite number of "extravagant opinions" and "absurdities" that conceal themselves under the cloak of religion. The justification of these beliefs and their accompanying practices depends upon the "crying up of faith in opposition to reason."[181] For those who wish to claim a rational foundation for their religious beliefs and practices, however, a simple reference to the dichotomy between faith and reason will not suffice. They must undertake to show more precisely the respective provinces of each in order not to fall prey, on the one hand, to mere enthusiasm and inspiration as a definition of religion, or on the other hand, to an acceptance of all the absurdities that religious authorities may be inclined to include within their view of religion where the acceptance of their authority with respect to matters of religion is equated with faith.

In laying down the foundation for a rationally grounded conception of religion, Locke suggests that we distinguish between "reasonings and deductions upon clear and perfect ideas" and the information supplied by the "evidence of our senses," and those phenomena whose acceptance or understanding requires the exercise of our faith. "Since our senses reach but a few of the matters of fact" we confront in our experience, faith supplies the defect of our knowledge "when our senses fail," and this is especially true with respect to those "things necessary to our salvation." The discussion does not proceed very far into the interior regions of this problem in these journal notes. Instead, Locke again invokes a theory of creationism, and his conception as to God's purposes in making us the kind of beings we are, in order to establish what he takes to be the boundaries between faith and knowledge, reason and revelation.

> Thus it seems to me that God has plainly set out the boundaries of our several faculties and showed us by which we are to conduct our-

[180] MS f.1, fols. 419–420; *ELN*, p. 276.

[181] "*Credo quia impossibile est*," Locke writes, may "pass for the mark of zeal" in religion, but it is the last rule "for men to choose their opinions by." That Locke especially associates the absurdities in religion with Catholic doctrine is indicated by his example of "transubstantiation," which, he argues, "is not a matter of faith but of philosophy," i.e., it is "a thing we exercise our senses and knowledge" about (MS f.1, fols. 420–421; *ELN*, p. 277).

selves; viz., by our senses in cognizance of sensible objects, by reason in deductions and discourses from perfect and clear ideas, and by faith in matters that the senses nor reason will not reach to. And though reason often helps our senses and faith our reason, yet neither the one nor the other ever invalidates the authority or destroys the evidence of the inferior and subordinate faculty.[182]

There is much more in a similar vein contained in Locke's journals—they continue for another three years—but it seems unnecessary to cite additional material from them here. The point I have tried to demonstrate through these citations taken from the notes in his 1676 journal is that when Locke did undertake to think seriously about the nature of the human understanding, he did so within a context in which a solution to the problem of tolerating a diversity of religious opinions forced him into a consideration of the structure of the moral universe and man's place within it, the nature of man as a rational being created by God, the limits of the civil magistrate's power over indifferent actions, the boundaries between faith and reason, the role of reason with respect to religion, the problem of knowledge and certainty in relation to the diversity of opinions, and a whole complex of issues that the debate over toleration provoked by Samuel Parker's *Discourse of Ecclesiastical Polity* caused others to consider seriously as integral aspects of their own defenses of toleration.

In addition to this intellectual response, Shaftesbury's discussion concerning toleration as reproduced in the *Letter from a Person of Quality* was presented to (or by) Locke in the clearest terms. The political meaning of a solution to the problem of religious toleration was made starkly evident to every reader of the *Letter*. Nothing less than the foundations of constitutional government and the rights of Englishmen were at stake in the practical debate with the "new party" of men determined to impose a system of popery and tyranny upon England.

In the state of war declared upon the Dissenters in the 1670s, survival depended not only upon the truth of one's reply, as John Owen had said, but also upon finding some practical means of resisting those who were prepared to wield the powerful machinery of Church and State to enforce their "dogmatic assertions." The intellectual and political foundations of Protestantism, so men believed, were threatened by a combination of clergy and Court in a "conspiracy" to restructure the social order of seventeenth-century England. Locke's association with Shaftesbury had not only prompted him to think about these problems, it had also placed him in the midst of the practical efforts to find a solution to them.

[182] MS f.1, fols. 426–427, fol. 422; *ELN*, pp. 279–281.

4

THE BASIS OF RADICAL POLITICS

LOCKE'S presence in France was fortuitous, not only in respect of his timely departure from England, but also because he was in a position to continue his political service on behalf of Shaftesbury and the opposition party. In 1677–1678, in an attempt to pressure France into signing a peace treaty with Holland, Charles II threatened to declare war on France. To this end, he asked Parliament for money, and began to raise recruits for the army. However, some members of the Country Party suspected that Charles' threats were merely a ruse, and that if the money were voted by Parliament, the king would decide not to declare war on France, but he would then have both the funds and a standing army at his disposal—and perhaps, French subsidies as well—sufficient for him to rule without calling Parliament into session again.[1] These suspicions were far from groundless, especially in light of the cumulative effect produced by the assertions by various individuals that there was a conspiracy afoot to establish an absolute monarchy in England. The most recent reaffirmation of this charge was contained in Andrew Marvell's popular work, *An Account of the Growth of Popery and Arbitrary Government.*[2]

In these circumstances, it was imperative for the leaders of the parliamentary opposition to gather as much intelligence as they could with respect to the designs of French foreign policy, and to ascertain, if possible, whether any secret arrangement did exist between Charles II and Louis XIV along the lines they suspected. In addition to this specific objective, Shaftesbury, Buckingham, and others were still pressing for a dissolution of the Cavalier Parliament. In fact, Buckingham, Shaftesbury, Wharton, and Salisbury attempted to raise the issue in the House of Lords as to

[1] Dalrymple, 1:190; J. R. Jones, *Country and Court: England, 1658–1714*, Cambridge: Harvard University Press, 1978, p. 110; Lois G. Schwoerer, *No Standing Armies: The Antiarmy Ideology in Seventeenth-Century England*, Baltimore: Johns Hopkins University Press, 1974, pp. 115–132. In the parliamentary debates, one member observed, "If we have not a war with the French king, there is no man but will tell you what will come of this army." Another added that, "for ought I know, these men are raised for an imaginary war. These red coats may fight against Magna Charta" (Grey, 5:233, 287).

[2] Marvell's *Account of the Growth of Popery and Arbitrary Government* was a continuation of the conspiracy theory of politics presented in the *Letter from a Person of Quality* (Andrew Marvell, *The Complete Works*, 4 vols., 1872, 4:248ff.; Haley, pp. 391, 438). Locke owned Marvell's tract (*LL* #1935).

whether a Parliament that had been prorogued for more than a year—as it then had been, from November 1675 to February 1677—was not, ipso facto, dissolved, according to some statutes of Edward III, never rescinded.[3] These efforts earned them imprisonment in the Tower, where Shaftesbury remained throughout 1677, even after his colleagues had been released.[4]

Notwithstanding their imprisonment, Buckingham and Shaftesbury had been in contact with the French ambassador, Barrillon, and his agent, Ravuigny, in an attempt to gain French assistance in forcing a dissolution of Parliament.[5] It was in Louis XIV's interest to preserve the neutrality of England with respect to his war with the Dutch. He also had his own reasons for wanting to prevent Charles from becoming as absolute and independent in his actions as the latter would have liked. The French monarch, therefore, was willing to cooperate with the parliamentary opposition in order to block the appropriation of funds for a war—real or imaginary—against France.[6] This cooperation, however, had to be maintained under the strictest secrecy, both because some members of Parliament accepted bribes from the French king which they had no wish to acknowledge, and also because Louis XIV sought to maintain ostensibly friendly relations with his cousin.[7] Thus, in addition to their intelligence-gathering operations, leaders of the opposition party were involved in secret intrigues with the French designed to frustrate Charles II's suspected aims to establish himself as an absolute monarch.

Beyond these sketchy outlines, the picture becomes darkened to the point of imperceptibility. During 1677–1678, various agents of Shaftes-

[3] The statutes were 4 Edw. 3, c.14, and 36 Edw. 3, c.10. Aaron Smith, later a participant in the Rye House Plot, also got into trouble with Parliament for defending this position (Cobbett, 4:825). Smith was one of Shaftesbury's attorneys when he applied for a writ of habeas corpus in 1677 (W. D. Christie, *A Life of Anthony Ashley Cooper, First Earl of Shaftesbury*, 2 vols., 1871, 2:238).

[4] The four lords were sent to the Tower in February 1677. Wharton, Salisbury, and Buckingham were released in July; Shaftesbury was released in February 1678.

[5] Haley, p. 444; Lacey, pp. 87, 91; Dalrymple, 1:185.

[6] On March 24, 1678, Barrillon wrote to Louis XIV: "I beg your Majesty to believe that I omit nothing which appears to me to be proper to fortify the party that is opposed to the court in parliament" (Dalrymple, 1:188).

[7] Throughout 1677, there were secret negotiations between Louis XIV and Charles about a sum of money to be paid by the French king in return for Charles' promise to prorogue Parliament (Dalrymple, 1:150, 164–169, 184–192). For an account of Barrillon's disbursement of money to various Whig leaders (not Shaftesbury), including Sidney, Russell, and Buckingham, see Dalrymple, 1:380–383; Keith Feiling, *A History of the Tory Party, 1640–1714*, Oxford: Clarendon Press, 1924, p. 171. Nevertheless, Russell lied on the floor of the House of Commons in response to accusations of his accepting bribes, declaring, "I defy any man alive to charge me with any dealing with the French" (Feiling, *Tory Party*, p. 174).

bury and Buckingham—including the latter himself—crossed the English Channel in disguises on mysterious missions with equally mysterious results. "I am confident," the English ambassador to France, Ralph Montagu, wrote to Lord Treasurer Danby in January 1678, "that some of the discontented Parliament men have been intriguing with the French ambassador, Mr. Barrillon."[8] This confidence, however, was not supported by any detailed information. As one historian of these events observed,

> There is so much of design in all the State letters of these times, and the politics of the several courts from whence they came shifted so often, almost daily and hourly, that it is scarce possible to reduce them to any consistency, or draw any solid inference from them . . . we must thread the whole maze of perplexities.[9]

Unfortunately, that task, described in this comment written more than two hundred years ago, still remains to be carried out. None of the biographies of Shaftesbury, Buckingham, Locke, or of any of the other principals involved have shed much light on what these secret intrigues accomplished, who the participants were, and what particular roles they had in the affair. Hence, while Locke was in a *position* to act as Shaftesbury's agent, the extent to which he did so, and to what purpose, is difficult to determine. What follows, therefore, is not so much an attempt to unravel the tangled threads of intrigue as to indicate something of the circumstances surrounding the last two years of Locke's stay in France.

Someone who was certainly acting as a spy was a Colonel John Scott, though he often used other aliases.[10] In several depositions later filed in a legal case involving Scott, it was charged that during 1677–1678, he had acted as an agent for the French government, gathering information on the English fortifications at Portsmouth and Plymouth. Scott was accused of making maps of the English coastline, smuggling information containing estimates of ships and men out of the Navy office, drawing up accounts of various castle fortifications, and so forth.[11] One witness testified that Scott was seen at Poole, taking notes on the military installations there, in the company of Major Wildman and Sir Robert Clayton. This information, it was alleged, was to be passed on to Lord Shaftesbury.[12] Although the allegation appears doubtful at least insofar as Scott was not

[8] James Ralph, *The History of England*, 1744, p. 342; Dalrymple, 1:191.

[9] Ralph, *History*, p. 343.

[10] One section of Wilbur C. Abbott's *Conflicts with Oblivion* (Port Washington, N.Y.: Kennikat Press, 1969, pp. 281–386) deals with Scott. The only full-length biography is Lilian T. Mowrer, *The Indomitable John Scott*, New York: Farrar, Straus and Cudahy, 1960.

[11] MS Rawlinson A 175, fols. 163–164.

[12] MS Rawlinson A 175, fol. 173.

likely to do his spying in crowds, it does, nevertheless, contain a kernel of truth. Through the influence of Lord Arlington, Scott had been appointed to the post of Royal Geographer in 1668.[13] Thereafter, he seems to have translated this official duty into the decidedly unofficial occupation of drawing up maps of English coastlines and fortifications, and selling them to the highest bidder.[14]

Scott was a world-class adventurer whose colorful and bizarre exploits are too numerous to detail here.[15] He seems always to have placed himself in the midst of the underworld of spies and intelligence agents. In the early 1670s, Scott resided in Holland in company with various English agents, mostly former Commonwealthmen living in exile.[16] At the same time, he was made a captain general in the Dutch military forces, eventually rising to the rank of colonel of the infantry.[17] During the Third Dutch War, Scott worked as a double agent, reporting on the activities of Peter Du Moulin, and other English and Dutch spies.[18] When England withdrew from the war, Scott moved to Paris, where he sought a new market for his maps and intelligence services.[19] The charge that Scott sold maps and information pertaining to English naval fortifications and ships to the French, therefore, while difficult to prove, does not seem ill grounded in light of the information we do have concerning his activities.

Another part of the accusation that was certainly true was that Scott

[13] The fact that Scott was in the Gatehouse prison at the time of his appointment is only one of a myriad of intriguing incidents in his life (*CSPD*, 8:189, 493; Abbott, *Conflicts*, pp. 331–332).

[14] Scott was alleged to have sold the Dutch maps and plans of the defenses of English harbors at the time of the Third Dutch War (Abbott, *Conflicts*, p. 341). Later, he sold maps to the French (Mowrer, *Scott*, p. 254; Douglas C. Greene, ed., *Diaries of the Popish Plot*, Delmar, N.Y.: Scholars' Facsimiles and Reprints, 1977, p. 66—this work includes a reprint of a journal for 1679 by James Joyne, a friend of Scott).

[15] The degree to which Scott is known to us at all is in large part due to the fact that he was a chief witness against Samuel Pepys before the Committee of Enquiry into the Miscarriages of the Navy, where he testified that the Treasurer-General of the French Navy had showed him maps of the English coastline, and various other items of intelligence, all of which "were signed by Pepys." Pepys testified that the very papers described by Scott were found in the latter's lodgings (Grey, 7:303, 307). Subsequently, Pepys sent out agents and wrote numerous letters in an effort to dig up every piece of information—especially incriminating information—against Scott that he could find. Two volumes of documents pertaining to Scott are included in the collection of Pepys manuscripts at Cambridge (Abbott, *Conflicts*, p. 367). Another large collection of documents by Pepys is in the Bodleian Library.

[16] Abbott, *Conflicts*, p. 339; Mowrer, *Scott*, pp. 216–222.

[17] Mowrer, *Scott*, pp. 197–198.

[18] Mowrer, *Scott*, pp. 221–222. Scott returned to England on June 3, 1672. Peter Du Moulin and another Dutch agent were arrested and sent to the Tower on August 1, 1672 (*CSPD*, 13:432, 683). William Carr, Locke's friend, was also serving as a double agent, as was (Lord) Howard of Escrick (*CSPD*, 14:221, 234, 270, 629, 631; Mowrer, *Scott*, p. 229).

[19] Mowrer, *Scott*, p. 254.

was closely associated with Major Wildman, with whom he sometimes lodged.[20] This association, in turn, brought Scott into the Duke of Buckingham's circle. In 1677, Major Wildman paid off a debt owed by Scott for £75, and in doing so, he was almost certainly acting on behalf of Buckingham.[21] Colonel Scott not only corresponded with Ellis Leighton, Buckingham's chief agent, but he also made frequent visits to the Tower in 1677 to see Buckingham while the latter was a prisoner there.[22] Subsequent to these visits, Scott spent a considerable amount of time crossing back and forth between England and France on missions of an indeterminate nature for Buckingham and the parliamentary opposition. During 1678, Scott worked closely with Shaftesbury's agent in Paris, John Harrington, who was there in disguise under the name of Benson.[23] Harrington was receiving payments for his expenses from Shaftesbury as the latter's "cousin in Paris," but the precise nature of the intelligence he and Scott were to provide for the leaders of the parliamentary opposition remains a mystery.[24]

Locke reenters the discussion at this point because he certainly knew Scott and had some contact with him during the period both men were in France. In Locke's journal, there is a notation indicating that he met with Scott.[25] In addition to Harrington (Benson), Scott's main contact in France was with Sir Ellis Leighton, who was Buckingham's chief agent in

[20] Greene, *Diaries*, pp. 57, 60, 68, 82. Scott thought of himself as a Commonwealthman. Besides Wildman, he was friends with several ex-Cromwellian officers, including Captain Newman, who in the late 1670s, was the proprietor of a London coffeehouse. Scott belonged to a club that met at the coffeehouse every night to discuss politics. He also associated with Richard Goodenough, who acted as his attorney. In 1680, Scott became a member of the Green Ribbon Club (Mowrer, *Scott*, pp. 359, 364).

[21] MS Rawlinson A 175, fol. 169. Besides handling various financial matters for him, Wildman exercised power of attorney for Buckingham (Add. MS 27872, fol. 24).

[22] MS Rawlinson A 175, fol. 193; Haley, p. 521n. Scott may have been part of Buckingham's entourage as early as 1672, but he was certainly close to him by 1677–1678 (Mowrer, *Scott*, pp. 225, 285).

[23] Abbott, *Conflicts*, p. 352. On November 8, 1678, the king ordered Scott to be apprehended and his papers seized whenever he next landed at Dover (Add. MS 19399, fol. 128).

[24] Greene, *Diaries*, p. 64; Haley, p. 521n.; MS Rawlinson A 178, fol. 57. Mowrer says that Scott also worked with a man named Butterfield, who was a friend of Locke and who is mentioned in his journal; see John Lough, *Locke's Travels in France, 1675–1679*, Cambridge: Cambridge University Press, 1953, pp. 161, 180, 195. Another individual working with Shaftesbury's agent (Harrington) was John Freke, later Locke's friend (unknown to him at this time, I believe) and a participant in the Rye House Plot. Freke had attempted to visit Buckingham in the Tower in 1677, but was not permitted to see him (Frank H. Ellis, "John Freke and *The History of Insipids*," *Philological Quarterly*, 44, no.4 [October 1965]:476).

[25] MS f.28, fol. 72.

Paris.[26] Locke seems to have known Leighton, for at the end of August 1677, he wrote to a friend that, in response to a summons from England, Leighton had voluntarily returned to England and surrendered himself to the authorities, whereupon he was promptly committed to the Tower.[27] It is also a curious fact, though it may be no more than that, that Scott's London correspondent in the early 1670s during the period of his intelligence activities and with whom he retained a friendship was Locke and Shaftesbury's friend, Sir John Banks.[28]

In July 1678, William Blathwayt wrote from France to an unidentified correspondent in England:

> I have been diligent in the search of all things relating to the business . . . I have got a very large map done by the hand, describing all the coasts, roads, and soundings of France with a particular designation of all the jurisdictions of the French admiralties.[29]

Evidently, Scott's maps of the English coast and naval installations were not the only charts crossing the Channel. Blathwayt wrote this letter while he was in residence at Mr. Brisbane's house. Brisbane was Charles II's agent in France for merchant affairs.[30] He was also an acquaintance of Locke. It was Brisbane who assumed custody of Locke's books and arranged their shipment and delivery to Locke after the latter's return to England.[31] In the letter from which I have cited, after a reference to a book concerning the French Admiralty, Blathwayt writes that he has compiled a good collection of books and pamphlets relating to trade and the plantations.[32] This piece of information is quite interesting in view of Locke's extensive book buying in France in these areas, the fact that these books passed through Brisbane's hands, and that Shaftesbury had a special interest in such material. Locke himself sent the earl some maps of France

[26] Abbott, *Conflicts*, p. 346.

[27] *Correspondence*, 1:510. Locke's correspondent was William Courten, living in France under the assumed name of William Charleton. I do not know when Leighton was released from the Tower, but he was back in Paris in January 1678 (Haley, p. 437n.).

[28] Mowrer, *Scott*, p. 229.

[29] MS PWV 51 (July 1, 1678). Scott was known to have sold his maps to a member of the Trade and Plantations Committee of the House of Lords, and Blathwayt appears to be writing to that committee or its chairman (Mowrer, *Scott*, p. 257).

[30] Payments to Brisbane of £500 and another of £100 were made in September 1676 and March 1677, respectively (All Souls MS 233, pt. 1, fols. 230–231). It is impossible to tell from these sums whether Brisbane also acted as an intelligence agent, though he did report the presence of Scott as Buckingham's agent in France (Mowrer, *Scott*, p. 302).

[31] Locke refers to Brisbane as his friend (*Correspondence*, 1:593; cf. ibid., pp. 546–547; MS b.2, fol. 20; MS f.4, fols. 141–142).

[32] MS PWV 51 (July 1, 1678).

(drawn by Scott?), and other material pertaining to French military forces.[33] In another letter written from France, Blathwayt inquires after Shaftesbury's steward and close associate, Colonel Rumsey, to whom Blathwayt sends his regards.[34] Blathwayt, like so many other of his countrymen then in France, was probably on an intelligence-gathering mission, but to what end, for whom, and what degree of cooperation (if any) he received from Locke are questions whose answers are not disclosed by the evidence available to us.

Sometime in 1678, Buckingham made a secret trip in disguise to France. "How long he will stay or conceal himself," the English ambassador wrote, "is as great a secret as why he came."[35] Buckingham was accompanied on that trip by Major Wildman. Through some unexplained circumstance, Henry Neville (another Republican and longtime friend of Wildman, Algernon Sidney, and James Harrington) was also in Paris at this time.[36] No one at the time could explain what Wildman, Neville, and Buckingham were up to, nor has anyone since clarified the nature of these secretive comings and goings. In February 1678, Locke's friend in Montpelier informed him that Wildman "and another English man" whose name he did not know, had arrived in that city.[37] It is possible that Wildman journeyed to Paris sometime before July 9, 1678, when Locke left that city, but given the clandestine character of almost everyone's behavior from the moment they set foot on French soil, and the absence of an accurate account of Wildman's movements, this is only a speculation. Buckingham and Scott, however, did hold secret meetings, and later, after both individuals had returned to England, Scott was dispatched to France by the duke with a letter and an oral message for Louis XIV.[38]

[33] *Correspondence*, 1:511–512. These maps were sent by Sir Thomas Armstrong's daughter (p. 517); MS f.2, fols. 279, 286; cf. MS f.3, fol. 64. It is not known whether she was the daughter—he had three daughters—who married Captain Matthews, who, along with Armstrong, was deeply involved in the Rye House Plot.

[34] MS PWV 51.

[35] *Savile Correspondence*, Camden Society Publications, vol. 71, 1858, p. 69 (Henry Savile to George Savile, August 27, 1678). None of Buckingham's biographers provide an adequate account of his whereabouts, and he may have been in France for some time prior to this report.

[36] Maurice Ashley, *John Wildman: Postmaster and Plotter*, London: Jonathan Cape, 1947, p. 217. Ellis Leighton was also in Paris meeting with Buckingham (*Savile Correspondence*, p. 69).

[37] *Correspondence*, 1:546. Charleton, author of the letter, frequently passes along political news to Locke, and the implication of his reference seems to be that Locke knows Wildman.

[38] Abbott, *Conflicts*, p. 350; Mowrer, *Scott*, pp. 297–299. Buckingham made another secret trip to Paris in April 1679, and was there again in October of that year (Dalrymple, 1:313; *Savile Correspondence*, p. 123).

While Ralph Montagu, the English ambassador to France, was keeping an eye on "the discontented Parliament men" flitting in and out of Paris, it is possible that they, in turn, were keeping an eye on him. On December 2, 1677, Locke received a summons to treat the ambassador's wife as her physician.[39] Montagu's wife was the Countess of Northumberland, a person Locke had known for almost ten years. He had traveled with her briefly in France on a holiday in the autumn of 1672.[40] Several other friends and correspondents of Locke were part of the countess's household, including Mrs. Blomer, who was Lady Northumberland's constant companion.[41] Locke was present in or had access to the ambassador's household throughout the month of December 1677.[42] It was precisely at this time that the French were making offers of money to Charles II in return for a guarantee of England's neutrality, and were also sending their agents to England to make contact with the parliamentary opposition leaders. Montagu's correspondence in December 1677 discusses both of these moves by the French.[43] As Cranston remarks, if Locke had been acting as an agent for Shaftesbury and the Whigs in their attempts to gain intelligence, he could not have been better placed.[44]

During the same period, the English government had decided to keep an eye on Locke while he was in France. Sometime following Shaftesbury's imprisonment in the Tower in 1677, Charles II summoned a young clergyman from Durham, Denis Grenville, to a meeting. Grenville was temporarily relieved of his clerical duties, provided with some money, and sent into France on a special mission. As he boasted in a letter to Archbishop Sancroft—who was obviously not informed that Grenville had left his post at Durham—he had undertaken this assignment with the personal encouragement of the king and his brother, James.[45] Whatever else Grenville was supposed to do, he immediately initiated a correspond-

[39] *Correspondence*, 1:525.

[40] Cranston, p. 145.

[41] Cranston, pp. 134–140; *Correspondence*, 1:326ff. In addition to Mrs. Blomer, Locke knew her sister, Anna Grigg, also a member of the ambassador's household (*Correspondence*, 1:334).

[42] Both before and after his medical visit in December, Locke occasionally received his mail through the ambassador's residence.

[43] Andrew Browning, *Thomas Osborne, Earl of Danby*, 3 vols., Glasgow: Jackson, 1951, 2:299–342.

[44] Cranston, p. 174. Locke was certainly in frequent contact with Shaftesbury and/or his circle of associates as to his friend's political situation. He copied in his journal Shaftesbury's speech in the King's Bench (June 29, 1677) in support of his application to be released on bail from the Tower. As von Leyden observes, this was one of those instances in which Locke's use of shorthand was meant to conceal the material (*ELN*, p. 250).

[45] MS Tanner 40, fol. 181. He was not in France, as De Beer says, because of his debts (*Correspondence*, 1:468).

ence with Locke, ostensibly to discuss matters of philosophy (of which Grenville knew very little), but probably with the intention of keeping track of Locke's movements.[46] Locke was not fooled by this, and he sometimes consciously misled Grenville as to his plans or whereabouts. Grenville then tried to join Locke in person, but the latter kept moving, changing his residence, and remaining one step ahead of the pursuing Grenville.[47] Their correspondence, and subsequent cat-and-mouse chase across France has the flavor of a comic opera about it, but Grenville's seriousness of purpose is evident from the diary he kept during his mission in France. At one point, he records a meeting with "Mr. Finch" and others, and their discussion of "the present dangers" with respect to the political situation in England.[48] Interspersed with notes of the letters he is to send to Locke are Grenville's comments about the dangerous consequences of a dissolution of Parliament, and other political reflections that clearly reveal for which side, at least, he was acting as a spy.[49]

Other curious items in Locke's journals include a note he made in 1677 on a secret way of writing, which allows "real" sentences to mean something else when the key to deciphering their meaning is a phrase agreed upon by the correspondents.[50] Also interesting are several references to William Waller, son of the parliamentary general, who was soon to assume a prominent role in the prosecution of the popish plot.[51] Because so many pieces of the whole puzzle are missing, however, it is virtually impossible to reconstruct the general political context within which Locke's

[46] Fox-Bourne found it "strange" that Grenville, a clergyman, should be writing to Locke for advice on questions of devotion and God's purposes for man (Fox-Bourne, 1:397). Grenville may have had a "weak noodle," as he confessed to Locke in one of his letters, but he was, even at this point, a rabid Royalist engaged in a jejune correspondence with the most intimate friend of the imprisoned leader of the opposition. Strange indeed! Not only did he later become a Jacobite, but Grenville had no hesitation in "using my utmost zeal" in his "public sermons" to preach directly on political issues, going so far in 1681 as to urge his parishioners to vote for the Court candidates in a parliamentary election (Denis Grenville, *Miscellanea: The Works and Letters*, Surtees Society Publications, vol. 37, 1861, p. 67; Thomas Comber, *Autobiographies and Letters*, Surtees Society Publications, vol. 157, 1947, pp. 44n., 122–123). Little wonder that "both of their Majesties [i.e., Charles and James] were pleased to give me encouragement from their mouths to undertake this present journey" to France (MS Tanner 40, fol. 181).

[47] Grenville wrote to Locke that "though I cannot catch your person," I will still call you my friend, in spite of the fact that you "run away as far as you please from me" (*Correspondence*, 1:633; Cranston, pp. 181–183).

[48] MS Rawlinson D 851, fol. 29 (this is Grenville's diary for the period he was in France). I do not know to which "Mr. Finch" Grenville is referring.

[49] MS Rawlinson D 851, fols. 74, 76.

[50] MS f.2, fols, 164–165.

[51] Locke was clearly well known to Waller, and vice versa (MS f.1, fols. 483, 487, 523, 526; *Correspondence*, 1:515).

activities might be seen to have particular significance. Still, taking into account what we do know of his activity for Shaftesbury in the periods before and after his sojourn in France, it is unlikely that Locke was so far removed from the political scene as some later writers would have us believe.

Locke returned to England at almost exactly the same time as Colonel Scott.[52] Scott had been arrested the day before, questioned, and searched for papers he was suspected of carrying, while Locke was allowed to pass into England unmolested.[53] Scott was held in prison at Dover, and he promptly wrote a letter to Shaftesbury, requesting the latter's assistance to obtain his release.[54] The England that greeted Locke, however, was imprisoned in its own nightmare. For several months, the country had been in the throes of the popish-plot crisis.

There is no easy path across the terrain of the next two years, covered as it is by an undergrowth of perjured testimony, forged documents, lies, sham plots, and judicial murders. Several scholars have written detailed accounts of the popish plot, exposing—or better, cataloging—the falsehoods that were generated by a stable of disreputable witnesses, and I will not attempt to summarize their findings here.[55] Although some parts of the testimony of Titus Oates, Israel Tonge, and others were known to be perjuries by their contemporaries, other parts of their stories were true, which made it quite difficult for most people to cast aside entirely the notion of a plot by the Catholics, even if that plot did not match in every detail what the informers alleged. In part, this was a consequence of years of suspicion and crying wolf about a Catholic conspiracy that, even in the absence of any specific evidence, many people had already come to accept as the truth. And, in part, a few people had obtained evidence, acquired quite independently of any offered by the popish plot informers, which they believed confirmed the existence of a conspiracy. Shaftesbury was clearly in possession of information regarding the intentions and designs

[52] Add. MS 15642, fols. 92–93. The day before Locke left Paris, Brisbane added a postscript to a letter from him to Secretary of State Henry Coventry, which Locke delivered to the latter (Fox-Bourne, 1:409).

[53] Scott, traveling under an alias, was arrested at Folkestone on April 28, and sent to Dover, where he was imprisoned (MS Rawlinson A 188, fols. 127–143; Abbott, *Conflicts*, p. 353).

[54] MS Rawlinson A 188, fol. 139; Haley, p. 521n. He was released a few days later on orders from Secretary Coventry. From this point on, Scott seems to have drawn closer to Shaftesbury, assisting him in the prosecution of the popish plot (Mowrer, *Scott*, pp. 307, 346, 364).

[55] John Pollock, *The Popish Plot*, London: Duckworth, 1903; John Kenyon, *The Popish Plot*, London: Heinemann, 1972; John Miller, *Popery and Politics in England, 1660–1688*, Cambridge: Cambridge University Press, 1973.

of Charles II and the Duke of York that was not available either to Oates or to the general public. The extent to which this fact guided his actions during the popish plot agitation is difficult to determine. Even if Shaftesbury was not so cynically manipulative in his use of the witnesses or of the plot as a whole as some contemporaries alleged, the possibility cannot be discounted that he lent support to the dubious revelations of Oates in order to bring out into the open, or to force a serious consideration of other more substantial evidence of a conspiracy.

Yet, even positing a clear-cut distinction between cynicism and belief seems misleading as an angle from which to view the popish plot. For, the atmosphere of uncertainty and confusion that prevailed is inadequately expressed by such a formulation. The plot itself in its barest outline was simple: It was alleged that there was a conspiracy by Catholics to kill Charles so that his brother, a Catholic, would succeed to the throne. But the various means by which this end was to be accomplished cast up so many multifarious details, and unleashed such a torrential outpouring of names of persons whose relationship with one another was impossible to fathom—often because there was no relationship—that the most profound and general effect produced by the popish plot was one of confusion and fear. As one contemporary put it, the popish plot has given us "such sensible apprehensions of future troubles and calamities, that we enjoy not what we have," nor can we find "ease or satisfaction in anything which we as yet possess." Everything had become "unsettled and uncertain," leaving us with an overriding apprehension of the future and a deep sense of "the instability of the times."[56]

While the hysteria surrounding the popish plot has received its due attention, it should not be forgotten that there were longstanding and well-grounded suspicions of a popish conspiracy involving the Duke of York, some high-ranking ministers of state, Catholic courtiers, some members of the Anglican church hierarchy, and perhaps the king himself. It is not easily determinable, therefore, whether the popish plot ought to be viewed within the context of this conspiracy, or whether the latter ought to be viewed within the context of the popish plot. Yet, in terms of how one assigns proportions of "rationality" or "hysteria" to the political behavior of individuals between 1679 and 1681, much depends upon one's answer to this question.

To complicate matters further, the "false" and the "real" Catholic conspiracies, as they are sometimes denoted, crossed and joined each other at several points. The most important of these junctures was provided by the correspondence of Edward Coleman, the private secretary to the Duke

[56] William Outram, *Twenty Sermons*, 1682, pp. 2ff.

of York. Coleman's letters, some of which were detroyed before the remainder were discovered, certainly contained inflammatory, and probably treasonable, statements.[57] He had written of "the great design . . . to undermine the intrigues of that company of merchants who trade for parliament and the religion, and to establish that of the associated Catholics in every place." He also spoke of bringing about "the utter ruin of the Protestant party." Some measure of Coleman's zeal can be gathered from the following frequently cited passage:

> We have here a mighty work upon our hands; no less than the conversion of three kingdoms, and by that perhaps the subduing of a pestilent heresy which has domineered over a greater part of this northern world a long time. There were never such hopes of success since the death of Queen Mary, as now in our days.[58]

Throughout the correspondence, there are references to the need for money from sources other than Parliament, with the declared object of dispensing altogether with a reliance upon that body. There are also assertions of the "King's power to command his subjects service against all acts of parliament." In other words, Coleman's letters confirmed the political suspicions of English Protestants as to the designs of Catholics to establish an absolute monarchy in England, through which they hoped to restore Catholicism as the national religion. The inference that Coleman was not expressing such views on his own, but was rather acting for James and with his knowledge, was difficult to resist, especially since Coleman himself had referred to James' unmatched "zeal and piety" in the service of bringing about the religious conversion of Britain.[59]

"The discovery of Coleman's papers," wrote one contemporary, "made as much noise in and about London, and indeed all over the nation, as if the very Cabinet of Hell had been laid open . . . People's passions would not let them attend to any reason or deliberation on the matter . . . so as one might have denied Christ with more content than the plot."[60] But one did not have to be guided by passion to decipher the intent of Coleman's correspondence. Charles II, who had his own reasons for re-

[57] This was the view of the Lord Chancellor in his report to the king (Kenyon, *Popish Plot*, p. 75).

[58] Cobbett, 4:xci. Two of Coleman's letters were published as a separate pamphlet, *Mr. Coleman's Two Letters to Monsieur l'Chaise*, 1678. This work is printed by Cobbett as appendix 8 to his parliamentary history.

[59] Cobbett, 4:xc. Coleman confessed that James knew and approved of his correspondence (G. M. Trevelyan, *England under the Stuarts*, London: Methuen, 1965, p. 373).

[60] Roger North, *Examen*, 1740, pp.177–178. "Oates's plot and Coleman's were universally confounded," and the evidence of the latter inspired a belief in the former (Cobbett, 4:1013).

maining generally skeptical about much of the evidence that surfaced during the popish plot, conceded that the letters "contained plainly a design to introduce Popery."[61] Coleman's correspondence was the most important, but not the only evidence that helped to convince even Catholics that some high-level "design" to undermine English constitutional government was not merely a conveniently invented political fiction. In a sense, therefore, as Ogg observed, Coleman's plot represented an extension or endorsement of the original design to institute Catholicism in England incorporated into the Treaty of Dover.[62]

By the time Locke returned to England, in other words, the country was enshrouded by a pervasive atmosphere of suspicion, mistrust, and fear directed against the king and his brother, Louis XIV and France, and the defenders of Catholicism. These were the crucial elements of the constricting framework within which Shaftesbury, Locke, and the Whigs formulated their political ideas. As Shaftesbury put it, there was "a secret universal Catholic league" whose object was "the utter extirpation of the Protestant religion out of the world." This design, he was convinced, could only succeed with "the full concurrence of the English Court."[63] Locke shared his patron's view on this, as on virtually all other political issues. *Coleman's Two Letters* was among the many tracts on the popish plot he purchased, and Shaftesbury, Locke, or someone in the earl's "family," made a number of notes on this pamphlet.[64]

The meanings attached to these beliefs viewed in relation to this conspiratorial political consciousness, and the general importance of the latter in structuring the political debate in the 1680s will be considered in the following two chapters. For the remainder of this chapter, I will be concerned with delineating the basis for the creation of a political movement by Shaftesbury and other leaders of the opposition. In that context, the important point is that all of the aspects of the popish plot, both the legitimate evidence it produced as well as the apprehension and fear it generated, are crucial ingredients in any explanation of the political behavior of the movement's participants. There is no question but that antipopery feeling was the glue that held together the various constitu-

[61] Arthur Bryant, *Charles II*, London: Longmans, Green, 1931, p. 273.

[62] Ogg, 2:572.

[63] Though not in his handwriting, the document is very likely by Shaftesbury (Haley, p. 502).

[64] *LL* #807. In 1681, Locke bought forty pamphlets dealing with the popish plot (MS b.2, fol. 35). Many of these were purchased for his friend, Dr. Thomas, but on Locke's pamphlet buying during the exclusion crisis, see Richard Ashcraft, "Revolutionary Politics and Locke's *Two Treatises of Government*," *Political Theory* 8, no. 4 (November 1980):440–441. The notes on Coleman's letters were among the documents confiscated at the time of Shaftesbury's arrest in 1681 (PRO 30/24/6A/349).

encies comprising the political movement that emerged during the exclusion crisis. Anti-Catholicism crossed class lines, and expressed a deeply held and widespread prejudice. It was capable, as the pope-burning demonstrations proved, of serving as a powerful instrument for mobilizing people.[65] What the popish plot provided, specifically, was an intensely experienced sense of uncertainty and apprehension of the future. It gave people the feeling of living in a world that had suddenly become unstable. What Shaftesbury and the Whigs offered as a response to this recognized crisis was some means of effectively expressing both the longstanding prejudice and the feelings of intense anxiety through the medium of collectively organized political action.

From this phrasing, it might be inferred that the Whig political movement was merely a cathartic response to a short-term convulsion in the body politic. To view it in these terms would be a mistake. Despite the obvious importance of the popish plot as a catalyst, it should not be forgotten that the opposition to Charles II's administration had been growing throughout the 1670s. This opposition fused economic, political, and religious grievances into an intellectually sophisticated and politically persuasive framework that increasingly found its expression in the political pamphlets published during the 1670s. Equally important, patterns of political alliance and cooperation began to develop; the circles of men with common practical concerns widened, overlapped, and merged. The practical experience of being in opposition to the government's policies that these men shared provided a solid ground upon which to build a political movement.

The first formal and informal signs of a political organization among the opposition began to appear during the tempestuous parliamentary session in 1675. The fight over Danby's Test Bill included a concerted propaganda counterattack by the parliamentary opposition. The pamphlets they published were distributed, read, and debated in the coffeehouses that had recently sprung up all over London. These coffeehouses thus became a locus for political gatherings, planned and spontaneous. They were popularly identified with the political opposition's viewpoint, although this representation underestimates their popularity with the public at large.[66] Both of these characteristics became evident when the

[65] Miller, *Popery and Politics*, pp. 70–71, 171. "Anti-popery was the strongest, most widespread and most persistent ideology in the life and thought of seventeenth-century Britain" (J. R. Jones, *The Revolution of 1688 in England*, London: Weidenfeld and Nicolson, 1972, p. 75).

[66] Government pamphleteers attacked those who "brew and run up sedition and treason" in the "seditious schools in London, and . . . most of the cities and boroughs of the nation." These coffeehouses, it was charged, are the places where pamphlets are written and dis-

government issued a proclamation at the end of 1675 ordering the suppression of all coffeehouses. The general uproar caused by this edict soon forced the government to back down and withdraw its demand.[67]

Meanwhile, a stream of dissidents was flowing through Shaftesbury's house during 1675–1676. On two consecutive days in 1676, he held meetings with the Earl of Salisbury, Robert Peyton, Thomas Littleton, Samuel Barnardiston, Thomas Papillon, and Robert Clayton—individuals whose political opposition to the Court was already well known. These names are available to us because the government had someone watching Shaftesbury's house, recording its visitors, for those two days.[68] This action followed an attempt by the king, through an emissary, to order Shaftesbury out of London on the grounds that, according to Charles II, he was engaged in political activity from which he should refrain. Shaftesbury stood firm, protested his innocence, and replied that he was merely pursuing his business interests. Given the names of the individuals cited above, this answer was perfectly plausible, for virtually all of them were financial magnates or merchants in the City of London. Nevertheless, Charles II's suspicions were equally plausible, for a significant proportion of the business and trading community of London had become politically alienated from the Court and the king's policies. During the 1670s, an increasingly close connection developed between the parliamentary opposition and a group of influential merchants.[69] In 1676, both Buckingham and Shaftesbury moved their residences into the heart of the City of London, for the purpose, it was alleged by some contemporaries, of building a network of political and financial alliances among the Dissenters and commercial groups who constituted a large proportion of the inhabitants of that part of London.[70] This may be reading too much

---

cussed, lectures are given, and political strategies are hatched (Fabian Phillips, *Ursa Major and Minor: or, a Sober and Impartial Enquiry into Those Pretended Fears and Jealousies of Popery and Arbitrary Power*, 1681, p. 47). For William Petty's participation in "several clubs and meetings" at coffeehouses in Dublin where "advices" were drafted against popery, see *The Petty-Southwell Correspondence, 1676–1687*, London: Constable, 1928, p. 73.

[67] William C. Sydney, *Social Life in England from the Restoration to the Revolution, 1660–1690*, 1892, pp. 410ff.; Ogg, 1:76, 101–102.

[68] Haley, pp. 404–405.

[69] Margaret Priestley, "London Merchants and Opposition Politics in Charles II's Reign," *Bulletin of the Institute of Historical Research* 29, no. 80 (November 1956):205, 218–219; C. D. Chandaman, *The English Public Revenue, 1660–1688*, Oxford: Clarendon Press, 1975, p. 18; Jones, pp. 76, 198. Sir Patience Ward, Locke's friend and later fellow exile in Holland, was one of those city magnates who began associating with the opposition to the Court about this time (C. E. Whiting, "Sir Patience Ward of Tanshelf," *Yorkshire Archaeological Journal* 34, pt. 135, (1939):245–268; cf. ibid., pp. 250–251.

[70] Haley, p. 411; O. W. Furley, "The Pope-Burning Processions of the Late Seventeenth Century," *History* 44, no. 150 (February 1959):16.

into the intentions of either Shaftesbury or Buckingham, but it is certainly accurate as an after-the-fact assessment of what did occur between 1676 and 1679.

By the time the parliamentary session began in February 1677, there were already people wearing the green ribbons that soon came to symbolize the most militant wing of the opposition party.[71] Considering that these ribbons signified a rather direct link with the Levellers, the fact that those in opposition to the government had fashioned a political identity for themselves drawn from the past represents an important advancement in terms of their organizational development. A further indication of this development is provided by the formation of the Green Ribbon Club at about the same time. The precise date of its origin, and many of the details as to its nature, remain obscure, but it seems reasonable to suppose that the formal nature of the club evolved out of the frequent informal coffeehouse gatherings of political dissidents.

The Green Ribbon Club constitutes a very interesting stage in the process of the emergence of a revolutionary political movement in the 1680s. Like the latter, the club's membership reflected a cross-section of society. Individuals from all social classes were "permanent members" of the Green Ribbon Club.[72] The ease with which Buckingham and Shaftesbury personally associated with individuals from the lowest to the highest classes in society, previously noted as a characteristic of their attitudes and personalities, now found its institutional embodiment in this political club. As an anonymous opponent wrote of Shaftesbury, "he keeps open house for entertainment of all state-malcontents, without consideration of quality or qualifications." Not only "the sons of the old nobility," but also "the meanest and basest of the people . . . he bewitches to associate with him."[73] This, in itself, was sufficient to amaze and worry some of Shaftesbury's contemporaries, but as a distinct organization, with rather strict rules of admission along ideological lines, and a secret membership, the Green Ribbon Club was the source of far greater alarm.

Some historians have maintained that the club's importance has been exaggerated.[74] This may be so, but the fact is that we still possess almost

[71] Haley, p. 412; J. R. Jones, "The Green Ribbon Club," *Durham University Journal* 49, no. 1 (December 1956):17–20; David Allen, "Political Clubs in Restoration London," *Historical Journal* 19, no. 3 (September 1976):561–580.

[72] J. R. Jones, "Green Ribbon Club," pp. 19–20; George Sitwell, *The First Whig*, 1894 (this is an erratic, not always reliable, but interesting account of the Green Ribbon Club's activities).

[73] *The Character of a Disbanded Courtier*, 1682, p. 3.

[74] For example, Miller, *Popery and Politics*, p. 183. Ogg devotes only one sentence to the club (2:541).

no detailed information as to the club's membership or its activities.[75] Nevertheless, numerous Green Ribbon Club members were participants in the Rye House Plot and Monmouth's Rebellion. This says a great deal about their ideological commitment and the extent to which they were prepared to act upon their political convictions, even to the point of armed resistance. From which it seems plausible to deduce that the Green Ribbon Club was no less active with respect to more lawful political activities, such as gathering petitions, distributing political literature, marshaling voters for elections, and so on. In other words, the Green Ribbon Club deserves its designation as a kind of party headquarters for the Whigs and as the locus of its party activists.

Much attention has been given to the Club's sponsorship and organization of the massive pope-burning demonstrations.[76] These were political spectacles on a truly impressive scale. Hundreds of thousands of individuals marched peacefully through the streets of London to register their protest against the popish conspiracy. Yet in the last analysis, it may be that the Green Ribbon Club's other activities were more important in terms of their lasting influence in shaping the contours of English political life. It was at the Green Ribbon Club, for example, that political activists from the lower classes could hear reports of parliamentary debates and other matters of political intelligence. On January 13, 1679, one of the government's spies reported that the club's discussions were about the nations being "sold to the French, that . . . popery and arbitrary government is intended" by some of the king's advisers.[77] It must be remembered that little reliable political information was available to the public, and that the publication of parliamentary debates was viewed as an act of sedition. The Green Ribbon Club thus provided a forum for the transmission of political information to a wider audience, outside the boundaries of those who held public office. Whig party strategy for future parliamentary action was debated at the club. Collections were made there and a common purse was established to finance party activities. The

[75] Membership estimations vary. A list of 162 names in the Pepys manuscripts was probably obtained from various individuals arrested after the discovery of the Rye House Plot (Allen, "Political Clubs," p. 567). I wish to thank Professor James R. Jacob for sending me a copy of this list. Jones says there were 177 "permanent members" (J. R. Jones, "Green Ribbon Club," p. 19).

[76] Furley, "Pope-Burning Processions," pp. 16–23; Sitwell, *First Whig*, pp. 96–120. Sheila Williams, "The Pope-Burning Processions of 1679, 1680, and 1681," *Journal of the Warburg and Courtald Institutes* 21, no. 1 (1958):104–108. In addition to writing a number of exclusion tracts, the playwright Elkanah Settle designed the pageants for the 1679 and 1680 pope-burning demonstrations (F. C. Brown, *Elkanah Settle*, Chicago: University of Chicago Press, 1910, pp. 21–22).

[77] *CSPD*, 21:21.

latter included publication and dissemination of political literature, and the coordination of a national electoral campaign.[78] In short, the Green Ribbon Club assumed the role, in embryo, of a political party.

At the end of January 1679, Charles II announced the dissolution of the Cavalier Parliament, a decision that owed much to his secret intrigues with France. It remained to be seen, however, whether the king or Shaftesbury would benefit most from this action in the wake of the anti-popery agitation and the impeachment of the Earl of Danby. For the first time in nearly twenty years, there were to be parliamentary elections. Was the opposition sufficiently organized to overcome the barrier posed by the considerable number of M.P.'s who were "Court-pensioners" and who generally voted accordingly, through the election of new members sympathetic to the Country Party's political perspective? Between 1679 and 1681, the Whigs were provided with three opportunities to answer this question.

Only recently have scholars begun to give serious consideration to the question of what the characteristics were of the electorate who participated in these elections. The answer to this question deserves our careful attention, not only because of the surprising results disclosed by this research, but also for its obvious relevance to the discussion in Chapter 5 of the kinds of ideological arguments that were formulated to appeal to this electorate. The starting point for a description of the latter is, of course, the 1429 statute establishing the county franchise in the owners of a forty-shilling freehold. Equally obvious as a fact of importance is the consequence of two centuries of inflation in effectively increasing the size of the electorate while this legal requirement remained unchanged. "It is well known," the Earl of Ailesbury wrote near the end of the seventeenth century, "what a difference there is between forty shillings now, and what that sum was four hundred years and more since."[79] Although he recorded this remark in his *Memoirs* in the midst of a discussion of the parliamentary elections of 1679–1681, there is no suggestion from the Tory earl that this inflationary enfranchisement of "the common unthinking people" ought to be reversed by raising the threshhold of property ownership for the franchise concomitantly with inflation. In other words, there was a rather surprising level of acceptance as a fact of political life of the economic effects that had reshaped the nature of the electorate. This is not to say that there were not political challenges and debates as to the exercise of the vote. There were, although not so many nor

[78] North, *Examen*, pp. 572–573; Trevelyan, *England*, p. 378; Iris Morley, *A Thousand Lives: An Account of the English Revolutionary Movement, 1660–1685*, London: Andre Deutsch, 1954, p. 124.

[79] Thomas, Earl of Ailesbury, *Memoirs*, 2 vols., 1890, 1:60.

were they so frequent as one might have assumed. In this respect, as in several others, the Putney debates are unique in their direct and extended discussion of the franchise.

The effects of inflation and commercial expansion are not, of course, experienced equally by all social groups. And this, too, is a detail of specific importance relative to the electorate in 1680. For tradesmen, artisans, shopkeepers, merchants, and most freeholders prospered quite dramatically following the Restoration of Charles II, at the expense of middle-size landowners and the small gentry.[80] This fact was also noticed and commented upon by contemporaries.[81] Yet, it was not until the exclusion-crisis elections that its political significance, measured in terms of the shifts in the social composition of voters in parliamentary boroughs, could be fully appreciated. Thus, there were both long-term and short-term economic tendencies that extended the franchise to thousands of shopkeepers, artisans, tradesmen, and small farmers, resulting in "a massive numerical" expansion of the electorate during the Restoration period.[82]

The franchise was not, however, simply a matter determined by the outcome of economic tendencies. As J. H. Plumb has pointed out, it was a fact of great importance to the future of English politics that Parliament decided, at the beginning of the seventeenth century, that it would assume the role of final arbiter over all disputes arising out of contested elections. In doing so, Parliament demonstrated, through a series of case-by-case decisions in the 1620s, that it generally subscribed to the view that all inhabitants paying scot and lot, or all inhabitant householders,

[80] The growth in shipbuilding, the expansion of trade, and especially the rebuilding of London after the Great Fire provided employment for numerous artisans and tradesmen. Coupled with a sharp decline in the prices of goods purchased by the ordinary consumer between 1650 and 1690, real wages for artisans and skilled workers rose, reaching their peak for the century between 1680 and 1690 (D. C. Coleman, *The Economy of England, 1450–1750*, Oxford: Oxford University Press, 1977, pp. 100–103; K. G. Davies, *The Royal African Company*, London: Longmans, Green, 1957, p. 55). Inflation brought the franchise to "thousands of small farmers, shopkeepers, craftsmen" and others previously excluded (J. H. Plumb, *The Origins of Political Stability, 1675–1725*, Boston: Houghton Mifflin, 1967, p. 27).

[81] See Sir Richard Temple's reflection that previously, by statute, only freeholders had votes, but now (1675) freemen, scot-and-lot payers, and other categories of individuals exercised the suffrage (Grey, 4:3; Ailesbury, *Memoirs*, 1:60). For comments from an earlier period, see Derek Hirst, *The Representative of the People?*, Cambridge: Cambridge University Press, 1975, pp. 30ff.

[82] Lawrence Stone, "Social Mobility in England, 1500–1700," in *Seventeenth Century England*, ed. Paul S. Seaver, New York: New Viewpoints, 1976, pp. 26–70; cf. ibid., p. 61; J. H. Plumb, "The Growth of the Electorate, 1660–1715," *Past and Present*, no. 45 (1969):90–116.

were to be regarded as having the right to vote.[83] This general principle was clearly articulated in the case involving a contested election at Cirencester in 1624:

> There being no certain custom nor prescription who should be the electors and who not, we must have recourse to common right, which, to this purpose, was held to be, that more than the freeholders only ought to have voices in the election; namely all men, inhabitants, householders, resiants within the borough . . . ought to have voices in the election.[84]

Not only freeholders, but all residents of the borough had the common right to vote. In case after case, this principle was invoked and consistently upheld by Parliament. The Committee on Privileges, containing more than fifty members, which ruled on disputed elections, declared that both "common prescription" and "the general liberty of the realm" supported the view that in any election "the greatest numbers of voices that reasonably may be had" ought to provide the standard for any decision regarding the franchise. Moreover, the Committee on Privileges did not require any positive proof that the franchise ought to lie with the wider constituency; rather, the absence of any specific proof to the contrary was sufficient to uphold the principle of the extended franchise. Thus, the burden of proof was placed upon those who wished to restrict voting to demonstrate that such restrictions did not violate the common right of individuals, and as already noted, this viewpoint was not easily defensible within the House of Commons.[85]

As the reference to the "liberty of the realm" intimates, extension of the franchise rested upon some assumptions relating to the body politic viewed as a collectivity, and not upon claims grounded in individually exercised rights. For it was the Commons' conviction that a wider franchise operated as a restriction upon the king's, or the Court's, influence over elections in the choice of its members. Its corporative identity as an independent body and branch of the government, in other words, was tied to the principle of an extended franchise as a defensive weapon against the

[83] Plumb, "Growth of Electorate," p. 98; Hirst, *Representative*, pp. 11–12; Richard L. Bushman, "English Franchise Reform in the Seventeenth Century," *Journal of British Studies* 3, no. 1 (November 1963):38–39; John Cannon, *Parliamentary Reform: 1640–1832*, Cambridge: Cambridge University Press, 1973, p. 4.

[84] Plumb, "Growth of Electorate," p. 100.

[85] "I well know," said Royalist Sir Bevil Grenville, "that the opinion of the Parliament house hath ever been, that all the inhabitants being free men have a voice, and too I have known it often adjudged" (Hirst, *Representative*, pp. 65–66).

Court.[86] Over and above the specific facts in particular cases, and a strong legal argument in general, it is this political conviction that doubtless accounts in large part for the consistency of Parliament's decisions in the application of its interpretation of the common right to vote in the cases of disputed elections it considered. The conclusion that clearly follows is that the more reasonable the presumption that the Court might interfere with the outcome of elections, the more likely was Parliament to uphold and apply the extended-franchise principle. Thus, the still radical-tinged and uncertain Convention Parliament of 1659 reaffirmed the standard in its decisions, while the Cavalier Parliament that met in 1661, in the wake of "the happy restoration" of the king, reversed this policy. The exclusion parliaments, however, restored the general presumption, since the prospects of Court influence over its members were by then not only obvious, but the fact had itself become a major issue in the elections.[87]

More historical research needs to be done before we can claim with confidence to be in possession of something approaching a total picture of what, in fact, the seventeenth-century electorate looked like, or how it behaved from election to election in various parts of the country. The evidence uncovered thus far, however, is sufficiently striking in its implications to guarantee the value of further investigation. Perhaps the most surprising fact disclosed by the evidence is how widespread the practice of voting was in the seventeenth century. In Coventry, Bristol, and Dover, for example, all freemen could vote in elections; that is, all those who were not servants or receiving public relief.[88] This was also true in Exeter, Cambridge, Hull, Liverpool, Norwich, Newcastle, Oxford, Worcester, and nearly a score of other cities and towns.[89] London had a franchise that was virtually manhood suffrage in the election of its city officials and parliamentary representatives.[90] In Warwick, Northampton, and Preston, all inhabitants could vote; in Abingdon, inhabitants paying scot and lot could vote; in Ailesbury, all householders; in Bedford, all freemen and householders.[91] And so it went. Of course, there were "rotten boroughs," like Old Sarum, where, it was said, only the shepherd and his dog voted. There were other boroughs where a select number of burgesses or magistrates (for example, mayor, aldermen, and members of the common

[86] Bushman, "Franchise Reform," pp. 41–43; Hirst, *Representative*, pp. 67–68; Plumb, *Origins of Stability*, p. 39.

[87] Plumb, "Growth of Electorate," p. 109. For an example of the application of this principle to an exclusion crisis election, see James Walker, "Records relating to a Seventeenth-Century Parliamentary Election," *Yorkshire Archaeological Journal*, 34, pt. 133 (1939):25–34. The Whigs' attack on Court pensioners is discussed in Chapter 6, below.

[88] MS Add. D.44, fols. 49, 69; Hirst, *Representative*, p. 213.

[89] MS Add. D.44, fol. 250; Hirst, *Representative*, pp. 213–215.

[90] Jones, p. 198.

[91] MS Add. D.44, fols. 1, 3, 15, 167, 194; Hirst, *Representative*, p. 215.

council) chose their parliamentary representatives. These types of boroughs, however, chiefly because they were widely complained of, have been known for a long time. What has been much less appreciated is the rather extensive *practice* of voting by members of classes we might be inclined to assume were excluded from political participation in the seventeenth century. The evidence that has so far emerged indicates that this assumption is in need of drastic revision, and that both the economic and political tendencies of seventeenth-century England, especially following the Restoration, encouraged very wide electoral participation indeed.

In those cities and towns where freemen could vote, the level of creation of freemen through admissions to the guilds or corporations tended to fluctuate in response to the immediate political situation. In a study of Norwich between 1660 and 1713, for example, it was discovered that the greatest number of admissions of freemen in the city—and hence, the creation of new voters—occurred during the years of the popish-plot crisis.[92] If this was true for other cities as well, then the antipopery fear could be added to the list of factors that produced a substantial widening of the franchise, thereby helping the Whigs in their efforts to organize the "meanest" of people as part of a political movement. Both the fact of their organization of such individuals and the nature of the political propaganda the Whigs directed toward them raised cries from contemporaries that Shaftesbury was attempting to revive the Leveller movement.[93]

For some time now, a controversy has raged amongst scholars as to the nature of the franchise advocated by the Levellers.[94] Were they committed to manhood suffrage or to something less than this, with some level of property ownership as the threshold of voting? This controversy merits our attention for its bearing on three aspects of the argument I wish to make. The political context within which the Leveller debate on the fran-

[92] Penelope Corfield, "A Provincial Capital in the Late Seventeenth Century: The Case of Norwich," in *Crisis and Order in English Towns, 1550–1700*, ed. Peter Clark and Paul Slack, Toronto: University of Toronto Press, 1972, p. 279.

[93] Though contemporaries did not always do so, I am drawing a distinction between the general ideological accusation that Shaftesbury or the Whigs were "Commonwealthmen" and the more specific and class-oriented charge that they were stirring up the "Leveller" elements of society.

[94] Aside from Macpherson's book, the relevant items are Iain Hampsher-Monk, "The Political Theory of the Levellers: Putney, Property and Professor Macpherson," *Political Studies*, 24, no. 4 (December 1976):397–422; Keith Thomas, "The Levellers and the Franchise," in *The Interregnum: The Search for a Settlement 1646–1660*, ed. G. E. Aylmer, London: Macmillan, 1972, pp. 57–78; Peter Laslett, "Market Society and Political Theory," *Historical Journal*, 7, no. 1 (1964):150–154; C. B. Macpherson, "Servants and Labourers in Seventeenth-Century England," in *Democratic Theory: Essays in Retrieval*, Oxford: Clarendon Press, 1973, pp. 207–223; A. L. Morton, *The World of the Ranters*, London: Lawrence and Wishart, 1970, pp. 197–219; J. C. Davis, "The Levellers and Democracy," *Past and Present*, no. 40 (July 1968):174–180.

chise occurred, in terms of the actual level of electoral participation by individuals from the lowest social classes in the 1640s has not been sufficiently emphasized. Apart from whatever light an exploration of this context might shed on the meaning of the Levellers' political ideas, it is important to recognize that, even in the absence of a direct defense of those ideas with respect to suffrage, the fact of widespread voting by "mean" or "indigent" persons in the 1680s evoked a recollection of Leveller principles in the political consciousness of individuals. Second, the distinctive characteristics of the Levellers' political language and the form of the argument that they developed as a defense of their position on the franchise needs to be stressed. While there has never been much doubt regarding the social composition of the audience to whom Leveller arguments were directed, the degree to which this audience identification with certain concepts or types of arguments imposes restrictions upon the intentions and political objectives of those who employ that language has not received the attention it deserves with respect to the radical political literature of the 1680s. Finally, as a specific corollary to the last point, the relationship of Locke's argument in the *Two Treatises* to the language used by the Levellers merits much more serious consideration than it has heretofore been given by interpreters of Locke's political ideas.

The focus of the controversy to which I have alluded is the interpretation of the Levellers' writings by C. B. Macpherson in his *Political Theory of Possessive Individualism*. In approaching Macpherson's argument, let me begin with a consideration of the last of the three points mentioned above: the relationship between Locke and the Levellers. The standard and almost universally accepted view among Locke scholars has been, and continues to be, that there is no relationship between Locke's political ideas and those of the Levellers. Since there is no evidence that Locke ever read any Leveller tracts, it is not surprising that no case has been made linking Locke's position with that of the Levellers. Macpherson was virtually alone in suggesting that such a connection did exist, although in advancing this argument, he downplayed the radicalism of the Levellers, thus bringing them much closer to establishment Whigs like Locke than previous commentators on the Levellers had assumed. "The Levellers," Macpherson wrote, "paved the way, unwittingly, for Locke and the Whig tradition," and, in particular, their own ambiguities on the relationship between property and democracy provided the framework for a full-scale defense of "possessive individualism," such as Macpherson believes Locke to have endorsed.[95]

[95] C. B. Macpherson, *The Political Theory of Possessive Individualism*, Oxford: Oxford University Press, 1962, pp. 158–159.

I will return later to the issue of whether there are grounds for asserting that a relationship exists between the ideas of Locke and those of the Levellers, but I have begun with Macpherson's formulation of the problem because it reveals the weaknesses that beset his argument generally. For Macpherson, history is moving inexorably though "unwittingly," in accordance with the model of possessive individualism he has constructed, and according to which he assesses the cogency and importance of various political thinkers of the seventeenth century. Whether any such historical development is in fact taking place, however, depends to a much greater extent than Macpherson's methodology makes allowance for upon some means of determining what the actual historical trends were as well as upon a deeper appreciation for the ability of political actors to articulate their consciously intended meanings.

Thus, although his argument was presumptively based upon historical-sociological evidence, in fact Macpherson made no effort to determine whether the kinds of franchise demands the Levellers were making were unrealistic or were merely reflective of the actual trends of voting with respect to individuals from those classes that provided the political support for the Leveller movement. He writes simply that "whether they had ever in fact exercised the franchise is not known." He is then free to assume that the forty-shilling-freeholder provision in the statute corresponds to existing electoral practices.[96] This is merely one of a number of mistaken and unhistorical assumptions that structure his argument. In fact, not only did wage earners, copyholders, and male inhabitants vote in elections, there are a number of instances in which almsmen were assumed by contemporaries to be included within the common right of suffrage. In one 1640 election, for example, 77 of the 245 electors were reported to be almsmen (some of them were even residents of the almshouse).[97] Prior to the Putney debates, there was a significant number of boroughs where male householders or male inhabitants were entitled to vote, and they did so.[98] Because of these widespread departures from the freeholder restriction, the size of electorate was considerably larger than Macpherson assumed. Indeed, Derek Hirst's research suggests that

[96] Macpherson, *Possessive Individualism*, pp. 112–113.

[97] Thomas, "Levellers and the Franchise," p. 65. Nor was this an isolated instance, as both the legislative efforts to restrict the practice, and the Commons' decisions upholding the right of almsmen to vote prove (Hirst, *Representative*, pp. 102–103; Ogg, 2:473).

[98] As Hirst shows, there were 26 boroughs in 1641 with an inhabitant franchise, which meant what it said: adult male suffrage (*Representative*, p. 99). Macpherson claims that none of the Levellers' demands for inhabitant suffrage in their writings prior to the Putney debates is "at all specific" (*Possessive Individualism*, p. 119). It is difficult to see how one could be more specific if we take them to mean, as the electoral practices in these boroughs mean, adult male suffrage.

by 1641 the electorate may have represented as much as 40 percent of the adult male population.[99] Since Macpherson begins with the assumption that only 20 percent of that population were voters, and argues that the Levellers sought merely to double that figure, it is little wonder that he is able to portray them as conservatives.[100] If, however, we began with actual voting practices and applied the notion that the Levellers were seeking to enlarge the electorate by a factor of two, they would undoubtedly appear to be the radicals and advocates for adult male suffrage their opponents took them to be.

As several of Macpherson's critics have noted, he paid as little attention to the parliamentary tradition with respect to the franchise as he did to the electoral practices of boroughs. Yet for nearly thirty years prior to Putney, parliamentary as well as particular local decisions were overwhelmingly in favor of the broadest possible extension of the franchise. It is a mistake, therefore, to view the Leveller position as a radical demand generated by their temporary political strength in the army; rather, this plank—and it was only one of many—in their platform represented the continuation of several decades of political agitation for a wider suffrage.[101] As Plumb observes,

> When the Levellers demanded a vote for all inhabitants, this arose from their experience of county elections, from what they had seen and heard, not from abstract theory. They were carrying to a logical conclusion the policy introduced by the puritan leaders in the house of commons between 1614 and 1628.[102]

[99] Hirst, *Representative*, p. 105.

[100] Macpherson estimates the total male adult population as 1,170,400 and the electorate as 212,100, or slightly more than 18 percent (*Possessive Individualism*, p. 291). I have not bothered criticizing Macpherson's numerous contortions with Gregory King's figures, since they amount to nothing more than guesses piled upon guesses mixed with dubious assumptions at every step, but for some critical comments on this part of his argument, see Thomas, "Levellers and the Franchise," p. 71; Morton, *Ranters*, p. 213.

[101] Macpherson, *Possessive Individualism*, p. 119. As Hirst shows, there were numerous local political and economic struggles between the freemen in the towns and landed oligarchs in the 1620s and 1630s in which an extension of the franchise was the outcome of the former's victory. (*Representative*, pp. 52–57). Even in the particular instance of Putney, it seems more plausible to conclude that it was not the Levellers, whose position on the franchise had been a matter of record in a number of tracts published in the previous two years, but rather Ireton who chose to make the franchise "a preeminent issue." There can be little doubt that, if it had been put to a vote in the army as a whole, the Leveller position, and not that of Ireton, would have been upheld.

[102] Plumb, "Growth of Electorate," pp. 108–109. The Levellers' ideas "were formed in the communities in which they lived and worked, and the democracy which they advocated for the nation was still a working reality in their own local communities" (Brian Manning, review of *Leveller Manifestoes of the Puritan Revolution*, ed. Don M. Wolfe, *Economic His-*

It is true, one cannot simply impute a full knowledge of either existing voting practices or prior parliamentary debates to the participants at Putney.[103] Nevertheless, some of the Levellers came from those areas where voting participation went far beyond the boundaries that Ireton and the army grandees were prepared to defend. And, from this standpoint, the degree to which the latter's conservatism represented a retrogression from or betrayal of the political gains already achieved by artisans, tradesmen, and wage earners needs to be appreciated in order to evaluate the seriousness with which the Levellers pressed their case. Similarly, the Levellers may not have pieced together all the parliamentary decisions since the 1620s favoring a broad franchise, but their leaders were reasonably well informed men with respect to the activities of the Parliament, past and present.[104] In 1641, for example, there were debates on election petitions and a bill to regulate elections in which several members of the Commons argued on behalf of the right of all inhabitants to vote. Indeed, in words later repeated almost verbatim by Lilburne in one of his tracts, and by Colonel Rainborough at Putney, Simonds D'Ewes maintained that "it was the birthright of the subjects of England" that "the poorest man" should have a vote as well as the richest or greatest man in England.[105]

In addition to his failure to pay attention to the general political context of the debate over the franchise, Macpherson not only slighted the spe-

---

tory Review, 2d ser. 22 [1969]:132). Thomas dismisses this too curtly as an exaggeration, but I think not ("Levellers and the Franchise," p. 61).

[103] Hirst's remark that both sides at Putney were somewhat confused as to how to make use of existing voting practices in the defense of their theoretical positions is apt (*Representative*, pp. 22–23).

[104] Even if they had known of all the parliamentary precedents, there would probably have been some reluctance on the part of the Levellers to cite them on behalf of their case because of their ambivalent attitude toward the role of Parliament with respect to the franchise. That is, on the one hand, the Levellers sought a law "paramount" to all Parliaments that established a "free and equal" representative legislature, but on the other hand, they urged that "all obstructions to the freedom and equality of the people's choice of their representors, either by patents, charters, or usurpations, [or] by pretended customs be removed" by the existing Parliament. Both positions are presented in *The Case of the Army Truly Stated*, 1647, a tract closely linked with the debates at Putney (Don M. Wolfe, ed., *Leveller Manifestoes of the Puritan Revolution*, London: Frank Cass, 1967, pp. 212–213). Both aspects of this argument show that the Levellers reproduced the reasoning underlying the earlier parliamentary decisions, since it is the "obstructions" to the "ancient liberty" and "common right" of manhood suffrage that require some positive justification, and not the extension of the franchise as such.

[105] Thomas, "Levellers and the Franchise," p. 63. John Lilburne, *The Charters of London*, 1646, cited in Wolfe, *Leveller Manifestoes*, p. 14; Thomas Rainborough in *The Clarke Papers*, ed. C. H. Firth, 4 vols., Camden Society Publications, 1891, 1:301. Rainborough's father was a member of the Long Parliament until his death in 1642 (H. N. Brailsford, *The Levellers and the English Revolution*, London: Cresset Press, 1961, p. 198).

cific political dimensions of the Putney debates, he also consistently imposed upon the speakers his assumptions as to what they must have meant. Yet, an examination of the details of the debate suggests that the participants understood their opponents to be saying something quite different from what Macpherson imputes to them.[106] The most serious instance of this is his fastening upon one particular interpolation in the debate, which he not only applies as a standard of meaning for all previous statements in the debate by any and all Levellers, but also to all previous tracts extending back to several years prior to Putney. And if this were not enough, Macpherson supposes on the basis of this one statement a homogeneity of outlook among *all* the Levellers on the point in controversy. The passage in question concerns Cromwell's attempt to get the protagonists to come to some agreement on the suffrage, which he hopes will include the exclusion of servants and almsmen. Petty, one of the Levellers, agrees that servants and "those that take alms" could be excluded. This is the first such admission by any Leveller in the debate, but, Macpherson concludes, "it appears that the Levellers had been assuming the exclusion of 'servants' all along, and this was understood by the Levellers' opponents as well."[107]

Now, this conclusion is not even consistent with Macpherson's own presentation of the debate, for as he correctly noted, both Ireton and Cromwell understood the Levellers to be defending manhood suffrage.[108]

[106] The most thorough treatment of the specific context of the Putney debates is Hampsher-Monk, "Political Theory of the Levellers." For a discussion of the political evolution of various versions of the *Agreement of the People*, which Macpherson treats rather indiscriminately without regard to the political circumstances of their composition, see John Gough, "The Agreements of the People, 1647–49," *History*, n.s. 15, no. 60 (January 1931):334–341.

[107] Macpherson, *Possessive Individualism*, p. 122. The exchange between Petty and Cromwell occurs in *Clarke*, 1:341–342.

[108] Macpherson, *Possessive Individualism*, p. 126. Macpherson adds that if the Levellers recognized that a claim for manhood franchise was being imputed to them, they "did not trouble to contradict it" because they were so busy refuting the charge that this would put an end to all property (p. 127). I find this a dubious reading of the record. From the outset (i.e., Rainborough's reply to Ireton's first statement of this allegation), the Leveller speakers regarded the property issue as a red herring (along with the charge of anarchy), which they especially resented because they did not believe that Ireton and his supporters really believed that the Levellers held such views. Again and again, their replies stick to the issue of manhood suffrage, about which they recognize that there is a real disagreement among the parties. The only serious response to the property issue I can find, aside from a reference to the commandment that "thou shalt not steal" as an injunction of natural law (cited by Macpherson), is (1) that "the chief end of this government is to preserve persons as well as estates," with the presupposition that the former takes precedence, and hence the priority of the suffrage issue over that of property in land, and (2) that no argument has been presented in favor of property except a defense of existing political institutions, which are the very things to be reformed (*Clarke*, 1:320).

Ireton's initial response to the provision in the *Agreement of the People* that referred to the distribution of representatives "according to the number of inhabitants" is that it made him think "that the meaning is, that every man that is an inhabitant is to be equally considered, and to have an equal voice in the election of the representors . . . and if that be the meaning" of the passage, then he will speak against it. Far from disabusing Ireton of this interpretation (and thus mollifying at the outset a powerful opponent), Colonel Rainborough's response that "the poorest he" in England or that "every man" has a right to vote, only confirms Ireton's understanding of his opponents' position.[109] And it is on that basis—as an argument for or against manhood suffrage (no exclusions having been conceded)—that the debate then proceeds. Even after several hours, it is clear that "the grand question of all is, whether or no it be the property of every individual person in the kingdom to have a vote in election."[110]

However, the participants and the audience are becoming increasingly restless. "We have been a great while upon this point," Colonel Rich observes, and Sexby adds his plea "to come to a determination of this question."[111] Nevertheless, Ireton continues to speak against the point, prompting Cromwell, as the chair, to say, "Let us not spend so much time in such debates as these are," while also suggesting a compromise—the inclusion of a "very considerable part of copyholders by inheritance"—as a means of bringing the issue of the franchise to a close. If some such compromise is not accepted, he foresees "our debates are endless." Another expedient he suggests is to send the whole matter to a committee.[112] The Levellers react rather sharply to this attempt "to put off" the question of suffrage, as Sexby puts it, and demand that the matter be put to an immediate vote.[113] But the debate continues, with Ireton seconding Cromwell's suggestion about sending the question to a committee.[114] Obviously, the participants are sharply divided not only on the substance of the issue, but also as to the method by which their differences are to be resolved, which (not surprisingly) itself reflects the point—whether every soldier will have a vote, or a select committee will decide. As Cap-

[109] *Clarke*, 1:299–301. Clarke's notes are somewhat garbled, but the speech by Ireton is clearly premised on his understanding that the Leveller speakers (Petty and Rainborough) have responded to his question with a defense of manhood suffrage, to which he now replies.

[110] *Clarke*, 1:331. As Hampsher-Monk points out, this question is stated at least six times between the opening remarks by Ireton and the intervention by Cromwell cited by Macpherson ("Political Theory of the Levellers," p. 399).

[111] *Clarke*, 1:321, 323.

[112] *Clarke*, 1:328.

[113] This motion for a vote is seconded by Rainborough (*Clarke*, 1:330, 335).

[114] *Clarke*, 1:334.

tain Audley remarks wryly, "I see you have a long dispute, that you do intend to dispute here till the 10th of March."[115] Still the debate continues, prompting Captain Rolfe to plead for the importance of the "preservation of unity in the Army" that seems to him to require some sort of compromise on the issue of "an equal as well as of a free representative." He suggests some "medium or a composure" on the subject "in relation to servants or to foreigners." Lieutenant Chillenden then moves for "a speedy end to this business" because "if we take this course of debating upon one question a whole afternoon," both the army and the country will be exposed to danger from their enemies long before we come to an agreement among ourselves, a point seconded by other speakers.[116] Nevertheless, the debate goes on, with Ireton making yet another speech against the notion that "any man shall have a voice in election." It is at this point that Cromwell finally intercedes to try for an agreement on the exclusion of servants and almsmen in order to bring the discussion to a close through some agreed upon compromise. But, even after Petty's acceptance of Cromwell's point, the debate proceeds, with Ireton again arguing against the original phrasing of the *Agreement* ("according to the number of inhabitants"), indicating that he, at least, has *not* understood Petty to be speaking for *the* Leveller position, as Macpherson assumes.[117] In fact, the issue is left unresolved, at least according to the record available to us, and the debate gradually drifts into other areas with no explicit recognition by any spokesman for either side that a compromise on the question has been reached.[118] Still, we know that some agreement was reached to exclude servants and beggars, and I do not understand how, reading the whole record, one can see this compromise, and Cromwell's

[115] *Clarke*, 1:331.

[116] *Clarke*, 1:337–338.

[117] *Clarke*, 1:345. Moreover, Petty was a relatively obscure Leveller, neither a leading spokesman within the army as was Colonel Rainborough, nor the author of any of the major Leveller tracts. Why Macpherson should so easily assume that his one statement represented the agreed upon position of Leveller leaders when he can find no evidence to support this conclusion in their speeches and writings is more than a little puzzling (J. C. Davis, "Levellers and Democracy," p. 175). And, in general, as Howell and Brewster emphasize, the Levellers were a more heterogeneous body in their views on this issue than Macpherson makes them out to be (Roger Howell, Jr., and David E. Brewster, "Reconsidering the Levellers: The Evidence of the *Moderate*," *Past and Present*, no. 46 [February 1970]:68–86).

[118] The Levellers subsequently asserted in *A Copy of Letter Sent by the Agents of Several Regiments* that a vote was taken at Putney and that the proposition—apparently the one excluding servants and beggars—was approved with only three dissenting votes. The vote was probably held on one of the days when Clarke was not present (Wolfe, *Leveller Manifestoes*, p. 61).

intercessions as the chair, as being anything other than responses to the urgent demands from supporters on both sides that they reach agreement on *something* so that other issues can be considered.

Now, as Macpherson points out, Leveller pamphlets and petitions subsequent to Putney do exclude servants and beggars.[119] His suggestion that this was the position of the Levellers all along imputes to the speakers at Putney a level of obtuseness and an unwillingness to mention any specific concessions that would move the discussion to a compromise that seems far more implausible than the supposition that, faced with a prolonged and stubborn opposition to manhood suffrage, the Levellers struck a realistic political bargain with their opponents to exclude servants and beggars.[120] This bargain was made palatable both by its reconcilability with the general principle according to which they defended manhood suffrage, and because of the practical allowance of the franchise to all soldiers and sailors, *regardless* of whether they were servants or beggars. Since the army was the most immediate and important political audience for

[119] Macpherson, *Possessive Individualism*, p. 118. Macpherson jumbles together "beggars" and "those receiving alms" in a manner quite unjustified in terms of the evidence and his own interpretive standards. For, when Petty, on whose statement he otherwise places such interpretative weight, explains what he means by the exclusion of "those that take alms" he defines them as "those that receive alms from door to door," or individuals who, in the seventeenth century would have been called beggars (*Clarke*, 1:342). This clarification is dropped by Macpherson in all his subsequent references to almsmen, however, because as he states in his appendix (pp. 286–287), whereas there were approximately 10,000 beggars in England, there were 343,000 individuals on public relief. By lumping the two terms together, he is able to exclude a very large number of individuals from the franchise, but if only beggars are excluded, the Levellers' position moves much closer to manhood suffrage. In support of his view, Macpherson cites the two most conservative versions of the *Agreement*, which were compromise documents drafted with Independents and advocating a ratepayer franchise, thus ignoring the political context governing the identification of almsmen in them. But in the tracts written by the Levellers themselves, some of which are cited by Macpherson, they generally refer simply to "beggars" as being excluded. As Thomas shows, Cromwell certainly understood the Leveller position to have included as electors those who received alms, for he reported this fact to the Commons several weeks after the Putney debates (Thomas, "Levellers and the Franchise," pp. 69–70). There is also some evidence that the party paper, the *Moderate*, assumed that almsmen were included in their franchise proposals (Howell and Brewster, "Reconsidering the Levellers," p. 78).

[120] In *Legal Fundamental Liberties*, 1649, Lilburne provides a detailed narrative of just such a political struggle between the Levellers and the Independents to reach a compromise agreement. He writes of "a long and tedious tug we had with Commissary General Ireton only, yea sometimes whole nights together . . . [and] for peace sake we condescended in to please him" (Wolfe, *Leveller Manifestoes*, p. 419). Since Ireton played the same role at Putney, standing out almost alone against the Leveller position, it seems more than likely that the Levellers made their concessions on servants and beggars "for peace sake . . . to please him" in that instance as well.

the Levellers, even this compromise could be read as a political triumph for their position.[121]

As a number of critics have observed, Macpherson's general assumption that "servant" in the seventeenth century "meant wage-earners, anyone who worked for an employer for wages," is not borne out by the evidence. In fact, as Keith Thomas notes, none of the three seventeenth-century writers Macpherson cites in support of his general assertion equates day-laborers or wage earners generally with "servants."[122] As Thomas further shows, the Statute of Artificers of 1563 incorporates a categorical distinction between "servants" who contract their services to a particular master for a year or more and "artificers and laborers being hired for wages by the day or week." The former are called servants; the latter, day-laborers.[123] It is simply a fiction of Macpherson's creation to propose a generally accepted identification of servant with wage earner de facto. Usage of the term was variable and loose, and if one had to depend upon a general survey of references, it is more likely, as Morton argues, to have meant a "personal servant" to a particular master than a class of wage earners.[124] This is not to say that "servant" might not be used generically to refer to anyone receiving wages, but the presence of this particular meaning does not, ipso facto, establish it as the generally accepted

[121] The Levellers' general principle that no individual should be dependent upon the will of another in the exercise of his free judgment could be interpreted to exclude servants and beggars because of their dependency. Macpherson treats the inclusion of soldiers in the franchise as a political expedient, though he recognizes that the Levellers had always insisted upon the right of every soldier to vote (*Possessive Individualism*, pp. 135–136, 297. This underestimates the extent to which, in the Levellers' eyes, the private soldier, without any social qualification whatsoever as to his status, is *the* archetypal individual claiming his natural rights, including the right to vote, as Sexby, for example, makes poignantly clear at Putney (*Clarke*, 1:322–323, 329–330). The aim of "securing the native rights of the Army and all others" advanced by the authors of *The Case of the Army Truly Stated* also puts the point in its proper framework (Wolfe, *Leveller Manifestoes*, p. 202). See note 140 below. The reaction of the Levellers' opponents seems to confirm this reconciliation of a principled position with a tactical victory. The author of *The Case of the Army Soberly Discussed*, 1647, a reply to the tract cited above, understands the Levellers to advocate extending the franchise to "all servants," and he complains that "very many in the Army" are "servants and prentices not yet free" who would therefore be entitled to vote (cited in Gordon J. Schochet, "Patriarchalism, Politics and Mass Attitudes in Stuart England," *Historical Journal* 12, no. 3 [1969]:422). If this is true, the Levellers managed to include "very many" servants within the franchise, although they were nominally excluded by the compromise.

[122] Macpherson, *Possessive Individualism*, p. 107n.; Thomas, "Levellers and the Franchise," pp. 70–71; Hampsher-Monk, "Political Theory of the Levellers," p. 412. Also, see the exchange on this issue between Laslett and Macpherson in the references cited in note 94 above.

[123] Thomas, "Levellers and the Franchise," p. 71.

[124] Morton, *Ranters*, p. 214.

meaning for the whole society. Moreover, Macpherson made another gigantic leap when he assumed that the Levellers, as a body, subscribed to this identification. Even if someone in seventeenth-century England held the view that Macpherson universalizes, he made not the slightest effort to demonstrate that the Levellers, in particular, made this identification in their writings. Yet, his entire argument rests upon this supposition.

If seventeenth-century documents are difficult to interpret as to their authors' presuppositions, this is no less true for a modern interpreter of Macpherson's text. For it appears that all of his general pronouncements assume that "anyone who worked for an employer for wages" could be called a servant.[125] Merely entering into a "wage contract" placed an individual within this category.[126] The difficulty, as Macpherson tacitly recognizes, is that this general proposition cannot be reconciled with the Levellers' specific references to the occupations of their constituents. That is, they speak of the rights of cobblers, tinkers, broom men, weavers, chimney sweeps, carpenters, and so forth. As Wildman explained, his defense of the right of "all freemen" or "every man" to vote placed that right with "coopers, tallow-chandlers, or other manual occupations," which clearly included wage earners.[127] If these individuals were persons who "alienated the use and direction of their capacities (i.e., of their labor) by entering a wage contract," as Macpherson puts it, thereby accepting the identification of "servant," then I fail to see how this construction can logically be reconciled with the Levellers' own references to such individuals as having the right to vote without, at the same time, making them defenders of "servants" as an inclusive category in their conception of the franchise, and thus making them defenders of manhood suffrage. I said that Macpherson tacitly recognizes the difficulty because at one point he speaks rather oddly of cobblers or chimney sweeps possessing the "working capital" that prevents them from being classified as mere wage earners.[128] Indeed, this is more than odd; it is preposterous in terms of any understanding of the economic activities of the members of these "manual occupations" in seventeenth-century England.[129] And, even if there is some necessity for Macpherson to convert a broom into "working capital" (what a laugh Marx would have had at that!) in order to avoid

[125] Macpherson, *Possessive Individualism*, pp. 107, 282–283.

[126] Macpherson, *Possessive Individualism*, p. 144.

[127] John Wildman, *London's Liberties*, 1651, p. 35. This tract is of some particular interest, not only because it is by Wildman or because it presents a relatively late restatement of the Leveller position, but also because it was reprinted in 1682. For Overton's view, see Wolfe, *Leveller Manifestoes*, p. 12.

[128] Macpherson, *Possessive Individualism*, p. 149.

[129] Morton, *Ranters*, p. 213; cf. ibid., p. 184.

recognizing that the Levellers did include wage earners in their notion of the franchise, there is no reason to foist this fiction upon the consciousness of the political actors themselves. In short, when the Levellers excluded servants from their post-Putney writings, they clearly were not thinking of the thousands of miners, the weavers receiving piece-rate wages, seamen or soldiers, or the forty thousand laborers working in the shipyards; it was the personal servant within a household they had in mind, and even here there must be some question as to how, in practice, the exclusion standard was to be applied to these individuals.[130] At most, these individuals represented not two-thirds of the male population, as Macpherson estimates, but approximately 15 percent, including beggars.[131] In other words, even after their pragmatic concessions, the Levellers could view themselves as defenders of the enfranchisement of 85 percent of adult males. Moreover, if I am right about the meaning the Levellers and their opponents gave to their statements, then any resuscitation of political activity, and especially electoral participation, among the working class was bound to revive a discussion of "Leveller" principles, such as in fact did occur during the exclusion crisis.

It would be anomalous to speak of Leveller tracts being published in the 1680s—although one or two were reprinted—just as it would be to speak of Puritans as an identifiable group during that period. What survived the Levellers' organizational defeat in the 1650s was the political language they employed in their writings. In the analysis of the Putney debates too much attention has been given, perhaps, to the specific issue of the franchise, and not enough to the form of the argument the Levellers developed to support that and other reforms. For, although Ireton was prepared to make practical concessions as to who could vote, he was totally

130 The exclusion of those "receiving wages from any particular person" in some of the more conservative documents seems to apply to a specific master/servant relationship, and not to the case of a carpenter hiring himself out to many different persons. The 4,000 Derby lead miners who lent their support to the Leveller cause certainly did not think themselves excluded because they were wage earners (H. N. Brailsford, *Levellers*, pp. 565–567). Also, the *Moderate* shows no reluctance in addressing itself to "day-laborers," nor does it draw the distinction or apply the language of "servant" in the manner that Macpherson suggests (Howell and Brewster, "Reconsidering the Levellers," p. 77). Moreover, from the lord's standpoint, everyone working for him, from his houseboy to his secretary or steward was his "servant." Yet Wildman, who became Buckingham's steward and servant did not think himself as being disenfranchised through such service. A number of individuals in service living in the family of lords like Shaftesbury owned small property or stock, were attorneys or doctors, or members of Parliament (e.g., Thomas Stringer and Wildman). The point is that even in the case of household or "in-servants," as Gregory King classifies them, franchise exclusion could never have been applied in an indiscriminate and abstract fashion to any and all servants as a general category, as Macpherson assumes.

131 Thomas, "Levellers and the Franchise," p. 73.

opposed to the Levellers' invocation of a natural rights argument as the theoretical foundation for their political program. From the outset, he perceived that the Levellers "must fly for refuge to an absolute natural right" position in order to defend their claims to manhood suffrage, and to this form of the argument, he and the others who sided with him were resolutely opposed.[132] The chief and most telling consequence of this appeal to the Law of Nature, according to Ireton, is that it will put an end to all property rights.[133] What is interesting, however, is that Ireton knows that this is not the avowed intention of his opponents. Yet so convinced is he that this consequence follows from the very language they use that he simply cannot disassociate the two. For, if "by the right of nature, we are free, we are equal, one man must have as much voice as another, then . . . I would fain have any man show me their bounds where you will end."[134] To this Rainborough objects that Ireton has accused the Levellers of favoring anarchy, which is not their position. Cromwell intercedes to assure Rainborough that "no man says that you have a mind to anarchy," but he, too, shares Ireton's belief that "the consequence of this rule tends to anarchy" because there are no certain and practical boundaries or limits set by natural law that allow for the kinds of social, economic, and political distinctions that Cromwell and Ireton are attempting to defend.[135] Without such positive lines of authority and privilege, civil societies and constitutions would dissolve into a state of natural equality—which, in their view, must be equated with anarchy. What the Independents seek, therefore, is some guarantee that this will not occur.

The form of the Leveller argument is quite different. As Rainborough explains early on, "I say, that either it must be the law of God or the law of man that must prohibit the meanest man in the kingdom to have this benefit" of voting. Since he can find nothing in the Law of Nature justifying such a prohibition, the latter can only be a consequence of the existing law of the kingdom. But—and this is the crucial point—that law can be changed, especially if one begins with the notion that "the foundation of all law lies in the people."[136] It does not make sense to the Lev-

[132] *Clarke*, 1:301.

[133] *Clarke*, 1:263–264, 306–308, 314.

[134] *Clarke*, 1:308. "I am afraid and do tremble at the boundless and endless consequences" of an appeal to the Law of Nature, Ireton confesses, because to him it means a reliance upon "that wild or vast notion of what in every man's conception is just or unjust" (1:263–264). The basic framework for every critique of political radicalism in the seventeenth century, from Hobbes to Samuel Parker, can be found in Ireton's speeches at Putney.

[135] *Clarke*, 1:309.

[136] *Clarke*, 1:304.

ellers that anyone should feel such a deep attachment to the existing law, just because it is the law. As Rainborough exclaims,

> I think that the law of the land in that thing is the most tyrannical law under heaven, and I would fain know what we have fought for, and this is the old law of England and that which enslaves the people.[137]

To Rainborough and other Levellers, the reluctance of Ireton to move ahead with reforms signifies his identification with the status quo, and it jeopardizes what the army fought for by leaving in place the tyranny of laws which, in their view, are no longer in force, since political power has returned into the hands of the people.[138] The latter are therefore free to reconstruct a form of government more in harmony with the principles of natural law than the old one, but there is no reason, Rainborough insists, to call this position an anarchical one. Ireton understands this, and his reply restates the crux of the matter. "If I had said, that I would not wish that we should have any enlargement at all of the bounds of those that are to be the electors," he explains, then you might have rightly objected. But that, he insists, is not his position. He is willing to go beyond what he conceives to be the present restrictions upon voting. What he is not willing to grant is the enlargement of the franchise "beyond all bounds."[139] And, so long as the principle of suffrage is tied to a natural law defense, Ireton cannot see that any specific boundaries can be established.

[137] Clarke, 1:311.

[138] Lilburne states the point in a number of tracts, but Overton is even more cogent in arguing that a forfeiture of the trust dissolves the existing government, returning political power to the people who now exist in a state of nature governed by natural law (Wolfe, *Leveller Manifestoes*, pp. 19, 33, 160–163; Hampsher-Monk, "Political Theory of the Levellers," p. 417; H. N. Brailsford, *Levellers*, pp. 137–138, 236–237, 259). It is sometimes asserted that the Levellers did not use the concept of the state of nature, but this confuses the specific concept with its meaning (Harro Hopfl and Martyn P. Thompson, "The History of Contract as a Motif in Political Thought," *American Historical Review* 84, no. 4 [October 1979]:940). In the precise sense of the term as defined above, which is also the political meaning given to it by Locke, the Levellers certainly had a conception of the "state of nature," though they did not call it that. They spoke of "dissolving" society into the "original law of nature." But see the statement by Lilburne that the dissolution of the government "reduced us into the original state of chaos or confusion" (cited in D. B. Robertson, *The Religious Foundations of Leveller Democracy*, New York: King's Crown Press, 1951, p. 80). From this political theoretical standpoint, we can see not only why the Levellers wanted their proposals and constitutions submitted to the people and not to Parliament, but also why they were so strenuous in their appeal to natural law at Putney; that is, for them, but not for Ireton, the political authority claimed by the "old constitution" and Parliament had already "dissolved," leaving the army free to decide its own fate (see note 140 below).

[139] *Clarke*, 1:313–314.

In other words, there is a rather classic confrontation here between a reformist and a revolutionary position, understood by participants on both sides, and explicitly linked to the usage of certain concepts and language. Thus, when Ireton tries to elicit some agreement that they acknowledge the law or "civil constitution" as the basis for their discussion, Wildman intervenes to return the question to "what is just," a proposition that must be pursued not in terms of existing laws (which, in any case, "were made by our conquerors"), but "according to the just rules of government." And the latter, Wildman argues, prescribe that "all government is in the free consent of the people," which, if that is granted, means that "there is no person that is under a just government . . . unless he by his own free consent" puts himself under that government. This in turn means that "every person in England hath as clear a right to elect his representative as the greatest person in England."[140] Not only has Wildman tried logically to deduce this proposition from the language of the natural rights/natural law argument being made by the Levellers, but he now puts the question back to Ireton: Why, if the consent of every individual is required for the legitimacy of government, should we regard existing laws, to which we have not consented, as being legitimate? This is a telling point, but Ireton is able to field it precisely because he is not committed to the language and form of argument employed by Wildman. He replies straightforwardly that "a man ought to be subject to a law that did not give his consent," and this reply is again tied to the defense of a "permanent interest in the land" as a basis of the legitimacy of laws.[141]

Other examples, both from the debates and from the political literature could be cited to illustrate the point, but enough has been said, I believe, to make it clear that the revolutionary natural law position, with appeals

[140] *Clarke*, 1:316–318. Wildman's reasoning is the same as that employed by Lilburne in one of his tracts where, after observing that the government had "dissolved into the original law of nature," he links this situation to the natural rights claim that "every individual private soldier . . . ought freely to have their vote, to choose the transactors of their affairs" (H. N. Brailsford, *Levellers*, pp. 236–237). In his *Memorial from the English Protestants to Their Highnesses . . . Prince and Princess of Orange*, 1688, Wildman employs the same language and reasoning, defending the "natural right" of "every subject's free consent" to the laws, which "the freemen of the cities and towns" of England have been denied by James' tyranny. On the other side, the anti-Whig paper *Heraclitus Ridens* also understands the linkage between a natural rights argument and manhood suffrage. For, if the privilege of choosing representatives to Parliament "were a natural right, all persons who are born in England would have a vote at elections" (May 17, 1681).

[141] *Clarke*, 1:319. When Petty later argues from a natural law position that any unjust constitution "should be annulled," Cromwell interjects that it is precisely this mistake of believing that the people can create a "better constitution in that paper" (i.e., *Agreement*) than "that which is" (i.e., the existing constitution), which lies at the heart of the entire dispute over the franchise (*Clarke*, 1:336).

to equality, freedom by natural birth, political power in the hands of the people, the free consent of every individual, and so forth, was a distinctively radical language associated with the Levellers and tied to a defense of manhood suffrage (as well as "anarchy" and the end of property). This language is explicitly repudiated by Ireton and Cromwell. It is not the Law of Nature, they argue, that gives a person property, but the civil constitution. Hence, "we ought to keep to that constitution" which we have now, because the alternative would lead to anarchy.[142] Quite apart from their disagreement on the specific issue of the franchise, therefore, there is, as Ireton puts it, the question of "the validity of that argument" being advanced by the Levellers.[143] If historians have tended to forget just how much the form of the Levellers' argument rankled their opponents, this is no excuse for supposing that when the same concepts and language reemerged in the radical Whig political tracts of the 1680s, they had somehow become the common property of an amorphous body of moderate Whigs.[144] On the contrary, as I will try to demonstrate in Chapter 6, both the form of the argument and the social composition of the audience to whom such arguments were directed, suggested to contemporaries that the Shaftesbury-led Whigs were attempting to revive the Levellers' movement.

As this last statement suggests, I have throughout this work placed

[142] The repeated and explicit rejection of the language of natural rights and of natural law as a ground of their political theory by Ireton and Cromwell has not received sufficient attention, either for what it says about their position or for what it reveals about the distinctive radical dimensions of the Levellers' political theory (*Clarke*, 1:263, 308, 310–311, 314, 322, 325, 327, 337). A notable exception to this generalization is G. P. Gooch's observation that Ireton's vigorous attack on "the philosophical argument" of the Levellers and "the whole theory of natural rights" is crucial to an understanding of his own position, especially with respect to the franchise (*English Democratic Ideas in the Seventeenth Century*, 2d ed., New York: Harper and Row, 1959, pp. 137–138).

[143] *Clarke*, 1:326.

[144] It is worth stressing this point since one might gain the impression from reading some of the secondary literature on Locke, or the exclusion tracts of the 1680s, that this language of natural rights, equality, consent of individuals, right of resistance, power in the people, etc., was simply the common coin of political thinkers. This is not the case. As I have tried to show in chapters 6 and 11, the radical argument that employed these concepts and terminology was aimed at a particular audience and was recognized by contemporary critics to be addressed to that audience. Both the social composition of that audience and the substance of the argument was directly linked in the minds of the critics (and in the minds of at least some of the radicals) with the Levellers. Given Locke's association with the radicals, his political objectives, and his familiarity with the radical tracts that employed the language he uses, I am arguing that, from the standpoint of a historically grounded approach to the meaning of political theory, there is a presumptive link between Locke and Levellers in the form of a social practice of theorizing through the use of a socially identifiable language.

Locke in much closer proximity to the Levellers and to the radical political theory they developed than has previously been supposed. In the absence of evidence indicating a direct link through Locke's reading of particular Leveller tracts, this can only be a suggestive general proposition for reorienting the way in which we approach the meaning of the arguments of the *Two Treatises*.[145] Yet, the more weight one places upon the decision of an author to identify himself with a particular political language selected from among a range of available choices, and the more one thinks in terms of the appeal that a specific political vocabulary has for specific social groups, the more plausible it becomes to think of Locke's political theory in terms of this association. In succeeding chapters, I have tried to reinforce this general presumption through considering particular arguments from the *Two Treatises* in relation to the Levellers' position when, for the reasons indicated above, this seemed to me to be appropriate in terms of Locke's own political associations and intentions.

It is sometimes alleged that the lack of initiative with respect to franchise reform indicates how much Shaftesbury and the Whigs were committed to the defense of an oligarchy of large property holders. Or, on the other hand, the same meaning is read into a proposal drafted by Shaftesbury that would have restricted the suffrage to property holders of £200 or more.[146] What is conveniently forgotten in the case of the latter, however, is that this proposal was drafted in 1679 at the height of the Whig campaign against the bribery of voters being practiced by the Court's supporters. Hence the attempt by the Whigs to counter this practice by raising the stakes through this redefinition of the electorate. Though it may seem paradoxical to us, this was, in fact, a response adopted by various radicals before and after Shaftesbury.[147] In any event, as it became clear

[145] Locke's library included more than 600 pamphlets and tracts stored loosely in boxes, only a very small proportion of which were included as specific titles in his library catalog (*LL*, pp.51–54). Whether any Leveller tracts were among this collection—which may even have been much larger—is anyone's guess, but the possibility cannot be so easily dismissed as it generally is in the secondary literature. It is also worth noting that Benjamin Furley, with whom Locke lived during his last two years in Holland, included a substantial collection of Leveller tracts in his library, to which Locke had constant access. Not only the works of Lilburne, Overton, Walwyn, and other Levellers, but also what appears to be a fairly complete collection of Gerrard Winstanley's writings were in Furley's library. In addition to the Levellers and Diggers, Furley owned numerous tracts by Ranters, Muggletonians, and other radical sectarians (*Bibliotheca Furleiana*, 1714). In the end, however, Laslett's observation (Laslett, p. 75) that it was "from conversation and casual contact, not from documentary acquaintance, that Locke inherited the fruit of the radical writings of the Civil War," is, I believe, the most accurate statement of the matter.

[146] Ogg, 2:481–482; Cannon, *Parliamentary Reform*, p. 19.

[147] Jones' discussion (pp. 53–54), however, focuses upon the object of this franchise pro-

to the Whigs that they could defeat the Court through their organizational skills, this reform proposal was dropped and not revived. Indeed, this last point explains the silence of the Whigs on the question of electoral reform. That is, they felt little need to supply a theoretical defense of a franchise already exercised by hundreds of thousands of artisans, tradesmen, shopkeepers, merchants, and small farmers who were, overwhelmingly, the electoral base of the Whig Party. The irony is that the theoretical demand for suffrage rights in the eighteenth and nineteenth centuries owes much to a reversal, or at least a dramatic slowing, of the dominant trends in the seventeenth century. The turn toward oligarchy and an increasing dominance of large property holders within the electorate is a distinctive feature of the eighteenth century, and not of the Restoration period.[148] In fact, seen in a total context in which voters are a proportion of the whole (adult male) population, or in terms of the proportion of voters from the various social classes, the late seventeenth century was a high-water mark of democratic participation, not achieved again in England until the mid-nineteenth century.[149]

If we turn to a consideration of a few specific reports on the exclusion elections, we can perceive some of the effects of the general tendencies discussed above. The elections themselves often assumed the form of quasi-military demonstrations of power. In one contest in Essex, Colonel Mildmay, the Whig candidate, appeared "with about 1000 gentlemen and freeholders," and he was supported by Lord Grey with "about 2000 horse attending him." These two forces joined with other supporters and proceeded to march through the town with "not less than 6000 men." On

posal, which was to prevent and punish bribery and corruption, rather than to create a Parliament of "plutocrats," as Ogg suggests. As Hampsher-Monk remarks, what really gave the radicals at Putney pause to reflect was not the assertion that the poor would outvote the rich, but that the rich would buy the votes of the poor and thus possess even more power than they had under the present suffrage (Hampsher-Monk, "Political Theory of the Levellers," p. 402). Later, in *Some Remarks upon Government, and Particularly upon the Establishment of the English Monarchy relating to This Present Juncture*, 1689, Wildman raises the problem of electoral corruption, providing a catalog of the various ways in which votes are purchased, to which he demands that criminal penalties be attached. In this context, he suggests that a £40 requirement might be established as the basis of the franchise. For a discussion of Wildman as the author of this tract, see Mark Goldie, "The Roots of True Whiggism, 1688–94," *History of Political Thought* 1, no. 2 (June 1980):212ff. Yet, Wildman also believes this to be consistent with his defense of "every subject's" natural right to give his consent to the law, asserted simultaneously in another tract (see note 140 above).

[148] Cannon, *Parliamentary Reform*, pp. 36–37; Plumb, "Growth of Electorate," p. 116.

[149] Plumb, "Growth of Electorate," pp. 115–116. As Cannon notes, in 1754 the electorate was approximately 10 percent of the total adult male population. In addition, the number of contested elections declined dramatically between 1702 and 1832 (*Parliamentary Reform*, pp. 30, 49).

the other side, the Court candidate appeared with several thousand supporters, including "most of the knights and gentlemen throughout the county, together with 200 of the clergy."[150] In another election in 1679, the Duke of Buckingham marshaled six thousand men at whose head he rode to the place of election, with Major Wildman riding at his side.[151] At the election of Sir William Waller in 1681, one witness wrote, "notwithstanding the coldness of the weather, the exceeding high winds, and the violent driving rain," between two and three thousand men turned out for the poll.[152] Even if Oliver Heywood's estimate of thirty thousand men present at the 1679 election at Lancaster seems wildly improbable—although two men were trampled to death by the crowd—it is nevertheless true that many elections involved the turnout of thousands of individuals, many of whom were participating in the electoral process for the first time.[153] These elections were frequently boisterous affairs—the Whigs at Essex shouted abuse at the clergy—replete with banners, chanted slogans, marches, and so forth. Moreover, individuals willing to stand for hours in a violent rainstorm in order to register their votes offer another example of men guided by hardy ideological convictions.

Even in those boroughs in which a more restricted franchise prevailed, one can see the effects of the tendencies toward popular participation. Thomas Bruce, Lord Ailesbury, stood for election in the Tory stronghold of Marlborough, where there were only 37 voters, all of them members of the town council. This situation accorded with Bruce's Tory views, since he did not like the fact that in other boroughs "the common unthinking people have a voice equal to a man of the best estate. I mean such as have but forty shillings per annum, and many have it not."[154] On election day in 1679, Bruce was duly elected by the 37 magistrates, but a crowd of more than 120 persons, "a party of alehouse keepers, poor and indigent persons," suddenly appeared at the polling place and demanded to have their votes counted on the grounds that they were inhabitants of the town, and therefore had a right to vote. The mayor refused their demand, but he did agree to record their names, whereupon the crowd

[150] Mrs. Eric George, "Elections and Electioneering, 1679–81," *English Historical Review* 45 no. 180 (October 1930):588–559.

[151] Mrs. George, "Elections," p. 562. At Sir Robert Peyton's election in 1679, some shots were fired and swords were drawn, but no one was hurt (*Domestick Intelligence*, September 9, 1679).

[152] *A Faithful Account of the Manner of Election of Sir William Poultney, and Sir William Waller*. . . (1681), p. 2. The previous election, the author remarked, had "cost us seven or eight days tedious attendance upon an irregular and ill-governed poll" (p. 1).

[153] Oliver Heywood, *Diaries*, 4 vols., 1882, 2:259.

[154] Earl of Cardigan, *The Life and Loyalties of Thomas Bruce*, London: Routledge and Kegan Paul, 1951, p. 51.

claimed that their candidates, Sir James Hayes and Major Wildman, were the true elected representatives for Marlborough.

Ailesbury's "poor and indigent persons" were probably not literally so (that is, on public relief), but were simply men of less than "the best estate," and a forty-shilling freehold belonging to the class of tradesmen, artisans, and shopkeepers. Beneath the partisan epithets directed against "the common unthinking people," one can find the recognition by Ailesbury that the Whigs drew their strongest support from those cities and boroughs "where all have votes that doth not receive alms."[155] Another Tory offered a reasonably fair account of the sources of Whig support, drawn primarily, as he said, from "the meanest but most numerous part of the freemen and freeholders." The Whigs were able to turn out the "most numerous part" of the freemen and freeholders because they had party agents "riding night and day about the villages and trudging about the corporations" rounding up voters. The Whigs, he maintained, had less success with "the gentry and magistrates," who "were never to be wrought over generally to them," although they did manage to make some inroads among "the weakest of the gentry." And in general, the author concluded, the Whigs relied upon "the moderate and discontented gentlemen, burgesses, and tradesmen" for their electoral strength.[156] In the city of Oxford, when the Tory candidate attempted to secure his own return through a mass creation of freemen, they promptly turned against him and exercised their newly won right of suffrage to elect the Whig candidate.[157]

Tory opponents, therefore, had a relatively clear perception of the sources of Whig political support, and the few who did not were liable to be disabused of their illusions through practical experience. It is true that "many of the yeomanry and freeholders were zealous for the church and government," but the general drift of voting among these groups (and among artisans, shopkeepers, and merchants) favored the Whigs in the exclusion-crisis elections.[158] Algernon Sidney's judgment that "the party that is most averse to the Court seems to prevail in the counties and great corporations, as the other doth in many of the small boroughs," appears to be an accurate reading of the election results.[159]

Charges of electoral corruption and abuse were hurled by partisans on

[155] Cardigan, *Thomas Bruce*, p. 52; Ailesbury, *Memoirs*, 1:60.

[156] Edmund Bohun, *The Second Part of the Address to the Free-Men and Freeholders of the Nation*, 1682, pp. 2–5.

[157] Jones, p. 164.

[158] Bohun, *Second Part*, pp. 2–6; Jones, p. 162.

[159] Alex Charles Ewald, *The Life and Times of the Hon. Algernon Sydney*, 2 vols., 1873, 2:138.

both sides, but even the nature of their respective allegations reinforces the general point. Tories were accused of "buying" votes by providing free food and drink for the voters, and perhaps outright money payments as well.[160] This was less likely to occur in boroughs with thousands of voters than in those with a franchise restricted to a small number of town officials. Whigs were accused of making "fraudulent conveyances for twenty-four hours of the freehold lands and tenements to their neighbors" in order to create "twenty mushroom voters"; that is, voters who were transformed overnight from freemen into forty-shilling freeholders.[161] In many cases, even this practice was unnecessary, since the (presumably, Whig) sheriff only required the prospective voter to swear on the Bible that he was, in fact, eligible to vote in the election. Tories accused the Whigs of circumventing the forty-shilling freehold requirement through perjury or fraudulent land transfers, but these allegations may simply indicate that the Tories had a different interpretation than the Whigs of the meaning of the "common right" to vote.[162] Doubtless there were instances on both sides where the charges were not without foundation, but the point I am making is that the Whigs had every reason to support the broadest possible interpretation of a freeman's right to vote (even if they sometimes had to convert him temporarily into a forty-shilling freeholder) as a guarantee against the corruption of Court pensions or the bribery of large landowners, while the Tories were shocked by the number of "meaner" individuals who were permitted, justly or unjustly, to participate in these elections.

Naturally, there were also cruder forms of electoral corruption in the seventeenth century. In Durham, where freemen could vote, of the 838 votes cast, 27 votes were by individuals who were not freemen, 6 of the voters were underage, and three men voted twice.[163] These errors may or may not have been partisan inspired, but there is less doubt about this in the election at Abingdon, where "three considerable persons in the Cor-

[160] *A Character of Popery and Arbitrary Government*, 1681, p. 6; William Penn, *England's Great Interest in the Choice of This New Parliament*, [1680], pp. 3–4; idem, *The Certain Way to Save England*, 1681, p. 13.

[161] Edmund Bohun, *An Address to Freemen and Freeholders of the Nation*, 1682, p. 25; idem *Second Part*, p. 4. It was alleged that prior to the 1680 election of Patience Ward as Lord Mayor of London, 1,300 freemen had been created in the London livery companies specifically for the purpose of insuring his election (Whiting, "Patience Ward," p. 251).

[162] J. H. Sacret, "The Restoration Government and Municipal Corporations," *English Historical Review* (April 1930), pp. 232–259; cf. ibid., p. 245; E. Lipson, "The Elections to the Exclusion Parliaments, 1679–1680," *English Historical Review* (January 1913), pp. 59–85; cf. ibid., p. 60.

[163] C. E. Whiting, *Nathaniel Lord Crewe, Bishop of Durham (1674–1721)*, London: Society for Promoting Christian Knowledge, 1940, p. 96.

poration" obtained a list of all those who were tenants on city-owned property. The three individuals visited the tenants a few days before the election, "promising them great immunities" if they would vote for the Court candidate, and "threatening them severely if they would not." They also warned the tenants "that they should be raised in their fines, and taxed at greater rates than they were before, and to some said, they should never renew their leases any more." When even this pressure failed to have its effect, the corporation officials threatened to arrest and imprison the supporters of the Whig candidate for indebtedness. In any event, although the Whig won, by 297 to 171 votes, the mayor nevertheless proclaimed the Court candidate the victor.[164]

Landlords in other parts of the country engaged in similar attempts to exert pressure on their tenants during the exclusion elections. Servants in the Oxford colleges were threatened with dismissal if they did not vote for the Court candidate.[165] These examples could be multiplied several times. They are hardly surprising, given what we know about the nature of elections, then and now. Pressure applied by the socially prominent gentry or by aristocratic landowners undoubtedly had its effects on some voters—of both persuasions—but the evidence seems to indicate that the exclusion elections were much more open in the sense that voters were less subject to this form of control than they had been in past elections. Indeed, this is a fact sometimes complained of, mostly by Tories. The Whigs, of course, applied their own form of electoral pressure. In several villages and towns, it appears that they threatened to institute an economic boycott by local tradesmen if the area voted against the Whig candidate.[166] Economic pressure exercised by the landlords or by tradesmen thus constituted a part of the electoral struggle between the two political parties.

What might be termed ideological pressure was also applied. The clergy, generally speaking, could not vote.[167] Nevertheless, they were frequently marshaled for an appearance at the elections, sometimes numbering in the hundreds, as supporters for the Court candidate. Their pres-

[164] *A Letter from a Friend in Abingdon to a Gentleman in London Concerning the Election of Burgesses for the Ensuing Parliament*, 1679, pp. 2–3.

[165] Jones, pp. 201–205; Lipson, "Elections," p. 83. The majority of voters, Baxter thought, were "ruled by money; and therefore by their landlords" (Richard Schlatter, *Richard Baxter and Puritan Politics*, New Brunswick, N.J.: Rutgers University Press, 1957, pp. 97–98).

[166] Andrew Browning, "Parties and Party Organization in the Reign of Charles II," *Transactions of the Royal Historical Society* 30 (1948):34.

[167] Bishop Crewe of Durham could vote as a freeman because he was a member of a merchant guild (Whiting, *Crewe*, p. 96). For a discussion of the controversy over the clergy's voting, see Hirst, *Representative*, p. 240.

ence at the poll was intended to have its authoritative impact upon the minds of those parishioners inclined to vote contrary to their minister's political viewpoint. On the other hand, the Whigs also brought nonvoters to the election, in the form of the common people who provided a cheering section for their candidate, keeping up the morale of the Whig voters. In an account of one election contest (again, supplied by a Tory witness) between a Court aristocrat and Sir Samuel Barnardiston, a Whig merchant, the effects of these nonvoters are described. The Court candidate, the author writes,

> had the gentry of the country, and all the church and loyal party entirely; the other had, as entirely, all the dissenters, sectaries, and factious people of all sorts, who were generally manufacturers, traders, and rabble. The election was looked upon as a trial of strength of parties; and both sides mustered all their forces, but the latter had the adjunct of the non-voting mob, who made more noise and stir than all the rest.[168]

This "non-voting mob," we subsequently discover, consisted largely of a crowd of seamen, who appear, on this occasion at least, to have been more impressive in their effect upon the outcome of the election than were the "non-voting mob" of assembled clergymen.

The mayor of Abingdon, whose arithmetic was impaired by his ideological convictions, offers an example of blatant official corruption, but there were many subtler forms of manipulating election results. The sheriff, whose duty it was to name the site and time of the polling, was free to designate any town or village in the county as the place of election. Clearly, he could appoint a location that might make it difficult for the supporters of a particular candidate to journey to the poll. The sheriff might withhold the exact time of the election until the very last minute, to the inconvenience of one side or the other; he might even change the location of the election; or he simply might not make an announcement of its details at all (though this was technically a violation of the rules). Official corruption was not limited to the magistrates of one political party, but since these were mostly Court-appointed officials, this form of electoral abuse, on the whole, probably favored the Tories.[169]

Many other Tories probably shared Lord Ailesbury's preference for an electoral system in which "the gentlemen agree beforehand" on the outcome, "and they only meet at the place of election for form sake," but the

[168] North, *Examen*, pp. 516–517.

[169] One striking instance is the manipulation of election results in order to prevent Algernon Sidney from claiming a seat in the Parliament (Ewald, *Sydney*, 2:54–56, 60).

exclusion elections, in general, were anything but mere formalities to be decided by a few "gentlemen."[170] For, "by the end of the Exclusion Crisis more men had become involved in Parliamentary politics in the constituencies than ever before in the history of Parliament."[171] That political participation attained such levels was due not merely to the political and economic forces that guaranteed a potentially large electorate; it was, more specifically, the consequence of a vigorous organizational effort by Shaftesbury and the Whigs. As Plumb remarks, the new electorate, both in size and social composition, "called into being new methods of propaganda and electioneering."[172]

Everyone, from contemporaries to modern historians, agrees that the Whigs possessed an impressive political organization that they employed to great effect during the exclusion elections. Yet on the level of detailed information as to the operations of this organization, the evidence remains scanty. Political propaganda, for example, was an important factor in the mobilization of large numbers of voters. But exactly how its publication was organized, who wrote many of the tracts, what network of distribution existed, and so on, are questions to which we possess only a glimpse of the answers. Some clues are supplied by the reflections of a radical Whig on his own political activity during the 1680s. He wrote that he

> travelled several times through England, to inform himself with the greater certainty of the state of the kingdom, and to know the inclinations of the people, and by frequenting all public companies, had obtained such a perfect knowledge not only of the general bent and turn of the minds of the commonalty, but of the temper and disposition of the most considerable gentry. He did not neglect at the same time to inquire who were the most considerable and leading tradesmen in boroughs and corporations, and to take down their names and dwelling places.[173]

This may be an exceptional example of intelligence gathering, but contemporaries claimed that the Whigs "had correspondents in all parts of the kingdom of the most active and greatest credit," and perhaps they did.[174] If so, and if the Whigs in London were supplied with the kind of information gathered by George Speke, it would explain why they could be so strikingly successful in distributing so quickly to all parts of the

170 Cardigan, *Thomas Bruce*, p. 51.

171 Plumb, *Origins of Stability*, p. 47.

172 Plumb, *Origins of Stability*, pp. 29, 34–35.

173 George Speke, *The Secret History of the Happy Revolution in 1688*, 1715, p. 42.

174 Dalrymple, 1:390.

country the political tracts printed in London. Speke had even included in his notes a record of the movements of coaches and wagons and their departure times between London and the country. Opponents observed that "every coffee house, every town, city, and corner of the land is full of these treasonous and disloyal papers" printed in London, from whence they are "speedily carried unto too many gentlemen and farmers' houses."[175] One such Whig "correspondent" in the country was Locke's close friend, Dr. David Thomas. Thomas wrote several times to Locke requesting that Locke purchase and send to him certain pamphlets on the popish plot.[176] In general, London Whigs and country gentlemen were urged to "buy a parcel" of tracts "for your country people."[177] That this was a common practice, and that bundles of pamphlets were purchased by the wealthier Whigs for distribution—often gratis—to their less wealthy supporters is evident from the frequent complaints lodged against the practice by Tory opponents. With what effect is more difficult to assess. Reflecting upon the proliferation of political pamphlets during the exclusion crisis, one contemporary wrote that it was "an age, wherein if two cartload of pamphlets could have made one convert, we had been all of one mind in England before this."[178] Still, this propaganda did have its effects, and it reached down to members of the lowest social classes in its appeals, a fact that caused the Tories much anxiety. Why are so many Whig tracts addressed to "the multitude"? one of them asked. There is no fear that they will accept popery: "There's no need of convincing *them* of the truth of the plot." Nor, he concluded, is there any need to call upon their assistance in the suppression of popery, since that is the government's business, in which "the multitude" can have no part.[179] Nevertheless, people did gather in the local taverns and coffeehouses, or at the county markets to hear the latest pamphlets or sermons discussed. Indeed, one of the most important purposes served by Whig political propaganda was to counter the influence of the clergy, whose sermons were often the source from which common people otherwise gained their information and formed their opinions about politics.[180]

Another intrusion into the political arena by "the multitude" came

[175] *Memoires of the Life of Anthony, Late Earl of Shaftesbury*, 1683, p. 7.

[176] *Correspondence*, 2:323, 337.

[177] See, for example, Penn, *Certain Way*, where this suggestion is made. In his reply to this tract, the author of *England Bought and Sold*, 1681, registers a complaint against this practice (pp. 2–3); George, "Elections," p. 572.

[178] *Reflections upon the Controversy about the Oath of Allegiance, Occasioned by the Letter in Answer to English Loyalty*, 1682, preface.

[179] Roger L'Estrange, *An Answer to the Appeal from the Country to the City*, 1681, pp. 32–33.

[180] Jones, p. 94.

through the medium of petitions. Shortly after the bill to exclude the Duke of York from succession to the crown was introduced in Parliament in the middle of May 1679, Charles II dissolved Parliament. The newly elected Parliament was scheduled to meet in October, but the king postponed its meeting until the end of January 1680. In response to these delaying tactics, the Whigs mounted a campaign of gathering petitions directed to the king, requesting that Parliament be allowed to assemble. Shaftesbury was sometimes accused of personally directing the propaganda effort, so that Whig political pamphlets "were written and dispersed by his direction and approbation."[181] Even in the absence of any solid information concerning such matters, these reports are exaggerated estimations of Shaftesbury's degree of control over either the Whig party machinery in general or its ideological spokesmen in particular. The petitioning campaign in 1679–1680, however, does appear to have been Shaftesbury's "new project" to put greater pressure on Charles II to accede to the Whig political demands.[182]

The Whigs "designed to have the hand or mark of every voting freeholder, citizen, and burgher in England . . . to sign one of these petitions for the sitting of Parliament." In order to realize this objective, they had hundreds of blank petitions printed, "and these were put into the hands of agitants and sub-agitants in the counties about, branching forth so nice as into hundreds of towns and villages. . . . And these agitators, being choice party men, and well-instructed, went to every free voter" for his signature.[183] On one of these petitions is appended a note from a Whig organizer to one of his county "agitants":

> By the next coach I'll send you down fifty of these petitions, being thought to be the easiest and best form and what London and Middlesex both subscribe to, so that you may send them about where you think fit.[184]

The Whigs canvassed house to house in the towns with these petitions; they set up tables in taverns and at county fairs and markets. One petition

[181] Haley, p. 499; O. W. Furley, "The Whig Exclusionsists: Pamphlet Literature in the Exclusion Campaign, 1679–81," *Cambridge Historical Journal* 13, no. 1 (1957):20–21. It was said that Shaftesbury had a printing press at his constant disposal, so that any tract could be printed and ready for distribution within twenty-four hours.

[182] Burnet, 2:248; Narcissus Luttrell, *A Brief Relation of State Affairs*, 6 vols., 1857, 1:27–28; Ailesbury, *Memoirs*, 1:45.

[183] North, *Examen*, p. 542; *The Dissenter Unmaskt, with Respect to the Two Plots*, 1683, p. 1; Add. MS 29572, fol. 173.

[184] *CSPD*, 28:478.

was estimated to have been one hundred yards long.[185] Through this tactic, the Whigs brought thousands of individuals, including nonvoters, into the political process for the first time in their lives. At the other end of the social scale, Shaftesbury, along with some other lords, personally presented a petition to Charles II.[186] Also, various county magistrates and corporation officers sent in petitions. One of the few surviving letters between Locke and Shaftesbury contains a report by Locke on a petition presented to Charles II by the Lord Mayor and Common Council of London.[187] In short, all levels of English society were engaged in Shaftesbury's "project." The efficiency and mass participation achieved in this petitioning campaign was unequaled during the eighteenth century.[188]

Such discussions of the Whig party activities as do exist in the secondary literature are mainly preoccupied with the personalities of various leaders and the personal interrelationships between them. As I have tried to demonstrate, however, the significance of the Whigs as a political movement lay in their ability to unite people across class lines around the antipopery issue while also mobilizing large numbers of voting and nonvoting members of the lower classes as political participants. As a party, therefore, the Whigs were much more organized and disciplined than a mere alliance established among a few aristocratic leaders and their immediate followers would suggest. Nor can the Whigs be properly viewed as merely a coalition of extended familial groupings based upon kinship relations among various politicians. In addition to the ideological unity the Whigs attempted to create through their political literature, which will be discussed in Chapter 5, there was a solid economic and social basis to the conflict engendered by the exclusion crisis, which helped to unify the opposition forces.[189] There were numerous outcries from the local gentry and aristocratic landlords in various parts of the country over the fact that their electoral provinces were being taken away from them by "the meaner freeholders," who had suddenly become a powerful political

[185] Jones, pp. 116–119. One such individual was arrested in 1681 for "dispersing seditious pamphlets" by riding "about to fairs and markets." Prior to his arrest, he had already distributed nearly 1,400 copies of a particular tract (*CSPD*, 22:237).

[186] Add. MS 29577, fol. 211.

[187] *Correspondence*, 2:226–227.

[188] Jones, pp. 114–116.

[189] As Keith Feiling noted, the "economic drift" of the seventeenth century "was undoubtedly towards a sharper demarcation of classes" (*Tory Party*, p. 20; Stone, "Social Mobility," p. 38). On the direct rivalry between "the commercial magnates" of the towns and "the landed interest of the country" during this period, see Sacret, "Restoration Government," p. 245. By the time of the 1681 election, "the country was more sharply divided" along party and class lines than at any time since the 1640s (Jones, p. 159).

force through their participation in the exclusion elections.[190] "Worthy and landed men," it was said, were being "jostled to make room for . . . monied men but without estate."[191] Even Halifax warned "the gentlemen, the knights of the shire," that they "may be kicked out by mechanics, by citizens and burgesses" if their boroughs voted for the Whigs. He complained that the Whigs had gone too far in their efforts to reach the masses; they had "infected the generality of the kingdom, the common traders and dwellers in cities and corporations and the unthinking and illiterate part of the gentry with hatred against monarchy and the Church of England."[192] The remark reflects not only a difference in ideological viewpoint between Shaftesbury and Halifax, but also how far removed the latter was from the Whig party machinery or party strategy in its efforts to reach precisely "the common traders" of the nation.[193] In addition to these objections against the class biases of the Shaftesbury wing of the Whig party, complaints were voiced against the centralized aspects of the party organization, particularly the efforts by the London Whigs to "interfere" in areas that had heretofore lain within the province of locally controlled boroughs.

Only after we have some appreciation of the scope and magnitude of the political organization created by the Whigs is it useful to turn to a consideration of the handful of individuals who supplied the leadership of the movement. Of this group, Shaftesbury was unquestionably the single most important figure. He "showed himself extraordinarily successful in combining and unifying all elements of opposition."[194] As we have seen, Shaftesbury was in a sense a living embodiment of the antipopery feelings of seventeenth-century Englishmen coupled with a sympathy for toleration and the advancement of trade. He was a natural rallying point for those in opposition to the government's policies. Shaftesbury was also extremely shrewd in his assessment of political tendencies, and remarkably resolute in the pursuit of his political objectives. If he was less engaging as an object of popular affection than Buckingham or the Duke of Monmouth, he was a person capable of making far bolder, and at the same time, more impressively reasoned, political decisions than either of them.

[190] Mrs. George, "Elections," p. 572.

[191] Ailesbury, *Memoirs*, 1:60. Morley, *A Thousand Lives*, p. 124.

[192] George Savile, *A Seasonable Address to Both Houses of Parliament Concerning the Succession, the Fears of Popery, and Arbitrary Government*, 1681, p. 11; cf. ibid., p. 5.

[193] Jones, pp. 17, 162; Bohun, *Second Part*, pp. 2–5. Halifax's importance, both as a thinker and as a party leader, has been grossly overexaggerated. Macaulay loses no opportunity to extol his virtues, either because Halifax was the only Tory he could admire or because he was as conservative a thinker as was Macaulay (Macaulay, 1:225–228).

[194] Jones, p. 7.

These traits gained for Shaftesbury a level of respect from his contemporaries that neither Buckingham nor Monmouth could command.

Shaftesbury and Buckingham had worked together for nearly a decade prior to the popish-plot crisis. In addition to their personal and social interaction, and their policy agreements on many issues, the two men frequently served together on the same parliamentary committees, including the one appointed to investigate the popish plot. In short, they had a working political relationship that can certainly be described as friendly.[195] Shaftesbury's relationship with Monmouth is a bit more puzzling, and yet—during the period from 1679 to 1682—more intimate than was his association with Buckingham. Historians have tended to view this relationship in terms of Monmouth's simple-mindedness, functioning as the tool of Shaftesbury's clever designs, or alternatively, it has been suggested that the latter assumed the role of a surrogate father figure for the younger man. These explanations are superficial and reflect rather too much on the specific influence of Dryden's *Absalom and Achitophel*. Even in the period when Monmouth did not support the Whig policy of exclusion, he was nevertheless a constant visitor at Shaftesbury's house and part of his political circle of friends.[196] Giving due account to Monmouth's popularity with members of the lowest classes and the importance of that fact to the overall strategy of the Whigs (and of Shaftesbury, especially), still Shaftesbury's friendship for Monmouth was a great deal more sincere and firm than that of some of the latter's so-called friends, like Halifax, who did not hesitate to intrigue against him.

Lord Russell was a man whose widely respected judgment had earned him a place as one of the leaders of the House of Commons. Russell and

[195] The Shaftesbury-Buckingham relationship is often characterized by remarks upon their differing temperaments and a struggle for political leadership between the two men; or Buckingham's retirement from politics during the exclusion crisis in disgust at Shaftesbury's tactics is cited as proof of the distance between them. There is a kernel of truth in all these observations, but alongside them must be placed the fact, for example, that as late as the end of 1681, Buckingham publicly acknowledged his deep respect and admiration for Shaftesbury. In his critique of Dryden's *Absalom and Achitophel*—a "national libel"—Buckingham defended Shaftesbury's "deep and apt intelligence" and the leadership qualities of "this great little man." It was Shaftesbury, not Dryden, he argued, who represented the honor and best qualities of the nation. Buckingham's unsolicited praise of Shaftesbury's "sublime judgment," "his clear discussions," and his "genius" at a time when the former was no longer closely involved with the leadership of the Whig party certainly deserves to be part of the total record in any assessment of the relationship between the two men (Buckingham, *Poetical Reflections on a Late Poem Entitled Absalom and Achitophel*, 1681).

[196] Haley reports the political differences between Monmouth and Shaftesbury (Haley, pp. 466–467), but omits any discussion of their frequent and friendly social contact. In April and May of 1680, for example, it was noted that they were meeting virtually every night (John Reresby, *Memoirs*, 1734, p. 99).

Shaftesbury established an extremely close alliance for developing and coordinating Whig party strategy in the two houses of Parliament. This alliance was made more effective by the fact that their homes were virtually next to one another, and this enabled the two men to engage in daily meetings.[197] Such other Whigs as Lords Grey, Salisbury, and Wharton are sometimes referred to as Shaftesbury's lieutenants, which, if it is not taken too literally, is an adequate description of their relationship to Shaftesbury personally and to the execution of Whig party policy generally.[198] The Earl of Essex, whose connection with Shaftesbury was initially respectful, but somewhat distant, seems to have gradually drifted closer to him as the exclusion crisis wore on, even as Buckingham was simultaneously gradually moving out of Shaftesbury's orbit. Of course, there were differences of opinion between Shaftesbury and all of these individuals at one time or another, and even a few well-reported disagreements. It would be unreasonable to suppose that in a political movement involving thousands of participants and struggling to maintain itself against powerful opposing forces over a three-year period, there would not arise some personality conflicts among its leaders or that there might not be a few important differences on matters of policy and party strategy. What amazed their contemporaries was the fact that, despite these differences, the Whigs were still able to maintain an impressive level of party discipline.

Much has been made of the antipathy between Shaftesbury and Algernon Sidney, for example.[199] It is possible that Sidney's dislike for Shaftesbury stretched as far back as their contact during the Interregnum, or even to the Civil War itself. Sidney's feelings of friendship for and subsequent contact with Edmund Ludlow—no friend of Shaftesbury—when both men were living in exile no doubt reinforced this prejudice.[200]

[197] Haley, p. 353; Julia Cartwright, *Sacharissa: Some Account of Dorothy Sidney, Countess of Sunderland,* 2d ed., 1893, pp. 239–240; Reresby, *Memoirs*, p. 99.

[198] Haley's tendency to understate Shaftesbury's party leadership is countered by Dorothy Sidney's remark that "all the several parties" in opposition to the Duke of York "are by all called, but my Lord Shaftesbury's followers" (*Some Account of the Life of Rachel Wriothesley, Lady Russell,* 1819, p. 343).

[199] None of those who write about Sidney speaks favorably of Shaftesbury, and Haley notes that "Sidney and Shaftesbury were at no time on good terms" (Haley, p. 718; cf. ibid., p. 508n).

[200] Shaftesbury and Sidney had served together on a commission on legal reform in 1652–1653 (Haley, pp. 68–69). Though Shaftesbury had led some forces assisting General Ludlow in relieving the siege at Taunton during the Civil War, the antipathy between the two men dates at least from the period 1653–1654, when they headed opposing lists of candidates in a Wiltshire election (pp. 82–83). On the curious fact that passages from Ludlow's *Memoirs* hostile to Shaftesbury were copied from the manuscript by Locke and omitted from its published version, see A. B. Worden's introduction to *A Voyce from the Watch*

Nevertheless, in addition to Wildman, Sidney's friends were drawn from a group of nonaristocratic Republicans in the city of London, virtually all of whom were strong supporters of Shaftesbury.[201] It was thus possible, despite personal animosities, to effect a significant level of cooperation between the two men through commonly shared associates. Even the extent of the personality differences between them may have been exaggerated by historians. It is true that sometime in late June or early July 1680, there was an angry exchange between Shaftesbury and Sidney in the course of which the former accused the latter of being a French pensioner and a spy for Lord Sunderland.[202] This is interesting because, as a matter of fact, Sidney was one of those being paid money by the French, which says something about the quality of Shaftesbury's political intelligence. On the other hand, this particular falling out between the two men was patched up in a very short time. Several weeks later, Sidney's mother wrote, "I have told you how my Lord Shaftesbury and Mr. Algernon have railed at one another. Now messages pass between them, I believe by Mr. Hampden." And, she added, Sidney, Monmouth, Shaftesbury, and Hampden were once again cooperating with one another.[203] Since she was not sympathetic to Shaftesbury or his policies, this did not please her. And, several months later, with the cooperation between Shaftesbury and her son still being maintained, she declared that the fact that Sidney was "well with Lord Shaftesbury" was a "thorn in my side."[204] Since there is no one among the leaders of the Whig party who is reputed to have had a greater personal dislike of Shaftesbury than Sidney, these statements ought to give us pause. At a minimum, they suggest that rather too much emphasis has been given to personality conflicts among a few leaders at the expense of gaining a better understanding of the dynamics of a disciplined and cooperative mass political movement.

When the year began in 1677, the Green Ribbon Club was a fledgling attempt at organization, most of the Country Party opposition leaders were in prison, and those who were not were deeply involved in secret intrigues with the French government. Throughout the following year, these negotiations continued, while the Green Ribbon Club increased its

---

Tower, Part Five: 1660–1662, by Edmund Ludlow, Camden Society Publications, 1978, pp. 3, 56.

201 Among Sidney's close friends, for example, were Wildman, Slingsby Bethel, Lord Howard, and John Hampden, all of whom worked closely with Shaftesbury. Another friend who disliked Shaftesbury was Sir William Jones, while William Penn probably stands somewhere between the two extremes (Cartwright, *Sacharissa*, pp. 201, 276, 278).

202 Cartwright, *Sacharissa*, p. 274; *Lady Russell*, p. 354.

203 Cartwright, *Sacharissa*, pp. 281–282; *Lady Russell*, pp. 365–366.

204 Cartwright, *Sacharissa*, p. 296.

membership, extended the scope of its political activities, and developed contacts with similar clubs in other cities in England. The popish plot and Charles II's own intrigues with France brought about a dissolution of Parliament, and the necessity of elections. Social and economic forces not directly within their control provided the Whigs with a potentially large electorate, but it was due to their collective efforts that these contingent realities were transformed into a powerful political force. By the end of 1679, the Whigs had become a political party with "a wide popular appeal, stimulated and maintained by a large-scale propaganda machine."[205]

[205] Jones, p. 2.

5

THE FORMATION OF WHIG IDEOLOGY

THERE are two perspectives from which the political literature of the exclusion crisis is generally viewed. The first maintains that the political tracts produced during this period were so preoccupied with the issues of immediate concern and generally governed by the hysterical dimensions of the popish plot that they contain little of interest for the historian of political thought. The second view accords this political literature more importance, but it does so by characterizing it as a prelude or introduction to the great triumphs of Whig political philosophy in the wake of the Glorious Revolution of 1689. Exclusion political writings constitute a dress rehearsal for a more profound and important later performance by such political theorists as Locke.[1]

"The hysteria, the lies, the betrayals and injustices of the Popish plot," it is said, "concern the historian of ideas only in so far as they affect the reputation of some important party politicians."[2] This is the vantage point from which the politics of that period has generally been studied. In *The First Whigs*, J. R. Jones maintains that "issues were what mattered during the exclusion crisis . . . political issues," although this assertion does not lead him to consider the political theory formulated by the Whigs, which he regards as being superficial, incoherent, and valueless. Thus, he writes,

[1] J. R. Jones (*First Whigs*) concentrated on parliamentary politics, and seems to have read little of the political literature. F. S. Ronalds, on the other hand, cites numerous titles, but simply fits them into his chronological account and offers no interpretation of the political debate (Francis S. Ronalds, *The Attempted Whig Revolution of 1678–1681*, Illinois Studies in Social Sciences, vol. 21, nos. 1–2, Urbana: University of Illinois Press, 1937), Carolyn Edie offers a confusing general review of exclusion arguments that is not very helpful in gaining an understanding of the contending political theories that supplied the foundations for this pamphlet literature ("Succession and Monarchy: The Controversy of 1678–81," *American Historical Review* [January 1965], pp. 350–370). The standard reference is O. W. Furley, "The Whig Exclusionists: Pamphlet Literature in the Exclusion Campaign, 1679–81," *Cambridge Historical Journal* 13, no. 1 (1957):19–36. Furley focused upon some important tracts, but his propensity to present the debate in terms of "the uniformity of Whig propaganda" (p. 21) makes it difficult to appreciate the political importance of the tensions and complexities within the Whig political movement.

[2] Caroline Robbins, *The Eighteenth Century Commonwealthman*, Cambridge: Harvard University Press, 1959, p. 27.

> The Whigs had no developed, definite, or coherent political philosophy. . . . Intense preoccupation with immediate political issues produced the superficial character which marked Whig thought and writing during the crisis. Whig pamphleteers and debaters were primarily polemical and controversial.

On this basis, Jones concludes that "none of the Whig political writings produced during the crisis bear close and critical examination."[3] This declaration supplies the rationale for the indifference shown to this literature in *The First Whigs*, which instead concentrates its attention upon describing the intrigues of Charles II and the actions of a few parliamentary leaders. Thus, "preoccupation with immediate political issues" becomes a judgment registered against the political thought of the 1680s, thereby discouraging the historian of political theory from engaging in further investigation.

At the same time, Jones also endorses the second viewpoint. That is, he observes that "it was to be left to Locke to publish . . . after 1688 the classical Whig exposition of the origin, nature, and purpose of political institutions."[4] In another study of the exclusion-crisis literature, the author concludes that the Whigs' "ideas of government, tempered though they were in the fierce heat of the Exclusion Contest, became the norm for the Whig party of the future, and the Whig apologists of the Revolution found that they could add little."[5] In both instances, the political ideas of the exclusion crisis are pictured as flowing imperceptibly into a "classical Whig" theory of constitutional government, frequently identified with Locke's position in the *Two Treatises of Government*.[6] Clearly, there is some truth in this view; one could not reasonably expect to discover an absolutely rigid line separating Whig political ideas of the 1680s from those of the 1690s. Nevertheless, the more closely one is prepared to examine the social composition and the political objectives of the Whigs in the 1680s as a large-scale popular movement, the less satisfactory this approach to their political thought becomes. The historical relationships between the radical political ideas cast up by Shaftesbury's attempt to organize a revolution and the Whig orthodoxy of the Glorious Revolution that sought to build upon and take into account its consensual foundations are both more complicated and more interesting than these interpretive attempts to present a homogenous Whig political theory make

[3] Jones, pp. 3–4, 214–215.

[4] Jones, p. 215.

[5] Furley, "Whig Exclusionists," pp. 35–36.

[6] Harold Laski, *Political Thought in England from Locke to Bentham*, London: Oxford University Press, 1920, p. 29.

it appear. Not only must these divergent tendencies within Whig political theory reflecting differing alignments of social classes with differing political objectives be kept in mind for the sake of historical accuracy in any discussion of the political thought in England during the last quarter of the seventeenth century, but it is also true, I believe, that these tendencies and ideas are structurally important to the radical/conservative axis around which liberalism as a political perspective developed in the succeeding three centuries. Liberal political theory, in other words, embodies certain internal tensions that have their historical roots in the political conflicts of the seventeenth century. The importance of this fact tends to be obscured if we insist upon viewing the political theory of the exclusion crisis as a prelude to, or as being identical with, the defense of a bloodless oligarchical coup.

Neither of these conventional frameworks for approaching the political thought of the exclusion crisis has stood up well in the face of recent historical research. With respect to the first standpoint, the problem is that both Locke's *Two Treatises of Government* and Sidney's *Discourses Concerning Government* were largely written during the exclusion crisis. To these should be added Henry Neville's *Plato Redivivus* and James Tyrrell's *Patriarcha non Monarcha*, both of which are impressive and sophisticated works of political theory. These writings are neither superficial nor incoherent attempts at political theorizing, and their emergence during this period of political struggle provides a prima facie reason for taking a much closer look at the political writings of their contemporaries. For, if we accept that "basic issues had to be resolved . . . during the Exclusion crisis," issues that "raised questions of more fundamental importance than any the eighteenth century was to experience," then we should not be surprised to discover that some individuals were able to rise to the occasion by offering a serious consideration of these profound issues.[7] The problems of determining the origins of government, the demands of political obligation, and the prospects of revolution were the central topics of political debate in the 1680s. Moreover, it was a debate marked by a bitterness and intensity not seen in England again until the end of the eighteenth century. In other words, in terms of the specific works of political theory it generated, as well as with respect to the nature of the political problems to which those works and others sought to provide the answers, the exclusion crisis does not deserve its classification as a historical period characterized by superficial political thinking.

The second approach, which rests upon an assumption of "the uniformity of Whig propaganda," fares no better when the historical evi-

[7] Jones, pp. 3–4.

dence is examined closely.[8] For as recent studies have shown, the Whigs who came to power in the wake of the Glorious Revolution did *not* rush to embrace the ideas of Locke and Sidney, nor did they claim their writings as the canon of a "classical Whig" doctrine. On the contrary, most Whigs in the 1690s went to considerable lengths to disassociate themselves from the "dangerous" opinions contained in the *Two Treatises* and the *Discourses Concerning Government*, just as they preferred to forget any association some of them might have had with Shaftesbury and his political objectives in the 1680s.[9] And with respect to the latter, it must be emphasized that the radical Whig viewpoint was, even in the 1680s, a minority position. In other words, rather than an approach to the political theory of the Whigs that is premised upon a consensus, we require a framework that highlights and explains the importance of a majority/minority split within Whig political theory in the 1680s and 1690s.

It is, therefore, misleading to take the works of Locke and Sidney as typical statements of the Whig position merely because, from the standpoint of philosophical criteria, they are adjudged to be major texts of political philosophy. Such an interpretation subordinates their importance as historical and political documents to an ahistorical conception of political theory. At the same time, precisely which arguments and concepts in these works were generally shared by those who identified themselves as Whigs cannot be determined merely from a reading of these two texts, nor even from a handful of other contemporaneous writings. In this chapter and the one following, I shall attempt to deal with the last point by indicating some of the basic precepts that characterized the Whig political perspective in the 1680s. That is, the emphasis will be upon demonstrating the extent to which Locke's political theory was deeply indebted to the same presuppositions that shaped the political thinking of thousands of his associates in the Whig political movement. As Peter Laslett observed nearly thirty years ago, it is odd "that the parliamentary issues and events of the years of the Exclusion Controversy have not been noticed in the constitutional discussions" of the *Two Treatises*.[10] It is this

[8] Furley, "Whig Exclusionists," p. 21.

[9] J. P. Kenyon, *Revolution Principles: The Politics of Party, 1689–1720*, Cambridge: Cambridge University Press, 1977; Julian Franklin, *John Locke and the Theory of Sovereignty*, Cambridge: Cambridge University Press, 1978. For a reevaluation of the political thought of the 1670s and 1680s, see Corinne Comstock Weston and Janelle Renfrow Greenberg, *Subjects and Sovereigns: The Grand Controversy over Legal Sovereignty in Stuart England*, Cambridge: Cambridge University Press, 1981, and the works by Daly, Schochet, and Goldie cited in note 16 below.

[10] Peter Laslett, "The English Revolution and Locke's *Two Treatises of Government*," *Cambridge Historical Journal* 12, no. 1 (1956):48. Dunn attempted in some measure to fill this gap in the literature, devoting one chapter of his study to the consideration of the *Two*

neglect that the next two chapters seeks to remedy. On the basis of a reading of hundreds of exclusion tracts, I will try to indicate the basic structure of the political debate in the 1680s, the shared premises of the Whig position as well as some of the differences internal to that position, and the relationship of Locke's *Two Treatises of Government* to both. Only after these broader cultural dimensions of Whig political theory have been sketched is it useful to turn to a consideration of those specific areas of departure from a position held by a majority of Whigs which characterized the radical Whigs, including Locke.

As I indicated in the Introduction, there is another reason that a broader survey of the political literature of the 1680s is necessary in order to supply a contextual meaning for the argument of the *Two Treatises*. That is, within the framework of a political movement, there are various levels on which the political thought of the movement's participants finds its expression. Many historians of political theory have a tendency to focus on the most abstract statements of political thought. Intentionally or unintentionally, this conveys the impression that other forms of political thought are, relatively speaking, without significance. Yet, as I shall try to show, the political objectives of the Whigs in the 1680s were embedded in a network of arguments that extended in many different directions, ranging from Biblical scholarship, to anthropological data contained in reports of travelers to the New World, to interpretations of Aristotle, to an analysis of the basic factors that produce economic wealth, to a comparative assessment of different European political systems, and so forth. The intriguing aspects of the political debate of the exclusion crisis, which form the focus for the discussion in this chapter, are the ways in which various writers drew together these themes in order to advance the particular political argument they were making. Viewed as a whole, I shall argue, there is a social language, very broadly characterized, which the Whigs drew upon for support for their political ideas in the 1680s.

As a political movement seeking mass support, the Whigs structured their political arguments around the slogans No Popery, No Slavery and Liberty and Property. The first indicated their opposition to the succession of the Duke of York, while the second identified their positive commitments. Underlying each of these catchwords was a multidimensional and sophisticated political argument, the key features of which were only slightly less widely known among the political pamphleteers of the movement than the slogans themselves. In this chapter, I will outline some of

Treatises as an exclusion tract (John Dunn, *The Political Thought of John Locke*, Cambridge: Cambridge University Press, 1969, pp. 43–57). His conclusion, however, that the work is either a piece of "conventional constitutionalism" or "a notably ham-fisted" exclusion tract is, I believe, mistaken on both counts (pp. 53, 57).

the connections between these simple ideological declarations and the larger and more complex arguments employed by the Whigs, with particular reference, of course, to the arguments contained in the *Two Treatises*. In Chapter 6, I will indicate the relevance the issues in the political debate of the exclusion crisis had for specific socioeconomic groups in the context of the parliamentary elections of 1679–1681.

It might be supposed that the focus of the political conflict—the exclusion of James—is too narrow and the theoretical dimensions of that controversy too circumscribed to retain much interest for the student of political theory. And as we have noted, this is in fact the prevalent opinion among scholars. To the participants, however, the situation appeared quite differently. The "great question of succession," it was conceded on both sides, involves "a change in the very fundamentals of our government."[11] "I must confess," Roger L'Estrange declared, "that our lives, liberties, and the religion of the government . . . lie all at stake."[12] More important for its determination of the structure of the political debate was the recognition that "not only the frame and constitution of the English laws, but likewise those of Nature" lay at the heart of the controversy.[13] Parliament, it was alleged, had no right to interfere with the succession of the monarchy by excluding James because the king's authority is not derived from statutes, but from God. Hence, "the immutable Law of Nature" supplied the foundations for the political controversy, since it was according to that law that the validity of all claims to political authority was to be assessed.[14] Because kingly power is granted to individuals within the framework of the Law of Nature, Filmer argued, there can be "no inferior law to limit" that power.[15]

Since Filmer figures so prominently in Locke's argument, it seems appropriate at this point to say something regarding his position in the general context of the political debate. Recently, much has been claimed—and disclaimed—for Filmer's authority and his writings, especially *Pa-*

[11] B. Thorogood, *Captain Thorogood His Opinion of the Point of Succession, to a Brother of the Blade in Scotland*, 1680, p. 1. For Locke, "the very foundations of human society" were at issue (*FT*, par. 3). And see his reference to "the great question" of succession (*FT*, pars. 94, 106, 122).

[12] Roger L'Estrange, *The Character of a Papist in Masquerade . . . in Answer to the Character of a Popish Successor*, 1681, p. 62; Grey, 7:142.

[13] *Three Great Questions Concerning the Succession and the Dangers of Popery*, 1680, p. 3 (*LL* #2802).

[14] *A Letter from a Gentleman of Quality in the Country to His Friend, upon His Being Chosen a Member to Serve in . . . Parliament*, 1679, p. 4.

[15] Filmer, p. 96.

triarcha, with respect to the Royalist position.[16] Both the defenses of monarchy in terms of divine right or as an extension of patriarchal authority predate the publication of *Patriarcha,* and both arguments relied upon an appeal to natural law. What is particularly interesting about Filmer's position is that he joined these two defenses, which were frequently advanced independently of one another, into one unified argument for the king's absolute authority. Moreover, he stressed at some length the natural law basis of this argument. These two aspects of *Patriarcha* were sufficiently striking to insure the work a prominent place in the political debate of the 1680s. Beyond that, it is not especially worthwhile to venture, for it is not true that the Royalist position depended upon Filmer's argument. Royalists were quite content to defend the king's authority through the citation of a few specific passages from the Bible, or more often, simply from the standpoint of general and vaguely stated claims relating to God's designs as to the government of His subjects. On the other hand, Filmer's viewpoint was easily assimilated into the Royalist perspective, and by a much wider audience than can be reconstructed by merely counting the number of those authors who, like Robert Brady, repeated specific passages from Filmer's works in their own political tracts. For most of those who read Filmer, it was sufficient to insist, as one of them put it, that God gave Adam the power of being king, "and from this I date the original of government. It was patriarchal, founded in the very Law of Nature."[17] As another writer declared,

> Adam, the first father, had not only simply power, but power monarchical . . . for by the divine appointment, as soon as he was cre-

[16] Gordon Schochet regards Filmer's theory as the "bedrock" of royal absolutism, claiming that in the 1680s "the Filmerian position very nearly became the official state ideology" (*Patriarchalism in Political Thought,* New York: Basic Books, 1975, pp. 139, 193). This view has been challenged by James Daly, who maintains that Filmer's ideas were largely unknown and unused by Royalist writers (*Sir Robert Filmer and English Political Thought,* Toronto: University of Toronto Press, 1979, pp. 9, 124, 146). One need not go so far as Schochet in order to see that Laslett's original pronouncement in his introduction to Filmer's *Political Works* (p. 36) that "Filmer's name is constantly recurring in the pamphlets and journals of the period" is much closer to the truth than Daly's rather peculiar attempt to force a premature burial upon Filmer. If, to cite only one example, Daly cannot find that L'Estrange used or cited from Filmer (Daly, *Filmer,* p.181), it is because he did not read the December 24, 1681 issue of the *Observator,* in which L'Estrange defends Filmer against the attack of Thomas Hunt (Roger L'Estrange, *Observator,* December 24, 1681). Later, L'Estrange defended Filmer's theory against Sidney in the January 5, 1684 issue. A good, well-balanced treatment of Filmer in the context of royalist political theory is Mark Goldie, "John Locke and Anglican Royalism," *Political Studies* 31 (1983):86–102.

[17] E. Foreness, *A Sermon,* September 9, 1683, pp. 3–4.

> ated, he was monarch of the world . . . yet, by the right of nature it was Adam's due to be Supreme or Governor over all his posterity.[18]

These pithy references hardly do justice to what Locke called "the windings and obscurities" of Filmer's "wonderful system," but they do encapsulate what for many were the essential points of his argument.[19] In establishing patriarchal and divine authority through Adam, God was providing the latter with the authority necessary for "an execution of the natural law."[20] It was just this question—How can the commands of natural law, and hence, the moral obligations of individuals as they pertain to politics, be fulfilled?—which so desperately required an answer, especially in times of political crises. Apart from its other attractions, the answer that this problem was best seen as lying within the province of the king's responsibility was clearly the most emotionally easing response available to individuals whose consciences were already burdened with the weighty concerns of providing for their own personal salvation. This position also had the practical effect of admonishing the populace at large to refrain from active participation in political life.

Since Filmer had insisted that his theory did not allow for any infringements upon the king's authority by inferior laws passed by Parliament, there was little point in appealing to such laws or precedents as the basis for a Filmerian perspective. I do not intend "to search the rolls in the Tower," Thomas Gipps advised the reader of *The Nature of Subjection to the Civil Magistrate*; the king, he declared, has a claim to authority grounded in the Law of Nature that is as convincing as any claim advanced by those who cite that law in defense of the people's authority.[21] Robert Brady also recognized the strategic advantages of occupying the higher ground in the political battle with the Whigs. "I must confess," he

[18] *A Letter from Winchester . . .* , 1681, p. 1. John Brydall, who refers to Sir Robert Filmer's "two pieces lately published," nevertheless presents a similar simple statement of the theory (*Jura Coronae: His Majesty's Royal Rights and Prerogatives Asserted*, 1680, pp. 23, 136–139). L'Estrange, who read Filmer's works but rarely cites from them, also eschews a detailed or elaborate defense of the divine right/patriarchal theory of government (L'Estrange, *Papist Masquerade*, p. 78). For other glosses on Filmer, see Robert Constable, *God and King: or Monarchy Proved from Holy Writ*, 1680, p. 3; John Vesey, *A Sermon Preached before the King*, 1684, pp. 11, 18, 32; John Northleigh, *The Triumph of Our Monarchy over the Plots and Principles of Our Rebels and Republicans*, 1685. This last work is extremely scarce, but it was reprinted in 1699 under the title, *Remarks upon the Most Eminent of Our Antimonarchical Authors and Their Writings*, and I have used this copy (pp. 616–617).

[19] *Two Treatises*, preface.

[20] *The True Protestant Subject, or The Nature and Rights of Sovereignty Discussed and Stated*, 1680, p. 38.

[21] Thomas Gipps, *The Nature of Subjection to the Civil Magistrate*, 1683, p. 70.

wrote, "I have no great opinion of an argument drawn from matter of fact." And though he immediately launches into a historical account of the succession of kings, it only leads to the conclusion that "the Kings of England do derive their titles from God and Nature only."[22] Brady argues that "the true state of the question" (the exclusion of James) must be resolved in terms of a political theory that incorporates the precepts of natural law.[23] In so doing, he was following the path set by Filmer, for it was the latter's *Patriarcha*, I am arguing, which acted as a catalyst in forcing the ideological battle onto the terrain of natural law.[24]

Locke, for example, certainly grasped this point.

> 'Tis true, the civil lawyers have pretended to determine some of these cases concerning the succession of princes; but by our [author's] principles, they have meddled in a matter that belongs not to them. For if all political power be derived only from Adam . . . this is a right antecedent and paramount to all government; and therefore the positive laws of men, cannot determine that which is itself the foundation of all law and government, and is to receive its rule only from the Law of God and Nature.[25]

In responding to this challenge posed by Filmer's theory, in other words, Locke, Tyrrell, and Sidney were not introducing philosophical issues or language into an otherwise legalistic discussion; rather, the Whigs were compelled to counter a natural law argument with one of their own in order to defend "the fundamentals of government."[26] If Fil-

[22] Robert Brady, *The Great Point of Succession Discussed*, 1681, pp. 1, 2–19.

[23] Brady, *Great Point*, pp. 25ff.

[24] G. R. Cragg, *From Puritanism to the Age of Reason*, Cambridge: Cambridge University Press, 1966, pp. 170–171.

[25] *FT*, par. 126; cf. ibid., pars. 123, 124. Thus, municipal laws "are only so far right, as they are founded on the Law of Nature, by which they are to be regulated and interpreted" (*ST*, par. 12). Also, see Algernon Sidney, *Discourses Concerning Government*, 2 vols., 1805, chap. 2, sec. 4.

[26] In his classic work, *The Ancient Constitution and the Feudal Law* (New York: W. W. Norton, 1967), John Pocock noted "how exceptional was Locke in omitting any discussion of English legal or constitutional history from the *Two Treatises of Government*" (p. 188). Given that Pocock was primarily interested in the origins of historiography and the development of a historical consciousness in seventeenth-century England, it is perhaps not so surprising that Locke should not have figured prominently in either undertaking. If we ask, What is the significance of Locke's omission of legalistic historical arguments from the *Two Treatises* in relation to the political debate of the 1680s? the answer must be that this fact has very little significance. Only if one assumed that this debate was structured around a historical approach to the political problems of exclusion and the limits of political obligation would Locke's decision to approach these issues from a natural law perspective have some significance for our understanding of that debate viewed as a whole. Pocock did not directly address himself to this issue, but his remark (p. 237) that "the attempt to under-

mer's adherents could not demonstrate either "by Right of Nature or a clear positive Law of God" who had the right to succession, then the people, acting through Parliament, were at liberty to decide this question however they pleased, so long as that decision was made in accordance with the principles of natural law.

> All human laws whether they relate to the kinds of government, or the ways in which persons shall succeed unto it, they suppose an antecedent right in men of protecting their lives and liberties . . . and the design of all human laws is to secure those antecedent and natural rights.[27]

In the last analysis, therefore, both opposing political theories rested upon an interpretation of the Law of Nature.

The Whigs developed their position around three major tenets of natural law theory: (1) the Law of Nature was given by God to mankind in order to preserve the common good; (2) natural law requires the keeping of agreements and contracts; and (3) the community and (secondarily) individuals have a right to preserve themselves against the unauthorized use of force. All of these points were employed repeatedly in the propaganda war waged by the exclusion Whigs. As Thomas Hunt phrased it,

---

stand English politics through the history of English law was an all but universal pursuit of educated men in the seventeenth century" might lead others to conclude that this was the most important framework for a consideration of the issues raised by the exclusion controversy. This is the position adopted, for example, by Weston and Greenberg, *Subjects and Sovereigns*, p. 135 and passim. What needs to be emphasized is that in the development of the political consciousness of seventeenth-century Englishmen, the historical framework was only one, and not necessarily the most important, of several perspectives from which to view political problems. A great many political writers adopted the natural law approach to these problems, in terms of which a custom-oriented legalistic argument was either irrelevant or of secondary importance. Thus, even some of those writers cited by Pocock—Sidney, Brady (in the work cited above), and Tyrrell (who included historical references)—recognized that the fundamental issues of the debate rested upon the ground of natural law. In this respect, they were following or responding to the natural law argument advanced by Filmer. The vast majority of political writers in the 1680s simply ignored the history-of-English-law approach to political problems. They did not all, of course, resort to a natural law framework, though there were scores of tracts and sermons that did, but that is the point I am making: The exclusion political debate, viewed as a whole, was one in which many different types of arguments coalesced. Within that context, the historical legalistic argument constituted one small part of the whole, and its importance should not be exaggerated. And from *this* standpoint, Locke was not an exceptional political writer in his rejection of a legalistic approach.

[27] *A Letter from a Gentleman in the City, to One in the Country, Concerning the Bill for Disabling the Duke of York to Inherit the Imperial Crown of This Realm*, 1680, pp. 12–13; Locke, *FT*, par. 119. The people "have by a Law antecedent and paramount to all positive laws of men, reserved that ultimate determination to themselves" to judge when their rights and liberties are endangered (*ST*, pars. 168, 135, 222).

God gave "to all mankind . . . the Law of Nature. . . . This law was given or declared to all mankind, when they were in a state of nature, before governments were constituted, and by that Law of Nature obliged to form themselves into societies, to enter into mutual obligations."[28] "All the Laws of Nature, or Reason," Tyrrell declared, "are intended for one end or effect, viz., the common good and preservation of mankind."[29] Government, which Tyrrell argues is founded in the consent of the people, must be instituted in accordance with this natural law precept. This proposition, Edmund Hickeringill wrote in his *History of Whiggism*, is the meaning of "the old Whiggish maxim, Salus Populi, Suprema Lex."[30] Since, Sidney reasoned, "it cannot be imagined that men should generally put such fetters upon themselves, unless it were in expectation of a greater good thereby to accrue to them," it follows that, in leaving the state of nature, men "voluntarily enter into these societies, institute them for their own good, and prescribe such rules and forms to them as best please themselves."[31] In another exclusion tract, the author observed, "nothing is so entirely, perfectly, and abstractly civil, as government, the perfect creature of men in society, made by pact and consent . . . and therefore most certainly ordainable by the whole community, for the safety and preservation of the whole."[32] Thus, "government being for the preservation of every man's right and property . . . for the good of the governed . . . the positive laws of the society" must be "made conformable to the Law of Nature for the public good."[33]

But, the Whigs asked, what is to be done in the case of a prince who not only acts contrary to the common good but who intends "the destruction of those that are to be governed and protected"?[34] That James harbored such intentions was attributable to his Catholic beliefs, because, it was argued, from the standpoint of that religion, "it is not only lawful for such

[28] Thomas Hunt, *The Great and Weighty Considerations relating to the Duke of York*, 1680, p. 8.

[29] James Tyrrell, *Patriarcha non Monarcha*, 1681, p. 15 (*LL* #2999).

[30] Edmund Hickeringill, *History of Whiggism*, 1682, in *Works*, 2 vols., 1716, 1:43.

[31] A. Sidney, *Discourses*, chap. 1, sec. 12; cf. *ST*, pars. 131, 164.

[32] Thomas Hunt, *Mr. Hunt's Postscript for Rectifying Some Mistakes in Some of the Inferior Clergy*, 1682, preface (*LL* #1533); Henry Booth, Lord Delamere, *Works*, 1694, pp. 4–11. Most of the speeches and essays in Delamere's *Works* are not dated. Some are responses to the issues of the Glorious Revolution, but the greater part appear to date from the period of the exclusion crisis.

[33] *FT*, par. 92; cf. *ST*, pars. 3, 131, 135, 163, 165, 171, 229; A. Sidney, *Discourses*, chap. 3, sec. 16.

[34] Hunt, *Great and Weighty Considerations*, p. 6. What security is there "against the violence and oppression of . . . a declared enemy to society and mankind?" (*ST*, par. 93; A. Sidney, *Discourse*, chap. 2, sec. 27).

a prince to destroy those of his subjects who disagree from him in faith and worship, but it is an indispensable duty upon him to do it."[35] Thus, another writer warned, "by their laws and principles," Catholic kings "are always under an obligation utterly to exterminate Protestants," although, for obvious prudential reasons, they sometimes conceal this objective from their subjects so "that they might have the better advantage . . . when they have an opportunity to destroy us."[36] The simple fact is, Charles Blount wrote, that you can never believe in the words or trust in the promises of "a Popish successor" to the crown.[37] "Treason in papists," one minister preached, "is like original sin in mankind; they all have it in their natures."[38] On that level of the argument, at least, there could be no answer, nor were there any mitigating circumstances to be taken into account.

The suspicion and distrust prompted by fears of a Catholic conspiracy that had seaped into the mainstream of political life during the 1670s now appeared as an open and clearly delineated threat to the health of the body politic. The Whig response to that threat was an equally clear refusal to place in the hands of a Catholic king the trust necessary for the maintenance of the government or the common good for which it was established. Coleman's letters about James' presumed intentions "to extirpate the pestilent northern heresy" merely supplied the literal confirmation of a proposition that secretly guided the political actions of all Catholics.

Furthermore, James, as a Catholic, would be subservient to the pope, and would therefore "alienate his kingdom," that is, "give it up into the hands of another sovereign power."[39] In the *Two Treatises*, Locke specifically argues that no "oaths to any foreign power whatsoever" can discharge an individual from his office of trust or his obligation to obey the laws of the kingdom. And, he adds, "the delivery also of the people into the subjection of a foreign power . . . [is] a dissolution of the government."[40] In short, a Catholic on the throne meant the abandonment of "the whole kingdom to bondage and popery."[41] Hence, if James "be so disposed as to destroy the *reason of government*, he likewise loses the

[35] *Letter from a Gentleman in the City*, p. 3.

[36] David Clarkson, *The Case of Protestants in England under a Popish Prince*, 1681, p. 26.

[37] Charles Blount, *An Appeal from the Country to the City*, 1679, p. 2 (*LL* #356; it should be noted that Locke bought this tract after the exclusion crisis, although it is possible, of course, that he was replacing a copy he had previously owned but lost).

[38] William Payne, *A Sermon*, September 9, 1683, p. 20.

[39] Hunt, *Great and Weighty Considerations*, p. 6. "A papist is looked upon as a person that has a Sovereign somewhere else than in England" (Grey, 3:186).

[40] *ST*, pars. 134, 217, 220.

[41] *Letter from a Gentleman in the City*, p. 1.

reason of right to succession in government."[42] Locke reaffirms this point.

> For all *power given with trust* for the attaining an *end* . . . whenever that *end* is manifestly neglected, or opposed, the *trust* must necessarily be *forfeited,* and the power devolve into the hands of those who gave it, who may place it anew where they shall think best for their safety and security.[43]

By virtue of his designs and intentions to pursue a policy so contrary to the public good, James is simply "incapable to attain the end of government, the general welfare."[44] "That the Duke of York succeeding to the Crown," another Whig writer declared, "is inconsistent with the welfare of the nation, is even confessed by the opposers of the [exclusion] bill."[45]

In other words, when the ends of government cannot be attained, individuals are placed in a condition "as if they had none."[46] In that state of nature, the people are at liberty to institute a new form of government, one that will promote the common good. Popery, it was asserted, undermined the very concept of constitutional government, and "when the whole frame of the government is out of order . . . Nature teaches self-preservation."[47] In such a situation, one was returned to a reliance upon the foundation of all political theory, the precepts of natural law.

Even if there were no precedents and laws to support the case for the exclusion bill, one member of Parliament insisted, still "the Law of Nature . . . would afford us sufficient arguments" for its passage.[48] For no civil laws or constitutions can "restrain and limit us in such things which we have a right unto by the Law of Nature. That is . . . they could not deprive us of . . . a right to protect and defend ourselves from our declared adversary. So that if the people of England be but acknowledged to have a right to preserve their lives, maintain their properties, or secure their religion, it is lawful for them to disable the Duke of York to inherit the imperial crown of this realm," since he has "proclaimed by his actions

[42] *Two Great Questions Determined by the Principles of Reason and Divinity,* 1681, p. 8.

[43] *ST,* par. 149 (italics in original); cf. ibid., par. 222.

[44] *Two Great Questions,* p. 10.

[45] *A Dialogue at Oxford between a Tutor and a Gentleman, Formerly His Pupil, Concerning Government,* 1681, p. 19 (*LL* #1296).

[46] *Two Great Questions,* p. 10; *ST,* par. 94.

[47] Grey, 8:163.

[48] *An Exact Collection of the Most Considerable Debates in the Honorable House of Commons . . . October, 1680,* 1681, p. 47; *A Letter from a Person of Quality to His Friend Concerning His Majesty's Late Declaration,* 1681, p. 4 (*LL* #667).

that he is an open enemy to every one of them."[49] The anonymous author of *A Word in Season to All True Protestants* asserted that by his evident inability to promote the common good, James had "*ipso facto* forfeited all right of succession." And, he asked, "what people that are not mad will swear allegiance" to a prince who designs "the destruction of his subjects? . . . That principle of self-preservation which God hath implanted in the very nature of all his creatures is a sufficient warrant from the God of Nature to all mankind to refuse subjection in such cases."[50]

To the question, "Can the government be safe without a power to exclude a person . . . principled to destroy it?" the Whigs responded in the negative, with an argument that was structured around the concepts of the Law of Nature, the common good, and the state of nature, and that provided the justification for viewing the people as the original source of political power.[51] Since the people had expressed their will in support of excluding James from the throne in three successive national elections, this argument carried with it a substantial practical resonance. Whig political theory thus claimed for its adherents that they represented the voice of the people expressed through parliamentary elections, as the institutional embodiment of the dictates of natural law; and the basic precepts of that law, as the Whigs interpreted it, were in turn repeatedly emphasized in their campaign literature addressed to the electorate.

Despite the considerable electoral successes achieved by the Whigs through this strategy, the latter was not without its problems, most of which were traceable to the inner tensions of a political theory that attempted to reconcile the extremist rhetoric of its appeal to the masses with the specific, limited, and legalistic practical objectives of the party. The Whigs sought to combine an antipopery propaganda campaign with a defense of the legal authority of Parliament, both of which were ultimately grounded in an appeal to natural law. But while the most violent imagery directed against Catholics might be useful as an inducement to voters to refuse to give their support to any parliamentary candidate suspected of favoring Catholicism, this imagery was not so easily reconcilable with the parliamentary strategy of the Whigs who sought by legal means to exclude someone for whom, according to their own political pamphlets, parliamentary statutes had no real meaning. If James was as thoroughly treasonable as they presented him as being, what possible safety could the Whigs expect to gain from the passage of a law to which they, but not he, had consented?

[49] *Letter from a Gentleman in the City*, p. 14.

[50] *A Word in Season to All True Protestants* (I have cited from the unpaginated manuscript copy of this tract in the Shaftesbury papers: PRO 30/24/43/63).

[51] Hunt, *Great and Weighty Considerations*, p. 5.

In appealing to the Law of Nature on behalf of self-preservation and the common good as the realizable ends of government, the Whigs were also forced to accept the moral dimensions implicit in that appeal, as they applied to papists. As Locke phrased the general point in the *Second Treatise*,

> In transgressing the Law of Nature, the offender declares himself to live by another rule, than that of reason and common equity, which is the measure God has set to the actions of men, for their mutual security; and so he becomes dangerous to mankind . . . one of those wild savage beasts with whom men can have no society nor security.[52]

Such a transgressor of natural law was "a declared enemy to all mankind."[53] Yet it was continuously drummed into people's consciousness during the exclusion crisis that "the papists are enemies to all mankind."[54] It may be true, Bishop Fowler conceded, that there are some "honest or good natured persons" among the rank-and-file Catholics, but it "may safely be said that, whoever is thoroughly instructed in the popish principles and acts accordingly . . . has totally cast off all *humanity*."[55]

References in numerous exclusion tracts to "popish beasts of prey," "blood-thirsty monsters," to a papist as "a companion fit for brutes and savages," and so on, were barely disguised expressions of the feelings of terror and hatred directed against the Duke of York.[56] In *The Character of a Popish Successor*, Elkanah Settle maintained that James as king would be "the most terrible and the most dangerous of England's enemies" imaginable. His reign would be marked by an "inflexible invincible enmity" between the king and his subjects.[57] In this regard, it is useful to recall that, in the *Two Treatises*, Locke's concept of a state of war is not

[52] *ST*, pars. 8, 11; cf. ibid., pars. 10, 16, 172, 181, 182, 207, 230. Locke applied this general proposition to Catholics in his 1664 lectures on natural law, criticizing them for subscribing to a set of beliefs that "breaks the great bond of humanity," i.e., the Law of Nature (*ELN*, p. 175; cf. Tyrrell, *Patriarcha non Monarcha*, pp. 63, 115; A. Sidney, *Discourses*, chap. 3, sec. 19).

[53] *ST*, par. 93.

[54] Grey, 8:35.

[55] Edward Fowler, *A Sermon Preached before the Judges . . . in the Cathedral Church at Gloucester*, 1681, p. 23; D. Clarkson, *Case of Protestants*, p. 6.

[56] Elkanah Settle, *The Character of a Popish Successor*, 1681, pp. 17–18 (*LL* #659); *A Word in Season: or, A Letter from a Reverend Divine to a Justice of the Peace in London*, 1679, pp. 4, 7; Christopher Ness, *A Protestant Antidote against the Poison of Popery*, 1679, p. 113.

[57] Settle, *Popish Successor*, p. 13.

defined in terms of the numbers of people actually engaged in armed conflict, but rather, it consists in "declaring by word or action" an "intention" or "a sedate settled design" by any individual that he professes "enmity and destruction" toward others.[58] This definitional notion of a state of war was certainly being applied to James as a Catholic, and especially to the situation that would obtain should he become king. As one of Locke's contemporaries put it, James as king would be "the mortal enemy of both us and our estates."[59] Given the manner in which James' accession to the throne was portrayed in the political pamphlets, as well as the implications attached to anyone's willful transgression of natural law, there can be no doubt that the impression being transmitted through this political literature was that a Catholic ruler would exist in a state of war with his Protestant subjects. "No Popery," therefore, signified in its most essential meaning an avoidance of this state of war and a defense of those natural law limitations under which any legitimate political society was presumed to exist—both of which depended upon the exclusion of Catholics from the exercise of political authority.

The extremist rhetoric employed to emphasize this point, however, created an atmosphere in which people were drawn inevitably to the conclusion that they would "have no moral security" for *anything* they valued—life, liberty, property—under a popish king. Locke articulated this feeling when he asked, What security is there "against the violence and oppression of . . . a declared enemy to society and mankind?"[60] Or as one leading Whig summarized the point,

> I would fain see how it is possible to live in quiet with a people whose religion obliges them to destroy all converse or human society, to murder their neighbors, assassinate their king, and subvert the government . . . brutes and christians can never live and converse together.[61]

How, indeed, was one to find a political bridge across this moral chasm?

Radical Whigs were not inclined to look for a bridge. Their response was to advocate violence under the justification of self-defense against the actions of the "noxious beasts" or "willful transgressors" who had abandoned their "humanity" by living outside the boundaries established by

[58] *FT*, par. 131; *ST*, pars. 16, 17.

[59] *Letter Concerning Declaration*, p. 4.

[60] Grey, 7:140; *ST*, par. 93.

[61] Delamere, *Works*, p. 134; *A Collection of the Substance of Several Speeches and Debates Made in the Honorable House of Commons, relating to the Horrid Popish Plot*, 1681, p. 7.

natural law.[62] Most Whigs, and even more, most anti-Catholics, were not willing to sanction this political conclusion as following from the premises of the generally accepted moral argument. Even the radicals, as we shall see in Chapter 7, did not immediately embrace the notion of armed resistance. They were more or less reluctantly led down that path as the exclusion crisis dragged on and Charles II's intransigence became increasingly obvious.

For virtually all Whigs until 1681, and for the majority of them thereafter, notwithstanding the extremist antipopery language, their political policies were frequently presented in moderate tones. "Shall not we be allowed to use such legal means, as are consistent with and warranted by our Constitution, to hinder a papist from ascending the legal throne of this kingdom?" one writer asked.[63] "We desire and endeavor by law," proclaimed another, "to disable a professed enemy both to our religion and government from getting into the throne." This was an entirely "legal method" of self-protection: to "tie up" James "by such rules and laws, as will put it without his power to effect the dreaded mischief" of endangering the lives, liberties, and religion of the people. But having done this through parliamentary action, the people "have done all that *lawfully* they may."[64] For most of the exclusion-crisis period, this legalistic, constitutional approach to the problem of a future Catholic monarch reflected the dominant Whig perspective. It was supported by appeals to previous parliamentary statutes, historical precedents, and to the general authority of Parliament as a legislative and representative institution, backed ultimately by references to the very purposes and origins of government as sanctioned by the Law of Nature.

Nevertheless, the uneasy murmurs of doubt and skepticism as to the efficacy of this solution to the problem were present among the Whigs from the outset of the crisis. As the author of *England's Concern in the Case of His Royal Highness, James Duke of York* reminded his countrymen, even if the exclusion bill were passed, the act "falls to the ground of itself, in the moment" James becomes king. At the time of the introduction of the exclusion bill, John Hampden rose to tell his fellow members of the Commons that "for us to go about to tie a popish successor with laws for the preservation of the Protestant religion, is binding Sampson with withes; he will break them when he is awake." At the same time,

[62] The importance of this language to the radicals in the specific context of the Rye House Plot is discussed in Chapter 8 below. For L'Estrange's satirical response to the imagery of "lions, bears, tigers, and wolves" as part of the Whig strategy of frightening the common people, see the October 1, 1681 issue of the *Observator*.

[63] *Letter from a Gentleman in the City*, p. 2.

[64] Hunt, *Great and Weighty Considerations*, p. 7; *Two Great Questions*, p. 12.

another member asked, "How little security have we that this exclusion of the Duke . . . shall not end in a civil war?"[65] The fears expressed by Hampden and others were never quelled; on the contrary, they grew to frightening proportions by the time a significant section of the Whigs—including Hampden—decided to abandon their legal approach to exclusion. As Settle asked his readers, "How is an arbitrary absolute popish tyrant any longer a lawful successor to a Protestant established and bounded government, when lawfully succeeding to this limited monarchy, he afterwards violently, unlawfully, and tyrannically overruns the due bounds of power, dissolves the whole royal constitution"?[66] It is a poignant piece of historical information that Settle himself had no convincing answer to this question. Faced with the conclusion that such a tyrant as he had just described must be resisted with force, Settle retreated; he recanted his Whig political beliefs, and subsequently wrote a scurrilous commentary on Algernon Sidney's dying speech, printed at the time of the latter's execution for his participation in the Rye House Plot.[67] Settle, however, was far from alone in having to face up to the political dilemma which, in part, he had helped to create through his own writings.

The problem of reconciling Whig political rhetoric with Whig political policy can be viewed from several angles. In the first place, the Whigs were never successful in getting a bill of exclusion passed through both houses of Parliament. They achieved no measure of political success that might have served, temporarily at least, to moderate the tone or the effect of their propaganda. Even if the bill had passed the Lords, however, it would almost certainly have been vetoed by the king. In retrospect, therefore, what seems difficult to understand is why the skepticism regarding the legislative approach to exclusion was not very much greater than it was. Perhaps, on the most practical level, exclusion really meant the banishment of James out of the kingdom, where, removed from all of his military and civil offices, he might find it difficult to return to claim the throne following Charles II's death, even if the latter had never ac-

[65] *England's Concern in the Case of His Royal Highness, James Duke of York*, 1680, reprinted in the Second Collection of *Somers Tracts*, 4 vols., 1750, 3:249; Grey, 7:243, 246. Hampden is here objecting to Charles' offer to place certain legal limitations upon his successor, arguing instead in favor of the exclusion bill. Nevertheless, the same general point applies to the latter.

[66] Settle, *Popish Successor*, p. 20.

[67] Elkanah Settle, *Remarks on Algernon Sidney's Paper, Delivered to the Sheriffs at His Execution*, 1683. Settle also attacked Shaftesbury and Russell, and wrote a panegyric to George Jeffries: *A Dialogue between the Earl of Sh——y, E. Settle, and Dr. Oates at Parting*, 1682; *Some Succinct Remarks on the Speech of Lord Russell*, 1683; *A Panegyrick on the Loyal and Honorable Sir George Jeffries*, 1683. For a general confession of his having been deceived by Whiggism, see *A Narrative*, 1683, epistle dedicatory.

tually given his consent to a bill of exclusion. In any event, the legal approach was a far more rock-strewn path than many people imagined; and simultaneously with its pursuit through the difficult channels of English constitutional government, its theoretical credibility was constantly being undermined by the atmosphere of moral insecurity stressed in the Whig propaganda. This tension existed at the interstices of Whig theory, where the level of its moral argument intersected with its political claims, because both features of that theory were advanced as self-characterizations of what it meant to be a Whig.

A second aspect of the problem arose on the level of specification. The more the details of this intersection were spelled out, the more difficult it was to minimize the inherent tension contained in the political perspective as a whole. Once people began to see more clearly the concrete political applications of the general moral argument they professed, the harder it became to effect a reconciliation between the two. Viewed over a period of several years, and as the cumulative effect produced by thousands of political tracts and sermons, the process of specification of the implications of their argument helped to bring about a transformation in the political consciousness of many Whigs.

The general assertion that Catholics are not obligated to keep faith with heretics, for example, carried with it a very definite picture of what the future political relations between James and his Protestant subjects might be like. It is not the "delusive, ridiculous, and romantic doctrines of transubstantiation, purgatory," and so forth, of the Catholics that are the problem, one Whig wrote, but their "holding that no faith is to be kept with those they call heretics, and that the murdering of such is meritorious, with other like principles destructive of all morality."[68] Since Protestants were "heretics" from the Catholic standpoint, there could be no "contract" between a Catholic king and a Protestant people; their relationship could only be one of conquest and slavery.

> Seeing a papist successor can be obliged by no contract or oath, therefore he cannot succeed by contract. And if he succeed not by

[68] Slingsby Bethel, *The Interest of Princes and States*, 1680, p. 175; Blount, *Appeal from the Country*, p. 2; A. Sidney, *Discourses*, chap. 3, sec. 19. For a typical summary of these beliefs, see Thomas Barlow, *Popery: or the Principles and Positions Approved by the Church of Rome*, 1679. "These pernicious doctrines," William Cave declared, "are not mere scholastic subtleties, dry and barren speculations, but impregnated with life and power" (*A Sermon Preached before the Lord Mayor . . . of London*, November 5, 1680, p. 23). What seventeenth-century Englishmen feared, in short, was Catholicism as a political doctrine (John Miller, *Popery and Politics in England, 1660–1688*, Cambridge: Cambridge University Press, 1973, pp. 70–71).

> contract, then he will succeed by conquest; for there are but two ways of succession, either by contract, or by conquest.

But, the author argued, if the ruler succeeds by conquest, he will present himself as being "above all human laws." This situation makes every subject "a slave to be destroyed at pleasure, by a cruel, unjust, and lawless will" of the prince. And, he asked, "what commerce or human society can there be had with those who hold such views?"[69] In *The Case of Protestants in England under a Popish Prince,* the author also elaborated upon the political consequences that flowed from the Catholic doctrine. Protestant subjects under a Catholic king, he argued, as heretics would be subject to the penalties for heresy—legally, a form of treason—for which the severest punishment is death.

> So that the papal authority being introduced among Protestants, they are forthwith traitors by law . . . and are exposed to the penalties which the highest treason is judged worthy of.[70]

Under such conditions, it would be impossible to have Parliaments, since Protestant candidates could by law be excluded from holding office, and Protestant voters could be barred from voting. This was a point echoed by many other pamphleteers.[71] It is well known, one writer noted, that the Duke of York "hates our Parliaments with an implaccable hatred . . . therefore, if he succeed, adieu to all Parliaments," and we can "expect to be ruled by force."[72]

Not only would a Catholic king intervene in parliamentary elections, William Lawrence asserted, but he would also "seize on the power of public offices," creating sheriffs, mayors, military officers, bishops, and judges, thereby subverting the very foundations of representative gov-

[69] William Lawrence, *The Right of Primogeniture,* 1681, p. 148 (*LL* #1694); Grey, 8:330. What have we to do "with a sort of people that cannot be bound by any law or contract whatsoever? Much less can their words or promises be depended on" (*Exact Collection,* pp. 36–37; Settle, *Popish Successor,* p. 21). For Locke's contrast of consent and conquest, see *ST,* par. 175. As this debate makes clear, the meaning of "conquest" was not limited to its historical association with William the Conqueror, nor to a foreign invasion. Since popish kings ruled by conquest and not contract, their defenders, in the eyes of the Whigs, were supporters of a conquest theory of government. This point needs to be understood in order to appreciate the prevalence of the attacks on the conquest theory in the Whig political literature, including the *Second Treatise.*

[70] D. Clarkson, *Case of Protestants,* pp. 3–4.

[71] D. Clarkson, *Case of Protestants,* p. 5; Lawrence, *Right of Primogeniture,* p. 179; Thomas Hunt, *A Defence of the Charter, and Municipal Rights of the City of London,* 1683, p. 34 (*LL* #1534).

[72] *A Most Serious Expostulation with Several of My Fellow-Citizens in Reference to Their Standing So High for the Duke of York's Interest at This Juncture of Time,* n.d., p. 4.

ernment.[73] For, Locke argued, when the prince "employs the force, treasure, and offices of the society, to corrupt the representatives, and gain them to his purposes . . . by solicitations, threats, promises" and attempts to tell them "what to vote, and what to enact," the legislative power is altered. This is also the case "when by the arbitrary power of the prince, the electors, or ways of election are altered, without the consent, and contrary to the common interest of the people." Thus, Locke concludes, "to regulate candidates and elections, and new model the ways of election, what is it but to cut up government by the roots," which is Locke's description of "conquest."[74]

In other words, the Whigs developed an argument in which No Popery, No Slavery meant that a Catholic king intended to rely upon the army and the use of force, rather than upon elections and Parliament to support his policies. For "the king must govern either by a parliament or an army."[75] Charles Blount warned his readers that all popish kings governed by an army rather than through Parliaments.[76] "From popery," Sir Henry Capel observed, "came the notion of a standing army and arbitrary power."[77] Shaftesbury had emphasized these points in his parliamentary speeches. As early as 1675, when he was already thinking of the Duke of York's succession, Shaftesbury declared:

> If ever there should happen in future ages (which God forbid) a King governing by an army without a Parliament, it is a government I own not, am not obliged to, nor was born under.[78]

Throughout the exclusion crisis, the Whigs attacked Charles II for maintaining a standing army, whether it was the six thousand troops assisting the French in 1679, or the twenty-two thousand soldiers in Scotland that the Second Militia Bill had placed at the king's disposal. An insistence upon no standing army, therefore, was second in importance only to the antipopery theme in the Whig campaign for exclusion, and the two themes were frequently intertwined. Thus, one aspect of the meaning of "popery and arbitrary government" referred to the propensity of Cath-

[73] Lawrence, *Right of Primogeniture*, p. 179; Hunt, *Defence of the Charter*, p. 5; Grey, 8:279.

[74] *ST*, pars. 216, 222. See also Chapter 8 below for a discussion of "conquest" in the context of Locke's political argument in the *Two Treatises*.

[75] Cobbett, 4:1271.

[76] Blount, *Appeal from the Country*, p. 2.

[77] Grey, 7:149; Hickeringill, *Works*, 1:159.

[78] Shaftesbury, speech (October 20, 1675), in *Somers Tracts*, 3:209. Shaftesbury asked the author of the *Letter from a Person of Quality* to consider what would happen if "a popish prince" should come to power, "which was not a thing so impossible, or remote, as not to be apprehended" (Locke, *Works*, 9:207).

olic monarchs to rule by "force," that is, through a standing army, rather than by "consent" through a Parliament.[79]

The second—economic—component of the accusation charged that James would confiscate the property and estates of Protestants "and divide the spoils amongst the papists."[80] In the Commons debates of 1680, it was argued with reference to a future government run by Catholics, that since "we are heretics, they will burn us, and damn us. For our estates, they will take our lands, and put monks and friars upon them."[81] It was frequently asserted that James intended to reclaim those lands which had formerly belonged to the Catholic church.[82] However far-fetched this threat may appear to us, for practical reasons alone, it was taken seriously, especially by the small and moderate gentry, many of whom were the owners of such land. James himself went to great lengths to deny this particular charge. As late as 1687, even after two years as king, he thought it necessary to commission a tract, *The Assurance of Abbey and Other Church Lands*, the purpose of which was to reassure his subjects that their property rights would be respected.[83]

Nevertheless, apart from the specific fears of owners of property previously held by the Catholic church, there was a general sense of insecurity regarding the property rights of Protestants should James become king. "If popery come in," it was alleged, "not only the church-lands, but all the lands we have" will be confiscated.[84] Even before the exclusion crisis, Andrew Marvell had warned in his *Account of the Growth of Popery and Arbitrary Government* that "the alteration of religion" from Protestantism to Catholicism "would necessarily introduce a change of prop-

[79] Blount, *Appeal from the Country*, p. 2; *Exact Collection*, p. 245. "Many have mistaken the force of arms for the consent of the people," which leads to the substitution of conquest for contract (*ST*, pars. 175, 176). Laslett seems unable to figure out what this reference means (Laslett, p. 403n.), but in the context of the debate over James' succession to the throne, given the association of Catholic monarchs with absolute power, a standing army, and their rule by "force" or "conquest," its meaning is very clear. For this reason, I cannot agree with Lois Schwoerer's assertion that "the standing army question was almost completely ignored" during the exclusion crisis (*No Standing Armies: The Antiarmy Ideology in Seventeenth-Century England*, Baltimore: Johns Hopkins University Press, 1974, p. 132). Neither Laslett nor Schwoerer looked for the meaning of "conquest" or a "standing army" in the context of the antipopery literature, which in the 1680s is where the arguments are to be found.

[80] Lawrence, *Right of Primogeniture*, pp. 116–118.

[81] Grey, 7:400.

[82] D. Clarkson, *Case of Protestants*, p. 7; *A Character of Popery and Arbitrary Government*, 1681, p. 7; Blount, *Appeal from the Country*, p. 7.

[83] Miller, *Popery and Politics*, p. 71.

[84] *Exact Collection*, p. 114.

erty. . . . It would make a general earthquake over the nation."[85] As one exclusion author summarized the point: "As soon as the papacy is admitted, all title and property is lost and extinct among us."[86] Popery, therefore, meant slavery in the form of a loss of one's property rights. "Can anyone say the king" may "take away all, or part of the land," or "the goods or money" from any individual "at his pleasure?" Locke asked. "If he can, then all free and voluntary *contracts* cease and are void . . . and all the *grants* and promises of *men in power* are but mockery and collusion."[87] Clearly, it was important for the Whigs to stress—as Locke does throughout the *Two Treatises*—that property cannot be taken from an individual without his consent, and that force conveys no title to property.

What was being constructed by the Whigs in their political literature was a detailed account of what life would be like under an absolute monarchy. For, it was commonly asserted, "popery never can nor will grow but by absolute government."[88] Hence, "it is not to be doubted," it was remarked during the House of Commons debates, "but that popery and arbitrary government are so near of kin as cannot be separated."[89] This was a crib of Shaftesbury's famous statement that "popery and slavery, like two sisters, go hand-in-hand," a saying repeated in numerous exclusion tracts.[90] Popery, William Lawrence wrote, represents "a most lawless arbitrary power" exercised by kings against their subjects "to dispose of their lands, goods, persons, liberty and property, at their [kings'] pleasure."[91] In short, popery would plunge the nation into a "bottomless pit of arbitrary power."[92]

If this was insufficient to convince people of the dangers posed by a Catholic sovereign, there were more lurid scenes laid before the readers of exclusion literature. That Catholicism was a "religion of blood" and persecution was an accepted commonplace of seventeenth-century English thought. There is not a single instance in history, one anonymous author declared, where this linkage between popery and absolute monarchy did not result in "the most outrageous cruelties" committed

[85] Andrew Marvell, *The Complete Works*, 4 vols., 1872, 4:260.

[86] D. Clarkson, *Case of Protestants*, p. 10.

[87] *ST*, par. 194 (italics in original).

[88] Grey, 8:34.

[89] *Exact Collection*, pp. 160–163; *Popery and Arbitrary Government*, p. 2.

[90] Shaftesbury, speech in the House of Lords (March 25, 1679), p. 1.

[91] William Lawrence, *Marriage by the Moral Law of God Vindicated*, 1680, p. 324 (*LL* #1693).

[92] Cited in George F. Sensabaugh, *That Grand Whig Milton*, Stanford: Stanford University Press, 1952, p. 81.

against subjects.[93] Catholicism's means of converting Protestants, it was alleged, was that of "scourging, and wracking, and boiling them into the fear of God." Visions of "dark dungeons," "the shrieks of the tormented," cannibalistic priests with a propensity "to ravish grave matrons," and much more were conjured up from the depths of the nightmarish imaginations of exclusion pamphleteers.[94] The history of Protestant subjects living under a Catholic king, as they presented it, was one long "dismal story of murder and massacre," and it lost nothing in the telling. The reign of Bloody Mary was repeatedly invoked as a historical reminder of the story's relevance to the English past.[95] Those whose imaginations had been dulled by the passage of time were advised to "read the Book of Martyrs, if these things so easily slip your mind."[96]

Of no less emotional force, but with a slightly higher level of evidential support attached to it, was an argument that attempted to provide a comparative assessment of the English political system in relation to those of European countries ruled by Catholic princes. One example cited by a Whig writer discussed Philip of Spain's attempt to establish his "absolute dominion" over Belgium, which he intended to rule "arbitrarily according to his own will and pleasure." Philip not only "designed the total subversion" of the people's liberties and religion, he intended to confiscate their property as well. The fact that he failed in this attempt, forcing the people "to fly to the natural right of self-preservation," and resistance served, in the author's view, "to show to all princes, what a small people made desperate may do, and will be a matter of admiration to posterity."[97] But the most obvious and relevant example for the Whigs was, of course, France. Numerous writers pointed to the "poor and miserable" condition of the inhabitants of France, maintaining that this was a direct consequence of a political system of "absolute rule founded in [the] arbitrary will and pleasure" of the king.[98] "There are but two sorts of mon-

[93] *Letter from a Gentleman in the City*, p. 4; *Debates relating to Popish Plot*, p. 7; Ness, *Protestant Antidote*, pp. 104, 107–116; A. Sidney, *Discourses*, chap. 3, sec. 43.

[94] Ness, *Protestant Antidote*, pp. 107–108.

[95] Ness, *Protestant Antidote*, p. 104.

[96] *Serious Expostulation*, p. 3.

[97] Bethel, *Interest of Princes and States*, pp. 123–124.

[98] Bethel, *Interest of Princes and States*, p. 215; cf. ibid., pp. 180–181; *Popery and Arbitrary Government*, p. 2; A. Sidney, *Discourses*, chap. 2, sec. 21; ibid., chap. 3, secs. 5, 6, 39; Henry Care, *English Liberties: Or, The Free-Born Subject's Inheritance*, [1682], pp. 1–2, 206. This last work has generally been attributed to Care, but see Winthrop S. Hudson's case for Penn's authorship. "William Penn's *English Liberties*: Tract for Several Times," *William and Mary Quarterly* 26, no. 4 (October 1969):578–585. Hudson associates the tract with the Rye House Plot, which—if true—would make Penn an extremely unlikely candidate for its author, since his political views had long since diverged from those of Shaftesbury, and there is no evidence that Penn was involved in or had any knowledge of Shaftesbury's plans for an insurrection. It is more likely that *English Liberties* was written

archy in the whole world," Sir Henry Capel declared, "one absolute without limitation, as that of France, whose subjects are at the disposal of the king for life and limb . . . and all to support absolute monarchy," and the other a constitutional or limited monarchy, such as that of England.[99] The author of *A Character of Popery and Arbitrary Government* develops this point at some length. "Your neighbors in France, Spain, and other Popish governments," he informed his fortunate English readers, "have no other security either for their estates or beings, save the grace or favor of their prince; which renders them perpetual vassals to the crown." Then, expressing this relationship through its economic consequences, he wrote:

> There you may see the poor tenant ground to beggary, betwixt the tax-gatherers on the one hand, and the gyping landlords on the other. There you may behold the merchants, tradesmen, and artifacers, paying excessive . . . excise . . . for every egg or bit of bread they put in their mouths. Their very labors are not their own. . . . These and a thousand more inconveniences are incident to absolute monarchy, and absolute monarchy incident to popery.[100]

So strongly did France serve the Whig cause as the paradigmatic illustration of the connection between popery and absolute monarchy that, even after the Glorious Revolution, Bishop Burnet could remind the House of Lords:

> When I have named France, I have said all that is necessary to give you a complete idea of the blackest tyranny over men's consciences, persons, and estates, that can possibly be imagined, where everything that the subject possesses is at the mercy of a boundless power . . . and by which subjects are treated with as much cruelty, as enemies are with barbarity.[101]

---

in connection with the dispute over the 1682 London sheriffs election. Even the date of its publication has been difficult to determine, but an advertisement for it in the September 2–6, 1682, issue of *The True Protestant Mercury* (no. 174) makes it likely that it appeared in late August of that year. Penn sailed for Pennsylvania in mid-August 1682 (ibid., no. 168), which does not rule out his authorship, but an advertisement for Penn's *No Cross, No Crown* in the October 21, 1682, issue (no. 187) refers to it as "the last book he wrote before his departure from England." (This is the second edition of the work originally published in 1669.) Hudson's argument is interesting, but I have retained the attribution to Care. Nevertheless, he does demonstrate the ideological importance of this tract to Anglo-American political thought.

[99] Grey, 8:264; cf. ibid., 3:136.

[100] *Popery and Arbitrary Government*, p. 2; William Petyt, *Britannia Languens*, 1680, p. 287 (*LL* #2967).

[101] Gilbert Burnet, *A Sermon Preached before the House of Peers*, November 5, 1689, p. 29.

The general implications for political theory of the example of France were clearly understood by the Whigs. As a form of government, a French-type absolute monarchy was as "uncivilized" in the world of politics as papists were supposed to be within the realm of morality. Since Locke, Sidney, and other Whigs defined slavery as the condition of an individual being subject to the arbitrary will of another, absolute monarchy, as the political system of slavery, violated the moral conditions of civil society.[102] Or to put it another way, because no one can legitimately consent to slavery, and hence to absolute monarchy, the latter must be viewed as a government by "conquest," in which subjects have only the status of "slaves."[103] This was a direct refutation of Filmer's assertion that "we see the principal point of sovereign majesty and absolute power to consist principally in giving laws unto the subjects without their consent."[104] For the Whigs, absolute monarchy, in William Penn's words, was "not properly a government."[105] "Hence it is evident," Locke wrote, "that absolute monarchy, which by some men is counted the only government in the world, is indeed *inconsistent with civil society, and so can be no form of civil government at all.*"[106] Thus, the choice was starkly presented: freedom versus slavery, a limited versus an absolute monarchy. To Locke's contemporaries, a Catholic king represented "the subversion of our religion, laws, and properties, the introducing of popery and a tyrannical arbitrary government by an army, our common and statute laws to be abolished and annihilated, and a mixture of military and civil law introduced . . . [in] our courts of justice."[107]

[102] "This freedom from absolute, arbitrary power, is so necessary to, and closely joined with a man's preservation, that he cannot part with it. . . . For a man . . . *cannot,* by compact, or his own consent, *enslave himself* to any one, nor put himself under the absolute, arbitrary power of another" (*ST,* par. 23; cf. ibid., pars. 24, 57, 135, 149, 172; Tyrrell, *Patriarcha non Monarcha,* pp. 64, 104–105; A. Sidney, *Discourses,* chap. 1, sec. 5; ibid., chap. 3, sec. 16).

[103] As Settle put it, kings must come to power either through the consent of the people or by conquest. In James' case, it could only be by means of the latter, which meant that his government would be a tyranny, and his subjects slaves (*Popish Successor,* pp. 21, 163). See also Hunt, *Great and Weighty Considerations,* pp. 19ff.; Lawrence, *Right of Primogeniture,* p. 148; *Dialogue at Oxford,* p. 5; Grey, 8:330.

[104] Filmer, p. 320.

[105] William Penn, *England's Great Interest in the Choice of This New Parliament,* 1680?, p. 2.

[106] *ST,* par. 90; cf. ibid., par. 137. "Absolute dominion, however placed is so far from being one kind of civil society, that it is as inconsistent with it, as slavery is with property" (ibid., par. 174).

[107] Cited in Ronalds, *Attempted Whig Revolution,* p. 13n. "Our religion . . . will then be totally overthrown . . . The execution of old laws must cease . . . The most sacred obligations of contracts and promises . . . will be violated . . . The lives, liberties, and estates of all such Protestants . . . will be adjudged forfeited" under a popish successor (The Commons Address in Answer to the King's Speech [December 30, 1680] in Cobbett, 4:1257).

From this perspective, it is not surprising that the exclusion political debate was perceived as revolving around "the very fundamentals" of English government. "The very essence of a popish successor," Settle exclaimed, "is the greatest plot upon England since the Creation."[108] Doubtless this relegation of original sin to a secondary place in God's designs for England was not greeted with universal approbation by Settle's contemporaries. Nevertheless, many of them were prepared to believe that the prospects of a Catholic sovereign signaled "the greatest mischief that ever threatened this kingdom."[109]

In the political literature of the 1680s, the exclusion of James from the throne was presented as the focal point of a struggle to preserve a whole way of life from an impending catastrophe. What the Whigs attempted was to build a mass movement around a deeply ingrained cultural prejudice against Catholicism, and to a lesser degree, a widely shared suspicion of James' political intentions in particular, which was expressed in its most general form as a moral argument. Catholicism, they maintained, violated the moral conditions necessary for legitimate government, as dictated by the Laws of Nature. Although the Whigs gained positive benefits from the employment of this strategy, in the form of a broad political alliance of various social groups, the intensity and the clarity of the moral choices their argument presented to the nation left them, as a political party, with increasingly fewer political options the longer the exclusion crisis persisted. In emphasizing the moral condemnatory aspects of the Whig position, therefore, Locke, far from adopting a philosophical style as a means of detaching himself from the specific issues of the political debate, was in fact pressing home the most radical political course possible within the general framework of the Whig argument. For, on this level of the political controversy, there were only two forms of practical activity through which a mass movement could express its political power: through elections or through a revolution. Since, following the dissolution of the Oxford Parliament in March 1681, no further parliamentary elections were planned or held, the moral choice between freedom and slavery could, from a political standpoint, lead in only one direction.[110]

The Duke of York stood for the "interests" of popery and absolute monarchy. To these were contrasted the "interests" of Protestantism and Parliament, or "your own freedoms and liberties."[111] In their positive delineation of the meaning of "Liberty and Property," the Whigs collated a diverse bundle of specific claims under the general heading with which

[108] Settle, *Popish Successor*, p. 22.

[109] Hunt, *Postscript*, p. 30.

[110] As Delamere put it, "there is no middle state betwixt slavery and freedom" (*Works*, p. 620).

[111] *Serious Expostulation*, p. 2.

they identified themselves. Not everyone, of course, agreed with some particular pamphleteer's interpretation of liberty, but it is fair to say that there was a large measure of tolerance shown among the Whigs for the various representations of their viewpoint in the political literature. Whig writers did not rush into print in order to refute the overextended claims of a misguided ally, nor was there an attempt by anyone—certainly not by Shaftesbury—to impose a rigid ideological uniformity upon the Whig movement. It is likely that such an attempt, had it been made, would have failed. But it is a point worth stressing that, in addition to various practical considerations that helped to preserve a diversity of viewpoints among the Whigs, much of the substantive argument of the Whig perspective depended upon a de facto acceptance of the diversity of opinion among individuals as an existentially given condition of social life. This presupposition provided an umbrella under which various claims for liberty were advanced.

In *English Liberties: or, the Free-Born Subject's Inheritance,* Henry Care insisted that "each man [had] a fixed Fundamental Right born with him, as to freedom of his person, and property in his estate, which he cannot be deprived of" except by his consent or his commission of some crime.[112] William Penn elaborated upon this claim in one of his exclusion tracts. The first of our "fundamental rights," Penn wrote, is the right to property; "that is, right and title to your own lives, liberties, and estates: in this every man is a sort of little Sovereign to himself." The second great fundamental right is "the power of making laws," by which, he explained, he meant that no law could be enacted "without your own consent" as given through Parliament. The third fundamental right, according to Penn, is the right of the people to share in the execution of the laws, the chief example of this being through the institution of a trial by a jury of their peers.[113] These points were also made in the House of Commons debates, where one member declared:

> The two great pillars of the government are parliaments and juries; it is this gives us the title of free-born Englishmen: for my notion of free Englishmen is this, that they are ruled by laws of their own making, and tried by men of the same condition with themselves.[114]

The phraseology of the Whig argument is interesting, for on the one hand, the claim is made for "fundamental rights," and on the other, it is advanced on behalf of "free Englishmen." The former was generally as-

[112] Care, *English Liberties*, pp. 2, 206.

[113] Penn, *England's Great Interest*, p. 2.

[114] *Debates relating to Popish Plot*, p. 4.

sociated with a natural rights/natural law position, while the latter employed the concept of the "ancient constitution" as a means of justifying the rights of Englishmen. Most Whigs were quite content to advocate both types of argument as the occasion demanded, and in fact, to regard the notion of "English liberty" simply as a specification of a general claim they wished to make about the natural freedom of all individuals. This was clearly Shaftesbury's position. In one parliamentary speech he could refer to the fact that "all the Northern countries have, by their laws, an undoubted and inviolable right to their liberties and properties."[115] In another speech, he could appeal to the Magna Charta as a source of English liberty.[116] And in other speeches, Shaftesbury did not hesitate to affirm that it was "the Law of Nature" that guaranteed the liberties and properties of individuals and that also supplied the basic framework for "the Constitution of our government."[117]

In *Plato Redivivus*, Henry Neville asserted that "the people by the fundamental laws, (that is, by the constitution of the government of England) have an entire freedom in their lives, properties, and their persons."[118] This is not simply a historical claim for English liberty. In any case, Neville's admission that "government is more ancient than history" would make this view a difficult one to defend.[119] For, when Neville argues for the people's "exercise of that power, which is fallen to them by the law of nature," he establishes a clear priority for natural law claims.[120] In the second part of his *History of Whiggism*, Hickeringill declared that "*the very essence* of the government" or "the *common law*" could be appealed to, and that such an argument "is of *more value than any statute*; and of which *Magna Charta* and other statutes are but declaratory."[121] And, if a bridge were required to connect these two arguments, Hickeringill referred his reader to Coke and to the author of the *Mirror of Justice* who, he maintained, had demonstrated the inseparable link between a natural law and a statute law viewpoint.[122] Similarly, the anonymous author of *Fundamental Law the True Security of Sovereign Dignity and the*

[115] Shaftesbury, speech (March 25, 1679), p. 2.

[116] *The Case of Anthony Earl of Shaftesbury*, 1679, p. 14; Shaftesbury, speech (October 20, 1675), p. 210.

[117] Shaftesbury, speech (October 20, 1675), p. 205.

[118] Henry Neville, *Plato Redivivus*, 2d ed., 1681, in *Two English Republican Tracts*, ed. Caroline Robbins, Cambridge: Cambridge University Press, 1969, p .130. Though it is not included in his final library catalog, Locke did own a copy of *Plato Redivivus*, which he lent to Tyrrell in 1681 (MS c.1, fol. 412).

[119] Neville, *Plato*, pp. 84–85.

[120] Neville, *Plato*, p. 145.

[121] Hickeringill, *Works*, 1:131.

[122] Hickeringill, *Works*, 1:144.

People's Liberty observed that the Magna Charta was merely a specific declaration of the freedoms to which English subjects were entitled according to the Law of Nature. Thus, "the Fundamental Law of England" to which "every Free-born Englishman" could appeal on behalf of his liberties was unquestionably grounded upon a natural law guarantee that such an appeal was a valid one.[123]

In other words, instead of preoccupying themselves with establishing ancient constitution or natural law arguments as Weberian ideal types that are then abstracted from the context of the political debate as it actually existed at a particular time, historians of political thought would be better advised to treat the differences between the two approaches in terms of the tactical advantages to be gained from the employment of one or the other of these rights claims in a particular instance. This question, however, cannot be answered except by specifying what, concretely, the advantages to be gained were, and by what social groups or segments of a political movement. In the exclusion crisis, as I have already intimated, there was a drift in the debate away from a legalistic defense of Parliament's statutory right as part of the ancient constitution to pass a law excluding the Duke of York toward a greater emphasis upon the natural law foundation for this exercise of parliamentary power. In part, the Whigs were forced onto this ground by the ideological position developed by their Royalist opponents, especially after the publication of *Patriarcha*, and in part, more of them adopted the language of natural law because the extremity of the practical dangers posed by a popish conspiracy compelled them to defend themselves with the ultimate weapons of political warfare supplied by a natural law perspective. Indeed, the metaphor is an apt one, since virtually no one doubted the existence of a natural law deterrent that could be employed against one's political opponents if conventional arguments failed to convince, but whether the former ought to be resorted to depended very much upon the nature of the ideological warfare prevailing at the time. Thus, while it is perfectly legitimate to speak in terms of a shift of emphasis or a tendency to rely more upon one form of the Whig argument than the other, it is misleading to posit a dichotomy between the two. One reason the natural law argument supporting the radical Whig position was so powerful was that it could never be wholeheartedly rejected, even by those who preferred to identify their own perspective with the language of the ancient constitution argument. Moreover, some radical Whigs (Robert Ferguson, for example) never did see

[123] *Fundamental Law the True Security of Sovereign Dignity and the People's Liberty*, 1683, pp. 95ff., 141. Delamere was another radical who believed that "the Saxon principles" of the Constitution and the Law of Nature were merely two expressions of the same point (*Works*, p. 560).

any reason not to put forward both arguments simultaneously, perhaps on the consciously recognized grounds that this was, in fact, the way in which most Whigs thought about their "liberties."[124]

One part of the English Constitution, it was suggested, affirmed that "any free subject hath a fundamental liberty to choose knights and burgesses; and accordingly to inform them of their grievances, and petition them for redress."[125] The first half of this statement was, potentially, a contentious claim, since it could have produced a serious division within the ranks of the Whig supporters. Sir William Jones, for example, told the Commons that those who were "not able to pay towards the charge of the government . . . ought not to have liberty of choice of representatives . . . I would have substantial men choose representatives."[126] Jones was answered immediately, however, by another Whig, who insisted that "by common right, all ought to have voices of election in boroughs *sui juris*. He that is worth twenty shillings is as much rated, according to his proportion as he that is worth twenty thousand pounds. . . . It is not what the man pays" toward the maintenance of government, which is merely an accident of his condition, but rather, his common right by nature that defines the meaning of this fundamental liberty.[127] Jones based his argument upon the legalistic appeal to the statute enfranchising forty-shilling freeholders, while his interlocutor appealed over the head of that statute to a common right. For reasons already suggested, both viewpoints expressed the Whig position, and this direct exchange on the suffrage was an exceptional departure from the prevailing ambiguity concerning the

[124] According to Ferguson, our rights and liberties might be more "distinctly expressed" through the Magna Charta or parliamentary statutes, but these were only "acknowledgments . . . of what we had reserved unto ourselves in the original institution of our government"; that is, the rights individuals could claim in a state of nature from natural law (Robert Ferguson, *A Brief Justification for the Prince of Orange's Descent into England*, 1688, pp. 12–13). It was also Wildman's view that the Magna Charta was "only declarative" of the rights established by the Law of Nature, which was superior to all forms of law (John Wildman, *London's Liberties*, 1682, pp. 8–9). Later, in a radical defense of the Glorious Revolution, the same point was reaffirmed. The Magna Charta and other "legal expressions of the Constitution" are really "modifications" or expressions of the "Original Contract" of government. Thus, the author insisted, these two ways of referring to the Constitution "strengthen one another," and are mutually compatible (*The Revolution Vindicated*, in *A Collection of State Tracts*, 1705, 3 vols., 3:716). See below, Chapter 11, note 183. Indeed, the more one appreciates this viewpoint and its association with the radical tradition, the more clearly one can understand Locke's decision not to pursue the historical or legalistic approach to the rights claims he was defending in the *Two Treatises*.

[125] *The Nation's Address to the Committee of Grievances in Parliament for the Taking off the Corporation Oath*, 1680, in the Second Collection of *Somers Tracts*, 3:237.

[126] Grey, 8:127–128.

[127] Grey, 8:128.

question of who was entitled to participate in the political process. It was this ambiguity, I am arguing, which helped to preserve the practical unity of the Whig political movement; and the practical demands of organization, in turn, reinforced the ease with which the two types of theoretical arguments about liberty and rights were able to coexist among the Whigs.

Whatever divisions might have arisen over the issue of suffrage, had this brief exchange between individual Whigs become a matter of party debate, the "common natural right" of individuals to petition for a redress of grievances was a much more consensually accepted proposition, one to which the majority of the House of Commons was willing to lend its support.[128] Other rights claimed included the freedom of the press and the right to religious toleration. "Liberty of the press," one writer asserted, would bring "very great benefits and advantages to the people."[129] As for toleration, it hardly requires an extensive discussion here in order to make the point that a very large proportion of the Whigs viewed this objective as an essential aspect of their definition of liberty.

Aside from an elucidation of particular liberties due freeborn Englishmen, what was being claimed in the Whig political literature was that only certain forms of government were capable of guaranteeing the rights of liberty and property. This, too, was potentially a contentious issue if the divergence between Whig and Republican conceptions of government had grown as large as some later commentators have incorrectly assumed that it did.[130] What the Whigs were agreed upon was that liberty and

[128] Grey, 7:388. Sir Francis Wythens was expelled from the House of Commons for having denied the subject's right to petition (Grey, 7:391).

[129] Lawrence, *Marriage by Moral Law*, pp. 166–167.

[130] Because they have focused so exclusively upon models of government, none of the writers on republicanism have provided a clear line of demarcation between Republican and Whig political theory that, nevertheless, is capable of taking into account the actual variations and differences within each group. Fink's effort to separate "classical republicanism" from the Whig theory of the mixed constitution makes sense only if we note that during the heyday of classical republicanism (the 1640s), there were no Whigs, while following the triumph of the latter, virtually all Republicans believed in the theory of the mixed constitution (Zera S. Fink, *The Classical Republicans*, Evanston, Ill.: Northwestern University Press, 1945, pp. x, 183–185). No matter how she defines the "eighteenth-century commonwealthman," Caroline Robbins cannot dispose of Locke, especially since many of these Comonwealthmen display a propensity for quoting from him. She is certainly as wrong in attempting to place Locke "in direct descent" from "a long English legalist tradition" as she is in claiming that Sidney was more insistent upon the people's right to make a revolution than was Locke. The latter has no textual warrant whatsoever, and Robbins' own contextual discussion of the American revolutionaries shows that it has no historical basis either in any distinction between the two writers that *they* drew (Robbins, *Commonwealthman*, pp. 63–65; idem, "Algernon Sidney's *Discourses Concerning Government*: Textbook of Revolu-

property could not be secured under an absolute monarchy, and that a constitutional or limited government was the necessary alternative to this condition. Within this constitutional system, the legislature (Parliament) ought to have a very large—at least, a preponderant—share of the law-making power, the latter being rooted, of course, in the popular consent given by the electorate. Beyond that, opinions as to whether this was a Whig or a Republican definition of government, whether Parliament ought to have all the legislative power, whether "the people" included an identifiable collectivity that was larger than the electorate, whether the latter should be enlarged, and so on, depended upon whom one asked. And to repeat the point, the Whigs, for obvious political reasons, were not themselves especially eager to be drawn into a discussion of these particular questions. As we shall see in the next chapter, it was an important tactic employed by their Tory opponents to try to force or taunt them into articulating more specific answers, in the clear expectation that this would have the consequence of fostering the growth of sectarian ideological divisions within the Whig movement.

A constitutional government, the Whigs maintained, was one in which an individual was "preserved in an undisturbed possession of his civil rights."[131] This required not only "a just and equal constitution" or some form of express limitations upon the exercise of political power and some balance among the various components of the government, but also, it depended upon a broader set of social relations that supported the existence of a balanced government. Just as absolute monarchy was portrayed by the Whigs not merely as a perverse political system but as an oppressive way of life extending into every sphere of the subject's existence, so there were social institutions and practices that were more or less supportive of specific political claims to civil rights. For, as one Whig put it, "lib-

---

tion," *William and Mary Quarterly* 4 no. 3 [July 1947]:267–296). Similarly, the propensity of Weston and Greenberg, in *Subjects and Sovereigns*, to force all political debate into their dichotomous models of "the order theory of kingship" or the "community-centered view of government" (p. 22) not only obscures the complexities of the political debate in the 1670s and 1680s, but it also makes it particularly difficult to understand the position of Locke and the radicals, since either they are merged indistinguishably with all other "community-centered" Whigs or else they are omitted altogether from the discussion. In short, the attempt to understand the dimensions of Locke's political thought through a dichotomous framework that posits that he subscribed to a theory of "limited monarchy," while being "repelled by the republican theories of such men as Milton and Harrington," simply will not do (Sterling P. Lamprecht, *The Moral and Political Philosophy of John Locke*, New York: Russell and Russell, 1962, p. 140). Though I do not share his view of Locke, the most successful attempt to clarify the dimensions of Whig and Republican political thought is J.G.A. Pocock, *The Machiavellian Moment*, Princeton: Princeton University Press, 1975.

[131] William Penn, *One Project for the Good of England*, [1680], p. 2; Delamere, *Works*, pp. 467–468; Tyrrell, *Patriarcha non Monarcha*, p. 147.

erty is the foundation of virtue and industry; what does anything else signify without it?"[132] One reason a division between Whigs and Republicans cannot be pressed too far is that when constitutional government is viewed in terms of the wider socioeconomic context within which it was presumed to function, there was fairly wide agreement among exclusion Whigs as to what the ingredients of that context were and how, historically, the context itself had come about.

We have thus far examined the Whigs' rejection of absolute monarchy as an adjunct of the religious doctrines of Catholicism, and vice versa. However, absolute monarchy not only violated the moral conditions requisite for the maintenance of legitimate government, but, the Whigs insisted, it was also a form of government totally unsuited to the socioeconomic conditions of seventeenth-century England. The formulation of this argument can best be understood, I believe, if we ask ourselves why it was that Locke and other Whig critics of *Patriarcha* were willing to make such huge concessions to the historical claims of their opponents on the issue of absolute monarchy as the first form of government. The answer is that this concession was made as part of a historical argument that the Whigs developed in order to demonstrate that although Filmer's principles and the political institutions that they supported might have been suited to the socioeconomic conditions of primitive societies, they could not be adapted to the very different circumstances of contemporary England. In a sense, the Whigs were employing one maxim drawn from Aristotle's *Politics*—that political institutions must conform to the socioeconomic institutions—against their opponents who relied upon another proposition from that text—that monarchy was the original form of government, having arisen from an extension of the family under the rulership of a father.[133]

[132] Delamere, *Works*, p. 486.

[133] On the citation of Aristotle to support a patriarchal or divine right theory of government whose origins lay in the family, see for example, Jonathan Kimberly, *Of Obedience for Conscience-sake*, 1683, p. 4; Matthew Rider, *The Power of Parliaments in the Case of Succession*, 1680, p. 16; *True Protestant Subject*, pp. 6ff., 19; Brady, *Great Point*, p. 29. Other examples are discussed by Schochet (*Patriarchalism*, pp. 22–28), who also shows how other writers, such as George Lawson, following Hooker's interpretation of Aristotle, defended the view that more complicated forms of government were necessarily rooted in mutual consent (pp. 52, 160–161, 182). Northleigh cites Aristotle on the relationship between monarchy and the family, but notes, as Hobbes had before him, that "some of our democratics" have also "adored some part of his [Aristotle's] political observations," while ignoring the citations on monarchy (*Remarks upon Antimonarchical Authors*, p. 634). One of those authors, Peter Allix, makes it very clear that he is citing Aristotle's *Politics* specifically in order to demonstrate that different forms of government must be suited to the choice and different conditions of the people (*Reflections upon the Opinions of Some Modern Divines Concerning the Nature of Government in General, and That of England in Particular*, 1689, p. 11 (*LL* #1297).

Regardless of how many times the Tories repeated the proposition that in primitive times kings exercised absolute power, Whig critics could undermine the force of the assertion by agreeing with it, and by incorporating it into their own argument. In *The Power of Kings from God*, the Filmerian author observed:

> That patriarchal government, or the ruling of the father or eldest of the family over the rest was the first form of government in the world, I think is generally owned.[134]

Indeed it was, by virtually all of the exclusion Whigs. Absolute monarchy, James Tyrrell conceded, is "the primitive government of the world."[135] Tyrrell went on to say that although "it is likely that commonwealths were first instituted by fathers of families, having wives, children, and slaves under their domestic government," this proposition did not lead to a conclusion supporting the legitimacy of absolute monarchy, as Filmer supposed it did.[136] William Penn provides a summary account of this consensus:

> If the true ground and rise of government be considered . . . all lawyers and statesmen derive the first grounds of government from the posterity of Noah's sons after the Flood, and do show how through necessity, reason and the Law of Nature led them thereunto . . . and this all lawyers generally acknowledge was the first foundation of civil government, in the joint agreement of several families. . . . Now as in the first part of government in families, the authority stood in one, viz., in the father of the family, so they usually chose one for the government of joint families, who thence were called kings; and this was the original of monarchy.[137]

This point is restated by Locke in the *Two Treatises*:

> I will not deny, that if we look back as far as history will direct us towards the original of commonwealths, we shall generally find them under the government and administration of one man. And I

[134] Paul Lathom, *The Power of Kings from God*, 1683, p. 27; *True Protestant Subject*, p. 25; Brady, *Great Point*, pp. 27ff.; Thomas Comber, *Religion and Loyalty Supporting Each Other*, 1681, pp. 10–12; Adam Littleton, *Sixty-One Sermons*, 1680, pp. 36, 233; Filmer, pp. 79, 107, 231, 304.

[135] Tyrrell, *Patriarcha non Monarcha*, p. 259; cf. ibid., pp. 47, 60, 73–74, 83; *Three Great Questions*, p. 5.

[136] Tyrrell, *Patriarcha non Monarcha*, pp. 35, 60, 83, 95.

[137] William Penn, *The Great Question to Be Considered by the King and This Approaching Parliament*, [1680], p. 2 (*LL* #2255a). See also John Pettus, *The Constitution of Parliaments in England*, 1680, p. 1; William Temple, *An Essay upon the Original and Nature of Government*, 1680, pp. 63, 67.

> am also apt to believe, that where a family was numerous enough to subsist by itself, and continued entire together, without mixing with others, as it often happens, where there is much land and few people, the government commonly began in the father.[138]

After pointing to "the people of America" as an example of individuals living under such conditions as he has described, Locke concludes:

> Thus, though looking back as far as records give us any account of peopling the world, and the history of nations, we commonly find the government to be in one hand. . . . But this having given occasion to men to mistake, and think, that by nature government was monarchical, and belonged to the father, it may not be amiss here to consider, *why* people in the beginning generally pitched upon this form . . . [of government].[139]

The fact that "no other sort of government did prevail in the world for the first three thousand years, but monarchy," was not, for the Whigs, the salient point.[140] Their argument maintained that "the increase of mankind, and necessity of commerce," the development of a money economy and different forms and amounts of property, and the growth of cities led to an increase in "controversies" among people, which required for their settlement a more complicated political system than that provided by absolute monarchy. "In ancient times," before the growth of cities, wrote the author of *The Constitution of Parliaments in England*, the making and executing of laws was a relatively simple matter that might be entrusted to an absolute monarch, but the growth of society necessitated "greater forms of government." Specifically, he argued, with the growth of cities the act of legislation became so complicated "there was a necessity to constitute a supreme council of the chiefest and wisest men selected from the multitude."[141] In *Three Great Questions Concerning the Succession and the Dangers of Popery*, the author writes that whether one accepts Aristotle's view or whether one begins from Scripture, "it will evidently appear that in all parts of the world Empire must have been monarchical at the beginning." However, he observes, "in the beginning the burden of a Crown was not so heavy, nor the cases so many," nor did the people have "written constitutions." But with "the great increase and spreading of mankind," it became necessary "to distribute some part of their [the kings'] power" to the people at large. Pop-

[138] *ST*, par. 105.

[139] *ST*, par. 106 (italics added).

[140] Foreness, *Sermon*, p. 7; Brydall, *Jura Coronae*, p. 140.

[141] Pettus, *Constitution*, pp. 1, 305; *Three Great Questions*, pp. 5–6.

ulation growth and a more complicated set of social relations among people thus marked the death of the "primitive institution" of absolute monarchy, where the prince's "will was their undisputed law."[142] "The paucity of people in the . . . first monarchies," William Petty wrote, made it easy to establish absolute monarchy as the first form of government. But with the growth of population, the rise of "great cities," and advancement in the arts and sciences, he asserted that the inappropriateness of this form of government becomes increasingly obvious to everyone. This, Petty informed his correspondent, was also the view of his friend, William Penn.[143] Indeed, in *The Great Question to Be Considered*, the latter had affirmed that "when the primitive simplicity and integrity of those first ages began to wear out, kings did extend and advance the authority they derived from their predecessors, but lost their equity and justice. . . . Thus monarchy degenerated into tyranny . . . which gave rise, as many judge, to the institution of commonwealths."[144]

To be sure, there is a moral tone to this condemnation of monarchy, shared by other Whigs, but the causal explanation they provided for the rise of this degeneration is clearly socioeconomic. In an account strikingly paralleled by Locke in the *Two Treatises*, Tyrrell explains that in primitive and "thinly peopled" societies, where subsistence is produced "only by the labor of the inhabitants in hunting, fishing, and the like employments" and the people have no need or desire of "superfluous things, . . . there is no need of enclosing or appropriating any more land than they really make use of." Since their possessions are scanty, there are few controversies, and so, little need for government to act as an umpire in deciding them.[145] Referring to the Indians in America, as Locke did, to illustrate these "first ages" of human existence, Tyrrell argues that since "they have no distinct property in land . . . where land is worth nothing every man enjoys, by a tacit consent, a living . . . from hand to mouth, and taking care only to provide mere necessaries of life, as they never have any superfluities, so they have no disputes about them . . . so that one of the main ends of a supreme power among us, viz., to decide controversies about property, and punish thieves, are there of no use."[146]

This was also the argument employed by William Temple in *An Essay upon the Original and Nature of Government*. Monarchy, he wrote, derives from the tacit consent of members of a family to be governed by a father, but it can only arise in thinly populated areas where the people are

[142] *Three Great Questions*, p. 6.

[143] *The Petty-Southwell Correspondence, 1676–1687*, London: Constable, 1928, pp. 93, 153–155, 166–168.

[144] Penn, *Great Question*, p. 2.

[145] Tyrrell, *Patriarcha non Monarcha*, p. 153.

[146] Tyrrell, *Patriarcha non Monarcha*, p. 120.

poor and possess little or no property. Under such conditions, they exhibit little ambition or avarice, since they rarely have more than the bare necessities of life. Temple also instances the Indians in America to illustrate this point. Hence, he adds, they "examine not the nature or the tenure of power and authority."[147] Life is very different in commonwealths, Temple argues, which are based upon "rich and populous cities" governed by assemblies of some form. Within this political system, people are conscious of the need to protect themselves and their property from "arbitrary rules" laid down by a monarch. Thus, Temple contends, there are two kinds of governments in the world: those based upon popular consent (commonwealths) and those based upon the arbitrary rule of one man (absolute monarchy). Although there still remain some instances of the latter in the seventeenth century, it is the clear intent of Temple's *Essay* to demonstrate that the absolute monarchy he has described is a product of certain historical and sociological conditions that no longer prevail, at least in the "civilized" part of the world. At best, this form of government might have met the needs and conditions "of the old British nation," but it is wholly unsuited to the present conditions of seventeenth-century England.[148]

History, in other words, was divided into two rather sharply distinct stages. In the first, the population was small, men "wandered freely up and down," possessions "would not be very large," human needs and desires were confined, "so that it was impossible for any man, this way, to entrench upon the right of another, or acquire, to himself, a property to the prejudice of his neighbor"; and thus, "there would then be no reason of quarreling about title . . . no room for controversy" about property.[149] For Locke, therefore, "the equality of a simple poor way of living confining their desires within the narrow bounds of each man's small property made few controversies and so no need of many laws to decide them." In this primitive form of society, the "first care" of the people was security against foreign invasion rather than the settling of domestic disputes. For this reason, monarchy was a "simple and most obvious" political solution to this problem, especially since the people "had neither felt the oppression of tyrannical dominion nor . . . the inconveniencies of absolute power," which is a danger endemic to a monarchy.[150] Not only were there no "express conditions limiting or regulating his [the king's] power," but there was no need in general for a "multiplicity of laws."[151] "In the in-

[147] Temple, *Essay*, pp. 49–52.

[148] Temple, *Essay*, pp. 47, 66–67.

[149] *ST*, pars. 36, 39, 51, 108; cf. ibid., par. 31.

[150] *ST*, pars. 107, 110–112.

[151] *ST*, par. 112. See also *Three Great Questions*, p. 6.

fancy of governments," Locke concludes, "when commonwealths differed little from families in number of people, they differed from them too but little in number of laws. . . . A few established laws served the turn, and the discretion and care of the ruler supplied the rest."[152]

In his chapter on property in the *Second Treatise*, Locke draws a sharp dividing line between the stage "where there is plenty of peopling under government, who have money and commerce," and an unequal distribution of landed property, and that stage "in the beginning and first peopling of the great common of the world," when "it was quite otherwise."[153] The turning point, of course, was "the invention of money, and the tacit agreement of men to put a value on it."[154] In accounting for this phenomenon, Locke writes,

> As families increased, and industry enlarged their stocks, their possessions enlarged . . . till they incorporated, settled themselves together, and built cities, and then, by consent, they came in time, to set out the bounds of their distinct territories, and agree on limits between them and their neighbors, and by laws within themselves, settled the properties of those of the same society.[155]

Coupled with this demographic shift in social existence, Locke argues, it is "commerce with other parts of the world" that both explains and justifies the invention of money and the enlargement of possessions beyond the boundaries of need or subsistence.[156]

When Locke speaks, therefore, of the "unforeseeing innocence of the first ages" or "the innocence and sincerity of that poor but virtuous age," these moral characterizations are premised upon the socioeconomic observation that "want of people and money gave no temptation to enlarge their possessions of land, or contest for wider extent of ground," which, in turn, meant that there was "no contest betwixt rulers and people about governors or government."[157] Without the "temptation" associated with

[152] *ST*, par. 162.

[153] *ST*, par. 35.

[154] *ST*, pars. 36, 48–50.

[155] *ST*, pars. 38, 45. Dunn is mistaken in his contention that Locke never specified various forms of social or political relationships "in terms of empirical criteria of social simplicity or complexity," or that he had no interest in providing historical examples or putting forward a sociological argument as part of his theory of the origins of government (John Dunn, *Political Obligation in its Historical Context*, Cambridge: Cambridge University Press, 1980, pp. 32, 46).

[156] *ST*, par. 48.

[157] *ST*, pars. 94, 108, 110, 111. In the first ages, "there could then be no reason of quarreling about title, nor any doubt about the largeness of possession it gave. Right and conveniency went together" (*ST*, par. 51).

a developed commercial economy, virtue and absolute monarchy might very well coexist. With the invention of money, expansion of trade, and growth of cities, however, political power must concomitantly undergo an expansion.

Thus, in his attack upon Filmer's historical account of the development of government, Locke adheres to the principle that the expansion of political power is a direct consequence of the increase in wealth.

> Those who were rich in the patriarch's days, as in the West Indies now, bought men and maid servants, and by their increase as well as purchasing of new, came to have large and numerous families, which they made use of in war and peace, can it be thought the power they had over them was an inheritance descended from Adam, when it was the purchase of their money?

Political power is gained, Locke concludes, not by "descent and inheritance," but rather, "by bargain and money."[158] This is an important point, and it is a direct refutation of Filmer's assumption of an indistinguishable and unchanging unity between political and economical forms of power. Filmer refused to accept that there could be any distinction between the two such that changes in one form of power could produce or necessitate changes in the other. Economical power, he argued, does not "really and essentially differ from political" power. Since "the kinds of power are not distinct," it followed for Filmer that any political power granted to Adam remained unaffected by the "accidental difference by the amplitude or extent of the bounds of the one beyond the other," for example, by the growth of a commercial economy, cities, and so forth.[159]

The form of government that Locke wishes to defend, however, is a specific outgrowth of a theory of history and politics that presupposes that the economical development of mankind produces its own natural tendencies or causal forces that redirect individuals' attitudes and activities with respect to political institutions. And, in particular, this development finds its material expression in the changing forms of property.

> The preservation of property being the end of government, and that for which men enter into society, it necessarily supposes and requires, that the people should *have property*.[160]

The author of *Fundamental Law* . . . presents the commonplace picture of "the primitive ages of the world," which were "void of all extravagant desires," when the people could live simply, following the dictates of the

[158] *FT*, par. 130.
[159] Filmer, p. 78.
[160] *ST*, par. 138.

Law of Nature, and so on. However, when "the world was vastly stored with people" whose "stocks" and property had "greatly increased" as well as the people's "ambition" and "profit," then, he argues, "there was an absolute necessity of written ordinances and constitutions." Thus, the people "began . . . to think of framing laws and ordinances for the better government of so numerous [a] commonweal." That is, they "made laws and constitutions for the safety and security of right and property," which they had now acquired as a consequence of their socioeconomic development. The latter, in short, supplied the material foundations for all "well-constituted governments."[161]

To summarize the argument: Because people have unequal amounts of property and accumulated capital (money), because there are controversies over titles and property rights and disputes arising out of contractual arrangements established by bargain and money, because trade and commerce now play an important role in the advancement of civilization, power *must* shift away from the monarch into the hands of a representative assembly in order to provide that security and protection for property which is the rationale for the institution of civil society. As Locke explains this transition,

> [When] the negligent and unforeseeing of the ages . . . [ended and time] had brought in successors of another stamp, the people finding their properties not secure under the government, as it then was, (whereas government has no other end but the preservation of property) could never be safe nor at rest, *nor think themselves in civil society*, till the legislature was placed in collective bodies of men, call them Senate, Parliament, or what you please. By which means every single person became subject, equally with other the meanest men, to those laws, which he himself, as part of the legislative had established.[162]

Locke reiterates this point several times in the *Second Treatise*; a "well-ordered commonwealth" is, by definition, one in which the lawmaking power is in the hands of an elected representative assembly.[163] Moreover, as noted earlier, Locke is equally insistent upon the fact that "absolute monarchy is inconsistent with civil society," and therefore it is no form

[161] *Fundamental Law*, pp. 7-8, 25, 36–37.

[162] *ST*, par. 94. The alternative to absolute monarchy is a political system in which there is a "balancing [of] the power of government, by placing several parts of it in different hands" (*ST*, par. 107).

[163] *ST*, pars. 143, 153, 159, 213, 222. In a number of places, Locke simply presupposes the existence of an elected representative assembly and free elections as the basis for constitutional government.

of government at all.[164] Absolute monarchy, in other words, cannot provide that protection and security of property gained through bargain and money because it represents a form of political power that is not itself bounded by contractual limitations. Constitutional government, on the other hand, provides just such a limiting framework for political power, and that constitutional structure is supplied by the lawmaking or legislative power in the hands of the people being placed with an assembly of their elected representatives who act on their behalf. This political outcome is not only in itself morally desirable; it is also historically and practically necessary when political institutions are viewed within the broader social context within which they function. Thus, it is axiomatic for the Whigs that absolute monarchy simply cannot supply the basis for improvement in the "arts and sciences, and the conveniencies of life," nor for the expansion of riches and trade, which Locke assumes are desired goals for his countrymen.[165]

William Petty thought there was a kind of natural law at work underlying this development that would make the objective of establishing an absolute monarchy "(whatever the King of France may think) . . . grow every century more and more difficult by the course of nature."[166] Defoe later stated the point poetically in his *Jure Divino*:

> While in the infant-ages of the King
> Nature to first paternal rule confirmed
> The men untainted, and their number few
> The patriarchal government might do
> . . . There can be no pretense of government
> Till they that have the property consent.[167]

Henry Neville, following Harrington, presents the economic argument for this position more or less directly, without the anthropological dimension employed by Locke and other Whigs. In *Plato Redivivus*, Neville begins by citing the "basic principle" that the form of government changes whenever the distribution of land changes. He concludes that, because more and more land has passed from the aristocracy into the hands of "the lesser gentry and the commons" during the last two centuries, "it has made the country scarce governable by monarchy."[168] In-

[164] *ST*, pars. 90, 137, 174.

[165] *FT*, pars. 33, 41.

[166] *Petty-Southwell Correspondence*, p. 93.

[167] Cited in Schochet, *Patriarchalism*, p. 216.

[168] Neville, *Plato*, pp. 88, 94–95, 144. Algernon Sidney also makes the point, noting that the "ancient nobility" have lost their position in society, and hence, their political power. Now they are simply individuals with "empty titles . . . deprived of all privileges such as

deed, the king, having suffered the same fate as the rest of the landowning aristocracy with this shift in economic power, is *already* exercising more political power than his status as a property owner would warrant, according to Neville. In his dependency upon Parliament for grants of money, it was evident to Neville that the king "must have a precarious revenue out of the people's purses."[169] It was precisely on the basis of such realistic assumptions regarding the distribution of economic and political power that the Whigs believed that their withholding of parliamentary grants of money to Charles II would eventually force him to agree to their exclusion bill.

Algernon Sidney, who also incorporated much of Harrington's argument into his *Discourses*, generalized the Whig attitude toward the distribution of political power. All human institutions, Sidney wrote, need to be revised and adapted to changing circumstances.

> Changes therefore are unavoidable, and the wit of man can go no farther than to institute such, as in relation to the forces, manners, nature, religion or interests of a people.[170]

Political institutions, John Somers declared, must be "molded into several forms agreeable to [the people's] interests and dispositions," and in accordance with "the variety of accidents in several ages" that have shaped those interests and dispositions.[171] Numerous exclusion pamphlets repeated this argument, both in its general and in its specific formulations. To the Whigs, it was obvious that changes in the socioeconomic conditions of a people required concomitant changes in political institutions. As Hickeringill stated the point pithily in the *History of Whiggism*, different men and different manners require different constitutions.[172] "If it be lawful for us . . . to build houses, ships and forts, better than our

---

were common to them with their grooms. Such a stupendous change being in process of time insensibly introduced, the foundations of that government which they had established were removed, and the superstructure overthrown." Thus, the old "balance" of power is broken, and the real battle is now between the king and the Commons. It is this shift in the distribution of economic resources, Sidney argues, that explains "the perpetual jarrings" between the respective socioeconomic interests, and the division of the nation into conflicting factions (*Discourses*, chap. 3, sec. 37).

[169] Neville, *Plato*, pp. 135, 175.

[170] A. Sidney, *Discourses*, chap. 2, sec. 13, 17. Thus, "the laws that may be good for one people are not for all, and that which agrees with the manners of one age, is utterly abhorrent from those of another" (chap. 3, sec. 25).

[171] John Somers, *A Brief History of the Succession*, 1681, pp. 15–16; J.D., *A Word Without Doors Concerning the Bill for Succession*, n.d., pp. 4, 8 (*LL* #3185a; I have used the copy in the British Library, Add. MS 22589).

[172] Hickeringill, *Works*, 1:7.

ancestors . . . and to invent printing," Sidney asked, "why have we not the same right in matters of government?"[173] That, indeed, was the central point, for it was changes in population growth, forms of property, and trade and commerce that were the crucial factors underlying the need for a form of government other than absolute monarchy, whose suitability the Whigs willingly limited to the primitive ages of human existence.

Directly or indirectly, therefore, the Whigs tied their defense of parliamentary power to the peculiar socioeconomic characteristics of a commercially developed society. For them, the latter social context, which they identified with seventeenth-century England, ruled out any possibility of establishing absolute monarchy as a form of government. Whatever the challenges on the level of moral obligation posed by Filmer's appeal to natural law, his political theory, in its historical and practical dimensions, was, according to the Whigs, a piece of quaint nostalgia for a way of life that had long since disappeared.

Thus, a broad, multidimensional, and interwoven political theory supplied the contextual meaning for particular arguments, seen as elaborations of the political slogans No Popery, No Slavery and Liberty and Property used by the Whigs during the exclusion crisis. As Roger L'Estrange remarked, the exclusion debate brought together arguments from nature, Scripture, law, history, custom, and reason.[174] The arguments against Catholicism were joined with those against absolute monarchy, just as arguments against the latter were linked with a defense of private property, trade, and the power of Parliament. Within a rather widely understood framework, there flowed a social language, which served to knit together the stated and unstated presuppositions and arguments of particular books and pamphlets for the audience caught up in this political conflict.

There is a very interesting illustration of this "social language" in a series of unpublished letters exchanged during the exclusion crisis between two friends, one of whom was a Whig and the other a Tory. The correspondence is instructive not only because it restates many of the points and arguments discussed in the preceding pages, but also because, although these letters are focused upon the issues of the exclusion debate, they incorporate a consideration of the problems central to the controversies over epistemology, toleration, and the nature of religion, discussed in Chapters 2 and 3. The correspondence evidently begins with a

[173] A. Sidney, *Discourses*, chap. 3, secs. 7, 25.

[174] Roger L'Estrange, *The Case Put, Concerning the Succession of His Royal Highness, the Duke of York*, 1679, p. 1.

letter (not included in the collection) from Mr. Codrington, a Whig at Bristol, to his friend, White Kennett, at Oxford, referring to a book that had been highly recommended to him by various friends as an excellent refutation of Filmer's *Patriarcha*. The first letter in this correspondence, recorded in Kennett's letterbook, is the latter's reply to Codrington's inquiry. Kennett wrote to his friend that the work to which he referred "is I suppose a late pamphlet-like treatise entitled *Patriarcha non Monarcha* in opposition to the learned endeavor of that incomparable politician, Sir Robert Filmer."[175] As to the argument itself, Kennett defends the patriarchal theory of government against what he calls the "Republican" notion of a mutual compact. He also takes a few passing swipes at Hobbes' "unaccountable whimsy of a state of war." The latter he regards as being an affront to God's dignity and the Christian version of man's creation, although Kennett does not shrink from cribbing a Hobbesian definition of "anarchy," which, he insists, is the alternative to an acceptance of the patriarchal theory of the origins of government.[176] Codrington replies, brushing Hobbes aside, with a disclaimer that society is born out of the necessity of conflict—a war of all against all. On the contrary, he argues, man is sociable by nature and is originally a member of a natural moral community. The individual is capable of exercising his reason, and of providing for his self-preservation according to the Law of Nature. Though he does not mention Hooker by name, Codrington certainly intimates that he is following the path marked out by that thinker, especially when he describes the establishment of civil society as "the best use and improvement of our rational faculty." Codrington defends the view of government as instituted "by the mutual consent of the people," which, he maintains, is more consonant with the dictates of natural law than is the argument based upon paternal authority. After stating the Whig theory of government, Codrington moves on to raise a question as to what extent human laws can be presumed to oblige an individual's conscience to obedience.[177]

Kennett replies that "you have succinctly epitomized the whole scope

[175] Landsdowne MS 960, fols. 45–48 (January 11, 1682). There are a number of Codringtons from the Bristol area, but this individual is probably Richard Codrington. He was at Oxford between 1678 and 1682, and received his B.A. on March 9, 1682 (Joseph Foster, *Index Ecclesiasticus*, 1890). A Reverend Richard Codrington (probably a relative) is mentioned in the will of Christopher Codrington, who was a friend of Locke (Vincent T. Harlow, *Christopher Codrington, 1668–1710*, Oxford: Clarendon Press, 1928, pp. 99–100, 219).

[176] Landsdowne MS 960, fols. 46–48. In the fall of 1680, Kennett's tutor had advised him to read "Sir Robert Filmer's incomparable Treatise [*Patriarcha*]" (G. V. Bennett, *White Kennett, 1660–1728*, London: Society for the Promotion of Christian Knowledge, 1957, p. 5).

[177] Landsdowne MS 960, fols. 48–49 (February 6, 1682).

of the question" regarding the nature and origins of government. This topic, however, is left at its existing state of development and is not further pursued. Instead, Kennett takes up the issue of the individual's obligation to obey the law. To this problem, he observes, three possible answers, or grounds of obligation are generally offered: A papist holds to the prudential, self-interest view; the orthodox Anglican position requires complete obedience (the grounds of which are not spelled out); and the Dissenters argue for a satisfaction of individual conscience.[178]

From a consideration of this problem, the discussion quite logically proceeds to the subject of natural law, and the origins of moral standards. It is at this point that Kennett attempts bring in the "judicious Hooker" on his side of the argument. There is a not very successful attempt by Kennett to reconcile his belief that "the rules of good and evil are so wholly dependent on God's will that he can alter the nature of each at his pleasure" with the proposition that "things themselves are so essentially and unalterably" good and evil because there is a standard of eternal reason that has established this distinction.[179] From the nature of God, morality, and natural law, the correspondence moves on to the problem of accounting for the diversity of opinions among individuals respecting matters of religion. The correspondents are especially concerned with finding some boundary line between faith and opinion, and this raises the question, What is knowledge? In order to answer this question, Kennett maintains, we must have some clear conception as to the nature of "the understanding" and how it relates to our acquisition of knowledge. He concedes "the metaphysical intricacy of the question" he has raised, but he argues that there can be no doubt as to its importance and its relevance to the discussion of toleration and to the general argument between himself and Codrington.[180]

The latter agrees as to the importance of the major topics that must be dealt with, and, he argues, in the course of discussing the nature of human understanding, we need "to distinguish between the difference of a certainty concerning religion, and those things that respect our faith, and those objects about which our senses are conversant."[181] The problem thus is to find that formulation which will clearly delineate the dimensions of human existence accessible to reason, faith, and sense experience, within a generally acceptable framework of Christian belief. Codrington goes on to offer his own views on the nature of the universe, the eternity of matter, the proof of God's existence according to the argument from

178 Landsdowne MS 960, fols. 50–53 (March 23, 1682).

179 Landsdowne MS 960, fols. 56–59 (May 4, 1682).

180 Landsdowne MS 960, fols. 67–70 (July 3, 1682).

181 Landsdowne MS 960, fols. 70–72 (July 18, 1682).

design, and several more "metaphysical intricacies." Interestingly, slightly bewildered by the scope of the problems now being addressed, Codrington observes that anyone who could make his way through the "labyrinth of difficulties" these issues raise for philosophy (which, he maintains, Descartes' philosophy has failed to do) would certainly perform a considerable service for the advancement of human knowledge.[182]

My account of the correspondence between these two intelligent and highly articulate individuals is necessarily an exceedingly schematic one. But it does indicate, I think, how the issues of political theory extended easily and imperceptibly into the discussion of toleration, matters of morality, theology, epistemology, and philosophy. As Kennett remarks in one of his letters, toleration and liberty of conscience in religion "are as plausibly cried up as liberty and property in the state, and indeed each from the same cause and with the same effect."[183] In this respect, the debate concerning toleration, especially as it was formulated during the 1670s, merged with the political debate over exclusion in the 1680s. It is perhaps of no little interest to note that at the end of Kennett's letterbook is an abstract he made of Samuel Parker's *Discourse of Ecclesiastical Polity*, whose arguments he obviously regarded as being useful and relevant to his correspondence with Codrington.[184]

[182] Landsdowne MS 960, fols. 89–91 (October 18, 1682).
[183] Landsdowne MS 960, fols. 67–70.
[184] Landsdowne MS 960, fols. 148–150.

6

CLASS CONFLICT AND ELECTORAL POLITICS

SINCE there were three national elections held during the exclusion crisis—more than were staged during any two-year period in English history—the Whig arguments discussed in the previous chapter were primarily, though not exclusively, addressed to the electorate. When these arguments are viewed as part of an election campaign, they take on a sharper and more polemical character than can be conveyed merely from a consideration of the substantive nature of these shared presuppositions as expressed in the political literature of the Whigs. As election propaganda, these Whig tracts and sermons attempted to establish a linkage between particular intellectual arguments and the interests of members of specific socioeconomic groups for whom these arguments were assumed to be especially salient. Moreover, it is possible, when these arguments are seen within the polemical context of an electoral struggle, to gain some appreciation of the efficacy of particular arguments with respect to their appeal to various groups of voters, especially if one takes into account the kinds of responses formulated by Tory opponents seeking to neutralize the effects of such appeals.

Referring to the two main political slogans of the Whig movement, the author of *Achitophel's Policy Defeated* observed that "under the guise of property and public good," Shaftesbury hoped to "prevail with those to come over to the party, who were honest and industrious," while the attacks on popery and arbitrary government were especially aimed at the landed gentry and the "well descended."[1] Though from a critic, this is a shrewd and accurate description of the bifurcated strategy adopted by the Whigs. They wanted to forge an alliance between merchants, tradesmen, artisans, shopkeepers, *and* yeoman farmers and the gentry. As their critics were to argue, and as events were to demonstrate, this proved to be an exceedingly difficult task, especially when the movement, under Shaftesbury's leadership, moved further and further in the direction of revolution.

In their election propaganda, the Whigs openly appealed to freeholders and burgesses to choose "men of industry and improvement," that is,

[1] *Achitophel's Policy Defeated*, 1683, p. 18.

"laborers to propagate the growth of the country."[2] William Penn warned that if the interests of "trade, populacy, and wealth" were not looked after, it would mean "the utter ruin of thousands of traders, artifacers, and husbandmen."[3] Henry Care, addressing himself to the citizens and freemen of cities and corporations, used exactly the same phrases in his advice on electing representatives to Parliament.[4] Representatives, it was urged, should be chosen to represent "your qualities as well as your persons."[5] "It being natural to all men to seek their own profit," another Whig advised, cities, market towns, and corporations ought to elect representatives who will protect their interests, rather than country gentlemen, "who will be sure to prefer their particular interests before that of trade."[6] Hence, in the coming election, towns should choose as representatives only those men "who live and subsist by trade, and whose interests are bound up with it." For how can individuals "be supposed to understand perfectly the particular interest of these towns in which perhaps they never set foot but at elections? What reason have tradesmen to hope that strangers, not concerned in trade, should be more concerned for their good, than men of their own body, obliged by the same interest?" The author thus appealed to his readers to choose tradesmen rather than members of the nobility or gentry as their representatives.[7] Numerous exclusion pamphleteers urged their readers to pay special attention to "the private interests" of the candidates.[8] And at the same time, they endorsed the selection of those individuals who would defend the interests of trade and of those who "live by trade."[9] The general message was clear: Individuals follow their private interests, the interests of trade and commercial expansion must be defended, and Whig candidates must therefore be elected.

[2] William Penn, *England's Great Interest in the Choice of This New Parliament*, [1680], pp. 3–4; idem, *The Certain Way to Save England*, 1681, p. 11. "The traders of a nation ought to be most encouraged," since commercial expansion is the key to a country's greatness or wealth (Slingsby Bethel, *The Interest of Princes and States*, 1680, pp. 2–3).

[3] William Penn, *An Address to Protestants upon the Present Conjuncture*, 1679, pp. 196–197.

[4] Henry Care, *English Liberties: or, The Free-Born Subject's Inheritance*, 1682, p. 109. This point might be cited in favor of the claims of Penn's authorship of this tract, but see note 8 below.

[5] Penn, *Certain Way*, pp. 8–9.

[6] Bethel, *Interest of Princes*, p. 15.

[7] *Considerations Offered to All the Corporations of England*, 1681, pp. 3–5.

[8] *A Character of Popery and Arbitrary Government*, 1681, p. 5; Care, *English Liberties*, p. 108. The same wording and phrase is used in both tracts. Other instances of plagiarism relating these two works (recorded in notes 36, 62, 103, and 104 below) lead me to believe that Care is the author of both works.

[9] *Considerations Offered to Corporations*, p. 3.

Against Parker's attack in the *Discourse*, John Owen had defended the relationship between the advocacy of trade and a dissenting viewpoint in religion. This relationship became a frequently voiced platitude of social life (though not always with favorable connotations) in the exclusion tracts and sermons. Richard Baxter's view that "freeholders and tradesmen are the strength of religion and civility in the land" found many willing defenders among the Whig pamphleteers.[10] "Tradesmen," it was argued, "are a very substantial and useful part of a nation, and their way of living seems preferable to the living of gentlemen and husbandmen, as requiring more industry than the former, and more ingenuity than the latter."[11] "Dissenters," one Whig declared in an election tract, "have a great share in the trade, which is the greatness of this kingdom."[12] He did not actually ask the voters to elect a Dissenter to Parliament, but he was certainly defending the right of Dissenters as voters to send someone there who would look after their interests. The importance of toleration to trade was incorporated into the general Whig argument on behalf of "good" or "constitutional" government. For, "the chief things that promote trade and make it flourish are . . . freedom from arrests, certainty of property and freedom from arbitrary power"; in short, "a free and good government."[13] Since "trade must be the principal interest of England," another writer declared, it followed that "the traders of a nation ought to be most encouraged." But, he observed, "the advancement of trade . . . cannot be improved without liberty." Thus, "nothing makes countries rich but trade, and nothing increases trade but freedom."[14]

A very large proportion of Whig political propaganda, therefore, was aimed at "the common traders and dwellers in cities and corporations" who were expected to defend their own "civil interests" by supporting the claims of Parliament against the designs of the king and the Court.[15] Given "the vast number of cities, boroughs, and corporations . . . in comparison of the shires," it was not surprising to their opponents that

[10] Richard B. Schlatter, *The Social Ideas of Religious Leaders, 1660–1688*, London: Oxford University Press, 1940, p. 158.

[11] Schlatter, *Social Ideas*, p. 161.

[12] Penn, *Address to Protestants*, p. 199.

[13] Carew Reynell, *The True English Interest*, 1679, pp. 6, 71. "We have a particular high advantage over France in the nature of our government; under which liberty and property are by law, and public constitutions secured, which must be a vast encouragement to trade and traders" (William Petyt, *Britannia Languens*, 1680, p. 287; cf. ibid., pp. 3, 103, 141–142, 292).

[14] Bethel, *Interest of Princes*, pp. 2–3, 162.

[15] George Savile, *A Seasonable Address to Both Houses of Parliament Concerning the Succession, the Fears of Popery, and Arbitrary Government*, 1681, pp. 5, 11.

the Whigs had so large a number of active supporters.[16] As the Whigs claimed, and as their opponents conceded, it was "the trading part of the nation"—L'Estrange referred to merchants as the "cash-keepers to the tyrants at Westminster"—who formed the heart of their political movement.[17]

The Tories responded to the Whig arguments and to their general appeal to the commercial classes in a variety of ways. While it would be an oversimplification to assume that, as a group, Royalists were opposed to trade or commercial expansion in general, there was, nevertheless, a strong tendency in their writings to emphasize the negative features of commerce. In part, this was due to the fact that many of them associated trade with popular government, dissent, and sedition. "The Athenians," Filmer had written, "sold justice as they did other merchandise." Echoing Plato, he referred to popular government as "a fair where everything is to be sold."[18] Against this way of life, Filmer extolled the virtues of "a quiet and peaceable life in all godliness and honesty."[19] He then proceeded to show that popular commercial societies (Rome, Venice, and Holland, for example) did not foster or exhibit these virtues.[20] In this sense, there was a built-in predisposition in Filmer's political theory against the furtherance of the interests, values, and way of life of those groups and classes from which the Whigs drew so much of their support. Robert South spoke with open contempt of "the sober, industrious, trading part of the nation" because, like Samuel Parker, he saw them as fanatic opponents of the established order in the Church and State.[21] Other Tories referred to the "spiritual merchants" and "zealous hucksters" whose supposed concern for religion was merely a disguise for their real interests: "the care of their wealth and estates."[22] It was not so much that Anglicans or Royalists were against trade or commercial wealth as such; obviously, they were capable of recognizing the material advan-

[16] Thomas Comber, *Religion and Loyalty Supporting Each Other*, 1681, p. 7.

[17] *A Letter from a Student at Oxford to a Friend in the Country, Concerning the Approaching Parliament*, 1681, pp. 1–2; Roger L'Estrange, *An Answer to the Appeal from the Country to the City*, 1681, p. 15; Savile, *Seasonable Address*, p. 5; Schlatter, *Social Ideas*, pp. 158–169, 172; Jones, pp. 76, 162.

[18] Filmer, p. 89.

[19] Filmer, p. 207.

[20] Filmer, pp. 207–222.

[21] Schlatter, *Social Ideas*, p. 167. Even Robert Southwell, who William Petty said talked "like a man wedded . . . to the rural life," was suspicious of the growth of commerce, wealth, and cities because it would lead to a "melting down" of "the order of superiors among us and bring all towards levelling and Republican" values (*The Petty-Southwell Correspondence, 1676–1687*, London: Constable, 1928, pp. 235–236).

[22] Thomas Gipps, *The Nature of Subjection to the Civil Magistrate*, 1683, p. 57.

tages these activities brought to the nation. Rather, what disturbed them was the connection they perceived between a decline of the values to which many of them subscribed and the increase of the members of the "trading classes" who did not appear to respect or to share those values. As one Anglican clergyman put it, it was true that trade was "hugely advantageous to the public," but, he argued, at the same time, its pursuit seemed to produce in individuals what he called a "latitude of conscience" with respect to matters of religion. Although he had no wish to abolish the activities associated with commerce, even if this were possible, still he could not help but recognize that religion in general and the Anglican church's status in particular had been better off when "the more simple way of agriculture was attended to."[23]

Other Royalists, however, pursued more "progressive" lines of argument. They tried, for example, to expose the hypocrisy of the Whigs' attack upon arbitrary power exercised by the king by maintaining that this form of power was a common feature of various aspects of social life. In *The Complaint of Liberty and Property against Arbitrary Government*, John Nalson remarked that "to cry out against arbitrary government . . . has been set up as a mark and estimate of a true Protestant." Yet those "who make all this noise about it, are the most arbitrary principled persons in the world."[24] In denouncing the Whigs' reliance upon the principle of majority rule, some critics suggested that Whigs ought to apply this principle to their own family relationships in order to discover its unworkability.[25] Since the analogy between a family and a kingdom was a common one, Tory writers used it as part of an elemental appeal on behalf of "fatherly authority" against the democratic rhetoric of "obstinate children."[26] The Whigs were attempting to draw sharp distinctions between types of authority, as Locke, for example, does at the beginning of the *Second Treatise*.[27] Tories, however, were inclined to view authority as pyramidic, with an analogical—if not direct—relationship among the

[23] Schlatter, *Social Ideas*, pp. 164–165.

[24] John Nalson, *The Complaint of Liberty and Property against Arbitrary Government*, 1681, p. 1.

[25] Paul Lathom, *The Power of Kings from God*, 1683, p. 20; Roger L'Estrange, *The Interest of the Three Kingdoms*, 1680, p. 13. Sidney actually responds to this criticism in the *Discourses*: "For the question is not concerning the power that every householder in London hath over his wife, children, and servants; but whether they are all perpetually subject to one man and family; and I intend not to set up their wives, apprentices, and children against them" (Algernon Sidney, *Discourses Concerning Government*, 2 vols., 1805, chap. 2, sec. 9).

[26] *A Vote for Moderate Counsels*, 1681, p. 14; John Cave, *The Duty and Benefit of Submission to the Will of God in Afflictions*, 1682, pp. 6–7.

[27] *ST*, par. 2.

various levels of the pyramid. From that perspective, to argue for majority rule on one level of authority relationships but not on the others was inconsistent.

In the world of business, Fabian Phillips argued, arbitrary power is exercised daily by merchants, tradesmen, bankers, and artisans in their business dealings or over the membership of guilds, companies, or corporations. Something is wrong, Phillips complained, "when all the trades of London and Westminster . . . can by an unreasonable and arbitrary power . . . impose and put what price they please upon their work and commodities," and, "at the same time make heavy complaints against the king . . . and in all their discourses make hue and cry against arbitrary power." In tones that anticipate a later Tory radicalism, Phillips attacked the "sinful liberty and arbitrary power" exercised by "rich tradesmen" for "the raising of their prices . . . starving the workmen." And, more generally, he condemned the arbitrary power "daily made use of . . . [by] the rich over the poor."[28] In effect, these critics, recognizing the negative implications and appeal of the Whigs' assault upon arbitrary or absolute power in the political realm, were attempting to outflank their opponents by demonstrating that arbitrary power was exercised in other areas of social life (family relations, business) even by the Whigs themselves.

Some Royalists, recognizing that "foreign trade is the great support of England, and does so universally influence all men's estates, that we see they rise and fall in proportion with the actions of the merchants," asked, "what will then become of the East India, Guinea, African . . . companies, and of all the fraternities, guilds, and companies of trade in London . . . whose very essence and being depends upon the monarchy," if the Whigs are successful in weakening the power of that institution?[29] It is precisely the unsettled political situation, attributable to the disruptive politics of the Whigs, Edmund Bohun argued, that is most damaging to trade and economic investment. Because merchants are careful "to lodge their fortunes or a considerable part of them, in places that are better secured" than is England at the moment, not only have trade and investment declined, but, Bohun maintained, millions of pounds of capital have been exported out of the country. The Whigs, therefore, are responsible for the fact that "the wealth of the nation"—which they endeavor to identify with the realization of their own political policies—has been "insensibly wasted."[30] Thus, accepting the importance of trade, merchants,

[28] Fabian Phillips, *Ursa Major and Minor: or, A Sober and Impartial Enquiry into Those Pretended Fears and Jealousies of Popery and Arbitrary Power*, 1681, pp. 22–29, 46.

[29] *The Character of a Rebellion, and What England May Expect from One*, 1681, p. 13.

[30] Edmund Bohun, *The Second Part of the Address to the Free-Men and Freeholders of the Nation*, 1682, pp. ii–iii; *England's Concern in the Case of His Royal Highness, James*

commerce, and industry, some opponents of the Whigs sought to reverse the thrust of the Whig argument by associating these activities and the political stability necessary to their advancement with the power exercised by the king rather than with that claimed by Parliament.

The class-oriented arguments employed by the Whigs, which associated liberty and constitutional government with a defense of parliamentary power and the advancement of trade, were not only directed to their urban "bourgeois" supporters; they were also directed *against* a bankrupt, idle, and corrupted aristocracy, supported by a sycophantic clergy. It was one thing, the Whigs contended, to engage in the honest pursuit of one's private interests (commerce, for example), but it was quite another matter to be bribed or bought by the king as an instrument of his interest. The practice was not only morally offensive and deceptive; it also undermined the independence of Parliament and in effect, cheated the people out of their representative. A fierce attack was mounted by the Whigs against these "pensioners," which included the publication of a list containing their names.[31]

The Whig critique of the aristocracy as such, however, was a muted one, and it was generally expressed through indirect references. This was partly because not all pensioners or courtiers were aristocrats, and partly because many of the Whig leaders were members of this class. Still, in *An Address to Protestants upon the Present Conjuncture*, it was argued that the industry and wealth of the nation have to be defended against the excess, luxury, and waste indulged in by the sinful. The latter are not otherwise identified, although they are contrasted with the productivity and usefulness to the kingdom of the "traders, artifacers, and husbandmen."[32] Another Whig writer warned voters not to support those individuals who "are desperately in debt," even though they may be gentlemen or members of the nobility.[33] Trading corporations were urged to choose one of their own members as a representative rather than a member of the aristocracy.[34] Although the frequently offered warning to beware of those candidates who indulge in bribery or who spend money lav-

---

Duke of York, 1680, reprinted in the Second Collection of *Somers Tracts*, 4 vols., 1750, 3:252.

[31] *A Seasonable Argument to Persuade All the Grand Juries in England to Petition for a New Parliament*, 1677. This is a list of Court pensioners, which appeared prior to the exclusion elections, but was, of course, made much use of by the Whigs in their campaign. It is printed as appendix 3 in Cobbett, 4:xxii–xxxiv; *Popery and Arbitrary Government*, p. 6; Penn, *Certain Way*, p. 13; idem, *England's Great Interest*, p. 3. Also, see E. S. De Beer, "Members of the Court Party in the House of Commons, 1670–1678," *Bulletin of the Institute of Historical Research*, 11, no. 31 (June 1933):1–23.

[32] Penn, *Address to Protestants*, p. 33.

[33] *Popery and Arbitrary Government*, p. 6; Care, *English Liberties*, p. 100.

[34] *Considerations Offered to Corporations*, passim.

ishly upon voters cannot be taken as being exclusively aimed at the aristocracy, since its members were not the only persons who engaged in the practice, nevertheless, the general implication that Tory aristocrats are the primary targets of these warnings seems borne out by the frequency of their appearance in the Whig campaign literature and by the evidence relating to election practices in those parliamentary boroughs from which Tory aristocrats were most likely to seek election. As one Tory writer complained, the attack on the nobility had become so fierce in the pamphlet literature that it is difficult for some members of that class to be elected to Parliament.[35]

Occasionally, France was cited as an example of a country wholly dominated by the king and a court-directed aristocracy, with thinly veiled implications that this peril was closer to the shores of England than some might suppose.[36] Not everyone would have shared Sidney's blunt characterization of France as a country in which the produce "gained by the sweat of so many millions of men" is "torn out of the mouths of their starving wives and children" in order to feed the lusts of the French aristocracy and to support "those luxurious courts" maintained by them.[37] Still, the undertones of a disposition to view the aristocracy as a socially useless and economically exploitative class can be found in the Whig exclusion tracts. The exclusion elections produced a greater polarization of the nation along class-divided lines than anything had done since the Civil War itself.[38]

In addition to their direct attacks upon "the meaner sort of people," and the "pert tradesmen" who supported the Whigs, the Tories launched a more sophisticated (though no less class oriented) assault upon the fundamental assumptions of Whig political theory. One objective of the Tory critique was to undermine the effectiveness of Whig claims that their party in Parliament could speak on behalf of the people of the nation. As the Whigs put the point in one of their pamphlets,

> For if elections of members to serve in Parliament be the best standard to judge the disposition of the kingdom by, it is not so long since we had an opportunity of feeling the pulse of the nation, but that we

[35] Matthew Rider, *The Power of Parliaments in the Case of Succession*, 1680, p. 39.

[36] *Popery and Arbitrary Government*, p. 2; Care, *English Liberties*, pp. 1–2; Henry Neville, *Plato Redivivus*, 1681, 2d ed., in *Two English Republican Tracts*, ed. Caroline Robbins, Cambridge: Cambridge University Press, 1969, pp. 136–137.

[37] A. Sidney, *Discourses*, chap. 3, sec. 39. Locke did, however, record in his journal during his travels in France the observation that the landed nobility was largely exempt from paying taxes; hence the overwhelming burden of taxation fell upon the merchants and artisans—the producers of wealth (Fox-Bourne, 1:350). Also, see note 170 below for Locke's critique of the "luxuries of courts" and the "rich and noble."

[38] See Chapter 4, note 189, above.

may reasonably conclude, that all other things remaining as they did, the temper and complexion of the generality of the people is also much the same.[39]

In an effort to counter this identification of elections, Parliament, and "the generality of the people," the Tories sought to turn the Whig rhetoric of consent and representation against them. Those who subscribe to the view that political power is originally and radically in the people, George Hickes declared, cannot tell us "whether the supreme power belongs to all the people promiscuously, that have the use of reason, without any regard to sex or condition, or only to qualified persons, to men only, and men of such a condition and sort." And if men only are electors, by what right, Hickes asked, are women excluded? Moreover, are rich and poor to have equal shares of power? These "troublesome questions," as Hickes called them, had not been explicitly dealt with by the Whigs.[40] It is "obvious" to everyone, another writer noted, how "intolerable the mischief would be if all the freemen were admitted to a right of suffrage," or "if all the people or the freeholders of England were actually to have a vote in the passing of every law."[41]

In *Patriarcha non Monarcha*, Tyrrell had written that those "without any property in goods or land, had no reason to have votes in the institution of the government." At the same time, he asserted that, "as for all others who possessing no share in the lands or goods of a kingdom, yet enjoy the common benefits of the government, I conceive they are likewise to obey and maintain it." Tyrrell concedes that for those who presently exist in a state of poverty, obedience to government may "appear inconvenient for them, and the property now established contrary to their interests, as having perhaps little share in either lands or goods," but, he argues, they must nevertheless obey the constituted government, because to disturb the peace would violate natural law and introduce a state of war and anarchy.[42] Locke's argument in the *Two Treatises*, and the position adopted by most other Whigs, is much more ambiguous in its discussion of "the people" than is Tyrrell's statement. Instead of the latter's direct and rather conservative response, the Whigs generally formulated a perspective that, while incorporating the emphasis upon prop-

[39] *An Impartial Account of the Nature and Tendency of the Late Addresses in a Letter to a Gentleman in the Country*, 1681, pp. 7–8 (*LL* #23).

[40] George Hickes, *A Discourse of the Sovereign Power*, 1682, pp. 22–24; Rider, *Power of Parliaments*, pp. 3–4.

[41] John Turner, *A Sermon Preached before Sir Patience Ward . . . 1681, with Additions*, 1683, epistle dedicatory.

[42] James Tyrrell, *Patriarcha non Monarcha*, 1681, pp. 84, 86–87, 147; cf. ibid., pp. 76–77.

erty ownership as a rationale for political participation, also left indeterminate the membership status of individuals in the propertyless class. The specification of the nature of the political power in the hands of "the people," was, as Hickes perceived, a troublesome question for the Whigs. Not surprisingly, they preferred to remain unresponsive to the kinds of specific questions put to them by Hickes and other critics.

By far the most direct and effective attack upon the Whigs' ideological position was one aimed at separating the people from Parliament, with an argument that the latter could not in any meaningful sense be said to be "representative" of the former. As one critic observed,

> The Commons does not represent one sixth of the nation, their electors being only such freeholders as are worth 40s a year, or upwards, together with the freemen of incorporated places; these are far short of the body of the people; and for them to fetter the rest, who have none or less estates, is to make themselves lords and tyrants, and the others not servants, but slaves and villains.

Thus, those "whom we commonly call representatives are either not so at all; or if they be, do not derive their power from a third part of the nation."[43] One critic elaborated upon the basis for denying that Parliament could claim "an actual or virtual deputation or commission from every individual person" in the kingdom:

> For none have votes in elections but freeholders of at least forty shillings a year, and citizens and burgesses. . . . The greatest part of the clergy, all soldiers, and seamen in general, most the young servants, artifacers, and tradesmen . . . are totally excluded. . . . And what can be more unequal, not to say unjust, than that a numerous and . . . the far greatest part of the nation, that are passengers in the great ship of the commonwealth, as well as the rest, should be debarred their right of choosing a master or pilot to whose skill and care they commit their common safety? Have they not their liberty, their property, their religion . . . and must this, all this be left to the arbitrary power and discretion of such, as by chance . . . perhaps more

[43] *Three Great Questions Concerning the Succession and the Dangers of Popery*, 1680, p. 12; Lathom, *Power of Kings*, p. 21; B. Thorogood, *Captain Thorogood His Opinions of the Point of Succession, to a Brother of the Blade in Scotland*, 1680, p. 3; Rider, *Power of Parliaments*, p. 4. Filmer had made this argument in a general way in *Patriarcha* (*LL* #1122) and in his *Observations upon Aristotle's Politics*, pp. 118–119, 223ff., 252 (*LL* #1121). In the *Anarchy of a Limited or Mixed Monarchy*, however—a work with which Locke was familiar even before the republication of Filmer's works in 1679–1680—Filmer made the specific argument reproduced by later writers during the exclusion crisis (Filmer, p. 290).

> than merit, have acquired the possession of some land, or are free of boroughs and cities.

Furthermore, it was argued, in a representative government there ought to be some "proportion and equality" in the system of representation. Yet "we see no such thing, for the meanest borough, for example, Old Sarum, deputes as many men to serve in Parliament, as the greatest county in England." And, the author continued,

> Cornwall which is the two and fiftieth part of the kingdom, makes above an eleventh part of the House of Commons; and yet London, Southwark, and Westminster, which in the power of men and riches, is judged to be a sixth of the whole nation, is in the representative but the sixty-fourth part. And this solecism alone in the very constitution of the government will make it forever impossible to have the people represented in any just and rational manner.[44]

Thus, against the Whigs their critics repeatedly stressed these facts, concluding that "whoever weighs this inequality, must find out a new signification of words if he calls the Parliament the representative of all the commons of England."[45] Seen in perspective, and in relation to the reality of who "the people" of England actually were, the Tories argued that it was absurd to identify the former with "any artificial or fictitious majority of a quorum, as in the House of Commons."[46]

Nor were the Whigs insensitive to such criticisms. Locke, for example, makes a direct reply—albeit a partial one—to this Tory attack. Noting the "constant flux" of trade, riches, population, and wealth, Locke argues that shifts in these socioeconomic conditions explain why "representation becomes very unequal and disproportionate to the reasons it was at first established upon." He then cites the same facts and notorious example used by the Whigs' critics, conceding that this situation "everyone must confess needs a remedy." Obviously, "a fair and equal" system of representation is consonant with the public good. But, Locke asserts, the executive, through his prerogative to act for the public good, is just as capable of effecting electoral reform to achieve this "fair and equal" system

[44] Thorogood, *Captain Thorogood*, pp. 3–4. As noted previously, the language of natural rights, equality, and popular sovereignty was associated in the minds of Locke's contemporaries with inhabitant or manhood suffrage. Tories, therefore, were eager to push Whigs as close as possible to this Leveller position, which in their view meant that "any porter, cobbler, or tinker" had an equal right to make political decisions with "the greatest peer in the realm" (Rider, *Power of Parliaments*, pp. 3–4, 6, 29).

[45] *Three Great Questions*, p. 13.

[46] *England's Concern in the Duke of York*, p. 248.

of representation as is the legislature. In thus shifting the burden of reform to the king, Locke is attempting to expose the insincerity of the Whigs' critics, none of whom, of course, was pressing Charles II or James II to institute the fair and equal system of representation that they used as a standard for criticizing the Whig defense of Parliament and popular sovereignty.[47]

In the political debate of the exclusion crisis, the Whigs' opponents naturally did not attempt a defense of Catholicism, but they did try to undermine the effectiveness of the Whig attack on arbitrary power and absolute monarchy with appeals to history, business practices, and family relationships; they sought to demonstrate the compatibility of monarchy with commerce; they showed that "consent" served as a mask for the protection of an unequal distribution of property, that "the people" were excluded from participation by a restricted suffrage, that "representation" was disproportionate and unequal, and that, therefore, a defense of Parliament could not be equated with a defense of the people. The Tories also sought through their own petition campaigns in 1680–1681 to give a practical basis to their own claims to represent the political thinking of their contemporaries. In all these respects, the Whigs' critics were responding to what they perceived to be the most important and widely understood political assumptions accepted by the participants in the Whig political movement.

None of the Whig opponents, however, had so clear or comprehensive a grasp of Whig political theory as that shrewd and seasoned defender of the established order, Roger L'Estrange. L'Estrange understood the importance of the Harringtonian argument to the Whig position, and in linking together their political, economic, and social presuppositions in his critique of that position, he produced an impressive and effective counterargument. This island, L'Estrange declared, is governed "by the subordinate influence of the nobility and gentry, who live plentifully, and at ease upon their rents, extracted from the toil of their tenants and servants; every one of them acting the prince within the bounds of his own

[47] *ST*, pars. 157, 158. In fact, Shaftesbury and the Whigs had introduced a bill in Parliament in 1679 to effect a reform of the franchise and the electoral districts (Jones, pp. 53–54; Ogg, 2:481–482). The irony of Locke's argument (*whoever* brings the people "a fair and equal representative," acts for the public good) as a reply to Tory criticism has been completely missed by commentators on this passage (see, for example, Sterling P. Lamprecht, *The Moral and Political Philosophy of John Locke*, New York: Russell and Russell, 1962, pp. 141–142). A literal reading of it, however, in the face of the king's quo warranto proceedings against boroughs and corporations, which was specifically undertaken in order to remodel and restrict the franchise, is simply nonsensical in terms of Locke's political views, and his criticism in *ST*, par. 216.

estate, where he is in a manner absolute. His servants and laborers are as vassals, his tenants indeed are free, but yet in the nature of subjects. . . . The more his manors are . . . the larger is his territory, and the more awful are his commands." Moreover,

> Into the rank of gentry do our officers, citizens, and burghers aspire to be enrolled. So that no sooner by arms, office, or trade, do they acquire a competent stock, but forthwith for land it is disposed; and then, disowning the title of soldiers, citizens, or burghers, they take to themselves the degree and name of gentlemen. . . . For by gentry I understand not such only as are so in blood, but in quality also.[48]

This straightforward appeal to the gentry and the concession, *pace* Harrington, of their importance to English society, laid the groundwork for L'Estrange's rejection of the republicanism he attributed to the Whigs.

> Now, as the agrarian or interest of land, is principally in these two ranks, so also is the consequence thereof, power and command; which emboldens them to such a height of spirit . . . that they are too apt to undervalue persons of inferior condition (burghers and merchants) with whom to intermarry.[49]

It is especially the Whig rhetoric that all men are by nature free and equal that L'Estrange wishes to show is, on socioeconomic grounds, absurd. His argument, however, is not premised upon taking these assertions, as made by Tyrrell, Penn, Ferguson, and others (and indirectly by Locke and Sidney), merely as metaphysical declarations and then citing the facts necessary to prove them false. Though L'Estrange, like other Whig critics, does do this, his attack is a far more subtle one, for he wants to show that, given such initial assumptions, there would inevitably be a *tendency* on the part of the Whigs to *act* on such assumptions, should they emerge victorious in their power struggle with the king. Hence, for L'Estrange, the Whigs represent a movement toward the realization of social and political equality, a movement that would radically subvert the principles of hierarchy and status that support the existing social and political institutions. It is, in other words, the political ramifications of the

[48] L'Estrange, *Interest of Three Kingdoms*, pp. 5–6; Roger L'Estrange, *The State and Interest of the Nation, with Respect to His Royal Highness, the Duke of York*, 1680, pp. 3–5. L'Estrange's views were widely disseminated. Not only was he editor of the *Observator*, which appeared three or four times a week beginning on April 13, 1681, but it has been estimated that 64,000 copies of pamphlets bearing his name were in circulation in London between 1679 and 1681 (Violet Jordain, ed., *Selections from the "Observator,"* Los Angeles: Augustan Reprint Society, 1970, p. i).

[49] L'Estrange, *Interest of Three Kingdoms*, p. 6; idem, *State and Interest*, p. 5.

Whigs' theoretical framework which, in L'Estrange's view, are most dangerous. For, "it [is] of the very essence of a commonwealth, to reduce all degrees to a parity. For as titles and honors are incident to kingship, so also are equality of place and birth to democracy," and within the latter political system, everyone is reduced in status "to the condition of the vulgar."[50] Now, L'Estrange asks, can anyone "imagine that our nobility and gentry (as now in power) will ever be induced to admit a parity: will level their degree and domination to a proportion with their copyholders? Nay, will renounce the *wearing* of a sword, and learn to *make* one?"[51] Another Whig critic, writing after the publication of L'Estrange's pamphlets, and perhaps influenced by them, echoed this point, with specific reference to the Harringtonian argument employed by the Whigs. He did not challenge the empirical connection between property ownership and political power; instead, he focused upon what he called the "absurd consequences" that would follow if such a tendency were allowed to go unchecked. For, he reasoned, this doctrine, in practice, means that "meaner persons must have greater share too in public adminstration as soon as they grow mightier in possessions."[52] Such an outcome, he felt sure, was obviously unacceptable to the majority of his readers.

In an approach that anticipates Montesquieu, L'Estrange emphasizes the importance of "the public spirit" of a nation, to which, in the long run, forms of government must correspond.[53] Since the gentry are the keystone of the social order, the force of L'Estrange's argument rests upon his showing how alien to this class are the political ideas of popular government, equality, and republicanism. Most republics, past and present, he observes, have been dominated by great cities, "the nobles and gentlemen being purely tributary to the chief city."[54] London, of course, is such a city, but L'Estrange passes over this obvious fact in silence, perhaps ironically, in the sense of stressing by his silence the dangers faced by the gentry if they should ever become "purely tributary" appendages to this Leviathan. Instead, he reasserts the point that the country at large is under the governance of the nobility and gentry, and adds,

> It falls not within my memory that there ever was, or at this day is, a free-state in the whole world, that is managed by the gentry inhabiting at large.

[50] L'Estrange, *Interest of Three Kingdoms*, pp. 7, 9.

[51] L'Estrange, *Interest of Three Kingdoms*, p. 10 (italics in original).

[52] John Northleigh, *Remarks upon the Most Eminent of Our Antimonarchical Authors and Their Writings*, 1699, p. 174.

[53] L'Estrange, *Interest of Three Kingdoms*, p. 12.

[54] L'Estrange, *Interest of Three Kingdoms*, p. 10. Filmer had also made this argument (p. 187).

It is this ignorance of the facts of social and political history, L'Estrange argues, that places Whig political theory in the same category with the "fantasies" of Plato or of More's *Utopia*.[55]

Besides, L'Estrange observes, republics do not necessarily or universally promote the advancement of commerce and industry, as the Whigs claim. During the late republic (1649–1660), he maintains, the excise and customs taxes were high, and "our trade fell to nothing."[56] Even if there is some correlation between republicanism and commerce, L'Estrange adds, we are not like the Dutch, who are "addicted only to traffic, navigation, handicrafts, and sordid thrift." Rather, as he has already noted, Englishmen have a deep desire to become gentlemen. It is difficult to see how the Whigs, who have committed themselves so thoroughly to the advancement of trade and manufacturing, can adequately appreciate "the laws, genius, and interest of this nation"—that is, its "public spirit"—which rests upon a different set of interests, values, and life style. More to the point, how could the political institutions that *they* would establish possibly be made to conform to that public spirit?[57]

L'Estrange understood very clearly that such Whig concepts as the state of nature, the equality of individuals, consent, popular sovereignty, and so on, were tied to practical political objectives, and that these, in turn, were formulated in terms of their appeal to particular socioeconomic interests or classes. What he sought to bring out into the open was the incompatibility between the political objectives of the Whigs and the socioeconomic interests of the nobility and gentry, for whom the Whig political slogans might otherwise have some appeal. In other words, like Dryden, L'Estrange perceived the "contradictory" interests united in the Whig political movement, and he hoped to break apart the unity of the movement by showing that some classes (tradesmen and merchants) would benefit greatly at the expense of others (nobility and gentry) if the Whigs achieved their political objectives.

L'Estrange's special merit, it should be stressed, does not lie in his noticing that Whig political arguments were aimed at specific classes; that, as we have seen, was quite obvious to everyone. Rather, his critique was radical because it eschewed appeals to Scripture or a principled defense of absolute monarchy in favor of a historical, sociologically grounded defense of existing political institutions. It therefore attempted to challenge the Whigs upon their own (Aristotelian/Harringtonian) methodological ground, and to do so in a manner that was comprehensively and polemi-

[55] L'Estrange, *Interest of Three Kingdoms*, pp. 10–11; idem, *State and Interest*, p. 7.

[56] L'Estrange, *Interest of Three Kingdoms*, pp. 13–14.

[57] L'Estrange, *Interest of Three Kingdoms*, pp. 15–16; idem, *State and Interest*, pp. 8–10.

cally opposed to their political theory. To which it should be added that L'Estrange fully appreciated that the practical success of the Whig political movement—certainly insofar as the electoral process was concerned—depended upon their winning a significant portion of the gentry over to their side.

In attacking the Whigs, more than one Tory warned that it is "in at this country man's door" that "all mischief is like to creep."[58] Another writer estimated that there were approximately ten thousand manors in England and Wales, "whereof the lords are as it were little kings among their tenants," and the former "have their dependency upon, and must run the same fate with monarchy; if that stands, they stand, if that falls, they must fall also."[59] This association was evident to the Whigs as well. The gentry, Henry Neville observed matter-of-factly, are "more tractable" subjects, and therefore provide a more reliable basis of support for a monarchy "than a wealthy and numerous commonalty."[60]

In addressing their election propaganda to the gentry, the Whigs hoped to win the support of the members of that class, which depended upon the successful pursuit of three ideological objectives. First, they had to alienate the gentry from the Crown. This they largely accomplished by playing upon the gentry's fears of popery and pointing out the real and suspected Catholic influence at Court. As one Whig critic complained, men of "little fortunes" had stirred up the country against popery and arbitrary government, and by doing so, "they have gained too much credit amongst the gentry."[61] (Since the arguments associated with this strategic aim have already been considered in Chapter 5, I will confine my discussion here to the other two Whig objectives.) Second, the Whigs had to alienate the gentry from the influence of the Anglican church. As Henry Care lamented, the gentry "are governed by their more impertinent chaplain, or the parson of their parish . . . [who] set[s] up absolute monarchy to be *jure divino*."[62] Among other things, the execution of this strategy necessitated a direct attack upon Filmer's ideas, and in general, upon a scriptural defense of monarchy. Third, the Whigs had to alienate the gentry from the landowning aristocracy and, if possible, show the benefits of an economic alliance of the gentry's interests with those of the merchants, tradesmen, and artisans in the cities and towns. This the

[58] *Advice to the Nobility, Gentry, and Commonalty of This Nation in the Qualifications and Election of Their Knights and Burgesses, Their Representatives in Parliament*, 1680, p. 1.

[59] *Character of a Rebellion*, p. 13; Filmer, p. 97.

[60] Neville, *Plato*, p. 138.

[61] *Plain Dealing Is a Jewel, and Honesty the Best Policy*, 1682, p. 10.

[62] Care, *English Liberties*, p. 93; *Popery and Arbitrary Government*, p. 4.

Whigs attempted to do by comprehending the labor employed to cultivate and enclose acreage under the general label of "the industrious," to which they opposed the idle, luxurious, and useless large landowners who allowed their property to go to waste.

Normally, the interests represented by the Tories could have expected to receive the support of a large majority of the gentry. Tory writers openly addressed themselves to "my country neighbors, who being otherwise employed have not had the leisure that was necessary to reflect upon these things."[63] Such condescending tones were not always well received, however. The country gentry, though obviously interested in news of what was happening in Parliament and in London generally, tended to be wary of the missives directed at them by the writers—including Tories—in London. As one Lancashire minister remarked, the people in the north "are not so diligent to enquire out, and furnish themselves with such learned treatises" as are those individuals in London who are wont to send them to us. Nor, he added, do "the learned sermons preached in the city" have much influence upon "the remote country congregations." But, he advised, if a local clergyman should restate the plain truths regarding the individual's duty to obey the magistrate, even if such truths were not novel or cleverly phrased, the country people would listen to and follow his advice.[64] Country ministers were especially eager to disassociate themselves from the Court, though not from a position that supported the government. The author of *Obedience to Magistrates Recommended* proudly proclaimed that, despite the orthodoxy of his political argument, he lived "in an obscure country town" and was "no Court parasite."[65] Others also insisted that it was not simply "Court parasites" or "a few of the younger and meaner sort of the clergy" who advocated the theory of the divine right of kings; rather, that was the established doctrine of the Anglican church.[66] The message sent back from the country, therefore, was that they did not require "learned sermons" or treatises, or instructions from Court-appointed bishops to preach to them about loyalty or dutiful obedience to the magistrate. Country people understood such simple truths, and in any case they would follow the advice of their local clergyman.

That, of course, was the point so far as the Whigs were concerned.

[63] Edmund Bohun, *An Address to the Freemen and Freeholders of the Nation*, 1682, p. ii; John Inett, *A Sermon Preached at the Assizes held in Warwick*, 1681, epistle dedicatory.

[64] Gipps, *Nature of Subjection*, preface.

[65] [John Clapham], *Obedience to Magistrates Recommended*, 1683, preface.

[66] E. Foreness, *A Sermon*, September 9, 1683, p. 9; Comber, *Religion and Loyalty*, p. 59. For Locke's reference to Court parasites as the champions of Filmer's doctrine, see *FT*, par. 5.

Echoing Henry Care's comments, cited earlier, one Whig pamphleteer denounced the country gentry's subjection to "the designs of some idle, covetous and sycophant clergymen . . . [who] set up absolute monarchy to be *jure divino*."[67] In *The Reformed Papist, or High-Church Man*, the author accused the Anglican clergy of promulgating the belief that "the unlearned cannot rely upon any other people than the authority of their pastors expounding to them the substance of a Christian's duty." But, he warned the reader, if the clergy's word were allowed to carry such weight with respect to a discussion of political duties, one would, in the end, be led to believe that he is a Christian only "because the Church (meaning the clergy) tells you so."[68] The Anglican clergy, another Whig caustically observed, "have nothing else to do, but live at ease, keep their coach and horses," and engage in "railing against the Whigs and fanatics."[69]

Hence, when Tyrrell singled out the gentry and the clergy as the primary audience to whom he was addressing his critical remarks, he was stating what was politically obvious to his contemporaries: that if the gentry could be won away from supporting the notion of a monarchy instituted by divine right, the Whigs' pressure upon the king to agree to the exclusion of James would become too great for him to withstand. In the preface to *Patriarcha non Monarcha*, Tyrrell explained that it was necessary for him to write this book against Filmer's ideas because the "notion of the divine and patriarchal right of absolute monarchy has obtained so much [credit] among some modern churchmen, who cry it up as their Diana."[70] Locke, in his own preface to the *Two Treatises*, repeats this point, declaring that he would not have written the work "had not the pulpit, of late years, publicly owned [Filmer's] doctrine . . . principles which they preached up for Gospel . . . and made it the current divinity of the times."[71] It was obvious, Sidney wrote in the *Discourses*, that Filmer's doctrine in support of absolute monarchy has "been lately brought into the light again, as an introduction of a popish successor."[72] That was, in fact, the message that the Whigs wished to put across to the gentry,

[67] *Popery and Arbitrary Government*, p. 4. This anticlerical attack, with the object of undermining their influence among the gentry, was actually launched by Shaftesbury (Locke?) in 1675 in the *Letter from a Person of Quality* (*Works*, 9:201–202, 208). Also see another "Shaftesbury" pamphlet, *A Letter from a Parliamentarian to His Friend*, 1675, in *State Tracts*, 1689, pp. 70–71.

[68] *The Reformed Papist, or High-Church Man*, 1681, p. 3.

[69] Care, *English Liberties*, p. 94.

[70] Tyrrell, *Patriarcha non Monarcha*, preface.

[71] *Two Treatises*, preface; *ST*, par. 112. See also Haley, p. 724.

[72] A. Sidney, *Discourses*, chap. 3, sec. 43. The same point was made by Thomas Hunt, *Mr. Hunt's Postscript for Rectifying Some Mistakes in Some of the Inferior Clergy*, 1682, p. 6.

with or without the accompaniment of an extensive critique of Filmer's writings, such as was produced by Tyrrell, Locke, and Sidney.

Nevertheless, the Whigs never developed a clearly stated party line on the best means of counteracting the clergy's influence over the gentry. Some Whigs, like Henry Care, who characterized "blind obedience" to the clergy in matters respecting religion and politics as a popish principle, were inclined to be rather scathing in their criticisms of the clergy. Moreover, this criticism frequently spilled over to include "the country people" themselves, who, according to Care, were willing to "sell all that they have for a little roast beef . . . and a pot of ale."[73] Other Whigs, like Tyrrell, despite his reference to "unthinking country gentlemen" and theologians who were deceived by Filmer's ideas, were, on the whole, more respectful and moderate in tone in their efforts to criticize the beliefs held by the gentry. Thus, within the Whig movement there was a split between those who simply dismissed the gentry as politically unreliable and intellectually backward country squires, and those who were actively attempting to win the support of the gentry for the Whigs. This division, in turn, was reflected in the political literature between those writers who attacked the clergy so vehemently as to alienate the gentry from the Whigs, and those who, like Tyrrell, tried to defeat the clergy on their own ground with reasoned arguments.

Next to the attack upon the clergy through a critique of Filmer, property was the most important and troublesome issue for the Whigs in their effort to gain the support of the gentry. Specifically, members of this class required some assurance as to the security of their property rights. Yet, Whig propaganda did much to foster the belief that those rights were in jeopardy in the event of a Catholic king. Tories, on the other hand, argued that the ten thousand manors of the gentry depended upon the maintenance of the king's (Charles II's) authority, and they threatened the gentry with the loss of their property if the Whigs were successful in weakening that authority, and perhaps, in establishing a republic. The result would be a "levelling" of men's estates.[74] The gentry, in other words, were threatened by both sides with the loss of their property if the other side won the battle between king and Parliament. The propaganda war of the exclusion crisis must have indeed produced feelings of intense anxiety among country gentlemen concerning their estates.

Most historians have tended to discount altogether the accusations of "levelling" imputed to the Whigs. At best, it is said, the charges can be viewed as an excess of campaign rhetoric, but they are patently absurd as

[73] Care, *English Liberties*, pp. 93, 95.

[74] Rider, *Power of Parliaments*, p. 6; Schlatter, *Social Ideas*, pp. 168–169.

a characterization of the Whigs' political commitments or intentions. Although I was initially inclined to agree with this viewpoint, I now believe it is mistaken—or at least misleading—in two important respects. First, it tends to underestimate the strength of the Whig support drawn from tradesmen, artisans, and shopkeepers, who were, after all, the same people from whom the Levellers had drawn their support. This fact could not have escaped the attention of contemporaries, and as we have seen, it did not. Having lived through the experience of the Civil War, some of them reasoned (quite plausibly) that the Whigs might find themselves, as the Puritan grandees had found themselves forty years earlier, faced by "a many-headed monster" that they had helped to create but could no longer control. Once the ties of authority were loosened, no one could be quite certain what the end would be or to what extent the fabric of society might come unraveled.

Historians have concentrated far too much upon deciphering Shaftesbury's aims—no easy task—or those of the other Whig leaders, in terms of which any "levelling" accusations do appear to be ridiculous. What contemporaries wanted to know, however, was what was Major Wildman doing riding at the side of the Duke of Buckingham and running for election to Parliament? Wildman, after all, following the deaths of Colonel Rainborough and Lilburne, undoubtedly epitomized the Leveller movement in the eyes of his contemporaries. Moreover, he was well known to the king and several others in the government from his intrigues with the Royalists during the 1650s.[75] Also, why was Shaftesbury surrounded by old Commonwealth officers like Colonel Rumsey and Captain Walcot? Major Manley, Colonel Danvers, Colonel Mansell, and many others were deeply involved with Buckingham and Shaftesbury in the prosecution of the popish plot.[76] Why had the city of London elected Slingsby Bethel, a known Republican and former member of Cromwell's Council of State, as one of its sheriffs?[77] What was Algernon Sidney doing running for a

[75] In addition to his close association with Lilburne following the Putney debates, Wildman made financial investments on behalf of Colonel Rainborough's widow (Maurice Ashley, *John Wildman: Postmaster and Plotter,* London: Jonathan Cape, 1947, p. 73). On Wildman's intrigues with the Royalists during the 1650s, including his "close correspondence" with Charles, see ibid., pp. 100–120; David Underdown, *Royalist Conspiracy in England 1649–1660,* New Haven: Yale University Press, 1960, pp. 192–193. Wildman's friendship with Buckingham, also involved as a conspirator, dates from this period.

[76] Colonel Mansell and Colonel Danvers both did some interviewing and managing of popish plot witnesses for Shaftesbury. Major Manley appears to have been active in organizing Shaftesbury's "brisk boys" in Wapping for demonstrations (Douglas C. Greene, ed., *Diaries of the Popish Plot,* Delmar, N.Y.: Scholars' Facsimiles and Reprints, 1977, p. 100; PRO 30/24/43/63).

[77] One civil servant wrote to the English envoy in Brussels of the "abundant zeal" of "the

seat in Parliament after having spent twenty years living in exile?[78] Major Breman, an old army agitator, had also been elected to the exclusion Parliament. Breman, along with Colonel Richard Rumbold, had worked with Wildman in the Leveller movement.[79] Colonel Scott, previously mentioned, had been sent by Shaftesbury as an advance man, making arrangements for the Duke of Monmouth's 1680 progress through the countryside, designed to stir up Whig support among the gentry.[80] Colonel Rumsey and others had been sent to Bristol to organize voters there.[81] When one Whig critic wrote that old Commonwealth army soldiers and officers "now all took the field again" during the exclusion-crisis elections, the charge was very far from being merely a piece of rhetoric.[82]

Even more foreboding than their electoral activities, however, was the fact that some of these individuals had actually participated in the abortive attempts to overthrow Charles II in the early 1660s, for which they had been pardoned.[83] Nevertheless, no one doubted for a moment that

---

fanatics" in choosing such "a rank antimonarchist" as Bethel as sheriff (MS English Letters d.72, fol. 1, Bodleian Library). Both Buckingham and Monmouth campaigned for Bethel in his unsuccessful attempt to win a seat in Parliament (MS Carte 222, fol. 248, Bodleian Library).

[78] William Penn served as Sidney's election agent, but Colonel Danvers was also involved in Sidney's campaign (Doreen J. Milne, *The Rye House Plot, with Special Reference to Its Place in the Exclusion Contest and its Consequences Till 1685*, Ph.D. diss., University of London, 1949, p. 66).

[79] Major Breman (his last name is variously spelled) was the leader of "the factious party" in Rye, and a member of the three exclusion parliaments (MS Tanner 149, fol. 128). In addition to having been an agitator, he was court-martialed for his involvement in "Overton's Plot" against Cromwell in 1655 (Charles H. Firth and Godfrey Davies, *The Regimental History of Cromwell's Army*, 2 vols., Oxford: Clarendon Press, 1940, 1:144, 155). For Wildman's association with Breman and this plot, see Ashley, *Wildman*, p. 88; for Rumbold's association with the Levellers, see ibid., p. 69.

[80] Scott's activities in this capacity so impressed John Trenchard that he sponsored Scott's membership in the Green Ribbon Club. Scott also appears to have been involved with Ferguson in the "black box" campaign regarding Monmouth's legitimacy (Lilian T. Mowrer, *The Indomitable John Scott*, New York: Farrar, Straus and Cudahy, 1960, p. 364).

[81] Colonel Rumsey had been a customs collector in Bristol. Following his capture after the defeat of Monmouth's Rebellion, Nathaniel Wade said in his confession that he first met Rumsey during 1680 when, along with Shaftesbury, Monmouth, Robert West, Richard Goodenough, John Trenchard, "and several other gentlemen" he assisted Wade in organizing the Whigs in Bristol (Harleian MS 6845, fol. 266). It may be that Locke, who also made a trip to Bristol early in 1680, was one of these "other gentlemen" who Wade met at this time (*Correspondence*, 2:160–161; MS f.4, fol. 41).

[82] Bohun, *Second Part*, p. 4.

[83] Breman was arrested in 1660 for his suspected complicity in Lambert's projected rising (Firth and Davies, *Regimental History*, 1:162–163). He was arrested again in May 1662 for his part in a rising against Charles II and sent to the Tower. Wildman was also in prison at the time (*CSPD*, 2:376, 456; cf. ibid., pp. 197, 460). Colonel Danvers was arrested in 1667

they were dangerous men. Now they were once again in the thick of the opposition to the king. What did it all mean? And, come to that, Shaftesbury himself had once been a Commonwealthman. Who could vouchsafe that his own designs did not run in that direction? This was not an easy question to answer. Even after three centuries of scholarship, Shaftesbury's political aims are very far from being clear. My point, however, is that it is not necessary to believe that Shaftesbury wanted to establish the republic he was so often accused of aiming at in order to grant the plausibility of the fears being expressed on behalf of the gentry that Commonwealthmen and Levellers were beginning to reappear in the political arena.

The second reason for taking the Republican-Leveller accusations more seriously is that it helps to explain why the issue of property loomed so large in the political debate of the 1680s, and why the Whigs were compelled, even in the midst of arguing for a revolution (for example, in the *Two Treatises*), to come to its defense. In the petitions, or "addresses," to the king gathered by the Tories, the "old commonwealth principles" of the Whigs were repeatedly denounced.[84] We know, said the authors of one petition, that without the king to protect our property rights, "we shall not be able to enjoy anything as our own . . . but shall relapse into the misery of having mean men and servants to bear rule over us."[85] Addressing himself to "the interest of the gentry," a Tory supporter warned that the country was threatened by those who "would revive Lilburne's name in a new race of Levellers" in order "to parcel out [the gentry's] estates and level their persons with the common crowd."[86] Apart from the resonance provided by Civil War memories, these accusations must have drawn some of their force from the fact that in some areas of the country "mean men" had already proven themselves capable of winning power through elections at the expense of the local gentry. Moreover, as L'Estrange and others pointed out, why was there all this talk about natural equality and the freedom of all individuals, the "native rights of freeborn Englishmen," and government being founded in the consent of the people, if the Whigs did not actually believe that greater equality and

(*CSPD*, 6:545). Breman, Danvers, Rumsey, Walcott, Manley, Rumbold, and a number of other Commonwealth officers were involved in the Rye House Plot.

[84] *Vox Angliae: or, the Voice of the Kingdom*, 1682, p. 9; O. W. Furley, "Whig Exclusionsists: Pamphlet Literature in the Exclusion Campaign, 1679–81," *Cambridge Historical Journal* 13, no. 1 (1957):31.

[85] *Vox Angliae*, p. 16. This is the result intended by "our designing Levellers" (Rider, *Power of Parliaments*, p. 6).

[86] John Inett, *A Sermon in Warwick*, p. 19; Christopher Wyvill, *A Sermon*, March 8, 1686, p. 6.

freedom ought to be instituted? To the Tories, that meant elevating the status of members of the lower classes. As one writer stated the point, if the Whigs believe all that they profess, "and all this notwithstanding a surviving king or protestant successor, how near this would have come to the nature of a commonwealth, I submit to the determination even of those men that think all republican designs at this time so ridiculous and impossible." But, he argued, if one takes their arguments seriously, then the consequences will be that "the very rabble" will be "set up for the sole magistrates and legislators."[87] In the end, that will put the kingdom at the mercy of the Levellers, and it will encourage every poor man to "plunder his wealthy neighbor. . . . And then by *property* can never be meant the keeping of their possessions in quiet."[88]

Of course, the Whigs denied such charges. Even the Levellers had denied these imputed intentions. Yet the Whigs, like their predecessors, were forced to respond to these accusations. The author of *A Character of Popery and Arbitrary Government* reassured his readers among the nobility and the gentry that they had no reason to fear the assumption by Parliament of a greater power. They would not, as a consequence, find their houses or estates "resolved" into a "commonalty."[89] Property rights, they were told, would remain secure. Other Whigs tried to supply this reassurance by generally disavowing "democratic principles," in favor of "rectifying an ancient monarchy" as a statement of their true aim.[90] In his preface to *Patriarcha non Monarcha,* Tyrrell merges these two responses. It is possible, he concedes, that when Filmer's ideas were originally put forward, they may have served a useful purpose as a counterweight to some "levelling" notions about property that were then current.[91] However, in the present context (in 1680), Tyrrell argues, this

[87] John Northleigh, *The Parallel: or, the New Specious Association an Old Rebellious Covenant,* 1682, pp. 21, 34; J. Turner, *Sermon before Ward,* epistle dedicatory.

[88] Northleigh, *Parallel,* p. 22; Phillips, *Ursa Major,* p. 31.

[89] *Popery and Arbitrary Government,* p. 3.

[90] Neville, *Plato,* p. 195; Robert Ferguson, *A Just and Modest Vindication of the Two Last Parliaments,* 1681, p. 44 (*LL* #2208); *A Letter From a Person of Quality to His Friend Concerning His Majesty's Late Declaration,* 1681, p. 8 (*LL* #1725); *Popery and Arbitrary Government,* p. 3; *Impartial Account,* p. 37.

[91] Tyrrell, *Patriarcha non Monarcha,* preface. Tyrrell's assumption that Filmer wrote *Patriarcha* in response to the Levellers' arguments is interesting and has recently been reaffirmed by John Wallace in "The Date of Sir Robert Filmer's *Patriarcha,*" *Historical Journal* 23, no. 1 (1980):155–165. Laslett's dating of the work between 1635 and 1642 (p. 3) seems far too early for the type of arguments against which Filmer believes he is contending. It is true that he designates certain schoolmen as his opponents, and their arguments could certainly have been answered during this period, quite apart from the political situation in England. On the other hand, that is the point—that is, if *Patriarcha* is not merely a speculative treatise, but is meant to be a work of political theory addressed to the problems

cannot serve as a mitigating excuse for their appearance, since the Whigs obviously (to Tyrrell) have no such designs on property. Furthermore, Filmer's ideas go much too far in the opposite direction by refusing to recognize the legal and contractual limitations upon the king's authority, for, he emphasizes, these are also the safeguards of the subject's property. Hence, Tyrrell proclaims, although he is very far from being "a commonwealthman" or someone who wishes to "set up a democracy amongst us," nevertheless, he must undertake this critique of Filmer's perspective in order to show how individual property rights can be secured according to the Whig theory of government. Since Locke's argument in the *Two Treatises* closely parallels in many respects Tyrrell's position on property, this framing of the problem and the rationale for his treatment of the issue of property rights is particularly interesting.[92] It is especially instructive, I believe, in explaining why the chapter on property is accorded such prominence in the *Two Treatises.* The Whigs needed some means of reconciling the language of equality, natural rights, and the view that all property was originally given to mankind "in common" with a justification of individual property rights in order to defend themselves against the accusation of a design to level men's estates, which the Tories repeatedly hurled at them in their exclusion sermons and pamphlets.

It is important to recognize that this defensive posture was not to be adopted at the expense of an abandonment of the natural rights lan-

---

facing England in the 1640s, then a relatively late date (1648) for its composition is, I believe, more likely. The statement on which Laslett rests his case (p. 95) is much more ambiguous than his interpretation of it makes it appear (Filmer could mean that "only twice *before*" have civil wars wasted the kingdom). Especially appropriate to Tyrrell's reading of Filmer are the arguments associating natural rights claims with the question of the franchise (pp. 118–119). This is not conclusive since, as was argued in Chapter 4, parliamentary leaders had made such claims prior to 1640; nevertheless, the political importance of that argument was certainly associated with the Levellers from 1646 on. Nothing in the argument I have advanced in the text rests upon the dating of *Patriarcha,* but there is a symbiotic relationship between the political situations of the 1640s and the 1680s that is suggestive: namely, the more contemporaries perceived a political drift toward the return of "the Levellers," the more they turned toward Filmer's extreme defense of patriarchalism and divine right.

[92] One scholar has suggested that, in fact, Locke collaborated with Tyrrell specifically with respect to the treatment of property in *Patriarcha non Monarcha,* at a late stage in its printing (Richard Tuck, *Natural Rights Theories: Their Origin and Development,* Cambridge: Cambridge University Press, 1979, p. 169n.). This is an interesting suggestion, but it can hardly be more than that simply on the basis of the interruption and repagination of Tyrrell's work while it was in press. Having said that, however, it would explain why there is such confusion in Tyrrell's discussion of property, which combines arguments based upon labor with those based upon occupancy. It could also be related to my suggestion (Chapter 9, note 221 below) that the chapter on property was a separate manuscript that came into Tyrrell's possession sometime during the early 1680s.

guage—at the price of alienating the Whig supporters among artisans and tradesmen, for whom such appeals and language found a very strong resonance. If a practical alliance between the country gentry and the urban tradesmen was to be effected, therefore, the theoretical problem of property rights had to be confronted and resolved in a manner that would satisfy both groups. The theoretical solution to the problem of property, I am arguing, was formulated by Locke and Tyrrell, and especially by the former, within the framework set by this political alliance.

Naturally, the Whigs also had to be responsive to their opponents' views on the origin and nature of property rights. Here they were helped by the lack of any clearly orthodox position. Most Royalists held that in some form or other, the king was sovereign with respect to the subject's property rights.[93] In fact, technically speaking, a property "right" was something that "none can have in any lands or tenements, but only the King in right of his Crown, because . . . all lands within this realm were originally derived from the Crown; and therefore the King is Sovereign Lord . . . of all, and every parcel of land within the realm."[94] For good measure, the Royalist author of this tract throws in an appeal to Sir Edward Coke in support of this view. Still other Royalists treated this proposition (that all land in the kingdom belongs to the king) as a historical truth, maintaining that once some parcel of land had been granted by the king to a particular subject, then the property ownership of that subject was thereafter protected by conventions or customs that effectively limited even the king's right to reclaim what had originally been his.[95] Notwithstanding these variations, there was a general underlying theme: The king was the proprietor of the kingdom. Thus, "Tory thinking tended to make the monarch essentially a landowner," such that "an attack on monarchy was an attack on landownership."[96]

[93] For a brief statement of the ideological framework within which the Tory view of property was placed, see H. T. Dickinson, *Liberty and Property: Political Ideology in Eighteenth-Century Britain*, London: Methuen, 1979, pp. 13–27.

[94] John Brydall, *Jura Coronae: His Majesty's Royal Rights and Prerogatives Asserted*, 1680, p. 92.

[95] For a developmental account of the king's voluntary diminishment of his prerogative in order to provide security for property rights that incorporates a version of the two-stages-of-society argument, see *Protestant Loyalty Fairly Drawn*, 1681, pp. 28–30. The author also invokes the authority of Coke in support of his position (p. 31). The king's voluntary grants of property, as Nathaniel Johnston put it, had become "mounds and boundaries" hedging in the subject's property rights from any absolutist or tyrannical pretensions on the part of the monarch (James Daly, *Sir Robert Filmer and English Political Thought*, Toronto: University of Toronto Press, 1979, p. 189; cf. ibid., pp. 53–54; Schlatter, *Social Ideas*, pp. 92–95).

[96] J. R. Western, *Monarchy and Revolution: The English State in the 1680s*, London: Blandford Press, 1972, p. 31.

The question of property rights, therefore, could not be disentangled from the whole complex of issues cast up by the exclusion crisis. Their status appeared to be especially closely linked to one's attitude toward the status of parliamentary power. This was, of course, a point much stressed by the Whigs in their political literature. The issue, in its simplest form, can be stated as a conflict between two views, one of which maintained that Parliament's existence, as well as such incidentals as the Magna Charta, represented "concessions" by the king drawn from the well of his absolute authority. These institutions or practices were acts of "grace" and not juridical claims of "right" to which a subject might appeal.[97] This argument preserved the notion of the king's absolute authority, but it placed property in the same limbo as other "rights" claimed by the king's subjects. The other extreme viewpoint, advanced by the Whigs, has already been discussed at length. In this drama constructed out of the language of natural rights, natural law, common good, and equality, the king does not have a leading role, and must make his way across the stage in the company of individuals who already own more property than he does.

On the whole, Tory writers said surprisingly little about property. One author sneeringly observed that there is a "principle now on foot, *that dominion is founded on property*."[98] Yet he neither challenged this Whig precept by offering a counterargument nor attempted to show how property might relate to the king's authority, which he was defending. One Whig critic, specifically attacking Neville's contention that since property ownership had shifted, so must political power shift toward the people, replied that property holdings were always in a state of transition and that no political conclusion could be drawn from this fact one way or another.[99] Another of the king's supporters conceded that individuals had "the undoubted right" to property on the basis of first occupancy, but, he suggested, this right was easily lost in a Hobbesian state of war, to which the establishment of a monarchy was the best remedy. Hence, it was also the best guarantor of property rights.[100] Given these differing opinions and responses among those engaged in defending the divine right of monarchy, it is not an exaggeration to speak of the problem of property rights or ownership as existing in a state of some theoretical confusion.

Moreover, the language necessary to the defense of an absolute monarchy did not make it easy to provide the gentry, or anyone else, with the

[97] *England's Concern in the Duke of York*, p. 243; Weston and Greenberg, *Subjects and Sovereigns*, p. 184.

[98] Gipps, *Nature of Subjection*, p. 25.

[99] *Antidotum Britannicum: Or, a Counter-Pest against the Destructive Principles of Plato Redivivus*, 1681, pp. 32–33.

[100] J. Turner, *Sermon before Ward*, epistle dedicatory.

reassurances about property rights that many Englishmen in the 1680s had come to regard as an important factor to be taken into account in determining to whom they ought to pledge their political loyalties. This is possibly one reason the Tories so infrequently addressed themselves to the issue of property, for as the exclusion crisis wore on, they rose to an increasingly strident defense of absolutism and the theory of divine right.[101] It is no wonder, then, that the Whigs fastened upon Filmer, who is both an absolutist and a theorist with a great deal to say about property. What better way to expose the implicit contradictions inherent in the Tory position? Divine right and patriarchalism might have some appeal to the country gentry, but would they really accept the tenuousness of property rights held by grace of the king, especially by grace of a (future) Catholic king?

Though he certainly did not wish to see such privileges and liberties as Englishmen enjoyed destroyed, nevertheless, in Filmer's view, there could be no such thing as limitations upon the sovereign's will in any shape or form whatsoever. Hence, there could be no property rights for a Filmerian. Any claims for property were, in the words of one scholar, "thoroughly insecure and retractable emanations of a sovereign will."[102] It was this position that the Whigs consistently attacked in their political literature, whether or not the viewpoint was specifically identified with Filmer's writings.

The clergy, one pamphleteer remarked, "teach that men have no property either in their lives or goods, but during the prince's pleasure."[103] Care criticizes the same proposition in *English Liberties*.[104] Locke's argument is distinguished in this respect only by the relentlessness with which he pursues Filmer across the propertyless expanse of absolutism. For most Whig writers, it was sufficient to remind the gentry that if they conceded their property rights to the arbitrary will of a Catholic king, they deserved to lose their estates; but if they were not willing to do so, they had better align themselves with a Whig position that advocated strong limitations upon the king's power.

The Whigs, however, had their own problems with respect to the issue of property rights. They were arguing for government based upon consent, but in what sense could property ownership be said to be based upon consent? And the consent of whom? It was difficult to imagine that the unequal distribution of property, especially as it existed all over the world, had ever, in fact, received the consent of individuals. On the other hand, if they accepted Halifax's position that "property is not a funda-

[101] Burnet, 2:216, 290.

[102] Daly, *Filmer*, p. 54.

[103] *Popery and Arbitrary Government*, p. 4.

[104] Care, *English Liberties*, p. 94.

mental right," but only "an innovation introduced by laws," could they really provide an adequate defense of property rights against the king's ability to alter the law through an act of will?[105] Moreover, their increasing reliance upon the language of natural rights and the state of nature seemed to push the Whigs toward the assertion that property had originally been held in common. Their opponents recognized this, and attacked the "pernicious" doctrine that "a community of all things" once existed, a proposition they lost no opportunity in linking with the Levellers.[106] But if property began in common, how did it come to assume its present form? This is the interrogatory Tyrrell set out to answer in *Patriarcha non Monarcha.* "Supposing the earth and fruits thereof to have been at first bestowed in common on all its inhabitants," he wrote, this assumption did not conflict with the view that "the personal possession of things" arose from the first occupancy of the land by an individual and from his "use" of objects to satisfy his natural needs.

> So that though the fruits of the earth, or beasts, for food were all in common, yet when once any man had by his own labor acquired such a proportion of either as would serve the necessities of himself, and family, they became so much his own, as that no man could without manifest injustice rob him of these necessities of life.[107]

On the basis of some not very clear mixture of labor and occupancy, therefore, Tyrrell rested the individual's initial claim to remove "personal possessions" from the common stock granted to mankind. This original right, he argued, was subsequently confirmed through the consent given by individuals when they established civil society. Thus, all property in the state of nature is the consequence of "occupancy or possession," but the "absolute propriety in things . . . arises from compact in a commonwealth."[108] Tyrrell reconciles the juridical claims—derived

[105] H. C. Foxcroft, *The Life and Letters of George Savile*, 2 vols., 1898, 2:496.

[106] *The True Protestant Subject, or the Nature and Rights of Sovereignty Discussed and Stated*, 1680, p. 17; William Payne, *A Sermon*, September 9, 1683, p. 14. The extent to which this assumption was subjected to political attack in the 1680s is generally ignored by commentators who assume that it is merely a traditional assumption made by Locke's contemporaries. Whatever we may think, for Englishmen in the 1680s, the authority of Grotius or the early Christian fathers did not simply set aside the tarnishment this proposition had received from having been incorporated into a number of Leveller and Digger tracts in the 1640s.

[107] Tyrrell, *Patriarcha non Monarcha*, p. 140. That Tyrrell does not place the same emphasis upon "labor" that Locke does, even in this passage, is evident from his statement of the same point in terms of "occupancy." Thus, he observes that "occupancy . . . confers a right in the state of nature to such things as are merely necessary for a man's subsistence" (p. 65). At the same time, however, he speaks of the individual's "natural right" to those things he can "make use of" (p. 153; see note 92 above).

[108] Tyrrell, *Patriarcha non Monarcha*, p. 49.

from natural law and consent—by associating the first with the "bare necessities" of life, while the latter component of the notion of property already presupposes that, as Locke put it, individuals "have property" that they wish to protect.[109] Of course, these two claims to property exist on different planes of moral justification, but it can also be said that, placed within the framework of human history, they presupposed two different types of societies. The argument that there are two stages of social existence, in other words, was quite important to the Whigs' general defense of property rights. For, it enabled them to posit a natural rights claim on behalf of any individual (and the means of susbsistence necessary to maintain himself and his family), and yet at the same time imply that the actual exercise of this right belonged to persons who lived in the distant past, in a society where there was virtually no property beyond the level of subsistence. It is true, Tyrrell (and Locke) argued, that "in a case of extreme necessity," the natural right to subsistence could still be claimed, even within modern societies. Thus, an individual retained a right to "make use of some of the superfluous necessaries of life which another man may have laid by for the future uses of himself, and family, and that were without his consent, if it can by no other means be obtained."[110] This is a significant exception, but it is an exception all the same.[111] It stands on the same plane as the individual's right to kill a thief in certain circumstances within modern society where the normal appeal to the law is not possible.[112] Neither Locke nor Tyrrell envisioned a collective body of starving vigilantes plundering their neighbors' superfluities. Tyrrell was especially careful to rule out the possibility, and, in the process, he all but withdrew even the individual's claim to "make use" of someone else's property.

In a civil society established by the consent of those who wished to preserve their property, Tyrrell wrote, even propertyless individuals are obliged "to maintain it, being once instituted." For, "since the common

[109] Tyrrell, *Patriarcha non Monarcha*, p. 149; *ST*, par. 138.

[110] Tyrrell, *Patriarcha non Monarcha*, p. 151; *FT*, par. 42; cf. *ST*, par. 183; Hunt, *Postscript*, preface.

[111] On the one hand, this argument is rooted in Christian theology. Aquinas, for example, wrote that "it is not theft, properly speaking, to take secretly and use another's property in case of extreme need" (Richard Schlatter, *Private Property*, London: Allen and Unwin, 1951, p. 53). At the same time, it should not be forgotten that Ireton associated the Levellers' use of this natural rights argument that the individual had a right to "meat, drink, clothes, to take and use them for his sustenance" with an *attack* upon property, and he therefore did not make this concession to subsistence (*The Clarke Papers*, ed. C. H. Firth, 4 vols., Camden Society Publications, 1891, 1:307). Ireton obviously thought this an important line of attack on the Leveller position, for he later repeats the challenge to Rainborough (p. 314).

[112] *ST*, pars. 18, 19; Tyrrell, *Patriarcha non Monarcha*, p. 63.

good of mankind is the highest end a man can propose to himself," and this is identified in practice with "the common good of the city or commonwealth where he lives," it followed for Tyrrell that no individual was "at liberty to resist the government, and to change the course of this property already established." This restraint, Tyrrell believed, was evident once it was conceded that "no man can disturb the general peace of human society for his own private advantage or security, without transgressing the natural law of God."[113] Hence, while the Law of Nature might, in extreme cases, sanction the appropriation of the means of subsistence by an individual, it very definitely proscribed any attempt at the "levelling" of property.

Tyrrell believed he had successfully defended an absolute natural rights claim to limited property, while at the same time providing a nearly absolute guarantee for the security of unequal property distribution. Moreover, his explicit rejection of any claims by the propertyless "to change the course of this property already established" seemed to provide the kind of reassurance against levelling designs on the part of the Whigs that the gentry required. "I hope this great difficulty" regarding the origins and rights of property in relation to government, "which has puzzled some divines is now cleared," Tyrrell declared confidently.[114] Yet it was not "cleared," and not only in the eyes of Tory clergymen; Locke, evidently, was not entirely satisfied with Tyrrell's solution to the problem of property.

Much could be said concerning the intellectual antecedents of Locke's treatment of property, but since there is an extensive body of literature that discusses that subject, I will not pursue that topic here.[115] Rather, I shall focus upon the political context within which Locke's arguments on property are advanced. In that regard, there are three aspects of his treatment of property to which I wish to draw particular attention. The first point, drawn from his attack upon Filmer in the *First Treatise*, emphasizes the theological origins of property rights; the second concerns Locke's attribution of a social and political significance to the meaning of "labor" as a "title" to property; and the third relates to Locke's integra-

[113] Tyrrell, *Patriarcha non Monarcha*, p. 147.

[114] Tyrrell, *Patriarcha non Monarcha*, p. 156.

[115] Schlatter, *Private Property*, pp. 1–150; James Tully, *A Discourse on Property: John Locke and His Adversaries*, Cambridge: Cambridge University Press, 1980, pp. 1–94; Paschal Larkin, *Property in the Eighteenth Century*, 1930; reprint ed., New York: Howard Fertig, 1969, pp. 1–53; Tuck, *Natural Rights*; Karl Olivecrona, "Locke's Theory of Appropriation," *Philosophical Quarterly* 24, no. 96 (July 1974):220–234; idem, "Appropriation in the State of Nature: Locke on the Origin of Property," *Journal of the History of Ideas* 35, no. 2 (April–June 1974):211–230.

tion of the political objectives of his discussion of property into the political objectives of the *Second Treatise* as a whole.

To consider Locke's position on the relationship of labor to property divorced from its theological underpinnings is not only a serious interpretive mistake in terms of the intentional structure of Locke's intellectual commitments in the *Two Treatises*, it also misrepresents through omission a crucial dimension of the political radicalism that work expresses. Far from endorsing a secular and conservative attitude toward property ownership, the *Two Treatises* incorporates many features of a critical attack upon the private appropriation of property formulated within the framework of traditional Christianity.[116]

In his lectures on the Law of Nature, Locke described the individual's relationship to God and the moral duties derivable from that relationship in terms that were subsequently restated in his later writings. We are subject to God's authority, he argued, by "the right of creation, as when all things are justly subject to that by which they have first been made and are also constantly preserved."[117] Hence, man's obligation to obey God's will derives not merely from the divine wisdom of the lawmaker, but also "from the right which the Creator has over His creation."[118] On this point, Locke never changed his mind, and the argument reappears in both the *Essay Concerning Human Understanding* and the *Two Treatises of Government*.[119] At the beginning of the *Second Treatise*, for example, Locke declares that:

[116] For a brief discussion of the importance of various propositions concerning property by Christian writers and the similarity of their position to Locke's theory of property, see Schlatter, *Private Property*, pp. 33–76; A. J. Carlyle, "The Theory of Property in Medieval Theology," and H. G. Wood, "The Influence of the Reformation on Ideas Concerning Wealth and Property," in *Property: Its Duties and Rights*, 2d ed., ed. J. V. Bartlett, London: Macmillan, 1915, pp. 119–132 and 135–167, respectively. In general, it seems more accurate to say say that the Christian paradigm of property is a radical/conservative one, unstable at its core. It justifies an original state of common property with individual use, and this standard can be invoked in cases of extreme individual necessity or a general economic crisis (and sometimes on religious grounds for those who live closest to the dictates of natural law) in order to override the claims of private ownership. At the same time, the paradigm provides a defense for private property, not only as an integral part of an Aristotelian conception of the family or household, but also as a badge of that lost innocence which makes the institution of government necessary. The latter is especially useful as a defense against external interference as a means of restricting the claims of temporal power by the king or the pope over individuals, while the former relies upon the social bond of the community to unite individuals in the pursuit of the common good.

[117] *ELN*, p. 185; cf. ibid., pp. 155, 157.

[118] *ELN*, pp. 183, 187; *ECHU*, 2:28, 8.

[119] For a discussion of the importance of creationism to Locke's thought, see Tully, *Discourse on Property*, pp. 40–42, 58–59.

> For men being all the workmanship of one omnipotent, and infinitely wise Maker; all the servants of one Sovereign Master, sent into the world by his order and about his business, they are his property, whose workmanship they are, made to last during his, not one anothers pleasure.[120]

This is a clear statement of the theory of creationism, which we considered in Chapter 2 as part of the Dissenters' response to Parker's attack on nonconformity. In that context, the theory functioned not only as a means of reconciling reason and will as the constitutive elements of the individual's moral obligations to God, it also assumed an indirect role in the Dissenters' rejection of the claims for the absolute authority over matters of religion advanced by the Anglican church. In the *Two Treatises*, this aspect of the theory, as a critique of absolute political authority, assumes a much more central place in Locke's argument. Creationism is employed by Locke as the primary axis for his rejection of Filmer's definition of political authority. It also establishes the moral boundaries for his discussion of property rights.

Both of these points can be illustrated, I believe, from a consideration of the implications that follow from the statement of the theory of creationism, as formulated by Richard Baxter. God, Baxter wrote, is more than "our creator"; he is also "our *owner*." Thus, "our obligation is founded in our being His creatures, and so His *own*."[121] As another writer put it, God is the great proprietor of the earth and "man has only the use, and stewardship, and employment of these things which are committed to him, by the allowance of God's providence."[122] Creationism, therefore, not only sets forth the reasons for our obedience to the Law of Nature, it also describes the individual's relationship to God as part of a theory of property. To his description of individuals as the property of God, Locke adds a characterization of the latter as the "sole Lord and Proprietor of the whole world."[123] Since, for Locke, the Deity is the Great Property Owner, it is possible to construct a model of the appropriate uses of property in terms of God's intentions and His relations with man. This model can

[120] *ST*, par. 6; cf. *FT*, par. 53; *ECHU*, 4:3, 18.

[121] Cited in Tully, *Discourse on Property*, p. 42; cf. *Life of Richard Baxter*, ed. Matthew Sylvester, 1696, p. 22; Richard Schlatter, *Richard Baxter and Puritan Politics*, New Brunswick, N.J.: Rutgers University Press, 1957, p. 154; H. G. Wood, "Influence of Reformation," pp. 154–156; Hunt, *Postscript*, p. 67.

[122] M.S., *Submission to the Will of God in Times of Affliction*, 1683, pp. 13–14. This sermon was dedicated to Lady Russell, following the execution of her husband. In view of the argument's similarity to Baxter's own statements, M.S. is probably Baxter's close friend and editor, Matthew Sylvester. See also Schlatter, *Social Ideas*, pp. 125ff.

[123] *FT*, par. 39. All property belongs to God (*ELN*, p. 203).

then be employed as a critical standard according to which all other proprietors are assessed in light of their uses of property.

From the standpoint of Locke's critique of Filmer's conception of political authority, the most relevant aspect of property ownership is the owner's right to use his property even to the point of "destroying" the object through its usage. Such a proposition may appear innocuous enough when applied to nuts and berries and other articles of consumption, but its religious significance restates the kernel of terror at the heart of Calvinist theology.[124] In the *Two Treatises*, however, this owner/object relationship functions as a prohibitive injunction against any humanly advanced claims to exercise a right of destruction over God's "property," at least in the absence of any direct divine order to do so. In putting the problem in this way, it becomes clear why Filmer's argument presented such a fundamental challenge to Locke's own viewpoint; for Filmer claimed precisely that God had delivered a definite, positive instruction to man (Adam) that conferred on him the absolute political authority necessary to treat other human beings as his property.[125] Moreover, Filmer was willing to generalize this grant of authority so that all fathers, as creators of their children, could rightfully exercise a (potentially) destructive power over them.[126] This Locke denies, and he suggests that in attributing to fathers such a creative role with respect to their children, Filmer is guilty of a form of blasphemy. Those who subscribe to such a view "are so dazzled with the thoughts of monarchy," that they have forgotten that it is not human beings, but God "who is the author and giver of life."

> To give life to that which has yet no being, is to frame and make a living creature, fashion the parts, and mold and suit them to their uses, and having proportioned and fitted them together, to put into them a living soul. He that could do this, might indeed have some pretence to destroy his own workmanship. But is there any one so bold, that dares thus far arrogate to himself the incomprehensible works of the Almighty? Who alone did at first, and continues still to make a living soul, He alone can breathe in the breath of life. . . . he is indeed Maker of us all, which no parents can pretend to be of their children.[127]

[124] *FT*, pars. 39, 92. Locke's relationship to Calvinist theology is extremely elusive, but with respect to the obligation the individual owes to God by "the right of creation," this is an expression that occurs in Calvin's *Institutes*, as von Leyden notes (*ELN*, p. 185n.). For a discussion of the general importance of Calvinism to Locke's thought, see John Dunn, *The Political Thought of John Locke*, Cambridge: Cambridge University Press, 1969.

[125] *FT*, pars. 8, 9.

[126] *FT*, par. 52.

[127] *FT*, par. 53.

In this passage the political message of Locke's commitment to creationism is starkly clear: Neither monarchs nor fathers have a right to destroy God's workmanship, since such a right belongs to the maker of the property. In view of the social composition of the audience to whom Locke's political message in the *Two Treatises* was addressed, this artisanal image of the Deity is rather interesting.[128] In any event, it is the existential and moral framework provided by creationism that sanctions Locke's rejection of the belief that "men were made as so many herds of cattle, only for the service, use, and pleasure of their princes," the position he attributes to Filmer and to all defenders of political absolutism.[129] Locke argues that "there cannot be supposed any such *subordination* among us, that may *authorize us to destroy one another*, as if we were made for one another's uses, as the inferior ranks of creatures are for ours."[130] This, if we may put it this way, is the negative contribution to Locke's theory of property stipulated by his theological argument against Filmer. Our freedom and equality with respect to one another is a function of our being the servants and the property of a higher Being.

There is, however, also a positive side to Locke's religious approach to property. Early in the *First Treatise*, Locke informs the reader that he intends to show that God did not give Adam "private dominion over the inferior creatures," and that, as a consequence, property was given to mankind "in common."[131] This point is repeatedly asserted by Locke throughout the work, and it has received prominent attention in the secondary literature on the Lockean concept of property. Yet the failure of Filmer to establish a claim for a positive proprietary grant from God, and the consequent reversion of property to a communal status, does not exhaust Locke's discussion of property in the *First Treatise*. For as we have seen, his defense of our right to be treated as free and equal beings is framed in terms of our obligations to a higher authority. Before turning to the political implications of Locke's conjunction of labor and property, it is important to place the former concept within the same framework of higher moral obligations. The labor of individuals that vouchsafes for them a claim to property, in other words, represents the positive fulfillment of a divine command. For Locke, if God is the Lord Proprietor of the world, then we are his productive tenants.

God not only "furnished the world with things fit for food and rayment and other necessaries of life," he also "directed" individuals "to make use of those things that were necessary or useful to his being." Thus, "man

[128] Tully, *Discourse on Property*, pp. 4, 9, 33–36, 40.

[129] *FT*, par. 156; *ST*, par. 163.

[130] *ST*, par. 6.

[131] *FT*, par. 24

had a right to a use of the creatures, by the will and grant of God."[132] This directive receives an even sharper phraseology in the *Second Treatise*. There Locke declares that God "commanded man also to labor," and that it was "in obedience to this command of God" that man "subdued, tilled and sowed any part" of the land, and "thereby annexed to it something that was his property, which another had no title to, nor could without injury take from him."[133] As Locke restates the point several paragraphs later,

> So that God, by commanding to subdue, gave authority so far to appropriate. And the condition of human life, which requires labor and materials to work on, necessarily introduces private possessions.[134]

In short, if labor serves as a title to property, it does so, according to Locke, within a juridical structure in which the authority to appropriate objects is received by human beings in the form of a command to labor. Through their laboring activity, individuals are fulfilling an obligation to obey God's commands. This should not appear surprising since the command to labor is simply a specific manifestation of God's designs that govern the relationships posited by the theory of creationism. "It does not seem to fit in with the wisdom of the Creator," Locke observes, "to form an animal that is most perfect and ever active, and to endow it abundantly above all others with mind, intellect, reason, and all the requisites for working, and yet not assign to it any work."[135] It is clear to Locke that "God intends man to do something," to be active; in short, to labor.[136] The particular mandate to do so is exemplary of the fact that we are "sent into the world by his order and about his business," and are "subservient to his designs."[137] Hence, property, as envisioned by Locke is totally enshrouded in a network of moral obligations. Nor should the religious characterization of labor as a "calling" be overlooked, since from Locke's perspective, the question of what place within God's designs for man may be claimed by those who do not labor has, potentially, socially radical implications. It is, therefore, a mistake to proceed directly from human labor to property, disengaged from the theological structure that Locke em-

[132] *FT*, pars. 85, 86.

[133] *ST*, par. 32. It is within this theological framework that M.S., for example, endorses the proposition that "whosoever makes anything by his own proper art and labor . . . is counted to have a full right to it, and a full power to dispose of it" (*Submission to the Will of God*, p. 13).

[134] *ST*, par. 35.

[135] *ELN*, p. 117.

[136] *ELN*, p. 157.

[137] *ST*, par. 6.

ploys in the *Two Treatises*. Not only does such a viewpoint neglect the political resonance of Locke's critique of Filmer, but it also fails to appreciate the stewardship limitations upon property rights when the latter are interpreted in light of a reading of God's intentions. This point is applicable both in a negative sense (that is, what individuals cannot do with their property) and in the positive sense of a recognition of productive labor as a sign of obedience to God's demands.[138] As we shall see, this religious perspective is quite capable of supporting a radical theory of the uses and ownership of property.

Quite apart from the neglect of the religious premises of Locke's discussion of property, interpreters of his thought have displayed an inordinate propensity to regard labor as a metaphysical concept.[139] The point Locke repeatedly emphasizes throughout his chapter on property, however, is that it is laboring activity that is important. It is "the labor of those who broke the oxen, who digged and wrought the iron and stones, who felled and framed the timber," and "the ploughman's pains, the reaper and thresher's toil, and the baker's sweat" that provides the "useful products" for "the benefit of mankind."[140] The social implications of Locke's stress upon the value of "human industry" to society (or individual labor seen in a social context) has not received the attention it deserves. Too often commentators have contented themselves with a consideration of Locke's resolution of an intellectually constituted problem of explaining the relationship between the individual and his property.[141] Certainly, this was a genuine theoretical problem, for Locke as well as for many other writers. That he set out with the intention to resolve it cannot be denied. Nevertheless, this problem arose during the exclusion crisis within the precincts of a political debate, and that debate demanded

[138] Though it has received little attention from commentators, there is no question but that Locke did accept the "stewardship" conception of property. As he put it, we are all keepers of "the treasure of which God has made us the economists" (King, 2:58; see also *ELN*, p. 203; and Lady Masham's statement that Locke regarded individuals as "but stewards" of the property they possessed, cited in Fox-Bourne, 2:536). J. Dunn does not mention stewardship, but he does discuss the "calling" as a concept applicable to property ownership, which belongs to the same tradition (*Political Thought of Locke*, pp. 252ff.).

[139] Olivecrona, for example, maintains that the individual's "spiritual ego was infused into the object," and that Locke's theory of property seems "to make sense only on this interpretation" ("Locke's Theory of Appropriation," p. 226). And for a methodologically metaphysical treatment of the philosophical problem of property, see J. P. Day, "Locke on Property," *Philosophical Quarterly* 16 (1966):207–221.

[140] *ST*, pars. 32, 42, 43.

[141] Sabine's discussion is a classic example of the interpretation of Locke's theory of property in terms of the individual's egoistic interests (George Sabine, *A History of Political Theory*, 3d ed., New York: Holt, Rinehart and Winston, 1961, pp. 525ff.; see also Leo Strauss, *Natural Right and History*, Chicago: University of Chicago Press, 1953, p. 248).

that property ownership be viewed as a constituent element of "the common good," at least so far as the Whigs were concerned. Whether laboring activity or human industry was necessary for the solution of the theoretical problem, this social view of labor was clearly essential to the political argument Locke wished to make regarding property ownership.

When Locke writes that "justice gives every man a title to the product of his honest industry," this appears to be a reasonable, if trifle innocuous, statement.[142] Yet the encouragement of "honest industry" could, under certain circumstances, take on a polemical and more sharply political meaning than is evident from its definitional association with justice. The chapter on property in the *Second Treatise*, I shall argue, has precisely this intentional objective: to provide a defense of "the industrious" and trading part of the nation—the constituency to whom the Whigs addressed their appeals—against the idle, unproductive, and Court-dominated property owners. Locke's argument, in other words, has the ring of much of the Whig election propaganda in its appeal to the nation to support "the industrious" rather than the "court parasites" or "pensioners."[143] If the overall political objectives of the *Two Treatises* are considered, this can hardly appear surprising. But I believe that with respect to his treatment of property, Locke's political aims can be more specifically stated.

"As much land as a man tills, plants, improves, cultivates, and can use the product of," Locke declares, "so much is his property." As we noted, this commandment to till the earth was a divine injunction, but, Locke adds, introducing the critical component of his teleological reading of God's intentions, man was commanded "to subdue the earth" in order to "improve it for the benefit of life, and therein lay out something upon it that was his own, his labor."[144] In Locke's view, God has a wider purpose in mind than simply providing for the individual's self-preservation; rather, individual labor is seen as a contributory action to the improvement and benefit of life, taken in a collective sense. Again, this should not surprise us, for Locke's view of natural law is that it is designed to provide

[142] *FT*, par. 42.

[143] *Popery and Arbitrary Government*, pp. 6–7; Penn, *England's Great Interest*, pp. 3–4; Bethel, *Interest of Princes and States*, p. 15. As framed by John Phillips, the contest was between "the industrious part of the nation" versus "the voluptuous" aristocracy and Court sycophants (*The Character of a Popish Successor . . . Part II*, 1681, p. 31 (*LL* #660); Thomas Hunt, *A Defence of Charter, and Municipal Rights of the City of London*, 1683, p. 45). Owen's defense against Parker's criticisms of the "honest industry" of those associated with "the trading interest" of England should also be kept in mind (John Owen, *Truth and Innocency Vindicated: in a Survey of a Discourse Concerning Ecclesiastical Polity*, 1669, pp. 78–80).

[144] *ST*, par. 32.

for the common good, and the benefit of mankind, and that it is given as a standard to individuals who exist as part of a "natural community."[145] It is within this teleological framework, I am arguing, that the entire discussion of property in chapter 5 of the *Second Treatise* must be viewed. In the passage immediately following the one cited above, Locke restates the same point in negative terminology: "Nor was this appropriation of any parcel of land, by improving it, any prejudice to any other man."[146] The fulfillment of God's intentions not only contributes to the common good, but it does no particular injury to any other individual. Moreover, Locke's reading of God's purposes—that "nothing was made by God for man to spoil or destroy"—is specifically applicable to the use of land.[147] Thus,

> God gave the world to men in common, but since he gave it to them for their benefit . . . it cannot be supposed he meant it should always remain common and uncultivated. He gave it to the use of the industrious and rational . . . not to the fancy or covetousness of the quarrelsome and contentious.[148]

Not only are God's designs realized by the industrious, the practical social benefits are both immense and, in a general sense, shared in common.[149] The empirical dimensions of this position seem self-evident to Locke. As he observes,

> The provisions serving to the support of human life, produced by one acre of enclosed and cultivated land, are . . . ten times more, than those which are yielded by an acre of land, of an equal richness, lying waste in common. And therefore he that encloses land and has

[145] *ST*, pars. 7, 128, 134, 135, 182; cf. Tyrrell, *Patriarcha non Monarcha*, pp. 15, 17, 29. "If the preservation of all mankind . . . were everyone's persuasion, as indeed it is everyone's duty, and the true principle to regulate our religion, politics, and morality by," we should all be much better off than we are (*STCE* #116).

[146] *ST*, par. 33.

[147] *ST*, par. 31. "No man in the state of nature, has a right to more land or territory than he can well manure for the necessities of himself and family" (Tyrrell, *Patriarcha non Monarcha*, p. 154).

[148] *ST*, par. 34.

[149] Locke applies the same reasoning, from the standpoint of the public good, to his argument for the institution of political society, wherein the individual "is to enjoy many conveniencies from the labor, assistance, and society of others in the same community" (*ST*, par. 130). This point is reaffirmed in the *Letter Concerning Toleration*, where Locke argues that the "honest industry" of every individual can be preserved through the "mutual assistance" of others to secure "the things that contribute to the comfort and happiness of this life," which can only "be procured or preserved by pains and industry" of all the members of society (*Works*, 5:42).

> a greater plenty of the conveniences of life from ten acres, than he could have from a hundred left to nature, may truly be said to give ninety acres to mankind.[150]

From our perspective on property rights as expressions of self-interest, this passage appears oddly phrased, if not downright disingenuous. That an individual would have the benefit of mankind in mind as the outcome of his enclosure and cultivation of land can, at best, be said to be a rather naive reading of human motivations. But Locke is plainly not interested in *individual motivations* for property development; rather, what concerns him are the moral and social uses to which property (and labor) can be put. It is quite true that, even under this view, particular individuals may be able to acquire considerable wealth as the outcome of their productive and beneficial actions, but to suggest that Locke ever sets men free from their natural law obligations such that wealth may be accumulated solely because individuals desire to do so and without any social constraints on its employment is to reverse completely the thrust of his argument in the *Second Treatise*, not to mention the political rationale of the Whigs' claim to represent the common good against the arbitrary self-interest of an individual (the king).

Since it would be a mistake to convey the impression that the critical edge of Locke's attitude toward property is merely a response to the contingencies of the exclusion crisis, I want to place the argument of the *Two Treatises* within a broader perspective, one subscribed to by Locke both before and after he wrote the chapter on property. I have already alluded to the importance of the theological framework as a specific response to Filmer's formulation of the problem. There is, however, another, socially rooted conception of labor and property that Locke, at least from the time of his association with Shaftesbury, incorporated into his understanding of political society. This view supplies a positive endorsement of laboring activity, productivity, and commercial expansion, and a corresponding critique of idleness and waste, however these attributes are expressed in any particular social context.[151] Seen from this vantage point, Locke's

150 *ST*, par. 37. These lines were added to a later edition of the *Two Treatises*, but the argument, with respect to the benefits to mankind of cultivated land versus "waste in common" was already present in the chapter (cf. ibid., pars. 36, 42).

151 Locke's attitude toward "waste," for example, is not merely a convenient attribute of his characterization of the early stage of social existence. "Waste of anything," Lady Masham wrote, Locke "could not bear to see," and she especially associated this character trait with his attitude toward property. Thus, "he often found fault" with proprietors who thought they could do anything they pleased with their property (Fox-Bourne, 2:536). "People should be accustomed from their cradles," Locke argued, "to spoil or *waste* nothing at all." The "spoiling of anything to no purpose" is nothing less than "*doing of mischief*"

chapter on property simply expresses through a specific formulation a general attitude characteristic of Locke's thought since the 1660s.

In his manuscript and subsequently in the published work on the lowering of interest, Locke defended "the sober and industrious" individuals who labor for the benefit of society.[152] These "industrious and thriving men" are identified with those who contribute to the manufacture of goods and to the expansion of trade.[153] He is especially concerned to identify the interests of artisans, manufacturers, and tradesmen with "the wheels of trade."[154] Locke's argument is directed, as we have seen, against the bankers who hold a disproportionate share of the kingdom's money in their hands, to the detriment of the public good.[155] Nevertheless, some of the blame must fall upon the foolish country gentleman or aristocrat who has "carried his money to London" and put it in the hands of the bankers.[156] This remark is part of a muted critique of landowners that runs as a leitmotif throughout the *Considerations*. For example, when Locke raises the question as to why land is sold on the market, he suggests two basic causal factors, neither of which reflect favorably upon landowners: The first, "general ill husbandry," is self-explanatory; the second is indebtedness. This condition, of course, might befall almost anyone, regardless of his personal virtues, but Locke is especially concerned with the relationship between "debauchery" or a "depraved education" and indebtedness. Both of these characteristics are associated with the belief, held by many landowners, that it is "fashionable for men to live beyond their estates."[157] This "costly itch after the materials of . . . luxury from abroad" is one cause for the scarcity of money and the consequent decay of trade.[158] The latter, in turn, leads to a decline in rents for the land-

(*STCE*, #116; italics in original). Since this is the way in which Locke viewed goods and property in general, not only does the prohibition against waste not disappear in the course of his discussion of property, but it can hardly be branded an "irrelevant" part of that discussion, as Plamenatz, for example, labels it (John Plamenatz, *Man and Society*, 2 vols., New York: McGraw-Hill, 1963, 1:242).

[152] *Works*, 4:20. "The industrious and frugal" (p. 72); cf. ibid., p. 75.

[153] *Works*, 4:39.

[154] *Works*, 4:8–9, 14–15, 28, 39. "All encouragement should be given to artifacers." Also, "manufacture deserves to be encouraged" (pp. 28–29).

[155] *Works*, 4:8–9, 28.

[156] *Works*, 4:9. "If money were more equally distributed . . . into a greater number of hands, according to the exigencies of trade," most of the problems addressed by Locke would be resolved (p. 64).

[157] *Works*, 4:53. Locke's observation that the "industrious" individual who accumulates wealth through manufacturing is shrewd enough to invest in land near enough to his businesses that "the estate may be under his eye" might be regarded as a subtle critique of absentee landlordism (p. 39).

[158] *Works*, 4:72.

owner, and thus to his indebtedness. So whether or not he realizes it, the country gentleman must take a much greater interest in trade—and a correspondingly diminishing interest in the conspicuous consumption of imported goods—not only to free himself from this cycle of indebtedness, but also in order for the country as a whole to prosper.[159] Locke's message, therefore, is that "if ill husbandry has wasted our riches," then only the practice of "general industry and frugality, joined to a well-ordered trade" will restore the wealth of the nation.[160] Locke is thus able to contrast the social values of "sobriety, frugality, and industry" associated with trade with the "debauchery" and "expensive vanity" of "lazy and indigent people" who "waste" their resources through extravagant living.[161]

This aspect of Locke's argument has been little noticed. Much more attention has been paid to Locke's recognition of the fact that the laboring class lives from hand to mouth, an observation that is often cited as though it represented a derogatory judgment on Locke's part.[162] But this is not Locke's view. On the contrary, these individuals, whatever the paucity of their temporal rewards, are at least fulfilling the divine injunction given to all individuals to labor—and to labor, moreover, for the common good. "We ought to look on it as a mark of goodness in god," Locke argues, "that he has put us in this life under a necessity of labor." For, it is the "ill men at leisure" who are likely to commit "the mischiefs" that distress others. Thus labor preserves us "from the ills of idleness."[163] "I think," Locke wrote to a friend, "everyone, according to what way providence has placed him in, is bound to labor for the public good, as far as he is able, or else he has no right to eat."[164] As Dunn observes, anyone

159 *Works*, 4:54–55.

160 *Works*, 4:61, 55.

161 *Works*, 4:53–55, 72–75.

162 *Works*, 4:71. C. B. Macpherson, *The Political Theory of Possessive Individualism*, Oxford: Oxford University Press, 1962, pp. 224ff.; Strauss, *Natural Right*, pp. 242–243. The context of Locke's description, which is almost universally ignored, is the removal of the working class from "the usual struggle and contest" over economic goods, which "is between the landed man and the merchant." Locke, in other words, is noting that laborers as a "body of men" have no "time or opporunity to . . . struggle with the richer" classes in society, except when "some common and great distress" has the effect of "uniting them . . . as one common interest" and makes them de facto participants in the "struggle and contest" between classes. Not only is the meaning of Locke's observation generally distorted (with talk about rationality, which is not mentioned at all in the passage), but it is far from clear that the nonparticipation by the laborers in the class struggle is not, in Locke's view, a socially positive comment about their behavior.

163 Cited in J. Dunn, *Political Thought of Locke*, p. 232.

164 Locke to William Molyneux (January 19, 1694), *Works*, 8:332.

who fulfilled his "calling" in these terms executed his obligations under the Law of Nature.[165]

We can appreciate the socially critical dimensions of this general admonition if we attend to Locke's application of it to various social groups within his society. Here again, great emphasis has been given to the harshness of his attitude toward "the idle poor." Certainly, they are a problem with respect to the injunction both to labor and to pursue the common good. But they are not the only social group that poses a problem, and it could be argued that, unless their numbers grow exceedingly large, the poor are not even the primary example of idleness in Locke's society. In notes on trade he made in 1674 for Shaftesbury, Locke divided society into two groups: "those that contribute in any way" to trade, and those who are "idle" or who do not advance the wealth of society. In the first group Locke placed those who worked in the mines, the clothing industry, as well as artisans and farmers. In the second group, are those "retainers" employed by landowners (and logically, the landowners themselves) who simply consume the commodities produced by others.[166] Here the laboring class is certainly included among those who "contribute in any way" to trade and the public good, while the idle gentry are negatively assessed by Locke. Later, in some journal notes, he suggests that "gentlemen" ought to spend at least three hours a day "in some honest labor," by which he means "manual labor." The consequence of this slightly utopian demand would be an improvement of the condition of "all mankind," and hence, a truer fulfillment of the precepts of natural law than presently exists in society.[167] These notes, it is true, are somewhat fanciful, but the underlying attitude that they express is not, and it reappears in Locke's correspondence with Clarke in the 1680s, and subsequently in *Some Thoughts Concerning Education*, which is based upon that correspondence. Thus, Locke will not allow "a gentleman's calling" to be defined except in a manner that includes his learning "a manual trade, nay two or three."[168] Moreover, he appeals to the "ancients" who "understood very well how to reconcile manual labor with affairs of state" and even "great men" did not regard laboring activity as a "lessening [of] their dignity."[169]

Locke contrasts the "honest labor in useful and mechanical arts" favorably with "the luxury of Courts," the "idle and useless employ-

[165] J. Dunn, *Political Thought of Locke*, p. 253.

[166] MS c.30, fol. 18. I say that Locke wrote these notes for Shaftesbury because, like the *Essay on Toleration*, they are written with respect to "your" (Charles') kingdom.

[167] Cited in J. Dunn, *Political Thought of Locke*, pp. 231–232.

[168] *STCE* #201; *Correspondence*, 3:343–353.

[169] *STCE* #205.

ments'' of ''the rich and noble'' whose ''pride and vanity'' have led them to regard such laboring activity as a ''disgrace.''[170] Those who inherit ''a plentiful fortune'' may be ''excused from having a particular calling in order to their subsistence in this life,'' but they are not excused from being ''under an obligation of doing something'' in order to carry out the precepts of ''the law of God'' to labor for the benefit of mankind.[171] Laboring activity, in other words, is never detached from its conjunction with the advancement of the public good.[172] Political society is instituted for the latter purpose, and even if Locke did not have a more than slightly suspicious attitude toward ''the rich and noble'' and the possession of wealth, there is no way in which he could be supposed to have conceptualized political society in a manner that, in effect, excluded ''the laboring class,'' as Macpherson suggests.[173] On the contrary, Locke's general attitude toward manual labor, toward ''the necessity of labor,'' and toward those who worked in the mines or textile industries, as I have tried to demonstrate, was overwhelmingly positive. His attitude toward idle landowners, the ''useless employments'' of the ''rich and noble,'' and those of inherited wealth who do nothing to advance the common good, on the other hand, is decidedly negative. This framework, I am arguing, through which Locke perceived the activities of various groups within his own society, is one he developed prior to (and retained following) his writing of the *Two Treatises*. It ought, therefore, to be kept in mind as the prism through which the activities described in the chapter on property in the *Second Treatise* are reflected and evaluated.

Returning to the argument of that chapter, we have seen that to this point, Locke's theoretical and political objectives in his treatment of property have jointly reinforced the importance and natural law endorsement of those who cultivate the land and so benefit mankind. At this juncture,

[170] Cited in J. Dunn, *Political Thought of Locke*, pp. 232–233.

[171] King, 1:181.

[172] See Locke's discussion in his journal (1677) of the labor we expend ''to procure new and beneficial productions . . . whereby our stock of riches . . . may be increased, or better preserved,'' which is written from the standpoint of our divinely constituted natures and the ''concernment mankind hath'' in our fulfillment of our capacities for labor (King, 1:162–166).

[173] ''Locke recognized . . . that the members of the laboring class . . . were unfit to participate in political life'' (Macpherson, *Possessive Individualism*, p. 230). Apart from the fact that Locke never said anything of the sort, this statement must be measured against the fact that Shaftesbury and the Whigs were busily engaged in organizing members of the laboring class (including apprentices) to sign petitions, engage in political demonstrations, and even vote, and hence they contributed more to the integration of laborers into participation in political life than any other force in the seventeenth century, except, perhaps, the Levellers.

however, the theoretical argument takes a crucial turning, with the invention of money, but (and this is the point I wish to emphasize) Locke's *political* attitude remains unchanged. Throughout the chapter on property, Locke insists that those who cultivate the land contribute to the common good, while those who do not do so are wasteful landowners and, from the standpoint of society, useless individuals. The invention of money, along with certain other demographic factors, changes the form of the society within which this contrast takes on a distinct social importance, but it does not at all mitigate the forcefulness of Locke's moral and political argument. The invention of money, and commerce with other parts of the world, in other words, may themselves be justifiable practices if they are viewed as being consonant with the natural law command to provide for the common good—which is the way Locke views them—but they provide no justification whatsoever for the "wasteful" use of landed property.[174]

"A thousand acres . . . without any improvement, tillage, or husbandry," Locke argues, is not worth "ten acres" of "well-cultivated" land in Devonshire. The former is simply an "uncultivated waste" and contributes nothing to "increase the common stock of mankind."[175] The contrast here is presented with the "wilds" of America, but Locke displays the same attitude toward the thousands of acres of uncultivated land in seventeenth-century England. "Even amongst us," he maintains, "land that is left wholly to Nature, that hath no improvement of pasturage, tillage, or planting, is called, as indeed it is, waste; and we shall find the benefit of it amount to little more than nothing."[176] Locke's approval for the individual who "by his labor does . . . enclose [land] from the common," is a major theme throughout the chapter on property in the *Second Treatise*.[177] And conversely, he insists, "the extent of ground is of so little value without labor" that it qualifies only as "wasteland."[178] It is true

[174] Strauss's contention that "the natural law prohibition against waste is no longer valid in civil society" (*Natural Right*, p. 241) is mistaken not only in terms of the text (of *ST*, chap. 5), but also for the reasons given in note 151 above.

[175] *ST*, par. 37.

[176] *ST*, par. 42. This is the way such land is referred to in, for example, the Calendar of Treasury Books.

[177] *ST*, pars. 30, 32, 37, 40, 43. There is no warrant for Tully's conclusion that Locke is attacking the enclosure of land. The passage he cites (par. 35) is simply a defense of the requirement of the consent of commoners before anyone can enclose *their* land; it is certainly not an attack upon the enclosure of "waste" land. Nor, in my view, is there any basis for his conclusion that "the only form of property in land which [Locke] endorses in the *Two Treatises* is the English Common" (Tully, *Discourse on Property*, pp. 153–154, 169). See note 199 below.

[178] *ST*, pars. 36, 37, 38, 42, 45.

that, within civil society, where "the laws regulate the right of property, and the possession of land is determined by positive constitutions," no one can enclose the commons "without the consent of all his fellow commoners." Hence, "the law of the land . . . is not to be violated" merely for the sake of enclosure.[179] Yet in those instances in which the law is doubtful (as in Spain) or is nonexistent (as in America), Locke endorses enclosure even to the point of arguing that if someone has already enclosed the land but allowed it to remain uncultivated, then the land, "notwithstanding his enclosure, was still to be looked on as waste, and might be the possession of any other."[180] It seems strange that this rather radical endorsement of the claims of labor over those of land ownership has been so little commented upon by those who are so eager to award Locke the honor of having formulated the modern defense of the private ownership of property.

Obviously, Locke was not advocating the return of the Diggers, though his attitude toward property is not so far removed from theirs as is generally assumed.[181] Nevertheless, except in cases of extreme necessity, covered by the divine command to practice charity, individuals could not appeal to the Law of Nature to override the legally established property limits within society.[182] Even so, by framing his argument in such a way

[179] *ST*, par. 35.

[180] *ST*, pars. 36, 38. Thomas Hunt also endorsed the natural right "to break the civil enclosure of property" if the choice were between productive subsistence and idle ownership (*Postscript*, preface). Hunt was a radical Whig lawyer who may or may not have been privy to the Rye House conspiracy; he did, however, leave England to become one of the exiles in Holland sometime after the discovery of that conspiracy. According to Winstanley, "God made the earth for the use and comfort of all mankind" and because "we have a right to the common ground" derived from both the Law of Nature and Scriptures, "the common and waste grounds belong to the poor" (cited in Lewis H. Berens, *The Digger Movement in the Days of the Commonwealth*, London: Holland Press and Merlin Press, 1961, pp. 150–151).

[181] It should be recalled that the Diggers maintained that they did not intend "to meddle with any man's property nor to break down any . . . enclosures." Rather, they were merely claiming the right to cultivate "what was common and untilled" in order "to make it fruitful for the use of man." This argument presupposed that every individual had the natural right to produce his own subsistence (Berens, *Digger Movement*, p. 37; see also David W. Petegorsky, *Left-Wing Democracy in the English Civil War*, London: Victor Gollancz, 1940, pp. 163, 204–205). Whatever else may be said about the differences between the thought of Winstanley and that of Locke, the two men shared these fundamental assumptions. For other specific phrases and assumptions common to both thinkers, see *Left-Wing Democracy*, pp. 140–141, 147.

[182] *FT*, par. 42. This does not mean, however, as Strauss and Macpherson maintain, that the duties of charity are abandoned within civil society, or that "individuals can pursue their productive-acquisitive activity without obstruction" (Strauss, *Natural Right*, pp. 246–248; Macpherson, *Possessive Individualism*, p. 221). Speaking of those within society, Locke declares that "common charity teaches that those should be most taken care of by the law, who

as to knit together "labor," "cultivated land," and "the common good," Locke produced a powerful natural law critique of those individuals in society who neither labored nor contributed to the common good of society. Indeed, Locke's chapter on property is one of the most radical critiques of the landowning aristocracy produced during the last half of the seventeenth century. A qualification of this statement, as was suggested earlier, is needed in order to distinguish between the aristocracy as such and those who were merely the useless members of that class. Locke makes this point clear when he notes that it is not "the largeness of his possession" in land, but rather the allowing of it or its products to perish "uselessly" that is the critical standard to be applied to landlords and landownership. So long as a landowner "made use of" his land in such a way as to benefit others, "he did no injury" to mankind through the mere "largeness" of his possessions.[183] Still, Locke has no doubt that, in general, "numbers of men are to be preferred to largeness of dominions" as a standard for the economic and social development of society.[184] Labor

---

are least capable of taking care for themselves" (*Works*, 4:11). Nor is this merely a pietistic endorsement of a system of poor relief. The harshness of the treatment accorded to the idle poor in Locke's draft proposal for the Board of Trade has been much remarked upon; what has received little notice, however, is the provision that makes it a *crime* for any parish to allow any individual to die of starvation within its precincts (Fox-Bourne, 2:390). Not only is every individual entitled by the claims of charity (and the natural right to subsistence) to meat, drink, clothes, shelter, and heat, whether he works or not (p. 382), but Locke presses the issue further: It is an offense "against the common rule of charity" for one individual to "enrich himself so as to make another perish." Indeed, to take advantage of another in the marketplace by accumulating goods in such a fashion that "by reason of extortion" or the exploitation of another's "necessity" the individual suffers is, at a minimum, a form of robbery and, in the extreme instance, it is "murder" ("Venditio," Locke's journal note, published in John Dunn, "Justice and the Interpretation of Locke's Political Theory," *Political Studies* 16, no. 1 [1968]:85–86; cf. Jean Le Clerc, *An Account of the Life and Writings of John Locke*, 3d ed., 1714, p. 25).

[183] *ST*, par. 46. Olivecrona thus misses the point altogether by taking "appropriation" rather than use as the standard of property. In reversing Locke's emphasis, he not only gives precedence to enclosure over the cultivation of land, but he also places Locke unproblematically within that part of the natural law tradition which grants priority to occupation as a title to property rather than labor (Olivecrona, "Locke's Theory of Appropriation," p. 228). Similarly, Lamprecht's assertion that Locke's treatment of property is written from the standpoint of the aristocratic governing class represents a failure to understand the political context of the argument Locke is making in the *Two Treatises* (Lamprecht, *Moral Philosophy of Locke*, p. 125). It is certainly not based upon any evidence supplied by members of that class which indicates that this is the standpoint from which they read that work, nor, so far as I am aware, is there any such evidence to be found until well into the eighteenth century, when the political context for reading the *Two Treatises* had changed considerably.

[184] *ST*, par. 42. It is "plenty of people and money in proportion to . . . land" that is the pathway to wealth (MS e.8, in William Letwin, *The Origins of Scientific Economics*, London: Methuen, 1963, p. 274; *Works*, 4:63). "Riches consist in plenty of moveables . . . but

has an infinitely higher social value than does land for Locke. That is why "the right employing" of land—through the application of labor to it—"is the great art of government." For unless government encourages the productive, useful employment of land, unless it supports the "honest industry" of its subjects, society as a whole will suffer the consequences.[185] Again and again, the point was made by various writers that it was only the "laborious and industrious people" of the kingdom, such as butchers, brewers, drapers, mercers, bricklayers, carpenters, and productive farmers, who contributed to the advancement of trade; these efforts at "improvement" were contrasted with the behavior of "the landed and lazy," as William Petty called them.[186]

Thus far, I have presented Locke's argument in its negative terms, as a critique of a certain type of landowner among the aristocracy. There is, of course, a positive side to the argument as well. Here Locke's point is to establish an alliance among all those engaged in activities that do contribute to the advancement of the common good, and that are therefore in conformity with natural law commands. We have already seen Locke's admiration for the socially productive labor of those who "digged and wrought the iron" or "who felled and framed the timber," along with those who cultivate the land. These laboring activities clearly fulfilled the commands of God and the Law of Nature to employ labor "for the benefit of life." The case to be made for the use of money, however, is more problematic, and it rests directly upon "the tacit consent of men" rather than upon a divine injunction. Nevertheless, if the invention and use of money can be shown to be compatible with the advancement of the common good of mankind, then it, too, will fall under the authoritative endorsement of natural law. This is the point Locke sets out to prove midway through the chapter on property.

---

especially in plenty of gold and silver" and "power consists in numbers of men and ability to maintain them" (MS c.30, fol. 18). Thus, it is a large laboring force that is essential to "the riches of every country and that which makes it flourish" (MS f.3, fols. 198–199). For other contemporary opinions stressing the importance of industrious labor over land, see William Penn, *One Project for the Good of England,* [1680], p. 2; *Petty-Southwell Correspondence,* pp. 153–155; Reynell, *True English Interest,* p. 18; E. Lipson, *The Economic History of England,* 6th ed., 3 vols., London: Adam and Charles Black, 1961, 3:66; Joyce Oldham Appleby, *Economic Thought and Ideology in Seventeenth-Century England,* Princeton: Princeton University Press, 1978, pp. 133–134, 155. On the socioeconomic implications of this perspective, see D. C. Coleman, "Labor in the English Economy of the Seventeenth Century," in *Seventeenth-Century England,* ed. Paul S. Seaver, New York: New Viewpoints, 1976, pp. 112–138; T. E. Gregory, "The Economics of Employment in England, 1660–1713," *Economica* (January 1921), pp. 37–51.

[185] *ST,* par. 42. It is the labor of the landlord's tenant that gives the land its value (MS e.8, fol. 21).

[186] Appleby, *Economic Thought,* pp. 133–134, 155, 183.

It is useful to recall from our earlier discussion of the Whigs' defense of the two stages of social existence (which Locke endorsed in the *Two Treatises*) the fact that a congeries of social and economic relationships constitute the developed form of society. Thus, in the chapter on property, Locke places the invention of money in the context of the creation of this developed society, which is itself being defended by the Whigs as a normative model for the realization of the common good. In other words, such justification as can be claimed for the invention of money must be made in terms of its *social* benefits. It decidedly cannot be morally defensible on the grounds of hoarding by an individual.

It is true that Locke begins his discussion by conceding that the invention of money allows men to "enlarge" their possessions.[187] His aim, however, is not to supply a justification for the enlargement of possessions as such, but to show how "the disproportionate and unequal possession of the earth" has come about without the "express consent" of men, and to demonstrate that this transition and its consequences are in accordance with the dictates of natural law. Locke first mentions the invention of money in paragraph 36 of the chapter on property, but promises that he will consider the subject "more at large . . . by and by."[188] And, except for a passing reference in the following paragraph, Locke does not again take up the subject until paragraph 45. Between these references, Locke describes the conditions that explain the necessity for "the invention of money." From a subjective standpoint, the latter is rooted in "the desire of having more than men needed," but this fact alone could never explain the use of money, and, even if it could, it could not supply the necessary moral grounds to justify its use.[189] In paragraph 38, Locke writes:

> But as families increased, and industry enlarged their stocks, their possessions enlarged with the need of them; but yet it was commonly without any fixed property in the ground they made use of, till they incorporated, settled themselves together, and built cities, and then, by consent, they came in time, to set out the bounds of their distinct territories, and agree on limits between them and their neighbors, and by laws within themselves, settled the properties of those of the same society.[190]

[187] *ST*, par. 48.

[188] *ST*, par. 36.

[189] *ST*, par. 37. "Covetousness, and the desire of having in our possession . . . more than we have need of, being the root of all evil" (*STCE*, #110; cf. ibid., #105; *ELN*, pp. 205–215).

[190] *ST*, par. 38.

The enlargement of families, the establishment of cities, and leagues or treaties with neighboring cities, and so on, are associated with the "enlargement" of men's possessions. "Associated" is, I believe, the proper word, since I wish to avoid—as I believe Locke does—positing a causal relationship as to the invention of money. There is, rather, a convergence of the psychological and sociological conditions in Locke's account of the latter. Commentators have generally focused their attention on the psychological, individual/object, aspect of Locke's discussion of property. But that Locke means to stress the importance of sociological conditions is evident from his repetition in paragraph 45 of the point cited above when, as he had promised, he takes up the subject of money "more at large."

Now he once again observes that "the increase of people and stock," the fact that "several communities settled the bounds of their distinct territories, and by laws within themselves, regulated the properties of the private men of their society, and so, by compact and agreement, settled the property which labor and industry began," and the fact that "leagues . . . have been made between states and kingdoms," are all associated "with the use of money."[191] In short, there is clearly a type of society "where there is plenty of people under government, who have money and commerce" and in which property regulations are based upon consent and laws that emerges at some point in history and does so in the form of a complex of interrelated factors, of which the invention of money is one.[192]

I will return to this point in a moment, but there is another aspect to Locke's treatment of property that is discussed in the hiatus between his first mention of money and his subsequent consideration of the subject that merits our attention. Most of the paragraphs between 36 and 45 are concerned to demonstrate that well-cultivated land is capable of producing much more than any one person or family could possibly consume. Hence, "an acre of land that bears here twenty bushels of wheat" produces a thousand times more "profit" for its owner than does an acre of land in America produce for its user, an Indian. What is especially interesting about this comparison (which, like all the others Locke makes in the chapter, is designed to emphasize the value of labor) is that Locke never suggests that the Indian's acre is not sufficient to support his existence. Nor does he suggest that the English landowner consumes himself the twenty bushels of wheat he produces. Rather, the comparison is stated in monetary terms and with reference to its social benefits. Thus,

[191] *ST*, par. 45.
[192] *ST*, par. 35.

"the benefit mankind receives" from the English acre "in one year, is worth £5 and from the other possibly not worth a penny, if all the profit an Indian received from it were to be valued, and sold here."[193] The "useful products" of this piece of well-cultivated land, in other words, are seen in terms of the "profit" that accrues to the landowner who sells them in exchange for other goods, and through him, "the benefit mankind receives" that this sale and exchange of commodities passes on to other members of society. This fact of social existence, arising from the technical application of labor to land and the consequent productive surplus of goods that flow from cultivated land is simply carried forward by Locke and incorporated into his discussion of money beginning with paragraph 45.

In fact, that discussion begins with the presupposition that productive labor generates a surplus of goods, for, Locke argues, one individual was entitled "to give away" part of this surplus to another individual, and that if he did so, it could not be denied that he had "made use" of his property within the definitional limits set by the Law of Nature. The same principle applies, Locke maintains, "if he also bartered away" part of his surplus in exchange for some other useful product. This action could not be viewed as a waste of "the common stock" of property.[194] Immediately following this point, Locke applies the same reasoning to the exchange of goods for money.

> And thus came in the use of money, some lasting thing . . . that by mutual consent men would take in exchange for the truly useful, but perishable supports of life.[195]

Money, as Locke elsewhere emphasizes, is a commodity of exchange, an instrument for the development of trade. Indeed, this is its primary and its most socially beneficial role.[196] It is in terms of this definition that

[193] *ST*, par. 43. The other side of this comparison is drawn between "a king of a large and fruitful territory" in America who "is clad worse than a day laborer in England" (par. 41). In his clarification of this point in the following paragraph, Locke refers to the value of "human industry" that produces clothes, bread, and the other items that explain why the day-laborer is better off (par. 42). In other words, the reference is not simply to the laboring activity of the individual(s)—even if the Indian chief worked harder than the day-laborer, his expenditure of effort would not affect the comparison—but between the social consequences of "labor and industry" within different types of societies.

[194] *ST*, par. 46.

[195] *ST*, par. 47. According to "the universal consent of mankind," individuals have agreed to accept money as a medium of exchange (*Works*, 4:22).

[196] Money is "a universal commodity" and as "necessary to trade as food is to life" (*Works*, 4:7, 14). It is the "standing measure" of all other commodities because individuals have agreed to accept it as a medium of exchange for all commodities (p. 44; MS b.3). Locke

Locke provides a justification for the invention of money in the *Second Treatise*. "For supposing an island, separate from all possible commerce with the rest of the world," he asks the reader, "what reason could anyone have there to enlarge his possessions beyond the use of his family, and a plentiful supply to its consumption?" Without money and "commerce with the rest of the world," Locke argues, an individual would have no reason "to enlarge his possessions."

> For I ask, what would a man value ten thousand, or an hundred thousand acres of excellent land, ready cultivated, and well stocked too with cattle, in the middle of the in-land parts of America, where he had no hopes of commerce with other parts of the world, to draw money to him by the sale of the product?[197]

Interestingly, he also remarks that, in these circumstances, the land "would not be worth the enclosing," indicating how closely linked in Locke's mind the value of land itself, and especially cultivated land, was to the existence of commerce and a money exchange economy.[198] The view that "the encouraging of tillage" was "the surest and effectualest

---

says this so often that the point would hardly be worth noting, except for the fact that Macpherson blithely discounts this social function, arguing that "the characteristic purpose of money is to serve as capital. . . . Indeed its function as a medium of exchange was seen as subordinate to its function as capital" (*Possessive Individualism*, pp. 206–207). Macpherson derives this odd conclusion from the fact that Locke recognizes that, in addition to serving as a medium of exchange, money can yield income through interest (*Works*, 4:33). It is, one might have thought, a rather long historical step from interest-bearing capital to a justification of "unlimited capitalist appropriation," such as Macpherson suggests Locke had in mind (p. 221). Locke had no particular objections to the interest function of money, but everything he ever wrote on that subject subordinated that function *entirely* to the advancement of trade, and hence to the importance of the function of money as a medium of exchange. He wrote of money "considered in its *proper* use as a commodity passing in exchange," and not in terms of Macpherson's conception of capitalist appropriation (*Works*, 4:42; italics added). After he has drawn the comparison between the "use" of money (which yields interest) and the use of land through labor (which yields rent), both of which are a consequence of unequal distribution, Locke argues that more "use" can be gained from employing money in trade—this is the whole point of his essay—than through any other means (Letwin, *Origins*, pp. 285–288). At best, one might say that Locke recognizes the need for circulating capital, but this is not an argument for the priority of "real" capital that Macpherson imputes to him. For a critique of Macpherson's argument along these lines, see Karen Ivarsen Vaughn, *John Locke: Economist and Social Scientist*, Chicago: University of Chicago Press, 1982, pp. 53–54, 102. Hence, if such a thing as capitalism were to arise from the ashes of Locke's argument, it would have to emerge from the accumulation of merchants' capital, and not by way of the circuitous route of interest, which Macpherson takes to be the basis for Locke's endorsement of capital accumulation.

[197] *ST*, par. 48; cf. ibid., par. 26. Tyrrell also makes this point (*Patriarcha non Monarcha*, p. 153).

[198] This point was stressed, for example, by Petyt, *Britannia Languens*, pp. 10–14; Reynell, *True English Interest*, pp. 18–20, 41.

means of promoting and advancing any trade," especially with respect to the "great quantities of land within this kingdom . . . lying in a manner waste and yielding little" was certainly one shared by Shaftesbury and Locke.[199]

The point Locke believes he has demonstrated is that "a man may fairly possess more land than he himself can use the product of" if he lives under those social conditions in which "by receiving in exchange for the overplus, gold and silver," he is able to "make use of" his land through engaging in "commerce with other parts of the world."[200] This exchange not only does no injury to anyone, it is positively beneficial to society, and it explains why land in England is so much more profitable than land in America. It should be noted that it is in this context of Locke's discussion of money as an exchange commodity that he states that "largeness of possession" of land does not, in itself, exceed "the bounds of . . . just property."[201] Largeness of landownership, in other words, is tied to an exchange of its "useful products," so that whatever its actual size, productive use (that is, cultivation and exchange) remains the critical factor

[199] The quotation is taken from a 1663 statute on the exportation of corn (Lipson, *Economic History*, 2:451). The subject of enclosures in seventeenth-century England is too complicated to be dealt with here. Suffice it to say that there was no simple pro or con position on enclosure because there were various types of enclosure, undertaken by different classes of landowners, with differing benefits to the public. As Lipson points out, enclosure "to promote better methods of tillage . . . enlisted general approval," especially among those social groups which comprised the political constituency of the Whigs, while the enclosure of arable land for pasture or for parks, which depopulated the countryside, was "generally condemned" (pp. 397, 406). Which of these two types of enclosure could provide the greater number of examples for the Restoration period is not easy to say, but the most spectacular example of land redevelopment was certainly the reclaiming of large expanses of wasteland in eastern England (Barry Coward, *The Stuart Age: A History of England, 1603–1714*, London: Longman Group, 1980, p. 13; cf. W. H. R. Curtler, *The Enclosure and Redistribution of Our Land*, Oxford: Clarendon Press, 1920; E. C. K. Gonner, "The Progress of Inclosure during the Seventeenth Century," *English Historical Review* 91 [July 1908]:477–501). In the general process of reclamation of wasteland, it was the small and middle gentry, or yeomen, who played the leading role, not the aristocracy or larger landowners (John Clapham, *A Concise Economic History of Britain*, Cambridge: Cambridge University Press, 1963, p. 206; Charles Wilson, *England's Apprenticeship, 1603–1763*, London: Longman, 1965, pp. 151–153). In a memorial drafted in 1669 among the Shaftesbury papers, it is argued that the wealth of the kingdom depends chiefly upon a large industrious labor force and the "enclosing of wastes and manuring them to tillage." Though both Christie and Cranston assumed Shaftesbury to be the author of the memorial, Haley disagrees, on the basis of certain statements contained in the document (Haley, p. 258). Haley may be right, though in this case I find his arguments weak and I am inclined to agree with Christie. In any case, I would argue that the document certainly expresses Shaftesbury's views on the points I have cited. The work is printed as appendix 1 in W. D. Christie, *A Life of Anthony Ashley Cooper, First Earl of Shaftesbury*, 2 vols., 1871, 2:vi–ix.

[200] *ST*, par. 50.

[201] *ST*, pars. 49, 50, 51.

in assessing its value. To put the point another way, it could be said that while Locke's evaluative criterion—productive labor—remains constant, its meaning changes according to the nature of the social context within which this activity finds expression. Hence, once productive labor applied to land has produced a surplus that exceeds the limits of familial consumption, that labor must, in order to retain its productive character, be viewed in relation to the extended world of commerce. Macpherson's statement that Locke's argument justifies "unlimited appropriation" of property is an ill-chosen phrase, since it is not land nor its appropriation that Locke wishes to justify, but rather the extension of trade. And although limitless commercial expansion cannot be simply equated with capitalist appropriation, nevertheless in terms of the political and economic attitude underlying Locke's general argument about property, as well as in terms of the historical relationship between commercial expansion and the development of capitalism, perhaps Locke's position is not so far removed from what Macpherson has in mind as some of the latter's critics have argued.[202]

[202] It is striking how many of Macpherson's critics have accepted the basic dimensions of his argument. Isaiah Berlin, for example, has no qualms in proclaiming that Macpherson has established "Locke's claims to be regarded as the spokesman of unlimited capitalist appropriation," and this point is seconded by Geraint Parry, and by Strauss (Isaiah Berlin, "Hobbes, Locke and Professor Macpherson," *Political Quarterly* 35, no. 4 [October–December 1964]:461; Geraint Parry, *John Locke*, London: George Allen and Unwin, 1978, p. 123). As Dunn, Tully, E. J. Hundert ("The Making of *Homo Faber*: John Locke Between Ideology and History," *Journal of the History of Ideas* 33, no. 1 [January–March 1972]:3–22), and others have argued, not only did Locke not set out with the intention of providing such a justification, but Macpherson's inattention to what Locke was trying to do obscures the extent to which the chapter on property in the *Second Treatise* functions as a critique of existing property relationships. I trust it is clear that in this debate I have sided with Macpherson's critics, both on general methodological grounds and with respect to particular substantive suggestions. In the first category are the significance of the actor's intentions as a guide to the meaning of his actions, and the sociological evidence necessary to establish what type of social structure exists (both in reality and in his consciousness). In the second category are the theological assumptions about labor, property, and the calling, and Locke's critical attitude toward landownership and wealth. Having said this, I nevertheless think that some of Macpherson's critics, and Dunn especially, have implied that the very objective of providing a rationalization for the social structure as a whole represents a serious misconception on the part of the interpreter as to the kind of action a political theorist like Locke could have taken. I cannot accept this position, either in general with respect to political theorists as historical individuals or with respect to Locke in particular. More concretely, if Macpherson had not fastened so precipitously upon "capitalist appropriation" as the construct through which he views Locke, a pathway leading from "productive labor"—tying together artisans, merchants, laborers, and small farmers—might, in the end, have eventually led him, as it did Adam Smith and other eighteenth-century thinkers, to perceive that the seeds for a justification of a new order were indeed embedded in the ideological critique of an unproductive landowning aristocracy.

In any event, Locke's examples, both hypothetical and real, are intended to illustrate the obvious (to the Whigs) point that trade does benefit society as a whole. And, incidentally, it also increases the value of land. Thus, the invention of money and the institution of commerce are practices that are within the compass of natural law commands to provide for the common good of mankind. To summarize, I have tried to show that, in its negative application, Locke's chapter on property in the *Second Treatise* constitutes a radical critique of a wasteful section of the landowning aristocracy, and that, in its positive formulation, Locke's argument attempts to prove that laboring activity, the cultivation of land, and commercial exchange are all beneficial activities for the development of English society. The political message of the chapter was clear enough: Artisans, small gentry, yeoman farmers, tradesmen, and merchants were all productive members of society and ought, therefore, to unite in the pursuit of their interests against an idle and wasteful landowning aristocracy in order to establish that kind of society in which all sections of the social structure could work together for the realization of the common good.

Prior to this extended discussion of Locke's treatment of property, I had suggested that the Whigs very much needed a theory of property rights that would appeal to the gentry, reassuring them as to the security of their property, without, at the same time, abandoning the language and defense of property rights in terms that appealed to the urban commercial classes of Whig supporters. If we place Locke's discussion of property within this political context, we can appreciate how admirably he fulfilled these requirements while also resolving the theoretical problem of property that had preoccupied Grotius and Pufendorf. Moreover, if we compare Locke's treatment of property with that of Tyrrell, we can see why, despite the numerous parallels and similarities that exist between the two arguments, Locke's is not only the superior theoretical formulation, it is also far more radical in its political implications.

Though Tyrrell gives prominence to the relationship of labor to property, he confuses the issue by also allowing "occupancy"—which was also the criterion of Pufendorf and Grotius—to supply a claim for property rights.[203] Occupancy, however, carries with it no necessary injunc-

[203] All property in the state of nature, Tyrrell argues, "being but occupancy or possession" (Tyrrell, *Patriarcha non Monarcha*, pp. 49, 65, 139, 149–150). Richard Cumberland also argued for occupancy as the basis for the right to property in the state of nature. Tyrrell subsequently published *A Brief Disquisition of the Law of Nature, According to the Principles and Method laid down in the Rev. Dr. Cumberland's Latin Treatise on that Subject*, 1692, which, as the title suggests, indicates how closely he followed Cumberland's approach. Burnet also regarded occupancy as the source of a title to property (Burnet, 2:36, 38).

tion to improve the land, and the concept could therefore be easily stretched to include a justification of the aristocratic landowner's occupancy of land that, in Locke's terminology, would be adjudged wasteland. This was probably not Tyrrell's intention; he was, after all, a "disaffected" Whig. Yet, some Royalists were willing to use occupancy in their accounts of the origins of property, and they were certainly not embarked upon a critique of aristocratic landownership.[204]

Second, Tyrrell is so terribly conscious of the necessity to refute the accusation of levelling imputed to the Whigs that much of the emphasis of his argument is defensive in tone. He is so eager to disassociate himself from any intention of advocating a "change" in "the course" of property as it is "already established" that his argument amounts to a wholesale endorsement of existing property relations, whatever their form or social utility. Without his advocating that any individual in civil society could actually be deprived of his property—and in fact reaffirming several times that this cannot happen within societies based on consent—Locke, nevertheless, is able to convey an altogether different tone in his discussion of property, one that is much more radical and hostile in its attitude toward a certain form of "established" property than anything to be found in *Patriarcha non Monarcha*.

Third, Locke's argument supporting the need for labor, cultivated land, and commerce—and their concomitant interests—to unite in defense of their common interests is much more clearly formulated and tightly knit together in its theoretical structure than is Tyrrell's effort to realize the same general objectives. This last point, to return to the discussion of Whig election propaganda, was one the Whigs wished to convey to the electorate, but in fact, only a few attempts were made to construct a bridge between the gentry's economic interests and those of "the trading part of the nation." Possibly more efforts were not undertaken owing to the difficulty in dealing with the theoretical problem of property, or perhaps many individuals genuinely did not see how the gentry's interests could be rendered compatible with those of the urban trading classes. There are, however, a few references in the exclusion literature that reveal, on a purely pragmatic level, the basis for this alliance between members of the various social classes. William Petyt, for example, spoke of "a concatenation and sympathy between the interest of land and trade," and he affirmed the proposition that the value of land increased as a consequence of the advancement of trade. The growth of trade, Petyt reasoned, would lead to a higher level of domestic consumption of agricultural products, and in order to accommodate this growth in demand, the land

[204] J. Turner, *Sermon before Ward*, epistle dedicatory.

would have to "receive an inevitable improvement": that is, cultivation undertaken by the "industrious members" of the landowning classes.[205] As another writer put it,

> The more a country is enclosed, and the less waste grounds, commons, and forests there are, the more populous, wealthy, and full of trade it will be. And the smaller estates the land is divided into, the better for the nation.[206]

In this regard, Locke's attack upon primogeniture deserves mention, since the abolition of this practice would have undercut the rationale for many of the then existing large landed estates, and thus would have produced the consequences advocated in the citation above.[207] In this respect, too, as well as in some of the language he used, Locke's views on property are much closer to those of the Levellers than we have generally been led to believe.[208] It may not have been Locke's intention, or one to which the Whigs generally wanted to give prominent attention, but as the radical author of one Civil War tract had observed, the effect of this encouragement of industrious labor, enclosure of waste, and the elimination of primogeniture was that "the wealth of the land is more equally distributed amongst the natives."[209]

Other Whigs, following what I believe was Shaftesbury's view of the matter, argued that the encouragement of trade would not only bring material benefits to the nation as a whole, but it would also foster a general spirit of "industry" among the people. According to the author of one tract, this would, for example, help to discourage the "idleness" that

[205] Petyt, *Britannia Languens*, preface, pp. 13–14.

[206] Reynell, *True English Interest*, pp. 20, 41.

[207] Locke makes a direct and sustained attack on primogeniture in the *First Treatise*. His argument is that all children of the father have "the same title" to his property as a consequence of their natural rights claim and his natural law obligation to provide for their nourishment. Moreover, Locke makes it clear that since this is "a right not only to a bare subsistence but to the conveniences and comforts of life, as far as the conditions of their parents can afford it," the rights claim of the children extends to *all* the property owned by the father (*FT*, pars. 87–98, 111, 112, 119; Tully, *Discourse on Property*, p. 169).

[208] For the Levellers' attack on primogeniture, see Petegorsky, *Left-Wing Democracy*, p. 109; Margaret James, *Social Problems and Policy during the Puritan Revolution 1640–1660*, London: Routledge and Kegan Paul, 1966, pp. 26, 97–99. Tully emphasizes the extent to which Locke is willing to make the "community of goods . . . mutual assistance, and maintenance" of all its members an essential part of his definition of the family (*ST*, par. 83; Tully, *Discourse on Property*, pp. 133–134). Locke also endorsed the need for a national land registry of titles, another demand the Levellers had put forward (*Works*, 4:75; Haley, p. 245).

[209] Appleby, *Economic Thought*, p. 113.

characterized the social behavior of many landowners.[210] As more than one writer argued, "tradesmen are a very substantial and useful part" of the nation, and they exemplify "more industry" in "their way of living" than do gentlemen and the nobility.[211]

It is, of course, difficult to assess the efficacy of these Whig arguments, but judged purely in terms of the prevailing economic situation in the last quarter of the seventeenth century, they should have carried some force among the gentry. The latter were under considerable economic pressure exerted against them by large landowners who were attempting to increase the size of their estates through a consolidation of small parcels of land. Hence, throughout this period, the small landowner was being squeezed—economically and politically—out of the marketplace.[212] This situation did not automatically push him into the waiting arms of the urban bourgeoisie, nor did it necessarily make the Whig ideas of equality or resistance any less unpalatable than they had been during his most prosperous days. Nonetheless, there was a real economic basis for the political strategy of fomenting an ideological opposition between the small gentry and the large landowning aristocracy. Without discounting the primary importance of the antipopery issue, it seems likely that some measure of the success as the Whigs did achieve in getting their message across to the gentry—which surprised even their opponents—was due to the ideological appeals the Whigs addressed to their "country neighbors" that were grounded in extolling the virtues of "honest industry."

On reflection, the electoral struggles of the exclusion crisis amounted to something of a high point in the success of the Whig political movement. The Whigs created an efficient party organization and mounted an effective propaganda campaign. They won each of the three elections, gaining increasingly larger majorities in the House of Commons. And that body passed the exclusion bill and steadfastly refused to grant Charles II any money until the bill had received the royal assent. From the standpoint of a purely electoral movement, and in relation to the po-

210 Bethel, *The Interest of Princes and States*, p. 3. Shaftesbury had frequently emphasized the importance of "the industrious part of the nation" to the social and economic welfare of England (Haley, p. 254).

211 Cited in Schlatter, *Social Ideas*, p. 161.

212 By the end of the seventeenth century, land was becoming "more and more concentrated in the hands of the larger farmers" (Joan Thirsk, "Seventeenth Century Agriculture and Social Change," in *Seventeenth Century England*, ed. Seaver, pp. 80–81; Lawrence Stone, "Social Mobility in England, 1500–1700," in ibid., p. 36; L. A. Clarkson, *The Pre-Industrial Economy in England, 1500–1750*, London: Batsford, 1971, pp. 63–64, 218; D. C. Coleman, *The Economy of England, 1450–1750*, London: Oxford University Press, 1977, pp. 125, 128; G. E. Mingay, *English Landed Society in the Eighteenth Century*, London: Routledge and Kegan Paul, 1963, pp. 15, 50).

litical institutions of Restoration England open to their influence through electoral success, it is difficult to see what more the Whigs could have hoped to have accomplished. But, of course, the Whig political movement was not a purely electoral undertaking, and as the remaining obstacles to the achievement of their aims appeared to be oblivious to the effects of petitions, elections, and Commons' votes, a more treacherous and perilous path lay before Shaftesbury and his followers.

7

FROM RESISTANCE TO REVOLUTION

THROUGHOUT 1680, Shaftesbury and the Whigs maintained a high level of political pressure directed against the king. The petitioning campaign, begun in the winter of 1679, continued into the following year. As late as August 1680, Locke was reporting to Shaftesbury the presentation of a petition to Charles II by the Lord Mayor of London, which asked the king to call Parliament into session.[1] New witnesses revealing an Irish extension of the popish plot were presented to the nation in the early spring, to the further alarm and anxiety of the populace.[2] In July and August, the Duke of Monmouth was sent on a progress, or tour, of the west country to stir up popular support for the Whigs and to prepare their supporters for the sitting of Parliament, which was expected to meet in the autumn. At one point on the duke's progress, an estimated twenty thousand people turned out to greet him.[3] The Whigs, in other words, were pursuing their constitutional strategy, grounded in the mobilization of popular support.

The king, on the other hand, exercised his prerogative in defensive counterattack. In addition to his frequent announcements of the postponement of Parliament, which had been scheduled to meet at the end of January 1680, Charles II initiated a systematic purge of Whigs from their offices as magistrates or deputy lieutenants in the counties.[4] The government also considered interfering with the election of the London sheriffs, but in the end, it backed down in the face of the almost certain riot that would have resulted if it had attempted to set aside the election results.[5]

[1] *Correspondence*, 2:227.

[2] Haley, pp. 575, 594–595.

[3] Bryan Little, *The Monmouth Episode*, London: Werner Laurie, 1956, pp. 47–50. Dalrymple's figure of 30,000 seems a bit inflated (Dalrymple, 1:274).

[4] Individuals "were dismissed from their magistracies in numbers unheard-of since 1661, and this purge continued after the dissolution of the Oxford Parliament in 1681" (J. P. Kenyon, ed., *The Stuart Constitution, 1603–1688*, Cambridge: Cambridge University Press, 1966, p. 495; MS Carte 228, fol. 146).

[5] Secretary Jenkins outlined the government's options in a memorandum that apparently circulated among several ministers. We could, he wrote, allow the election to take place and order the sheriffs to declare the Court candidates elected "whatever they find the books to be," or, alternatively, we could have the Whig candidates declared ineligible by the Court of Aldermen (presumably on the grounds that they were Nonconformists). "The first way is extremely dangerous to the King's affairs," and the sheriffs would not follow the second

In February, Charles summoned his brother back from exile, an action that gave considerable encouragement to the king's supporters. So did the petitioning campaign of the Tories, a collection of "addresses" abhorring the Whigs' petitions for presuming to advise the king as to how to use his prerogative with respect to summoning parliaments. The meeting of that Parliament, when it finally did take place, gave every indication of promising a showdown between the Whigs and the Tories.

Despite the fact that Parliament had not met for over a year, the Whigs entered the battle in reasonably good order, so far as party unity and discipline were concerned. Deprived of a convenient forum and meeting place, they had nevertheless kept in frequent communication with one another through informal meetings. In April and May, for example, it was reported that Shaftesbury, Russell, Monmouth, and others were engaged in meetings that "shifted every night from house to house" in an effort to escape government surveillance.[6] In July 1680, Locke accompanied Shaftesbury and Monmouth to the former's country home, where they outlined the strategy for Monmouth's forthcoming progress.[7] In September, Monmouth, Grey, Russell, and other Whig leaders had gone off on a "hunting trip."[8] These quasi-political social gatherings—attendance at horse races was another popularly-disguised political meeting—helped to keep up party morale, and to keep the channels of communication open among the Whig party leaders. In preparing for their confrontation with the king's supporters in the fall, the Whigs retained their confidence because, as Burnet wrote, "they were sure of the nation, and of all future elections, as long as popery was in view."[9]

Nevertheless, an electorally based strategy had its limitations, and in the context of seventeenth-century English government—and Charles II's secret financial dealings with Louis XIV—these limitations were formidable. The Whigs, of course, were well aware of this fact. The other, darker, side of their direct appeal for popular support consisted of a threat

---

course, since the eligibility of the Whigs has already been conceded by the aldermen. Court interference with the election, Jenkins warned, "may bring us within the hazard of a tumult, which being once begun on such a popular account . . . nobody can tell where it will end." In the end, he concluded, "though the danger be great," it is probably safer to allow the Whigs to be elected than to engage in any "illegal or arbitrary" action to prevent that result (*CSPD*, 21:558).

[6] John Reresby, *Memoirs*, 1734, p. 99.

[7] Cranston, p. 195; Haley, p. 585.

[8] Since this gathering occurred immediately following Monmouth's successful progress through the country, it is likely that the question of how to translate that success into political action when Parliament met in October was among the topics discussed (MS Carte 39, fol. 214).

[9] Burnet, 2:266.

that a civil war would follow if the effort to enact an exclusion bill failed. In the previous year, some Whigs had raised the question as to whether the exclusion of James might not lead to a civil war. Now, in October and November 1680, they were in a much more defiant mood. The query had been transformed into a definite threat. "When a popish king comes to the crown," John Trenchard warned his colleagues in the Commons, "either we must submit, and change our religion, or resist."[10] Another member of the House swore he was willing to lose his life in defense of his religion, and argued that if the exclusion bill could not be passed, "we must either submit, or defend our religion by a sharp contest."[11] Other Whigs affirmed that "we are not afraid of war . . . let it be so, if there is no other way to prevent popery. Let us . . . be in a condition to fight for our laws and religion."[12] As Henry Booth put it,

> So that the case in short is this: Whether we shall sit still and put it to the venture of having a popish successor, then we must either submit our heads to the block, or fight and be rebels.[13]

In any event, most Whigs, and certainly most members of Parliament, chose to "sit still." But in the fall of 1680, Whig strategy depended upon hovering close to the brink of civil war as a means of encouraging doubtful allies, especially among the gentry, to lend their support to the exclusion bill.

In the *First Treatise*, Locke echoed this viewpoint, charging that acceptance of Filmer's defense of monarchy would have the effect of laying "a sure and lasting foundation of endless contention and disorder."[14] To subscribe to his political theory, Locke warned, "dissolves the bonds of government and obedience."[15] The choice, as posed by Locke in the *First Treatise*, and by the Whigs in their parliamentary speeches, was between a politics based upon "election and consent" or a politics whose outcome would be "tyranny and usurpation."[16] To move toward the latter, the

[10] Grey, 7:413.

[11] *An Exact Collection of the Most Considerable Debates in the Honorable House of Commons . . . October, 1680*, 1681, p. 250.

[12] Grey, 7:406. Calamy spoke for many when he reflected that in 1680 "things looked very generally as if the nation was running into a new civil war" (Edmund Calamy, *An Historical Account of My Own Life*, 2 vols., 1829, 1:90).

[13] Henry Booth, Lord Delamere, *Works*, 1694, p. 95; Grey, 7:426.

[14] *FT*, par. 106; cf. ibid., par. 72: The choice is between lawful government and "disorder, tyranny, and usurpation." "The great danger these three protestant kingdoms lie under," William Lawrence wrote, "is if any papist should again . . . kindle a civil war," which could occur "if the succession of the crown should . . . become contentious" (*Marriage by the Moral Law of God Vindicated*, 1680, pp. 335–336).

[15] *FT*, par. 105. It "subvert[s] the very foundations of human society" (par. 3).

[16] *FT*, par. 148.

Whigs argued, would "lay a foundation for perpetual disorder and mischief, tumult, sedition, and rebellion."[17]

Notwithstanding an impassioned speech from the king's "great asserter of monarchy" according to divine right, Leoline Jenkins, that the exclusion bill was "contrary to natural justice . . . and tends to the overthrow of the very being and constitution of our government," the House of Commons passed the bill on November 11, 1680, and sent it to the Lords.[18] A great deal of dramaturgical nonsense has been written regarding the so-called great oratorical confrontation between Shaftesbury and Halifax during the Lords' debate of the bill.[19] Oratory had little or nothing to do with the bill's outcome, and if it contributed anything at all, the advantage was probably on Shaftesbury's side, judging by the final result. There was never the slightest prospect that the House of Lords would exclude James from the throne. Prior to the debate, Charles reaffirmed his resolute opposition to exclusion, and he "took pains to speak to almost every Lord himself to dissuade him" from supporting the legislation, indicating that no matter what the Lords did, "he would never suffer such a villainous bill to pass."[20] As Lawrence Hyde had asked the Commons the week before, "Does any man think that this bill will pass

[17] *ST*, par. 1. This is Locke's summary of his argument in the *First Treatise*.

[18] Burnet, 2:257; Grey, 7:418–420, 447. Jenkins made two speeches, on November 4 and November 11. Both are printed in his biography, which is interesting for its disclosure that Jenkins' Royalist sympathies were rooted in the activities of a group of conspirators against Cromwell led by Dr. John Fell during the 1650s, and for the light it sheds on his continuing association with Cavaliers and his connections with Archbishop Sheldon and Samuel Parker following the Restoration (William Wynne, *The Life of Sir Leoline Jenkins*, 2 vols., 1724, 1:ii–xi, xlviii, xcix–ciii; 2:689).

[19] Macaulay is chiefly responsible for the creation of this myth. Halifax's eloquence, he wrote, "struck the opposition dumb" (Macaulay, 3:27). It is hardly surprising that Halifax's biographer should have enlarged upon Macaulay's imagination, but the silliness of characterizing the "breathless suspense" of the Halifax/Shaftesbury debate is much more widespread than that (H. C. Foxcroft, *The Life and Letters of George Savile*, 2 vols., 1898, 1:246–248; G. M. Trevelyan, *England under the Stuarts*, London: Methuen, 1965, p. 396; Elizabeth D'Oyley, *James, Duke of Monmouth*, London: Geoffrey Bles, 1938, p. 176; Nesca A. Robb, *William of Orange: A Personal Portrait*, vol. 2, *The Later Years, 1674–1702*, New York: St. Martin's Press, 1966, p. 160). This fiction made its way into the Locke literature through Fox-Bourne, 1:419. So far as is known, there is only one set of contemporaneous notes on this debate. They are printed in E. S. De Beer, "The House of Lords in the Parliament of 1680," *Bulletin of the Institute of Historical Research* 20, no. 59 (November 1943):22–37. What they show is that although Halifax spoke frequently, he said very little that impressed the writer sufficiently to record his remarks. That he would have liked to have quoted Halifax more seems indicated by the fact that the notetaker wrote down Halifax's name when the latter rose to speak, but virtually all of these notations are followed by blank spaces. So much for his "masterpieces of reasoning, of wit, and of eloquence"! (Macaulay, 1:240). The remarks of other speakers, however, are recorded, including some comments by Shaftesbury.

[20] J. S. Clarke, *The Life of James II*, 2 vols., 1816, 1:553, 615.

the Lords and the King too?"[21] The answer was obvious, and even James, who always assumed the worst, never had any doubts that the upper House would stand by him. Just in case there were any wavering voters, or Lords who imagined they might not have to honor their assurances to the king, Charles came down to the chamber and sat through the entire debate. The final vote was 63–30 against the exclusion bill.[22] Considering that, from the beginning of the exclusion battle, Shaftesbury had never mustered more than twenty peers on his side, it is not the defeat of the bill but the size of the opposition that is surprising. As Burnet observed,

> The country party brought it nearer an equality than was imagined they could do, considering the king's earnestness in it, and that the whole bench of the bishops was against it.[23]

Indeed, the fact that the bill had even reached the House of Lords was significant. Previously, Charles had prorogued or dissolved Parliament as a means of halting the bill's legislative progress. Now, in allowing it to run its parliamentary course, he had also demonstrated clearly and irrevocably the the extent of his own opposition to the exclusion of James, and his refusal to be persuaded otherwise. In the face of the king's determined opposition, the Whigs were forced to reconsider their strategy. Sometime after the House of Lords vote, Monmouth, Russell, and Grey met at Shaftesbury's house to discuss their next move. Shaftesbury argued that they had evidently misjudged the degree of Charles' opposition, and "that we had committed a great error in being so long a screen between the king and the house of commons." Instead of trying to protect the king, or sidestep the issue of his complicity in the "conspiracy" while directing their fire at James, they would from now on have to pursue a more frontal attack on the king. It was acknowledged by the group that Charles would never give his assent to the exclusion bill "unless compelled to it." At the same time, it was also recognized that if James should become king, the Whig leaders had already gone so far in their opposition to him that, despite their having followed a constitutional path, they "were marked out for destruction." Both the need to "compel" the king and the necessity to defend themselves against James' vengeance meant that they now had to give some serious consideration to "the taking up of arms."[24]

[21] Grey, 7:402.

[22] J. P. Kenyon, *Robert Spencer, Earl of Sunderland, 1641–1702*, London: Longmans, Green, 1958, pp. 64–65; Clarke, *James II*, 1:615.

[23] Burnet, 2:259. As De Beer notes, contemporaries understood that the exclusion bill would never pass the Lords ("House of Lords," p. 29).

[24] *Secret History*, pp. 9–11. That Charles had used James as a screen to hide his own intentions was a point echoed in Robert West's confession (Add. MS 38847, fol. 92).

According to one of those present at this meeting, the subject was not pursued further, but the prospect of armed resistance had been placed on the agenda, and in the not too distant future it would inevitably have to be discussed as an alternative to the Whigs' parliamentary strategy.

Meanwhile, Parliament was still in session. Following the Lords' rejection of exclusion, a bill to establish an "association" was introduced in both Houses.[25] As introduced in the Lords, the bill would have encouraged the nobility "to associate themselves in defense against popery."[26] The ostensible object of a Protestant Association was to protect the king from an assassination by papists. Since such an association had been created to ensure Queen Elizabeth's safety, there was an established precedent for the action.[27] Charles II, however, contemptuously dismissed any need for an association, whose real purposes he rightly suspected might turn out to be much more sinister. When the bill came up for debate in the Commons, it was described as "an association of all his Majesty's Protestant subjects," since not only the king's life, but also "the lives, liberties, and properties of all his Majesty's Protestant subjects are in apparent danger of being destroyed."[28] One member of the House suggested that the bill ought to be amended so that, by its provisions, "any man may take arms against a popish successor" and that those on the other side who attempted to defend his claims to the throne would be guilty of a felony.[29] Another member, alluding to the Duke of York's supporters, declared that "there is no way left for us to oppose this party, but by a rebellion." This was the declarative rephrasing of a question Shaftesbury had put to the opposition in the November 15 House of Lords debate.[30] The bill for association was still in the preliminary stages of its legislative journey when the Parliament was prorogued, and a few days later, dissolved by the king.

The question of a Protestant Association—to which we shall return later—raised, directly and indirectly, the prospect of defensive armed resistance by subjects. Nominally, the association was an expression of loyalty to the king, but its real object, as everyone knew, was to prevent

[25] Laurence Echerd, *The History of England*, 1720, pp. 998–999; James Ralph, *The History of England*, 1744, pp. 544–545; Cobbett, 4:1247ff.

[26] Burnet says that the motion for an association "was agreed to in a thin house" of Lords (Burnet, 2:265).

[27] Parallels to the Elizabethan Association and passages from its authorizing resolution were cited in the Commons debate. William Jones, while accepting the idea of an association, argued that the Elizabethan precedent could not serve as a model for their own objectives (Grey, 8:166–167, 273).

[28] Echerd, *History*, p. 998.

[29] Grey, 8:167.

[30] Cobbett, 4:1247; De Beer, "House of Lords," p. 35.

James from becoming king. But could a subject take up arms against a king, even a Catholic king? For the moment, this was a hypothetical question, but no one doubted that it would soon become a matter of political urgency to have a clear answer to this interrogatory. It seems appropriate, therefore, to consider the state of resistance theory as it presented itself to Whigs and Tories in 1681, for as in the case of "property," there was both a general and a specifically formulated theoretical problem to be resolved.

The simplest position on this issue was one that denied the legitimacy of any form of resistance by the subject against the magistrate on any grounds whatsoever. Whether this viewpoint was reinforced by a few scriptural homilies, a grand theory of divine right, or patriarchal authority, or simply by reminders of the practical destruction caused by rebellion, is immaterial, since from whatever perspective such exhortations to avoid rebellion were hurled, they add little to our understanding of the theoretical problem. There are two important exceptions to this statement, however.

One theme of the nonresistance argument, which became especially prominent in scores of sermons preached during 1682, maintained that "private" individuals were not entitled to make, much less act upon, public pronouncements. "The Divine Wisdom" of God, it was preached, "is seen in fitting every man for the business of his station and . . . in disposing all men to be content in the places wherein God has set them."[31] Individuals should "sit still and be quiet . . . mind their own duties in their proper sphere and station . . . and not . . . meddle with public government."[32] In addition to reinforcing a hierarchical view of society and the universe, this admonition enlisted the Protestant idea of a "calling" on the side of nonresistance. As several ministers put it,

> Everyone of us should first and chiefly mind his own private duty, that belongs to him in that station God's Providence has placed him in here . . . everyone should keep his own proper rank, and follow his own work and calling . . . leaving public affairs to those who have authority and ability to manage them.[33]

[31] Paul Lathom, *The Power of Kings from God*, 1683, p. 6; Nicholas Claggett, *A Persuasive to Peaceableness and Obedience*, 1683, p. 14.

[32] [John Clapham], *Obedience to Magistrates Recommended*, 1683, pp. 26, 32; John Owen (not the Independent), *The True Way to Loyalty*, 1684, pp. 5, 18, 20–21; Philip Browne, *The Sovereign's Authority, and the Subject's Duty*, 1682, pp. 27, 36.

[33] Benjamin Calamy, *A Sermon Preached before the Lord Mayor*, 1682, p. 17; cf. ibid., pp. 13, 19; John Walker, *The Antidote: Or, A Seasonable Discourse on Rom. 13:1 . . . with an Account of the Divine Right or Original of Government*, 1684, pp. 29–30; Henry Dove, *A Sermon*, 1682, p. 3; Samuel Freeman, *A Sermon Preached before the Lord Mayor*, 1682, pp. 18, 20.

Now, although this point was urged on behalf of a "quiet and peaceable subjection to the government," it rested upon a premise that the advocates of resistance did have to take into account: that when Parliament was dissolved, or was not in session, even M.P.'s were returned to their status as "private individuals."[34] It is "the wild conceit of some city mechanics," one Tory wrote, which endorses the "strange opinion" that "disbanded members" of Parliament, having been "reduced by the breath of a king into their primitive stations," nevertheless still retain some public authority, as if a representative could "carry his power with him wherever he goes."[35] There was, in other words, a relatively sharp and clearly understood dividing line between holders of public office and private individuals. The plea for nonresistance drew upon this commonplace distinction for support, but any argument for resistance would either have to defend the right of private individuals to take up arms, or else it would have to find some means of conferring a public status upon them.

The second important aspect of the nonresistance argument concerns the Tories' use of Hobbes. The relevant point here, recalling the earlier discussion of Samuel Parker's ambivalent attitude toward that philosopher, is that the alternative to absolute obedience to the magistrate's will was portrayed as a condition of Hobbesian anarchy—a war of all against all. It is not at all surprising that defenders of the established order should have conceived of anarchy as the consequence of civil disobedience or resistance; the point I am making, however, is that they quite explicitly made use of *Hobbes'* picture of anarchy to enforce their argument. Either the Tory position was accepted (that individuals should not "intermeddle with public affairs of state"), or "we must unavoidably lapse into the Malmesbury Philosopher's state of nature."[36] Nor was this merely the viewpoint of some country parson. Robert Brady, L'Estrange, and Dryden all specifically insisted that it was "Hobbes' state of war" that was threatened by the Whigs' policies.[37] Like Parker, the Tories in the 1680s

[34] Thomas Somerville, *The History of Political Transactions and of Parties from the Restoration of King Charles the Second to the Death of King William*, 1792, p. 132. Buckingham, for example, in his parliamentary speech of February 15, 1676, argued that according to "the ancient constitution of parliaments," representatives "become private men again" when they return to their homes (*State Tracts*, 1689, p. 237). Locke incorporates this meaning when he refers to the dissolution of the legislature, "rendering them private persons" again (*ST*, par. 218). The distinction was specifically maintained, employing the Calvinist notion of the calling, by the sixteenth-century Continental theorists of resistance. See the work by Franklin cited in note 42 below.

[35] John Northleigh, *The Parallel: or, The New Specious Association an Old Rebellious Covenant*, 1682, pp. 19–20.

[36] John Walker, *Antidote*, pp. 80, 126–128. Political society will be "levelled into Mr. Hobb's [sic] state of nature" (Roger L'Estrange, *Observator*, May 30, 1683).

[37] The Whigs, according to Brady, were leading the country into "Hobbes' senseless no-

were quite willing to second Hobbes' description of the breakdown of orderly government when it suited their purposes to do so. A Whig theory of resistance, therefore, was necessarily forced to present itself in clearly defined terms as an *alternative* to this Hobbesian imputation.[38]

If total nonresistance is accepted as one extremity, the middle ground, occupied by some Tories and most Whigs, conceded that an individual, under certain conditions, was entitled to exercise force as an act of self-defense. These conditions varied, but it was generally granted that in some form of prepolitical situation, "every man has a right of resistance, to repel an injury from himself"—to fend off an attack by an aggressor. Yet, this is "his private power," and is not to be confused with any right to resistance by him as "a member of a commonwealth."[39] Some holders of this view of private-law resistance argued that this power was wholly given up to the sovereign once the individual became a citizen of the commonwealth.[40] Others maintained that while this self-defensive use of

---

tion of a state of war" (Robert Brady, *The Great Point of Succession Discussed*, 1681, p. 25). The same charge is made by Roger L'Estrange, *An Answer to the Appeal from the Country to the City*, 1681, p. 30; John Dryden, *His Majesty's Declaration Defended*, 1681, p. 10; Northleigh, *The Parallel*, pp. 11–12; and see E. Foreness, *A Sermon*, September 9, 1683, pp. 12–13, 18; Josias Pleydell, *Loyalty and Conformity Asserted in Two Sermons*, 1682, pp. 6-8; John Turner, *A Sermon Preached before Sir Patience Ward . . . 1681, with Additions*, 1683, p. 24; Thomas Pomfret, *Passive Obedience Stated and Asserted*, 1683, p. 2; Thomas Gipps, *The Nature of Subjection to the Civil Magistrate*, 1683, pp. 69, 75–76; David Jenner, *The Prerogative of Primogeniture*, 1685, pp. 2–4; Christopher Wyvill, *A Sermon*, March 8, 1686, p. 9; John Byrom, *The Necessity of Subjection*, 1681, pp. 1-2.

[38] For a discussion of the extent to which Locke and other Whigs did attack Hobbes, taking pains to distinguish between the state of nature and the state of war, see Richard Ashcraft, "Revolutionary Politics and Locke's *Two Treatises of Government*," *Political Theory* 8, no. 4 (November 1980):443–445.

[39] Pomfret, *Passive Obedience*, pp. 10–11. Another theme that frequently appeared in the exclusion literature maintained that since "no man has a right to dispose of his own life . . . he cannot have, as a private person, this right over another; and . . . neither can he transfer it to another" (John Vesey, *A Sermon Preached before the King*, 1684, pp. 15–16). The Whigs, and Locke, accepted the first premise as part of the suicide taboo. Nevertheless, I have not classified this as a problem to be dealt with because, in my view, it could only have qualified as such if the logical conclusion of the argument had been that *no one*, therefore, had the right to kill anyone else, whereas what was concluded, explicitly by Vesey and more ambiguously by others, was that God gave the king the power to kill. The arguments in defense of this proposition are thus most consonant with Filmer's theory of political authority, and have already been discussed. However, it is precisely this question (How do private individuals ever come to have the power to take someone else's life?) that is answered by Locke's "strange doctrine" derived from his interpretation of natural law (*ST*, pars. 7–9, 13).

[40] Dove, *Sermon*, pp. 19–23; *A Letter from Winchester . . .*, 1681, p. 2; Pomfret, *Passive Obedience*, p. 11. J. Turner actually cites Hobbes on this point (*Sermon before Ward*, p. 24).

force might be appealed to even within society under special conditions (as against a highwayman), it did not apply in the case of the magistrate. He was a public officer, not a private individual. The resort to resistance against him "would be destructive of public good and injurious to the peace and welfare of mankind."[41] Here, too, one confronted the distinction between private individuals and the public magistrate.

There was a resistance argument developed by Continental theorists of the sixteenth century that supported action taken by "lesser magistrates," who were, of course, publicly constituted authorities.[42] The conflict thus remained wholly within the public realm, between competing claimants for public authority, acting on behalf of the people. The latter were, at best, adjuncts to a dispute in which they possessed no juridical right to intervene directly and act for themselves. This theory was widely known, but based upon my reading of the political tracts of the 1680s, it does not appear to have had much influence upon the development of resistance theory in this period. Still, from one standpoint, the Protestant Association itself could be viewed as an expression of this perspective.[43]

[41] Gipps, *Nature of Subjection*, pp. 61–63; *Two Great Questions Determined by the Principles of Reason and Divinity*, 1681, pp. 11–13; William Payne, *A Sermon*, September 9, 1683, p. 27. Despite the fact that individuals are endowed by God with a natural "right of self-defense against murderers and robbers," Richard Baxter wrote, "private men may not defend their lives or other rights by any act injurious to the honor or power of the king, much less by a war against him." This was a recantation of a more revolutionary opinion he had once held, and it is contained, interestingly enough, in a letter he wrote to Dean Fell commending the latter's condemnation of "dangerous" and "traitorous" principles upon the occasion of the public book burning at Oxford in 1683. Baxter's *Holy Commonwealth* was one of the books burned, and in his remarkable letter, Baxter wrote, "I do consent to your decree for the burning of it" (Baxter MS IV, fols. 61–62, Dr. William's Library, London; cf. Richard Schlatter, *Richard Baxter and Puritan Politics*, New Brunswick, N.J.: Rutgers University Press, 1957, p. 154).

[42] Julian Franklin, ed., *Constitutionalism and Resistance in the Sixteenth Century*, New York: Pegasus, 1969; J. H. M. Salmon, *The French Religious Wars in English Political Thought*, Oxford: Clarendon Press, 1959; Quentin Skinner, *The Foundations of Modern Political Thought*, 2 vols., Cambridge: Cambridge University Press, 1978. Skinner is especially useful in tracing the antecedents of the private-law theory of resistance and in showing its relevance to Locke's argument (2:125–127, 174–178, 203–204). Locke bought the *Vindiciae contra Tyrannos* in May 1681, and he owned most of the other major works of Continental resistance theory (LL #2054c).

[43] Baxter specifically rejected the notion that inferior magistrates had any right to take up arms, but by the 1680s he appears to have repudiated any form of resistance theory (Richard Baxter, *The Second Part of Nonconformists Plea for Peace*, 1680, pp. 57–59). Skinner observes that Milton employed the argument in his *Tenure of Magistrates*, and it is used by Samuel Johnson in one of his tracts: *The Opinion Is This: That Resistance May Be Used, in Case Our Religion and Rights Should Be Invaded*, 1689. But, in general, defenders of revolution, including Locke, relied upon the private-law theory, and the arguments of such writers as George Buchanan, as their critics duly noted. See, for example, John Northleigh,

Neither were straightforward defenses of parliamentary sovereignty of much assistance to the revolutionary Whigs, both because Parliament was an institution divided against itself on the issue of exclusion, and also because there was great uncertainty within the ranks of the radical Whigs regarding the fate of monarchy in general, Charles II in particular, and the identity of his likely successor. The conflict, in short, was anything but a clearly delineated one between king and Parliament. Therefore, despite many similarities on general points that they shared with their predecessors, the Whigs in the 1680s could not simply reproduce the resistance arguments of the Civil War tracts. To this generalization, there are, again, one or two important exceptions, as we shall see.

Two pathways toward resistance remained open to the Whigs. The first was well marked, and owed much to respected authorities who were not generally sympathetic to resistance. This argument maintained that while resistance to the king was not permissible, there were certain conditions under which a king ceased to act as such. In these cases, he could be considered to have forfeited his kingship, returning to the status of a private individual, and as such he was subject to a defensive act of force exercised by the people. This was the view of Barclay, Bracton, and some other early theorists, all of whom were frequently cited by the Whigs in support of their position.[44]

Remarks upon the Most Eminent of Our Antimonarchical Authors and Their Writings, 1699, p. 355. Apart from whatever theoretical defects the argument of resistance by lesser magistrates may have contained, one very good practical reason that it would have been futile to employ it in the 1680s is that the king (both Charles II and James II) was busily engaged in replacing the lesser magistrates throughout the kingdom with individuals who were more pliant to the Court's objectives.

[44] Bracton is most often cited. See, for example, Robert Ferguson, *A Just and Modest Vindication of the Two Last Parliaments*, 1681, pp. 43–44; Edmund Hickeringill, *Works*, 2 vols., 1716, 1:130; *An Impartial Account of the Nature and Tendency of the Late Addresses in a Letter to a Gentleman in the Country*, 1681, p. 15; Henry Care, *English Liberties: or, The Free-Born Subject's Inheritance*, [1682], p. 3; *The Nation's Address to the Committee of Grievances in Parliament for the Taking Off the Corporation Oath*, 1680, in the Second Collection of *Somers Tracts*, 3:283 (misprint); *A Letter From a Person of Quality to His Friend Concerning His Majesty's Late Declaration*, 1681, p. 4; Samuel Johnson, *Julian the Apostate*, 1682, pp. 82–83. The passage was cited so often by Whigs that the government tried to get intellectuals like Stillingfleet to come up with a different reading of it. See his letter to Halifax discussing "the passage in Bracton which those who plead for the lawfulness of resistance make use of," and his alternative interpretation of it, which places all legal power in the king (Tanner MS 34, fol. 102). Barclay was less frequently quoted, but in many respects, he was the shrewder choice, for as Locke points out, he was an avowed champion of absolutism and the opponent of Buchanan, on whom many resistance theorists were relying for their arguments. Nevertheless, this was also a well-trod path prior to the *Second Treatise* (see *Nation's Address*, p. 239; *Letter Concerning Declaration*, p. 4; and the discussion in J. H. M. Salmon, *French Religious Wars*, p. 137). On the importance of Bu-

When Locke, for example, takes up the question, "May the commands then of a prince be opposed?" he begins by repeating the Tory charge that an affirmative answer would "unhinge and overturn all politics, and . . . leave nothing but anarchy and confusion,"—a Hobbesian state of nature.[45] This general condition of disorder cannot result, Locke argues, if we first distinguish between the king's "person" and his authority. As a single person, the king can do little damage to the political order, but the belief of his subordinates that it lies within the king's power to authorize them to take actions that the law does not sanction can undermine the public peace and cause great destruction to society.

> For the King's authority being given him only by the law, he cannot impower any one to act against the law, or justify him, by his commission in so doing. The commission, or command of any magistrate, where he has no authority, being as void and insignificant, as that of any private man.[46]

Locke then, with the aid of Barclay, applies this doctrine to the king himself. Barclay denies that the people can exercise any power over the king, "unless he does something that makes him cease to be a king. For then he divests himself of his crown and dignity, and returns to the state of a private man, and the people become free and superior." In certain circumstances, therefore, "a king, *ipso facto*, becomes no king; and loses all power and regal authority over his people." The two circumstances under which this might occur, according to Barclay, are (1) when a king "endeavors to overturn the government" or has a "design to ruin the kingdom and commonwealth"; or (2) "when a king makes himself the dependent of another" and "alienates" his kingdom into the hands of a foreign nation. Locke evidently believed that both conditions were applicable to the argument he was making, and he quotes from Barclay at some length on these points. As Locke proclaims, even "the great champion of absolute monarchy" (Barclay) is thus forced to admit that when a king "ceases to be a king," he may be resisted by the people "as they would any other man, who has put himself into a state of war with them."[47] The loss of public authority, in short, returns one to the status of a private

---

chanan to seventeenth-century theories of resistance, see Skinner, *Foundations*, vol. 2, and Francis Oakley, "On the Road from Constance to 1688: The Political Thought of John Major and George Buchanan," *Journal of British Studies*, 1, no. 2 (May 1962):1–31. Buchanan's work is available in an English translation by Charles Ardwood, *The Powers of the Crown in Scotland*, Austin: University of Texas Press, 1949.

[45] *ST*, par. 203.

[46] *ST*, par. 206.

[47] *ST*, pars. 237–239.

individual. The same distinction upon which the Tories based their appeal for quiet submission could thus be turned against the king or lesser magistrates for the advantage of a theory of resistance.

The second route open to the Whigs presented them with much greater theoretical difficulties. Basically, the problem lay with establishing *who*, exactly, was to exercise the awesome power of "the people." Once one moved beyond recognizable institutional boundaries (parliaments, courts, magistrates), what, precisely, did "the people" look like? If we begin with the Tory response to this question, we can appreciate some of the difficulties the Whigs faced in developing their own answer. "According to our antimonarchical sectaries," one author declared, "all by native right are equally equal born with a like freedom." Even if this proposition were accepted as true, he argued, it would make "the people" nothing more than "a headless, a disordered multitude." Indeed, the Tories asked, what could the language of natural rights, equality, and popular sovereignty mean, except a defense of "the sovereignty of the rabble" or "the dregs of mankind"?[48] To grant the individual the right of "being his own judge and assertor of his own privileges," the Tories insisted, would produce "an independent herd of licentious and ungovernable men . . . not a compact body of citizens united together."[49] Thus, "to talk of the people in the multitude, or of placing the government there," it was argued, was to strike at the root of government.[50] Moreover, "what can be the end of setting up the rabble for judges," except to drive them toward some desperate act?[51] The Tories, in other words, identified appeals to "the people" with "a disordered multitude" or "the rabble," and they challenged the Whigs to distance themselves from this identification of the term with the lowest classes in society.

In one sense, of course, all of these arguments were familiar as counterattacks upon the Whigs' defense of the contractual origins of political society, the assumed social conditions in the state of nature, and so forth. But whereas the Whigs could reply by specifying that individuals lived in familial relationships, that contractual government emerged historically out of paternal monarchy, that a certain type of property ownership characterized the social and political status of the people, and so on, in order to defeat the charge of their having presupposed the existence of "a dis-

[48] John Maxwell, *Sacro-Sancta Regum Majestas: or the Sacred and Royal Prerogative of Christian Kings*, 1644; reprint ed., 1680, pp. 75, 137; L'Estrange, *Observator*, July 30, 1681; October 12, 1681; December 7, 1681; Matthew Rider, *The Power of Parliaments in the Case of Succession*, 1680, pp. 2–3; Wyvill, *Sermon*, pp. 10, 25.

[49] Gipps, *Nature of Subjection*, p. 22.

[50] L'Estrange, *Observator*, September 21, 1682; T.L., *The True Notion of Government*, 1681, pp. 12, 33.

[51] L'Estrange, *Observator*, July 19, 1682.

ordered multitude" as the basis of popular government, these qualifications and arguments were of little use in the construction of resistance theory. Tyrrell, for example, could maintain that in the beginning "the people or heads of families have a freedom of setting up what kind of government they please, either monarchical or other."[52] This may have been an effective means of placing Aristotle within the contractual tradition, but no one was suggesting—least of all, Tyrrell—that resistance could then be carried out by the people defined as the "heads of families." Tyrrell concedes that, within a family, a son has the right to defend himself against "the unjust violence of his father" in extreme cases, but he certainly has no right to organize other "children" in order to make a collective rebellion against "fathers."[53] In other words, the Whig argument for the origins of political society, precisely because it did *not* accept the atomism imputed to it by Tory critics (and by later historians of political thought), replied to these critics by drawing out the social, economic, and political relationships that characterized individuals or the people as the Whigs viewed them. While this was an intelligible refutation of the Tory critique, as the latter applied to the question of the origins of political society, it was no answer at all with respect to the problem of revolution. It was, in fact, the very point at issue in the resistance debate: What was the social or economic status of the people who were supposed to carry out the armed resistance?

When it came to revolution, even a Whig like Burnet wanted nothing to do with "the wildness of ungoverned multitudes" or "the madness of lawless men" such as he believed "the people" to be.[54] As the Earl of Anglesey, another Whig supporter, phrased the problem in discussing "the present licentious paper war" that raged during 1681–1682, there is, he wrote, a "mustering of parties" in the conflict between the Whigs and the Tories, and "appeals are made to the people, who can neither meet nor judge in a body." In Anglesey's view, without Parliament "where the collective body of [the] people meet by representation," it was extremely dangerous to direct appeals to an entity ("the people") who could "neither meet nor judge" as a distinct collectivity.[55] When L'Estrange asked

[52] James Tyrrell, *Patriarcha non Monarcha*, 1681, p. 118; cf. ibid., pp. 35, 47, 77, 83.

[53] Tyrrell, *Patriarcha non Monarcha*, p. 26.

[54] Gilbert Burnet, *A Sermon Preached at the Coronation of William and Mary*, 1689, pp. 9–10; idem, *An Exhortation to Peace and Unity*, 1689, p. 7. These are late sermons, but they were preached during the most radical period of Burnet's life. He expressed the same attitude toward the rabble in 1681, and throughout his life (see *A Sermon*, January 30, 1681, p. 15; Burnet, 2:328).

[55] *The Earl of Anglesey's State of the Government and Kingdom* (published in 1694, but the date of the MS is April 27, 1682), pp. 13–14. In his attack upon Thomas Hunt's appeal to the "People" or to the "community," L'Estrange asked, "How is it possible to get 'em together?" (*Observator*, January 20, 1683).

why so many Whig tracts were addressed to "the multitude," he not only denied that the latter had any legitimate role in the political arena, he also argued that such appeals constituted prima facie evidence that the Whigs were "preparing" the masses for some form of armed uprising.[56] In *Vox Angliae: or, the Voice of the Kingdom*, what the country feared, it was alleged, was "the insupportable tyranny of an armed multitude."[57] The persuasive force of the Tory critique of "a disordered multitude," in other words, was much more difficult to defuse when one was advocating popular resistance than it was when one was defending the popular origins of government. This was especially true when one could not refer to an easily recognizable or publicly constituted authority, such as Parliament, subordinate magistrates, or a social group such as the nobility. As one radical Whig claimed, in setting aside Parliament, political power in the English political system "does still lie in the body of the people; and the meaning of a parliament must never be construed so as to destroy that liberty. . . . That which belongs to everybody . . . cannot be taken away from any by a law," or by any parliamentary majority.[58] This described the situation in which the radical Whigs found themselves in 1681–1682: wishing to defend individual rights without having to appeal to a parliamentary majority. It was therefore essential to give some meaning to "the body of the people" as the locus of this constitutional power, upon which their case for resistance necessarily rested.

Who were "the body of the people"? Even if one staked a claim for legitimacy upon the principle of majority rule, when this precept was applied more or less literally to the people, it clearly placed the reservoir of political power in the hands of members of the lowest classes in society. As one Whig critic wrote, " 'Tis insufferable for the multitiude, whose duty it is to be governed, to concern themselves in public affairs, as if they were sharers in the government itself." The social implications of the political theory he was attacking were clear, for in the "multitude" he saw simply "the scum and dregs of the people."[59] But, as the Tories never tired of pointing out to their Whig opponents, did they really mean to lodge this ultimate power with "every pert tradesman, that can but make

[56] L'Estrange, *Answer to the Appeal*, pp. 32–33. The irony in L'Estrange's observation is that, as he explains in the preface to the collected volumes of the *Observator*, he addressed the paper to "the common people" or the multitude precisely because the government needed "some popular medium for the rectifying" of the "poisoned" doctrines the Whigs were advancing at "that turbulent and seditious juncture" (April 1681).

[57] *Vox Angliae: or, the Voice of the Kingdom*, 1682, p. 3.

[58] *The Case of the Sheriffs, for the Year 1682*, pp. 24–25. The same arguments were used by Thomas Hunt in his *A Defence of the Charter, and Municipal Rights of the City of London*, 1683.

[59] Wyvill, *Sermon*, p. 25; cf. ibid., pp. 9–10.

a shift to spell out a *Gazette*" or "every capricious brain, and vulgar understanding"?[60] Clearly, most Whigs would have replied in the negative. Even those Whigs who had no qualms about extending the suffrage to the lowest levels of society would have balked at a lower-class-based resistance theory. Voting for one's betters was one thing; revolting against them was quite another.[61]

Yet Whig opponents were relentless in pressing home this issue. The extreme language of the natural rights/resistance argument was, they insisted, addressed to "the meanest of cobblers" or "any porter, cobbler, or tinker."[62] "All your appeals . . . to the rabble," a Whig critic observed, "are only a slyer way of setting up tinkers, and broom-men, with this cobbler, for gentlemen and judges," according to the political theory that makes kings and their ministers "but the trustees of the multitude, which they can displace, or punish at pleasure."[63] This is not the language of the lords and gentlemen of the Whig party, L'Estrange observed, but of the "factious mechanics" and "cobblers."[64] It was an appeal to the liverymen of London, but, he asked, who made them a part of the government? How did this confused multitude suddenly become the "community" of which the radical Whigs spoke so often?[65] In short, the "ignorant and confused multitude" was composed of weavers, shoemakers, butchers, and carpenters.[66] Neither the allegation nor the conception of "the rabble" was novel, but it is for that very reason worth recalling that when someone like Richard Baxter referred to "the rabble" in his writings of the 1680s, he was repeating his usage of that term as he had applied it against the Levellers and their supporters among the artisans and tradesmen in the 1640s.[67] In the 1670s, Parker did not have the Levellers to rail against, but when he spoke of "the inconsiderate rabble," he meant the "arrogant mechanics" and members of the lowest social classes who constituted "the

[60] B. Calamy, *Sermon before the Mayor*, pp. 18–19.

[61] This point was explicitly recognized by Shaftesbury; see note 76 below.

[62] Rider, *Power of Parliaments*, pp. 2–3. Penn also referred to "illiteral [*sic*] cobblers and tinkers" being championed by the Whigs in 1681 (Mary Maples Dunn, *William Penn: Politics and Conscience*, Princeton: Princeton University Press, 1967, p. 75n.).

[63] L'Estrange, *Observator*, July 31, 1682.

[64] L'Estrange, *Observator*, July 30, 1681; December 14, 1681. Ferguson speaks of the resistance movement as being composed of "very many of all ranks" (*Ferguson*, p. 414).

[65] L'Estrange, *Observator*, July 13, 1682.

[66] References to the rabble or the multitude obviously included members of the laboring class, but as I have tried to show, they also included tradesmen, members of the livery companies of London, those who live by their trades, and those who "should be in their shops" as well (L'Estrange, *Observator*, July 19, 1682; B. Calamy, *Sermon before the Mayor*, pp. 18–19).

[67] *Life of Richard Baxter*, ed. Matthew Sylvester, 1696, p. 43; Schlatter, *Baxter*, pp. 26–28, 87, 89.

multitude."[68] This is clearly the contextual meaning being applied to the radical Whig argument in the 1680s, especially in the period following the dissolution of the Oxford Parliament. The language directed against the rabble had become so current that Dryden, for example, pauses in the middle of a work to interject a discussion of the question, Who are the rabble?[69] And on the other side, some Whigs, as we have noted, felt compelled to disassociate themselves from the rabble, both in theory and in practice. In *Vox Patriae*, the author notes that some people "have lately spoken contemptuously of the populace, calling them the rabble . . . the dregs of mankind." These terms are applied to "persons without estates" who are also assumed to be without "reason and judgment," but, he argues, he is writing on behalf of "men of large estates, well-bred gentlemen, merchants, . . . and rich and substantial yeomen and freeholders."[70] The point, therefore, is that without such a qualification, or without some reference to "the rabble" as a term of distance in one's own writings, it was perfectly plausible, and in accordance with the prevailing meaning, to assume that unqualified references to "the people" in the context of a natural rights/resistance argument were, in fact, directed toward "persons without estates."[71]

This was certainly the view taken with respect to Shaftesbury's political activities in 1681–1682. Increasingly, he became the focal point for the radicals who "were mostly obscure men of comparatively humble origins."[72] Or as Shaftesbury's contemporaries put it, he was "the little head of the Great Rabble," the "idol of the crowd."[73] To be sure, Shaftesbury sought to bring as many of his colleagues among the nobility as possible into his plans for an insurrection, but the more they excused themselves or wavered in their resolution, the more he placed his trust in the obscure radicals and "brisk boys" of Wapping. Some leading men, L'Es-

[68] Samuel Parker, *Discourse of Ecclesiastical Polity*, [1669], pp. 263, 283; idem, *A Defence and Continuation of the Ecclesiastical Polity*, 1671, pp. 688, 709.

[69] John Dryden, *The Vindication: or the Parallel of the French Holy League and the English League and Covenant*, 1683, pp. 14–15. As the title suggests, this was an attack on Shaftesbury's "association."

[70] *Vox Patriae: or, the Resentments and Indignation of the Free-Born Subjects of England against Popery, Arbitrary Government*, 1681, preface.

[71] For a general discussion of the usage of this terminology, see Christopher Hill, "The Many-Headed Monster," chap. 8 in *Change and Continuity in Seventeenth-Century England*, London: Weidenfeld and Nicolson, 1974.

[72] Jones, p. 15.

[73] That is, "the meanest and basest of the people" (*The Character of a Disbanded Courtier*, 1682, pp. 3–4; *An Elegy on the Right Honorable Anthony, Earl of Shaftesbury*, 1683; *Animadversions upon a Paper, Entitled, the Speech of the Late Lord Russell*, 1683, pp. 1–2; Elkanah Settle, *A Panegyrick on the Loyal and Honorable Sir George Jeffries*, 1683, pp. 6–7).

trange wrote, "betake themselves to the rabble for sanctuary," like a wounded deer running with the herd.[74] In a 1682 tract written in defense of Shaftesbury, the author had attacked the nobility and the gentry in rather sharp language, and in an immediately published reply, these words were quoted back to Shaftesbury. "You tell the world, my Lord, that . . . the greatest part of the nobility and gentry have lost" their senses, while the yeomen and plain countrymen have kept theirs. This amounts, the author charged, to an appeal "to the rabble." "For a person of quality to set up clouted shoes for the oracles of law and government" and to turn out the nobility and gentry, is "to introduce new articles of faith, and of state; and, in effect, an appeal from the privy-council to the bear-garden."[75] Indeed, according to one associate, Shaftesbury clearly understood that "the rich men of [London] would vote for elections, but it could hardly be expected they should stand by them in case of a disturbance; for they valued their riches more than their cause." On the other hand, "the rabble about Wapping and Aldersgate," he believed, were definitely on their side in the event of "a disturbance" or revolt.[76] As one contemporary observed, the area of Wapping "is inhabited by the refuse and dregs of the people, porters, seamen, bargemen, butchers, cobblers, curriers, ropers, and all kinds of ordinary mechanics."[77] Thus, when a spy reported to the government that "the leader of the fanatic apprentices in London" had drafted a version of the association proposal for circulation among the apprentices that he showed to Shaftesbury who approved of it, we can just barely glimpse something of the degree of apprehension his auditors must have felt when they used the term "rabble" in conjunction with resistance theory.[78] It makes no sense, I am arguing, in terms of the social meaning attached to the language employed in the *Two Treatises* by contemporaries in 1681–1682, in terms of Shaftesbury's own

[74] L'Estrange, *Observator*, July 24, 1682. The author of *The Knot Untyed: or, the Association Disbanded*, 1682, specifically applied this wounded-deer simile to Shaftesbury (p. 10).

[75] *A Letter from a Friend to a Person of Quality in Answer to a Letter from a Person of Quality to His Friend, about Abhorrers and Addressors*, 1682, p. 1. The Shaftesbury pamphlet, named in the last part of the title, provoked several other replies; see Haley, pp. 691–692.

[76] *The Complete Statesman, Demonstrated in the Life, Actions, and Politics of That Great Minister of State, Anthony Earl of Shaftesbury*, 1683, p. 142. This elegiac and favorable defense of Shaftesbury's life, which incorporates conversations with the earl or discussions at which the author was present, was written by someone who shared his general viewpoint.

[77] Samuel Parker, *History of His Own Time*, 1727, pp. 403–404. From internal evidence, Parker's manuscript appears to have been written in 1685–1686 (cf. ibid., p. 11).

[78] *CSPD*, 23:327–328.

political purposes and activities, or in terms of the social composition of the audience receptive to an argument for resistance to assume that Locke could only have imagined "members of the aristocracy" as the social actors implementing his theory of revolution.[79]

Most often, of course, Locke's theory of revolution has been discussed by scholars as an abstract problem—as a political issue divorced from any specific context of social relations.[80] It is true that any assertion of the people's "right" to revolution in the 1680s would certainly have met with

[79] John Dunn, *Political Obligation in its Historical Context*, Cambridge: Cambridge University Press, 1980, pp. 60–61, 64; H. T. Dickinson, *Liberty and Property: Political Ideology in Eighteenth-Century Britain*, London: Methuen, 1979, p. 78. If there was one point on which the radical Whigs and their critics were in agreement, it was that a revolution "levels the parties" and "cancels all former relation of reverence, respect, and superiority" that previously governed the political relationships between the opposing parties (*ST*, par. 235).

[80] See Martin Seliger, "Locke's Theory of Revolutionary Action," *Western Political Quarterly* 26, no. 3 (September 1963):548–568. Thus the attempts by Sabine and others to deny that Locke was "a radical," and to portray him as "a cautious" or "conservative" advocate of revolution, or indeed, as someone who was not really committed to revolution at all, notwithstanding "his insistence on the right of revolution" (George Sabine, *A History of Political Theory*, 3d ed., New York: Holt, Rinehart and Winston, 1961, pp. 535ff.; John Gough, *John Locke's Political Philosophy*, Oxford: Clarendon Press, 1956, pp. 113, 120–135; Robert A. Goldwin, "John Locke," in *History of Political Philosophy*, ed. Leo Strauss and Joseph Cropsey, Chicago: Rand McNally, 1963, pp. 478–485; Harold Laski, *Political Thought in England from Locke to Bentham*, London: Oxford University Press, 1920, p. 29; Caroline Robbins, "Algernon Sidney's *Discourses Concerning Government*: Textbook of Revolution," *William and Mary Quarterly* 4, no. 3 (July 1947):291; Sterling P. Lamprecht, *The Moral and Political Philosophy of John Locke*, New York: Russell and Russell, 1962, p. 149). Thus Seliger writes that "the apathy of the masses is a factor of stability and attains the stature of a civic virtue," concluding that "the *Second Treatise* does not support the repeated and extremist recourse to the right to revolt" (Martin Seliger, *The Liberal Politics of John Locke*, London: George Allen and Unwin, 1968, p. 320). And Lamprecht speaks of "the non-revolutionary motive behind Locke's discussion of the right to revolution" (*Moral Philosophy of Locke*, p. 150). These attempts to divorce Locke from the political context within which he was writing, and through which his contemporaries would have viewed his arguments, merge with the remarks cited in the previous note. Plamenatz, whose general treatment of Locke is sufficiently abstract to place him with the other sources named above, thinks that "only the well-to-do" could have taken revolutionary action in the 1680s. Hence, "it seemed natural to [Locke], as it seemed to nearly all his contemporaries, that the right to resist rulers who have abused their authority should in practice be confined to the educated and propertied classes" (John Plamenatz, *Man and Society*, 2 vols., New York: McGraw-Hill, 1963, 1:250). We are therefore offered the choice between Locke's abstract defense of revolutionary action by anyone in general divorced from any real revolutionary movement or a real revolution carried out by the aristocracy, if they deign to undertake it; in either case, Locke's theory of revolution must not be allowed to seep down into the ranks of tradesmen, tinkers, or cobblers, which, in the 1680s, is where it existed. If I have dwelt overlong on this point, it is because, surely, this ranks as *the* single most unhistorical proposition in the secondary literature on Locke.

an equally abstract denial that such a right existed. That level of confrontation, however, barely exposes, let alone exhausts, the theoretical difficulties attached to a popular resistance theory. Indeed, so long as the people could be identified with Parliament, the House of Commons, property holders, or some similar group, there were many Whigs who were willing to subscribe to an abstractly formulated endorsement of the people's power. It is when these social groupings and political institutions are no longer available that, as I have tried to show, the real theoretical problems of providing a defense of popular resistance are exposed to view. Seventeenth-century thinkers were well aware of this, and, therefore, to press the issue of resistance in the absence of any socially definable boundaries to the people was to adopt, quite consciously, an extremely radical position, one from which most Whigs in the 1680s unequivocally disassociated themselves.

Nevertheless, this is the viewpoint defended by Locke. He begins, like other radical Whigs, by setting aside claims of parliamentary sovereignty as the ultimate extension of popular resistance. This is necessary because, first, Parliament may not be in session, and hence, would not be in a position to redress the people's grievances, as it was not in 1681–1683. Locke's second reason, however, is more radical: Even the legislature, he argues, is capable of acting contrary to the people's interests, and should it do so, it ought to be resisted by them. Thus,

> The Legislative being only a fiduciary power to act for certain ends, there remains still in the people a supreme power to remove or alter the Legislative, when they shall find the Legislative act contrary to the trust reposed in them . . . the trust must necessarily be forfeited, and the power devolve into the hands of those who gave it, who may place it anew where they shall think best for their safety and security. And thus the community perpetually retains a supreme power of saving themselves from the attempts and designs of any body, even of their legislators, whenever they shall be so foolish, or so wicked, as to lay and carry on designs against the liberties and properties of the subject.[81]

Unlike Tyrrell, Burnet, and many other Whigs, Locke makes no effort whatsoever to distance himself from the rabble or the disordered multitude. Indeed, Locke goes to some lengths to defend the people taken broadly and in a literal sense. If the government is dissolved, he argues, "every man" has a right to judge what is best for all, and to engage in resistance in order to achieve that end. When Locke observes that this

[81] *ST*, par. 149.

"will seem a very strange doctrine to some men"—that "every man hath a right to punish the offender, and be executioner of the law of nature"—he identifies who the "some men" are and why they will think this argument "strange." "Those who make this objection" against every man having such a right, Locke observes, are the defenders of absolute monarchy. They do so, he suggests, because of their inability to imagine that individuals are capable of responsibly exercising such power, since in their view "nothing but confusion and disorder will follow" if such an assumption is made the foundation of political authority.[82] But that is just the point at issue. Not only are these men inclined to forget that, as an individual, an absolute monarch is no better or worse with respect to his rationality or self-interest than any other individual, but they seriously deprecate the rationality of most individuals. It is worth recalling here that during the early period of his political life, when he held similarly absolutist views, Locke had used the same terminology to describe the people, referring to them as an "untamed beast," and an "ignorant . . . confused multitude."[83] Nor is Locke unaware of the polemical importance of such language, for as he later observed in the *Conduct of the Understanding*, "the title of many-headed beast is a sufficient reason" for some men to conclude that no opinion held by the common people is worth anything.[84] It is easy, therefore, to dismiss out of hand particular beliefs simply by attaching this polemical label to them, and in no realm was this a more widespread practice than with respect to political opinions.

A defense not only of the people's opinions but of their right to take revolutionary action either had to absorb the full force of this polemical attack or else it had to deflect its impact by raising the concept of "the people" to a social status above the level of the multitude or the rabble. As one who had himself employed this political tactic and who clearly understood the social implications of a defense of a theory of popular resistance in the circumstances under which he was making it, Locke, I am arguing, like other radicals around Shaftesbury, chose not to minimize the force of their argument through the application of such terminology to the people. The latter, Locke argues, are not "so foolish" as certain

[82] *ST*, pars. 7–13. In the specific context of his refutation of the charge that the people cannot be trusted with the power of deciding when to revolt because they may be deceived by "ill affected and factious men," Locke repeats the point that even "where the welfare of millions is concerned," it is nevertheless the case that "*every man* is *judge* for himself . . . whether another hath put himself into a state of war with him" (pars. 240, 241; italics in original).

[83] *FTG*, pp. 158–159; *STG*, pp. 210–211.

[84] *Works*, 2:362.

"flatterers" of absolute monarchs make them appear.[85] On the contrary, "the people . . . have the sense of rational creatures," however much the Tories may portray them otherwise or label their defenders as "the voice of faction and rebellion."[86] The issue is joined in this extreme and direct fashion by Locke, I am arguing, because that is the way in which the political debate was structured in 1681–1682. No one, under those conditions, could offer a defense of armed resistance without placing the power squarely in the hands of "every man" as a private individual, of whatever station in society, because there were no other options available save a retreat from resistance itself, which of course is the option most Whigs in 1681-1682 in fact chose.

Thus, to the Tory contention that to place political power in the hands of individuals qua individuals would lead to a Hobbesian condition of "disorder and confusion," Locke replies with his "strange doctrine." In its defense, he must show not only that it does not necessarily entail these Hobbesian consequences, but he must also be willing to defend the individual on the lowest scale of social existence as an appropriate medium for the execution of natural law. For beneath the abstractions of "anarchy" and "disorder"—which in the actual political literature of the period are anything but disguised or esoteric terms—lurked the very real social threat posed by the rabble or the unthinking multitude, as viewed by seventeenth-century Englishmen, Whig and Tory alike. The question for most of Locke's contemporaries who accepted the general proposition of popular sovereignty was, How could this commitment to popular authority be hedged, or phrased in such a way as to restrain the socially subversive implications that the Whigs' opponents persistently read into or attached to their political ideas?

It is significant that Locke explicitly rejects Tyrrell's attempt to weasel out of his endorsement of the individual's right to resistance. Actually,

[85] *ST*, pars. 93, 94.

[86] *ST*, par. 230; cf. ibid., par. 93. Contrary to "what some men would have it," Locke argues, "the people . . . [are] rational creatures entered into a community for their mutual good" (par. 163). These are the same "some men," here crying up the king's prerogative and alluding to the people as "void of reason, and brutish," who Locke had earlier attacked as flatterers of absolute monarchs (*ST*, pars. 9–13). L'Estrange had characterized the radical Whigs in late 1682 as "the voice of a factious and divided multitude" (*Observator*, December 30, 1682). The point is that, far from being a speculative work, the *Second Treatise* is deeply rooted in the language of polemical debate, of which Locke shows himself to be extremely conscious. Yet, he concedes no ground to these attacks on the rationality of the people taken in the most literal sense. To put it in the starkest ideological terms, faced with the choice between softening his position or distancing himself from the people in order to appeal to more conservative or aristocratic readers at the price of losing some support among tinkers or cobblers, Locke invariably presses his argument forward as a hard-line radical.

Tyrrell has very little to say on the subject of resistance in *Patriarcha non Monarcha*, and, in one place at least, he states that he cannot "suppose" a situation in which the aggrieved subject could not find redress through the existing political institutions.[87] When later he did address himself to the problem, he wrote, "I do by no means allow the rabble or mob of any nation to take arms against a civil government," and all the evidence suggests that this was the view he held in 1681.[88] In *Patriarcha non Monarcha*, Tyrrell had written that it was not a matter of "giving every private person power, that thinks himself injured by the prince or his officers, to be his own judge and right himself by force, since that were contrary to the great duty of every good subject of endeavoring to preserve the common peace and happiness of his society, which ought to be preferred before any man's private interest."[89] Locke, on the other hand, reaffirms "the right of resisting" even "for one or a few oppressed men." He simply observes that, as a practical matter, this is unlikely to "disturb the government" to any great extent.[90] Another radical writing in late 1682, whose tract Locke owned, also defended the right of any single individual to prosecute those who violate the fundamental principles of the political community, even if the violators happen to be a majority.[91] This view certainly seemed as "strange" to L'Estrange as Locke suggests it will appear to "some men" in the *Second Treatise*, and the editor of the *Observator* lost no time in attacking it.[92]

Locke directly refutes the Tory assertion that "the people being ignorant, and always discontented," they cannot be presumed to be trusted with the responsibility of exercising the power of resistance. Here there can be little doubt that the reference is to "pert tradesmen" and shopkeepers and not to such property owners as might be members of Parliament. Locke denies that the people are of an "unsteady opinion" or an "uncertain humor." Quite the reverse, they "are not so easily got out of

[87] Tyrrell, *Patriarcha non Monarcha*, p. 231; Julian Franklin, *John Locke and the Theory of Sovereignty*, Cambridge: Cambridge University Press, 1978, p. 95.

[88] Cited in Dickinson, *Liberty and Property*, p. 78.

[89] Tyrrell, *Patriarcha non Monarcha*, pp. 211–212.

[90] *ST*, par. 208. One reason that the radical Whigs' conception of resistance reached down to the level of the individual was derived from their interpretation of the suicide taboo: that is, no one could authorize his own death. The political argument, as Hickeringill put it, maintained that the refusal to adhere to the natural law obligation to resist a thief or a murderer was, in effect, to consent to one's own death, and thereby become an accessory to murder (Hickeringill, *Works*, 1:85; cf. Johnson, *Julian*, pp.76–77). It was this belief that caused virtually all the radicals to be skeptical about the Earl of Essex's "suicide."

[91] Hunt, *Defence of the Charter*, p. 42.

[92] L'Estrange, *Observator*, January 20, 1683.

their old forms, as some are apt to suggest."[93] Indeed, the whole discussion of revolution in the final chapter of the *Second Treatise* is heavily laden with ironical statements about the "slowness and aversion" of the people to engage in resistance, the fact that "they are hardly to be prevailed with" to adopt such a course of action, that they "are not apt to stir" in order to "right themselves by resistance," and so forth.[94] Despite the fact that most commentators have overlooked the point, the irony is unmistakable, and seasoned with not a few traces of bitterness, considering that Locke had written the *Second Treatise* in the 1680s with the object of *urging* the people to engage in resistance. Much of the confidence with which he speaks of their not "stirring" themselves is born out of a reflection upon the experience of the fruitless attempts by Shaftesbury, and later by Monmouth, to convince the people otherwise.

In any event, the main point is that Locke refuses to accept "the people's wantonness" as imputed to them by the Tories. Instead, he is willing to "leave it to impartial history to determine" whether "the ruler's insolence, and endeavors to get, and exercise an arbitrary power over their people" is not more frequently the cause of "disorder."[95] Whatever the final decision of history, it is clearly the latter situation that describes the specific cause of disorder at hand, as it pertains to the actions of Charles II and James II. And in this case, one is returned to the general principle defended by Locke, namely, that "if *any* men find themselves aggrieved," they have the right to appeal to "the body of the people" on the issue of resistance to the magistrate.[96] There are no attempts on Locke's part to deny the literalness of this appeal or to modify its social implications. On the contrary, he is at some pains to refute the standard charges levelled against the rabble or the disordered multitude.

It is not only, as some scholars have noted, that Locke identifies himself as a radical political theorist through his affirmation of a constituent power resident in the people; he is also considerably to the left of his contemporaries in the specific context of the political debate of the 1680s by virtue of his refusal to qualify the social character of the people in such a way as to raise them above the level of artisans or tradesmen who, in the minds of most seventeenth-century Englishmen, comprised the rabble. For reasons to be developed more fully in Chapter 8, such individuals are

[93] *ST*, par. 223. The directness of this reply to the many writers, who like the author of *The True Protestant Subject, or The Nature and Rights of Sovereignty Discussed and Stated*, 1680, referred to "the ignorant and unsteady sort of people" who subscribed to the Whigs' political theory, is striking in the context of the political literature of the 1680s.

[94] *ST*, pars. 223, 225, 230.

[95] *ST*, par. 230.

[96] *ST*, par. 242.

clearly included by Locke within his definition of the people as executors of the right to resistance.

There is one additional point worth noting in Locke's treatment of the general theoretical problem of resistance. Since, unlike the parliamentary spokesmen or the Levellers who wrote on behalf of the army during the 1640s, Locke has no institutional expression of the people to defend, his theory of resistance is framed rather nebulously, in terms of a moral community rather than a distinctly organized expression of political power. In other words, one reason for the amorphous character of Locke's argument for resistance is that there is no constituted group—as opposed to a movement—that is in a position to execute effectively this right to resistance. Even a political party, if one prefers this characterization of the Whigs to my reference to them as a movement, could not have claimed, in the seventeenth century, to be the kind of entity that could speak for the people, or that could, with any semblance of theoretical legitimacy, assume the mantle of resistance on their behalf.[97] This practical difficulty of specifying the concrete form through which Locke's argument for popular resistance could find its social expression is, I am suggesting, one reason that such earlier writers as Philip Hunton and George Lawson had such a special appeal for Locke.[98] Both theorists maintained that there was a constituent power in the people, but at the same time, they viewed this as "a moral power."[99] The constituent power, that is, belonged to "the community" or "the body of the people"; but, Hunton declared, it was not "a formal authoritative power" because it had no "civil" (that is, political) status. He was compelled to call it a moral power because it was not exercised by a specially designated group to which he could refer the reader.[100] Similarly, George Lawson wrote that in a situ-

[97] Even "the best party," Halifax wrote, "is but a kind of conspiracy against the rest of the nation" (Foxcroft, *Savile*, 2:505).

[98] For a discussion of Hunton's thought, see C. H. McIlwain, *Constitutionalism and the Changing World*, Cambridge: Cambridge University Press, 1937, pp. 196–231. For Lawson, see A. H. Maclean, "George Lawson and John Locke," *Cambridge Historical Journal* 9, no. 1 (1947):69–77. Franklin discusses both thinkers in *Locke and Sovereignty*.

[99] Philip Hunton, *A Treatise of Monarchy*, 1643, reprint ed., 1680, p. 26 (*LL* #2013); Franklin, *Locke and Sovereignty*, pp. 69–70. Hunton's view of "a moral transcendent power" in the people was specifically attacked by several Tory pamphleteers (Northleigh, *Remarks upon Antimonarchical Authors*, pp. 519, 572; Gipps, *Nature of Subjection*, pp. 55, 71–72). His work was said to be in great vogue with those who adhered to "commonwealth and levelling principles" (Corinne Comstock Weston and Janelle Renfrow Greenberg, *Subjects and Sovereigns: The Grand Controversy over Legal Sovereignty in Stuart England*, Cambridge: Cambridge University Press, 1981, p. 58). It was burned at Oxford in 1683.

[100] Philip Hunton, *A Vindication of the Treatise of Monarchy*, 1644, reprint ed., 1689, pp. 70ff.; Franklin, *Locke and Sovereignty*, pp. 40–42. With the dissolution of government,

ation in which individuals found themselves confronted by the "dissolution of government," they owed their "allegiance" not to any specifically constituted entity, but to "the community."[101] Hence, for Lawson, every man remained under an obligation to enforce the standards of justice (natural law), even if it proved a difficult task for him, in the specifically political sense, to determine who, exactly, was "the just party" in the dispute.[102] In the historical situation in which Lawson and Hunton formulated their arguments, during the 1640s, when there were actually armies in the field and specific political institutions contending for political authority, their appeals to an amorphous community independent of all political identity carried with them something of an a-plague-on-both-your-houses tone, while preserving the basic ingredients necessary to a radical argument for popular sovereignty. For very different reasons, and in a different historical context, Locke found himself in a situation in the 1680s in which the theoretical formulations of these writers claimed a special relevance to his own argument.

Locke's theory of resistance, to summarize the discussion, extends the meaning of "the people" to the lowest social classes, and at the same time, endows them with a moral responsibility that cannot be described in terms of a concretely designated political group. This, I have argued, reflects Locke's response to the particular ideological debate concerning revolution that prevailed during the period he was writing the *Second Treatise*, and it also reflected a defense of the kinds of individuals with whom

---

Hunton argues, the "people are unbound, and in a state as if they had no government." Thus, with the demise of political power, the people may claim "a moral power, such as they had originally before the constitution of the government" (Hunton, *Treatise*, p. 26). Lawson's position is that the natural moral community of families and neighborhoods exists as a political community *in potentia* of free and equal persons. It has a corporate identity and is capable of making collective decisions through a qualified democratic suffrage, and its members are morally obligated to follow the dictates of the Law of Nature, but it is not a distinctly political entity until it institutes a particular form of government (George Lawson, *Politica Sacra and Civilis*, 1660, reprint ed., 1689, pp. 16–25 [*LL* #1695a]; Franklin, *Locke and Sovereignty*, pp. 69–74).

[101] Lawson, *Politica*, p. 24; Franklin, *Locke and Sovereignty*, pp. 72–75, 79–80.

[102] Franklin, *Locke and Sovereignty*, p. 80. The difficulty with this view, as Franklin notes, is that since neither party in the dispute—Parliament against king—was completely just in relation to the interests of the community, it might turn out that the "rational judicious party" was simply one that "desired the peace, welfare, and happiness of England." In subscribing to this view, Lawson was forced to admit that the community might have to submit to despotic rule for the sake of peace, thus confusing submission with allegiance (Franklin, *Locke and Sovereignty*, pp. 82–83). This appears to have been the theoretical price of Lawson's de-emphasis upon the political capacity of the community in favor of its moral qualities, and it is a consequential outcome that is proscribed at the outset by the structure of Locke's political theory.

Locke was himself associated in the Whig revolutionary movement, with respect to the latter's social composition and the nature of its political organization. Whether one considers this as a solution to the theoretical problem of revolution depends very much upon which side of the barricades one is standing on. A more specific characterization of the kind of organization that Locke had in mind as the conduit of revolutionary action will be discussed below.

However, in order to understand this aspect of his argument and to appreciate more fully the specific dimensions of the problem of resistance as it presented itself to Locke in 1681, it is necessary to return to the consideration of Shaftesbury's plans to "compel" Charles II to accede to the exclusion bill. At the end of December 1680, Shaftesbury made a speech in the House of Lords, which was subsequently printed and distributed as a pamphlet.[103] In this speech, Shaftesbury characterized, in candid language, the nature of the impasse at which the Whigs and the king had arrived. "My lords," he began, " 'tis a very hard thing to say that we cannot trust the king; and that we have already been deceived so often." But, whatever doubts one may entertain regarding the king, James' intentions are very plain; he aims to capture the throne and to defend it by surrounding himself with armed guards (that is, a standing army). The popish conspiracy, Shaftesbury alleged, was "plainly headed by the Duke" in whose interest the conspiracy was launched. Moreover, the Court, judging by its actions, has consistently promoted James' designs, against the express wishes of Parliament.

> The prorogations, the dissolutions, the cutting short of Parliaments, not suffering them to have time or opportunity to look into anything, hath showed what reason we have to have confidence in this Court.

The Lords have rejected the exclusion bill, and in the meanwhile, Shaftesbury observed, James "is in Scotland where he can raise an invasion army." All that appears to be lacking, he asserted, is the money necessary to set up a military government, "and then they shall have no more need of the people . . . but this I know, and must boldly say it and plainly, that the nation is betrayed if upon any terms we part with our money till we are sure the King is ours." In short, the Court must not "have money to set up for popery and arbitrary designs." Since Charles II was standing in the chamber at the time, Shaftesbury made what must have been for him

[103] Shaftesbury, *A Speech Lately Made by a Noble Peer of the Realm*, 1681. Francis Smith was arrested for publishing this tract, but the London Grand Jury returned a verdict of *ignoramus* (*CSPD*, 22:137).

a last-ditch plea to the king to "change your principles, change your Court, and be yourself."[104] Shaftesbury's speech was a sharp and biting critique of the government, in which only the immediate threat posed by James' command of the Scottish army was given precedence over the dangers to the nation presented by Charles II and his Court.

On January 18, 1681, the king announced the dissolution of Parliament and his intention to summon a new one to meet at Oxford in March. This decision was made by Charles in order to avoid any "tumult" staged by the London mob if, as seemed likely, he was once more compelled to dissolve Parliament.[105] The king now reopened negotiations with Louis XIV to obtain a subsidy that would allow him—as Shaftesbury had warned—to set aside Parliaments altogether. As Henry Sidney remarked a few days after the king's announcement, the Prince of Orange believed that Charles II had "taken measures with France"; and Sidney added, "so does everybody."[106] It seems reasonable to suppose that Shaftesbury, whose political intelligence was generally very good, may be included among the "everybody."

The Whigs were impressively successful in these parliamentary elections, although a few notable radicals failed in their bids to win seats. Still, the Oxford Parliament was certainly the most hostile and radically tinged group of legislators Charles II had to face during his reign. The confrontation was short-lived, however, and after six days, the king sent them all home with a dissolution that proved to be his final message to Parliament. Despite the impression he attempted to convey to the public that he was not "out of love" with Parliaments, Charles II had, in fact, resolved "never to call another."[107] This was a message the king conveyed privately to a few individuals, but, as several contemporaries wrote, it was "generally believed" that the king did not wish Parliament to meet and that he had no intention of calling a new one.[108] This was certainly Shaftesbury's conviction. As a consequence, the Whigs' parliamentary strategy had clearly come to the end of the road. The abruptness of the king's action caught the Whigs by surprise—though not by much—and

[104] Shaftesbury, *Speech by a Noble Peer*, pp. 1–2.

[105] Keith Feiling and F. R. D. Needham, eds., "The Journals of Edmund Warcup, 1676–84," *English Historical Review* (April 1925), p. 249; Clarke, *James II*, 1:667.

[106] Henry Sidney, *Diary of the Times of Charles the Second*, 2 vols., 1843, 2:161. It was part of the secret treaty Charles made with Louis XIV that he should call no more Parliaments (Dalrymple, 1:282, 285).

[107] According to the Earl of Ailesbury, Charles II told him that "I will have no more parliaments." This view was widely suspected to represent the king's true position, despite his public statements to the contrary (Thomas, Earl of Ailesbury, *Memoirs*, 2 vols., 1890, 1:21; Dalrymple, 1:370; vol. 1, pt. 1, bk. 1, p. 80; see note 106 above).

[108] Dalrymple, vol. 1, pt. 1, bk. 1, p. 3.

it would take some time to work out an alternative policy, but the prospect of armed resistance was now a matter deserving the most serious consideration.

According to Robert Ferguson, prior to the dissolution of the Oxford Parliament, "there was not the least conspiracy set on foot against the King's person nor the government."[109] This point is confirmed by the testimony of others.[110] As noted above, the issue was raised during the last few weeks of 1680, but it was left undeveloped. Following the dissolution of Parliament, however, Shaftesbury and a few other Whigs began to lay the foundations for a strategy of armed resistance. The specifically designated ground for this policy, as distinguished from the general threats of popery, arbitrary government, military rule, and so on, was the king's use of the prerogative to call and dissolve Parliaments in such a way as to defeat the purposes of representative government. In preventing Parliament from carrying out its constitutional duties vis-à-vis the people, Charles II had subverted the very essence of constitutional government, and had thereby violated the ends for which all government was established—the preservation and promotion of the common good. This was both an ancient constitution and a natural law argument. The first maintained that the government—king, lords, and commons—was "unbalanced" by the king's misuse of his executive power, while the second identified the exercise of legislative power and the common good with the ability of Parliament to carry out its functions. On either view, the government was "dissolved," and the people were now placed in a situation in which they would have to act to "restore" a constitutional government to England in the face of Charles II's opposition.

As Ferguson characterized Shaftesbury's and his own attitude following the Oxford Parliament, they considered "all the obligations they stood under to the King were become dissolved." And since these obligations were dissolved, "whatever the Laws of Nature, Nations, or the kingdom made lawful" in justifying their action in self-defense in resisting the king's actions could now be appealed to.[111] From the testimony of other radical Whigs, we know that this was the position adopted by Shaftesbury.[112] It was also the viewpoint reflected in the Whigs' political

[109] *Ferguson*, p. 412.

[110] "It was after the dissolution of the Parliament at Oxford," Nathaniel Wade declared in his confession, "that I first heard of any discourse about having recourse to arms" (Harleian MS 6845, fol. 266).

[111] *Ferguson*, pp. 67, 164, 414.

[112] *Secret History*, p. 23; *Complete Statesman*, pp. 144–145; Thomas Salmon, ed., *A Complete Collection of State Trials and Proceedings upon High Treason*, 2d ed., 4 vols., 1730, 3:610; *CSPD*, 23:236.

literature. A petition they gathered under the auspices of the Middlesex grand jury asked the king to call a Parliament into session because, the authors asserted, in the absence of its meeting, we find ourselves in a situation "tending even to the dissolution of the constitution of the government."[113] The "exercise of absolute power," Ferguson declared, "dissolves the government, and brings us all into a state of nature, by discharging us from the ties . . . we formerly lay under."[114]

When either the executive or the legislative "endeavor" to set up absolute power or their own arbitrary will "as the law of the society," Locke wrote, "they put themselves into a state of war with the people."[115] The latter "are thereupon absolved from any farther obedience" to the king or whoever makes such an attempt.[116] Hence, "when illegal attempts are made upon their liberties or properties" by "their magistrates," Locke argues, "the people . . . are absolved from obedience" to the magistrates. In this state, when the king has forfeited his trust, "all former ties are cancelled . . . and every one has a right to defend himself, and to resist the aggressor."[117] Both Locke's argument and the specific language he employs, in other words, state the position to which Shaftesbury and the radical Whigs had arrived following the dissolution of the Oxford Parliament.

Shaftesbury's speech, "by a Noble Peer of the Realm," had criticized the king and the Court for "the cutting short of Parliaments" through acts of dissolution that denied the legislature the "opportunity" to fulfill its constitutional role of redressing the people's grievances.[118] In the party instructions Shaftesbury drafted for the Whigs prior to the elections for the Oxford Parliament, it was demanded of Whig candidates and voters "that you insist upon an adjustment to be made, betwixt the King's prerogative of calling, proroguing and dissolving Parliament, and the rights of the people to have annual Parliaments." If this was not done, Shaftesbury warned, "our laws, liberties, lives, and estates should be-

[113] *The Presentment and Humble Petition of the Grand Jury for the County of Middlesex,* May 18, 1681, p. 2.

[114] Robert Ferguson, *A Representation of the Threatening Dangers,* 1688, p. 31.

[115] *ST,* par. 222; cf. ibid., pars. 155, 214.

[116] *ST,* pars. 151, 222.

[117] *ST,* pars. 228, 232; cf. ibid., pars. 211, 222.

[118] Shaftesbury had always held the view, as he put it in a 1675 speech, that "the greatest and most useful end of parliaments . . . is not to make new laws, but to redress grievances" (Cobbett, 4:793; cf. *Two Seasonable Discourses, Concerning This Present Parliament,* 1675, in *State Tracts,* 1689, pp. 65-66). In the Shaftesbury papers, there is a draft of an act to require Parliament to be called into session at least once each year "for the redress of grievances" (PRO 30/24/30/44).

come in short time at the will of the Prince."[119] The king's action in dissolving the Oxford Parliament had transformed this position from a hypothetical argument into a declarative accusation against Charles II. It is worth paying careful attention to the way in which the radical position is formulated by Shaftesbury, for it is not a simple demand for annual Parliaments. Shaftesbury insisted, on the one hand, only that "an adjustment be made" between the king's prerogative in calling Parliaments and the people's right to have annual Parliaments; on the other, he emphasized the functional importance of Parliament's ability to redress the people's grievances, regardless of how frequently the legislature was called into session. These two arguments are not the same and the fact that some particular author emphasized one or the other was not viewed by the radicals in terms of an internal disagreement within the revolutionary movement, whose common objective lay in taking whatever action was necessary to insure that a Parliament that would redress the people's grievences was assembled.

The position developed by Shaftesbury in his speech and in these party instructions became the dominant theme in the political literature representing the views of the radical Whigs. In *Vox Populi, Vox Dei: Or, England's General Lamentation for the Dissolution of the Parliament*, the author wrote that the people's hopes and confidence in Parliament's ability to "take action to save the nation from popery and slavery" had been shattered. We have been "cast down in a moment" by the king's action, and "our trust and our confidence is broken." He went on to observe that the "people" were "troubled" by the king's dissolution of Parliament.[120] Other pamphleteers, however, were willing to pursue the argument even further. In *Vox Populi: Or, the People's Claim to Their Parliaments Sitting . . .* , the author asserts that, according to the Law of Nature, "Parliaments ought frequently to meet for the common peace, safety and benefit of the people." Charles II's repeated dissolutions of Parliament have frustrated the execution of this natural law obligation.

[119] PRO 30/24/6b/399. In addition to exclusion of James, the other articles were to accept no standing army and to appropriate no money for the king until "complete security against popery and arbitrary power" had been provided for. The document bears the endorsement, "The original of this wrote in Mr. Lock's own hand," but, as Haley points out, this does not necessarily mean that Locke authored these instructions; he may simply have made a copy from the original letter for his own purposes (Haley, p. 627n.). On the other hand, there is no reason to assume that Locke did not endorse or share Shaftesbury's policy position as expressed in this document.

[120] *Vox Populi, Vox Dei: or, England's General Lamentation for the Dissolution of the Parliament*, 1681, p. 1.

> So that not to suffer Parliaments to sit to answer the great ends for which they were instituted, is expressly contrary to the common law, and so consequently of the Law of God as well as the Law of Nature, and thereby violence is offered to the government itself, and infringement of the people's fundamental rights and liberties.[121]

He defends Shaftesbury's view that Parliaments are "an essential part of the government," and "are so absolutely necessary in this our constitution, that they must then have their certain stationary times of session" in order to have the opportunity to redress public grievances. Thus, the author concludes, Parliaments must meet annually, and must not be dissolved by the king "before they have finished their work." If the legislature is dissolved before the people's grievances have been redressed, this is "nothing but . . . a striking at the foundation of the government itself, and rendering Parliaments altogether useless," which is the same thing as to have no Parliaments at all.[122]

In *A Just and Modest Vindication of the Proceedings of the Two Last Parliaments*, Robert Ferguson spoke of "the amazement which seized every good man, upon the unlooked for dissolution of two parliaments within three months." Although he conceded that the king has the power to call and dissolve Parliaments, still, he insisted, the people have a right to annual Parliaments. And, "abruptly to dissolve parliaments at such a time, when nothing but the Legislative power . . . could relieve us from our just fears or secure us from our certain dangers, is very unsuitable to the great trust reposed in the prince."[123] More ominously, Ferguson warned that James' coming to the throne would "force" the nation "into a war in its own natural defense."[124] The people have sought "under the authority of law" through the last three Parliaments to resolve the conflict between themselves and James, but the king and the Court have prevented this peaceful resolution of the conflict. "Let the people to whom the appeal is made," Ferguson declared, "judge then between them and us; and let reason and the law be the rules, according unto which the controversy may be decided. But if by denying this, they shall like beasts re-

[121] *Vox Populi: or the People's Claim to Their Parliaments Sitting*, 1681, p. 5 (*LL* #2218). This tract, a critic wrote, was a compendium of commonwealth arguments, and "a trumpet to rebellion" (*Vox Populi, Fax Populi*, 1681, pp. 2, 13).

[122] *Vox Populi . . . Parliaments Sitting*, p. 6. The same statutes of Edward III in defense of annual Parliaments that Shaftesbury had quoted in 1677 were cited by the author.

[123] Ferguson, *Just and Modest*, pp. 1–2.

[124] Ferguson, *Just and Modest*, p. 31.

cur to force," he warned, then that response will be met with force from the people.[125]

In the second part of his *History of Whiggism*, Hickeringill wrote that if the king used his prerogative to call Parliaments and then sent them home "and dissolve them as he list and when he list, without redress of grievances, then the fundamental Constitution and law of the government" were undermined and made "imperfect." This situation, according to Hickeringill, left the subject existing in a condition in which the "law" could only be identified with the king's arbitrary will. If there was no obvious and built-in constitutional remedy for this "defective" condition, then, he argued, an appeal must be made in terms of "the very essence of the government," and ultimately, to the Law of Nature.[126] "When parliaments are not suffered to meet and sit according to the usual times that the law or necessity of affairs do require," another radical Whig observed, then government becomes "entirely despotic." For the constant proroguing or dissolving of Parliaments is merely a means of "laying parliaments aside" altogether.[127] The consequence is that people are then subject only to the arbitrary rule of the prince. And "to govern a people any other way than by known and certain laws is to suppose mankind to be a company of brutes, and not reasonable creatures."[128] This was, from the Whig standpoint, a clear violation of the principles of natural law.

As we have seen, following the publication of *Patriarcha*, the Whig argument placed itself on the terrain of a natural law defense of the common good, but now that argument had reached its ultimate destination: a natural law defense of resistance. In the Commons debate on the bill of association, several members insisted that "when the whole frame of the government is out of order" or dissolved, "nature teaches self-preservation."[129] In a "Shaftesbury" pamphlet published following the dissolution of the Oxford Parliament, the author explicitly appeals to "the Laws of Nature" in the context of a defense of resistance, echoing Ferguson's position cited above.[130] Samuel Johnson used the natural law framework in conjunction with the private-law theory of resistance to defend the proposition that "it is every man's duty" to use defensive force to prevent

125 Ferguson, *Just and Modest*, p. 48.

126 Hickeringill, *Works*, 1:131.

127 Delamere, *Works*, pp. 38–39, 123; Cobbett, 4:1270–1271. This is also the argument of Hunt in *Defence of the Charter*, p. 9.

128 Delamere, *Works*, p. 388.

129 Grey, 8:163; *Exact Collection*, p. 47.

130 *Letter Concerning Declaration*, p. 4.

any "invasion" of "other men's rights." Because "all men have both a natural and civil right and property in their lives," Johnson argues, they cannot be supposed to have given up this right to society. Thus, under all conditions, "illegal force may be repelled by force."[131] There is no doubt that Shaftesbury had arrived at this conclusion, as several documents among the Shaftesbury papers clearly demonstrate.[132] It was equally clear to opponents that appeals to the Law of Nature in 1681–1682 were being made on behalf of a theoretical defense of armed resistance.[133]

Other examples could be cited to illustrate the prevalence of this viewpoint among the radical Whigs in the spring of 1681, but I think it is clear why Locke's argument in the *Second Treatise* is framed in terms of the condition of individuals living in the state of nature where the ties of government have been dissolved. They thus confront the possibility of a state of war brought on by the "designs" of a ruler who is attempting to claim absolute power and to identify the law with the exercise of his arbitrary will. In Locke's terminology, this is to exercise force "without authority"; it is, in other words, to act "like beasts [and] recur to force" in order to justify his power.[134] The people then have the right to appeal to the Law of Nature in defense of their resistance to such a tyrant. This, in its most cogent formulation, was Shaftesbury's view of the political situation in the period following the dissolution of the Oxford Parliament. The *Second Treatise* can, therefore, rightly be said to express that perspective and Shaftesbury's purposes.[135]

As a political tract, the *Second Treatise* sets out to provide a justification for the political authority of those who have decided to resist, on the grounds of self-defense (of their "lives, liberty, property and religion") the actions of a tyrant—one who exercises "force without lawful authority."[136] The question is raised in paragraph 155 of the *Second Treatise*, What if "the executive power" has employed "the force of the Common-

[131] Johnson, *Julian*, pp. 71–77, 86, 92; William Denton, *Jus Regiminis: Being a Justification of Defensive Arms in General*, 1689 (written several years before its date of publication), p. 55; *An Argument for Self-Defense*, reprinted in *Somers Tracts*, 3:525–532; a preceding note indicates that this tract was also written several years prior to the Glorious Revolution, though it was not published until after that event (pp. 527–529).

[132] There is a document by Thomas Stringer, Shaftesbury's steward, that defends his master's position on resistance on natural law grounds (PRO 30/24/6B/408; cf. *Complete Statesman*, p. 16). Other papers attempt to refute the charge that the insurrection plan was a "wild and impracticable" scheme (Haley, p. 723).

[133] Dryden, *His Majesty's Declaration Defended*, p. 12.

[134] *ST*, pars. 172, 181, 182.

[135] Laslett, p. 27.

[136] *ST*, pars. 202, 206, 207, 208, 232.

wealth" to "hinder the *meeting* and *acting* of the Legislative" power, contrary to both "the original Constitution" and to "the public exigencies" that "require" such a legislative body to be in session? For Locke, this is a paradigmatic instance of "exercising force without authority." He declares,

> I say using force upon the people without authority and contrary to the trust put in him, that does so, is a state of war with the people, who have a right to *reinstate* their legislative in the exercise of their power. For having erected a Legislative, with an intent they should exercise the power of making laws, either at certain times, or when there is a need of it; when they are hindered by any force from what is so necessary to the society, and wherein the safety and preservation of the people consists, the people have a right to remove it by force. In all states and conditions, the true remedy of force without authority, is to oppose force to it. The use of force without authority, always puts him that uses it into a state of war, as the aggressor, and renders him liable to be treated accordingly.[137]

The power of calling and dissolving Parliaments, Locke argues, "is a fiduciary trust," not an inherent attribute of monarchy. It is decidedly not "an arbitrary power" of the executive, "depending on his good pleasure"; rather, he must "make use of this prerogative for the public good."[138] Locke returns to this issue a few paragraphs later, declaring,

> The power of calling parliaments in England, as to precise time, place, and duration, is certainly a prerogative of the king, but still with this trust, that it shall be made use of for the good of the nation, as the exigencies of the times, and variety of occasions shall require.[139]

Like Shaftesbury and the radical Whigs, Locke adheres to a "purpose of government" critical standard, expressed as the common good, which may be framed either in terms of the customs and traditions of the English government, or as the fulfillment of the natural law.[140]

[137] *ST*, par. 155.

[138] *ST*, par. 156. For a direct reply to this viewpoint, and specifically to Shaftesbury's speech, see *A Letter from Scotland: Written Occasionally upon the Speech Made by a Noble Peer of the Realm*, 1681, reprinted as appendix 12 to Cobbett, 4:cxxii: "The calling, the proroguing, and the dissolving of parliaments, are so absolutely in the king, that they ought to be riddles to a subject"; cf. Weston and Greenberg, *Subjects and Sovereigns*, p. 208.

[139] *ST*, par. 167.

[140] This dualistic character of the radical argument (which on the one hand sometimes accepts the basic framework of the English government as established but maintains that it is not being allowed to function properly, and on the other hand appeals to the Law of Nature

Locke again raises the question, What can or should be done in case there is a conflict between the executive and the legislative powers? "The old question," he writes, "will be asked in this matter of prerogative, but who shall be judge when this power is made a right use of?"

> I answer: between an executive power in being with such a prerogative, and a Legislative that depends upon his will for their convening, there can be no judge on earth . . . The people have no other remedy in this, as in all other cases where they have no judge on earth, but to appeal to Heaven.[141]

That this is a central issue of Locke's argument is evident. He returns to the charge in his list of indictments against the king(s), which he offers as the grounds for resistance. "When the Prince hinders the Legislative from assembling in its due time, or from acting freely, pursuant to those ends, for which it was constituted, the Legislative is altered."[142] And, as he has explained, the government is thereby dissolved.[143] For, Locke argues,

> 'Tis not a certain number of men, no, nor their meeting, unless they have also freedom of debating, and leisure of perfecting, what is for the good of the society wherein the Legislative consists: when these are taken away or altered, so as to deprive the society of the due ex-

---

as the ground for making changes in the existing constitution itself) is responsible for the ambiguities on specific issues—such as the franchise, who constitutes a member of political society, and the relationship between the king and Parliament—that can be found in the radicals' writings. It is not true that radicals were *either* annual-Parliaments men *or* defenders of the king's prerogative in calling them. In fact, they espoused both positions simultaneously in the political tracts they wrote. These ambiguities may appear extremely frustrating to interpreters who want to sort radicals into neat categories of "good old cause" men and Whigs—categories that the radicals did not apply to themselves—but the point, as I have argued above, is that the political unity of the revolutionary movement in the 1680s, which was fragile enough in any case, depended precisely upon *not* drawing such ideological dichotomies, and it seems to me that this point was well understood by the participants themselves. It is of course especially difficult to pin down Locke on some of these issues, but for that very reason I would argue that the *Second Treatise* is a supremely shrewd political manifesto of the radical movement as a whole. For a discussion of Locke's ambiguous position on the issue of annual Parliaments, for example, see John Dunn, *The Political Thought of John Locke*, Cambridge: Cambridge University Press, 1969, pp. 55–56, though I do not accept his contention that Locke's position is an amalgamation of Whig and Tory viewpoints.

141 *ST*, par. 168.

142 *ST*, par. 215

143 This follows from the general assertion—for which paragraph 215 provides one of several examples—that whenever or however "the legislative is altered," civil society is dissolved (*ST*, par. 212).

> ercise of their power, the Legislative is truly altered . . . So that he who takes away the freedom, or hinders the acting of the Legislative in its due seasons, in effect takes away the Legislative, and puts an end to the government.[144]

Clearly, the king's actions in preventing Parliament from meeting to redress the grievances of the people through its passage of the exclusion bill was a violation of the "original Constitution." The result was that the government was now "dissolved," which meant that "the people are not therefore bound to obey" the king's commands. In this situation, the people were free to "constitute to themselves a *new Legislative*, as they think best, being in full liberty to resist the force of those, who without authority would impose anything upon them."[145]

Convinced as he was that Charles II intended to rule without calling any more Parliaments, and also that the king would now employ the full force of the executive power against his opponents, Shaftesbury constructed the argument for resistance upon the foundations of the right of the people to have their grievances redressed through their elected representatives. The king had abrogated that right, and in doing so, he had "forfeited his trust," and he could therefore be resisted as a private individual "without authority" by the people. This was the specific theoretical issue around which any argument for resistance in 1681–1682 was to be formulated. As Ferguson warned in a tract published in this period, "our lives and estates" are not to be "subjected to the arbitrary and despotic pleasure of a sovereign."[146] In acting against the law, Ferguson argued, the king thereby "cancel[s] all bonds by which subjects are tied to their prince . . . And whensoever laws cease to be a security unto men, they will be sorely tempted to apprehend themselves cast into a state of war, and justified in having recourse to the best means they can for their shelter and defense."[147] As we shall see, these theoretical arguments and specific demands constituted the core of the program formulated by the Rye House conspirators.[148]

[144] *ST*, par. 215.

[145] *ST*, par. 212.

[146] Robert Ferguson, *No Protestant Plot, Part Two*, 1682, p. 19 (*LL* #2352); Ferguson, *Just and Modest*, p. 44; cf. Johnson, *Julian*, p. 82.

[147] Ferguson, *No Plot, Part Two*, pp. 1–2.

[148] That the people were to elect an annual Parliament that could not be dissolved or prorogued without its consent before the grievances of the people were redressed was a central plank in the "scheme of fundamentals" drafted by Robert West and Nathaniel Wade. It is reaffirmed in Monmouth's Declaration (Sprat, appendix, p. 42; Landsdowne MS 1152, fol. 260; see note 191 below).

Charles II's interference with the constitutional functions of Parliament was not, of course, the only charge the radical Whigs proposed to bring against him, if and when they were ever in a position to enforce their natural law claims, but it was the keystone of Shaftesbury's plan to unite "the people" in a resistance movement. Unfortunately, the king retained a considerable reservoir of political power, which, as Shaftesbury correctly assumed, he was now prepared to use to crush the opposition. Secure in his financial arrangements, thanks to Louis XIV's subsidies, Charles II had decided to take "harsher" measures; or in the words of a more sympathetic contemporary, to effect certain "reforms" of the government.[149] He continued his policy, initiated prior to the meeting of the Oxford Parliament, of removing suspected Whigs from their offices as justices of the peace. He was also especially concerned, quite naturally, to remove any disaffected individuals from their commands of the local militia. Throughout 1681, Charles II set about carrying out these reforms in a systematic fashion.[150]

At the same time, the government launched the famous "quo warranto" attack upon parliamentary boroughs and city corporations, with the design of remodeling their charters from the king so as to insure election results that would be more favorable to the king in the future.[151] This action did not escape Locke's censure, and it, too, appears among his indictments in the final chapter of the *Second Treatise*:

> When by the arbitrary power of the prince, the electors, or ways of election are altered, without the consent, and contrary to the common interest of the people, there also the Legislative is altered. For if others, than those whom the society has authorized thereunto, do choose, or in another way, than what society hath prescribed, those chosen are not the Legislative appointed by the people.[152]

[149] Clarke, *James II*, 1:674.

[150] "By the end of 1681 the decision of no quarter for Whigs was taken at Court: 'not one man of them shall be employed . . . in any branch of the revenue, and even Whitehall will be purged of all the Whiggish party'" (Keith Feiling, *A History of the Tory Party, 1640–1714*, Oxford: Clarendon Press, 1924, p. 200; Jones, p. 199; David Allen, "The Role of the London Trained Bands in the Exclusion Crisis, 1678–81," *English Historical Review* [April 1972]:289–294).

[151] Two days after Shaftesbury's acquittal, Charles decided to proceed against the city charter of London with a writ of quo warranto (Arthur Bryant, *Charles II*, London: Longmans, Green, 1931, p. 327; Jennifer Levin, *The Charter Controversy in the City of London, 1660–1688, and Its Consequences*, London: Athlone Press, 1969, p. 23).

[152] *ST*, par. 216.

Charles II also removed judges, replacing them with men who were more likely to support his views or the Court's actions. The king thus "molded the judiciary into an instrument of personal power."[153]

A primary objective of the king's policy of reform was to capture control of the city of London. Charles II was determined "to wrest control over the City from the Whigs by all possible means."[154] The Court had previously considered, but rejected, the use of force and fraud to set aside the shrieval election results, but now, in 1681, they were more resolute in their determination. "Orders were sent to tradesmen" to vote for the Court-supported candidate for Lord Mayor, "on pain of losing all royal patronage." The Bishop of London and the clergy were instructed to exercise their influence on the laity in the Court's favor. "All keepers of ale and coffee houses were warned that their licenses would not be renewed unless they appeared and voted for the Tory."[155] Following the Oxford Parliament, London had become the last bastion and major rallying point for the radicals, and Charles II had decided to lay siege to the city.

The king's strategy was evident to Shaftesbury, and the latter had determined to make a fight for the control of London. At the beginning of May 1681, Shaftesbury was made a "freeman" of the city through his joining the Company of Skinners. Some weeks before, Buckingham had joined the Merchant Taylors Company, also becoming a freeman of London.[156] These actions, it was said, gave "great encouragement to a commonwealth disposition in the people, when they saw noblemen of the first order willing to rank themselves with tradesmen and citizens."[157] The government believed that the Whigs intended to elect Shaftesbury as a member of the London Common Council, and perhaps even as Lord Mayor of the city. The Whigs held a majority of the elected officials of the city, and it was feared they would use London as some kind of springboard from which to launch a republic.[158] This may or may not have been in Shaftesbury's mind, but it was not a far-fetched interpretation of his intentions. In one of the important tracts issued by, or through the auspices of, Shaftesbury at this time, it was asserted that the Lord Mayor and the Common Council of London represented "the general sense of the

[153] A. F. Havighurst, "The Judiciary and Politics in the Reign of Charles II," *Law Quarterly Review* (April 1950), pp. 246–249.

[154] Jones, p. 198. "It was visible the court was resolved by fair or foul means to have the government of the city in their hands" (Burnet, 2:338).

[155] Jones, pp. 201, 205.

[156] *CSPD*, 22:265; Haley, p. 641.

[157] Clarke, *James II*, 1:651.

[158] *CSPD*, 22:272, 274; Jones, p. 199. Hickeringill wrote that London had become "the asylum and sanctuary for Protestant patriots" in the period following the dissolution of the Oxford Parliament (*Works*, 1:24).

nation." Their views, as expressed in a petition to the king, asking him to recall Parliament, were "a copy of what all the nation would say." "In London, as in a glass," it was argued, "we see the face of the whole kingdom. For being the epitome as well as metropolis of the nation, whatsoever it says, is a compendious expressing of the sense of England."[159]

It may be that the radicals had adopted some such position as a last attempt to connect their views, and those of the people of England for whom they claimed to speak, with some recognizable public authority. Certainly, support of the magistrates and city officials of London would place some weight behind an appeal for popular resistance if one were to be made.[160] And, whatever encouragement the alliance of a nobleman like Shaftesbury with tradesmen brought to the latter, it indicated quite clearly the direction in which the argument for resistance was moving—toward the lower-class levels of society. Shaftesbury may or may not have always been a Commonwealthman at heart, but from 1681 on, he was both by conviction and circumstance the leader of a group of radicals, drawn from all classes, but especially and in significant numbers from among the class of artisans and tradesmen. It is no accident that, concomitantly, the appeals to natural rights and the Law of Nature became more frequent in these Whigs' writings, and the political language employed by the radicals became, generally, more strident in its tone.

At the same time, most of the Whig party was moving in the opposite direction. Various Whig lords made their separate peace with Charles II and resigned themselves to a life of quiet desperation in the country.[161] William Penn wrote a "plea for moderation," explaining why the "private concerns of family and estate" ought to take precedence over efforts to "look for trouble" in political affairs.[162] This, as we have already noted,

[159] *Impartial Account*, p. 40. When a petition was presented to the king by the Mayor and Common Council of London, Charles angrily told them, "you are not the Common Council of the Nation."

[160] In the debate over whether the king had the right to withdraw corporation charters, the attorneys for the Crown argued that if this authority were denied the king, cities would become "so many commonwealths by themselves, independent" of the Crown. The Court agreed, attacking in its judgment the legal theory that gave support to the creation of "little republics" (Levin, *Charter Controversy*, pp. 48–49).

[161] Jones, p. 208.

[162] William Penn, *The Protestant's Remonstrance against Pope and Presbyter: In an Impartial Essay upon the Times, or Plea for Moderation*, 1681, p. 34. This pamphlet has generally been attributed to Penn, although one recent biographer has demurred (M. M. Dunn, *Penn*, p. 75n.). Penn told Ormonde that he had "resolved to withdraw himself from all manner of meddling, since things to him appeared violent and irreconcilable" (Lacey, p. 136). Authorities disagree as to precisely when Penn did withdraw from Whig political activity, but it was sometime between late 1679 (following Sidney's campaign) and the end of 1680 (when Penn turned his thoughts toward colonization) (M. M. Dunn, *Penn*, p. 74; Ful-

was to become the main propaganda theme of the Tories throughout the next two years. Other Whigs, like Burnet, "went into a closer retirement" from politics after the dissolution of the Oxford Parliament.[163] The Whigs, as one Tory pamphleteer put it, were "now dropping off the spit," having "roasted" themselves by the fiery zeal with which they had espoused their "cause."[164] Equally apt was Dryden's simile of a shipwreck. Shaftesbury's "party," he wrote, "is mouldring away, and as it falls out, in all dishonest combinations, [the Whigs] are suspecting each other so very fast, that every man is shifting for himself, by a separate treaty, and looking out for a plank in the common shipwreck."[165]

Shaftesbury, however, had not given up. As one of his contemporary biographers put it in a tract published shortly after his death, "it was one branch of his character to undertake difficult attempts, and to persevere until he had brought to pass his designs." Shaftesbury "resolved never to desist until he had accomplished his aim."[166] He still hoped that many of the leading Whig politicians would support a policy of resistance to Charles II. But when, it is said, Shaftesbury proposed a "bold overture" at some of the meetings the Whigs held during this period, a number of the Whig grandees began to withdraw from any Whig councils, and severed their association with Shaftesbury in particular.[167] This did not deter Shaftesbury, but it did draw him closer to his supporters in the city and the "ten thousand brisk boys" in Wapping he claimed would stand by "their cause . . . in case there should be any disturbance."[168] It cannot be emphasized too strongly that, following the dissolution of the Oxford Parliament, "only a few Whigs began to turn to ideas of resistance. Most of those who had sat in the exclusion Parliaments, or had been prominent outside, found it expedient to subside into inactivity."[169] In this situation,

---

mer Mood, "William Penn and English Politics in 1680–81," *Journal of the Friends' Historical Society* 27 [1935]:3–21). Mood argues that the granting of a charter for the colony of Pennsylvania was, in part, a strategic move by Charles to drain off Shaftesbury's support among the Dissenters.

163 Burnet, 2:288.

164 *The Phanatic in His Colors: Being a Full and Final Character of a Whig*, 1681, p. 2; *CSPD*, 23:243.

165 Dryden, *His Majesty's Declaration Defended*, p. 20.

166 *The Fugitive Statesman*, 1683, p. 5.

167 Despite his close friendship with Lord Russell and his support for the bill of association, Lord Cavendish (Hobbes' pupil) was one of those who refused to lend his support to Shaftesbury's "bold overture." Sir William Jones was another exclusion Whig who withdrew after the Oxford Parliament (White Kennett, *Memoirs of the Family of Cavendish*, 1708, p. 21).

168 *State Trials*, 3:424; *Complete Statesman*, p. 142. Major Manley organized the Shaftesbury supporters in Wapping (*Secret History*, p. 12).

169 Jones, pp. 208–209.

we are therefore dealing with "the hard core of Whigs" who were prepared to engage in revolution. Of this group, Shaftesbury was unquestionably the acknowledged leader and the most vehement advocate of revolution.

It is in this context that Locke's association with Shaftesbury takes on a rather crucial importance, not only insofar as Locke's practical welfare was of immediate concern, but also with respect to his own political convictions, which (like those of Shaftesbury) were vehemently supportive of armed resistance. It is ridiculous in the extreme—not to mention historically absurd—to regard these views, as expressed in the *Second Treatise*, as summarizing the common-sense ideas of Locke's contemporaries. When they were not skulking around the Court in obsequious obeisance to the king, most of Locke's countrymen were in a deep retreat from politics enjoying the obscurity of country life. His intellectual contemporaries at Oxford consigned these views, and the books in which they were contained, to the flames of a gigantic book-burning bonfire, an event that Locke himself may even have witnessed.[170] Once and for all, the point must be lodged firmly in the minds of interpreters of Locke's political thought that, seen in the context of *his* contemporaries in general, and in relation to the Whigs in particular, Locke wrote the *Second Treatise* for a radical *minority* of individuals with whom he and Shaftesbury were associated, and not for some ex post facto fictional majority of politically conscious seventeenth-century Englishmen conjured up from the imaginations of later commentators and historians.

On the morning of July 2, 1681, Shaftesbury was arrested. After an interrogation before the king and the Privy Council, he was imprisoned in the Tower to await trial on the charge of treason. At the time of his arrest, Shaftesbury's papers were seized. Found among them was a draft proposal for an Association of Protestants to oppose the Duke of York. In itself, this document was not so legally damaging as the government could have hoped for, since it was undated and not in Shaftesbury's handwriting.[171] Nevertheless, at the indictment proceedings against Shaftesbury, the Chief Justice, referring to the proposal, admonished the grand jury to "consider that paper well . . . it seems to me to be of great consequence."[172] Then, too, a bill to constitute such an association had been introduced and debated in Parliament in December 1680, so that the pro-

[170] Laslett, p. 24.

[171] Haley, pp. 654–656. Although Essex had proposed a bill to form an association, Shaftesbury was one of those appointed to the subcommittee to draft it (p. 603). It is not surprising, therefore, that the paper, which was obviously such a draft, should be in Shaftesbury's possession.

[172] *State Trials*, 3:436–437.

posal lacked that degree of conspiratorial secrecy which might have made it more politically damaging to Shaftesbury's position. Still, the government and the Tories pressed this issue as far as they could, condemning the association as a "treasonable conspiracy."[173] More than a year later, Clarendon, Halifax, and others within the government were still working to draft a bill of indictment against Shaftesbury on the basis of this proposal for an association.[174] In 1683, after the exposure of the Rye House conspiracy, a contemporary noted in his journal that "the design appears to have been to prosecute the association."[175] Other contemporaries drew the same conclusion. The plan to form an association, one of them wrote, "was a scheme to form a rebellion and change the government by seizing the king's person and associating in arms."[176] In the sense that the plan to mount a revolution grew out of the rationale underlying the formation of the association, I believe that these assessments are correct. In his *Brief History of the Times*, published four years after the Rye House conspiracy, Roger L'Estrange also emphasized the connection. After reprinting the document, L'Estrange wrote that "the reader will find in this paper of Association . . . the sum of the whole cause, and of all they contended for . . . It lays open the rise, progress, and drift of a republican conspiracy."[177]

In its preamble, the proposal for the association declared that we have "endeavored in a parliamentary way by a bill for the purpose to bar and exclude the said Duke [of York] from the succession to the Crown," but these efforts have been "utterly rejected," leaving us "almost in despair" as to what action to take in order to provide for our "laws, estates and liberty." In response to this situation, "we have thought fit to propose to all true Protestants a union amongst themselves, by solemn and sacred promise of mutual defense and assistance in the preservation of the true

[173] Echerd, *History*, p. 1018; Reresby, *Memoirs*, p. 127. *The Knot Untyed*, pp. 24–26. Copies of the association paper were publicly burned at Durham in 1682, and at the 1683 Oxford book burning (C. E. Whiting, *Nathaniel Lord Crewe, Bishop of Durham [1674–1721]*, London: Society for Promoting Christian Knowledge, 1940, p. 119).

[174] Feiling and Needham, "Journals of Warcup," p. 258.

[175] John Lauder, *Historical Observes of Memorable Occurrents in Church and State*, 1840, p. 97.

[176] Add. *MS* 29577, fol. 401 (Hatton Correspondence, November 24, 1681); John Nalson, *Reflections upon Col. Sidney's Arcadia: The Old Cause, Being Some Observations upon His Last Paper Given to the Sheriffs at His Execution*, 1684, pp. 12, 15; L'Estrange, *Observator*, December 18, 1682; July 12, 1683; October 1, 1683.

[177] Roger L'Estrange, *A Brief History of the Times*, 1687, p. 27. L'Estrange prints the text of the association paper, from which the citations in the following paragraphs have been taken.

Protestant religion, his Majesty's person and royal state, and our laws, liberties, and properties." Subscribers to the association took an oath to "defend to the utmost of my power, with my person and estate" the Protestant religion against all efforts to introduce popery into England. They also pledged to defend "the power and privilege of parliaments, the lawful rights and liberties of the subject, against all encroachments and usurpations of arbitrary power whatsoever." Finally, members of the association were to bind themselves to a specific promise:

> I will never consent that the said James, Duke of York . . . be admitted to the succession of the crown of England: but by all lawful means, and by force of arms if need so require, according to my abilities, will oppose him, and endeavor to subdue, expel, and destroy him, if he come into England, or the dominions thereof, and seek by force to set up his pretended title, and all such as shall adhere unto him, or raise any war, tumult, or sedition for him or by his command, as public enemies of our laws, religion, and country. To this end, we and everyone of us, whose hands are here underwritten, do most willingly bind ourselves . . . in the bond of one firm and loyal society or association.

The association agreed to act under the leadership of "this present parliament whilst it shall be sitting, or the major part of the members of both houses subscribing this association when it shall be prorogued or dissolved."

The association, in other words, was the particular form in which, ultimately, an appeal to "the body of the people" was to be made on behalf of resistance. Its legal status, though dubious, was not without precedent. It was both a popularly directed and popularly constituted body, and yet it was under the guidance of members of the legislature. It was a "firm and loyal society" of individuals who had pledged their "joint and particular forces" to secure "the just and righteous ends of this association." In the following chapter, we will consider the extent to which these righteous ends were actually acted upon, and by whom. Before turning to that question, however, I want to conclude the discussion of a theory of resistance by viewing the aims and rationale of a Protestant Association in terms of the argument for resistance developed by Locke in the *Second Treatise*. Much of the ground necessary for understanding the contextual meaning of an "association" of self-defense against the use of "force" to establish "arbitrary power" has already been covered in our earlier discussion of Locke's theory of revolution. The one additional point that merits some emphasis is Locke's encouragement of individuals who find themselves facing this threat in a state of nature as a consequence of the dissolution of government to associate themselves in order to enforce the Law of Nature against those who are the "public enemies" of the community.

Not only does "every man" have a right "to punish offenses" against the Law of Nature, Locke argues, but "any other person who finds it just, may also join with him that is injured" by the violation of natural law. Everyone, therefore, has "the common right" to "assist him in recovering" what he has lost through the action of "the offender"—the transgressor of the Law of Nature.[178] Hence, "any one that joins with him in his defense and espouses his quarrel" becomes a party to the ensuing state of war between "the aggressor" and the "injured party."[179] The former "having renounced the way of peace . . . and made use of the force of war to compass his unjust ends," has "revolted" against the rational part of mankind, thereby sinking to the level "of beasts by making force . . . to be his rule of right." As a consequence, he "renders himself liable to be destroyed by the injured person and the rest of mankind that will join with him in the execution of justice."[180] This admonition occurs in the paragraph in which Locke is offering a definition of "despotical power," and it requires little exegesis to decipher its meaning within the political context within which it was written.

Since "want of a common judge with authority puts all men in a state of nature," and the exercise of "force without authority" defines "the state of war," it is clear that, in the absence of "the common judge" of Parliament, and faced with the "designs" of a king exercising "force without right," Locke has characterized the condition of England as he viewed it in 1681.[181] The people "living together according to reason,

[178] *ST*, pars. 10, 11. Speaking of the situation in which the magistrate, by acting against the purposes of the laws, "brings us back again to a state of nature," the author of *An Argument for Self-Defense* maintains (p. 529) that it is "the duty and interest of every one to assist the injured party against his oppressor," which, in this instance, is the magistrate.

[179] *ST*, par. 16.

[180] *ST*, par. 172; cf. ibid., pars. 16, 17.

[181] It should be noted that the arguments dealing with the state of nature and the state of war are part of an effort "to understand political power right" (par. 4), and this understanding is made necessary by the present political debate with the "followers" of Filmer's "hypothesis" (par. 1). Throughout the discussion, Locke interposes such phrases as, "it will perhaps be demanded" (par. 12), "it will be objected" (par. 13), "'tis often asked" (par. 14), "to those who say" (par. 15), and so forth, which indicate that Locke is directing his comments about the state of nature to his contemporaries and their political ideas. His effort to show them what the right use of political power is through the use of these concepts, in other words, places the entire discussion within the context of the political situation of England as it existed in 1681. In paragraph 17, Locke writes that "he who attempts to get another man into his absolute power, does thereby put himself into a state of war with him,"

without a common superior on Earth with authority to judge between them" are, with respect to one another, living in "the state of nature."[182] At the same time, between the people and a king with "a declared design of force" as the basis for his policies and actions, there is a state of war. Thus the king can, through his commission of "illegal acts," and "by actually putting himself into a state of war with his people, dissolve the government, and leave them to that defense, which belongs to everyone in the state of nature."[183] That Locke believed that Charles II had "actually" done just that we saw earlier in his treatment of the relations between the king and Parliament. The "injury" and the "crime" committed by an "aggressor" or one who exercises "despotical power" is a crime chargeable to Charles II in his "illegal" use of power against the people. The "injury" committed, as Locke has defined it, is thus not merely a "particular injustice" committed by a private individual against another private individual, but is rather an act of "oppression" whose "consequences seem to threaten all," and in opposition to which, every man has a "common right" to make an appeal to "the body of the people."[184] The "injury" is, in fact, the loss of the people's "legislative power," a loss that automatically dissolves the government. This loss can only be "recovered" when the legislature has been "reinstated" and the aggressor "punished."[185] This "punishment" and "reparation" may be administered against the aggressor by every man and "any other person who finds it just" and joins with him in their execution of the commands of natural law. Indeed, only through such joint efforts is it likely that justice can be done and the loss recovered.[186]

---

but he immediately places this argument in its political context as it appeared to Locke in 1681, by adding, "he that in the state of society, would take away the freedom belonging to those of that society or commonwealth, must be supposed to design to take away from them every thing else, and so be looked on as in a state of war" (*ST*, par. 17; cf. ibid., par.20).

[182] *ST*, par. 19.

[183] *ST*, par. 205.

[184] *ST*, par. 209.

[185] Those living under absolute power cannot regain their freedom "till they have recovered the native right . . . which was to have such a Legislative over them, as the majority should approve, and freely acquiesce in" (*ST*, par. 176; cf. ibid., par. 155). Those involved in the Rye House Plot, L'Estrange observed, had operated on the assumption that they could form "an association . . . for the recovery, or resumption of their pretended liberties" (*Observator*, July 12, 1683).

[186] *ST*, pars. 10, 16. These comments regarding the collective enforcement of natural law are specifically placed in the context of the political situation when, after discussing the despotical power exercised by an executive who hinders the meeting of the legislature, Locke applies the "aggressor" and "beastial" references of chapters 2 and 3 to this individual. Thus, "he renders himself liable to be destroyed by the injured person and the rest of mankind, that will join with him in the execution of justice" (par. 172).

That individuals should thus "associate" together in order to provide for their "mutual defense and assistance" against the king is the specific political message of Locke's natural law argument for resistance. The whole point of the *Second Treatise* is to demonstrate that "it is lawful for the people . . . to *resist* the king."[187] Moreover, there could hardly be an issue around which individuals ought to associate themselves "in the execution of justice" that could claim to be of greater importance than the defense of the people's right to have laws enacted by their freely chosen representatives. The whole foundation of "civil society," as defined by Locke in the *Two Treatises*, rests upon this proposition.[188] Or to put it another way, if *this* were not an issue around which a resistance movement ought to organize itself, the entire structure of Locke's political theory, as it is laid out in the *Second Treatise*, would collapse.

The association was pledged to "mutual defense and assistance" in support of "the power and privilege of parliaments" and "the lawful rights and liberties of the subject, against all encroachments and usurpations of arbitrary power whatsoever . . . by force of arms if need so requires." Both Shaftesbury's plans for an insurrection, culminating in the Rye House conspiracy, and the theoretical defense of those plans and of armed resistance, as expressed in the *Second Treatise*, I am arguing, were framed in terms of the specific context provided by this "association" for "the execution of justice." This connection seemed evident to many contemporaries, as the statements cited earlier linking the association with the Rye House conspiracy indicate. They did not, of course, know of the arguments contained in the *Two Treatises*, but they did have some idea of the arguments actually employed by those who were "associated" in the revolutionary movement. The author of *The Magistracy and Government of England Vindicated* replies to those arguments which he specifically identifies with the views of the Rye House conspirators. These revolutionaries, he wrote, constructed an argument to the effect that "the government was dissolved," whereupon everything was "reduced to its primitive state of nature," and "all power devolved unto individuals." In this condition, the people could "provide for themselves by a new contract." Since they were thus "absolved" from the bonds of obedience to the previous (existing) government, he argued, they sought to legitimize their "illegal" actions committed in this state of nature through the use

[187] *ST*, par. 232 (italics in original).

[188] Individuals "could never be safe . . . *nor think themselves in civil society*, till the Legislative was placed in collective bodies of men, call them Senate, Parliament, or what you please" (*ST*, par. 94; italics in original).

of this notion of a political dissolution. Other writers also attacked these doctrines, which they viewed as the rationale for the Rye House Plot.[189] Although the distinction between the private and public actions of the king was an ancient one, the author of *The Triumph of Our Monarchy over the Plots and Principles of Our Rebels and Republicans* singled out Shaftesbury as the individual responsible for the propaganda use of Bracton and Barclay against Charles II in order to "metamorphose him into a common man."[190]

Nor should we be content to trust entirely to the testimony of the radicals' opponents. In a letter apparently written by one of the Rye House conspirators, the author refers to "the design . . . to seize the king and Duke [of York]" as part of "the Association" which "is carried on with vigor" and which is organized with agents in every county in England. He goes on to describe "the Declaration" that the conspirators have prepared to justify their insurrection, which emphasizes the "ill usage of Parliaments" by Charles II: his "proroguing and dissolving them when they once touched upon grievances." The point of the declaration, of course, is an appeal to Englishmen "to assist against this tyranny" by joining in the armed resistance against the government.[191] And, in a remarkable tract published in Holland to justify the actions of those who did engage in resistance to Charles II, the author restates much of the argument and the phraseology of the *Second Treatise*, cited above. Here I shall pay particular attention only to that portion of the argument which illustrates the importance of a defense of parliamentary rights to a theory of

[189] Bartholemew Shower, *The Magistracy and Government of England Vindicated*, 1689, p. 36; L'Estrange, *Observator*, December 18, 1682; October 1, 1683; Elkanah Settle, *Remarks on Algernon Sidney's Paper, Delivered to the Sheriffs at His Execution*, 1683, p. 3; Dryden, *Vindication*, p. 8.

[190] Northleigh, *Remarks upon Antimonarchical Authors*, p. 266.

[191] This letter was printed in the *Observator*, August 4, 1684. The letter is dated May 30, 1683, and is from someone who is "privy to all [the Rye House conspirators'] actions, and may in time make myself known to his Majesty." The fact that this letter did not surface until more than a year after it was written, and that it was never made use of by the government as evidence in any of its prosecutions, so far as I know, is suspicious. On the other hand, L'Estrange did have access to documents seized by the government (which he sometimes printed in the *Observator*). Also, the details contained in the letter that give a more specific description of the declaration drafted by the conspirators than is found in the depositions or trial records and do not contradict any other available evidence lead me to believe that the letter is genuine. Captain Walcot did write a similar letter to Secretary Jenkins, offering to provide evidence, and it is possible that he is the author of this letter as well. Since Walcot was one of the first conspirators executed, this might explain why the letter, if it turned up following his death, was never used by the government.

resistance, as expressed in this work. The author begins with a brief enquiry into "the nature of government in general" and "the great and principal ends for which . . . [it] was originally instituted," in order to lay the groundwork for his discussion of the English government in particular.[192] Having stated that, according to the Law of Nature, all government is established to promote the common good of mankind, he argues that "whensoever princes cease to be for the common good, they answer not the end" for which they were instituted, and "become injurious to the community." Such princes thereby become "enemies," and may be treated as such by the community; "nor is it rebellion in any to resist him."[193] By taking such actions, a king "doth *ipso facto* depose himself, and instead of being owned any longer for a king, ought to be treated as a rebel and traitor . . . And to resist such, is not to oppose authority, but usurpation."[194] In language that recalls that of the association, the author defends "the righteousness and equity of their cause"—the attempt by his associates "who endeavor[ed] to repress the violence of rulers that persecute them."[195] Hence,

> When a ruler . . . seek[s] the ruin of a vast as well as innocent number of his people, he forfeits his right to reign, and the subjects are justifiable in defending and vindicating themselves.[196]

He quotes Bracton in support of this proposition, to the same purpose that Locke cites from Barclay in the *Second Treatise*. So that, when a king ceases to "be" a king, the people "are then absolved and freed from their fealty and allegiance" to him, nor are they "bound in anything to obey him." Since "he hath no tie upon his people" any longer, the power granted to the king, which was only "conditionally" given to him as a trust in the first instance, now returns to "the people," that is, to "the community."[197]

The people, he argues, "always retain a right and liberty to redeem and vindicate themselves" from kings who "tyrannize over them . . . when-

[192] [Robert Ferguson], *An Impartial Enquiry into the Administration of Affairs in England*, [1684], p. 3. For a discussion of Ferguson as the author of this tract, see note 207 below.

[193] *Enquiry*, p. 14.

[194] *Enquiry*, p. 4.

[195] *Enquiry*, p. 6. The same language, defending the 'righteous undertaking' of Monmouth's Rebellion, is used in the latter's declaration (Landsdowne MS 1152, fol. 259).

[196] *Enquiry*, p. 26.

[197] *Enquiry*, p. 28.

soever they shall think fit or see occasion." They may "enter their actions against invaders" of their rights "at what time soever they please."[198] Not only is it true that "by the Law of Nature it was lawful to resist tyrants," but appealing to English history, the author maintains that whenever "the former kings of this realm were found to invade the rights and liberties of their people, our ancestors not only thought it lawful but judged it their duty by force and arms to oppose and withstand them."[199] This is, of course, the primary point the pamphlet seeks to demonstrate and to justify, as a response to "the invasions of Charles the Second . . . upon all our laws and rights."[200]

Having established this general framework for his argument, the author sets out the specific case for the view that Charles II has "invaded" the rights and liberties of his subjects. "One of the chiefest parts of the present conspiracy of his Majesty, the Duke [of York], and the ministers against the kingdom," he observes, involves their "invasions upon the rights, privileges and jurisdiction of Parliaments." This is evident from the king's "frequent proroguing and dissolving them when the condition and state of the nation required their continuing to sit." In effect, the consequence of the king's action was "to rob and deprive" the people of their parliaments, and thereby to change the form of the government.[201] For Parliaments are "an essential part of our Constitution." Moreover, since "parliaments should be annually called, so by the Law they are not to be dissolved till all the matters and concerns of the nation be transacted and issued, for which they were called." In other words,

> To prorogue or dissolve parliaments while the condition and state of the kingdom requires that they should continue to sit is not only a failure in that duty which the king owes unto his people, but is a violation of the oath by which he is bound to them. For the power of calling and dissolving Parliaments is not a prerogative of the Crown, in the virtue of which he may do in this matter as he pleaseth; but it

[198] *Enquiry*, pp. 14–15.

[199] *Enquiry*, pp. 15, 29. Ferguson cites these precedents because he wants to show that "our predecessors . . . must abhor us as a degenerate offspring, in so servilely bowing to the yoke prepared for our necks, and so tamely surrendering the rights and franchises" of our liberties to Charles II. The apathy of the people, and their slowness to engage in revolution or resistance is thus being held up, with some bitterness and irony, by Ferguson against those who charge the people with being rash and unsteady.

[200] *Enquiry*, p. 29.

[201] *Enquiry*, p. 68.

is only an honorary trust, reposed in him, which he is obliged to apply and use for the good of his subjects.

If it were otherwise, and "the calling and dissolving Parliaments depended upon the arbitrary will of the Prince," then, as Locke argued, "parliament" would exist in name only, and "the having of them would be very insignificant and . . . [of] little worth."[202] The aim of this "brief survey of [the king's] invasion upon the freedom, authority and jurisdiction of parliaments," the author explains, is to illustrate the particular fact of Charles II's having "trampled upon the rights and privileges of parliament," culminating in the fact that he "contrived to lay them finally aside."[203] In so doing, the king acted "contrary to the trust reposed in him," and destroyed the constitutional structure of the English government.[204] According to the author, therefore, the "legal government is overthrown and dissolved." In this situation, nothing "but the vindicating our rights and redeeming ourselves from slavery" through resistance to Charles II can "restore us to our ancient honor" that we enjoyed as free subjects under a constitutional government.[205]

This is the argument of Shaftesbury, Locke, and of all those—for whom the author of this tract is speaking—who engaged in resistance to the tyrannical actions of Charles II. These arguments appeared in a pamphlet published in Holland by one of those in exile who managed to escape from England following the discovery of the Rye House Plot. It is a matter of some interest that the English envoy in Holland, Thomas Chudleigh, a graduate of Christ Church, Oxford, who knew Locke, wrote in one of his dispatches to the Secretary of State that, "I can think none more likely" as the author of this "horrid libel" against the king than John Locke. Locke, Chudleigh observed, shared the late Lord Shaftesbury's "spirit and his malice" toward Charles II's government.[206] While

[202] *Enquiry*, p. 66. "For it is not names [e.g., parliaments] that constitute governments, but the use and exercise of those powers that were intended to accompany them" (*ST*, par. 215).

[203] *Enquiry*, pp. 65, 76; cf. ibid., p. 68.

[204] *Enquiry*, p. 75; cf. ibid., pp. 66, 71–72.

[205] *Enquiry*, pp. 71, 73.

[206] Add. MS 41810, fol. 188 (November 11, 1684). Portions of this letter were printed by Cecil Price, "Thomas Chudleigh on John Locke, 1684," *Notes and Queries* 194, no. 24 (November 26, 1949):519. De Beer is thus mistaken in his remark that "Locke is not mentioned" in Chudleigh's correspondence after 1683 (*Correspondence*, 2:665n.). It would be even more erroneous to draw the inference that Locke's name does not appear in the dispatches of Chudleigh's successor, Bevil Skelton. As we shall see, he is mentioned more than a few times by the English envoy to Holland.

I would not dismiss this suggestion out of hand, from certain internal evidence, it seems more probable that Robert Ferguson was the author of this particular pamphlet.[207] Nevertheless, as I have tried to show, Chudleigh was not mistaken in supposing that Ferguson, Locke, and Shaftesbury all shared the same views respecting the English government.

[207] While I must forgo the detailed comparison of texts that I believe would strengthen the case for Ferguson's authorship of the *Enquiry*, the following points are, I believe, sufficient to establish the basis for my assignation of the tract to him. The author informs the reader both at the beginning (p. 2) and at the end (p. 88) that he is in possession of "the history of [Charles II's] life and reign," some of which he includes in the *Enquiry*, but much of which he has reserved until another time. From several documents in the Shaftesbury papers, we know that Shaftesbury had commissioned a "history of the times, a kind of diary drawn up by Ferguson" that recounted "the life and reign of his present Majesty (Charles II)" (PRO 30/24/43/63). The government, of course, tried very hard to get its hands on this manuscript, but Ferguson, obviously, carried it with him to Holland. Ferguson himself alludes to this register of "all the miscarriages of the government from the time of the Restoration." At one point, it was suggested that this manuscript should be published, with the design of embarrassing or indicting the king, but Shaftesbury scotched the idea (*Ferguson*, p. 411). This, nevertheless, is precisely the aim of the *Enquiry*—that is, to offer an unmasking of the designs of Charles and James (p. 2). The author of the letter printed by L'Estrange (see note 191 above) also refers to the declaration—which we know Ferguson drafted—which was prepared to justify the insurrection as a kind of history of Charles II's reign. Second, the *Enquiry* is a scurrilous personal attack on the king, in the tradition of the Marprelate tracts, which dwells on his "brutish and unnatural lusts" (p. 8) of rape, adultery, incest, (pp. 10–11) and extending even to the "unaccountable fondness" Charles had in his childhood for "a wooden billet" (p. 18). The author speaks of Charles' "wallowing in these impurities" (p. 13), which serve to "deprave the manners of the English people" (p. 10). The *Enquiry*, in other words, runs to the kind of excess in its list of personal crimes that is a distinctive feature of Monmouth's Declaration, which we know Ferguson wrote. One of Skelton's spies reported that Ferguson had written a scandalous book against Charles II, and from his description, the work referred to is almost certainly the *Impartial Enquiry* (Add. MS 41811, fol. 242). Third, there are excursions into Scottish history (pp. 8–9, 11, 16), which one often finds in other pamphlets by Ferguson. Fourth, there is a fairly detailed discussion of Essex's "murder," which repeats some of the material in the pamphlet *An Enquiry into, and Detection of the Barbarous Murder of the Late Earl of Essex*, 1684, which Ferguson wrote. The information on Essex's death was not available to the general public—the government was particularly energetic in its efforts to arrest anyone who attempted to make it so—and especially not to exiles in Holland. Yet, we know that Robert Cragg carried over the information from England to Ferguson, which allowed him to write his tract on Essex. (However, since we do not know the exact publication date of this tract or of the *Impartial Enquiry*, no sequential link between the two tracts can be established.) Finally, I have not cited phrases or arguments of a political nature that I believe link the *Impartial Enquiry* with Ferguson's other writings, but there is one distinctive and sarcastic phrase—"the king and his dearly beloved brother"—which Ferguson uses in both the tract on Essex and the *Impartial Enquiry*, which, added to the above, is sufficent proof that he was the author of both works.

8

THE LANGUAGE OF CONSPIRACY

HISTORIANS have for so long denied that there really was a Rye House conspiracy that an exploration of its empirical dimensions is necessarily a main objective of this chapter. From the standpoint of political theory, however, what I wish to show is the importance of the relationship between political ideas and political action, and specifically, how the former functioned as an organizational weapon against Charles II's government. I shall also try to show how the major precepts of the revolutionary political theory thus far discussed were understood by and formed part of the political consciousness of individuals from the lowest social classes in seventeenth-century England.

It is unusual, to say the least, to find oneself in the position of attempting to explain the significance of a nonevent. Yet for more than two hundred years, it has been a recurrent response among historians and biographers to deny that the Whigs ever engaged in a conspiracy against the government, let alone that they plotted to kill Charles II and his brother. John Oldmixon, an early Whig historian, maintained in his *History of England during the Reigns of the Royal House of Stuart* that the idea that the Whigs had conspired to kill or capture the king was simply "incredible." Not only was it beyond belief, it was a "devilish falsehood."[1] Nor was Oldmixon alone in his expression of incredulity.[2]

Even if something in the nature of a series of secret meetings were held by the Whigs, other scholars insisted, they amounted to no more than "discussions," which may have been critical of the government, but which could hardly qualify as a "conspiracy" or merit the punishment meted out to the participants in these meetings.[3] Those who conceded

[1] John Oldmixon, *The History of England During the Reigns of the Royal House of Stuart*, 1730, p. 680.

[2] Of the Rye House Plot, Maurice Ashley writes that "little evidence exists that it ever approached the realms of reality," and he regards it simply as a "myth" (*Charles II*, London: Panther Books, 1973, p. 309). This was also the view of Charles James Fox, *History of the Early Part of the Reign of James the Second*, 1808, pp. 158–160; cf. Barry Coward, *The Stuart Age: A History of England, 1603–1714*, London: Longman Group, 1980, p. 292.

[3] Iris Morley, *A Thousand Lives: An Account of the English Revolutionary Movement, 1660–1685*, London: Andre Deutsch, 1954, p. 150 ("vague talk," an "old rumour"); H. C. Foxcroft, *The Life and Letters of George Savile*, 2 vols., 1898, 1:390 ("this debating club"); Richard Lodge, *The Political History of England: From the Restoration to the Death of William III*, London: Longmans, Green, 1923, p. 224 ("futile discussions").

that plans for an armed rising might have progressed beyond the discussion stage nevertheless felt constrained to confine this excess of revolutionary fervor to "a few individuals," thereby exempting from the general feelings of revulsion engendered by the latter's actions all the important figures in the Whig pantheon of political immortality.[4] Still other historians, like Macaulay, advanced the view that there were two conspiracies, one designed to foment a general insurrection, and the other a plot to assassinate Charles II and James. The first was the outgrowth of Shaftesbury's attempts to organize a resistance movement among the leaders of the Whig party, while the second was a conspiracy "in which only a few desperate men were concerned."[5] Finally, it was argued that, even admitting the existence of such plots and conspirators, taking into account the fact that these individuals never actually carried out their proposed actions against the government, whatever the precise nature of their discussions and plans, they can hardly be regarded as being treasonable.[6]

"What wonder then," exclaimed Roger North as he set out to navigate his way through the details of the Rye House conspiracy, "is it that, at present, the current of history is muddy."[7] As a Tory, North was of course less deterred than others had been from plunging into an exploration of "the dark and dirty recesses" of Whig activities in the 1680s.[8] For their part, the Whigs sought to extol the virtues of the Glorious Revolution, and to forget any wilder schemes that may have been in the minds of Shaftesbury and "a few desperate men" in the 1680s; the latter could only be "remembered with disgust" so far as they were concerned.[9] Given the wide range of options available to the historian, between a denial that the event ever occurred and a portrayal of it as insignificant and

[4] "No hint of the plan was allowed to reach the recognized leaders of the Whig party" (Lodge, *Political History*, p. 224). If leaders like Monmouth and Russell were "implicated" in the conspiracy, it was simply because of their "proximity" to "the crazy underlings" responsible for the plot (G. N. Clark, *The Later Stuarts*, Oxford: Oxford University Press, 1940, p. 100).

[5] Macaulay, 1:247. The two plots were "unrelated" to each other because they were formulated "by men whose minds worked on a different plane" (W. C. Mackenzie, *Andrew Fletcher of Saltoun*, Edinburgh: Porpoise Press, 1935, p. 16; James Ralph, *The History of England*, 1744, p. 807; Robert Herbert Story, *William Carstares*, 1874, pp. 62–63).

[6] It became especially important to historians (e.g., Macaulay) to save Lord Russell from the charge of treason, although they were willing to apply that term to the activities of Shaftesbury and one or two others (Macaulay, 1:248; Cobbett, 4:1341; John Russell, *The Life of William Lord Russell*, 2d ed., 2 vols., 1820).

[7] Roger North, *Examen*, 1740, p. xi.

[8] North, *Examen*, p. 18.

[9] Thomas Somerville, *The History of Political Transactions and of Parties from the Restoration of King Charles the Second to the Death of King William*, 1792, p. 186.

inconsequential, it is something of an understatement to conclude, as the author of the only modern study of the Rye House conspiracy does, that "an aura of mystery surrounded it then, and has not been wholly dispelled since."[10] Naturally, much depends upon what is meant by "a few individuals," or the degree of rigidity one wishes to interpose in order to maintain the "separateness" of the "two plots," and so forth. The Rye House conspiracy, I shall argue, did encompass a scheme for a general insurrection as well as a plan of assassination, and, while it is true that thousands of individuals were implicated in the former who knew nothing about the latter, the number of persons who did know about the plot against the life of the king is far greater than has been generally assumed. That those engaged in both aspects of the conspiracy were, according to the law as it stood in the seventeenth century, guilty of treason is, I believe, a justifiable conclusion.[11] This does not mean, of course, that the English government invariably was correct in its prosecution, let alone its execution, of individuals, nor that it did not bend the law, or even abandon it altogether, in order to achieve its retributive purposes.

[10] Doreen J. Milne, *The Rye House Plot, with Special Reference to Its Place in the Exclusion Contest and Its Consequences Till 1685*, Ph.D. diss., University of London, 1949, p. 1. The Rye House Plot is "one of the most obscure affairs in the history of the period" (Morley, *Thousand Lives*, p. 149).

[11] This is still a matter of some dispute, but at Shaftesbury's grand jury hearing Chief Justice Pemberton explained the changes in the meaning of treason since it had been defined by 25 Edw. 3. There it was stated that imagining or compassing the death of the king or levying war against the king were acts of treason. But, Pemberton observed, by the more recent statute passed during Charles II's reign (13 Car. 2, st. 1, c. 1), it was made treason "to design, intend, or endeavor" any action that might bring the king "any bodily harm that might tend to his death, or . . . any restraint of his liberty, or any imprisonment of him." This change, Pemberton argued, "hath altered the former law greatly," because previously, treason had to be "declared by an overt act," whereas now, "the very design" of such acts, "whether they take effect or not" was sufficient to prove treason. Thus, "the very design, if it be but uttered and spoken, and any ways signified by any discourse . . . is made treason by this act," even if for any reason, the action itself should fail to be carried out. Conspiracy was therefore much easier to prove, because even in the absence of overt actions, "since this act, gentlemen, words, if they import any malicious design against the king's life and government . . . such words are treason now within this act" (Thomas Salmon, ed., *A Complete Collection of State Trials and Proceedings upon High Treason*, 2d ed., 4 vols., 1730, 3:415). It cannot be claimed either that Pemberton's interpretation of the law is merely the biased justification of the government's prosecution of the conspirators or that the latter were ignorant of this meaning of treason. In fact, Pemberton's speech to the jury is a very accurate rendering of the act, which is printed in W. C. Costin and J. Steven Watson, eds., *The Law and Working of the Constitution: Documents, 1660–1914*, 2 vols., London: Adam and Charles Black, 1952, 1:5ff. Moreover, two years before the Rye House conspiracy, Ferguson had complained of the existing statutes on treason "having made words treason" rather than simply overt actions (Robert Ferguson, *No Protestant Plot*, 1681, p. 15 [*LL* #2351]).

As in the case of the popish plot, it is necessary to issue a warning regarding the reliability of evidence available to us concerning the Rye House Plot. The efforts by individuals to disguise their intentions, conceal their political objectives, and create a language filled with ambiguity, irony, double meanings, and falsehoods, in order to protect themselves in a situation in which imminent death was likely to be the consequence of discovery or miscalculation have bequeathed to posterity a record that is, at best, opaque. Even with the greatest care possible given to ascertaining the accuracy of the statements of the individuals involved, no scholar, at this remove in time, can wade into the evidence with absolute confidence that his narrative will emerge unsullied by the traces of falsehood and deception that were constitutive elements of the revolutionary movement itself.[12] To say this does not diminish one's responsibility for the accuracy of the account that is presented to the reader. Even when the actions of particular individuals or the details of specific historical events remain obscure, what I believe can be realized is a portrayal of the kind of organization that the revolutionary Whigs created in order to achieve their aims.

As was mentioned earlier, not only was there no recognized right of individuals to organize themselves politically in the seventeenth century, but also, the government was not inclined to view itself as a disinterested party with respect to this issue. On the contrary, throughout the Restoration but especially during the 1680s, the thin line separating its intelligence-gathering activities from extralegal attempts to remove its opposition from the political arena was constantly being transgressed by officials within the government, extending even to the king himself. In an effort to achieve both objectives, the government dispensed considerable sums of secret service money to informers, double agents, and agents provocateurs.[13] In its instructions issued to an individual in the latter cat-

[12] It should also be pointed out, however, that the evidence is not all of one type: Some individuals confessed their guilt and were executed; others received a pardon for their confessions. Sometimes one witness was brought in to confront another, and notes of this encounter were made. Some individuals were not in custody and wrote their accounts for publication; others made private notations. Some discussed their activities with individuals they did not know to be informers; some evidence was intercepted and confiscated. And much evidence has come to light only recently and was not available to those in the seventeenth century. In short, the variety of circumstances pertaining to the evidence, numbers of individuals involved, and the types of evidence consulted provide some measure by which various statements can be checked for accuracy. Moreover, except in the instance referred to above, the government was generally careful in preventing witnesses in its custody from communicating with one another or allowing them to see the depositions of other witnesses.

[13] John Y. Akerman, ed., *Moneys Received and Paid for Secret Services of Charles II and James II*, 1851.

egory, he was advised to "help [the Whigs] forward in any plot against the government and then reveal it" to one of the ministers of state. Forging letters and documents that were then planted on Whig opponents was thought to be a particularly useful tactic.[14] These attempts, however, were often executed rather clumsily, and a few such efforts resulted in spectacular failures. In *No Protestant Plot*, the author complained that Shaftesbury's letters were regularly intercepted by the government, and forged documents of a treasonable nature were inserted, and the letters were then transmitted to government ministers.[15] The "meal tub plot" backfired when the details of the forgery and the planting of the documents were thoroughly exposed to the public by Whig pamphleteers.[16] Even more disastrous, from the government's standpoint, was its attempt to use an agent provocateur to persuade a Whig supporter to write a treasonable pamphlet, which the government hoped to use as the grounds for arresting a number of Whigs. Instead, the Whigs sprang a trap of their own, concealing witnesses behind a curtain where they could overhear the treasonable remarks of the agent. They promptly arrested him and sought, unsuccessfully, to have him arraigned before the House of Commons where his testimony would have fueled the Whigs' efforts to force Charles II to accede to their demands.[17]

[14] James Walker, "The Secret Service under Charles II and James II," *Transactions of the Royal Historical Society*, 4th ser. 15, no. 1 (1932):221.

[15] Ferguson, *No Protestant Plot*, p. 17.

[16] This forgery did, however, appear "to confirm the suspicions that there was a widespread plot to defame the opposition" to the Court (Haley, pp. 554–556; Maurice Petherick, *Restoration Rogues*, London: Hollis and Carter, 1951, pp. 183–263).

[17] Dalrymple, vol. 1, pt. 1, bk. 1, p. 7; Haley, pp. 629–631, 634–637, 642–651; Petherick, *Restoration Rogues*, pp. 264–324. Ferguson discussed the Fitzharris case in *No Protestant Plot* (pp. 19ff.), claiming to have seen a letter from Fitzharris to his wife confessing that he had been paid money to implicate Shaftesbury in a treasonable plot. The case provoked a notorious legal battle between the Commons, which wanted to impeach Fitzharris (and thereby make public the details of this sham plot), and the king, who wanted him summarily tried in the courts and executed. A number of tracts relating to various confessions and dying words of Fitzharris were published, including one by George Treby, *Truth Vindicated*, 1681, which, in addition to the Ferguson work, Locke owned (*LL* #1136). This is hardly surprising, since Shaftesbury and a number of his associates personally attended his trial and were deeply involved in the struggle over Fitzharris' fate. The forged pamphlet *The True Englishman Speaking Plain English* is printed as an appendix to Cobbett (4:cxxiii–cxxviii). It was published under the title *Treason in Graine*, [1682]; cf. *The True Protestant Mercury*, May 13–17, 1682. The tract itself is pathetic, and apart from the fact that Fitzharris received money through the Duchess of Portsmouth and other details that tend to substantiate the charges that he was an agent provocateur, it could hardly have been written by any Whig who *was* committed to revolutionary action, for as we have seen, their writings had a definite familial similarity in their style and in the justificatory basis of their arguments, which is simply not present in Fitzharris' tract (see the testimony of Mrs. Fitzharris, Grey, 9:180–182).

Mail was systematically intercepted—even mail from ambassadors—and opened.[18] Leading Whigs, including Locke, were more or less constantly kept under surveillance by government spies. In addition, there were spies and informers, some of them highly placed, within the ranks of the Whigs.[19] Nor was spying a purely domestic industry; the government extended its efforts into Holland, where, it was hoped, information could be obtained from the Whigs or their contacts in that country. As one minister of state put it in his correspondence with the English envoy in Holland,

> It is of absolute necessity that you should find emissaries to go among the fanatical Whig party of our own countrymen at Amsterdam or elsewhere by whom you may get better intelligence of their designs and contrivances, I mean in our country, than we can here.[20]

In order to deal with these tactics, the Whigs, of course, were compelled to take countermeasures. They frequently communicated with one another by personally delivered messages. When it was necessary to use the regular post, they wrote under pseudonyms, used mail drops, ciphers, or invisible ink, and so forth. The most widely used practice appears to have been to employ a "canting" language; that is, to write an ostensibly innocent letter with a double meaning, which the recipient would understand, but which, on its face, could not be regarded as incriminating if it were intercepted by government agents. They moved their meetings from house to house in an effort to escape surveillance, and, in general, they developed a network of safe houses where those individuals most wanted by the government (including Shaftesbury toward the end of 1682) found refuge. Naturally, the Whigs also tried to maintain a high level of secrecy concerning their plans, but in this endeavor, for reasons

[18] Walker, "Secret Service," p. 226. It was said that there were in London people who had "tricks to open letters more skillfully than anywhere in the world" (James Westfall Thompson and Saul K. Padover, *Secret Diplomacy: Espionage and Cryptography, 1500–1815*, New York: Frederick Ungar, 1963, p. 93).

[19] There were several paid informers in the lower ranks of the Whig party, but the most important government spy during the period under discussion appears to have been Sir James Hayes. He was close to Shaftesbury—he was especially friendly with his secretary, Samuel Wilson, and his banker, Peter Percival— and he provided the government with useful information (Add. MS 29572, fol. 174). Hayes also dined frequently with the Earl of Anglesey, and through him probably gathered information about Monmouth, since the latter was a close friend of Anglesey (Add. MS 18730, passim). For Hayes' reports to the government, see Stowe MS 186, fols. 39–46 (British Library); *CSPD*, 22:504–505).

[20] Add. MS 35104, fol. 53 (William Conway to Thomas Chudleigh, March 8, 1682). Specific individuals who served as spies for the government against the Whigs in Holland are discussed in later chapters, but Locke's college friend, William Carr, was one of those acting as an intelligence agent through his duties as consul in Amsterdam.

already suggested, they were not always successful. On the other hand, the Whigs, and especially Shaftesbury, possessed an impressive system of intelligence that kept them informed of the government's actions.[21]

In other words, the political battle between the Whigs and the government was fought out not only in the political literature that rained down upon Englishmen in the 1680s—and not only in the courts, grand juries, elections, and parliamentary debates—but also in the streets and back alleys of London and Amsterdam, or in the pubs of Bristol and Oxford. Political action might mean the delivery of a message, concealing a fugitive, hiding a printing press, or contributing money for the cause. In extreme circumstances, individuals might forfeit their lives—and some did—by engaging in such political actions. Yet in order for a revolutionary movement to survive, it must enlist the support of individuals willing to contribute their efforts on precisely this day-to-day level of action. Much of the information about the Whig movement the historian would like to have is, for obvious reasons, not available, but that which is confirms what contemporaries believed: that hundreds of individuals were participants in, and many more than that were sympathizers with, an organized attempt to resist Charles II in what they believed were his designs to institute Catholicism and an absolute monarchy in England.

Although they were moving toward developing a theory of armed resistance, the Whigs were still pursuing their strategy of putting pressure on Charles II to summon a new Parliament, through petitions and rallying their supporters in London, when on July 2, 1681, the king fired the first shot in the undeclared war by ordering Shaftesbury's arrest. Charles did not lack for supporters urging him to adopt a hard line against the "stiffnecked rebels" headed by Shaftesbury. As one of them put it in verse,

> Plain arguing but few converts will afford;
> No rhetoric will suffice but that of the sword,
> Their biased humors never will comply,
> Till force reduce them to loyalty . . .

[21] Shaftesbury's sources of intelligence are, for obvious reasons, not disclosed in the evidence available to us, nor are they likely to be discovered at this late date. His connections were so widespread, across all levels of society, that it is not even worthwhile to speculate on the subject. But Ferguson offers a couple of examples that illustrate the point. He writes that in the fall of 1682, Shaftesbury received "fresh intelligence from a friend at Whitehall that the Court . . . intended to seize and arraign him," and this information made him decide to leave England. Ferguson also says that he learned that a warrant for his arrest had been issued from a minister of the Church of England, who had heard it from a lord at Court, to whom James had confided the information (*Ferguson*, p.429).

Take up then British *Jove* thy thunderbolts
Of vengeance, and strike down such stupid dolts.[22]

Though the advice was not so bad as the poetry, it was nevertheless premature, at least so far as Shaftesbury was concerned. For the Whigs were still in control of London, and in particular, its two sheriffs were among the most radical members of the party. Since the sheriffs had the responsibility for raising juries, and possessed a good deal of latitude in deciding which individuals they would select, it was extremely unlikely that any Whig, let alone Shaftesbury, would be convicted by a London jury of charges brought against him by the Court.

There is no reason to suppose that, even had they existed, any plans to foment a rebellion were pursued during the period Shaftesbury remained a prisoner in the Tower. Since the government was desperately searching for incriminating evidence, including treasonable writings, to shore up its case against Shaftesbury, it would have been foolish in the extreme to have jeopardized his life by providing the king with precisely the material he lacked.[23] Rather, those closest to Shaftesbury directed their efforts toward securing his release. Locke was busy searching legal records in order to obtain material that could be used to quash the indictment when it was presented to the grand jury.[24] He also accompanied Shaftesbury's wife to a meeting with one of the king's ministers to enlist his help in securing his friend's release.[25]

Meanwhile, the king struck another blow by ordering the arrest of an ardent Whig, Stephen College. College was a "mechanic" and a popular leader of Shaftesbury's supporters among the London working class.[26] College was a pawn, though an important one, in the king's move against Shaftesbury. Pressure was applied to him and to several other associates then in prison—including a promise of a pardon—to persuade them to

[22] White Kennett, *The Humble Address of an Academic Muse to His Majesty*. It is printed as a postscript to *A Letter from a Student at Oxford to a Friend in the Country, Concerning the Approaching Parliament*, 168l, pp. 21–22.

[23] For the attempts to pressure Edmond Everard to turn informer, see PRO 30/24/43/63. In this case, the government succeeded, and Everard was granted a pardon in June 1681, just prior to Shaftesbury's arrest (All Souls MS 233, pt. 1, fol. 236). Attempts were made on other individuals, but I have named Everard because he figures prominently in the discussion in chapters 9 and 10 of the intelligence activities directed against the radicals in Holland after 1683.

[24] Haley, p. 656. On July 7, Locke paid Mr. T[yrrell?] "for searching records," to bolster Shaftesbury's legal case. On October 11, and again on October 22, Locke records his payments to Shaftesbury's attorneys (MS f.5, fols. 91, 137–138).

[25] Haley, p. 667n. Locke also visited Shaftesbury on September 16, when the latter paid him for bringing him some gazettes (MS c.1, fol. 132).

[26] Morley, *Thousand Lives*, p. 130; North, *Examen*, p. 585.

testify against Shaftesbury, but this tactic failed.[27] College was brought to trial on July 8, but after listening to a number of disreputable witnesses testify that he had spoken treasonable words and tried to incite rebellion at Oxford during the last meeting of Parliament, the jury threw the case out.[28] The government, however, refused to accept defeat, and decided to bring the case before the grand jury in Oxford, where the alleged crime had taken place, and where, incidentally, they could be sure of obtaining a loyal jury. This was an ominous move from Shaftesbury's standpoint; he was still awaiting his day in court, but even if, as he hoped, the London grand jury returned a verdict of *ignoramus*, he might still have to face a retrial in some other county where the forces at the Whigs' disposal in London would be of no assistance to him. College's case was therefore important to him, not only because the former was influential among the radical tradesmen and artisans, on whom much of the burden of executing a policy of resistance now rested, but also because College's fate was a portent of things to come with respect to the king's ability to crush the opposition. Accordingly, those most closely associated with Shaftesbury were deeply involved in the effort to provide a defense for College. Shaftesbury paid for College's attorneys, Robert West and Aaron Smith, though they were not permitted by the Court to assist him in preparing his defense.[29] Locke left London for Oxford the day after College's acquittal, and was informed a few days later by a correspondent that College's trial would be held in Oxford.[30] It is probable that he spent some time there making arrangements for some of those who were expected to accompany College to Oxford. It appears, for example, that he was responsible for finding accommodations for Robert West, and very likely for others as well.[31] Shaftesbury also sent his secretary, Samuel Wilson,

[27] Dalrymple, vol. 1, pt. 1, bk. 1, pp. 5–6.

[28] Narcissus Luttrell, *A Brief Relation of State Affairs*, 6 vols., 1857, 1:109. College created an entertainment—a kind of cartoon Punch-and-Judy show—for the Oxford Parliament, the allegorical essence of which was the deposition of Charles II by Parliament, with allusions to the prospects of a violent revolution. An interesting account of this "Raree Show" as presented at the home of Lord Lovelace for various Whig supporters is provided by North, *Examen*, p. 101. A fuller description of the show itself is given by B. J. Rahn, "A Ra-ree Show—a Rare Cartoon: Revolutionary Propaganda in the Treason Trial of Stephen College," in *Studies in Change and Revolution*, ed. Paul J. Korshin, Menston, York.: Scolar Press, 1972, pp. 77–98.

[29] *CSPD*, 22:431–432; Morley, *Thousand Lives*, p. 132.

[30] *Correspondence*, 2:424, 435.

[31] Edward M. Thompson, ed., *Letters of Humphrey Prideaux to John Ellis*, 1875, pp. 139–140. There are a number of papers and documents relating to College's trial at Oxford, including instructions for the defendant and a set of questions he should ask the judges, among the Shaftesbury papers (PRO 30/24/6B/433; PRO 30/24/43/63). Included among the latter manuscripts are some notations by Locke, made between the time of Shaftes-

to Oxford; Wilson was excellent at taking shorthand, and so could provide a transcript of the trial proceedings.[32] College's witnesses and some of his supporters met every night at the house of John Wallis, the Oxford mathematician.[33] Wallis was a good friend of Locke, and it was his house that Locke had arranged for Shaftesbury's residence during the Oxford Parliament.[34]

College's trial was scheduled for August 17. Though he made a valiant effort, he was not able, on his own, to stand against the Court and the government's lawyers. College invoked the claim of John Lilburne that every individual had a right to counsel, which he referred to as "the birthright of every Englishman."[35] This plea was rejected by the Court, and in his speech to the jury, George Jeffries—later Judge Jeffries—referring to College as a joiner, asked them, "What have such people to do to interfere with the business of the government?"[36] In the early hours of the eighteenth, the jury found College guilty, and he was sentenced to be executed. That same day, Locke left Oxford to return to London.[37] Shaftesbury's forces had lost this battle, and now the "family"—which included Locke, Wilson, and Thomas Stringer—would have to concentrate their efforts on insuring his safety. Charles II had told Barrillon, the French ambassador, that he intended to have some heads.[38] College's was only the first on the block, an early martyr to the Whig cause. The outpouring of grief and resentment at his death probably surprised the government; he was, after all, as Jeffries had sneeringly pointed out, merely a joiner. Yet, he was also a symbolic representation "of all that the term 'dissenting Whig' conveyed." It was, L'Estrange wrote, "as if in that single man the neck of the whole Protestant cause had been brought to the block."[39]

Shaftesbury was pressing the government for a writ of habeas corpus, which the Court, not altogether without qualms, denied.[40] Nevertheless,

---

bury's arrest and his grand jury hearing, indicating that he was to ask Shaftesbury whether he wanted someone other than West to be one of his attorneys for the proceedings.

32 *CSPD*, 22:428.

33 Anthony Wood, *The Life and Times of Anthony Wood*, 5 vols., Oxford: Clarendon Press, 1892, 3:133. Wallis also made a copy of College's dying speech, which the government tried especially hard to suppress (2:553n.; *CSPD*, 22:412).

34 Cranston, p. 199.

35 *State Trials*, 3:345.

36 *State Trials*, 3:405.

37 *Correspondence*, 2:435. Locke later sent his friend Dr. Thomas a tract on College's trial and some other papers (MS c.1, fols. 124, 167).

38 Haley, p. 663.

39 George Kitchin, *Sir Roger L'Estrange*, London: Kegan Paul, Trench, Trubner, 1913, pp. 289, 351n.

40 Haley, p. 665.

he would soon have to be brought to trial, and the government's case against him, even discounting the London jury, was extremely weak. The king's ministers decided to close in on the circle around Shaftesbury and to apprehend Thomas Stringer and Samuel Wilson.[41] The latter had been a particular object of surveillance of a double agent in the Whig camp. In a letter to the Secretary of State written in late September 1681, he recommended the "seizing" of Wilson, for "I do verily believe he will not die by keeping a secret to save any. Therefore . . . I do think that if you now lay hold upon him, it will be much for his Majesty's service." Apart from whatever evidence against Shaftesbury might be extracted from Wilson, the informant believed that the mere fact of his arrest would "certainly strike such a damp upon that party" (the Whigs) that they would be less inclined to challenge the Court's candidate for Lord Mayor in the forthcoming election.[42] On October 12, Wilson was arrested and interrogated by a battery of the king's ministers. Not only did he tell them nothing incriminating about his employer, but remarkably, he managed to smuggle a letter to his brother out of prison, in which he conveyed information about the kind of evidence the government was fishing for against Shaftesbury, and instructions to be given to Stringer and Locke, "our family," as to what to do about it. Locke's friend, Edward Clarke, an active supporter of Shaftesbury, was also arrested, but said nothing.[43] A few days following Wilson's arrest, Shaftesbury sent a message to Charles II, offering to leave England for America, where he could look after his plantations in the Carolinas, but whether this represented a worried reaction on his part to the evidence Wilson might give or was simply a ruse to obtain his release is unclear.[44]

Several weeks prior to Shaftesbury's appearance before the grand jury, an aggressive defense of his position was published. This tract, *No Protestant Plot: or, The Present Pretended Conspiracy of Protestants against*

[41] *CSPD*, 22:428. The warrant for Wilson's arrest was issued on October 10, 1681 (p. 504). There is a copy in the Shaftesbury papers (PRO 30/24/43/63). Stringer was not arrested until November 1682 (Haley, p. 725).

[42] Stowe MS 186, fols. 39–40. James Hayes was the double agent (see note 19 above). Hayes was a prominent alderman of London, whose sons Joseph and Israel were deeply involved in the radical movement, and later in Monmouth's Rebellion.

[43] Haley, p. 670.

[44] Haley (p. 667) says Shaftesbury's letter was written before Wilson's arrest, but two contemporary sources place it after his arrest, although they disagree as to its exact date. Morrice gives the date as October 20, while Luttrell says it was October 15 (Morrice, 1:319; Luttrell, *Brief Relation*, 1:136). According to Hayes, Wilson told him that Shaftesbury's friends were working on a "design" to get him out of the Tower, even to the point of the earl's making a false confession (Stowe MS 186, fol. 46). If Shaftesbury was indeed willing to go that far to regain his freedom, the possibility that the offer to go to Carolina was merely one such design cannot be dismissed.

the King and Government, Discovered to be a Conspiracy of the Papists against the King and His Protestant Subjects, attacked certain of the king's ministers, the credibility of the witnesses against Shaftesbury, and generally, the idea that Protestants would engage in a conspiracy against Charles II that would insure the succession of his brother, a Catholic. This "conspiracy," the author argued, was just another "sham plot" concocted by government agents, like the meal-tub plot, as an excuse for the imprisonment of Whig leaders.[45] *No Protestant Plot* was probably written by Robert Ferguson, but in putting the material together, he almost certainly relied upon the assistance of others in Shaftesbury's circle, including Locke.[46] It proved to be a very effective and timely piece of Whig propaganda. On the other side, a few days before Shaftesbury's trial, John Dryden's *Absalom and Achitophel* was published, one of the most powerful political poems ever written, which became an immediate best-seller. It was easily the best expression of the king's political perspective produced during the exclusion crisis, although it did not affect the outcome of Shaftesbury's case.[47] As expected, the grand jury returned a verdict of *ignoramus,* as several London juries had done previously in cases involving Whigs, and Shaftesbury was released on bail a few days later.[48]

On the day after Shaftesbury's acquittal, Charles II ordered his Attorney General to investigate whether the king could appoint the sheriffs,

[45] Ferguson, *No Protestant Plot,* pp. 17–19.

[46] Ferguson, as he subsequently claimed, was probably the author of this tract. However, one section of the work (pp. 28ff.) contains a detailed discussion of College's trial at Oxford, including citations from witnesses, comments on the court proceedures, and so forth. It was almost certainly written or compiled by someone who was present in the courtroom. Ferguson is not known to have been at Oxford—since he was a wanted man, he could not have appeared publicly as a spectator in the courtroom—and he therefore relied for at least this part of the pamphlet upon some other member of Shaftesbury's family. This might have been Samuel Wilson, who was sent to Oxford for the express purpose of providing an accurate account of College's trial, although Wilson himself was in jail in early October. The testimony of one of the witnesses against College (Dugdale) was impugned by his perjury about medical treatment he had (or had not) received from Dr. Lower. On this point, at least, it was most likely Locke who supplied the assistance to Ferguson. As L'Estrange noted, "I take for granted that the *Just and Modest Vindication* and *No Protestant Plot* were written by the same hand," although several people were probably involved in furnishing materials (*CSPD,* 22:532). In 1706, Ferguson supplied a list of tracts he wrote both before and after his Jacobite conversion. While this list is not exhaustive, it appears to be fairly reliable (Smith MS 31, fol. 30, Bodleian Library).

[47] Despite the temptation to make an exception of *Absalom and Achitophel* to my exclusion of literary sources as stated in the Introduction, I have stuck to the rule. The poem is the subject of a number of books and articles, and although I have found these discussions useful, I cannot do the work—or the political/poetical controversy it inspired—justice within the space I could allot to it here.

[48] Lord Russell, Sir William Cooper, John Sydenham, and Francis Charlton posted the bail for Shaftesbury (Luttrell, *Brief Relation,* 1:147).

thereby setting aside the Whigs' electoral control of London, which one way or another, he was determined to break.[49] Charles II had also decided to launch a more general attack to insure that the Whigs' electoral successes in the country at large would not be repeated in the future, if and when he should be forced to summon a new Parliament. This was his famous quo warranto campaign, recalling city and borough royal charters, with the object, as he put it in the case of the capital, to "take into consideration the abuses of the franchises of the City of London."[50] Referring to the latter's charter, one government minister wrote to his correspondent,

> When that is vacated, as I doubt not but it will be, the fanatical faction will be extremely broken and the consequence of that I need not enlarge upon.[51]

The government was still working on plans to rearrest Shaftesbury; meanwhile, it broadened its efforts to the extent that, if it were successful, the Whigs would not only lose their stronghold in London, but they would no longer be able to function as a political party in the rest of the country as well.

The year 1681 ended inconclusively: The Whigs had won the parliamentary elections, but the king had dissolved Parliament; the king had arrested Shaftesbury, but the jury provided for his release; the Whigs, generally, were on the defensive, but they still had not been defeated. Both sides were determined to raise the ante, and 1682 gave every promise of being a year of confrontation, a final showdown between the king and his enemies. The clergy, especially, threw their full support behind the government's propaganda campaign, urging private individuals to desist from meddling in political affairs.

> The pulpits resounded with the doctrine of passive obedience and non-resistance, which . . . was now universally preached. The clergy seemed to make it their business to surrender to the king all the liberties and privileges of the subjects, and to leave them only an unlimited obedience. According to the principles publicly preached, no Eastern monarch was more absolute than the king of England.[52]

[49] Milne, *Rye House Plot*, p. 40.

[50] Haley, p. 688; Jennifer Levin, *The Charter Controversy in the City of London, 1660–1688, and Its Consequences*, London: Athlone Press, 1969, p. 23. Charles reconstituted the electoral structure of the boroughs, "and filled them with electors agreeable to himself" (Dalrymple, vol. 1, pt. 1, bk. 1, pp. 22–23).

[51] William Conway to Bevil Skelton, [1681?], Add. MS 35104, fol. 38.

[52] Ralph, *History*, p. 961; Burnet, 2:290; Laurence Echerd, *The History of England*, 1720, p. 1017.

In addition, "addresses" were raised condemning the "treasonable conspiracy" of a Protestant Association.[53] The Whigs, however, continued to meet, notably through holding public dinners. Several such dinners with Shaftesbury, Monmouth, Essex, Howard, and Grey in attendance were held with the London sheriffs during March 1682.[54] But in April, when the Whigs attempted to stage a large banquet for eight hundred "loyal Protestant nobility, gentry, clergy, and citizens" as a means of "the preserving and improving mutual love and charity" among these "loyal" citizens, the king intervened and ordered the banquet canceled, calling up four companies of trained bands to enforce this order against an unlawful assembly.[55] He was not about to permit a meeting of the "Association" under any guise whatsoever.

On the basis of the testimony of several witnesses, one may conclude that the radical Whigs had, at this time, some form of contingency plan that could be put into action in order to block the immediate succession of James in the event of the king's death.[56] Precisely at what point a shift occurred, rendering a contingent response into an operational project, is difficult to say, although everyone agrees that by the summer of 1682, Shaftesbury and others were developing serious plans for an armed uprising.[57] It was obvious that matters were coming to head, for at the end of June, the new sheriffs of London were elected. A combination of Court-directed intrigues and Whig tactical mistakes succeeded not only in securing the election of two Tories, but the king arrested the Whig sheriffs and sent them to the Tower for presiding over a "riot."[58] The

[53] Echerd, *History*, p. 1018; cf. *The Knot Untyed: or, the Association Disbanded*, 1682, pp. 9, 24–26.

[54] Haley, p. 693.

[55] Haley, pp. 694–695.

[56] *Secret History*, p. 13.

[57] *Secret History*, p. 23. Lord Howard testified that he also first heard from Captain Walcot about the plans for the insurrection around the time of the sheriffs' election in 1682 (*State Trials*, 4:218).

[58] Haley, pp. 697–700. The government's determination to gain control of London is expressed in Secretary Jenkins' letters. To one correspondent he wrote, "*We* have certainly got" one sheriff, "and the other is legally elected" (Add. MS 35104, fol. 66; italics added). To another, he confided that "if the Whigs will be so obstinate as to dispute [the election] at law," the government would drag out the legal proceedings so that the Tory sheriff could "serve out his year before the controversy can be ended" (Carte MS 216, fol. 47). It is not absolutely certain that Jenkins wrote this letter, but other letters in this manuscript collection are signed by him, or are intelligence reports from correspondents addressed to him. The House of Commons committee that investigated the 1682 London sheriffs election following the Glorious Revolution reported that there had been an "invasion made upon the rights of the city of London in the election of sheriffs" (Reginald R. Sharpe, *London and the Kingdom*, 3 vols., London: Longmans, Green, 1895, 2:543). When the Whigs protested the

government now held all the cards, with the Lord Mayor and the two sheriffs on its side, and it would soon be in a position to make a final push against its enemies. The newly elected sheriffs did not assume office until mid-September, but after that date, they would be able to remove the only remaining obstacle—London juries—standing in the way of the king's prosecution of Shaftesbury and the other Whigs. The latter had every reason to be concerned about their safety to the point of taking up arms as a means of self-defense. In this regard, it should be recalled that, from the radical perspective, there had been a conspiracy of long standing on the part of Catholics, the Court, and the clergy to subvert the Protestant religion and constitutional government in England. And by 1682, there was a widespread belief that "the King as well as the Duke were in the conspiracy to alter the Constitution and overturn our religion."[59] From this standpoint, revolutionary action did not appear to be such a giant step, for it had to be acknowledged "that either we have conspired against the King, or that he and his dearly beloved brother have conspired against us; so that which remains to be decided, is whether the reproach and guilt of this conspiracy is to be laid upon them or to be imputed to us."[60]

In his confession, James Holloway, a Whig supporter at Bristol, said that he first heard of the "design" for a revolution in July 1682, from his friend Joseph Tiley, who had just come from London with the bad news about the sheriffs' election. Tiley told him that "if some speedy course be not taken we shall be all undone" by the actions the government would be able to take against them through the sheriffs and juries now at their command. Tiley informed Holloway that Shaftesbury and some others had resolved upon an insurrection to be organized in several parts of the country, and "therefore, said he, we must consider how to manage affairs in Bristol" in support of this action.[61] Sometime before this, Shaftesbury

---

government's tactics, the army was called out and 300 people were arrested and imprisoned for a month for causing a "riot" (Levin, *Charter Controversy*, p. 27). Locke bought several issues of the *Protestant Mercury* that carried the story of this riot and the proceedings at Guildhall (MS f.6, fol. 83). He also purchased one of the tracts written in defense of the Whig sheriffs (MS f.16, fol. 140).

59 [Robert Ferguson], *An Impartial Enquiry into the Administration of Affairs in England*, [1684], pp. 23, 37, 40, 45, 55.

60 *Enquiry*, p. 79.

61 *The Free and Voluntary Confession and Narrative of James Holloway*, 1684, p. 2. According to one estimate, nearly 100 people in Bristol were involved in the Rye House Plot (C. E. Whiting, *Studies in English Puritanism from the Restoration to the Revolution, 1660–1688*, London: Society for Promoting Christian Knowledge, 1931, p. 376). Wade was one the earliest recruits for Bristol. He had accompanied Ayloffe to a meeting with Shaftesbury, Grey, Monmouth, and Armstrong sometime before Monmouth's progress, where

had sent word to Captain Walcot in Ireland, and to several individuals in Scotland to return to London to assist in planning the insurrection.[62] It was during this same period—early summer—that Monmouth, Russell, Grey, and Thomas Armstrong met at Shaftesbury's house to discuss the "necessity of having recourse to arms." And Grey added, "we had many meetings after this," at which "tedious discourses, and innumerable proposals" were presented.[63] What they agreed upon was that Monmouth should make another progress through Cheshire in September, stirring up popular support for the Whigs, giving them some idea of what kind of strength they could muster for a revolution. Monmouth's trip, in other words, was to serve as a dress rehearsal for a mobilization of forces scheduled for November. Walcot went to see his friend Lord Howard to enlist his support, and the circle kept widening. The earls of Essex, Salisbury, Macclesfield, and Anglesey were brought into the plan. So were lords Brandon, Delamere, and Clare.[64]

---

plans were drafted for the insurrection. Prior to the duke's arrest, Wade returned to Bristol, where—along with his brother, Holloway, and some others—he purchased four small cannons and some powder and bullets, which were stored at Holloway's house (Harleian MS 6845, fols. 266–267).

[62] Add. MS 38847, fol. 88. The Scots were already in contact with Shaftesbury in July 1682 (Andrew Lang, *Sir George McKenzie: His Life and Times, 1636(?)–1691*, London: Longmans, Green, 1909, p. 237).

[63] *Secret History*, p. 23; *Ferguson*, p. 417.

[64] Salisbury was a friend and supporter of Shaftesbury, who had been with him in the Tower in 1677. Locke visited Salisbury in 1680 (Cranston, p. 194), and Stringer described him as a very zealous supporter of Protestantism (W. D. Christie, *A Life of Anthony Ashley Cooper, First Earl of Shaftesbury*, 2 vols., 1871, 2, appendix 8, p. cxxix). His wife was ill, however, and he was able to contribute little to the insurrection, though if it had been carried off in 1682, he would probably have given his support. Lord Howard said they had tried to add Salisbury to the Council of Six in 1683 (*CSPD*, 25:80). Anglesey is very likely to have been a major source of court intelligence for the radicals until he was replaced as Lord Privy Seal in August 1682. Throughout 1682, his diary shows him meeting with Essex, Monmouth, Howard, Alderman Wright, Macclesfield, Grey, and Francis Charlton. Moreover, although Anglesey was in London, there is a suspiciously unexplained break in the diary between November 6 and November 18—just when the plans for the insurrection reached their critical point. The regular entries resume on November 19, the night of Shaftesbury's departure, and during 1683, they show Anglesey meeting frequently with Russell and Monmouth. On the night of June 13, 1683, he dined with Russell, and between June 13 and June 19 there is another unexplained gap in the diary, precisely the time when the conspirators learned that the plot had been discovered. Anglesey left town and went into hiding; when he returned in July, he found that his house had been broken into and his papers searched. Though Anglesey appeared as a witness at the trials of Russell and Sidney, he was never arrested as a conspirator, though the evidence clearly suggests that he did at least know of the Rye House Plot (Add. MS 18730, fols. 98–108). Clare was another friend of Shaftesbury, and it was one of his tenants who gave information to the government in 1683 that Clare, Sidney, and others were engaged in a treasonous conspiracy (Ralph Thoresby,

On a different social level as participants were Colonel Rumsey, Major Wildman, John Trenchard, Sir Walter Yonge, John Freke, Robert West, Thomas Shepherd, Nathaniel Wade, Colonel Danvers, Major Manley, Robert Ferguson, Francis Charlton, Aaron Smith, John Ayloffe, Major Breman, Major Holmes, Richard Nelthorp, and many more. In addition to these, there was a group of Scotsmen—nobility, gentlemen, and clergy—who were privy to the plans for a revolution. The Earl of Argyll, who was a fugitive from Scotland, where James had tried to have him executed for sedition, had gone into hiding in London. He was being assisted by the underground network of the radicals, and was in contact with Shaftesbury regarding the role to be played by the Scots in the planned insurrection.[65] Other Scotsmen—George Campbell, John Cochrane, and William Carstares—began to drift into London on the pretense of consulting about their colonial interests in the Carolinas.[66] Slingsby Bethel's secret trip to Scotland at the end of September was undoubtedly part of the effort to coordinate the activities of the Scottish participants in the insurrection.[67]

As matters stood at the beginning of September, therefore, Shaftesbury was attempting to put together a three-pronged armed attack; there was to be a rising in the country simultaneous with a seizure of the king's guards in London, and on this signal, the Scots would mount some form of armed resistance of their own.[68] At the time Monmouth set out on his

---

Letters of Eminent Men, 2 vols., 1832, 1:23). Other individuals, such as William Ellis, the son-in-law of Richard Hampden and a close friend of lords Wharton and Stamford, as well as the latter himself (who had given Colonel Rumsey £800 under suspicious circumstances in June 1683), and Walter Yonge, Locke's close friend, were also implicated, though for one reason or another, they were not prosecuted. In short, as Monmouth told the king, there were many more individuals involved in the Rye House conspiracy than had been publicly named or arrested.

[65] William Veitch, whose release from prison in Scotland was due to Shaftesbury's intervention, guided Argyll to London and to an underground organization of old Commonwealth officers—Captain Lockyer, (a Republican and an associate of Colonel Blood) and Major Abraham Holmes (a former agitator)—and such sympathizers as Mrs. Smith (wife of a wealthy sugar-baker, and later the chief financial backer of Argyll's invasion) (*Memoirs of William Veitch and George Brysson*, 1825, pp. 99–140). According to Ferguson, there were at least two personal meetings between Shaftesbury and Argyll, and numerous messages passed between the two men (*Ferguson*, p. 415). Burnet says that Monmouth "had many conferences" with Argyll while the latter was in London (Burnet, 2:354)..

[66] Add. MS 38847, fol. 88; Burnet, 2:355; *Letters to Earl of Aberdeen*, 1851, pp. 58–59; Lang, *George McKenzie*, p. 237.

[67] The Bishop of Edinburgh gave orders for Bethel to be seized, but discreetly (*Letters to Aberdeen*, p. 82). Through James Stewart and others, the Scots had sent emissaries to Holland and from there to Scotland in order to mobilize support for the insurrection (HMC 15th Report, appendix, pt. 8, vol. 1, pp. 174–175).

[68] *State Trials*, 4:221.

progress, this project was still in the early stages of planning. Even so, a number of Whigs, including Shaftesbury, thought it prudent to absent themselves from London during some or all of the time Monmouth was in the countryside, just in case the king should take his progress as an excuse to have them all arrested. Shaftesbury held a secret meeting with Salisbury and Essex, at the latter's estate, on September 15, in the midst of Monmouth's tour, a meeting at which Locke was also present.[69]

In fact, the king, who received numerous intelligence reports from informants in the countryside, had a reasonably clear understanding of the purposes behind Monmouth's tour. At its outset, he reinforced a garrison of troops stationed at a castle in the area and put them on alert, as a hedge against any spontaneous uprising.[70] At the same time, Secretary of State Jenkins wrote to several people in Cheshire with orders from the king that they should engage in a surveillance of Monmouth and his supporters during the progress. Accordingly, reports "were sent hourly to court, by the spies who were sent to the country for that purpose."[71] Neither the progress, nor the accompanying horse races, both of which attracted huge crowds, were accepted at face value by the government. Thus Jenkins wrote to a correspondent that the king "knows the Association to be deep rooted and that those that contrived the rendezvous at Wallasea had other designs than those of horseracing in their heads, which he hopes in time to discover to the bottom."[72]

The government had good reason to be concerned. Monmouth was extremely popular with the lower classes and drew large crowds of admirers wherever he appeared. On this progress, however, he was also met at every stage by a number of lords—Macclesfield, Brandon, Delamere, Colchester, Russell, Grey, "and many others of the high gentry of the Whig party"—who greeted Monmouth riding "at the head of their tenants."[73] Alarmed by the size of the crowds and the fact that many individuals greeted Monmouth carrying arms, several government informants sent in reports describing "the riotous and dangerous concourse" of people and the "horrible tumult" caused by the "rabble" at Chester.[74] The king sent an order for Monmouth's arrest, though only on the misdemeanor charge of disturbing the peace.[75] Monmouth did not challenge

[69] Haley, p. 715; Burnet, 2:351.

[70] *Correspondence of the Family of Hatton*, 2 vols., ed. E. M. Thompson, 1875, 2:18; Elizabeth D'Oyley, *James, Duke of Monmouth*, London: Geoffrey Bles, 1938, p. 196.

[71] Dalrymple, vol. 1, pt. 1, bk. 1, p. 20; *CSPD*, 23:370.

[72] *CSPD*, 23:460; HMC 3d Report, 2:269.

[73] Dalrymple, vol. 1, pt. 1, bk. 1, p. 19.

[74] *CSPD*, 23:417; HMC 3d Report, 2:96.

[75] All Souls MS 241, fols. 160–162. This is a copy of the warrant for Monmouth's arrest, dated September 16, 1682 (cf. ibid., fols. 178–179).

the sergeant-at-arms who presented him with the summons ordering his return to London, but he sent his friend and companion Sir Thomas Armstrong ahead to obtain a writ of habeas corpus. According to Lord Grey, Armstrong also carried a message for Shaftesbury, whom he found at home with Colonel Rumsey. The message related to Monmouth's uncertainty as to whether he should obey the king's order and return to London or remain in Cheshire where the gentry had offered "to draw their swords and rise instantly" in his defense, which offer Monmouth was reluctant to accept without the approval of Shaftesbury, Russell, and Grey, since such an action might very well prove to be premature with respect to executing the overall plan for an uprising.[76] Shaftesbury immediately called a meeting at his house to discuss the matter with Grey and Russell, and argued, against Russell's strenuous objections, that Monmouth should remain in Cheshire and begin the revolution immediately. Russell pointed out, quite sensibly, that they did not yet have sufficient arms or money—even assuming that they had sufficient men—to engage the king's forces, but Shaftesbury seems to have believed that the king's misdemeanor charge was merely a subtle move by Charles II to force Monmouth to return to London where he, and the other Whig leaders, would be arrested on more serious charges. In this exchange, Russell's views prevailed; Monmouth returned, and was released on bail.[77] Shortly thereafter, there was another meeting at Shaftesbury's house with Grey, Russell, and Monmouth present, at which Shaftesbury urged that they speed up their efforts and if necessary, rely upon a rising in London by his "ten thousand brisk boys" in Wapping, even without the simultaneous support from those in the countryside. Russell again urged patience and more planning, but Shaftesbury was not convinced that time was on their side, and believed that, given the large number of individuals who knew of the proposed revolution, the plot would soon be discovered by the government, and they all stood to be executed without having accomplished anything.[78] It was around the time of this meeting that the new Tory sheriffs were sworn into office. That evening, Shaftesbury left his house and went into hiding, moving his residence to various safe houses in London, and concealing his identity under a false name.[79]

Sometime later, in October, there was a meeting at the house of Thomas Shepherd, the merchant.[80] Shaftesbury was not present, but sev-

[76] *Ferguson*, pp. 417–418; *Secret History*, p. 27.

[77] *Secret History*, pp. 29–30; Add. MS 38847, fol. 89.

[78] Haley, p. 713.

[79] According to West, Shaftesbury went into hiding on the night the new sheriffs were installed in office (Add. MS 38847, fol. 89).

[80] Sprat, p. 114.

eral of those who were in constant contact with him and who could act as his agents were. At a minimum, those in attendance included Russell, Monmouth, Grey, Rumsey, Ferguson, and Armstrong.[81] John Trenchard was supposed to be at the meeting, but when Grey and Armstrong stopped by his chambers to collect him, he declined to accompany them.[82] At this meeting, Ferguson read a "declaration," of which more will be said later, but the group also directed its attention to working out the specific details of the agreed-upon general plan. To this end, they set a definite date for the insurrection: November 19. This was a Sunday, when the shops in London would be closed and the element of surprise could be maintained. The government might be expecting trouble on November 17, the day on which the pope-burning demonstrations had traditionally been mounted by the Whigs, and the king would probably call up the trained bands to be in readiness against any tumult. But by the nineteenth, these troops would have been disbanded or reduced to a minimum. The plan, therefore, was to gather in small groups of unarmed men, and each group would make its way inconspicuously to various houses spread around the city where caches of arms were hidden. Once armed, the groups would reassemble just before midnight and launch the first strike "by attacking the train-bands at the Exchange," closing off that part of the city with a barricade, backed by three or four cannons. This position, it was expected, would receive the first counterattack from the king's guards. Meanwhile, another contingent would take command of London Bridge, in order "to cut off the correspondence between Whitehall and the Tower." It was estimated that these actions could be carried out with about two thousand men, who could hold their positions "till the rest were got together and in order." They then hoped to dispatch a thousand men, and whatever cavalry they could muster, under the leadership of Lord Macclesfield whose object was to "fall upon the rear of the King's forces" sent to quell the first disturbances. The general objective of this plan, according to Grey, was to force the king to flee London and establish himself at Portsmouth, though exactly what was to transpire from that

[81] These individuals are a minimum because it did not emerge until after Monmouth's Rebellion that ex-sheriff of London Henry Cornish had attended at least one of the two meetings at Shepherd's house, although Ferguson later testified that Cornish was not present when he read his declaration to the group (*Secret History*, p. 47; Landsdowne MS 1152, fol. 228; HMC 12th Report, appendix, pt. 6, p. 129). Although the motives for naming Cornish were far from pure, and certain embellishments were made by the witnesses at his trial, it is probably true that he was at one of the meetings, and even more certain that he was a knowledgeable participant in the Rye House conspiracy. That his name did not surface for two years makes it possible that the names mentioned were not an exhaustive list of those present.

[82] *Secret History*, p. 36.

point on, assuming everything else had met with success, was anyone's guess.[83] It is easy, in retrospect, to dismiss all this as wishful—and even reckless—thinking on the part of the radicals, but certain details in Grey's account, for which we have other supporting evidence, indicate, I think, that these discussions were devoted to planning a revolution in something of a more technical sense of that term than has sometimes been credited to these individuals by historians. Trenchard's absence at this meeting, however, was a crucial weakening factor in the forwarding of these designs, since he had promised to raise 1,500 men in Taunton for a coordinated uprising in the country.[84]

Nevertheless, a few days after this meeting at Shepherd's, Grey, Armstrong, and Monmouth went, at about midnight, to view the state of readiness of the king's guards at several posts, in order to present a report to the group at their next meeting regarding this aspect of their plan.[85] And at that second meeting at Shepherd's house, which was probably in early November, Monmouth gave an encouraging report on the unprepared state of the guards. But again, Trenchard was not present, and word had been conveyed from him that preparations in Taunton were not ready and that the rising would have to be delayed. This discouraging news was greeted with some anger, and not a little resentment directed toward Trenchard's cowardice, but it did, in fact, force a postponement of the revolution.[86] The rising in the west country was a key element in the plan, and, without question, Taunton was vital to its successful execution. More than one informant writing to the Secretary of State had singled out "the rebellious town of Taunton" as a center of resistance to the government. As one writer put it, "were this town brought down to obedience, all the West would be then very regular; for it is the nursery of rebellion in these parts."[87] It is not surprising, then, that the radicals staked so much upon a mobilization of forces from this "rebellious town," or that they reacted as they did to Trenchard's refusal to live up to his pledge to lead those forces.

All this was too much for Shaftesbury, still in hiding and dependent upon the reports provided him by those present at these meetings. He apparently interpreted their outcome as a reluctance on the part of his colleagues to act at all, and fearing for his own safety, he decided to leave

[83] *Secret History*, pp. 41–42; Add. MS 38847, fol. 112.

[84] Add. MS 38847, fol. 91; *Secret History*, p. 26.

[85] *Secret History*, p. 45. Later, in 1683, Walcot, Captain Gaunt, and James Burton went to observe the forces stationed in the Tower (*State Trials*, 4:145).

[86] *Secret History*, p. 46.

[87] *CSPD*, 23:98. Macaulay provides a brief account of the rebel history and tradition of Taunton (Macaulay, 1:525–526).

England for Holland, which he did on November 19, the evening of the projected revolution.[88] Shaftesbury's fears were both justified and understandable, but he was perhaps overhasty in his assessment of his fellow conspirators' intentions. They did not, in fact, abandon their plans for a revolution. They continued to meet long after Shaftesbury's exile and subsequent death. It is important to emphasize this point—that notwithstanding his intense commitment, influence, and organizational skills, the revolution was never simply Shaftesbury's personal project; it was rather a collective undertaking by a group of radical Whigs. As I shall argue later, Locke's participation in this undertaking was not merely an expression of personal loyalty to his friend and patron, but as with the others, the consequence of deeply held political convictions.

Before continuing with the narrative of the preparations for a general insurrection, following Shaftesbury's departure, however, I want to turn to a consideration of the second component of the Rye House conspiracy: the assassination plot. Since this part of the conspiracy was further developed after Shaftesbury's death, I will be concerned here only with the suggestion that such a scheme was formulated by, or with the approval of Shaftesbury himself. The primary, though not the only, source for this suggestion is Robert Ferguson. Sometime during his exile in Holland, Ferguson recorded his recollections of the Rye House conspiracy in a manuscript, later published as an appendix to his biography.[89] In this manuscript, Ferguson noted that sometime in the fall he heard from

[88] Shaftesbury's departure on the night set for the insurrection may be purely coincidental, but there was a large fire in Wapping that evening that effectively provided the cover necessary for his escape. West pretty clearly implies that the fire was deliberately set for this purpose (Add. MS 38847, fol. 94). Contemporary accounts of the fire also suggested arson as its cause (*A True Account of the Dreadful Fire, Which Happened on Sunday, the 19th of November . . . in Wapping*, 1682, pp. 2–3). The fire destroyed about 1,500 houses (Clark, *Later Stuarts*, p. 64).

[89] Ferguson began writing his account sometime after the defeat of Monmouth's Rebellion. At the end of his manuscript, he denies that this confession that "I have discovered to you" is designed to purchase the king's favor or his own life (*Ferguson*, p. 437). Nevertheless, despite the fact that he was specifically exempted from James II's general pardon in 1686, it may be that Ferguson did believe that he could secure his pardon through providing a history of the radicals' activities. This would date the manuscript from 1686–1687, precisely when many radicals in Holland were applying for individual pardons from James, and when the revolutionary movement was at its lowest ebb. On April 25, 1687, a bundle of ninety-three papers belonging to Ferguson was delivered to the Secretary of State, and it is possible that this manuscript was among them (*Ferguson*, p. 179n.; see also, *CSPD*, [James II], 3:396). There is no indication as to how the government came into possession of Ferguson's papers, but they were probably confiscated during one of the numerous raids on his various residences in Holland, since Ferguson was much too cautious a person to have left such a quantity of material in England when he went into exile.

Wildman that there was an assassination plot brewing.[90] This "enterprise to be made upon the person of the king and his brother," according to Ferguson, had been "fomented and entertained by many" individuals before he heard of it. Following his conversation with Wildman, Ferguson confronted Shaftesbury ("to whom I could at all time make my own access") with the rumor, and the earl told him "that he was resolved to try, whether it was not possible to save and deliver the nation by a few, seeing as there was no hope of effecting it by united councils and a combined strength."[91] From the tone of these remarks, it would appear that the assassination plan was Shaftesbury's response to the failure of the meeting(s) at Shepherd's house to produce the kind of results he had hoped for. Given the state of Shaftesbury's thinking at the time and his insistent demand for some action to be taken, Ferguson's account has a fair degree of plausibility attached to it.[92] Yet since he allows himself such a modest role in planning this undertaking—when both subsequent events and later confessions assigned Ferguson the leading part in the conspiracy—it is probably wise not to rely entirely on the credibility of his manuscript.

According to Robert West, Captain Walcot came to visit him around the middle of October 1682, and the two discussed the revolution, which, Walcot assured him, "had been well and long considered" by Shaftesbury and the other lords. Walcot also told him that Shaftesbury had another "design," which was the "cutting off the King and the Duke of York" on their return to London from the horse races at Newmarket, which was scheduled to take place later that month.[93] If this assassination were car-

[90] In his manuscript, Ferguson refers to the individual as "a gentleman that is at present at Amsterdam"—as Wildman then was—and a person "who is esteemed a great statesman and excellently versed in the laws of England, though never accounted very friendly to kingship," and someone with whom Ferguson had been "long acquainted." I agree with Ashley that there can be little doubt that Wildman is the individual to whom reference is being made (*Ferguson*, p. 419; Maurice Ashley, *John Wildman: Postmaster and Plotter*, London: Jonathan Cape, 1947, p. 241). It should be noted, however, that Ferguson says that Wildman was "the first man of note and consideration" from whom he heard about the assassination plot, not necessarily the first person to pass the information to Ferguson.

[91] *Ferguson*, pp. 418, 420. The assassination was also presented as "a more easy, cheap, safe, and compendious way for relieving ourselves, than that of an insurrection" (p. 419).

[92] During the period Shaftesbury was in hiding, he stayed at Ferguson's house for a week, during which time they held a number of conversations. According to Ferguson, Shaftesbury in these discussions reaffirmed his endorsement of the assassination scheme, partly as a consequence of the earl's growing disenchantment with monarchy, partly because of the difficulty of raising the money necessary for a general insurrection, and partly because of his dissatisfaction with the efforts of his associates (*Ferguson*, p. 422).

[93] Add. MS 38847, fol. 90; MS PWV 95, fol. 259. Robert West, *An Answer to a Late Paper, Entitled a True Copy of a Paper Written by Capt. Thomas Walcot*, 1683, pp. 1–2.

ried out, Walcot said, it "would prevent all danger" to the conspirators. According to West, Walcot "gave me no account by whom, or where this attempt was to be made, but only, that Mr. Ferguson had the management of it, and told me, though he thought it lawful, he looked upon it as base and ungenerous, and scorned to be concerned in it."[94] Later in his confession, West said that Colonel Rumsey told him that £600 had been raised by Shaftesbury and that this "sum was . . . deposited in a person's hand for carrying on the assassination designed in October."[95]

As it bears upon the credibility of this last statement and Shaftesbury's general commitment to the assassination plan, as well as upon the discussion of rebel finances in the next chapter, we ought to consider the question of how the radicals proposed to finance their undertakings. The Scots had presented an estimate of £30,000 as the amount needed to finance their participation in the revolution, though they eventually came down to a figure in the range of £10,000.[96] Between May 20 and September 30, 1682, Shaftesbury borrowed several thousand pounds from friends and business associates.[97] With some exaggeration, Sprat wrote that Shaftesbury "had more debt on his estate than the full value of it amounted to."[98] We cannot be certain as to what happened to the cash raised by Shaftesbury, but it appears that he did disburse several hundred pounds to various trusted associates, and this money was to be used for "the cause."[99]

Thomas Shepherd testified that Ferguson had informed him in October or November 1682 of the assassination scheme, and that Rumsey, West, and Wade came to his house one night to discuss the project.[100] William Carstares also recalled some conversations with Ferguson during this same period regarding the assassination.[101] Lord Howard later alluded rather vaguely to some "dark hints" he heard from Walcot, Goodenough, West, and Ferguson about killing the king at Newmarket. He said he discussed the proposed assassination with Monmouth.[102] What emerges from all this, I think, is a reluctance on the part of any of these individuals

[94] Add. MS 38847, fols. 90, 101. Ferguson maintained that Rumsey and West were "the chief instigators" of the assassination scheme (*Ferguson*, p. 429).

[95] Add. MS 38847, fol. 101; Sprat, p. 43.

[96] Add. MS 38847, fol. 111.

[97] Haley, p. 725. The amount of cash raised was between £9,000 and £22,000.

[98] Sprat, p. 14.

[99] Sprat, p. 59; appendix, p. 4. Ferguson later claimed that £3,000 had been raised to purchase arms (Sprat, appendix, p. 15).

[100] Sprat, appendix, p. 9.

[101] *The Tryal and Process of High Treason . . . against Mr. Robert Baillie of Jerviswood*, 1685, p. 51.

[102] Sprat, appendix, pp. 70, 72.

to take credit for the assassination plan—in some cases, for perfectly understandable reasons, since they were prisoners of the government at the time of their confessions—but a general agreement that some such plan did exist, and that Ferguson, Rumsey, West, and a number of others, including Shaftesbury and Monmouth, knew of its existence. Thus while the assassination itself was to be carried out by individuals who were by and large from the lower classes, it is highly unlikely that they, or Ferguson, would have agreed to do so without some sort of protective assurance from the "grandees," which, during the fall of 1682, meant Shaftesbury and Monmouth. Macaulay painted Ferguson as a wild-eyed fanatic, but the fact is, what made Ferguson such an effective organizer was his ability to remain in constant communication with his various constituencies. Shaftesbury, Monmouth, and others trusted Ferguson because they knew he would act to carry out their interests. If he had been as prone to launch improvident schemes on his own as some have suggested, he could never have retained their confidence as he did. Speaking of Ferguson's relationship to the leaders of the revolutionary movement following Shaftesbury's death, West wrote that "I know Mr. Ferguson wholly devoted to their service, daily conversant with them," and West was convinced that he would not and could not "carry on such a design without them." Nor was Ferguson unique in this respect. "I knew Col. Rumsey conversed frequently with the Duke of Monmouth and Sir Thomas Armstrong," West continued, and that he, too, "had more wit than to engage in a thing of this nature if he had not known it to be agreeable to their desires."[103] Since both Ferguson and Rumsey were closer to Shaftesbury than they were to those of whom West is here speaking, his observations apply with even greater force to the activities of 1682. To this should be added the fact that John Row later disclosed that Monmouth certainly knew of the assassination plan in the spring of 1683, and John Gibbons, his personal servant, may have volunteered to be one of the participants in the attempt.[104] In short, in terms of the resources available, the working relationship between the actual participants in or organizers of the assassination attempt and the leaders of the revolutionary movement, and the evidence provided independently by a number of witnesses, the assassination part of the Rye House conspiracy involved radicals from the highest to the lowest classes in society.[105]

[103] Add. MS 38847, fol. 106.

[104] Add. MS 41818, fol. 214; Add. MS 38847, fols. 93, 95; Sprat, appendix, pp. 20, 43.

[105] This must remain an open question, but as Grey relates, everything the conspirators did, or planned to do, was the result of numerous meetings and discussions, and I believe the assassination must be included within that working relationship among the various groups of conspirators.

Shaftesbury's departure, however, brought a temporary interruption to the planning for the general insurrection, because, Grey explained, Shaftesbury and Ferguson (who had accompanied the earl to Holland) had "managed the greatest part" of the plans for the uprising in London, and were in closest contact with its organizers. The other lords (Russell, Monmouth, Essex, and Grey), for whom total abandonment of the project never seems to have been a considered option, felt they had to go ahead with the revolution, since "we expected every day to be hanged," but they were not exactly sure at this point (December 1682) how they should proceed.[106] Meanwhile, Rumsey, West, Goodenough, John Row from Bristol, Edward Norton, Richard Nelthorp, and Joseph Tiley "had several meetings" in December, at which "both the assassination and the insurrection were discussed." Shortly after Christmas, Rumsey invited a number of individuals to dinner at his house in Soho, and they continued these discussions.[107]

News of these meetings appears to have reached Lord Howard (who was a good friend of West), who discussed the matter with his friend Sidney. Out of this conversation, the idea emerged that "the unadvised passions of a multitude might precipitate them into some rash and ill-guided undertakings unless they were under the steering and direction of some steady and skillful . . . Council," which could "give some steadiness to the motions" of these underlings.[108] Accordingly, a meeting was arranged at John Hampden's house in mid-January 1683, among Sidney, Howard, Monmouth, Russell, and Essex, where discussion of their previous plans for a revolution was resumed. This meeting led to another several weeks later at Lord Russell's house, at which it was decided to reopen negotiations with the Scots in order to enlist their participation. Aaron Smith was dispatched to Scotland with a message from the council to this effect, under the guise, formerly employed by Shaftesbury, of inviting the Scots to London for a meeting about their economic interests in America.[109]

At the same time (February 1683), Goodenough brought Colonel Rumbold to West's chamber in the Middle Temple, where they, along

[106] *Secret History*, p. 49.

[107] Add. MS 38847, fols. 94–95; Sprat, appendix, p. 23.

[108] Sprat, appendix, pp. 70–71; *State Trials*, 3:716–717. If one reads between the lines of Howard's statement, he seems to be saying that he learned that Rumsey, West, and others were still meeting and considering the assassination scheme. There was no possibility of their being able to effect a revolution without the aid of Russell, Monmouth, and others, but they just might be able to carry off the assassination. It appears, therefore, that it was the threat of the latter that gave the grandees the impetus to resume their meetings about the insurrection.

[109] Sprat, pp. 63–64; *State Trials*, 3:716–717; Add. MS 38847, fol. 98.

with Rumsey, considered by what means they could effect the assassination. This led to another meeting a week later at which it was agreed that they should send for Ferguson to return from Holland. After this meeting, West and Rumsey went to Thomas Shepherd's house, where the former wrote "a canting letter" to Ferguson, which Shepherd, who was in contact with him, sent.[110] It is very likely that, by this point, the actions of the two groups of conspirators merged, for Shepherd was also the key figure in the correspondence with the Scottish contingent, and he had frequent meetings with members of the Council, notably Sidney and Russell.[111]

Immediately upon Ferguson's arrival, there was a meeting at the Five Bells Tavern in the Strand, among him, West, Rumsey, Rumbold, and Goodenough, at which assassination was still the chief topic for consideration. Another meeting at a tavern in Fleet Street was devoted to a discussion of various alternative locations and means for executing the design, all of which were rejected except the original idea that the assassination should take place when the king was on his return to London from the horse races at Newmarket.[112] The group, which now included Captain Walcot, who had returned from Holland with Ferguson, decided to meet thereafter at West's chambers in order to avoid surveillance, and "several consultations were afterwards held there late in the evening." Rumbold offered his house at Rye as a place by which the king would pass on his journey, and where the road was narrow and offered opportunity for concealment behind a high wall.[113]

[110] Add. MS 38847, fol. 96; *Ferguson*, p. 431.

[111] Shepherd met with Robert Baillie, who was acting for Argyll. William Carstares also met with Shepherd on behalf of the Scots, and Shepherd passed the information on to Sidney and Danvers. Carstares and Russell subsequently met at Shepherd's house to discuss raising money and the role of the Scots in the insurrection. Carstares said he heard about the assassination plot from Shepherd (and Ferguson) (*Tryal of Baillie*, pp. 50–53; North, *Examen*, p. 383). West says that Shepherd promised to come to the meetings in West's chamber discussing the assassination, but he did not, although he received an account of what was discussed (Add. MS 38847, fol. 98).

[112] Add. MS 38847, fols. 98–100. Ferguson returned to England on February 21, 1683 (D'Oyley, *Monmouth*, p. 220). Immediately upon his arrival, Thomas Armstrong told Ferguson that the assassination plan had been "revived," and that some of its advocates "were more violent than ever" about seeing it executed (*Ferguson*, p. 431). Rumbold was one of those who supported the design in 1682 (p. 426).

[113] The plan was to allow the guards in front of the king's coach to cross a narrow bridge, and then to drag a cart across the road blocking their return. The attackers would be hidden behind a wall and would fall upon the rear guard. This plan had a very high probability of success, for the Rye House, "like a citadel, commands the road, which is a narrow pass," according to Mr. Airy who viewed it in the nineteenth century (Burnet, 2:361n; Allan Fea, *King Monmouth*, London: John Lane, 1902, pp. 139–140).

While these plans were being formulated with a view to their execution around the end of March, contact with the Scots had been reestablished. William Carstares, who had gone to Holland to meet with the Earl of Argyll and other Scots who had fled in exile after Shaftesbury's departure from England, acted as a go-between for them with Shepherd and the council. After receiving several letters from Shepherd, Carstares returned from Holland to meet with Sir John Cochrane and some other Scotsmen. Subsequently he, Cochrane, and Russell met at Shepherd's house to discuss the problem of raising money to finance the arms and supplies the Scots would need.[114] From all accounts, money seems to have been the sticking point in preventing any closer correspondence from developing between the English and Scottish conspirators. The English radicals set about to raise the agreed upon sum of £10,000.[115] Still, it seemed unlikely that the joint insurrection could be mounted much before June or July.[116] Nevertheless, according to Grey, Shepherd "received some thousands of pounds from my Lord Russell, to transmit to my Lord Argyle, just before the discovery of the plot."[117]

The assassination plan, however, was still going forward. Ferguson, Goodenough, and Rumbold agreed to try to raise the forty men needed for the ambush, and at one of the meetings in West's chambers, they brought the lists of individuals they had recruited.[118] At least three persons on those lists had already made a preliminary trip to Rye to inspect the area.[119] Ferguson was asked about the availability of money, and referred to an unused sum that had been deposited with someone as part of the assassination scheme in October. West wrote to John Ayloffe in the country and also to Wade in Bristol about the assassination, informing them that it was going ahead at the end of March, and that they should "get their clients together" in preparation for its outcome.[120] From his

[114] Sprat, p. 124; *Tryal of Baillie*, pp. 50–52; *State Papers and Letters Addressed to William Carstares*, 1774, p. 10. There were a number of meetings between Russell and the Scots (*Secret History*, p. 55).

[115] This money was passed through Shepherd and Ferguson to Holland, where "the arms lay ready provided." They were to be shipped from Holland to Edinburgh (Add. MS 38847, fol. 111; Sprat, appendix, p. 33).

[116] Add. MS 38847, fol. 112; Holloway, *Confession*, p. 3.

[117] *Secret History*, p. 74.

[118] Add. *MS* 38847, fol. 101.

[119] According to West, one of the three was Joseph Keeling (Add. MS 38847, fol. 109). In Sprat's account, Walcot is also said to have visited the Rye House (pp. 105–106). At their executions, Hone and Walcot confessed their participation in the conspiracy, and both men admitted that they were to have been members of the party of assassins (HMC 14th Report, appendix, pt. 4, p. 162).

[120] Add. MS 38847, fol. 107. West also wrote to Wade in the same terms, but in the latter's absence, this letter came into the hands of James Holloway (Harleian MS 6845, fol. 268;

meetings with Ferguson, Carstares also knew of the assassination plan, as did Shepherd, and through one or both of them, a number of Scots were also kept informed.[121] One of them, Alexander Gordon, received a letter from John Nisbet on March 20, 1683, which, though written "under the metaphor of trade throughout the whole letter," was actually about the insurrection and the assassination. Since "*trading* was very low here [in London]," Nisbet wrote, it "has made the merchants (such as they are) to think that *desperate diseases must have desperate cures*; and while they have some stock, it will be better to venture out, than to keep shop and sit still till all be gone, and then they shall not be able to act." He went on to refer to the fact that "our merchants" were "broke," characterizing the English conspirators, "most of them," as "fire-side merchants." But, Nisbet warned, there are "treacherous dealers in our trade," and "if any *strange thing* fall out this week or the next, I will again post it towards you."[122]

About ten days before the king's scheduled return from Newmarket, a fire broke out there, and on receiving this news, Ferguson dispatched messages calling for an immediate meeting of those involved in the assassination. It was the consensus of the group that the fire would probably force the king's early return to London. When they learned at a meeting on the following day (Saturday) that the king intended to remain at Cambridge over the weekend and return to London on Monday, they gave some consideration to completing their preparations to meet that deadline. It was doubtful that they could purchase the horses on a Sunday, though Ferguson borrowed forty guineas from Rumsey in order to

Holloway, *Confession*, p. 3). Row later said that Holloway showed him this letter from West, and that its contents were discussed in London with Ferguson and Aaron Smith. Row described the assassination scheme to Trenchard, who seemed to be startled by it, and he mentioned it to Monmouth. The latter angrily scolded Ferguson for having spoken to so many people about the assassination (Add. MS 41818, fol. 214).

[121] Carstares not only discussed the assassination with Ferguson, but he also heard about it from Shepherd, who told him that some individuals "were full upon it" (*Tryal of Baillie*, p. 52; *Carstares State Papers*, p. 10). Since at least some Scotsmen knew of the assassination plot, as Nisbet's letter to Gordon demonstrates, either Shepherd or Carstares, who were key figures in the communications between the Scottish and English conspirators, probably passed the information to others.

[122] The letter is printed in *A True and Plain Account of the Discoveries Made in Scotland, of the Late Conspiracies against His Majesty and the Government*, 1685, pp. 7–8. An almost identical letter of the same date was sent from John Ward to Alexander Pringle. It mentions Captain Gaunt and John Johnson (a pseudonym), and in addition to the phrases cited in the text, the author writes that they "endeavor the dispatching of the old rotten stuff" within the next week or two. The author asks his correspondent to write to him care of Mr. Meade's in Stepney, implying that Meade knew of the assassination plot (MS Tanner 34, fol. 286).

make the attempt.[123] Even with the failure of their specific plan, the radicals did not abandon the general objective of revolution. They resumed their meetings the same week the king returned to London, and at one of them at a tavern on Ludgate Hill, they agreed to purchase a stock of arms to be kept in readiness if a future opportunity for the assassination should present itself, or for use in the general insurrection. In addition to Ferguson, West, Walcot, Rumsey, Goodenough, and Rumbold, the group included Ayloffe, Edward Norton, and a man named Joseph Keeling, the last having agreed to be one of the assassins.[124] From this point on (April), there were frequent meetings with various participants, and I will not list them all.

West agreed to act for the group in purchasing the arms, since he owned a plantation in America, and could use the pretense of shipping them there as a covering excuse for the purchase. He ordered thirty cases of pistols, thirty carbines, and ten blunderbusses from a gunsmith he knew.[125] With Ferguson's assistance, West obtained the money (£100) for the purchase from Charlton.[126] By early May, the group had devised (or revived) a scheme for dividing London into twenty districts, each headed by one of the conspirators. Two hundred men would be raised from each district for the insurrection. Goodenough was in charge of recruiting most of these individuals; as a former undersheriff of London, he had many contacts in the city.[127]

Meanwhile, groups of Scotsmen had begun to filter into London, disguised as peddlers, or in connection with the plantations in America.[128] Carstares kept in touch with the Earl of Argyll through Major Holmes

[123] Add. MS 38847, fols. 108–109, 128. This is an example of the radicals' good intelligence, since the king's decision to delay his return to London until Monday represented a change in his original plans (*Savile Correspondence*, Camden Society Publications, vol. 71, 1858, pp. 273–274).

[124] Add. MS 38847, fol. 109.

[125] Add. MS 38847, fol. 110; Sprat, pp. 57–58; MS PWV 95, fol. 237. It is sometimes said (Milne, *Rye House Plot*, p. 151) that the conspirators had no arms or ammunition available to implement their plans, but this is not true. Quite apart from the arms purchased by West, there were small caches of arms scattered around London and the countryside. Two boxes of arms were found in Colonel Rumsey's house, and these were not part of West's supply (MS PWV 95, fol. 240). Some arms were seized at Thomas Wharton's house sometime before September 1683 (Carte MS 81, fols. 727, 730). A "good quantity of arms" was confiscated at Chester, "all new arms in chests" (Add. MS 29577, fol. 542). Nearly fifty muskets were confiscated from the Earl of Macclesfield, and more arms were found at the houses of other radicals (Fea, *Monmouth*, p. 134). And see Lord North's list of arms confiscated following the discovery of the plot (Add. MS 32519, fol. 36; *Examen*, pp. 388–389).

[126] Add. MS 38847, fol. 111; Sprat, appendix, p. 38.

[127] Add. MS 38847, fol. 115; Harleian MS 6845, fol. 268; Holloway, *Confession*, p. 5.

[128] Add. MS 38847, fol. 97.

and William Spence, who had developed a sophisticated cipher by which to conduct the correspondence.[129] Major Wildman, an active participant in planning the revolution and the assassination, also carried on a separate correspondence with Argyll.[130] As was noted earlier, the lines of communication between the Council of Six and the other conspirators were extremely fluid. Wildman, Ferguson, and Rumsey were in daily contact with some or all of the leaders, and they, in turn, kept their colleagues informed.[131] Moreover, since West and Walcot were close friends of Lord Howard with whom they held a number of meetings prior to late March, it seems clear that the council (to which Howard had by then been added as a member) was also kept well informed as to the existence of the assassination plan.[132]

Although the radicals had been fairly successful up to now in maintaining a high degree of secrecy, the government was hovering very close to a discovery of their plans. At the end of March, a report had been received that there was a plot afoot for "killing the King and altering the government," and that Sidney and others were involved in it. This report was not treated lightly. The Privy Council took up the matter, "and they were hard at it till ten of the clock," when they decided to turn the problem over to Secretary Jenkins (a person "well-skilled in plots"), ordering him to conduct further investigations.[133] In May, the government received an intelligence report that there were caskets containing nearly one hundred new muskets hidden in Lord Grey's house, another piece of information that was subsequently verified.[134] In addition, of course, officials from

[129] *Tryal of Baillie*, p. 5l. This correspondence, or some part of it, is printed in Sprat, appendix, pp. 110–115. Major Abraham Holmes was a Republican and one of those arrested in 1662 on suspicion of having been involved in one of the Fifth Monarchy conspiracies against the government (*CSPD*, 2:487; J. G. Muddiman, ed., *The Bloody Assizes*, London: William Hodge, 1929, pp. 84–85). Carstares also communicated with Argyll through James Stewart (*Carstares State Papers*, p. 10).

[130] Wildman conducted this correspondence under the name of "West," a fact that Robert West did not know until after the discovery of the plot by the government, and the humor of which he did not appreciate (Add. MS 38847, fol. 113).

[131] Add. MS 38847, fols. 105–106. Also, Wildman "was privately consulted upon all occasions" by the members of the Council of Six (*Ferguson*, p. 434). West, Rumsey, and the other conspirators often met at a tavern close to the house in which the members of the council held their meetings (J. H. M. Salmon, "Algernon Sydney and the Rye House Plot," *History Today* [October 1954], p. 702).

[132] Add. MS 38847, fols. 107–108; Sprat, appendix, p. 18.

[133] Thoresby, *Letters*, 1:23–24; Morrice, 1:362. Jenkins also received an anonymous, but well-informed, report on April 18, 1683, concerning the involvement of some ex-Army officers and others (e.g., Rumbold, Hone, Breman, Colonel Owen) who were being watched (*CSPD*, 24:184).

[134] Add. MS 28875, fol. 251; *CSPD*, 24:242.

time to time received surveillance reports on particular individuals, including Locke, who were suspected of being "plotters" against the government.[135]

The radicals were thus plagued by the fact that time was not necessarily on their side. Some of them had been engaged in and committed to making a revolution for almost a year, and the number of people with whom they had come into contact and who knew of their activities continued to grow. Sooner or later, if events dragged on inconclusively, someone would inform on them, and the bubble would burst, as indeed happened. Yet, if more individuals were to be recruited as participants, this was a risk that had to be taken. Some dissenting ministers, for example, knew of the assassination and the insurrection plots. These included John Owen, Stephen Lobb, Matthew Meade, George Griffith, John Hicks, and John Collins.[136] Monmouth implied in his confession that an even larger number

[135] Cranston, p. 221. Ferguson's house was more or less constantly watched (*CSPD*, 24:277). Monmouth's movements during 1681 were also under surveillance (D'Oyley, *Monmouth*, pp. 183–184). Captain Walcot told West that he was continuously watched by spies (*The Trials of Thomas Walcot, William Hone, William Lord Russell, John Rous, and William Blagg*, 1683, p. 12).

[136] According to West, Ferguson told him that Owen and Collins supported both the assassination and the insurrection, and that Meade and Lobb were zealous supporters of the general rebellion (Sprat, appendix, pp. 61–62; Colonel Owen, who was himself involved in the conspiracy, deposed that Ferguson used to stay with his brother and often preached at his meetinghouse during this period. Also, John Owen maintained a correspondence (lost) with Ferguson in 1682–1683 when the latter was with Shaftesbury in Holland (*CSPD*, 27:258; Peter Toon, *God's Statesman: The Life and Work of John Owen*, Exeter: Paternoster Press, 1971, p. 157). Zachary Bourne had spoken to Stephen Lobb, who was strongly in favor of the insurrection and promised to raise men for it from his congregation (Add. MS 38847, fol. 116). Bourne and Meade were arrested together trying to escape after the discovery of the plot (MS PWV 95, fol. 251). Carstares had told Meade, Owen, and Griffith of the plot, and they allegedly supported it. This point was confirmed by Monmouth in his private confession to the king (George Roberts, *The Life, Progress, and Rebellion of James, Duke of Monmouth*, 2 vols., 1844, 1:161; *Tryal of Baillie*, p. 52; Sprat, appendix, p. 136). When questioned about this, however, both Meade and Owen denied any knowledge of the conspiracy (Sprat, pp. 81–82; appendix, p. 121 [misnumbered]; *Tryal of Baillie*, p. 52). Ferguson later referred to the fact that, despite the "positive information given" against Meade, the latter, in his appearance before the king had sufficient "wit and presence of mind" to bluff or lie his way out of the charges (Robert Ferguson, *A Letter to Mr. Secretary Trenchard*, 1694, p. 19). It is possible that William Kiffin, whose son-in-law and two grandsons were participants in the revolutionary movement, also knew of the conspiracy. Kiffin was a former captain under Cromwell, and seems to have kept in touch with some old Commonwealth officers, such as Major Manley, who were involved in the conspiracy. The evidence in this case is a bit thin, but the fact that Kiffin's name was on a list of ciphered names in the correspondence between Colonel Holmes and Argyll, along with Monmouth, Russell, Essex, Baillie, and others, is suspicious (*True and Plain Account*, p. 14; *Carstares State Papers*, p. 109). Considering the extremely complicated nature of the cipher, and the amount

of Nonconformist ministers were aware of the conspiracy. Doubtless, some of them disapproved of it, though they were not prepared to inform the government. In short, beyond the hard core of active participants in the conspiracy, there was a much larger, and looser, protective network of sympathetic support for the radicals' objectives.

Sometime around the beginning of June, Joseph Keeling began to have second thoughts, which he confided to someone who, in turn, passed the information on to one of the radicals; thus suspicions began to arise that Keeling had informed on the conspirators.[137] He had, in fact, put out feelers through a friend of his who was on good terms with Lord Dartmouth about the possibility of a pardon in exchange for providing evidence about a plot. This discussion took place on Saturday, June 9, and, by the following Tuesday, the twelfth, Keeling had found his way to the proper person, Secretary Jenkins, with whom he spent five hours. Jenkins listened intently to the disclosures, but knew that he would need more evidence—at least two witnesses—in order to bring charges of treason against the conspirators, and he therefore advised Keeling to devise a means of obtaining this evidence. The latter took his brother (not an altogether willing accomplice) to a meeting with Goodenough, who had recruited Keeling into the conspiracy.[138] Goodenough freely discoursed about the assassination plot and the insurrection, and the Keelings proceeded directly from that meeting to another conference with Jenkins. The government now had its first solid wedge into the conspiracy, and within a week, arrest warrants were being distributed like leaflets around London.[139]

Partly as a consequence of the refusal of historians to venture into the thicket of confessions and depositions bequeathed to posterity by the conspirators or to accept that anything so un-English as regicide had ever actually been plotted, and partly as a consequence of their own preconceptions as what could be expected from "a philosopher" such as Locke, the

of torture Carstares and William Spence endured before revealing it, there is a prima facie case for the importance of this correspondence in connection with the plot. As an extremely wealthy merchant, Kiffin was probably being solicited for funds to buy arms for the Scots.

[137] Although the precise date is difficult to determine, it appears that around the end of May or in early June the conspirators "were alarmed with an intimation that all our designs were discovered," and Keeling was the suspected informant. He had told a friend of the plot, and word had reached Goodenough. The latter talked to Keeling, "and was eventually satisfied" that everything was all right (Add. MS 41803, fols. 55–56). Rumbold told West that he suspected Keeling had confessed two weeks before the actual discovery of the plot (*Trials*, p. 17).

[138] Add. MS 41803, fols. 55–58; Sprat, p. 66.

[139] The first batch of warrants were issued on June 21, "and the messengers [were] flying about the Temple" distributing them (Add. MS 38847, fol. 119).

latter's life was for many years encased within a myth of innocence with respect to his political involvement.[140] In some respects, this is a general problem, for Victorian England was awash with biographies (mostly by descendants) and histories that portrayed the Rye House conspiracy as a nonevent. Nevertheless, Locke was a special figure, and as Macaulay put it, it had to be assumed that Locke's "temperament" as a philosopher "preserved him from the violence of a partisan."[141] This view still persists among interpreters, though as Cranston has remarked, it is not on its face credible.[142] As Laslett, observed,

> [Locke] went much further towards revolution and treason than his earlier biographers knew, anxious as they were to present him as a man of unspotted personal and political virtue.[143]

It is just his close association with Shaftesbury, however, that is partially responsible for the maintenance of the myth. For during the last two years of his life (at least), Shaftesbury was someone the government desperately wanted to prosecute for treason. He was much too astute a politician to oblige his enemies by providing them with the evidence they could not obtain from paid witnesses or through the arrest of his servants and associates. Almost all of Shaftesbury's political correspondence (and more than likely a wealth of other information bearing on his political activities, especially in the 1680s) was destroyed, or at least has not come down to us. Moreover, most of Locke's own political correspondence, especially his letters to Shaftesbury, did not survive this period of political turbulence.[144] We are faced, therefore, with a black hole in the Locke-

[140] Not content with insisting upon Locke's innocence, Fox-Bourne went so far as to make up a relationship and conversation between Locke and Shaftesbury for which there was never the least shred of evidence. "Instead of taking any part in Shaftesbury's ill-planned and unwise conspiracy," he wrote, Locke "joined with others in vainly endeavoring to dissuade Shaftesbury from his rash action" (1:469–470). Did Fox-Bourne really believe that, having failed in this endeavor, Locke then set about to write a justificatory defense of a revolution to which he was opposed, and which had been "ill-planned" by Shaftesbury?

[141] Macaulay, 1:490.

[142] Maurice Cranston, "The Politics of a Philosopher," *Listener* (January 5, 1961), p. 18.

[143] Laslett, p. 31.

[144] From references in the correspondence and notations in his journals, we know that Locke wrote many letters that have not survived, and that his total correspondence must have been two or three times larger than its present size. Locke wrote and received many letters while he was in Holland that are lost or were intercepted by the government (or exist but are not known to be part of Locke's correspondence because of the several pseudonyms he adopted). See, for example, MS f.34, fols. 2–16 (May 1685–April 1688) compared with *Correspondence*, vol. 3. Of course, little can be said regarding these letters, but occasionally, from the circumstances and date, the inference that they form part of Locke's missing political correspondence seems justified. For example, the letter Locke wrote to a correspond-

Shaftesbury relationship, particularly during the period of their intense political activity: 1681-1683. Yet as we have already seen, Locke not only remained personally loyal to and a member of Shaftesbury's political family during these years, but he was surrounded by other close friends and associates who were also actively involved, at the peril of their lives, in the revolutionary movement.

In reconstructing this context, it is worth recalling an earlier point: We are dealing with the *historical* Locke, and not with someone to whom academic intellectuals might wish to impute the qualities of an ideal-type philosopher. We have become accustomed to seeing a tapestry in which Locke is pictured alongside Newton or Boyle. The historical Locke, however, was more often in the company of Ferguson or Wildman or some obscure tradesmen. One friend who knew Locke especially well made a particular point of emphasizing that he was *not* like most academic intellectuals—and since she was Ralph Cudworth's daughter, we may assume she had known a great many of them—nor did Locke feel himself aloof from members of the lower class. On the contrary, Lady Masham wrote, Locke

> suited his discourse to the meanest capacities . . . He conversed very freely and willingly with all sorts of persons . . . For even tradesmen would ask his advice, and were frequently instructed by him . . . [He] was very far from despising any one, though their persons were ever so mean.[145]

Pierre Coste, Locke's friend and secretary, was also struck by this facet of Locke's personality, and his ability to associate with "all sorts of men." "This condescension," Coste remarked, is "not very common among men of letters." Moreover, those who assumed from a reading of his

ent in Switzerland shortly after Monmouth's sailing from Holland (MS f.34, fol. 4) was almost certainly addressed to one of several conspirators then resident in Switzerland, since none of Locke's other acquaintances were in that country. Another illustration is provided by a letter written on March 26, 1681, filled with political news about the Oxford Parliament which had just been summarily dissolved by the king. Both Christie and Cranston believed this letter to be by Locke, but De Beer is probably correct in identifying its author as John Hoskins (*Correspondence*, 2:390–391). What De Beer failed to note, however, is that Locke's journal shows that he did write a letter—actually two letters—on March 26, and that one of them was so important and urgent that he paid the highest postal rate to have it delivered immediately (MS f.5, fol. 50). It is clear that this urgency was tied to the dissolution of Parliament, and that this particular letter should also be included in the lost political correspondence of Locke. There is a note in the Shaftesbury papers that a letter from Oxford, dated March 26, 1681, was confiscated at the time of Shaftesbury's arrest (PRO 30/24/6A/349). This may be the Hoskins letter, which was returned, or it may have been the letter from Locke, which was not.

[145] Jean Le Clerc, *An Account of the Life and Writings of John Locke*, 3d ed., 1714, p. 24.

writings that, because he was "one of the greatest philosophers of the age," Locke was like "one of those scholars . . . [who] are incapable of familiarizing themselves with the common sort of mankind" were grossly mistaken.[146]

In fact, one of Locke's best friends, Robert Pawling, was a tradesman. Pawling was active in the city politics of Oxford, having been elected during the height of the Whig agitation as its mayor, with the assistance of John Trenchard and other Whigs. Pawling was "a rank fanatic," always "talking against the King and government with the utmost malice." He was, however, Anthony Wood lamented, the popular leader of "our Whiggish townsmen" and was supported by "all the rabble of the town."[147] Pawling was also bitterly disliked by Bishop Fell of Oxford, who likewise regarded him as an outright "incendiary," and who more than once, conveyed his complaints in writing to Secretary Jenkins.[148] Yet, it was to Pawling's care and custody that Locke entrusted some of his papers and belongings when he went into exile. This fact did not go unnoticed by the government spies, one of whom wrote to Jenkins to report,

> It is taken notice of in Oxford that from Mr. Locke's chamber in Christ Church, that was a great confidant, if not secretary, to the late Earl of Shaftesbury, in a clandestine way several handbaskets of papers are carried to Mr. James Tyrrell's house . . . or to Mr. Pawling's, the mercer's house in Oxford.

Since both men were known to be "disaffected" from the government, Serjeant Holloway, the informer, felt sure that it would "conduce to his Majesty's service" if both men's houses, as well as "Mr. Locke's chamber" were searched by the king's deputies.[149] Nor was Holloway alone in holding this view. Both Wood and Humphrey Prideaux reported that, after the Rye House conspiracy was discovered, Locke had "conveyed away with him several letters and writings without being searched." But, if these materials had been confiscated, they argued, they would have revealed his involvement in that conspiracy. Prideaux, who spied on Locke more or less regularly between 1681 and 1683, wrote that

> Whiggism goes down apace, and the punishments of sedition and treason fall very heavy upon those that have so boldly been guilty of it in the late licentious times [i.e., the Rye House conspirators] . . .

146 Pierre Coste, "The Character of Mr. Locke," in Locke, *Works*, 9:165–168.

147 *Letters of Prideaux*, pp. 80, 84. Pawling held a celebration at his house when some of the Rye House conspirators were released on bail in November 1683 (Wood, *Life and Times*, 3:80).

148 *CSPD*, 25:325, 381.

149 *CSPD*, 25:109–110; Cranston, pp. 228–234.

> Our friend John Locke is likewise become a brother sufferer with them. As soon as the plot was discovered, he cunningly stole away from us, and in half a years time no one knew where he was.[150]

As for Pawling, it appears that his house was searched by the king's deputies, and later, at the time of Monmouth's Rebellion, he was arrested and imprisoned.[151] After the Glorious Revolution, he and Locke were reunited, and Pawling received a mention as a friend and legacy in Locke's will.[152] Nor was Pawling the only tradesman who was Locke's friend, nor even the only one involved in or sympathetic to the radical Whig movement.[153]

Ferguson, as was previously mentioned, first came to prominence as a spokesman for the Dissenter cause during the 1670s debate with Parker. He was then an assistant to John Owen, who remained his lifelong friend. During the period of the Rye House conspiracy, Ferguson spent much of the time in hiding at the house of Owen's brother, Colonel Henry Owen, who was one of those involved in the conspiracy.[154] If he did not become acquainted with Locke during the earlier period, Ferguson certainly knew him well by the 1680s, when both were members of Shaftesbury's inner political circle. In a letter to his wife at the time of Shaftesbury's death, Ferguson wrote of the loss of his "honorable friend" who had shown him great "fatherly love and care." Shaftesbury had also left Ferguson a leg-

[150] *Letters of Prideaux*, p. 139.

[151] Bishop Fell's complaints (note 148) were directed against Alderman Wright, a staunch Whig and an acquaintance of Locke, as well as of Pawling. Wright's house was searched in 1683, and on the basis of some papers found there, Pawling was arrested (Wood, *Life and Times*, 3:155–156). Wright's house was searched on June 25, and again on July 17 (pp. 59, 62). I have assumed that Pawling's house was searched following his arrest. If so, Tyrrell's transfer of some of Locke's manuscripts left at Pawling's house to his custody in October 1683 might have come too late (Cranston, p. 232n.). Was some part of the *First Treatise* confiscated or destroyed at this time?

[152] *Correspondence*, 2:579–580; Cranston, p. 475.

[153] Locke's cousin, John Bonville, with whom he kept in touch, was a small tradesman; another friend was John Cox, a member of the Soapmakers Company, and a common councilman of London. See *Correspondence*, 2:179, 215, 496, 602.

[154] *CSPD*, 24:282. Owen had been a Major in Cromwell's regiment (*The Correspondence of John Owen*, ed. Peter Toon, London: James Clarke, 1970, p. 4). Owen was arrested trying to flee to Ireland. He claimed that he had innocently left London at "the beginning of June," and was mistakenly arrested at Minehead as he was about to cross to Ireland, but even the dates and information supplied in his testimony indicate that he must have left London following the discovery of the plot, but before the warrants were issued (i.e., June 14–20), as Locke had. Goodenough named Owen as one of those involved in the conspiracy (Landsdowne MS 1152, fols. 122, 171, 227). Rumsey testified that Owen had contributed toward Smith's expenses as their emissary to Scotland (Sprat, appendix, p. 16).

acy of £40 in his will.[155] It was Ferguson who recorded that, in his conversations with Shaftesbury during the latter's final days in Holland, the earl had attributed his Socinian religious beliefs to Locke's influence and ideas.[156] Later, Anthony Wood noted that, after leaving England, Locke "kept company and was great with Robert Ferguson and Ford Lord Grey . . . which was complained of by Thomas Chudleigh," the English envoy in Holland.[157] In fact, Chudleigh, and his successor, Bevil Skelton, made numerous complaints, as we shall see in Chapter 9, about Locke's seditious activities and associations while he was living in exile in Holland. Locke's relationship to Monmouth and his rebellion will also be more fully considered there, but in a conference with Charles II, following the discovery of the Rye House conspiracy, Monmouth noted in his diary that the king "received me pretty well; and said Locke* and Ferguson* were the causes of my misfortune, and would ruin me. After some hot words against them," the interview ended.[158]

Locke was certainly well known to Monmouth. The latter's secretary, and a member of Parliament for Cambridge during the exclusion crisis, James Vernon, had been one of Locke's pupils at Christ Church.[159] Locke attended some important meetings between Shaftesbury and Monmouth, and he was undoubtedly present at countless others when Monmouth and all the Whig leaders met at Shaftesbury's house between 1680 and 1683.[160] He carried messages to Lord Russell for Shaftesbury.[161] Lord Grey was a friend of Locke, and he arranged the accommodations for

[155] *CSPD*, 24:23; PRO 30/24/6A/384 (Shaftesbury's will).

[156] Haley, p. 732.

[157] Wood, *Life and Times*, 3:117.

[158] Except for a few excerpts published by James Welwood, this notebook is lost, or more likely was destroyed. The passages cited appear in James Welwood, *Memoirs of the Most Material Transactions in England for the Last Hundred Years*, 1700, p. 374. The names in Monmouth's notebook were in cipher, which Welwood could not decipher. This was successfully accomplished by John Willcock, "The Cipher in Monmouth's Diary," *English Historical Review* 20 (1905):730–735. Willcock, however, was unclear as to who "Locke" was. But the only Locke remotely close to Monmouth, and the only one the king would have known sufficiently to attribute Monmouth's ruin to his ideas and influence upon his son was certainly John Locke.

[159] Shaftesbury also conveyed letters to Locke through Vernon (*Correspondence*, 2:354, 357).

[160] For example, Locke attended the meeting between Shaftesbury and Monmouth at the end of July 1680, when the two men were planning Monmouth's progress to stir up Whig support (MS f.4, fol. 143). From mid-April to the end of May 1680, Locke was at Thanet House when Shaftesbury, Russell, and Monmouth were meeting virtually every night (John Reresby, *Memoirs*, 1734, p. 99; Haley, p. 576; Cranston, pp. 194–195; MS f.4, fols. 77, 107).

[161] *Correspondence*, 2:227.

Shaftesbury and Grey, along with Colonel Rumsey, to lodge together during the Oxford Parliament.[162]

Locke had also arranged for accommodations for Robert West, during College's trial at Oxford, and it was alleged that Locke "transacted all affairs with West, and, therefore, as soon as he was secured [after the discovery of the Rye House Plot], he thought it time to shift for himself for fear West should tell all he knew."[163] Locke also knew another member of Shaftesbury's inner political circle—Francis Charlton—very well.[164] The latter had been a student at Christ Church when Locke was a tutor, as had Henry Cornish, another participant in the Rye House conspiracy.[165] Locke also knew and had transactions with John Ayloffe, Christopher Battiscombe, Aaron Smith, and Israel Hayes—all of them deeply involved in the revolutionary movement.[166] Wildman was also one of

[162] *Correspondence*, 2:180, 362, 382.

[163] *Letters of Prideaux*, pp. 139–140.

[164] Charlton was a close friend of Shaftesbury and a frequent visitor to his house. He put up a £1,500 bond as part of Shaftesbury's bail in 1681 (Haley, pp. 520, 682). He was, as Burnet notes, "a great enemy to the court and was devoted to Shaftesbury" (H. C. Foxcroft, ed., *A Supplement to Burnet's "History of My Own Time,"* Oxford: Clarendon Press, 1902, p. 116). Locke notes that he was at Charlton's house with Shaftesbury on April 30, 1680 (MS f.4, fol. 97). In another notebook, Locke records Charlton's address and an appointment with him at the Golden Lion (MS f.28, fols. 141, 177). Charlton was arrested in August 1683 for his part in the Rye House Plot (MS PWV 95, fol. 289). He was also a very close friend of Wildman.

[165] Cornish had been a prebendary of Christ Church under Owen in 1652–1653; he was ejected as a Nonconformist in 1662 (*Owen Correspondence*, p. 119n.; G. Lyon Turner, *Original Records of Early Nonconformity under Persecution and Indulgence*, 3 vols., London: T. Fisher Unwin, 1911, 2:827). Cornish, named as a conspirator by Goodenough, was arrested and examined in July 1685 (Landsdowne MS 1152, fols. 227–229; *State Trials*, 4:149). Grey says that Cornish was at one of the meetings at Shepherd's house, but left early. Nevertheless, Grey was convinced that Cornish knew of the insurrection and had promised his assistance (*Secret History*, p. 47). Another conspirator, Nathaniel Vincent, was a student at Christ Church (1651–1655, received his M.A. in 1657, and was ejected in 1662. He became a Nonconformist minister. Vincent was arrested and charged with complicity in the Rye House Plot and was sent to prison. He was later suspected of being involved with Monmouth's Rebellion and was sent to prison again in 1685 (Walter Wilson, *The History and Antiquities of Dissenting Churches*, 4 vols., 1808–1814, 4:305).

[166] John Ayloffe graduated from Oxford in 1662, and subsequently became an attorney. His name appears frequently in the Calendar of Treasury Books in the 1670s as the counsel for a number of individuals who appeared before the Treasury Lords, which included Shaftesbury. In this same period, Ayloffe was a member of the intelligence network run by Peter Du Moulin, with Trenchard, Lord Howard, Carr, Goodenough, and Carstares (K. H. D. Haley, *William of Orange and the English Opposition, 1672–1674*, Oxford: Clarendon Press, 1953, pp. 58ff.). If Locke did not know Ayloffe during this earlier period, he had become acquainted with him by 1679 when Locke records in his journal a favor done him by Ayloffe (Add. MS 15642, fol. 125). Ayloffe was executed in 1685 for his participation in Monmouth's Rebellion. Smith was one of College's attorneys and had accompanied him to

Locke's friends, at least as early as 1679–1680, when along with Locke and others, he was assisting Shaftesbury in examining witnesses during the popish plot. As was mentioned earlier, Wildman was an active electoral agent for the Whigs during the exclusion elections and he sat as a member of the Oxford Parliament. He maintained contact with Locke when both men were in exile in Holland.[167] Following the Glorious Revolution, Wildman, Locke, and Henry Neville, were all members of a club Locke had helped to form.[168]

One of Locke's best friends was Edward Clarke, another of Shaftesbury's strongest supporters, and also, as I will argue below, someone who was involved in the Rye House conspiracy. As a trustee for Shaftesbury's estate, Clarke was obviously someone in whom the former placed a great deal of confidence.[169] When Locke left England, he sent some of his papers and letters to Clarke, advising him,

> You will know how far and what occasions they are to be made use of better than I. What *you* dislike you may burn.

Clearly, Clarke was a person whose political judgment Locke also trusted. He devised a cipher that he left with Clarke so that the two could correspond safely, on the assumption that their letters were likely to be intercepted by the government.[170] Nor was Locke mistaken in this belief;

Oxford. He also had helped Shaftesbury with the popish plot witnesses (PRO 30/24/43/63). He was arrested in August 1683, and confessed his part in the conspiracy (MS PWV 95, fol. 305). Battiscombe was a friend of Locke and of their mutual friend, Dr. Thomas. Locke records several financial transactions with Thomas arranged through Battiscombe in 1681–1682 (MS f.5, fol. 105; MS f.6, fol. 10). Battiscombe was one of the guests (along with West) at Colonel Rumsey's Christmas gathering, when the assassination was discussed; he was later executed for his role in Monmouth's Rebellion (Sprat, appendix, p. 23). In the same notebook in which he recorded appointments with Charlton and meetings at the Green Dragon, Locke wrote down the pub in Cornhill at which he was to meet "Willoughby," sometime in 1681 (MS f.28, fol. 98). "Willoughby" was an alias used by Edward Norton, one of the Rye House conspirators, and a close friend of Ayloffe, Nelthorp, and Wade (Add. MS 41818, fols. 27, 49; Add. MS 41812, fol. 72). It was, however, also an alias used by Thomas Dangerfield, one of the popish plot witnesses. Which individual Locke was supposed to meet cannot be determined from the notation. The details of Locke's association with Israel Hayes, and the latter's role in the revolutionary movement, will be discussed in Chapter 9.

[167] On Wildman and Locke, see above, Chapter 4, note 37, and below, Chapter 10, p. 472.

[168] Caroline Robbins, ed., *Two English Republican Tracts*, Cambridge: Cambridge University Press, 1969, p. 18. See the reference to "Honest Wildman" in *Correspondence*, 3:636.

[169] Haley, p. 727; *Correspondence*, 2:479. Locke also knew William Clarke, Edward's brother, with whom he had some financial dealings (MS c.1, fol. 23).

[170] *Correspondence*, 2:600, 603.

Clarke was later arrested and charged with maintaining a correspondence with traitors in Holland.[171] I will return in a moment to an examination of the content of these letters, as they bear upon Locke's activity in 1682–1683. One of Clarke's lifelong friends was John Freke, who was also a good friend of Locke.[172] Freke was actively involved in the Rye House conspiracy, working with Ferguson, West, and Wade in developing the plans for the insurrection. As someone who visited Ferguson when the latter was in hiding, Freke was certainly part of a trusted circle of friends who helped to forward the radicals' designs.[173] Later, he was a supporter of Monmouth's Rebellion—"we knew [Freke] would be zealous to serve our design," as Grey put it—and like Clarke, he was arrested "for dangerous and seditious practices."[174] Sir Walter Yonge, another of Locke's friends who had been active in the Rye House conspiracy, was likewise counted on as a supporter of Monmouth's Rebellion.[175]

When Locke did arrive in Holland, he lodged at the house of Thomas Dare, another radical Whig and Shaftesbury supporter.[176] As Cranston remarks, "no 'disaffected person' in Amsterdam was more important politically or more notorious" than Dare. Dare's house was a frequent meeting place for the exiled radicals; it was, in fact, *the* headquarters of radicalism in Amsterdam.[177] It was at a meeting at Dare's house, for example, that Ferguson drafted and read for discussion among the gathering of exiles present the declaration of principles he wrote in support of Monmouth's Rebellion.[178] It was to Dare's house that Major Wildman sent his emissary from London to work out the plans for the invasion, and it was there that Monmouth and Argyll formulated these plans.[179] Throughout this period, Locke was receiving his mail at Dare's house and most of his

[171] A warrant for Clarke's arrest was issued on June 4, 1685 (*CSPD*, [James II], 1:178).

[172] *Correspondence*, 2:479. Locke left £100 in his will to "my good friend, John Freke."

[173] Freke knew of the assassination plan, since Carstares, among others, had discussed it with him (*Tryal of Baillie*, p. 52). Freke was involved with Ferguson, Wade, West, and Goodenough (*CSPD*, 25:100).

[174] *Secret History*, pp. 26, 112. Freke was so active that Russell sent him on a mission into the west of England to recruit other supporters for the rebellion (pp. 25–26). Later, he was one of those contacted by Cragg, Monmouth's messenger (p. 103; *CSPD*, [James II], 1:157).

[175] *Secret History*, pp. 24–26, 112, 130. As it turned out, Yonge was cooler toward Monmouth's Rebellion than the radicals had expected.

[176] Cranston, p. 248; Wade and Nelthorp had also gone directly to Dare's house when they fled England after the discovery of the Rye House conspiracy (Harleian MS 6845, fol. 269).

[177] Cranston, p. 249; Charles Chenevix Trench, *The Western Rising*, London: Longmans, 1969, p. 71.

[178] Roberts, *Life of Monmouth*, 1:232; Landsdowne MS 1152, fol. 242.

[179] *Secret History*, p. 100; Add. MS 41812, fol. 9; HMC 12th Report, appendix, pt. 6, p. 393.

finances were handled by Dare, who was also the financial conduit for Monmouth's Rebellion.[180] The government knew of Locke's whereabouts; its spies were keeping a watch on the movements of the radicals, and specific instructions were issued by the Court "to inquire after him."[181]

It would be tedious to list all the friends and associates of Locke who were, with him, active in the revolutionary movement during the period from 1680 to 1685, and some of these activities will be considered in greater detail in the next chapter. Suffice it to say that if Locke really wished to convey to the outside world that he was as politically innocent as some of his biographers have assumed, then, in selecting his numerous "disaffected" friends, Locke appears to have had the poorest judgment of any man who ever lived. The fact is that the majority of Locke's friends were political activists, and of these, the overwhelming majority had been members of the Green Ribbon Club and were participants in the Rye House conspiracy.[182] Clearly, Locke *could* have retired to Oxford to live a quiet nonpolitical life at any time during the eight months after Shaftesbury fled to Holland. He chose not to do so; instead, he remained in London and assisted in the planning for the projected revolution.

Mention was previously made of the trip Locke made with Shaftesbury in the fall of 1682 to the estate of the Earl of Essex at Cassiobury, when a secret planning meeting was held concerning the projected revolution. What seemed puzzling to Locke's biographers was a second trip Locke chose to make to Essex's estate in April 1683 after Shaftesbury was dead. Why, it was asked, should Locke have gone there "on his own"?[183] The answer is, Locke did not go there on his own. Essex was a member of the Council of Six, which was now directing the Rye House conspiracy. In his detailed account of the latter, Lord Grey wrote that about the end of April 1683, "it was thought necessary there should be a speedy meeting of the

[180] Cranston, p. 249; *Correspondence*, 2:623.

[181] *Letters of Prideaux*, p. 139.

[182] Besides Grey and Shaftesbury, Ayloffe, Goodenough, West, Rumsey, Dare, Freke, Battiscombe, Hoskins, Stringer, Anthony Shepherd, Colonel Scott, Waller, Trenchard, Smith, and Percival (banker for Locke, Shaftesbury, and Monmouth) were members of the Green Ribbon Club (George Sitwell, *The First Whig*, 1894, pp. 88, 197; Harleian MS 6845, fol. 282; Pepys MS Miscellanies 7, fols. 489–491). Almost all of these individuals were involved in the plans for an insurrection formulated by Shaftesbury, and most of them knew of or were participants in the assassination part of the conspiracy. The most interesting item on Wade's membership list is the names of two "Clarks," one of whom is not identified by his first name. The other Clarke is William. Since Wade had listed other brothers (e.g., Trenchards, Goodenoughs) together, this makes it very likely that the unnamed Clarke was William's brother, Edward, who was Locke's close friend.

[183] Laslett, p. 32.

cabal"(the Council), because the Scottish rebels were then in London and the plans for their participation in the insurrection had to be worked out. Therefore, "my Lord of Essex (who was then in the country) was sent for to be there."[184] In his diary, Locke records his trip from London to Essex's estate on April 24, returning to London the following day.[185] In other words, Locke did not go there on his own, but as a representative from the Council of Six to summon Essex back to London for an emergency meeting of the revolutionaries.

Another item that has puzzled Locke scholars is the strange manuscript in his papers that deals with the mysterious death of the Earl of Essex in the Tower while he was awaiting trial for his part in the Rye House Plot.[186] In the context of the radical movement, however, the manuscript takes on a particular significance. For, to a man, the radicals always insisted that Essex had not committed suicide; they maintained that he had been murdered either by or with the connivance of the government.[187] A number of tracts were published asserting this point, of which the most notorious was the one by Ferguson, *An Enquiry into . . . the Barbarous Murder of the late Earl of Essex.*[188] Some people suspected, incorrectly, that Locke was the author of this pamphlet.[189] They were not mistaken, however, in believing that he shared Ferguson's viewpoint, or that he did not accept the official version of Essex's death.[190] This is an instance in

[184] *Secret History*, p. 56.

[185] MS f.7, fol. 93.

[186] MS b.4, fols.61–67. Both Cranston and Laslett mention the manuscript (Cranston, p. 250; Laslett, p. 32n.).

[187] George Speke, for example, was one of those who undertook "making the discovery of the horrid murder" of Essex (George Speke, *The Secret History of the Happy Revolution in 1688*, 1715, p. 10). James Welwood also refers to "the barbarous murder of the Earl of Essex" in *A Modest Enquiry into the Causes of the Present Disasters in England*, 1690, p. 4. In short, the murder of Essex was a commonplace belief among the radical Whigs (*Ferguson*, p. 185).

[188] Robert Ferguson, *An Enquiry into, and Detection of the Barbarous Murder of the Late Earl of Essex*, [1684]. Ferguson's tract was immediately translated into French, Dutch, and Flemish and was publicly sold throughout Holland (Add. MS 41811, fol. 266; Add. MS 38847, fol. 122; *Letters of Prideaux*, p. 142). Almost as notorious was Lawrence Braddon's *Essex's Innocency and Honor Vindicated*, 1690, a copy of which Locke owned (*LL* #1069). Although not printed until after the Glorious Revolution, Braddon's manuscript created a sensation, and he was placed on trial by the government; John Freke was one of his defense attorneys (Harleian MS 1221, fols. 217–243; Morrice, 1:418). Colonel Danvers also wrote a tract alleging Essex's murder, which was published in 1684 (Luttrell, *Brief Relation*, p. 324; *Dictionary of National Biography*, s.v. "Henry Danvers").

[189] *Letters of Prideaux*, p. 142.

[190] Cranston, p. 250. Miss Milne expresses the view of virtually all modern historians when she writes that it "seems quite certain" that Essex's death was a suicide (*Rye House Plot*, p. 135). Not only was it far from certain that this was so in the 1680s, but certain de-

which an understanding of the reasoning behind this interpretation of and response to the facts is essential. It runs as follows: The radicals knew that the government had employed agents provocateurs, suborned and bribed witnesses, and forged documents in an effort to frame the political opposition; it rigged the sheriff's elections in London to gain control of the city and the juries; and it refused to honor certain legal procedures in its trials of the dissidents. What the "murder" of Essex "proved" to them was that there were no limits to which the government would not go—including violence against those in its custody—in its opposition to the radicals. This fact, as they viewed it, obviously legitimized the use of force against such a tyrannical regime. The murder of Essex, Ferguson argued, was a violation of the Law of Nature, because "the destroying one innocent person is construed as a threatening of all." Thus every sup-

tails of the case, including the government's marked refusal to investigate the matter, are more than a little suspicious. Milne dismisses too quickly the £50 in secret service money paid to Paul Bomeny, Essex's valet (Akerman, *Secret Services*, p. 84). It is possible, as she suggests, that this money was reimbursement for Bomeny's being a witness at Braddon's trial, though other witnesses were not only not paid, but were threatened by prosecutors in so far as their testimony did not support the government's official line. It is also possible, as Ferguson charged, that Bomeny was an accessory to murder. In any event, following Braddon's trial, Bomeny disappeared without a trace. Among the other suspicious aspects of the case is the fact that Essex's body was moved, washed off, and his clothes were changed before the coroner's jury was allowed to view the corpse. Certain wounds on his hands, as if fending off blows from the razor, were never explained in the official report (Thorseby, *Letters*, 1:35). Evelyn, a close friend of Essex, did not believe in the suicide theory, and noted in his diary that "there were odd reflections upon it" (John Evelyn, *The Diary of John Evelyn*, ed. E. S. De Beer, 6 vols., Oxford: Clarendon Press, 1955, 4:326–327). In his pamphlet, Ferguson argued, as did Evelyn, that suicide was "contrary to the frame and constitution of [Essex's] nature, as well as to all the intellectual and moral habits of his mind" (*Murder of Essex*, p. 5). Ferguson noted Bomeny's suspicious behavior and his correspondence with Secretary Jenkins, and accused him of being an accessory to murder. The real person Ferguson believed was behind the action, however, was Lord Sunderland (pp. 24, 41–42). It is intriguing, to say the least, therefore, that John Holland, a sometime servant of Sunderland, later wrote a letter professing to have information concerning Essex's death, and strongly implying that he had been asked by Sunderland to be a participant in the assassination. Not only had Holland obtained a pardon for all his previous crimes shortly after Essex's death through the efforts of Sunderland, but later, when Holland was again in prison, he received money payments from Sunderland. When Essex's death was investigated by a parliamentary committee after the Glorious Revolution, various witnesses were called to testify, and Holland's letter was incorporated into the record, but it does not appear that he was ever called to testify in person, although Morrice says that he was examined by the Privy Council (HMC 12th Report, appendix, pt. 6, pp. 22–28; Braddon, *Essex's Innocency*, pp. 8, 27–28, 45, 52–53; Morrice, 2:413, 440, 443, 466, 476, 541; *An Account of the Taking of Captain Holland*, 1689, p. 1). I do not profess to know whether Essex committed suicide or was murdered, but the circumstances of his death are far from "certain," and certainly the accusations of the radicals were not without plausibility in the context of what was known in the 1680s.

porter of "natural rights" is threatened by Essex's death, because "the laws that could not protect him, will be unable to defend you."[191]

The "murder" of Essex, in other words, was for the radicals not merely a cause célèbre; it also became part of their ideological creed. Accordingly, this charge against the government is repeated in every radical document and pamphlet written after 1683; it forms, in effect, part of the indictment against the government, and is thus incorporated into their justification for revolution. The charge appears, for example, in the declaration written to justify Monmouth's Rebellion.[192] In this respect, Locke's manuscript is really quite revealing as it concerns his political beliefs in 1683, and it provides one more piece of evidence that he shared this perspective with other radicals.

Locke read widely on a number of subjects, but some notes he made in his journal between 1681 and 1683 have a curious and I believe salient connection to this discussion. Suddenly, notes on political conspiracies, extracted from several authors, began to appear in his journals. In May 1681, he recorded an observation about the disastrous consequences that would befall England if it were ruled by "a prince tractable to prelacy" or "busy and audacious men." To this note he appended the query as to "whether there be any such thing," that is, whether this condition did not exist in 1681?[193] Locke made a number of extractions from Gabriel Naude's work on coups d'état and the "ruses" and "stratagems" adopted by rulers and opponents involved in such coups.[194] On March 3, 1683, Locke bought *A Conspiracy of the Spaniards against the State of Venice*, from which he made a long extract on the conspiracy in Venice.[195] In early May of that year, Locke copied out some passages from Rushworth's *Historical Collections*, which concerns a plot against the king, and the decision by some of the plotters to make a confession to the king.[196] Although these notes are largely recorded without comment by Locke, he did append next to one of them the letters *A.E.S.*, which I agree with Lord King signifies a reference to Anthony, Earl of Shaftesbury.[197] Between 1681 and 1683, in other words, there is a marked concentration of interest on Locke's part in political conspiracies, reflected in the appearance of these

[191] The crime against "the common ties . . . of mankind" is greatest when committed by those in whose hands the people have placed their trust (Ferguson, *Murder of Essex*, pp. 1–2, 5, 73–75).

[192] I have used a copy of Monmouth's Declaration in the British Library (Landsdowne MS 1152, fols. 258–261; the Essex charge appears on fol. 258).

[193] MS f.5, fol. 49; King, 1:223.

[194] MS d.10, fols. 111, 137, 140 (*LL* #2074a).

[195] MS f.7, fols. 24–27. I am uncertain as to whether this is the same work as the one listed by Laslett under a different title as entry *LL* #3064.

[196] MS f.7, fols. 97–98; MS f.4, fols. 203–205.

[197] King, 1:222.

notes in his journals. In one of them, Locke had followed Naude's discussion of Machiavelli's treatment of conspiracies in *The Prince* and the *Discourses*. It is interesting, therefore, that West reveals in his confession that he, too, was reading Machiavelli on conspiracies at this same time.[198] In addition to these reading notes, Locke has recorded several places where he was to keep an appointment or attend a meeting. The most intriguing of these appears under the heading, "Tanton" (Taunton?) and names "the Green Dragon tavern," which was, in fact, a frequent meeting place for West, Rumsey, and the other Rye House conspirators.[199]

It is also worth noting that as soon as the government discovered the Rye House conspiracy—even before the arrest warrants for West, Sidney, Russell, and the others had been issued—Locke hastily left London for James Tyrrell's house, where he began to make preparations to leave the country. He did not return to London until after the Glorious Revolution. Joseph Keeling's five-hour interview with Jenkins had been held on June 12, but the government issued no warrants or public announcement of its discovery of the conspiracy until June 21.[200] Locke, however, departed from London immediately after Keeling's confession.[201] In other words, at this time, only the government and the conspirators knew, or strongly suspected, that the plot had been discovered.[202]

Reference has already been made to the fact that the radicals carried on a correspondence with supporters in Holland, Scotland, and in various parts of England, and that in order to do so, they employed a canting language that disguised the letter's meaning in case it should be intercepted by the government. For, as one scholar has noted, "the secrecy of the post was violated on a greater scale during the seventeenth century than at any other time."[203] As one of the radicals explained, "Things were expressed under new words; so that indeed upon the matter it is a new language."[204] When West wrote to Ferguson in Holland, he wrote "a canting letter"

[198] Add. MS 38847, fol. 110.

[199] MS f.28, fol. 154; cf. ibid., fol. 98.

[200] Morrice, 1:370.

[201] Locke left London on June 14, 1683, the day of Keeling's second conference with Jenkins (MS f.7, fol. 111).

[202] The conspirators appear to have heard from their intelligence sources that Keeling had informed on them almost immediately following his discussions with Jenkins. Keeling, who was forced by the circumstances to continue associating with the conspirators, denied the accusations. Nevertheless, the delay by the government in issuing the arrest warrants against the conspirators placed Keeling's life in jeopardy, and he went to Jenkins "to hasten the warrants against us," because he feared for his life. And, West admits, Keeling would have been killed by the conspirators had he not gone into hiding (Add. MS 38847, fols. 117–119).

[203] Walker, "Secret Service," p. 226.

[204] *A True and Plain Account . . . in Scotland*, p. 18.

about his health.[205] Others wrote using medical or legal terminology. When Captain Walcot wrote to Lord Howard in the country about the insurrection, the latter explained, "The style of the letters was that of merchants, for so was the cant that I had given him."[206] The language of commercial transactions, as the letter cited above from John Nisbet about the assassination illustrates, was very popular among the radicals. They wrote about buying horses, corsets, books, tobacco, and so on. "Family" letters, discussing relatives and their health was another widely used style, through which to convey messages. Sometimes, when the radicals met in public places, taverns or coffeehouses, to discuss the revolution, they employed these linguistic codes (legal, medical, or commercial terminology) in order to disguise their intentions.[207] In this way, they could refer to the assassination as "executing a bargain and sale" or to the insurrection as "executing the conveyances." But the most frequent and widely used term to refer to the latter was "executing a lease and release." The terms "lease and release" were coined by Robert West at the post-Christmas dinner at Colonel Rumsey's house at the end of 1682, and West added, this way of referring to the revolution was accepted by the group, "and afterwards often made use of in discourse."[208]

In late February 1683, after Ferguson had returned to England and the meetings of the Council of Six as well as those in West's chambers were working concertedly to implement Shaftesbury's plans for an insurrection, Locke wrote several letters in a canting language to Edward Clarke. In them, he refers mysteriously to something being "put into her hands so that all that business will be as well as is possible, and I hope the event will be as successful as the beginning has been in all the parts lucky." In these letters, Locke refers to "Tregonil's lease and release."[209] Other letters to Clarke refer to two pseudonymous individuals, "Roberts and Sheldate," and the "business" Locke is ready to carry out in conjunction with Roberts.[210] From the depositions taken from three different Rye House conspirators, we learn that Ferguson at this time "went by the name of Roberts."[211] And according to the testimony of Thomas Shepherd, "busi-

[205] Add. MS 38847, fol. 96.

[206] *State Trials*, 4:218; Sprat, appendix, p. 67.

[207] Sprat, appendix, p. 7.

[208] Add. MS 38847, fol. 95; Sprat, appendix, p. 23.

[209] This phrase occurs in two letters to Clarke written February 20 and 22 (*Correspondence*, 2:582–583). There was a real Mr. Tregonil, a neighbor of Shaftesbury in Dorsetshire, but this does not affect the use of the key phrase (Christie, *Shaftesbury*, 1:8).

[210] *Correspondence*, 2:605. In this letter, Locke refers to a previous letter by him in answer to one from Clarke (both lost) discussing these two individuals. It is only a guess, but Sheldate might be Shepherd.

[211] Sprat, appendix, pp. 46, 50, 78; Add. MS 38847, fol. 98; Holloway, *Confession*, p. 3.

ness" was a common shorthand name for the revolution.[212]

Indeed, Locke's correspondence, or what survives of it from this period, and especially his letters to Clarke, merit a much closer examination in light of what we know about the radicals' propensity to rely upon a canting language. At the end of October 1682, Clarke wrote from London to Locke, then at Oxford, that

> I find your friends in the City are very desirous of your company . . . because I have reason to believe that all circumstances considered, they have as much need as ever of the best advice and assistance of their wisest and truest friends, in which number I am sure you deserve the first place.[213]

This letter was sent sometime after the first meeting at Shepherd's house, when the news of Trenchard's inaction caused the group to waver in its steadiness, and forced Shaftesbury into having to decide whether to proceed on his own, with an uprising in London, or to accept this delay and continue working with the Monmouth-Russell contingent. Locke was a natural person to turn to for advice at this time, since he was widely respected, and more important, he was trusted by individuals on all sides of this question. It may even be that Shaftesbury had it in mind to use Locke as a mediator, a role that could not be filled by Colonel Rumsey.[214]

In early 1683, after the revival of plans for the insurrection, Thomas Stringer wrote to Locke:

> My Lady doth own exceeding great obligations to Mr. Clarke for his kind offer to come out of Somersetshire hither.[215]

From other correspondence of the radicals, we know that Monmouth was referred to as a "Lady," and that the metaphor of a "child" was used for the revolution.[216] Clarke, in other words, had volunteered his assistance

[212] Examination of Thomas Shepherd, December 23, 1683, printed in *Tryal of Baillie*, p. 54. Shepherd knew a great deal more than he ever confessed, and could have accused "several of our best and ablest friends," which he did not do (*Secret History*, pp. 74–75).

[213] *Correspondence*, 2:556. A few days before this, Walcot had written to Lord Howard, then in the country, in a similar vein—namely, that his friends in the city desired his speedy return to London (Sprat, appendix, p. 67).

[214] It was at precisely this time that relations between those close to Shaftesbury and those associated with Russell and Monmouth were most strained. Ferguson writes of the need to effect a reconciliation within the party, and the individual he suggested as mediator was Francis Charlton. The latter did try to play this role, but, Ferguson notes, the result was an even greater estrangement than had existed before (*Ferguson*, pp. 422–423). Ferguson does not say so, but it may be that Locke was also proposed for this role.

[215] *Correspondence*, 2:578.

[216] For example, one of the letters written to Monmouth's supporters in England, informing them of the preparations for the impending invasion (April 15, 1685) adopts the cant of courting "the Young Lady" (Monmouth), and uses the pseudonyms for Nelthorp, Wade,

in "coming out of Somerset" on Monmouth's behalf. A week later Locke wrote that "we found Mas[ter?] very well and lusty and so he continues for such was the news Charles brought to Salisbury Court last night." It is in this letter that Locke expresses his hope that the "business will be as well as is possible, and I hope the event will be as successful as the beginning has been in all the parts lucky and as far as I can guess Mistris's mind is at rest about it." The last phrase is apparently a reference to Monmouth's decision to go ahead with the revolution against his father (the king), a matter that naturally from time to time caused other radicals some concern, lest he effect a reconciliation—Charles II loved Monmouth more than any of his other children—with the king, leaving them in the lurch.[217] Locke goes on to refer to the "lease and release," and concludes: "Your Lady and the rest of the company at Salisbury court are well." Two days later, Locke again wrote Clarke:

> The child is thriven since we saw it there, but yet your Lady has resolved to put it into Nurse Trents hands tomorrow who is also come to town with Mr. Hadley to leave him here, and that for these plain reasons. First because the thriving of the child since your last seeing of it, argues some neglect in the nurse before, which the dissatisfaction appeared in you for her not thriving has made her mend since . . . 2nd Tis agreed that Nurse Edeling has very little or no milk and Nurse Trent plenty . . . To which you must add a third no less considerable and that is that upon long experience your Lady can with more satisfaction and confidence trust Nurse Trents care than the other, who never gave her so much reason to suspect her neglect in two year as this has done in three months. This resolution I hope will be of good success to the child.[218]

Locke is here informing Clarke that Monmouth has reenlisted and decided to rely upon John Trenchard ("Nurse Trents") to organize the insurrection (or a part of it) in the west country, to which segment of the revolution Clarke was to make his own contribution. From the testimony of the Rye House conspirators, we know that in fact it was just at this time that Trenchard did reenter the project with a pledge to carry out his orig-

Rumbold, and Goodenough, among others (Add. MS 41812, fol. 30). And, in one of the canting letters confiscated when Monmouth's servant, John Gibbons, was arrested at Dover, "Sarah Hubbard" writes of her concern for her "child" in the context of informing the radicals in England of the exiles' plans for a revolution (Add. MS 41803, fol. 108). These and other similar letters are discussed more fully in Chapter 9.

217 There was, from time to time, some suspicion among West and others that Monmouth and the other members of "the superior council" might decide to make their peace with the king and leave the other conspirators to be hanged, but each time these doubts arose, Ferguson reassured them (Add. MS 38847, fols. 105–106; Sprat, appendix, pp. 14–15).

218 *Correspondence*, 2:582–583.

inally assigned role.[219] Hence, he has "mended" his ways since his default in November (about which Clarke seems to have been one of those who expressed his "dissatisfaction" at Trenchard for "not thriving"), and he is replacing a Mr. Edeling ("Nurse Edeling"), who was in fact a Rye House conspirator, and who later lent his assistance to Monmouth's Rebellion.[220] Everyone agreed that Trenchard had "plenty of milk," or support, around Taunton, which, if it could be mustered, would be vital to the success of the revolution ("the child"). At the end of 1681, for example, the government received an intelligence report that Trenchard and Sir William Waller were riding about Taunton "and other adjacent fanatic places of trade" in an effort to stir up about five hundred poor persons who were unemployed and in "discontented humors . . . so that they begin to be mutinous" against the government.[221] In the eyes of Ferguson and Monmouth, therefore, Trenchard was the man for "enrolling troops at Taunton" if he had indeed reaffirmed his "long experience" as one of the radicals, overcoming his "neglect" of the last three months (that is, since November).[222]

On May 27, 1683, James Tyrrell wrote to Locke:

> A dog fell mad last week, and has bit divers children and amongst the rest Jo: Clarks little boy, (a very pretty child) by the hand.[223]

[219] It was just at this time that Grey learned from Russell and Monmouth that "Mr. Trenchard had recovered his fright, and was very forward now to be in action" (*Secret History*, p. 52). In short, as Locke here informs Clarke, Trenchard told Monmouth (and Wade) that he was now ready to lead the forces at Taunton in the rebellion (Add. MS 38847, fol. 97; Harleian MS 6845, fol. 267). The reason this information would have some particular interest to Clarke is that he was associated with Trenchard and had considerable influence with the radicals in Taunton. In February 1685, it was reported that Clarke and Trenchard were "birds of one feather," and the "damnable crew" of fanatics would choose them as their parliamentary candidates from Taunton (*CSPD*, [James II], 1:54). Three years later, another government agent reported the same news to James II (MS Rawlinson A 139B, fols. 183, 186–198). Monmouth ("Your Lady") and Russell had primary responsibility for the insurrection in the west country, which included Taunton (Add. MS 38847, fol. 90; Sprat, appendix, p. 87).

[220] He appears to have been associated with William Disney, and perhaps with Wildman, who was Disney's cousin. Edeling helped Disney with the printing and distribution of Monmouth's Declaration (*State Trials*, 4:227–228). He may have been the same person as Henry Edeling, a Nonconformist minister (G. L. Turner, *Original Records*, 3:58).

[221] *CSPD*, 22:515.

[222] Grey, West, and the other participants all agreed that Trenchard's reneging on his promise to raise 1,500 men at Taunton for the revolution was the chief reason for its postponement in 1682 (Add. MS 38847, fol. 91; *Secret History*, pp. 26, 46). Russell was said to be so angry at Trenchard that he offered to go to Taunton to lead the troops himself (North, *Examen*, p. 381). Years later, Ferguson reminded Trenchard of his "constitutional cowardice and fear" when "your assistance was required" in the conspiracy (*Letter to Trenchard*, pp. 3, 10, 25).

[223] *Correspondence*, 2:596. Later, in the midst of a letter to Locke filled with political

I do not know to what specific action Tyrrell is here alluding, but the "mad dog" reference was used to denote the government, and the message could be a warning to Locke that some discovery of the "children" has been made. This was written in the period after the discovery of the guns at Lord Grey's house, for which he had been arrested, and around the time of Keeling's first disclosures of the plot to a minister and to a schoolteacher friend of his.[224] Locke must have received this letter on May 29, and he immediately moved out of Shaftesbury's house and went into hiding, in residence with his friend, Dr. Goodhall.[225] On the same day, the twenty-ninth, Ferguson's house was searched. His wife wrote to a friend that "so many spies are now about my lodgings that I dare not now send to your friend."[226]

Later, when Locke was making plans to leave the country, arranging real estate transactions in order to raise cash, and assigning a friend his power of attorney, he wrote to Clarke that silence should be maintained concerning Locke's whereabouts, "for I would be private at least till you hear from me again." It is in this letter that Locke gives Clarke permission to "burn" any of the "many papers" he has sent him, if the latter should think fit to do so. Then, he adds,

> There is another paper also sealed up which what it contains I suppose you will guess by the shape of it from what I have formerly told you. You may consider whether you think it best to lie there or no.

I agree with Laslett that this (and a subsequent reference in a letter to Clarke from Holland that he should send Locke the "*Tractatus de morbo Gallico*") refers to the manuscript of the *Two Treatises*, left in Clarke's custody.[227] In the same letter from which I have cited above, Locke writes:

> I would desire you to enquire of Mr. Bray, one of the storekeepers of the East India storehouse at Leadenhall, whether he hath had any

news, Freke inserted a sentence about the cure for the bite of "a mad dog" that Locke had once shown him (*Correspondence*, 3:325). "The common law of mankind," Hickeringill wrote, has "given every man a license to smite . . . a mad dog" (Edmund Hickeringill, *Works*, 2 vols., 1716, 1:339). I am not suggesting that Tyrrell had any specific knowledge of the Rye House Plot, merely that he may have heard something concerning Locke that prompted him to warn his friend.

[224] A warrant for Grey's arrest concerning the discovery of eighty muskets in his house was issued on May 11, 1683 (*CSPD*, 24:242; cf. Add. MS 28875, fol. 251).

[225] Cranston, p. 226.

[226] *CSPD*, 24:277. Ferguson also wrote to his wife on May 29, advising her to leave their residence in London and go into the country because of the danger caused by some people speaking too loosely (*Ferguson*, p. 169).

[227] Laslett, pp. 62–65. See Chapter 11, p. 536 below.

news from . . . [name missing] of anything concerning me, and to take order in that matter as it shall require.

The "storekeepers" or "merchants" were Locke's fellow Rye House conspirators, and the "news" concerning him, which he is so eager to find out about, relates to the confessions from those whom the government now had in its custody. The number of these individuals had, by August 26 (the date of this letter), grown considerably.[228] They included West, Sidney, Russell, Wildman, Rumsey, Walcot, Carstares, Major Breman, Shepherd, Lord Howard, Essex, Charlton, Trenchard, Hampden, and several others. Locke had good reason to be worried; Charlton and Carstares had been arrested in the second week of August; Shaftesbury's servant, Anthony Shepherd, was arrested the following week; and only a few days prior to his letter to Clarke, another member of Shaftesbury's "family," Mr. Hoskins, had been arrested, as had Aaron Smith, who it was said, had "made a large confession."[229] Mr. Bray may or may not have been one of the individuals named above, but since this pseudonym occurs in a later canting letter written during the preparations for Monmouth's Rebellion referring to someone actively involved in those preparations, Mr. Bray was clearly an individual who survived the Rye House executions.[230] In his most specific reference to the Rye House conspiracy, Locke instructs Clarke: "What news the Old Bailey affords from time to time I would gladly receive from you."

Some of the conspirators had by then been executed—notably Lord Russell—but most of them were still awaiting their day in the Old Bailey. Locke's anxiety concerning his personal fate in these circumstances is clearly evident in this letter. He tells Clarke to forgive a debt owed him by his "cousin Bonville" (a small tradesman in London) "if I die" before it is repaid. He asks him to consult with Dr. Thomas "about the best way of securing the books and goods in my chamber at Christ Church if there should be any danger." And finally Locke adds, "Upon consideration I have thought it best to make a will."[231] Obviously, as Shaftesbury had done before him upon fleeing the country, Locke is settling his accounts and getting his affairs in order in circumstances in which, given their life-

[228] *Correspondence*, 2:600–603. Argyll and other Scots had been in hiding in houses on Leadenhall Street. William Spence, Argyll's secretary, was arrested in a house on Leadenhall Street shortly before this letter was written (John Willcock, *A Scots Earl in Covenanting Times: Being the Life and Times of Archibald the 9th Earl of Argyll*, Edinburgh: Andrew Elliot, 1907, p. 312).

[229] Carstares was arrested on August 7; Charlton on August 9; Shepherd on August 18; Hoskins on August 21 (MS PWV 95, fols. 286–305; Add. MS 29582, fol. 51).

[230] Add. MS 4159, fol. 185.

[231] *Correspondence*, 2:603.

and-death consequences so far as he is concerned, have an air of finality about them.

Having offered this brief sketch of the Rye House conspiracy, and of Locke's relationship to the undertaking, I want to return to the subject of the political language invented and employed by the radicals, first as it relates to their efforts to produce some declaration or statement of their basic political principles, and second as they employed a special political language as a means of organization and as an expression of their ideological commitment. Finally, I will try to demonstrate the relationship that I believe exists between both these uses of the radicals' language and the arguments and terminology employed by Locke in the *Second Treatise*.

Aside from plotting, writing is the one thing that intellectuals are expected to be able to do better than anyone else. In this case, the radical intellectuals were expected to provide some appropriate document that would present and justify the objectives of the projected revolution. That no such manifesto, with one possible exception, appeared before 1685 was due, first to the postponement in 1682, and then to the discovery in 1683, of the conspiracy.[232] Nevertheless, it was neither for lack of interest among the participants in the revolutionary movement in having such a document, nor for want of effort on the part of those attempting to meet this demand, that this objective was not realized. "The most necessary thing of all in our undertaking," Lord Russell declared at one of the meetings in 1682, is "a Declaration" that would set forth their aims and reasons.[233] And, Grey recalled, "there was at one of our meetings, a paper read which Mr. Ferguson brought; it was designed for a Declaration." Grey is rather fuzzy about the details of what others described as "a pretty large paper," but he did "remember it began with some account of the ends of government in general," before going on to discuss a number of specific grievances lodged against the existing government.[234] Ferguson's declaration was directed to "inciting men's minds to the intended insurrection."[235] Later, at another meeting, Grey wrote that Sidney presented a discourse "with a long prologue of the necessity we were reduced to, of taking up of arms, and the lawfulness of it; and from thence descended to a particular account of their several proceedings and resolu-

[232] Ferguson's *Enquiry* (see Chapter 7, note 207 above) could be considered such a manifesto.

[233] *Secret History*, p. 30; Add. MS 38847, fol. 102.

[234] *Secret History*, pp. 47–48. In his letter, the anonymous Rye House conspirator also described the Declaration as "a large Declaration containing 8 sheets." To his correspondent, he wrote, "'Tis too long to tell you half the heads of it." On this document, see Chapter 7, note 191, above.

[235] *CSPD*, 26:227–228; *Trials*, p. 41; Sprat, p. 114.

tions."[236] Not everyone was satisfied with Sidney's discourse, and he agreed to present a revised declaration at a later meeting.[237]

I will take up in a moment the question of what these various declarations said. The point I am making is that there was an understood responsibility on the part of the radical theorists to develop some declaration of principles for the revolutionary movement and a demand on the part of the participants in that movement to have them do so. Major Wildman "was commissioned to draw up a new English Constitution," the draft of which has not survived.[238] This may be the same document to which Ferguson refers, though he describes Wildman's paper more as an expression and justification of the views of those who "were for vindicating the laws and liberties of the people, by a formed and joint rising in the two nations."[239] In any case, Wildman had confided in his friend, Colonel Rumbold, that he "intended to have [it] printed and dispersed among the people at the time of the intended insurrection."[240] At the same time, both Robert West and Nathaniel Wade were asked to draft similar justificatory declarations—"a scheme of fundamentals to be presented to the council of six for their approbation," is the way West put it.[241] Ferguson took this "project of government" drawn up by Wade and West in order to compare it with one that Sidney had composed, promising to "reduce them into an entire one."[242]

In other words, throughout 1682–1683, Ferguson, Wildman, Sidney, West, and Wade, were busily engaged in drafting papers, discourses, proposals, and declarations to be issued on behalf of the revolutionary movement.[243] In this regard, it is a fact of considerable interest that "my Lord Shaftesbury was preparing a Declaration to be published" in conjunction

[236] *Secret History*, p. 59.

[237] *Secret History*, pp. 63, 67.

[238] Ashley, *Wildman*, p. 227; *Ferguson*, p. 434.

[239] *Ferguson*, p. 435.

[240] This was in addition to "the Declaration to be published at the time of the insurrection" (Add. MS 38847, fol. 112).

[241] Add. MS 38847, fol. 96. West says Colonel Rumsey helped to draft these "few fundamentals."

[242] *Ferguson*, p. 132; Sprat, appendix, p. 17.

[243] Most of Sidney's *Discourses* was probably written "between the beginning of 1682 and his arrest in June 1683" (Foxcroft, *Savile*, 1:238n.). Ferguson told West that a few Nonconformist ministers did know of the assassination plot and supported it. "They and himself had prepared sermons ready, suitable to the occasion" (Add. MS 38847, fol. 105). Sometime around November 21, 1682—that is, coincidental with the date of the planned insurrection—a seditious pamphlet was seized from a bookseller. This material had reportedly been delivered to the printer by Thomas Stringer, Shaftesbury's secretary (MS PWV 95, fol. 51). Two weeks later, Stringer was arrested, and more pamphlets were confiscated, including one called *A Vindication of the Association* (MS PWV 95, fol. 63; *CSPD*, 23:581–582).

with the revolution planned in 1682.[244] Not only was Shaftesbury preparing such a document, but he was also actively encouraging others to do so. As Ferguson explained to West, Shaftesbury "thought it best that several persons should severally draw one" declaration, and then, "upon comparing them all together," the radicals could adopt or formulate the best one.

> For, says [Shaftesbury], I would have several people draw it, to pick one good one out of all. And he told me he had made some collections toward it, and showed me a paper . . . [describing the] attempts to introduce arbitrary government and popery.

By now, the reader will have determined that I intend to argue that Locke's *Second Treatise* represents an outgrowth of this process and of the necessity to supply a political declaration for the revolutionary movement. I do not find it credible that Locke was the only unemployed radical intellectual in the group, when he, after all, was the chief adviser to the leader of the movement, a leader who was actively commissioning such discourses and declarations from others. In my view, Locke's *Second Treatise*, like Ferguson's "Declaration," Sidney's *Discourses*, and the proposals by Wildman, West, and Wade, were all formulated in the context of the revolutionary conspiracy begun by Shaftesbury and carried on by the Council of Six. If we turn to a consideration of the content or argument of these documents, their relationship to one another, and to Shaftesbury's political perspective, I believe their familial similarities will become clearer.

As West recalled, the paper Shaftesbury showed him concluded that, in view of Charles II's attempts to introduce arbitrary government and popery,

> the government was dissolved, and they were free to settle another government. These, I perceived, were the topics my Lord Shaftesbury laid weight upon.[245]

Ferguson's declaration, according to Grey, laid "the destruction of the government" to the arbitrary and absolute actions of the king, and it demanded that a "free parliament" be called into existence immediately to

[244] *Trials*, p. 14; Add. MS 38847, fol. 91. Walcot told West that Shaftesbury had prepared a declaration in October 1682, and Ferguson said that "one had been well considered of, was prepared, and would be printed ready to be dispersed" at the time of the rebellion (Add. MS 38847, fol. 102). These may be two different documents, but it seems clear that Shaftesbury had at least one "declaration" ready to go to the printer in the fall of 1682. See also Sprat, appendix, pp. 7, 13, 16, 30.

[245] *Trials*, p. 14; Add. MS 38847, fol. 91.

redress the nation's grievances.[246] Sidney argued, in his presentation to the group, that "the King had broken the laws and his own oath," and that as a consequence, the people were in a position "to provide for the safety of themselves," and further, the necessary means of doing so was to "secure the settlement of the kingdom to a parliament."[247] As Ferguson explained the situation to Zachary Bourne, another Rye House conspirator, the king had broken the social contract, "so the people were again at liberty" to constitute a new government for themselves.[248] If, as West said, these were the issues Shaftesbury "laid weight upon," namely, that the arbitrary actions and claim for absolute power by the king represented a break in the social contract, leaving the people again in a state of liberty to constitute a new government for themselves, and especially one that rested upon parliamentary authority, then even in this cryptic formulation, the basic structure of the argument in the *Second Treatise* was clearly a widely understood theoretical expression of the objectives of the Rye House conspiracy, and of the revolutionary Whig movement.

Some radicals also drew up a list of fundamental grievances and specific demands. These included (1) the militia to be in the hands of the people; (2) annual Parliaments; (3) sheriffs to be elected in every county; (4) religious toleration; and (5) Parliament not to be prorogued or dissolved without its own consent.[249] There was also some talk of easing or eliminating certain taxes—especially the chimney tax—so that "the common people would fall in with them more readily."[250] But their primary objective, aside from removing or restraining the king, was to insure that a Parliament would be summoned, and most of the radicals were willing to leave the decision on these and other matters to that body.[251] Hence, while there were naturally differences of opinion within their ranks, there is little reason to reify this difference into the kind of rigid categories—"Republican" and "Whig"—employed by some scholars.[252]

[246] *Secret History*, pp. 47–48. This was the central point emphasized in the declaration, according to the author of the letter mentioned in note 234 above.

[247] *Secret History*, p. 63. This was also Essex's view (Burnet, 2:356).

[248] Sprat, appendix, p. 50.

[249] Add. MS 38847, fol. 96.

[250] *Trials*, p. 9; Add. MS 38847, fol. 102.

[251] At Russell's trial, Howard testified that the Council of Six had decided "to resolve all into the authority of the Parliament" (*State Trials*, 3:717). West also said that the general decision made by the lower level of conspirators was to leave matters to Parliament (Add. MS 38847, fol. 96; *Trials*, p. 16).

[252] As, for example, Robert Story does (*Carstares*, pp. 68–69; Jones, p. 15; Caroline Robbins, *The Eighteenth Century Commonwealthman*, Cambridge: Harvard University Press, 1959, pp. 29–30). This dichotomy as a general interpretive problem has already been discussed above.

Men like Ferguson—who was *not* a Republican—and Wildman could nevertheless work together closely as friends. The same is true for Locke and Sidney, though perhaps they worked together at a greater distance.[253] As one anonymous spy reported to the government, "the factious . . . though they hate one another, they combine against the government."[254]

But how did they manage to "combine" together against the government, always a risky undertaking at best? Soliciting participants for a projected revolution cannot be done with the openness of a charitable fund drive; as soon as one reveals the plan to someone, everyone involved in it becomes vulnerable to betrayal and prosecution. To deal with this problem, the radicals invented a code language. Certain key words and phrases were used by them, and *only* by them, since the use of these words revealed very clearly the ideological commitment of radicalism. This terminology spoke of an "invasion of rights," "usurpation," "tyranny," the king's "betrayal of his trust," his use of "violence and force against us," the fact that he had "degenerated into a beast," and so forth. It is, and it was meant to be, a violent language. It was intended to convey to others that a state of war already existed, launched by the king, who was therefore the true "rebel," "thief," or "traitor."

Of course, since this language is in itself quite revealing, there had to be some means by which one could be led into it gradually so that the conspiracy could be revealed piecemeal according to the willingness of the listener to demonstrate his own ideological commitment. "First their inclinations were to be tried by gradual insinuations, and plausible discourses at a distance, till they had gained a full assurance of their fidelity." The means by which this was accomplished was through focusing upon the key word "invasion." "They were to be asked, what they would or could do in case of foreign invasion?"[255] There are several accounts of tavern or coffeehouse conversations along the following lines: Goodenough asked Hone, a joiner, "if in case of invasion I would not be ready to stand up for the liberties" of the people, and when Hone replied that he would be willing to do so, Goodenough "afterwards told me that the invasion was already" in progress because the people's liberties had been

[253] Forster says that Sidney was "a great friend and correspondent" of Locke, but there is no evidence of which I am aware to support that statement (Thomas Forster, ed., *Original Letters of Locke; Algernon Sidney; and Anthony, Lord Shaftesbury, Author of the "Characteristics,"* 1830, preface, p. lxxvi). Locke's long-time friend, John Mapletoft, was a good friend of Sidney, and Locke had the opportunity to meet Sidney when both men were in France in 1675–1677, but there is no indication that the two did in fact meet, let alone correspond.

[254] *CSPD*, 22:334.

[255] Sprat, p. 43.

taken from them by the government, "and therefore it was lawful to rise."[256] In another version of this conversation, Thomas Lee asked John Rouse if he would be prepared to oppose any invasion of his liberties, but Rouse demanded to know what Lee meant by an invasion, "for I knew of none." Do you not know what I mean, asked Lee? "Is there not an invasion on all we have? . . . You see how we are every day invaded against our rights." To all this, Rouse says, "I was not a little startled and desired him to explain for, when I expressed my readiness to serve, I intended against a foreign invasion." That was, of course, the point. The phrase "invasion of rights and liberties" was, in the words of one conspirator, "the way to hook in persons" who might be sympathetic to joining the revolution.[257] If, in response to the initial question about an invasion, the individual indicated that he was prepared to assist "against any common enemy," then he would be asked what he could contribute (arms, money, persons), and eventually, as Thomas Sprat phrased it in his *History*, "the whole mystery of the villainy was to be frankly disclosed."[258] In this way, West wrote, many people "were insinuated" into the undertaking.[259] If the listener proved to be less sympathetic than was hoped for, it could always be claimed that a French "invasion" for the popish interest was being talked about, and the conversation could be reported to the government only at the risk of impugning the informer's own loyalty to England.

It is worth noting that this language of "invasion" was not merely a password through which entrance into the radical movement was gained; it also existed within a justificatory context that provided the radicals with a purposive theoretical framework in terms of which they viewed their political actions. They understood, that is, that the king's oppressive actions constituted

> an actual invasion on . . . [their] liberties, properties, and consciences; that the only obligation the subject has to the King, is a mutual covenant; that this covenant was manifestly broken on the King's part; that therefore the people were free from all oaths . . . and had the natural liberty restored to them of asserting their own

[256] *CSPD*, 24:383.

[257] *CSPD*, 25:47; *Trials*, p. 68. In his deposition, Thomas Lee, a dyer, said that Goodenough had instructed them to use the phrase "our rights and liberties were invaded," in a general discourse hinting at a foreign invasion, but that "if that took" with the individual, they might go further in laying out the details of the conspiracy (Sprat, appendix, p. 25).

[258] Sprat, p. 43; *State Trials*, 3:623.

[259] Add. MS 38847, fol. 115.

> rights, and as justly at least against a domestic as against foreign invaders.[260]

This understanding reached down to the lowest social levels, and the articulation of the political theory that gave meaning to these particular propositions was as likely to emerge from a coffeehouse discussion among artisans as it was from the more formal and systematic declarations produced by the radical intellectuals.

Nor, on the other hand, should it be supposed that the language of "invasion" was confined to individuals from the lower classes. Captain Walcot, who attended several meetings of the middle-level people (Ferguson, Sir Thomas Armstrong, Colonel Rumsey, West) indicated in a speech at his execution that he had been present "where some things were discoursed of, in order to the asserting our liberties and properties, which we looked upon to be violated and invaded."[261] In the paper drawn up by Wildman, "for vindicating the laws and liberties of the people," he, too, charged that "the King had invaded and subverted the laws," to which the people's "joint rising" was thus a legitimate response.[262] In his account of his conversation with Lord Russell while the latter was awaiting his execution, John Tillotson paraphrased Russell's position as "if our religion and rights should be invaded, as your Lordship puts the case." Russell believed that "a visible design to bring in popery and arbitrary power, which he took to be the present case, was sufficient to justify resistance." Tillotson and Burnet both tried, unsuccessfully, to convince him that it was not lawful "upon any pretence whatsoever to take up arms" against the king. But Russell replied that, in that case, he could not see what difference there was between "a legal and a Turkish constitution."[263] Lord Howard testified at Sidney's trial that, in defense of their revolution, the Council of Six had resolved "ourselves into such principles, as should put the properties and liberties of the people into such hands, as it should not be easily invaded by any that were trusted with the supreme authority of the land."[264] And according to Lord Grey, Shaftesbury had already adopted the language of invasion as early as 1681.[265] The point is that the

[260] Sprat, pp. 43–44.

[261] *Trials*, appendix, pp. 2–3.

[262] *Ferguson*, pp. 434–435.

[263] John Tillotson, *A Letter Written to My Lord Russell in Newgate*, 1683, printed as an appendix to *Trials*, p. 1. Locke owned a copy of Tillotson's letter to Russell (*LL* #2919; cf. Echerd, *History*, p. 1034).

[264] *State Trials*, 3:717.

[265] *Secret History*, p. 15. It is some measure of how far removed Bishop Burnet was from the radicals that, even in 1688, he felt compelled to dissociate himself from the word "invasion," whose usage, he said, naturally conveys a sense of horror to the listener (Gilbert

organizational unity of the radical movement was expressed through its use of a political language, and this language, in turn, reflected a widely shared ideological commitment among the participants in the Rye House conspiracy that found its way into the papers, declarations, and pamphlets written by the radical theorists of the movement.

Locke's argument in the *Second Treatise* is that it is the possibility of "the invasion of others" that makes the individual's enjoyment of life, liberty, or property "very uncertain" in a state of nature.[266] Therefore, anyone who "unjustly invades another man's right" becomes an aggressor, robber, or thief who may be resisted or killed. Moreover, "the injury and the crime is equal, whether committed by the wearer of a crown, or some petty villain."[267] Thus, whenever magistrates "invade" the liberties and properties of the people "contrary to the trust put in them," the people "are absolved from obedience" and may resist.[268]

> This I am sure, whoever . . . by force goes about to invade the rights of either prince or people, and lays the foundation for overturning the Constitution and frame of any just government is guilty of the greatest crime, I think, a man is capable of . . . And he who does it, is justly to be esteemed the common enemy and pest of mankind.[269]

These "pests," "noxious creatures," or "common enemies," Locke maintains, may be destroyed or killed. Locke observes that, with respect to foreign "invasions," the legitimacy of this remedy "is agreed on all hands. But that magistrates doing the same thing may be resisted hath of late been denied."[270] It is just this distinction Locke attempts to undermine, and in the course of doing so, he advances the argument that there is no essential difference between a foreign or a domestic invasion of the people's rights and liberties.

> The people's right is equally invaded and their liberty lost, whether they are made slaves to any of their own or a foreign nation.[271]

In other words, the *Second Treatise* defends revolutionary action by the people, employing the language of invasion in precisely the same manner

---

Burnet, *A Collection of Eighteen Papers relating to the Affairs of Church and State during the Reign of King James the Second*, 1689, p. 134).

[266] *ST*, pars. 123, 131.

[267] *ST*, par. 176.

[268] *ST*, par. 222.

[269] *ST*, par. 230.

[270] *ST*, par. 231.

[271] *ST*, par. 239. Although these lines were added to the second edition of the *Two Treatises*, they simply reaffirmed the point Locke had made in par. 231. The quotations from Barclay starting in par. 232 were designed to demonstrate that the same reasoning that supported resistance to a foreign invasion could be applied to the king and other magistrates.

that was used by members of the revolutionary movement in order to build its organizational structure.

As Locke's reference to "slavery" intimates, the radicals believed they were opposing a "tyrant" or a "usurper." Rather than be "tyrannized over in their consciences, persons, and estates, and to see slavery entailed upon their posterity," Ferguson declared, they undertook to "retrieve the liberties of which they had been robbed."[272] Elsewhere, he wrote that any ruler who "does invade and subvert the Fundamental Laws of the society does thereby *ipso facto* annul all the legal right he had to govern." And, Ferguson adds, this is the act of a "traitor" against the Constitution.[273] In the declaration they issued in support of Monmouth's Rebellion, the revolutionaries claimed that "our religion, liberty and lives are visibly and undeniably attacked and invaded." Hence, "the Fundamental Contract" had been "violated" by James II, who "was actually a traitor." In fact, there is an outpouring of this language in the declaration, referring to James' "having invaded the Throne, and usurped the title of a King," his having "ravished" our liberties and properties through the use of "fraud and violence," leaving us to exist under an "absolute tyranny." In short, James is "a popish usurper of the crown, traitor to the nation, and tyrant over the people."[274] The Earl of Argyll's Declaration distributed in Scotland in support of his contribution to Monmouth's Rebellion employs the same language; it speaks of James II's "having invaded our religion and liberties" and of "his usurpations and tyranny."

In Ferguson's *Impartial Enquiry*, written to justify the Rye House conspiracy, he premises his critique of Charles II's administration upon the latter's "invasion" of the rights and liberties of the people. Any king who engages in such action, he argues, "doth *ipso facto* depose himself, and instead of being owned any longer for a King, ought to be treated as a rebel and traitor." Since, according to "the fundamental Laws of Nature . . . all magistracy is appointed for the benefit of mankind and the common good," rulers who violate this principle "degrade" themselves and "become injurious to the community," placing its members "in a worse condition" than they were before the government was instituted. These rulers are plainly "enemies" to mankind, "and may be dealt with after the manner" of anyone or anything that threatens the people's safety.[275]

[272] *Ferguson*, p. 416.

[273] Robert Ferguson, *A Brief Justification of the Prince of Orange's Descent into England*, 1689, p. 9; idem, *A Representation of the Threatening Dangers*, 1688, pp. 30, 51–53. Locke owned the second tract, *Representation* (*LL* #2467), and there is an unidentified title listed as "of the Prince of Orange," which could be Ferguson's *Brief Justification* (*LL* #934).

[274] Landsdowne MS 1152, fols. 258–259.

[275] *Enquiry*, p. 4.

This argument continues for another sixty pages, and many of its statements could be laid side by side with those found in Sidney's *Discourses*, or in Locke's *Second Treatise*.

Locke, as we have seen, employs the language of invasion in the manner of his radical colleagues, and like them, he links its usage to his definition of "tyranny" and "usurpation." In his chapter, "Of Conquest," Locke elaborates upon the political significance of this language. He begins by reiterating an earlier point: that "polities" cannot "be founded on anything but the consent of the people." To this proposition he opposes the view of government founded upon "the force of arms," which is what he means by "conquest."[276] This definition he immediately places in the context of "the aggressor, who puts himself into the state of war with another, and unjustly invades another man's right," which makes him nothing more than "a robber." Since it does not matter whether he is a "great robber" or merely an ordinary thief, such action can convey no title to legitimacy. Moreover, if the consequence of this conquest is to destroy the people's legislative power, derived from their consent—as is frequently the case, since "conquerors' swords often cut up governments by the roots"—then the people always have the right to resist "till they have recovered the native right of their ancestors, which was to have such a Legislative over them, as the majority should approve, and freely acquiesce in."[277] Locke then takes up the harder case, supposing that justice is on the side of the conqueror, and he argues that even as the victor in a just war, there are serious limits upon what a conqueror can and cannot do with respect to property, wives and children of combatants, and the lives of noncombatants. One point these limitations serve to illustrate, according to Locke, is that even in the best of circumstances, conquest cannot justify a claim to "absolute power" over a conquered commonwealth.[278] Not only that, but whatever the justice of conquest, it can never extend to "the descendants" of those who were conquered. Viewed in light of the constraints of natural law and consent in defining the limits of legitimate government, conquest (even under its most generous meaning) is for Locke nothing more than a temporary and limited aberration in the course of political existence. Thus,

> The people who are the descendants of . . . those, who were forced to submit to the yoke of a government by constraint, have always a right to shake it off, and free themselves from the usurpation, or tyranny, which the sword hath brought in upon them, till their rulers

[276] *ST*, par. 175; cf. ibid., par. 112.
[277] *ST*, par. 176; cf. ibid., par. 211.
[278] *ST*, pars. 182, 183.

> put them under such a frame of government, as they willingly, and of choice consent to.[279]

And, Locke concludes,

> Whence it is plain, that shaking off a power, which force, and not right hath set over any one, though it hath the name of rebellion, yet is no offence before God, but is that, which he allows and countenances.[280]

That part of Locke's argument which establishes an identification between the "unjust invasion" of rights (the use of force by an aggressor to set up a government) and the general response one should adopt with respect to a robber—resistance—will, Locke believes, "be easily agreed [to] by all men, who will not think, that robbers and pirates have a right of empire over whomsoever they have force enough to master."[281]

Having laid this groundwork, Locke moves on to consider in the two following chapters first "usurpation," and then "tyranny." The former opens with the statement that "as conquest may be called a foreign usurpation, so usurpation is a kind of domestic conquest." There is, however, a difference, as Locke points out: that while there might be such a thing as a just war, and hence a just conquest, "an usurper can never have right on his side," since usurpation is the possession of something to which the possessor has no "right."[282] In other words, in treating this subject as a form of "domestic conquest," Locke is carrying forward only those points made in the previous chapter which apply to an "unjust" conquest, the basic elements of which are cited above. If a usurper is, then, an unjust conqueror, a tyrant is even worse, since he lays claim to "the exercise of power . . . which no body can have a right to." Moreover, he employs this power not for the welfare of the people, "but for his own private separate advantage . . . [in] the satisfaction of his own ambition, revenge, covetousness, or any other irregular passion." It is not the law, based upon consent, but "his own will and appetite" on which he relies for his authority.[283] But, Locke argues,

> Whosoever in authority exceeds the power given him by the law, and makes use of the force he has under his command, to compass that upon the subject which the law allows not, ceases in that to be a magistrate, and acting without authority, may be opposed, as any other man, who by force invades the right of another.

[279] *ST*, par. 192.
[280] *ST*, par. 196.
[281] *ST*, par. 176; cf. *FT*, par. 81.
[282] *ST*, par. 197.
[283] *ST*, pars. 199–200.

And linking this discussion of tyranny both to his general argument about the use of "force without authority" as introducing a state of war, and to his just concluded discussion of "unjust conquest," Locke declares that such an individual "may be opposed as a thief and a robber." The connection is reinforced by his repetition of the point made in that chapter that "exceeding the bounds of authority is no more a right in a great, than a petty officer; no more justifiable in a King, than a constable."[284] The remainder of the chapter on tyranny is then given over to a justification of resistance. What Locke has tried to demonstrate, therefore, to emphasize a point made earlier, is that there is no difference between a "foreign" and a "domestic" invasion, either in terms of the use of "force without authority" or with respect to the people's right to resist a conqueror or a tyrant.

The radicals also expressed these views through the use of a more colorful language, one that postulated the lawfulness of killing "wolves or tigers," destroying "noxious beasts," and so on. "It was never thought injustice," Ferguson argued, "to shoot or set traps for wolves and tigers."[285] In the Shaftesbury papers, there is a manuscript that, after citing Bracton on the duties of kings, remarks upon those who overstep their lawful boundaries:

> Such are not kings but tyrants, called wolves and lions in the Scripture, that deserve to be destroyed from the face of the earth, as being the destroyers of mankind.

And, if Bracton and the Bible are not enough, the author cites Seneca for good measure. That writer, he says, "makes them worse than beasts of prey."[286] In the *Second Treatise*, Locke makes extensive use of this language. One who uses "unjust violence" against another individual has, by that action, "declared war against all mankind, and therefore may be destroyed as a lion or a tiger, one of those wild savage beasts with whom men can have no society nor security."[287] Since "such men are not under the ties of the Common Law of Reason," they "may be treated as beasts of prey, those dangerous and noxious creatures" which a man may kill "for the same reason that he may kill a wolf or lion."[288] This language

[284] *ST*, par. 202; cf. ibid., par. 176.

[285] Add. MS 38847, fol. 102; *Ferguson*, p. 129. According to Ferguson, Wildman, who had been an early supporter of assassination, spoke of it "under the cant of killing . . . beasts of spoil" (p. 434). For an interesting discussion that links many of the arguments considered in this chapter with those pertaining to tyrannicide, see Oscar Jaszi and John D. Lewis, *Against the Tyrant: The Tradition and Theory of Tyrannicide*, Glencoe, Ill.: Free Press, 1957, pp. 3–110.

[286] PRO 30/24/43/63.

[287] *ST*, par. 11.

[288] *ST*, par. 16.

forms part of Locke's general argument concerning anyone who introduces a state of war, or who transgresses the Law of Nature. As we saw in Chapter 5, the argument could be used to characterize the moral relationship, as seventeenth-century Englishmen saw it, between Catholics and Protestants, and especially between a Catholic king and his Protestant subjects. But Locke also makes it clear that these references carry a distinctly *political* meaning, as Seneca suggested, applicable to magistrates, whoever they may be, who exceed the bounds of their authority. Thus Locke incorporates the language into his definition of "despotical power," the exercise of which makes one an "aggressor" or a "wild beast, or noxious brute."[289] He introduces it again in his discussion of conquest and the unjust conqueror as a "savage ravenous beast" who may be "destroyed."[290] Finally, in his concluding chapter justifying resistance, Locke makes it clear that he is speaking of "the ill designs of the rulers," the "oppresion" and "evil intention of their governors" against whom the people may revolt, and in so doing, they are entitled to treat such rulers as "the common enemy and pest of mankind."[291] If we keep in mind that, in using this language the radicals clearly had in mind its applicability to Charles II and his brother, their decision to mount an insurrection or to entertain thoughts of assassination may not appear quite so strange or far-fetched, given the presuppositions of the political theory within which such language found its significance and meaning.

We have, of course, no precise indication of the numbers of persons who employed this political language as a means of making sense out of their political experience and activity. Yet, the accounts we do have suggest that its usage, and the radical audience for whom it had a distinct meaning, were much greater than we could deduce simply from the failure of the Rye House conspiracy to achieve its practical objectives, or from the number of individuals that, in fact, the government managed to capture. In addition to the hundreds of individuals who fled into exile, primarily to Holland, many more than that were never discovered or prosecuted. As one of the conspirators reflected,

> This plot had been laid broader and deeper than I apprehended, and . . . it had been communicated to a great number of people, both in London and in the country.[292]

Monmouth said the same thing in his private confession to Charles II, namely, "that it was much wider and more dangerous than is mentioned

[289] *ST*, par. 172.

[290] *ST*, par. 181.

[291] *ST*, par. 230.

[292] Add. MS 38847, fol. 91. Holloway also believed that "many thousands" of individuals were concerned in the conspiracy (Holloway, *Confession*, p. 7).

in any printed relation" of the plot.[293] Other conspirators reaffirmed the point.[294] Certainly, a number of contemporaries believed that "great multitudes of men" were committed to this perspective, and that "these were not the desperate designs of a few," but that "the business was laid very broad."[295] As was said earlier, we may wonder what is meant by "a few individuals," or what meaning "broad" conveyed in these assessments. If the estimate of twenty thousand participants in Sprat's official history of the Rye House conspiracy errs on the high side, still there are good reasons for believing that a substantial audience did exist in 1682–1683 that was sympathetic to the views expressed by Ferguson, Wildman, West, Sidney, and Locke.[296]

Since most of their writings did not come to light until much later, and under very different political circumstances shaped by different political attitudes, this point cannot be pressed too far. Yet at Sidney's trial, the prosecution relied heavily upon his manuscript of the *Discourses*, which it had confiscated and introduced as evidence of his treason. Sidney's manuscript, the Attorney General argued, was intended

> to persuade the people, that the King was introducing arbitrary power, that he subverted all their rights, liberties, properties . . . The whole design of this treatise is to persuade the people of England, that it is lawful, nay, that they have a right to set aside their prince, in case it appear to them, that he hath broken the trust laid upon him by the people.

He went on to associate these principles with those of "the late rebellion": that political power "is originally in the people"; that the king's power is "derived from the people upon trust"; that "the King had invaded their rights, and therefore, . . . they might assume that original power they had conferred" on him, and that if they do engage in such resistance, "it is no rebellion." This argument, the prosecutor explained to the jury, was specifically grounded upon the assertion that the king, by dissolving so many Parliaments, which he had no right to do, "therefore he hath broken his trust, and invaded our rights," and the people had the

[293] Dalrymple, vol. 1, pt. 1, bk. 1, pp. 57, 114; Roberts, *Life of Monmouth*, p. 161.

[294] *State Trials*, 3:614 (Walcot). According to Ferguson, "vast numbers had arrived at some intimation of" the assassination plot, and it was approved of by some individuals "of more prudence and better quality than I could have imagined" (*Ferguson*, pp. 431–432, 418–419).

[295] Edward Pelling, *A Sermon*, September 9, 1683, pp. 19, 30; Thomas Wagstaffe, *A Sermon*, 1683, p. 3. This point is made in Lord North's notes on the Rye House conspiracy (Add. MS 32518, fol. 145; *Examen*, p. 394).

[296] Sprat, p. 19. James used the same figure, and this may be one of the alterations he made in Sprat's manuscript before its publication (Dalrymple, vol. 1, pt. 1, bk. 1, p. 162).

right to rid themselves of the "tyranny" thus imposed upon them.[297] Sidney maintained that this violation of the "contract" or trust had the effect of "dissolving the whole fabric" of government. And like Locke, he argues that "consent" is to be contrasted with "usurpation and violence" as the basis for government.[298]

These were the "pernicious" and "damnable doctrines" condemned in *The Judgment and Decree of the University of Oxford* issued to justify a gigantic book burning staged at Oxford following the discovery of the Rye House conspiracy.[299] They were repeatedly attacked in sermons celebrating the king's safety preached throughout the summer and fall of 1683.[300] The arguments and language we have examined in this chapter, in other words, were firmly associated in the minds of contemporaries with the ideas and activities of the participants in the Rye House Plot. Moreover, the latter was itself an outgrowth of Shaftesbury's design "to prosecute the association."[301] The conspirators, it was said, undertook the assassination or uprising on behalf of "the associating members of the last House of Commons."[302]

As one contemporary put it, individuals who frequent "seditious clubs and conventicles," where they are exposed to "continual discourses" that employ this political language, "will come to steep their language" with such terms. Hence, "by treasonable talk men slide and fall into actual rebellion." This language then becomes itself an active instrument for promoting a rebellion.[303] Thus a person might be a rebel "without taking up arms against the government, merely by justifying the lawfulness of so doing."[304] John Northleigh undertook to transform this observation into a work of nearly eight hundred pages, the essential thesis of which was that the "consults" and meetings of the Rye House conspirators were tied

[297] *State Trials*, 3:714.

[298] Alex Charles Ewald, *The Life and Times of the Hon. Algernon Sidney*, 2 vols., 1873, pp. 321–323.

[299] *The Judgment and Decree of the University of Oxford . . . against Certain Pernicious Books and Damnable Doctrines Destructive to . . . Government, and of All Human Society*, July 21, 1683.

[300] Edward Pelling, *A Sermon*, November 5, 1683, pp. 28ff.; Wagstaffe, *Sermon*, passim; Benjamin Calamy, *A Sermon*, 1683, pp. 33–34.

[301] John Lauder, *Historical Observes of Memorable Occurrents in Church and State*, 1840, p. 97. The association "was a scheme to form a rebellion and change the government by . . . associating in arms" (Add. MS 29577, fol. 401).

[302] *Trials*, p. 4. The conspirators, as Echerd put it, looked upon themselves as an "association of patriots for the defense of the invaded liberties and religion of the nation" (*History*, p. 1027).

[303] John Owen, *The True Way to Loyalty*, 1684, p. 16.

[304] John Fitz-William, *The Virtues of Fearing God and the King, and the Mischiefs of Change*, 1683, p. 6.

to a familiar litany of "those sophisticated . . . false opinions . . . [and] treasonable positions" of a number of antimonarchical authors upon whom all conspirators and revolutionaries have relied as sources of the justificatory principles for their actions during the last century.[305]

Prior to Sidney's trial, the Privy Council minutes show that the council adopted a resolution that the paper of association found with Shaftesbury's papers ought to be compared with "Algernon Sidney's book."[306] And, in his address to the jury at the trial, Chief Justice Jeffreys referred to the "meetings and debates" of the Rye House conspirators, insisting that Sidney's manuscript expressed "the general design of the rebellion they planned," for "their debates at their meetings were to that purpose. And such doctrines as these suit with their debates."[307] As the prosecutor put it, "the whole book is an argument for the people to rise in arms, and vindicate their wrongs."[308] Unquestionably, the echo from that courtroom must have had a special resonance for the exiled author of the then unpublished *Two Treatises of Government*.

[305] John Northleigh, *Remarks upon the Most Eminent of Our Antimonarchical Authors and Their Writings*, 1699, pp. 672–765, esp. p. 738; cf. ibid., p. 9.

[306] *CSPD*, 25:412. Sidney himself was brought before the Privy Council, but he refused to answer any of their questions (Dalrymple, vol. 1, pt. 1, bk. 1, p. 43).

[307] *State Trials*, 3:735.

[308] *State Trials*, 3:714. Sidney's dying speech, Settle wrote, was "a license for the people to rebel" (Elkanah Settle, *Remarks on Sidney's Paper, Delivered to the Sheriffs at His Execution*, 1683, p. 3).

9

EXILE AND REBELLION

THE discovery of the Rye House Plot and the confessions of several of its participants provided the government with the political leverage it needed to crush the Whig opposition. As James expressed it in a letter to William of Orange, "if the right use be made of this conspiracy . . . that which was designed to be the destruction of [the monarchy] will prove of great advantage to it."[1] Whatever ambivalent feelings Charles might have had concerning the punishment to be meted out to the conspirators as a consequence of Monmouth's participation in the undertaking, James showed little hesitation in taking advantage of the situation to remove his enemies from the political arena. He had always viewed the Whigs as closet Republicans, and the Rye House Plot only confirmed his longstanding belief that it was simply the weakness and irresolution of the English monarchy that permitted such individuals the freedom of action they enjoyed. Insofar as he could exercise any influence over his brother (and during the last two years of Charles' reign, this influence appears to have been considerable), James was determined to make every effort to transform the prosecution of the Rye House conspiracy into a justification for absolute monarchy.[2]

Most of the conspirators had managed to make their way, individually or in pairs, to Holland. They were assisted in their escape by the fact that the government did not make public its discovery of the conspiracy, nor did it issue arrest warrants for any of the participants, until June 21, a week after Keeling's second conference with Secretary Jenkins. Ferguson and many others were thus able to slip out of the country before the government could tighten its grip upon the ports and border areas. Locke may not at first have had it in his mind to leave the country, though he certainly was in hiding. He ceased recording his movements in his journal

[1] William R. Emerson, *Monmouth's Rebellion*, New Haven: Yale University Press, 1951, p. 72.

[2] It was not only the Whigs who believed this, but as early as July 23, Barrillon wrote to Louis XIV that James would attempt to use the Rye House Plot as the means to establish an absolute monarchy in England. The fullest discussion of this point is by Doreen J. Milne, "The Results of the Rye House Plot and Their Influence upon the Revolution of 1688," *Transactions of the Royal Historical Society*, 5th ser. 1 (1951):91–108. On James' influence over his brother during the last two years of Charles II's reign, see G. N. Clark, *The Later Stuarts*, Oxford: Oxford University Press, 1940, p. 111; Maurice Ashley, *Charles II*, London: Panther Books, 1973, p. 315.

on June 18, and it was later disclosed (by Lady Masham) that Locke spent a great deal of time hiding in the west of England, where he had a number of friends and where, coincidentally, the highest concentration of political dissidents resided.[3] The execution of Russell and the death of Essex in the Tower at the end of July, however, coupled with the arrests of an increasing number of his friends and associates, probably convinced Locke that he, too, would have to become an exile. Among the many problems posed by such a decision was the basic one of financial survival. How could Locke provide for his economic maintenance abroad?

Naturally, he did not face this problem alone. Hundreds of individuals had to find some means to maintain themselves as exiles in Holland, Switzerland, and other countries. Moreover, those who escaped imprisonment and execution in England did not abandon their political objective of overthrowing the government of Charles II. As exiles, they planned and attempted to carry out Monmouth's Rebellion, an invasion force of English and Scottish radicals who sailed from Holland. This, too, required funds to supply the expedition with arms, ships, and men. The transmission of money from England to Holland was therefore crucial to the maintenance of the revolutionary movement, and to the practical survival of the exiles themselves. Thus far, little has been said concerning the subject of finances, but this question merits careful consideration. For how the radicals managed to subsist, how they obtained money while in Holland, and how they acquired the funds to buy arms and equip several ships for the attack on England are matters of considerable interest, since they cast a further light on the nature of the organization of the revolutionary movement, and especially upon the role played by its members among the class of merchants and bankers.

If, as Shaftesbury said, bankers and wealthy merchants were not prepared to man the barricades, perhaps they were willing to make a contribution to the cause in other ways. It was alleged that the radicals had planned to make a run on the bankers as one element of the Rye House conspiracy.[4] And during Monmouth's Rebellion, there was such a run, which caused a number of bankers to fail, and the bankruptcy spread "like a plague" into the countryside. As one contemporary put it, although the rebellion itself "failed to subvert the government of the nation," financially, it "did strangely shake that of this City and blasted the credit" of

[3] Cranston, p. 229n. Somerset had more Dissenters than any other county in England (James Walker, "Dissent and Republicanism after the Restoration," *Baptist Quarterly* 8, no. 5 [January 1937]:277).

[4] William R. Scott, *The Constitution and Finance of English, Scottish, and Irish Joint-Stock Companies to 1720*, 3 vols., Cambridge: Cambridge University Press, 1912, 1:305.

the bankers, and of the government.[5] "The rich men in the city of London," another observer noted, "are very discontented, and so renders trade very dead, for the men of most wealth and money there, being ill affectioned [*sic*] to the present government, keep up their money, and will not let it circulate in trade, and care not for a while to lose their interest and profit."[6] The arrest of two hundred people, including "some merchants of great note," at the time of Monmouth's Rebellion did not improve relations between members of this class and the government.[7] The point is that if most of the revolutionary action in the 1680s was carried out by artisans and laborers, there was, nevertheless, a significant reservoir of support for the radicals among the London merchants, tradesmen, and shopkeepers that could inflict considerable damage upon the Stuart government.

It is not surprising, therefore, that the latter displayed a serious interest in the financial transactions of the exiles, and it repeatedly demonstrated its willingness to inflict severe punishment against anyone it caught aiding them.[8] In these circumstances, the transmission of money from England to Holland to a political exile like Locke, for whom a warrant for arrest and extradition had been issued, was far from being a simple or innocent transaction. Such actions were necessarily endowed with a political significance and were therefore surrounded by a wall of secrecy.

That we know as much as we do concerning Locke's income during this period is due to the fact that he was a meticulous record keeper. Locke's financial transactions, as well as his movements in Holland, are with a few exceptions faithfully recorded in his journals and notebooks. Locke's personal income has never received much attention or scrutiny from scholars, possibly because of its generally modest dimensions, and because it appears to be irrelevant to a discussion of his ideas and activities. But, as we shall see, Locke not only depended personally for his well-being upon the underground network of communication the radicals in Holland established with England, he also continued to play a role in the political activities of the revolutionary movement during his six years in exile. In

[5] Scott, *Joint-Stock Companies*, 1:309–310.

[6] John Lauder, *Historical Observes of Memorable Occurrents in Church and State*, 1840, p. 232.

[7] Macaulay, 1:534.

[8] Peter Earle, *Monmouth's Rebels*, London: Weidenfeld and Nicolson, 1977, pp. 151–152; James Walker, "The English Exiles in Holland during the Reigns of Charles II and James II," *Transactions of the Royal Historical Society* 30 (1948):121–123. The government threatened Joseph Hayes with severe punishment if he did not provide information concerning the radicals' financial network (John Oldmixon, *The History of England during the Reigns of the Royal House of Stuart*, 1730, p. 689). See note 59 below.

this chapter, we shall focus upon the way in which these two dimensions of Locke's political life intersected.

Upon the death of his father, Locke inherited some small landholdings, from which he received the annual rent. The latter never amounted to much; a reasonable guess would place the figure somewhere around (and quite frequently less than) £100 per year.[9] By far, the major part of Locke's income came from the salary he received as an officeholder, and from his financial association with Shaftesbury. This income, in turn, permitted Locke to make a number of investments in various commercial enterprises, and occasionally to lend money to others at 6 percent interest.[10] Yet, when he prepared to leave the country in the summer of 1683, Shaftesbury was dead and Locke had not been an officeholder for many years. As we saw earlier, Locke drew up a will and made a number of arrangements regarding his personal belongings that suggest that he understood that his period of exile might be of rather long duration. If so, he would need a substantial sum of money to maintain his existence. Where was the money to come from?

At the time of his departure from London coincident with the discovery of the Rye House Plot, Locke entered into a financial transaction with Edward Clarke, in which the latter agreed to pay Locke an annuity of £100

[9] Cranston, p. 70. Cranston estimates Locke's annual income from his property in 1670 to be £240, but the account figures for the six months in 1669 he reproduces do not come close to adding up to half that total (pp. 114–115). In 1680, for example, the half-yearly rent from this property was approximately £33. In 1683, it was less than £32. In 1696–1697, the yearly income was less than £60 (MS c.26, fols. 67, 78; MS c.19, fol. 21). The major portion of Locke's income came from the salary he received as a civil servant in various positions, but the latter were extremely short-lived in the period before 1689. Moreover, although he was supposed to receive £800 for being secretary to the Council for Trade and Plantations in 1673–1674, there is no evidence that he actually received a penny of it (Cranston, p. 156). From approximately this same time, however, Locke purchased an annuity from Shaftesbury for £800 that guaranteed him an annual income of £100. For the period from 1673 to 1683, therefore, Fox-Bourne's figure of £200 seems a reasonable estimate of Locke's annual income (1:432).

[10] In 1673, Locke invested £400 in the raw-silk trade; the following year, he bought £400 stock in the Royal African Company, which he sold in 1675. In that year, he invested £100 in the Bahama Adventurers, and sold it in 1676 for nearly £30 profit. At the same time, he lent Lady Windham £600 at 6 percent interest (Cranston, p. 115n.; K. G. Davies, *The Royal African Company*, London: Longmans, Green, 1957, p. 65n.). Since some of these transactions represent a reemployment of Locke's original capital, it is difficult to average in the income from his banking and commercial investments on a yearly basis with his other sources of income. None of the above transactions, however, appears to have produced any income for Locke between 1680 and 1690 (since they do not show up in his account books or journals), either because he had disposed of all of his stock holdings or because he found some other way in which to employ his money.

against some property in Somerset.[11] On August 2, Locke received the semiannual rent from his property, amounting to a little more than £30.[12] On August 15, Locke sold the deed to a farm left to him by Shaftesbury to his friend Dr. Thomas for £500.[13] Ten days later, Thomas paid Locke £50, which probably represented a half-yearly payment for the bond. On August 23, he received £50 from Lady Shaftesbury as payment according to the arrangements Locke had made with the earl some years previously.[14] One or two other financial transactions probably left Clarke, who served as Locke's chief political and financial agent in England, with several hundred more pounds to find "a fit place to lodge money in."[15] Although Locke commissioned his friends to sell some of his clothing and personal belongings, there are no instructions regarding the sale or transfer of his stock or commercial investments.[16] The best guess, therefore, is that Locke departed for Holland carrying around £200 in cash or bills of exchange and secure in the knowledge that he would receive a sum slightly larger than that for the next several years.

It is not known exactly where or when Locke left England. He could not have left before August 25, since he was still receiving money from his friends on that date. He recorded his arrival in Rotterdam on September 7, which makes it very likely that he sailed from England on August 26.[17] There is a curious item noted in the *Calendar of State Papers* that might possibly have some bearing on the matter. On August 23, a John and Luke Leader, soapmakers—Mr. Keeling's friends—were granted a pass to sail for Rotterdam. The entire entry is brisk with irony. Mr. Keeling's "friends" were not leaving the country; his enemies were, and specifically, those implicated in the Rye House conspiracy. At least two of them appear to have made their escape using this pass and false identification, and one of these individuals may well have been Locke.[18] Whether he

[11] *Correspondence*, 2:598–589. This transaction with Clarke was arranged on June 12 and 13, or before Locke left London on June 14. It is the first of a series of financial arrangements designed to provide Locke with cash, and they begin just at the time of Keeling's discovery of the Rye House Plot, and before its public announcement.

[12] MS c.19, fol. 21.

[13] MS b.5, fol. 8.

[14] MS c.1, fol. 184; MS f.7, fol. 124.

[15] *Correspondence*, 2:600.

[16] *Correspondence*, 2:603.

[17] Locke arrived in Rotterdam on September 7; and, allowing for the ten-day difference in New Style and Old Style dates, plus a day in crossing, he would have had to have departed from England on August 26 or 27.

[18] *CSPD*, 26:193. Individuals often adopted aliases close to their real names; e.g., Robert Ferguson became "Roberts," and John Locke became "Johnson," "John Lynne," and "Dr. Van Linden." Hence, while the supposition that he may have been "John Leader" is only that, it is an alias within the pattern that Locke in fact followed.

used this particular alias and means of escape, Locke almost certainly did depend upon the assistance of other radicals or sympathizers in making his way to Holland. Once there, he went directly to Amsterdam where he immediately made contact with the leaders of the radical exile community in Holland.

For reasons that will be elaborated later, the English radicals in Holland had created a tightly knit community, which provided financial support, safe houses, mail drops, aliases, and a number of other survival features for its members. The English radicals also depended upon a network of Dutch sympathizers and supporters—merchants, magistrates, burghers, and ministers who shared the radicals' dissenting religious beliefs or their republican political views. As we shall see, during his six years in exile, Locke was a member of, and was perceived by others—by spies for the English government, other English radicals in exile, Dutch sympathizers with the radicals, and radicals who made visits to Holland from England during this period—to be a member of this distinctly political community. Unlike Burnet, who, on his exile from England, consciously chose not to associate himself with the English or Scottish radicals, Locke placed himself in the midst of this underground community and lived both as a participant contributing to its survival and objectives and as someone who, as an individual, was in turn dependent upon its successful functioning. In this respect, Locke's decision to reside at Thomas Dare's house, to receive his mail there, and to deposit his money in Dare's hands represented a degree of mutual trust that neither individual would have demonstrated toward the other had they not shared the same political views. For Dare, who had worked closely with Shaftesbury during the exclusion crisis before he was forced to go into exile himself, was unquestionably the leading English radical in Amsterdam.[19] He was, as was mentioned earlier, the focal point of political activity for the English radicals in Holland.

Nor was Dare an isolated contact for Locke. He also had extensive financial dealings with Israel Hayes, and his brother, Joseph Hayes, two English merchants deeply involved in the revolutionary movement as financiers of Monmouth's Rebellion.[20] Another friend of Locke was Jacob

[19] Cranston, p. 249; Charles Chenevix Trench, *The Western Rising*, London: Longmans, 1969, p. 71. Dare had been a witness to Shaftesbury's will (Haley, p. 731).

[20] On October 9, 1683, shortly after his arrival, Locke recorded a transfer of money from England through Israel Hayes, "drawn by his brother Mr. Joseph Hayes" (MS f.7, fols. 126–127; cf. ibid., fol. 158). Other transactions are recorded in MS b.1, fols. 53, 142. Lord Grey and Thomas Armstrong also received their money through Israel Hayes (Cecil Price, *Cold Caleb: The Scandalous Life of Ford Grey*, London: Andrew Melrose, 1956, p. 139). Ferguson frequently stayed in Hayes' house (James Walker, "English Exiles," pp. 121–124).

Vandervelde, a bookseller in Amsterdam. Vandervelde's bookshop was the central place of information for the English radicals, where they frequently gathered, both publicly and secretly—and were watched by English spies—to receive the latest news from England, to buy pamphlets smuggled into Holland, and to draft plans for political action.[21] Several months after his arrival in Amsterdam, Locke exchanged residences with another English radical, John Wilmore, who had served as the foreman of the jury at the London trial of Stephen College, and who now lived, as did Locke, as a fugitive from the English government.[22] Early in December 1683, Locke executed a financial transaction with Israel Hayes through John Nisbet, one of those deeply involved in the Rye House conspiracy, whose name appears on several lists of the most dangerous radicals wanted by the English government.[23] The names of other radical exiles or Dutch supporters will emerge as the story proceeds, but enough has been said, I think, to indicate that Locke decided at the outset of his sojourn in Holland to plant himself firmly in the center of an already organized, secretive, and politically active community, and he, in turn, was accepted without question by them as a bona fide member of that community.

Locke not only placed himself in the hands of the radical exiles, he also placed a rather extraordinary sum of money in their hands. On October 5, 1683, Locke received approximately £100 that he had left in the care of a woman in London named Rabsy-Smithsby to whom he had entrusted some of his goods and papers upon leaving England. Mrs. Smithsby paid the money to Edward Clarke, who sent the bill of exchange to Locke drawn against Israel Hayes. This money seems well accounted for in the notes in Locke's journals made before his departure, and in his correspondence with Clarke. What is slightly more puzzling is the £300 Clarke paid to Joseph Hayes to Locke's credit, mentioned in the same notation in

[21] Vandervelde was "a notorious bookseller for the rebels' interest who harbored Argyle" (Add. MS 41818, fols. 79, 229; Cranston, p. 235). Locke sometimes stayed with Vandervelde (Add. MS 41817, fol. 218; MS f.8, fol. 98).

[22] MS f.7, fol. 142. On May 1, 1684, Locke paid Wilmore "for the use of his bed" (MS f.8, fol. 72). In Locke's library catalog there is a curious listing of John Wilmer, *Legacy* (*LL* #3167). Since neither Wing nor any other source lists Wilmer (or Wilmore) as having written anything, this reference is more likely to a legacy left to Locke in Wilmore's will, a copy of which he may have owned. Another name that appears in Locke's journal is that of Samuel Harris. Locke lent him money and engaged in other financial transactions with him (MS f.8, fols. 232–233). Wilmore, Harris, and John Starkey, another of Locke's associates in Holland, had been part of Shaftesbury's entourage helping with popish plot witnesses and the distribution of exclusion tracts (PRO 30/24/43/63). Harris and Starkey had been close friends of Stephen College. As Skelton's double agent put it, Harris was "a very dangerous man . . . [and] a strong republican, willing to die for his principles. He is an associate of Major Wildman" (Add. MS 41819, fol. 60).

[23] MS f.7, fol. 158; James Walker, "English Exiles," p. 112.

Locke's journal.[24] This could be the sum of money Locke had left in Clarke's care to be conveyed to him through some safe means, or it could represent Clarke's payment of the annuity agreement he and Locke had drafted. Two weeks later, however, Locke received from Clarke, by way of Mrs. Percival, £310, as well as a bill drawn on Henry Daems by Mr. Denew for £360. In other words, less than two months after his escape from England, Locke had received, and deposited with Thomas Dare, nearly a thousand pounds. It does not require a degree in mathematics to recognize that this total far exceeds the carefully noted (by Locke) financial arrangements concluded during the summer of 1683. The £360 is an especially suspicious figure, but it is not, as will become apparent, the only questionable entry in Locke's financial records. This money, Locke notes, was transferred to Dare, "which he credited in Bank."[25] Although the origins of these funds remain obscure, it is possible that this money may have been deposited by Shaftesbury with various individuals he trusted, of whom Clarke, an executor of his estate, and Peter Percival, his banker, not to mention Locke himself, must be at the top of the list.[26] According to several participants in the Rye House conspiracy, during 1682–1683 sums of money were deposited in the hands of various individuals for safekeeping and the procurement of needed supplies, and the Duke of Monmouth had, in particular, advocated the establishment of a "common bank" for the projected revolution.[27] In light of the fact that Monmouth's own banking arrangements were conducted with Percival in London and Thomas Dare in Amsterdam, and the fact that the latter sailed with and served as paymaster for the invasion force, it is not unreasonable to suggest that some of the money mentioned above formed part of the funds that had been collected by the radicals for the execution of the Rye House

[24] MS b.1, fol. 53. The date of the last transaction is October 19, 1683.

[25] Several of these bills of exchange were made out to and signed by Locke's pseudonym, "John Lynne" (MS b.1, fol. 53). Henry Daems was the agent for the Royal African Company in Amsterdam (Davies, *Royal African Company*, p. 175).

[26] We have no accounting of what happened to the several thousand pounds Shaftesbury borrowed from friends and business associates between May 20 and September 30, 1682 (Haley, p. 725), though some of it, as was noted in Chapter 8 above, was deposited with Ferguson, Charlton, and Goodenough. The sums mentioned in these cases, however, do not come close to approximating the total amount of cash raised by Shaftesbury; and Locke, Percival, and Clarke are among the most likely repositories of the remainder of this cash.

[27] Elizabeth D'Oyley, *James, Duke of Monmouth*, London: Geoffrey Bles, 1938, p. 214. Slingsby Bethel, for example, had given Henry Cornish, Charles Bateman, and Major Wildman each £500 to hold for him and the cause (Add. MS 41818, fol. 185). It was alleged in discussions among the radicals in Holland that Cornish's decision to keep the money and his refusal to contribute it to the financing of the revolution provoked Colonel Rumsey and others to testify that Cornish had been present at the meeting at Shepherd's house, which, in turn, led to Cornish's execution.

conspiracy, and that it was being transferred to Locke and through him to Thomas Dare to be used for its original purpose, should the occasion arise. Since we shall later have to take up the accusation that Locke contributed a substantial sum of money toward the equipage of Monmouth's Rebellion, it may be well to keep in mind that, from the time of his initial arrival in Holland, Locke had access to a very large amount of cash, not all of which may have belonged to him personally.[28]

At the end of November, Locke wrote a canting letter to Clarke requesting some news regarding the Rye House trials and any plans with respect to pursuing a policy of political resistance to Charles II's government. After making apologies for the "blunt confidence I have troubled you [with] in my affairs," Locke asks Clarke to "reflect upon my former letters" from which he will understand "the reasons that made it almost necessary for me to write to you in such a style." Having given this signal for the "style" of the cant that follows—which Locke had employed in his letters to Clarke the previous February and March—he writes:

> I could hold no longer, and I must tell you again I am in pain till I hear from you. I know that the painful hour must by this time have overtaken your Lady, and I long to hear that 'tis safely over: when you assure me of that, and that she and you and the little ones are well, I shall be at rest and be at much more ease than I am at present.

It is in this letter that Locke mentions "Roberts and Sheldate," and inquires whether the "Lady" "had still any business here" that Locke might carry out; "the person Roberts talked so simply of is ready to serve her." Since we know "Roberts" to be Ferguson, the latter's recommendation of Locke's service speaks volumes on the subject of Locke's political commitment. Locke adds that "if there be any occasion still, and she thinks still to employ him," he is willing to undertake the task, though he asks that it be kept private "even from Mr. Sheldate."[29] The "Lady" is the common name radicals applied to Monmouth, and apart from

[28] Based upon his estimate of Locke's annual income (see note 9 above), Fox-Bourne argued that it was "preposterous" to assume that Locke could have contributed several hundred pounds toward the expeditions of Argyll or Monmouth; had he done so, Fox-Bourne wrote, Locke would "have been reduced to poverty" (2:20). Given what Fox-Bourne knew about Locke's finances, this was not an unreasonable conclusion for him to draw, but in light of Locke's notations in his journals (to which Fox-Bourne did not have access), the basis for the objection can no longer stand. See note 72 below.

[29] *Correspondence*, 2:605. Locke notes that he wrote in his letter "about the middle of October" (lost) an answer to Clarke's advice "concerning Roberts and Sheldate," a letter that also has not survived. Hence, not only is there further missing correspondence discussing Roberts and Sheldate, but Clarke clearly knew Ferguson to be Roberts, a piece of information known only to the inner circle of radicals around Ferguson.

Locke's clarification of his own willingness to remain true to the cause, the general question being raised is whether Monmouth still has any "business" to pursue that involves the English radicals in Holland. That is, as Shepherd explained, whether the revolution as a project was still going forward. This was a crucial question precisely at this time because rumors were floating about that Monmouth, having confessed his part in the conspiracy, had been reconciled with his father and had been granted a pardon from the king—which, in fact, did occur at the end of November.[30] At the same time, Sidney was on trial for his life, an event that the exiles doubtless followed with great interest.[31] The question, therefore, was whether their leader had abandoned them to their fate by forsaking the revolution. At approximately the same time as Locke's letter, Ferguson wrote a letter to Monmouth, which the government intercepted. We do not know the contents of the letter, but since Monmouth himself characterized it as something that counted more in his favor than against him, and thus was likely to produce a favorable effect upon the king in deciding whether to grant him a pardon, it may very well be that Ferguson was berating Monmouth for not being active enough in the pursuit of the cause.[32]

Locke asked Clarke to retrieve from "Mr. Smith's hands" a work left in his custody, namely, the *Tractatus de morbo Gallico*, "for I have heard it commended and shall apply myself close to the study of physic by the fireside this winter." This appears to be a blind, and the *Tractatus* was almost certainly a draft of the *Two Treatises*. We cannot be sure that Clarke did send it, but in December Locke bought three quires of paper, which suggests that he was planning to write something.[33]

In view of the fact that the winter of 1683 was a relatively quiet period in Locke's political life, it seems appropriate to consider here the broader

[30] Add. MS 4159, fol. 81; *CSPD*, 26:108–109. As one government official observed at the end of November 1683, the Whigs did not know what to make of Monmouth's reconciliation with the king (Add. MS 28875, fol. 301). This reconciliation was short-lived, however, and two weeks later, Monmouth was in disgrace for having demanded back from the king his letter confessing his part in the Rye House conspiracy (fol. 311).

[31] As a measure of this interest, Sidney's paper given to the sheriff at the time of his execution was first printed in Holland, where it was widely read. Copies of it were smuggled into England, and it was such a notorious underground document that the government decided to have it printed (James Walker, "English Exiles," p. 124). As James explained in a letter to William, noting that the latter had already read Sidney's paper, although "it was a very treasonable and insolent [document], yet 'twas thought fit to have it printed, that the world might see what his principles were, and what he and the rest of the conspirators drove at" (Dalrymple, vol. 1, pt. 1, bk. 1, p. 117).

[32] James Welwood, *Memoirs of the Most Material Transactions in England for the Last Hundred Years*, 1700, p. 374.

[33] *Correspondence*, 2:606; MS f.7, fol. 163.

question of the nature of the political environment for English exiles living in Holland before discussing the way in which Locke fulfilled his pledge to be of "service" to Monmouth during 1684–1685. For Locke's political activities as a participant in the planning of Monmouth's Rebellion need to be understood not only within the context of the general conditions governing the political lives of the exiled radicals, but also with reference to the body of evidence that both describes that context and specifically details Locke's place within it.

Throughout the seventeenth century, Holland served as a place of refuge for English political and religious dissidents. From the 1680s, however, there was a constant stream of refugees flowing across the North Sea channel, and the number of exiles increased dramatically following the discovery of the Rye House Plot.[34] The English government, acting through its official and unofficial agents in Holland, attempted to maintain surveillance upon the activities of the most dangerous of these individuals, and generally, to gather intelligence that would prove useful in determining what kinds of links these exiles maintained with various dissidents living in England. This endeavor likewise took on an increased urgency after 1683, not only because of the concentration of numbers of English and Scottish radicals in the Dutch Republic, but also because most of them were deeply committed ideologically to armed resistance against Charles II and the Duke of York. They were dangerous men, and the English government not only wanted them watched, it instructed its agents to capture these individuals, by whatever means possible, and return them to England to face trial and execution as outlaws or traitors. These increased demands fell primarily upon the English envoy in Holland whose unenviable task it was to try to carry them out in the face of tremendous hostility and resistance from the local Dutch magistrates and general populace who, on the whole, shared a sympathetic outlook with the exiles. The envoy's only possible chance of success depended upon his being able to develop an espionage network that could penetrate the radical organization and provide him with the kind of specific intelligence that would be required to crack down on the propaganda and financial activities of the exiles, or to arrest particular individuals for extradition to England.

Thomas Chudleigh and his successor, Bevil Skelton, created an effective intelligence system, using paid informers, double agents, and occasionally, the local authorities, which placed serious constraints upon the

[34] During the 1680s, the English consul in Amsterdam wrote to Jenkins that "if the English tumble over so as they do now, this may be a little London in time" (Emerson, *Monmouth's Rebellion*, p. 1; James Walker, "English Exiles," pp. 111–125).

movement, communication, and political effectiveness of the radicals. Skelton's intelligence was particularly impressive, since much of it was supplied by a very highly placed and well-informed double agent. The political responsibility for destroying or neutralizing the effectiveness of the revolutionary movement in Holland clearly outweighed all others, so far as both the English government and Chudleigh and Skelton were concerned. Skelton, especially, made it his preoccupation—even a personal obsession—to capture Ferguson and, generally, to subject the English exiles to continuous harassment. It was not only the elusiveness of Ferguson about which Skelton complained to his superiors; he also felt the burden of the seemingly endless reports on the exiles' activities that he was forced to submit to the Secretary of State.[35] Between 1683 and 1686, the envoy in Holland dispatched reports to England on the average of three times a week. These letters are filled with intelligence information on the radicals in Holland. Sometimes the report is a summary of the information the envoy has received from his various informants; very often, copies of the information from these individuals as sent to the envoy are included as enclosures accompanying his own report. There is, in other words, a rather large body of detailed evidence pertaining to the political activities of the English and Scottish radicals in Holland. Although these manuscripts were deposited in the British Museum more than sixty years ago, relatively little use has been made of them by historians, and none at all by Locke scholars. Neither Cranston, Laslett, nor the editor of the Locke correspondence consulted these manuscripts. As we shall see, they contain a number of reports on Locke that confirm his membership in the radical community.

On September 14, 1683, Lord Sunderland wrote to Chudleigh,

> His Majesty commands me to signify to you that he would have you find out some discreet person who knows Sir Thomas Armstrong and Ferguson by sight, but is unknown to them and send him privately to Cleves to get what information he can about such of the conspirators who . . . are or have been lately there.

Chudleigh was also directed to "get very particular information (if you can)" as to who was with Lord Grey and Monmouth, and what their plans were.[36] Two months later, Chudleigh received a more blunt directive

[35] "I am so tired with sitting up and writing every day and every night of late, not having had time almost to ease or sleep that I scarcely know what I have said" (Add. MS 41812, fol. 106).

[36] Add. MS 61651, fol. 7.

from Sunderland "to discover and seize them" (Ferguson and Armstrong), an order that was repeated several weeks later.[37]

In addition to its desire to prevent any further political initiatives launched against England from Holland, one reason the government desperately needed to capture someone like Ferguson or Armstrong was that at the end of November 1683, a number of individuals—Charlton, Wildman, Brandon, Trenchard, Hampden—were being held in prison awaiting trial, but the government lacked sufficient evidence to prosecute them. Moreover, it was caught in a bind, since it could not afford to have one of these prisoners die in captivity, as another "suicide," with the kind of attendant criticism and publicity as had accompanied the death of Essex.[38] Neither could the government afford to proceed with a trial that twisted the law of treason as it had done in Sidney's case. Despite his extreme republican views, Sidney's trial had generated widespread criticism, and added measurably to the unpopularity of the government.[39] In other words, if it did not very quickly come up with another key witness whose testimony could be used to prosecute the prisoners still in its custody, the government would be forced to release them. Naturally it wanted Ferguson or Armstrong, who had detailed knowledge of all the aspects of the conspiracy, but it was willing to make deals with lesser figures. In October, Chudleigh was instructed to offer a pardon to Sir John Cochrane in exchange for the information he could provide regarding the Rye House conspiracy.[40] Cochrane was one of the leaders of the Scottish contingent and had from the beginning worked closely with Shaftesbury in his negotiations with the Earl of Argyll in drafting plans for the insurrection. Cochrane, however, proved unreceptive to this offer. Others were less sanguine about offering their services to the government. At the end of November, Ezekiel Everest, a former official in the Customs

[37] Add. MS 61651, fols. 10, 12. On January 15, 1684, Sunderland told Chudleigh, You are "to employ your utmost endeavors to have them secured and sent over in safe custody" (MS Rawlinson A 266, fol. 32).

[38] By the end of October 1683, the government was having such difficulty finding witnesses that Charles II conceded that "all the prisoners in the Tower must be discharged, for there was but one witness against them" (Lacey, p. 161). For a further discussion of this point, see Doreen J. Milne, *The Rye House Plot, with Special Reference to Its Place in the Exclusion Contest and Its Consequences Till 1685*, Ph.D. diss., University of London, 1949, pp. 192–193.

[39] Sidney's trial was "universally cried out on, as a piece of most enormous injustice" (Burnet, 2:403). Evelyn also thought Sidney had been given a "very hard measure" in his trial (John Evelyn, *The Diary of John Evelyn*, ed. E. S. De Beer, 6 vols., Oxford: Clarendon Press, 1955, 4:353; cf. Dalrymple, vol. 1, pt. 1, bk. 1, p. 55).

[40] Add. MS 41809, fols. 140ff.; MS Rawlinson A 266, fol. 29; Milne, *Rye House Plot*, p. 193. Cochrane was the person Aaron Smith had been dispatched by the Council of Six to see (Add. MS 38847, fol. 98).

House, wrote to Secretary Jenkins requesting a pardon in exchange for his testimony as an informer. Everest was far too obscure an individual to have had access to the kind of important information the government needed, a fact of which Jenkins was probably aware. Nevertheless, the reply was favorable, and it is interesting because it reveals something of the government's feelings of exasperation and desperation with respect to its endeavors to gather the legal evidence that would support what it suspected or knew about the conspiracy. Jenkins wrote to Everest:

> I laid your letter of 29 November at Rotterdam before his Majesty, whose answer was that he had not the fruit he expected from scarce any of the pardons he has granted, yet, in regard you have been formerly in his service, he gave me leave to assure you, you shall have his pardon of all misdemeanors you confess or can imagine yourself to be guilty of, but he expects you to do what you promise, that is to discover truly and fully what you know of the conspiracy and of every one concerned in it.[41]

Everest may not have known much concerning the conspiracy, although we shall have to return to this point later since his testimony has a bearing on our discussion of Locke's activities, but he performed a useful service for Chudleigh in Holland as an intelligence source reporting on the activities of the exiles.

Besides Chudleigh, James Hodgson, the English consul in Rotterdam, sometimes submitted his own reports on the radicals to Jenkins. In December, he sent the latter a list of fanatics and enemies that included the names of Benjamin Furley, John Nisbet, Israel Hayes, and Abraham Keck.[42] Furley, Hayes, and Keck were resident merchants assisting the exiles. Shaftesbury and Ferguson had stayed in Keck's house when the earl fled to Holland, and Keck was also instrumental in securing the status of burghers of Amsterdam for many of the radicals.[43] By this means, the individual attained a certain legal status that gave him the protection of the law and the local magistrates, thereby making it more difficult for the English government to institute proceedings against him. Locke, and many others, took advantage of this protection by becoming burghers.[44]

[41] *CSPD*, 26:136.

[42] Add. MS 41811, fol. 119.

[43] Shaftesbury and Ferguson became burghers of Amsterdam (W. D. Christie, *A Life of Anthony Ashley Cooper, First Earl of Shaftesbury*, 2 vols., 1871, 2:452; *Ferguson*, p. 92; F. A. Middlebush, ed., *The Dispatches of Thomas Plott and Thomas Chudleigh*, The Hague: M. Nijhoff, 1926, p. 195). Chudleigh sent Whitehall a list of radicals who became burghers of Amsterdam through the assistance of Abraham Keck (Add. MS 41809, fol. 206; Add. MS 41811, fol. 121).

[44] James Walker, "English Exiles," p. 118.

Aside from reports on the movements of Monmouth, Grey, Armstrong, Ferguson, and others, little political information was gathered during the winter of 1683 regarding the plans of the exiles, and this very likely is due to the fact that they had not formulated a specific course of action rather than to poor intelligence on the part of the authorities. Monmouth was again in favor with Charles; he was romantically involved with Henrietta (Lady Wentworth); and he seemingly had abandoned all plans for leading a revolution. The Scots, however, had not given up their revolutionary objectives. In December 1683, they held meetings in Utrecht to formulate plans for a rebellion led by the Earl of Argyll.[45] Argyll gathered around him a number of the English radicals, and by spring 1684, they were working on a modified version of the original plan of attack drafted by Shaftesbury.[46] During the period he was in hiding in London, Argyll had become good friends with Mrs. Smith, wife of a wealthy sugar-baker.[47] Mrs. Smith was an active political and financial supporter of the revolutionary movement. According to Nathaniel Wade, he received a letter in April 1684 from John Ayloffe in Utrecht—where Argyll and Mrs. Smith were residing—informing him of the planned invasion, and asking him to use his influence on Edmund Ludlow, with whom Wade was then staying in Switzerland, to persuade the general to come to Holland to assist in the undertaking. Instead, either on his own or as an emissary from Ludlow, Wade himself went to Holland in May, and conferred with the exiles in Utrecht.[48] Among those who were working closely with Argyll were Ferguson and Goodenough.[49]

[45] Sprat, appendix, pp. 122–124.

[46] John Willcock, *A Scots Earl in Covenanting Times: Being the Life and Times of Archibald the 9th Earl of Argyll*, Edinburgh: Andrew Elliot, 1907, p. 327; *Ferguson*, pp. 196–197; John Erskine, *Journal of Hon. John Erskine of Carnock, 1683–1687*, 1893, p. 179. Emerson notes Argyll's planning, but underestimates the support he received from the English radicals (*Monmouth's Rebellion*, p. 7).

[47] Mrs. Smith had provided a safe house for Argyll and other Scotsmen in London during 1682 through a network of old Commonwealth officers and radicals, which she appears to have directed. When the Rye House Plot was discovered, she convinced her husband to move to Holland in 1683, and thereafter she and Argyll lived together in Utrecht (*Memoirs of William Veitch and George Brysson*, 1825, pp. 136–137, 146). Mr. Smith died a few months after their arrival in Holland, leaving her a wealthy widow. His estate was estimated at £40,000 (Charles Wilson, *England's Apprenticeship, 1603–1763*, London: Longman, 1965, pp. 200–201).

[48] Harleian MS 6845, fol. 269.

[49] *Ferguson*, pp. 196–197; Emerson, *Monmouth's Rebellion*, p. 75. In the Bodleian Library, there is a diary (1684–1697) that provides a good illustration of the frequency of social contact among Macclesfield, Aaron Smith, Shepherd, Wharton, Wildman, Charlton, Yonge, Brandon, and others, and their communication with Keck in Holland during 1684 (MS English History C.711, fols. 5–22). The author of the diary, a Mr. Whitley, was prob-

Sometime around the beginning of May, there was a general gathering of radicals in Utrecht to discuss Argyll's plan. As Chudleigh noted in one of his dispatches, because there were so many rebels in the city, he had gone to Utrecht. And despite verbal promises from the local magistrates, and the opportunity to catch Ferguson and Goodenough, Chudleigh received no assistance from the authorities. But, he reported, the radicals "have bought up lately in a clandestine manner considerable numbers of ordinary arms fit only for common soldiers," and they have had several meetings and seem very busy of late, "as if some great matter were in agitation." He recommended that an especially close watch be kept on all passengers sailing from Scotland to Holland.[50]

In early May, Argyll and James Stewart went to Amsterdam to purchase arms for the rebellion, and to confer with the English radicals there.[51] It was just at this time that Monmouth and Grey learned of Argyll's planned invasion, though neither appears to have been too forward in involving himself in the undertaking.[52] Armstrong was sent to Brussels to persuade Monmouth to rejoin his comrades in arms.[53] Ayloffe was sent to London to try to raise money, but he returned to Holland without success.[54] Cochrane and other emissaries were sent to obtain promises of assistance from various European governments, but they, too, failed.[55] Reports from Scotland were also not encouraging, not least because the English government had gotten wind of the planned invasion and had arrested a number of suspicious individuals in Scotland.[56] As a consequence of these discouraging reports, the radicals decided to postpone until the following spring the rebellion that had originally been planned for the end of the summer of 1684.[57] This was only a temporary setback for the

ably Colonel Roger Whitley, in whose house more than fifty muskets were found during the searches conducted following the discovery of the Rye House Plot (*CSPD*, 25:294).

[50] Add. MS 41810, fols. 59–60.

[51] Erskine, *Journal*, p. 179.

[52] *Secret History*, pp. 79–80; Emerson, *Monmouth's Rebellion*, p. 75.

[53] Armstrong was accompanied by Henry Booth (Add. MS 41810, fol. 63; *Secret History*, pp. 81–82).

[54] Harleian MS 6845, fol. 269.

[55] Richard and Francis Goodenough went to Flanders (Add. MS 41810, fols. 60, 69; Add. MS 41811, fol. 226).

[56] Harleian MS 6845, fol. 269; Willcock, *Scots Earl*, pp. 327–328. An intelligence report in July 1684 indicated that the radicals in Utrecht were discouraged by the reports of their emissaries returning from Scotland, due to the arrests and their failure to gain financial support for the rebellion (Add. MS 41811, fol. 226).

[57] As Wade put it, preparations for the spring were undertaken "with very great privacy, because it had been observed that the last intended expedition had been talked of in London and that about the time it was intended, the King had appointed a rendezvous of his English

radicals who decided both to exercise greater caution in the disclosure of their plans, and also to lay them more broadly in order to enlist the aid of all those disaffected with Charles' government. Thus, while the invasion itself was postponed, the planning meetings continued throughout 1684.

Meanwhile, Chudleigh was in no position to ignore either the steady pressure or the specific directive from the English government for the seizure of Ferguson or Armstrong. With the help of Everest and some other spies, Chudleigh managed to capture the latter, shortly after his return to Holland from Brussels. Chudleigh placed Armstrong under heavy guard, and quickly put him aboard the yacht *Catherine*. These measures were necessary, Chudleigh wrote, because the people here "are much incensed at this seizure, as being against the ancient rules and practice of their country." Inhabitants of Rotterdam openly declared that if the seizure had taken place there, the people would have rescued the prisoner themselves. Even so, one hundred seamen volunteered to rescue Armstrong after he had been put on the yacht bound for England, if the magistrates of Rotterdam would give their approval to the rescue. In any event, under an armed guard of thirty-five men, Chudleigh sent Armstrong back to England where he was summarily executed as an outlaw, without benefit of a trial.

Chudleigh advised the Secretary of State that he should not count on a confession from Armstrong, since he was likely to persevere to the end in the manner of Sidney. Although this proved to be the case, the envoy had confiscated some letters and papers carried by Armstrong at the time of his arrest, which were forwarded to England, and which, Chudleigh believed, would throw considerable light on the late plot.[58] Among other things, these letters detailed financial transactions between Joseph Hayes in London and his brother Israel Hayes in Amsterdam, on the basis of which, the former was arrested and brought to trial for "high treason."[59] The government subjected Hayes to threats and intensive interrogation in order to discover the financial connections of the exiles in Holland. These efforts appear to have been unsuccessful, and Hayes was acquitted by the jury, to the great consternation of presiding Judge Jeffreys.[60] Nonetheless, the information in Armstrong's papers probably did provide confirmation of the fact that the radicals "designed to come for Eng-

---

forces near London and had caused several people in Scotland to be taken up and examined upon oath if they knew of any rebels or of any correspondence with my Lord Argyle" (Harleian MS 6845, fol. 269).

58 Add. MS 41810, fols. 92–97.

59 *CSPD*, 27:61–62. Burnet gives an account of Hayes' arrest and trail (2:445–446).

60 Oldmixon, *History*, p. 689.

land."[61] They also intensified the government's determination to break the financial links between the dissidents in England and Holland.

In February 1684, Locke added a postscript for Edward Clarke to a letter he had written to Mrs. Clarke that suggested that Locke might be in England "next summer," that is, at the time of the projected invasion, as the plans were then developing under Argyll's direction.[62] In mid-March, Locke sent Clarke a report on the progress (or lack of it) of the planning meetings for the rebellion. He alerted Clarke with the phrase, "if I should contrary to my custom write news," which indicated the ironic intent of the message (that is, the passages should be read "contrary" to Locke's "customary" position). He informs Clarke that

> People are writing against one another as hot as may be, and there are every day pamphlets published here that deserve as well to be burnt as the *History of the Growth of Popery*, or *No Protestant Plot*, or the like . . . Tares and divisions sowing everywhere, and methinks the tares take root and spread apace.

Since Locke decidedly did *not* believe at any time in his life that either Andrew Marvell's work or the tract that was a defense of Shaftesbury's position should be burned, it is absurd to read this letter as a literal communication on Locke's part addressed to someone who, after all, was a radical like him and who had also been one of Shaftesbury's staunchest supporters.[63] Locke adds a cryptic sentence concerning the "defence of Christendom against the great event of war with the Turk." As the references in the *Two Treatises* and also the language employed by the radicals in their communication with one another make clear, "the Turk" is a referential symbol for absolute monarchy, and therefore applicable to Charles II's (or James') administration.[64]

Locke tells Clarke that since his last letter, he has "inquired most particularly of a very skilful man concerning abele and lime trees. He tells me of the abele trees there is but one sort, and in them you cannot be mistaken. Of lime trees there be two sorts, but the best is that which they

[61] *CSPD*, 27:177.

[62] *Correspondence*, 2:609.

[63] *Correspondence*, 2:612. As De Beer does, for example.

[64] In *Julian the Apostate*, 1682, p. viii, for example, Samuel Johnson condemned the "Turkish doctrine" of complete submission to absolute monarchy. In his prison conversation with Burnet and Tillotson, Russell told the latter that if the English government was as absolutist as they had portrayed it, then he could see no difference between "a legal and a Turkish constitution" (Laurence Echerd, *The History of England*, 1720, p. 1034). In the *First Treatise* (par. 33), Locke identifies "the Turkish government" with absolute monarchy, and in the *Second Treatise* (par. 192), he refers to the "Turkish yoke" of "tyranny."

call the female lime tree." The "abele" trees whose intentions and convictions are not to be doubted are the Scots, while "the female lime tree" is Monmouth himself, the perennial "Lady" of the revolution. Locke reflects upon the fact that he is writing to his friend "of those innocent designs of building houses and planning walks: the latter is my theme at present." He has already referred in a previous letter to a "walk" next summer, and later letters make reference to a "walk" in the spring, or the postponed date of Argyll's revolution.[65] It is precisely the "planning" of "walks" ("revolution") that is the main theme of Locke's letter. The Earl of Argyll was widely known as an individual who was especially skillful and preoccupied with the planting of trees and the planning of walks. He had devoted considerable energy to these pursuits, even soliciting the advice of John Evelyn, who was one of the greatest experts on the subject.[66]

In April and May, or shortly after this letter was written, Chudleigh, through his spies, reported to the English government that messengers were being sent secretly to England, Scotland, and European countries on missions relating to "some great matter," which, as we know, concerned obtaining promises of political and financial support for Argyll's invasion.[67] In his dispatch of May 16, Chudleigh mentions Ayloffe, Ferguson, "the widow Smith," Thomas Dare, and the two Goodenough brothers, Richard and Francis, as being involved in the planning meetings in Amsterdam and Utrecht.[68]

Locke, it was later alleged, contributed several hundred pounds to buy arms and ships for Argyll's invasion, and if, as I believe, this charge should be kept distinct from the one that named him as a contributor to Monmouth's Rebellion, it may relate to some rather curious and interesting financial notations that Locke recorded in his journal during the very period the radicals were purchasing arms.[69] Locke's financial trans-

[65] *Correspondence*, 2:613.

[66] Willcock, *Scots Earl*, pp. 152–153. Argyll had visited Evelyn to see his garden in 1662 (Evelyn, *Diary*, 3:318). The tree metaphor was a commonly used reference to Argyll among the radicals. In Carstares' letters, his code name is "forrest," and in other letters he is "Mr. Birch" (*State Papers and Letters Addressed to William Carstares*, 1774, p. 108; D'Oyley, *Monmouth*, p. 215; an abele is a white poplar.

[67] Add. MS 41810, fol. 60.

[68] Add. MS 41810, fol. 69.

[69] Even those (e.g., Roberts) who have taken seriously the testimony of Wade, Grey, and others that Locke contributed funds to support Monmouth's Rebellion have not distinguished between the references to Argyll and those to Monmouth. Yet, both Wade and Grey's testimony and the evidence clearly show that they are speaking of *two* distinct enterprises: Argyll's rebellion, which was planned and equipped initially between March and May 1684, and Monmouth's Rebellion, a year later. Hence, there are two distinguishable periods of financial contribution, with different amounts given, and they correspond, as I have argued, to the periods of large money transfers recorded in Locke's notebooks.

actions with Dare or Israel Hayes that relate to his personal expenditures are always expressed in guilders and are in modest amounts, designed to carry him through periods of one to three weeks, which is the frequency with which he records a transaction with either individual. There is, in other words, a pattern established in Locke's notations, relating to frequency and amount of money. This pattern is occasionally interrupted by transfers of large amounts (£100 or more) of money in pounds, which sometimes represent credit transfers on Locke's behalf from England for his maintenance, but which on other occasions look suspiciously like money being funneled through Locke to pseudonymous individuals for political purposes. Thus, on March 20, 1684, Locke notes that he received 100 guilders from Hayes. On the following day, he received a note to pay £100 to Thomas Dare on behalf of "Madame the widow" of Daval and Company, "merchants in London."[70] And, on April 7, there is another notation of a bill on "the Widow Daval & Company" for £200. Locke records on April 8 that he has "writ off" in the "bank" that amount of money in "the account of Mr. Dare."[71] This seems to indicate that Dare is keeping two accounts for Locke, one for his personal expenses, and another as trustee for the radical organization, as its banker. The transfers on behalf of the Widow Daval are "writ off" from the funds in the latter account.[72] These transactions are distinct from those of March 29, when Hayes paid Locke 150 guilders, and April 27, when he gave him another

[70] This bill of exchange was endorsed by Dare to Peter Percival, and sent with instructions to Percival to place it in Clarke's account (MS f.8, fols. 37–38).

[71] MS b.1, fol. 54. In his journal, Locke records on April 7, 1684, "pay to Thomas Dare £200," with a notation of Madam Widow Davall and Company, with the amount given in guilders, which would seem to indicate that the bill had been cashed to be spent in Holland (MS f.8, fol. 56).

[72] In justification of this assertion, it could be said that Fox-Bourne's assumption must be reversed; that is, Locke was in possession of so much cash that it could not possibly have been consumed in his *personal* expenditures, of which he kept a minute account, during his period of exile (see note 73 below). And, of course, he kept receiving money from England throughout the six-year period he was in Holland. This, in itself, was a risky and foolish enterprise unless he needed the money for some purpose, for it could easily have accumulated interest in England in safe hands. Yet, even with his book buying, based upon his notations for rent and other living expenses, it is doubtful that Locke spent on himself in the entire six years as much as the thousand pounds he had in his possession in the first two months of his exile. Moreover, between October 1683 and May 1685, Locke received between £1,500 and £2,000. Hence the question, How did this money get spent? It is curious, to say the least, that almost all of these suspicious financial transfers occur in the period prior to Monmouth's Rebellion, giving Locke between 1683 and 1685 this extraordinary amount of cash. In his own accounting to Clarke for the money he received during this period, Locke seems particularly concerned with £800 that passed through Clarke and Percival (*Correspondence*, 3:107, 119). Was this the amount Shaftesbury had deposited with Clarke for the cause?

200 guilders.[73] If "the Widow Daval & Company" are widow Smith and the radicals around Argyll, then the £300 recorded here during the three-week period of March through April, does indeed represent a contribution to Argyll's planned expedition.

In addition to these financial transactions, Locke's journal during this period contains other items of interest. In December, for example, John Nisbet's name appears as someone associated with Locke.[74] Besides being one of those involved in the assassination plan, Nisbet had been a key liaison figure between the English and Scottish conspirators.[75] The appearance of his name just at the time when those lines of communication were being reopened by Argyll is an interesting bit of information. On May 1, Locke paid John Wilmore "for the use of his bed." On that same day, there is a reference to Daniel Le Blon.[76] Wilmore and Le Blon were two of the radicals in Amsterdam Argyll enlisted for his cause, and both appear to have been involved in purchasing arms for the projected rebellion. On May 12, during or just after Argyll's visit to Amsterdam, Locke made a brief trip to Haarlem, returning to Amsterdam three days later. The purpose of this trip is not known, but between May 15 and August 15, Locke's whereabouts in Holland became extremely secretive and mysterious, even by his normally cautious standards. For three months, there is no indication in his journals where he is or what he is doing. It was just at this time that Ayloffe, Cochrane, Armstrong, and others were sent on various missions to raise support for Argyll. There is only one surviving letter from Locke to Edward Clarke (July 19) during this period, and from the text, it is apparent that Clarke's previous letter of June 17 (lost) was not answered by Locke, and this is a reply to Clarke's letter of July 1. Locke thanks Clarke for "the hamper of wine" sent on the same day. More important, and perhaps identical with the "wine," Locke records in his journal the receipt from Clarke of £100.[77] He writes:

[73] MS b.1, fol. 53. A reasonable calculation, based upon his journal notations, would be that Locke's living expenses in Holland averaged £10–15 a month.

[74] MS f.7, fol. 158. Nisbet is the middleman in the conveyance of bills of exchange and cash between Locke and Israel Hayes, but it appears that it was Locke who sent Nisbet to Hayes to act as his agent.

[75] In addition to the intercepted letter from Nisbet about the assassination cited previously, he had written about the general insurrection in February 1683. This letter was read to a meeting of Scottish dissidents (Michael Shields, *Faithful Contendings Displayed*, 1780, p. 58).

[76] MS f.8, fols. 72–73. There is also a reference on May 4 to Vandervelde, with whom Argyll often stayed when he was in Amsterdam (fols. 74, 77). Locke stayed with Vandervelde in July (MS f.8, fol. 98).

[77] MS f.29, fol. 20. Clarke is listed under his pseudonym, "Somerton." From the payments he received from Dare or Hayes for living expenses on May 10, June 10, and on July

> Madam need not trouble herself to thank me for any public services nor for any private favors I have done her. In the matter of . . . [missing in the letter] between her and me, I can pretend to nothing but to be on the receiving side.[78]

Locke's movements, secrecy, and associations in 1683–1684 may be only coincidental with what we know from other sources about the relationship between Argyll and the English radicals and the revival of plans for a rebellion, but it may also be that he was one of those engaged in public service—service for the cause. Another explanation for Locke's disappearance or retreat into deep hiding is that the seizure of Thomas Armstrong the first week in June, and the fact that his papers exposed the role of Joseph and Israel Hayes as financiers of the radicals placed Locke in some jeopardy in view of his own dealings with those individuals, especially since one of them had been arrested and was awaiting trial in England.[79]

It was at this time, early July, that Chudleigh himself made a sudden trip to England, where he remained for almost two months. It is possible that, having gained more concrete information pertaining to the arms purchases of the radicals and the "great matter" about which they were agitated, Chudleigh went to report in person on the plans for the insurrection.[80] In any event, shortly after his arrival, two of Argyll's important aides, William Spence and William Carstares, were subjected to torture. Interrogation by torture was illegal in England, though allowable under the laws of Scotland.[81] Notwithstanding this, in mid-June 1684, the Secret Committee of the Privy Council had been instructed "to examine the matter of the late conspiracy by torture and other effectual means."[82] Prisoners were therefore sometimes shunted across the border

1, 11, 27, and 29, Locke was in Amsterdam for much of this period. But as the first two dates indicate, there is a rather large (and unusual, according to Locke's pattern) gap between May and June that makes it difficult to say where Locke was, or how he was living without some payment for expenses during that period. In mid-July, Locke changed his residence twice in a week (MS f.8, fols. 86–99; MS b.1, fols. 53–55).

[78] *Correspondence*, 2:625.

[79] *CSPD*, 27:177.

[80] Chudleigh's trip is usually explained in terms of William's angry reaction to Chudleigh's admonishments of his favorable treatment of Monmouth, and the personal dislike the prince felt for the envoy. Chudleigh provides an account of this exchange in his report of June 27, 1684 (Add. MS 41810, fols. 125–128). Hence, his return to England was in the nature of a recall by Charles II at William's insistence. This is an adequate though not, in my opinion, complete explanation for the trip.

[81] Ogg, 2:407.

[82] *CSPD*, 27:55. Robert Wodrow, *The History of the Sufferings of the Church of Scotland from the Restoration to the Revolution*, 4 vols., 1830, 3:471.

and tortured, out of sight, so to speak, of English common law. This practice was applied to Spence and Carstares.[83] A newsletter in September reported that both men "have by their torture made large confessions . . . but the confessions are kept so very close that most of the [Privy] Council know them not." The few individuals who were present at or who transcribed the confessions were "sworn deeply to secrecy."[84] At the time of his arrest, Spence was carrying a cipher and letters from Argyll to Major Holmes. Spence's arrest led to that of Carstares, who had served as an important link between the Scots and the London radicals in the Rye House conspiracy.[85] Carstares' papers included a key to the aliases for Kiffin, Cox, and Lock.[86]

Under severe torture, Spence finally confessed in August.[87] On August 15, Locke left Amsterdam for a trip through the country. Although he changed locations almost daily, most of his time was spent in or around Leewarden.[88] Argyll, who owned some property near Leewarden, had gone there to reformulate his plans, following the postponement of the invasion date.[89] We do not know whether Locke made any contact with Argyll or his representatives during the time he was in the vicinity of Argyll's estate, but Locke arrived in Utrecht at the end of September, just when there was a general meeting of the radicals in that city to discuss their situation and plans.[90] As Cranston points out, Macaulay was mis-

[83] Spence and Carstares had been arrested and interrogated in England. Not satisfied with the results of these interrogations, the government sent them to Edinburgh Castle, where they were tortured (Willcock, *Scots Earl*, p. 315; Dalrymple, vol. 1, pt. 1, bk. 1, p. 56). They had the dubious honor of being the first victims of a new device—the thumbscrew—which had just been introduced to Scotland (David Ogg, *England in the Reigns of James II and William III*, Oxford: Clarendon Press, 1955, p. 173). Erskine, who visited Spence and Carstares in prison, provides a graphic account of the torture applied to them (*Journal*, pp. 37, 60, 78, 81–82).

[84] *CSPD*, 27:147, 149. Carstares was given a pardon on September 27, 1684 (p. 156). He was released at the beginning of 1685 and went to Holland, where he was active in planning Argyll's rebellion (*Carstares State Papers*, p. 24).

[85] *A True and Plain Account of the Discoveries Made in Scotland, of the Late Conspiracies against His Majesty and the Government*, 1685, pp. 9, 15–16. According to Major Holmes, "many letters" passed between him and Argyll.

[86] *True and Plain Account*, p. 14. Cox may be Locke's friend, John Cox, the London soap maker and a dissenting Whig.

[87] *True and Plain Account*, p. 17; Milne, *Rye House Plot*, p. 280. Carstares confessed on September 8, 1684 (Sprat, p. 78).

[88] MS f.8, fols. 107–173.

[89] Willcock, *Scots Earl*, p. 322; Erskine, *Journal*, p. 180.

[90] Sir John Cochrane returned from his mission to Europe at the beginning of September, and he, along with a number of Scottish radicals from Rotterdam went to Utrecht for a meeting. Since the exact date of the latter cannot be determined from the evidence, Locke's arrival in that city on September 23 may have been before or after the meeting (Add. MS 41810, fol. 168; MS f.8, fol. 173).

taken when he assumed that Locke's "temperament" as a philosopher "preserved him from the violence of a partisan" and induced him to retreat from the violent schemes put forward by the exiles in Amsterdam to Utrecht, where "he quietly repaired."[91] In fact, the most important colony of Scottish radicals, gathered around Argyll and the widow Smith, lived in Utrecht. Most of these individuals were well known to Locke. Many of them had been associates with Shaftesbury in his Carolina or colonial interests, and had been brought into contact with Locke through that means and through his position as a secretary to the Council for Trade and Plantations.[92] Around the end of October 1684, Lord Louden Campbell, one of the leaders of the Scottish community, died and was buried in the English church at Leyden. This Scotsman, Chudleigh wrote to Middleton, was a friend of Locke.[93] Since he was in Leyden at the time of Campbell's death, it is likely that Locke was one of the mourners present at the funeral.[94] In any event, during the years he spent in exile, Locke appears to have maintained close contact with the Scots, and this may have led some spies to assume that he was a Scotsman.[95]

It was shortly after his return to Holland that Chudleigh discovered that *An Impartial Enquiry into the Administration of Affairs in England*

[91] Macaulay, 1:490–491; Cranston, p. 250.

[92] Patrick Hume, for example, "who kept correspondence with Shaftesbury many years," was now living in exile in Utrecht under an assumed name (Sprat, p. 27). Fox-Bourne describes Locke's close association with the Carolina affairs and his correspondence with others about the subject (1:286–289).

[93] Add. MS 41810, fol. 188; *Memoir of Sir James Dalrymple*, 1873, p. 189.

[94] Locke was in Leyden from October 15 to November 18. Campbell's funeral was held sometime between the first date and November 11 (Add. MS 41810, fol. 195). Locke's ostensible reason for staying in Leyden was to attend a book auction, which was held on October 31 (*Correspondence*, 2:661; MS f.8, fol. 209).

[95] In one report by an informer (not the double agent), for example, an individual is listed as "Mr. Lock, a Scotsman" residing in Utrecht, along with Trenchard, Colonel Danvers, and a number of Scotsmen (Add. MS 41820, fol. 87). Though undated, based upon the names of individuals included on the list and other information relating to their movements, this list was compiled at a time when Locke was in fact living in Utrecht. The other Lock (Nicholas) was then resident in Amsterdam, and I believe from the context therefore that the individual named by the informer was John Locke. This raises the question whether he might not, from time to time, have passed himself off as a Scotsman. Trenchard, for example, did try to pass for a Frenchman during much of the time he lived in exile (Add. MS 41818, fol. 13). And on at least one occasion, Locke assumed the disguise of a Jesuit (*Correspondence*, 3:231). But, whether this (mis)identification of Locke is due to his conscious design or merely his frequent association with the Scottish exiles, the point is that he was in close contact with them. Another informer's report identifies Locke as Shaftesbury's former secretary and associates him with Argyll, Stewart, Cochrane, and other Scotsmen. Indeed, the informant, who was providing a surveillance report on who he had seen on board Argyll's ships prior to their sailing, believed that Locke had actually sailed with Argyll's expedition (Add. MS 41817, fols. 5–6; I wish to thank Elizabeth Martinson for her assistance in the translation of this report from the Dutch).

was circulating among the exiles. As he modestly characterized it in his report to Middleton, it was "the most impudent and horrid libel" that "the malice of hell itself could possibly invent." Chudleigh was only able to procure a copy "with great difficulty," because the radicals were "so very cautious in the sale and dispersal" of the tract "that they will not part with any one . . . but only to such as they well know and have a confidence in that they will not betray them."[96] It was in this report, from which I have previously cited, that Chudleigh suggested Locke as the work's author. This was not, for reasons already discussed, a reckless accusation on Chudleigh's part. He was personallly acquainted with Locke from his days as a student at Christ Church, and it appears that he met with Locke on at least one occasion following the latter's arrival in Holland. Since he knew Locke to be a radical, Chudleigh was not deceived by his ostensible reason for coming to Holland ("he pretends to be come for the benefit of the air"). And, he wrote, "whether he be the author of [*An Impartial Enquiry*] or not, I do not see for what reason Mr. Lock should be so much indulged as to keep his place in Christ Church whilst he lives amongst the worst of our traitors." Such sinecures were "never intended for the maintenance and support of such as seek to overthrow the government."[97] Chudleigh also mentions that Richard Nelthorp, one of the Rye House conspirators, after spending some time in Amsterdam was now en route for Luxembourg in company with William Waller's wife. Chudleigh indicated that an attempt would be made "to seize him if it be possible." And, he added, "this Nelthorp was one of Lock's companions" in Holland.[98]

This remarkable letter produced an immediate response from Sunderland, who wrote to Dean Fell ordering the expulsion of Locke from his studentship in Christ Church. Much ink has been spilled over the arbitrariness and injustice of this action, but it must be remembered that Locke had obtained the position originally as a political appointment, and indeed, even his medical degree was granted only after the intervention

[96] Add. MS 41810, fols. 188, 194.

[97] Add. MS 41810, fol. 188. This part of Chudleigh's letter was printed by Cecil Price, "Thomas Chudleigh on John Locke, 1684," *Notes and Queries* 194, no. 24 (November 26, 1949):519.

[98] Add. MS 41810, fol. 188. Locke had inquired after Mrs. Waller in a letter to Mrs. Clarke earlier in the year (*Correspondence*, 2:616). It was just at this time, according to Wade, that William Waller secured the promise of protection from the Duke of Luxembourg, and he and some of the conspirators went there to make preparations for Argyll's invasion in greater secrecy (Harleian MS 6845, fol. 270). Because of a complaint by Charles II to the Elector of Brandenburg, Goodenough and Nelthorp had been forced to leave Cleves for safer territory (*Secret History*, pp. 84–85). Chudleigh's intelligence, therefore, that Nelthorp, Waller, and others had gone or were en route to Luxembourg was very good.

of the highest political authority—the king himself. This does not excuse the arbitrariness of the removal, but there was certainly a point to Chudleigh's argument that Locke's biographers, because they have generally proclaimed his innocence of politically subversive actions, have failed to recognize. Sunderland's initial letter to Fell was terse and businesslike:

> The king being given to understand that one Mr. Locke, who belonged to the late Earl of Shaftesbury, and has upon several occasions behaved himself very factiously and undutifully to the government . . . would have him removed from being a student, and that . . . your lordship would let me know the method of doing it.[99]

Fell never doubted the king's assessment of Locke. The latter, he wrote, is, "as your lordship is truly informed, a person who was much trusted by the late Earl of Shaftesbury, and who is suspected to be ill-affected to the government." The problem for Fell was that on the relatively few occasions Locke was at Oxford, he had been extremely cautious, refusing to be trapped into political discussions by the various spies, including Fell himself, who made it a practice to keep an eye on him. Fell discloses this fact not as a defense of Locke's innocence, but almost apologetically, in the sense that he is unable to contribute anything to the evidence against Locke, as he had against Locke's Oxford friends, Robert Pawling and Alderman Wright. "Notwithstanding that" (the lack of evidence in his hands), Fell explains that he has summoned Locke to return to England by January 1, which, if he does not, he will be expelled by the college, and if he does, "he will be answerable to your lordship" for his actions. Doubtless, Fell thought this a clever trap, though he probably suspected some impatience on the part of the government, because he added that "if this method seem not effectual or speedy enough, and his majesty . . . shall please to command his immediate remove . . . it shall accordingly be executed."[100]

Fell was correct in his suspicions, for Sunderland immediately dispatched a directive to him "by his majesty's command" that Locke be "forthwith" removed from his student's place in the college. Fell replied that "his majesty's command for the expulsion of Mr. Locke from the college was fully executed" and he received in return Sunderland's assurance that Charles II "was well pleased" with the Dean's speedy compliance with his order.[101] Though Fell had some respect for Locke's intelligence and the fact that he had been a student and lecturer in the

[99] *CSPD*, 27:198. Sunderland's letter is dated November 6, 1684.

[100] The exchange of letters between Fell and Sunderland on Locke's expulsion is printed in King, 1:278–282.

[101] *CSPD*, 27:206. This letter is dated November 11.

college, he was no friend of Locke, and the Dean was even less sympathetic to the radical Whig political position with which Locke was clearly identified. Despite the attempts of later writers to bridge the gap between the man who supported and aided Monmouth's Rebellion and the man who rounded up students at Oxford and was prepared to lead a company of them against Monmouth in the field, the fact is, Fell's response to Sunderland represents nothing more than, at best, an attempt to preserve the autonomy of university procedures from direct political interference.[102] In this brief encounter between two institutional authorities, the political fate of Locke as a pawn in the struggle was never in doubt by either party in the dispute. But what was Locke's view of the matter?

At the time of his expulsion, Locke was in Leyden, and was planning to go to Utrecht, where he intended to spend the winter.[103] He arrived at Amsterdam en route to Utrecht on November 18, and while there he received word that Bishop Fell had summoned him back to Oxford. If De Beer is correct in his surmise that Locke responded immediately to the news of his removal from his student's place by writing a letter to Pembroke, then Locke received Fell's letter or notification of his expulsion on December 8.[104] Locke's letter to the Earl of Pembroke, of which mention has previously been made, is (to put it mildly) a document fraught with troublesome questions. Since its first appearance in print, in Christie's *Life of Shaftesbury*, toward the end of the nineteenth century, the letter has constituted the bedrock upon which the assumption of Locke's political innocence has been grounded.[105] Yet, it is a rather shaky foundation, and both Cranston and Laslett have challenged the veracity of some of Locke's statements in the letter.[106] In view of its importance, both the contents of the letter and the allegations concerning its accuracy as a measure of Locke's political perspective and activities, merit a careful consideration.

After mentioning his receipt of the news of his summons to Oxford, Locke writes, "when I was preparing to comport myself to that citation as became me, the next post brings the news, that I am actually expelled."

[102] Charles James Fox recognized that Fell was not acting as Locke's friend, and he condemned the pettiness of the action, though he subscribed to the view of Locke's innocence of any seditious activity (*History of the Early Part of the Reign of James the Second*, 1808, pp. 38–39). A few days after Monmouth's execution, Fell wrote to a friend reaffirming his commitment "for the sake of the old cavalier interest" (Add. MS 29582, fol. 280).

[103] *Correspondence*, 2:661–662.

[104] *Correspondence*, 2:658. De Beer suggests that Locke wrote his reply "within a few hours of receiving . . . the news of his deprivation."

[105] Fox-Bourne specifically cites the letter as printed in Christie as the basis for his defense of Locke's innocence (1:336).

[106] Cranston, pp. 247–250; *Correspondence*, 2:661.

Did Locke really intend to return to Oxford to confront the charges against him, as some interpreters have assumed, and as he seems to imply here? It is difficult to accept such a conclusion in view of the fact that, for more than a year, Locke had employed various aliases, changed residences, concealed financial transactions, used ciphers and other means of preventing his correspondence from being understood or intercepted by the authorities—all in an effort to escape detection from the English spies in Holland. And now, when he was in more serious trouble than ever, as a result of the direct action of the king, Locke suddenly planned to appear in person at Oxford to preserve a studentship of which he was not likely to assume the residency in the midst of Tory Oxford? Moreover, if he were planning to return to England, he would certainly require some money for the trip. Yet his journal shows that he received 100 guilders from Thomas Dare on November 17, as he was leaving Leyden; Dare paid him again on November 30, the date on which Locke probably learned of Fell's initial notification, and then not again until late December.[107] In other words, Locke made no attempt during the period he was in Amsterdam after receiving Fell's summons and before writing the December 8 letter to withdraw any money from Dare, as he would have had to have done if he planned to leave the country. Nor did he issue instructions about packing or the care of his books, or pay his debts, including his rent. In short, there is no tangible evidence that Locke actually intended to leave Holland in December 1684, or that he altered his original intention of spending the winter in Utrecht.

After appealing to Pembroke to confirm his innocence of the charges, Locke writes:

> I appeal likewise to my Lord Bishop of Oxford whether my carriage in the college . . . carried in it any the least . . . appearance of turbulency, faction, or sedition.

As Cranston remarks, this appeal was shrewdly formulated, for even Fell had to concede that while Locke was "in the college" he had been extremely cautious with respect to political activities. To what degree the evidence of Locke's relations with his friends Robert Pawling and Alderman Wright (two leading "disaffected" Whig politicians in Oxford about whom Bishop Fell regularly complained to the government) or his activities during College's trial at Oxford and his association with Robert West (upon whose testimony so many arrests and prosecutions of the Rye

[107] MS b.1, fol. 55. Fox-Bourne wrote that upon receiving Fell's letter, Locke "resolved to return at once to England," but there is simply no confirming evidence of this resolution (2:16).

House conspirators had been predicated) could have been cited against this appeal to Bishop Fell is a question to which we will never know the answer. But as Locke himself must have known, the appeal largely misses the point, since the king was not responding to complaints about Locke's behavior in the college, but rather to his activities "on several occasions" outside the college.

Locke then reflects upon his association with Shaftesbury, and in the only extant instance in Locke's writings in which he characterizes that relationship in negative terms, he observes "how small an advancement of my fortune I had made, in so long an attendance" upon Shaftesbury, and how some of his friends have told him "that I had no great reason to brag of the effects of that kindness." Locke complains, therefore, "that having reaped so little advantage from my service to him whilst living, I should suffer so much on that account now he is dead."[108] The very fact that Locke's criticism of Shaftesbury's treatment of him, even in this relatively mild form, runs counter to everything Locke ever said or wrote about this relationship ought, in itself, to give the interpreter of this letter serious pause about relying upon this particular text as an expression of Locke's settled or general opinions. On the contrary, as De Beer suggests, the letter was written in great haste and extreme anger; it is certainly one of the most emotionally charged pieces Locke ever penned. It is, in other words, precisely *not* the example of Locke's writing to be used as a general rule, as the statement of his long-held, rationally arrived at conclusions. It is an angry reactive document, a response to the spiteful and petty reprisals taken by the English government against the exiles, of which Locke's removal from Christ Church is only one instance.[109]

Finally, Locke turns to the important issue, the specific charges against him: his having written seditious libels and his association with Rye House conspirators. Referring to the period when Shaftesbury was alive, Locke declares,

> I never did any thing undutifully against his Majesty or the government: I know nothing in my life scandalous, or am conscious of anything that ought to give any offence; I have never been of any suspected clubs or cabals, I have made little acquaintance, and kept little

[108] Even this criticism is equivocal, since Locke does not present it as his own, but rather, what "some of my friends . . . have thought" and told him.

[109] On May 19, 1685, for example, Skelton wrote Middleton that an English minister at Rotterdam was the holder of a sinecure granted him by Charles II. Since this individual was "ill-affected and factiously inclined" toward the government, Skelton suggested that his sinecure be ended (Add. MS 41812, fol. 82).

company in an house where so much came, and for that little my choice was of bookish not busy men.

Locke cites his past record because his actions then were "all exactly the same" as "they have been now." Thus, "as to the company I am said to keep at coffee houses" in Holland, Locke protests that he did not come to Holland to "keep company with men, whom every one that would be safe shuns, and who were never any of my associates in England, when they were under much better circumstances." As for "those who are particularly named for my companions, I assure your Lordship with the truth I would speak my last breath, I never saw out of England, nor in a long time before I left it.[110] Coffee houses it is well known I loved and frequented little in England, less here. I speak much within compass when I say I have not been in a coffee house as many times as I have been months here . . . and when I went there, which I remember I was once forced to do three or four times in one week, it was only to speak with some merchant I had business with." The difficulty with this part of the letter lies in distinguishing the half-truths it contains from the outright lies. For if, by "suspected clubs" Locke means the Green Ribbon Club, it is true that there is no evidence to show that he was ever a member of that organization. But as to the general charge of keeping company with disaffected individuals in Holland who ought to be "shunned" by "everyone that would be safe" from suspicion of sedition, Locke's answer is more than disingenuous; it is a simple lie. Not only Thomas Dare, Israel Hayes, John Nisbet, John Wilmore, Richard Nelthorp, Jacob Vandervelde (the bookseller), Daniel Le Blon (one of the merchants in Amsterdam active in the planning of Argyll's and later, Monmouth's Rebellion), but also many others were Locke's companions and associates in Holland, and all of them were radicals the English government wanted arrested for sedition.[111]

In dealing with this part of the letter, it is necessary to skip ahead in the story in order to introduce into the discussion evidence that has a bearing upon any assessment of the veracity of Locke's reply to Pembroke. The evidence consists of extracts from the voluminous intelligence reports submitted to the English Secretary of State by Chudleigh and Skelton. In

[110] This confirms, incidentally, the fact that Locke *did* know Ferguson and Grey, who were those particularly named as his companions.

[111] Daniel Le Blon (along with James Washington), were two of the principal fund-raisers for Monmouth's Rebellion—"rebellion-promoting merchants," Skelton called them (Allan Fea, *The Loyal Wentworths*, London: Bodley Head, 1928, p. 156; Earle, *Monmouth's Rebels*, p. 152). Le Blon also provided lodging at various times for Ferguson, Grey, Armstrong, Goodenough, and other radicals (*CSPD*, 25:444; 26:32). Locke's journal between 1683 and 1685 shows that he maintained frequent contact with Le Blon.

April 1685, there is a report on Locke's association with John Cochrane, James Stewart, and others involved in making the final preparations for Argyll's invasion. Grey, Ferguson, the widow Smith, and Monmouth are also mentioned in the report.[112] In May, "the secretary of Shaftesbury, Doctor Lock" is meeting in Utrecht with one of Argyll's most dedicated supporters and a key liaison figure between the Scottish and English radicals. Locke invited this individual, Walter Cross, to share his house.[113] Cross was a Nonconformist minister who had been deeply involved in the Rye House Plot.[114] He had also contributed some money to help equip Argyll's expedition.[115] Any arrangement between Locke and Cross, the double agent wrote, was being held in abeyance, pending "the first news of the success" of Argyll's expedition. Later reports confirm Locke's association with John Starkey, Mrs. Smith, Cochrane, John Howe, John Thompson, and other radicals involved in the Rye House Plot and Monmouth's Rebellion. The substance and circumstances of these intelligence reports will be discussed below in the context of their importance to the planning of Monmouth's Rebellion, but they are introduced here because they cast grave doubts upon the truthfulness of Locke's letter to Pembroke. It is true that all of these reports describe meetings and actions that occurred a few months after that letter was written, and we may therefore conclude either that Locke suddenly involved himself with radicals with whom he had not previously associated in Holland, or that these associations represent a continuing relationship with individuals, one that precedes the letter to Pembroke, and as we shall see, one that unquestionably postdates it and extends throughout the period of Locke's exile until his return to England in 1689. Taking all the evidence into consideration, I believe the latter is the correct conclusion. Chudleigh's complaints to the English government were, after all, based upon intelligence reports ex-

[112] Add. MS 41817, fol. 5.

[113] Add. MS 41812, fol. 70. Locke, who appears to have been staying at this time at the house of the double agent, acted as a go-between for Cross in conveying an offer from the latter to his landlord of four ducatoons per week for Cross and his servant to live and eat at his house. This offer appears to have been declined, or more likely, voided by the events that befell Argyll and his associates. Later, there is a financial transaction between Locke and Papillon involving Cross, and at one point Locke received his mail at Cross's residence, which may indicate that he was staying there for a time (*Correspondence*, 3:61, 126). Locke owned a book by Cross on the Scriptures (*LL* #892).

[114] As reported by the double agent in Utrecht (Add. MS 41812, fol. 222). Cross was arrested in July 1683, trying to escape from England with Matthew Meade and Zachary Bourne, who certainly were part of the conspiracy. Two other conspirators, including one who had provided a safe house for John Nisbet, were also arrested near where Meade, Cross, and Bourne were captured (MS PWV 95, fol. 251; E. M., *A Copy of a Letter Sent from a Person That Was Present at the Apprehension of Mr. Meade and Five More*, 1683).

[115] Add. MS 41812, fol. 222; Add. MS 41818, fol. 106.

actly like those I have cited, and it seems more reasonable to conclude that the original documents describing this period (1684) of Locke's activity in Holland, unlike those of 1685–1686, have not survived than to believe that Locke's commitment to Monmouth's cause and his active role in advancing it were merely last-minute decisions on his part.[116] In any event, what we are not entitled to conclude from Locke's letter to Pembroke is that it represents a statement of Locke's political innocence that accurately describes the entire six-year period of his exile in Holland, not to mention his previous years of association with Shaftesbury.

The charge laid against Locke about which he may have been able to speak with most confidence and least prevarication—and certainly the one for which evidence one way or another was and is most difficult to discover—pertained to his having written "seditious libels." Interestingly, Locke, though he feigns surprise at the allegation, acknowledges that this is not the first time such accusations have been made. Rather, he has for a number of years been suspected of being the author of various anonymous tracts. So frequently, in fact, has the charge been made that Locke is able to turn the accusation around by maintaining that the styles of these various pamphlets attributed to him were so different "that it was hard to think they should have the same author," much less himself. Thus, "it is a very odd fate, that I should get the reputation of no small writer, without having done anything for it." Apart from some youthful poetry obscurely published, Locke writes,

> I here solemnly protest in the presence of god, that I am not the author, not only of any libel, but not of any pamphlet or treatise whatsoever in print good bad or indifferent.

This protest is reaffirmed, at greater length, in a subsequent letter to Edward Clarke (January 1685). Locke repeats the "malicious" suspicions that have been raised against him concerning the authorship of various libels published in Holland. He insists that such writing as he has done (in manuscript) deals with speculations remote from politics and that he is not preparing "anything for the press here."[117] To which he adds:

[116] It was Anthony Wood who recorded that Locke "was expelled for Whiggism" for having kept company with Lord Grey and Robert Ferguson (Anthony Wood, *The Life and Times of Anthony Wood*, 5 vols., Oxford: Clarendon Press, 1892, 3:117). Wood's accuracy as a source is definitely open to question, and there are several mistakes in this particular note, but the fact that he refers as a source for his comment to Chudleigh's complaint to Middleton about Locke suggests that Chudleigh's letter about Locke cited in the text is neither the first nor the only complaint he forwarded to the Secretary of State, since neither Ferguson nor Grey is mentioned in that letter.

[117] *Correspondence*, 2:672.

> For I tell you again with that truth which should be sacred betwixt friends that I am not the author of any treatise or pamphlet in print good bad or indifferent and therefore you may be sure how I am used when people talk of libels . . . I am so far from writing any that I take care not to read anything that looks that way, I avoid all commerce about them and if a letter from a friend should have in it but the title or mention of any libel, I should think it a sufficient reason to burn it immediately whatever else of concernment there might be in it, and to quarrel with him that writ it and I desire no other usage for my letters or myself from my friends. . . . I have never any commerce of news with any absent acquaintance, and inquire not after it . . . I have scarce read so much as half a dozen gazette[s] since I have been here and those only when other people have put them into my hands . . . having resolved not to meddle in the least with any public affairs, I decline as much as I can the discourse of them and . . . I choose rather to converse [with foreigners] than with my countrymen.

If, as I suggested in Chapter 3, Locke viewed his role with respect to *A Letter from a Person in the Country* or *No Protestant Plot* as merely that of a contributor to these publications for which Shaftesbury or Ferguson were ultimately responsible as authors, then Locke's denial might very well stand. Even so, it should be kept in mind that we are speaking of any *published* "libel," for Locke had *written* at least one seditious tract—the *Two Treatises*—and another with James Tyrrell, which probably would have been regarded as such, at the time this letter was written.[118] In other words, insofar as we are concerned with Locke's intentions, and his frame of mind, politically speaking, these protestations of innocence have a Jesuitical cast to them when viewed as expressions of Locke's political perspective, which certainly was not then, or ever, that of an apathetic neutral.

The middle part of the passage cited above appears to refer to an earlier letter to Clarke (March 17, 1684) in which Locke himself discussed the "pamphlets published here that deserve as well to be burnt" as the two "libels" whose titles he included in his letter. For, the message to Clarke is that "if a letter from a friend [Locke] should have in it but the title or mention of any libel, I should think it a sufficient reason to burn it immediately whatever else of concernment there might be in it." There was reason, as we have seen, to burn that particular letter, for it was a report to Clarke on the planning of Argyll's projected invasion. It was, in short,

[118] This manuscript reply to a book by Stillingfleet is discussed in Chapter 10 below.

an incriminating document, should it fall into the hands of the government at this point, and therefore it deserved to be burned.[119]

As to the part of Locke's letter relating to news of England, this is a three-quarters truth. That Locke did not discuss "public affairs" with individuals with whom he did not have a relationship of great trust is true enough, and is even confirmed by the intelligence reports submitted by one of those individuals, who was a double agent. That Locke never inquired after news of England is not quite true, since he had specifically asked Clarke to send him news of the trials of the Rye House conspirators in the summer of 1683, and in ciphered form, other political news is contained in their correspondence.[120] In a later letter, Locke wrote that there was no necessity for Clarke to include in his letters the "public news which gazettes and newsletters tell of," the implication being that Locke could obtain for himself this news from the gazettes available to him in Holland.[121] And in his journal, Locke does record the purchase of gazettes, and also a number of occasions under the heading "spent with my countrymen," where the wine and food was paid for by Locke.[122] So much for his avoidance of discourse with his countrymen!

If Locke's statements in his letter to Pembroke must be read with more than a grain of salt, and in a context that relates its contents to a lifetime of political activity on Locke's part, nevertheless the case for Locke's authorship of any particular pamphlet is still difficult to prove. But unlike his Victorian biographers, I do not believe that his statements to Pembroke (and Clarke) absolutely close the door on this question. Given the personal and political circumstances he was in, it is absurd to assume that Locke was incapable of lying and therefore, in a sense, was less of a human being than any of us might be in the same situation. Lord Russell lied more than once to save himself, as did Sidney in denying to Shaftesbury that he was receiving money from the French.[123] This is a serious

[119] *Correspondence*, 2:612–613.

[120] *Correspondence*, 2:602.

[121] *Correspondence*, 2:606.

[122] MS f.34, fols. 3–5, 12–13.

[123] In his initial examination, Russell maintained that he had heard nothing about an insurrection, did not know whether Ferguson was at the meeting at Shepherd's, heard no discussion of Trenchard, Taunton, or the seizing of the king's guards, and knew nothing concerning the participation of the Scots (Sprat, appendix, pp. 131–132). Some of these denials were modified at his trial when Russell was confronted with the witnesses against him, but even that record contains a number of outright lies by Russell. His lie on the floor of the House of Commons about not receiving money from the French was discussed in Chapter 4 above. It is not my intention to impugn Russell's character; on the contrary, the point is that even so well respected and generally truthful an individual as Russell, whose integrity was universally conceded, might nevertheless protect himself through a falsehood.

charge to consider, and I have tried to weigh his statements accordingly. But, as I have suggested, precisely because of the problematic character of these statements, they cannot simply be read as being self-evidently true.

Chudleigh suspected Locke of having written two specific "libels": *An Enquiry into . . . the Barbarous Murder of the Late Earl of Essex*, and *An Impartial Enquiry into the Administration of Affairs in England.* Robert Ferguson was certainly the author of the first, and almost as certainly, of the second. Yet, Locke's own position on Essex's "murder," and the political arguments and terminology of the *Two Treatises*, are parallel to, and frequently identical with, those employed by Ferguson in these pamphlets. Even if we accepted entirely the truthfulness of Locke's denial, applied to these two treatises, that denial could never serve as the basis for an argument that Locke did not share Ferguson's political perspective.

Locke sent the letter to Pembroke as an enclosure in a letter (lost) to Clarke.[124] Laslett has suggested that Clarke retained the letter and that Pembroke probably did not see its contents.[125] This interpretation does not seem borne out by Locke's inquiries put to Clarke in his letter of January 1, 1685, which presuppose that Clarke and Pembroke have discussed the contents of the latter's letter.[126] Yet the January epistle does raise some doubts about the status of the earlier document. In the lost or destroyed letter to Clarke, Locke had ventured a guess as to the identity of the individual who had informed on him, which he now characterizes as a "useless conjecture which could serve to no purpose to be mentioned." Moreover, "had I heard then what I have [since] concerning" the reports on his political activity, "I should not have mentioned it nor troubled" Clarke with the business.[127] And, describing the conditions of his writing to Pembroke (and Clarke), Locke refers to the fact that "the circumstance of the time led my then perplexed thoughts into that conjecture," a perplexity that, I have suggested, seems a term applicable to the letter as a whole and not merely to one conjectural part of Locke's correspondence

[124] *Correspondence*, 2:661.

[125] Laslett, p. 41n.

[126] "Did E P [Pembroke] take notice to you of the postscript of my letter and express any willingness that I should send him any part of my discourse *De Intellectu humano*? . . . If he did I will find some way to send it" (*Correspondence*, 2:674).

[127] Whatever the source of Locke's information in the month-long interval between his letter to Pembroke and this one to Clarke, it is not indicated in his correspondence nor was it in the *Gazette*. This statement even seems to contradict one on the previous page (p. 673) where he says he never listens to or inquires after political news. The news of Locke's expulsion, however, was more widely known than De Beer implies (p. 658). George Hickes wrote to a friend at Cambridge (November 26, 1684) that he "was very glad to hear that Lock is turned out of Christ Church," since "his Majesty's enemies," such as he believed Locke to be, had no right to hold such positions (MS Ballard 12, fol. 2).

at that moment. The January letter also indicates that Locke has had "second thoughts" about his letter to Pembroke, which contains statements of which I "do not upon second thoughts so well approve as being not of a piece with the rest, and therefore pray burn them, saving them cannot be of any use."[128] Finally, Locke rejects any reliance upon "his Majesty's *great clemency*" on his behalf, and asks Clarke to prevent any of Locke's friends from interceding on his behalf with the king, since it is not yet "a proper time to move" from Holland.[129] He also advises his friend to make sure that he employs "a sure messenger" in the exchange of messages between them, since some of Locke's letters have been intercepted by the government.[130]

Apart from the second thoughts Locke experienced in the month following his letter to Pembroke, other dramatic developments had taken place that affected the plans and circumstances of the radical exiles in Holland. In November, Monmouth made a not-too-secret trip to England in order to confer privately with Charles II. He warned his father that James had a secret plan to kill him.[131] Charles was not especially surprised at the news, but he was impressed at the dangers to which Monmouth had exposed himself in order to convey it. The fact that the king was planning to make a "great change" in his administration, which involved sending the Duke of York to Scotland, recalling Monmouth to England (where his legitimacy as Charles' heir would be acknowledged), and placing Lord Halifax in charge of an essentially moderate administration was beginning to be widely suspected.[132] Charles had maintained a regular corre-

[128] Due to missing and illegible sections of the letter, Locke's phraseology here is a bit obscure and could be taken to refer to the short essays on education that he sent to Clarke from time to time. But it was simple enough for him to say so directly—i.e., I have revised my thoughts on X, and will send you a replacement. Instead, he speaks of the letter "that enclosed E P's long one and also in another to the same purpose" as the objects of his second thoughts. The first reference is to his letter to Clarke (lost), and the second, "to the same purpose," must be the letter to Pembroke itself, both of which Locke wants burned. Surely this is a drastic response to second thoughts on the relatively innocuous topics of education that he sent to Clarke (*Correspondence*, 2:674).

[129] *Correspondence*, 2:673. This discussion, which precedes Locke's instructions to burn his earlier letter to Clarke and indicates that Locke has changed his mind about pressing his case and that he has withdrawn his earlier conjectures about who was responsible for his trouble, provides, I believe, the context for the reference to "second thoughts" in connection with his letter to Pembroke.

[130] *Correspondence*, 2:675.

[131] Dalrymple, vol. 1, pt. 1, bk. 1, p. 65; Arthur Bryant, *Charles II*, London: Longmans, Green, 1931, p. 356.

[132] At the very time Monmouth made his secret trip to England, Chudleigh wrote to Middleton that he had heard through Monmouth's servants that the duke had been "called to a private conference with the king," who they said was about to name Monmouth the heir to

spondence with his son since his departure from England at the end of 1683, and Halifax acted as the chief intermediary between the two men.[133] By the end of 1684, James began to suspect that his brother might be trying to prevent his ascension to the throne. The suspicion that James might, in these circumstances, act to hasten the demise of Charles and Monmouth was not a far-fetched supposition.[134] While in England, Monmouth received the reassurance of his father that the plans for his recall were going forward, and that James would be asked to go to Scotland to preside over the opening of the Scottish Parliament.[135] Armed with this news, Monmouth left England to return to Brussels and Holland. During the first week of January 1685, he received a message from Halifax, which he copied into his diary:

> I received a letter from Halifax marked by the King in the margin . . . that in February I should certainly have leave to return. That matters were concerting towards it and that the Duke of York had no suspicion.

A few weeks later, just three days before Charles' death, Monmouth made this notation:

> A letter from Halifax that my business was almost as well as done; but must be so sudden as to leave no time for the Duke of York's party to counter-plot. That it is probable he would choose Scotland rather than Flanders of this country; which is all one to the King.[136]

On February 16, Monmouth received the news of his father's death. "O cruel fate," as he put it in his diary. All prospects for a peaceful or bloodless return to England for Monmouth or for the other exiles were now at an end, with James, a Catholic, on the throne.

Meanwhile, those close to Argyll had spent "the whole winter" making preparations for the Scottish invasion, planned for sometime in the

---

the throne (Add. MS 41810, fol. 189). An interesting and in many respects plausible account of these intrigues involving Charles, Monmouth, and James is provided by William Veitch (*Memoirs of Veitch and Brysson*, pp. 155–164; cf. H. C. Foxcroft, *The Life and Letters of George Savile*, 2 vols., 1898, 1:423–426). Charles II's proposed changes were widely known. See the references cited by Emerson, *Monmouth's Rebellion*, pp. 4, 73.

133 Dalrymple, pt. 1, bk. 1, p. 65; Leopold von Ranke, *History of England*, 6 vols., 1875, 4:200; David Jones, *The Secret History of Whitehall*, 1697, pp. 21–22.

134 According to David Jones, French agents warned Monmouth that James had ordered him seized and wanted to get the duke "into his clutches dead or alive" (*Secret History of Whitehall*, p. 29; cf. *Memoirs of Veitch and Brysson*, p. 165; *Secret History*, p. 92).

135 Bryant, *Charles II*, p. 356; *Memoirs of Veitch and Brysson*, pp. 155–164.

136 Trench, *Western Rising*, p. 76.

spring.[137] It has generally been assumed that Monmouth knew nothing of Argyll's plans until March 1685, and that his decision to join forces with Argyll in a two-pronged attack on England was not made until sometime in April.[138] These dates are, in my opinion, too late by about a month. What is true is that there were significant personality differences between Argyll and Monmouth, and a suspicion on the part of the former that his earlier plans for a rebellion had been betrayed by his English "allies," either in Holland or in London.[139] Hence, there was a certain amount of distrust, as there had always been, between the Scots and the English radicals, which inhibited their willingness to cooperate with one another. Yet, the real difficulty lies with the propensity of historians to read events so exclusively in terms of the actions of the "great men," and their personalities. A radical underground organization existed quite apart from the daily involvement in its affairs of either Argyll or Monmouth, and there were individuals in Holland and England who were committed to armed resistance against Charles II and James II. Naturally, these individuals understood the strategic necessity of the leadership and alliance of Argyll and Monmouth in the making of that rebellion, but their plans for that undertaking did not rise and fall in response to every whim or reaction on the part of either individual.

In early January 1685, it was reported that the English radicals held a general meeting in Utrecht.[140] The object of this meeting appears to have

[137] Harleian MS 6845, fol. 270; Erskine, *Journal*, pp. 179–180.

[138] Emerson is primarily responsible for placing the date in April—chiefly, I would argue, as a function of his interpretation of Monmouth's personality. He seems to have known little concerning the extent of Argyll's preparations or the degree of cooperation between Argyll and the English exiles. Moreover, the movements and activities of individuals in England and Holland were far more complicated than can be gathered from Cragg's testimony, on which he appears to have placed great reliance. Thus, for example, Gibbons was arrested on February 6, which means that these canting letters pertaining to Argyll's invasion were written prior to Charles' death. Since Gibbons was merely the messenger, and had been equipped with a cover story by Monmouth that the duke had dismissed all his servants (which was not true), the implication certainly seems to be that Monmouth must have been privy to the efforts of Argyll and the exiles to link up with the radicals in England. Moreover, Gibbons was traveling with William Spence (alias Tristam Butler), who was clearly acting on behalf of Argyll. Another of Monmouth's servants, who had also been sent on his mission prior to the king's death but by a more circuitous route, was arrested at Dover in mid-February. Four days after Gibbons' arrest, an informer reported to the government that "the dissenting party" were in possession of 500 arms that they were prepared to deliver to Monmouth, provided they could set up a meeting and work out the arrangements (*CSPD* [James II], 1:1, 6; Fox, *Reign of James*, appendix, p. xxxi).

[139] There was some ground for this belief that "the too large spreading of the secret amongst our own friends" in London had led to the discovery of the planned rebellion (see note 57 above).

[140] Count D'Avaux, *The Negotiations of Count D'Avaux*, 4 vols., 1754–1755, 3:160.

been to enlist the support of the radicals in England on behalf of Argyll. A number of letters and messengers were dispatched to England in early January in an effort to determine what financial and political support was available. How many letters were sent is not known, but since at least ten of them were intercepted by government agents, the total volume of communication between Holland and England and Brussels in this period was probably rather large.[141] They were, of course, written in a canting style, to and from aliases, which makes it difficult to identify either sender or receiver. Nevertheless, the contents of some of these letters are quite interesting, and taken together they indicate that the lines of communication established by the radicals as well as the plans for a rebellion were not so chaotic as some scholars have assumed.

In a letter from James Welsh to John Mason at Mr. Wood's house in London, dated January 13, the author writes that he has been "entreated by a good gentleman to send the enclosed [letter] unto Mr. Brown who is I believe known to you to convey it safely to him." Mr. Mason is advised to speak to Mr. Brown about the contents of the letter. "Mr. Brown" was a pseudonym used by Lord Delamere. And, on the basis of his later communication and arrangements with Lord Delamere relating to Monmouth's expedition, a reasonable guess would be that "Mr. Mason" is Major Wildman.[142] Another letter of the same period from Alex Davidson to Robert Maitland describes the sickness of the author, although he has improved since the last letter he sent. He refers to his "physician" who says that "the Spring and good walks will improve his appearance." Mrs. Kean sends her regards, and is better than she was, but is "not yet absolutely free of the pains in her heart." The letter also contains the names of Lord Grey, Chapman Bray, Robert Read, and "Mr. Green who lived near Shaftesbury House in the Strand."[143] This letter is of special interest not only because of its reference to a pseudonymous individual, Chapman Bray, whom Locke had mentioned in his letter to Clarke in connection with an inquiry concerning the Rye House conspirators, but also because of its use of a medical style, the reference to the "physician" who

[141] Some of these letters probably did reach Scotland, for, it was just at this time (January 1685), according to one of the Scottish exiles, that there was a meeting in Scotland of those sympathetic to Argyll to ascertain what support, if any, they were prepared to give to the undertaking (Shields, *Faithful Contendings*, p. 157).

[142] Add. MS 4159, fol. 191. In his examination on July 26, 1685, Delamere indicated that he used the alias "Brown" and admitted that he had met Wildman at his house sometime before May 22, when the Parliament convened. Delamere could not or would not be more precise as to the date or who else was at the meeting (Landsdowne MS 1152, fol. 294). "James Welsh" wrote several other canting letters in January—to Thomas Jones and William Paine—which were intercepted.

[143] Add. MS 4159, fol. 185.

may even be Locke himself, and the particular canting phrase of "walks" in the spring as a euphemism for the date of the revolution, which Locke had employed in his letters to Clarke. "Mrs. Kean" is also an interesting reference, since Keane was Locke's mother's maiden name.[144] The individual referred to under that pseudonym is, I believe, Monmouth, who suffers from "pains in her heart" because he is not yet absolutely convinced of the necessity of a revolution (and for the good reasons discussed above, which were unknown to the radicals).

These letters from Holland brought replies from England. Writing from London on January 12, Sarah Gibbons also made use of medical terminology, reporting that "I have been very ill all Christmas with fits, but I am somewhat better now. If it please God that you should come over, nothing can be more welcome to me. I have satisfied my Brother Mores concerning those things." And she adds, "the first opportunity I have I will send over some money to you to buy a corset and primmer for a particular friend of mine. Love to Cousin Hubbert and all our friends."[145] I do not know who Brother Mores or Cousin Hubbert were, but Sarah Gibbons was the wife of John Gibbons, Monmouth's personal servant, and a frequent messenger traveling on the packet boat between Holland and England. On January 20, 1685, Sarah Hubbard sent the following letter from Brussels to Mrs. Ann Mobury in England:

> I have not had any letters from you, though I have previously written. I'm sending this by Mr. Gibbons with some money to buy some tobacco for my father. I have all the things you left with Mr. Sparrow; send word where my keys and things are . . . if all things go well . . . I may see you this summer.

She also indicates that she is particularly concerned about the health of "my child."[146] There are two more letters from Sarah Hubbard, undated, which convey the message that his grace is well, and mention the subject of money. She pleads with her correspondent in England, "Pray send us word what is become of Mrs. Percival. We heard that she was gone away, but we long to hear how it is with her."[147] This, too, is an interesting reference in view of the fact that Mrs. Percival was a particular confidante of Locke, with whom he had left some of his belongings when he fled from

[144] Fox-Bourne, 1:4. Wade, for example, used the alias of his mother's maiden name (Bryan Little, *The Monmouth Episode*, London: Werner Laurie, 1956, p. 203). In a letter to Clarke at the beginning of April 1685, Chapman Bray is again mentioned by Locke (*Correspondence*, 2:707).

[145] Add. MS 41803, fol. 107.

[146] Add. MS 41803, fol. 108.

[147] Add. MS 41803, fols. 110–111.

England.[148] In a notebook that Locke had with him in Holland, there are some cryptic notations: "letter . . . Sarah Dear . . . Brother."[149] These look suspiciously like code words indicating the style of cant to be used, and they could easily be applicable to the letters from either Sarah Hubbard or Sarah Gibbons. From the location (Brussels) and the fact that she is "sending" Mr. Gibbons, "Sarah Hubbard" may well have been Monmouth himself. John Gibbons was someone Monmouth trusted, and through whom he often conveyed messages. In this instance, however, Gibbons was seized as he disembarked at Dover, and the letters he was carrying, all of them written in cant, were confiscated.[150] Nor was Gibbons alone, for in February, William Spence, alias Tristam Butler, was arrested at Harwich carrying five letters from the radicals in Utrecht and some letters and a trunk belonging to James Washington, a sympathetic resident merchant of Rotterdam.[151] Under examination, Spence admitted "he saw Mr. Wilmore, Israel Hayes, Thomas Dare, and Mr. Keck, who are all as great rogues as any in Holland." The English agent also reported that Spence had mentioned a house in Amsterdam where Ayloffe, the two Goodenoughs, Norton, Wilmore, and several others have been harbored.[152] Since Locke notes on several occasions that he stayed in the same lodgings as Wilmore or paid him for his bed, it may be that he was among the others harbored in this Amsterdam house.[153]

One of the confiscated letters appears to be from Thomas Papillon, formerly a London merchant and sheriff closely associated with Shaftesbury, now one of the exiled radicals in Holland.[154] He observes that he has previously written "my good friend Mr. Brown, but I am troubled and disappointed not to have an answer from him." Nor has he heard from

[148] Mary Percival had been a member of Shaftesbury's household from at least the 1670s, and was thus well known to Locke (Christie, *Shaftesbury*, 2:211; Fox-Bourne, 1:433). She is mentioned by Locke in his letters to Clarke, March–April 1685. Mrs. Percival is also mentioned in two letters that I believe are misdated by De Beer as 1686, but belong to 1685 (*Correspondence*, 2:770–791; 3:1–4).

[149] MS f.28, fol. 155.

[150] Add. MS 41803, fols. 123, 170; *CSPD* (James II), 1:1.

[151] Add. MS 41803, fol. 181. That Spence went by the name of Butler is provided by Major Holmes' testimony (*True and Plain Account*, p. 9).

[152] Add. MS 41803, fol. 191.

[153] MS f.7, fol. 142; MS f.8, fol. 72.

[154] Everest seized two letters, both of the same date (February 10, 1685). One of them, written under pseudonyms and in cant—cited in the text—he noted on the back was written by Papillon. The other was a letter signed "T.P." and addressed to Papillon's wife in Amsterdam. Since the handwriting is completely different, both letters cannot be by Papillon. Papillon lived in Utrecht, not Amsterdam, and was unlikely to sign a letter to his wife "T.P." I believe the latter, therefore, was a forgery—by no means the only one—written by one of Skelton's spies.

Mr. Grock(?), Mr. Clark, or Mrs. Laile(?).[155] Another letter for Elizabeth Croxton in Brussels, dated the end of January and addressed "Dear Mother," complains that this is the third letter she has written since coming here, but she has not heard from her. And, the author adds, "I hope to see England by Easter."[156]

I believe these letters indicate that Monmouth was more informed about Argyll's plans for a rebellion and at an earlier date than has been assumed. Yet, they also make very evident the difficulties faced by the radicals in Holland in raising the money they needed from their friends in England, as well as the problems of sending and receiving messages across "the long pond." Being informed about and being wholly committed to the undertaking are, however, two different things, and the correspondence cited above discloses the doubts entertained by Monmouth prior to Charles' death regarding the necessity of armed rebellion, at least so far as England was concerned. Monmouth was at The Hague when he learned of his father's death, and incidentally of an express message from James II asking William to arrest him. William himself showed Monmouth the letter and allowed him to escape. He went to Rotterdam, and then to Brussels.[157]

While at Brussels, Monmouth received a letter from Spence, informing him of the preparations for Argyll's invasion, and asking whether he intended to lend his support to it. Emerson dated this letter "around the end of March," and on that basis, argued that sometime between that date and April 21, "a great change" occurred in Monmouth's attitude toward the projected rebellion, which at the last minute he decided to join.[158] This assumption was used to support the argument that Monmouth moved from a state of indecision to plunging into a rebellion over which he did not have any organizational control; moreover, he did so on the basis of false intelligence fed to him by Ferguson and by his contacts in England.[159] Such is the portrayal of Monmouth's involvement in his rebellion as presented in the secondary literature. This picture, I believe, is at

155 Add. MS 41803, fol. 185. From the handwriting, with the exception of "Clark," it is difficult to make out the names. "Grock" is an approximation, and probably a pseudonym in any case. The other is probably Mrs. Lisle, who was a radical sympathizer, and who was subsequently executed for having given refuge to Richard Nelthorp and John Hicks at the time of Monmouth's Rebellion. "Clark" may be a pseudonym for Ferguson, who used that name during this period (Add. MS 41810, fol. 69). Or alternatively, it might very well refer to Edward Clarke.

156 Add. MS 41803, fol. 113.

157 *Memoirs of Veitch and Brysson*, p. 165; D'Oyley, *Monmouth*, p. 263.

158 Emerson, *Monmouth's Rebellion*, pp. 12, 69–70. The original letter to Spence is printed in Welwood, *Memoirs*, pp. 377–378.

159 Emerson, *Monmouth's Rebellion*, p. 13.

best misleading, and in some respects false. Neither Emerson nor most of those who have accepted his authority, such as Trench, consulted the Middleton manuscripts and certain other material that renders the sequence of events in their narratives implausible; and this, in turn, necessitates a reinterpretation of the meaning of those events and of Monmouth's intentions.

According to Grey, immediately after Monmouth left The Hague for Brussels (February 16 or 17), Ferguson came to him and asked him to arrange a meeting between Argyll and Monmouth. Grey told him that the latter was in Brussels. Ferguson informed Grey of Argyll's plans, indicating that a number of English radicals were involved, that arms and ammunition had been purchased, "and that all things were in that readiness for his design." If Monmouth did not speedily lend his support to the revolution, Ferguson declared, "there were those that would [act] without him."[160] A few days later, Grey learned from Dare that the Scots had sent to Monmouth and had received a favorable answer from him, indicating that a meeting between Argyll and Monmouth would take place very soon.[161] This means that Spence wrote to Monmouth and received a reply from him in late February, not March, and that Monmouth's participation in the project began a month earlier and with a greater commitment on his part than has generally been assumed.[162] Patrick Hume, one of the Scottish leaders close to Argyll, supports this view. In his narrative of Argyll's rebellion, Hume writes that the Scots invited Monmouth, then in Brussels, to come to Rotterdam, "giving in the letter some intimation of our business with him, who without delay came to us," and agreed to join with Argyll in the enterprise.[163] If Monmouth had not replied to the Scots' invitation until the end of March, Hume would hardly have characterized this as a response "without delay," especially considering the state of readiness of Argyll's forces at the end of February. And in any case, Monmouth was not allowed to remain in Brussels from mid-Feb-

[160] *Secret History*, pp. 92–95; *Ferguson*, p. 199.

[161] *Secret History*, p. 97.

[162] Monmouth writes that "I received both yours together this morning," which could mean either that Spence wrote two letters that arrived together, or that two separate individuals wrote to Monmouth on the same subject and his letter is in effect a reply to both persons. Since Hume did, in fact, write to Monmouth at the end of February, I am inclined toward the latter interpretation (Emerson, *Monmouth's Rebellion*, pp. 9–10). Hume says "we" invited Monmouth to come to Rotterdam, and that he replied "to us" affirmatively (Patrick Hume, *Narrative of Occurrences in the Expedition of the Earl of Argyle in 1685*, in *Observations on the Historical Work of Charles James Fox*, by George Rose, 1809, p. 9). Both Hume and Spence wrote not as individuals but on behalf of Argyll and the Scots, as Monmouth clearly understood.

[163] P. Hume, *Narrative*, p. 9.

ruary until the end of March. As Wade notes, by order of the Marquis de Grana, James obtained an order banishing Monmouth from Brussels and all Spanish territory within a very short time after his departure from The Hague.[164]

Thus, both in response to the letters he received and to his expulsion, Monmouth left Brussels at the beginning of March and went to Rotterdam. He sent his aide, Captain Matthews, to Amsterdam to arrange for lodging and to set up the meeting with Argyll. A day or two later, Monmouth went to Amsterdam and met with Patrick Hume and some other Scotsmen. They discussed the planned rising in Scotland, and within two days of this meeting, Monmouth and Argyll met at Dare's house. Argyll told him that he had around ten thousand arms, several field pieces, five hundred barrels of powder, that he was buying three ships and would be ready to sail in a fortnight, but that he would delay his sailing if a rising was being planned for England, in order to coordinate their efforts. It is obvious that, had Argyll received an indecisive response from Monmouth at this meeting, he was prepared to go it alone, and to sail for Scotland before the end of March. But as Monmouth later informed Grey, "he was abundantly satisfied with my Lord Argyle's design," to which he gave his positive support.[165] And accordingly, Argyll postponed the planned date of his sailing.

We can date this meeting between Argyll and Monmouth around March 7 or 8 because Robert Cragg, an emissary from Wildman, arrived in Amsterdam just as it concluded. The radicals in England had maintained their contacts with one another throughout 1684, and in the early months of 1685, they held meetings to consider the political situation.[166] Wildman's cousin, William Disney, sent Cragg to Holland at the end of February to find out Monmouth's plans because the English radicals knew

[164] Harleian MS 6845, fol. 270; *Memoirs of Veitch and Brysson*, pp. 166–167. Barrillon reported in his February 23 dispatch to Louis XIV that the Spanish ambassador had already asked James how Monmouth should be received in Brussels (Emerson, *Monmouth's Rebellion*, p. 76). On March 1, James II had an audience with the envoy from the Marquis de Grana, at which I believe he stated or (restated) his demand for Monmouth's expulsion. It is true, he had another audience with the envoy on March 15, but this was probably in the nature of a report that Monmouth had, in fact, left Brussels (*London Gazette*, March 2–5, 1685).

[165] *Secret History*, pp. 99–101; Harleian MS 6845, fol. 270; Thomas Salmon, ed., *A Complete Collection of State Trials and Proceedings upon High Treason*, 2d ed., 4 vols., 1730, 4:222.

[166] Whitley's diary shows that there was a good deal of activity among the English radicals in February 1685 (MS English History C.711, fols. 26–27). One of the individuals meeting with them and acting as a messenger for Argyll was Locke's friend, Walter Cross. On April 7, he left for Holland, but on April 15, he was back in England (fol. 30; Add. MS 41803, fol. 224).

of Argyll's planned invasion of Scotland and wanted to ascertain what role, if any, Monmouth had in that design. Cragg says he arrived at Amsterdam on March 7 or 8.[167] Wade brought the news of Cragg's arrival to Monmouth, as the latter was relating to Grey the results of the just-concluded meeting with Argyll. Monmouth agreed to see Cragg the next morning. Meanwhile, Ferguson spoke with Cragg, informing him in general of the results of the meeting between Argyll and Monmouth. Argyll had agreed to sail for Scotland in a month's time, and Monmouth would sail for England about two weeks after that. The rebellion was therefore scheduled for late April or early May.[168] Ferguson reported back to Monmouth that evening, and the next morning Monmouth met with Cragg, and sent him back to England to arrange for money and support.[169]

At the same time, Monmouth dispatched Captain Matthews to speak to his supporters in Cheshire, and Battiscombe to speak to Wildman and those in the west country.[170] Cragg made several trips between Holland

[167] Cragg says he was asked to go to Holland at the end of February; hence, his arrival there on March 7 or 8—i.e., late February in England (HMC 12th Report, appendix, pt. 6, p. 393). It is not always easy to determine whether the English or Continental date is being used for a particular document, but I have tried to give the local date for the events described in the chronology.

[168] HMC 12th Report, appendix, pt. 6, pp. 393–394; *Secret History*, p. 101. Emerson's charge that Ferguson's assurance to Cragg that Monmouth and Argyll were cooperating "was almost certainly a lie," and that this began a fateful chain of misleading information passed between Holland and England, is based upon his misdating of events (*Monmouth's Rebellion*, p. 11). Milne also advanced this view (*Rye House Plot*, p. 293n.). Grey's account, however, makes it very clear that Ferguson spoke with Cragg *after* the meeting between Argyll and Monmouth at Dare's house and that Monmouth (and Grey) met with Cragg the next day. Moreover, this was at the time of Cragg's first trip to Holland, because the reason Ferguson was meeting him was that Monmouth did not know Cragg or what he wanted. Hence, Ferguson's task was to find out and report back to Monmouth prior to the latter's meeting with Cragg, which is what happened. On his later trips to Holland, Cragg simply made direct contact with Monmouth.

[169] *Secret History*, pp. 102–103. In his 1689 account, Cragg never mentioned meeting with Monmouth on his first visit, but said he simply carried back Ferguson's instructions to Disney and others (HMC 12th Report, appendix, pt. 6, p. 393). Grey's account, however, written a few months after the meeting, at which he was present and put questions to Cragg, seems more reliable.

[170] *Secret History*, p. 108; Harleian MS 6845, fol. 271; HMC 12th Report, appendix, pt. 6, p. 393. Emerson maintained that "Monmouth's intelligence from England was based solely on the reports of one Robert Cragg" (*Monmouth's Rebellion*, pp. 14, 23, 77). This is not true. Had he consulted the Middleton manuscripts, Emerson would have seen that messengers from both Argyll and Monmouth were crossing between Holland and England several times a week between February and May 1685. During that period, Ezekiel Everest was stationed at Harwich for the express purpose of reporting on all passengers traveling to and from Holland. Some of his reports, with the names of all suspicious persons, are included in these manuscripts. He knew, for example, that "Robert Smith" was a suspicious person,

and England, but the radicals in London were poorly organized, and some of the country gentlemen were cool to Monmouth's plans for a rebellion. Nevertheless, despite Wildman's reluctance to accede to Monmouth's requests for financial assistance, Cragg did bring back some money from London on one of his trips, and Monmouth, in any case, was prepared to act without the full support of those in England.[171] Matthews had been gone almost three weeks before Monmouth received a letter from him, around the beginning of April, containing generally favorable news.[172] After receiving this letter, Monmouth conferred with Argyll, and the latter decided to get everything in a state of readiness such that he could sail at a day's notice. He called a general war council of his officers in Amsterdam.[173] At the same time, Monmouth sent his servants to England to spread the news that Argyll was about to sail.[174] Around April 14, there was a large meeting of Scots in Rotterdam, where the rebellion was openly discussed.[175] On April 17, another large meeting was held in Amsterdam, presided over by John Cochrane. At the Rotterdam meeting, they had discussed Argyll's Declaration, and in Amsterdam they compared that document with the draft of Monmouth's Declaration. After some discussion and amendments, the two declarations were more or less reconciled. James Stewart was asked to make a final copy of Argyll's Declaration to be ready in a few days.[176]

These large meetings in Rotterdam and Amsterdam, and the plans for the rebellion, were so openly discussed, Wade reflected, that "we expected every day to hear of it in their public gazettes."[177] In fact, Argyll

---

though not that this was the alias of Robert Cragg. There was also a spotter at Dover, but there are fewer reports pertaining to that port.

171 HMC 12th Report, appendix, pt. 6, pp. 393–394; Landsdowne MS 1152, fol. 268.

172 *Secret History*, pp. 118–119. Emerson dates Matthews' letter as April 21, and suggests that Argyll waited for this letter before calling his war council (*Monmouth's Rebellion*, pp. 15, 80). This makes no sense, since Grey plainly states that Argyll did not decide to call his officers together until after Monmouth had heard from Captain Matthews. Since that meeting was held on April 17, Matthews' letter could hardly have arrived four days later. Moreover, the notice for the meeting, judging by the reports on the movements of the exiles in Utrecht, Rotterdam, and Amsterdam, went out several days, possibly as much as a week, before the date of the meeting. This moves Argyll's decision even further away from a dependence on Matthews' letter unless, as I maintain, the letter arrived during the first week in April (which accounts for the three-week period following Matthews' departure, around March 9 or 10, not April 1, as Emerson says).

173 *Secret History*, p. 119.

174 Add. MS 41812, fol. 15.

175 Erskine, *Journal*, p. 112; P. Hume, *Narrative*, pp. 36–37; Add. MS 41812, fol. 17; Add. MS 41817, fol. 3; D'Avaux, *Negotiations*, 3:191.

176 P. Hume, *Narrative*, pp. 36–37; *Memoirs of Veitch and Brysson*, p. 311; *Ferguson*, p. 203; Wodrow, *Sufferings of the Church*, 4:284.

177 Harleian MS 6845, fol. 270.

received a message through Dare that his expedition "was so public at the Hague" that Skelton was about to ask the States-General to seize his ships. Upon receiving this intelligence, Argyll decided to set sail. He dispatched several messengers to Scotland and England with that news.[178] This decision was probably made around April 23, and on the 28th, Argyll's forces boarded their ships, which sailed from Amsterdam a couple of days later.[179] I will return in a moment to the chronology of the narrative as it concerns Monmouth's preparations for the rebellion during May, but first, I want to consider Locke's correspondence and activities in light of the events discussed thus far.

On February 6, 1685, Locke wrote a canting letter to Clarke discussing turnips and lime trees, the gist of which seems to be that the latter should be set up "20 foot" on either side of Clarke's house. Locke reflects:

> If I had your coat of Arms in colors I would get it done in glass to be set up somewhere at Chipley, being very well acquainted with a good glass painter here.

If the "glass painter" refers to Argyll, Clarke's responsibility appears to have been to supply forty foot soldiers to be set up in the neighborhood of Chipley. After mentioning some other "trees," Locke advises his friend to "examine the gardens and see how many of them were left last summer."[180] That is, after the government's discovery of Argyll's initial plans for an invasion and its arrest of some English radicals. In the same

[178] *Secret History*, p. 119; Harleian MS 6845, fol. 270; *Memoirs of Veitch and Brysson*, p. 148; Erskine, *Journal*, p. 112. Erskine saw Veitch, who was one of Argyll's messengers, on the eighteenth, so he obviously left after that date.

[179] Erskine, *Journal*, pp. 113–114; *Memoirs of Veitch and Brysson*, p. 313.

[180] *Correspondence*, 2:684–685. This letter appears to have been written with some urgency, since it was sent only three days after Locke had written Clarke, and before he received any reply. The reason he gives is that in the earlier letter, he forgot to say something "about your garden and trees," hardly a matter for urgent discussion, unless the references are allusive. February 3–10, however, was precisely the period in which Argyll and those around him began to move their preparations for a rebellion into high gear. This appears to have been in response to Charles' decision to call the Scottish Parliament into session. That Charles had made such a decision prior to his death was conceded by James. According to him, the Scottish Parliament was to have met sometime in March (Richard Lodge, *The Political History of England: From the Restoration to the Death of William III*, London: Longmans, Green, 1923, p. 234). News of Charles' intention reached Monmouth at The Hague on February 3, in the form of a letter from Halifax. If it reached Argyll and the other exiles at approximately the same time, it would explain why so many messengers and so many letters were sent from Holland during the first week of February. Erskine recorded in his *Journal* (p. 99) that the Scottish Parliament was scheduled to meet on March 10, 1685. As later discussions make clear, Argyll intended to land in Scotland before the Scottish Parliament met. In this context, Locke's letter does take on some urgency as to its news.

notebook previously mentioned, after Clarke's name Locke has written, Write to him of limes and turnips.[181] Again, this represents the recording of a cipher, a fact confirmed by Clarke's notation on Locke's letter, describing its contents as "an account of seeds, etc.: and some ciphers on it."[182]

Although the period between February and April is one of those in which Locke's movements are difficult to determine from his journal, on March 8 he was still receiving his mail at Dare's house, and was either staying there himself or was in frequent contact with Dare.[183] As we have seen, it was just at this time that Monmouth and Argyll met at Dare's house, when Ferguson delivered his reports there, and when Cragg came to see Monmouth there. Grey noted in his confession that Cragg not only carried a message from London, he also brought some money (or more likely, bills of exchange) with him for Ayloffe and others in Holland.[184] It was just at this time (the first week in March) that Locke recorded a financial transaction involving a bill on Van Tongaren for £300, a bill on Abarbanel for £100, and another for £100 on R. Hill.[185] This looks like another transmission of funds for the cause, and as we shall see, a few weeks after this, Locke is involved in the effort to purchase arms and ammunition for the rebellion.

On March 22, Locke wrote Clarke from Utrecht, advising him that "you should not think of your journey till the beginning of May at soonest" because of the various accidents "and incommodities of travel" that threaten a "relapse" if the trip should be made before then. Some of the difficulties of advancing the date of the revolution and Clarke's journey into the west country are recounted by Locke:

> The seeds I hope you have ere this but the trees we are very unlucky in, for when I believed them at Exeter I received a note that told me that they were not to be got where I was promised them and therefore I was advised this was the place I must furnish myself. I then presently sought the nurseries here, where I found none but what were . . . infinitely above the price I expected . . . I was loath to give

[181] MS f.28, fol. 141.

[182] *Correspondence*, 2:685.

[183] A letter to Locke from Nicolas Toinard, dated March 8, 1685, is addressed to him care of Dare (*Correspondence*, 2:696). Grey was staying at Dare's house in early March (*Secret History*, p. 100).

[184] Landsdowne MS 1152, fol. 268.

[185] Locke notes that these bills were sent by Clarke to Locke, through him to Dare, and processed through Percival (MS b.1, fol. 55). A few months later, Robert Hill was executed for his participation in Monmouth's Rebellion (George Roberts, *The Life, Progress, and Rebellion of James, Duke of Monmouth*, 2 vols., 1844, 2:263).

> £15 sterling for 200 Lime tree plants. . . . I advise you to furnish yourself among the gardeners and seeds men in and about London with the seeds.[186]

Other letters to Clarke refer to "turnips," "seeds," and "lime trees" and of Locke providing him with "another parcel of seeds" that "your gardener will take care to sow them so as to observe which genus will suit you," and so forth.[187] In the context of Locke's journal notations, the intelligence reports on his activities during this period, and the general preparations being made by the Scottish and English radicals, Locke's correspondence with Clarke in the early months of 1685 seems to be conveying information about the difficulty of obtaining "trees" (arms) in Holland because of the lack of money. Therefore, Clarke and the English radicals must "furnish" the "seeds" (money) from among the "gardeners and seeds men in and about London" (Wildman, Danvers, and the London radicals). On April 5, Locke wrote to Clarke:

> Mr. Bray you say in your last of 17 Mar [lost] yet hears nothing and I begin to think that I shall never hear anything of that I expected.

If Chapman Bray is a pseudonym for Wildman, Locke's message communicates the frustration of Monmouth and the English radicals in Holland with Wildman's reluctance to send them money, or even encouraging reports about the prospects for the rebellion.

The primary message Locke wants to get through to Clarke, however, and which he repeats over and over in his letters, is that the revolution has been set for, or at least is not likely to occur before, sometime in May.

> Yet let me prevail with you; not to venture upon that journey ["into the country"] till the warm weather of May.

And, a few lines later, Locke writes, "I therefore beg you not to think of your journey till the warm weather in May be steady and settled." This admonition to Clarke is reaffirmed in Locke's subsequent letters.[188]

At the end of March, Skelton reported to Middleton that Monmouth and Argyll were meeting in Rotterdam. A few days later, he complained that the rebels "swarm" together in various parts of Holland, and that Ferguson had grown bold enough to appear publicly on the streets of Amsterdam. On April 3, he wrote that the rebels "flock together at Rotterdam" and "are in continual consultations." In the same report, Skelton conveyed the news that Monmouth and Argyll were meeting at Dare's

[186] *Correspondence*, 2:696–697.
[187] *Correspondence*, 2:688–689, 707–710, 721.
[188] *Correspondence*, 2:707, 712, 718.

house in Amsterdam.[189] This meeting finalized the agreement between the two leaders on the two-pronged assault, and their respective responsibilities in the rebellion.[190] Locke's letter of April 5, subsequent to this meeting, thus is able to confirm the "steady and settled" date of May as the projected month of arrival of Monmouth in the west country of England.

On April 14, Skelton wrote to Middleton that at midnight on the previous Sunday, "an unknown person desired . . . to speak with me in private," pretending to have important information to disclose. All Skelton could discover was that Rumbold and Nelthorp were then at Amsterdam and were often with Monmouth, which the envoy said was no news to him, nor was he ignorant of what they designed. But this mysterious individual told Skelton how easily "his Majesty might be rid of a very ill and dangerous subject" (Monmouth), which for a price, he was volunteering his services. Skelton says he "expressed great detestation of so horrid a thing, assuring him that his Majesty would abhor the man that should make any such proposal to him." Yet he also concluded that the individual had in fact been sent by the rebel party in order "to discover whether any thing of that nature were intended" or would be embraced by the government. Skelton believed, correctly, that Monmouth suspected that James II had given secret orders to have him killed.[191]

Skelton was not speaking idly when he indicated to this suspected double agent sent by the radicals that he knew what they were up to. There was nothing wrong with his intelligence system, which was even more effective and accurate than the one employed by Chudleigh. On April 13, for example, Skelton notified his superiors that the rebels had three small ships being prepared to sail for Scotland. Not only that, he obtained a detailed list of those supplies, the number of barrels of powder, muskets, and so forth, which had been loaded onto the ships.[192] Also, in mid-April, he confiscated some letters, described as being extremely damaging to

[189] Add. MS 41812, fols. 2, 7, 9.

[190] This is probably the meeting at which Monmouth related the news he had received from Captain Matthews, although Matthews' letter might have arrived prior to their meeting in Rotterdam at the end of March (Add. MS 41812, fol. 2).

[191] Add. MS 41812, fol. 20. In fact, Chudleigh had written to a correspondent (probably Richard Bulestrode, the English envoy in Brussels) that "if you can seize and convey [Monmouth] safe to England it will be a piece of service that you shall be well thanked for; and therefore pray go about it if you find any hopes or opportunity for it, but do it discreetly, without letting anything of your design appear to any but such as will be assisting to you in it, and let it not be known that I have given you any such direction as this" (cited in Fea, *Loyal Wentworths*, pp. 151–152).

[192] Add. MS 41817, fols. 1, 7, 13.

Monmouth, which he forwarded to England.[193] It was around this time that Skelton managed to recruit a highly placed radical in Utrecht who agreed to inform on his associates. This individual is never named in the manuscript reports, but he is without question an unsuspected, well-informed member of the planning group with access to the decisions made at the highest level. More than two weeks prior to Monmouth's landing in England, for example, this spy had supplied Skelton with the exact location—Lyme Regis—where Monmouth's invasion force proposed to set ashore, a fact that even those on Monmouth's ships did not know until they were several days at sea.[194] Various radicals, including Slingsby Bethel, frequently stayed at the spy's house, or held their meetings there. On other occasions, he is clearly reporting the substance of meetings at which he was present.[195] He was, in other words, a key instrument in the English government's attempt to penetrate and neutralize the radical exile organization.

It is in this context that we must consider the intelligence reports that describe Locke's activities, for many, but not all, of them are supplied by this particular double agent in Utrecht who obviously knew Locke very well. On May 8, this informer reported where Ferguson was hiding in Amsterdam, and the various comings and goings of messengers between England and Holland, to which he added a note about "the secretary of Shaftesbury, Doctor Lock," describing his association with the radicals. In other reports, he comments on Locke's great secrecy in discussing public affairs, his adoption of several aliases, his hiding and taking refuge with other radicals, including Locke's staying with the double agent himself.[196] On May 22, the latter reported on the large gathering of rebels in Amsterdam, a final assembly of those sailing with Monmouth. The agent was leaving Utrecht that evening for Amsterdam, as did Locke.[197] Later reports give accounts of meetings between Starkey and Locke, or associate him with Mrs. Smith, Vandervelde, John Howe, Lord Wharton, and others. Since some of these intelligence letters were written months after the defeat of Monmouth's Rebellion, they will be considered in connec-

[193] Add. MS 41812, fol. 17.

[194] Add. MS 41817, fol. 142. It is therefore not true, as Wyndham states, that "Monmouth's actual place of landing, Lyme Regis . . . was kept completely secret from James II's spies" (Violet Wyndham, *The Protestant Duke*, London: Weidenfeld and Nicolson, 1976, p. 131; cf. D'Oyley, *Monmouth*, p. 274).

[195] One remarkable letter suddenly breaks off in mid-report because the radicals about whom the informant is writing "have just come into my house" (Add. MS 41812, fols. 154–155). Frequently, his reports were passed through two other spies, a husband and wife living in Utrecht, in order to increase his concealment.

[196] Add. MS 41812, fols. 70, 85.

[197] Add. MS 41812, fol. 77; MS f.8, fol. 273.

tion with the events of that period. What they make clear, however, is that the English envoy in Holland, and therefore the ministers in Whitehall, were well-informed regarding the specific plans and activities of the radicals, including Locke.[198]

On April 21, Skelton wrote that there was a gathering of English rebels in Utrecht, and that he planned to make a trip there to gather better intelligence. Three days later, reporting on his trip, the envoy gave an account of a meeting in that city of Ferguson, Papillon, Patience Ward, Starkey, and others, adding that he had learned that the radicals "intend very suddenly for England," and that some people in Amsterdam furnish the money to carry out their designs.[199] In May, one of Skelton's spies in Rotterdam provided information on the 60 great guns, 500 English and Scottish rebels, and ammunition for 5,000 men carried by Argyll's three ships, which had already sailed. He also observed that a number of the English merchants in Holland were "concerned in this affair," that is, equipping the expedition, and indicated that he could probably find out exactly "who furnished the money" for Argyll's invasion.[200] Another report in May mentions that the radicals in Amsterdam are suddenly in possession of a large amount of cash.[201] On April 16, Locke went from Amsterdam to Utrecht, possibly to attend the meeting alluded to by Skelton.[202] Sometime between April 16 and early May, £500 passed through Locke's hands, precisely at the time he was named as one of those purchasing arms for the rebellion.[203] This money, as well as the previously mentioned sums credited to "the Bank" in Thomas Dare's custody, thus appear to represent Locke's financial contribution to Monmouth's Rebellion, though what proportion of the total contribution was drawn from his personal income and what amount of money was funneled through his hands as a trustee for the cause is difficult to determine. Of Dare's role as a purchasing agent and financier for Monmouth's Rebellion there has never been any doubt.[204] Locke's biographers, however—including Cran-

[198] On May 22, 1685, Middleton wrote Skelton: "The good intelligence you had from Utrecht is particularly taken notice of and commended by his Majesty" (Add. MS 41823, fol. 16).

[199] Add. MS 41812, fols. 33–34.

[200] Add. MS 41817, fol. 13.

[201] Add. MS 41822, fol. 242.

[202] MS f.8, fol. 268.

[203] MS b.1, fol. 55. Monmouth's arms were purchased for a ship that was supposedly bound for Spain (Roberts, *Life of Monmouth*, 1:197). It is again curious that the names of "Mr. Henriquez" and "Antonio Rodriquez Marquis" appear on the bills of exchange being processed by Locke in the early months of 1685 (cf. *Correspondence*, 3:107, 119).

[204] Harleian MS 6845, fol. 264.

ston—have strenuously denied that he played this or any other role in the forwarding of Monmouth's Rebellion.[205]

The original allegation of Locke's involvement with the latter arose because both Lord Grey and Nathaniel Wade, who were captured following Monmouth's defeat at Sedgemoor, named Locke as a financial contributor to the rebellion in their respective confessions. Locke's Victorian biographers simply assumed that Grey and Wade were mistaken or that they were referring to some other Locke. This is also Cranston's position, although he did make an effort to identify this other Locke. Wade testified that it "cost about £9000" to equip Argyll's expedition, and that "£1000 was given by Mr. Lock and the rest I suppose by Madame Smith." In the case of Monmouth, Wade said the duke had pawned "all he had in the world" to raise the needed funds, and that besides this money, "as I remember £400 was given by Mr. Lock, £100 by William Rumbold, £500 by Sir Patience Ward."[206] Grey confirmed Wade's testimony in his own confession, indicating that Argyll had received money from Mrs. Smith and "near a £1000 from Mr. Locke." "The Duke of Monmouth," Grey said, "had money presented by Mrs. Smith, Mr. Lock," Daniel Le Blon, and some others, whose names he could not remember.[207] After citing this evidence, Cranston observes:

> The reader will notice that neither Wade nor Grey named Mr. *John* Locke; in fact I believe they were both referring to another man. The clue here is a deposition made by Ezekiel Everest on January 19 1683/4 informing the British government how Argyle with several Scotsmen "and one Smith and his wife with Lock a tobacconist of London had come to Cleves and then returned to Holland. Smith and his wife and Lock with some part of the company went to Utrecht, where they are now." Later, Everest mentioned the presence of Sir Patience Ward in Utrecht. Lock the tobacconist is thus connected with Argyle, the Smiths, Sir Patience Ward and Scotsmen; and for this reason I believe that their Mr. Lock is the tobacconist of London and not the subject of this biography.

[205] George Roberts is one scholar familiar with the evidence who inferred that Wade and Grey were obviously referring to Locke (Roberts, *Life of Monmouth*, p. 256).

[206] Harleian MS 6845, fols. 270, 272. John Erskine, one of the Scottish radicals who sailed with Argyll, also noted in his journal that "Mr. Lock . . . advanced a part" of the funds to finance Monmouth's Rebellion (*Journal*, p. 180). Apart from a number of mutual friends and acquaintances among the radical exiles, one reason that Erskine was in a position to know who Locke was is that he, like the latter, frequently attended book auctions (pp. 110, 177).

[207] *Secret History*, pp. 120, 126.

To which Cranston adds the gratuitous remark, "I should not have expected the philosopher to give money to the rebel funds: he was not a giving man."[208]

Before taking up the clue offered by Cranston, which is a far more complicated issue than he knew, two important points need to be emphasized. First, Wade and Grey, through their association with Shaftesbury and the Rye House conspiracy, were well known to and were friends of Locke. When they named Locke as a contributor in their confessions, with a knowledge of the amount of his contributions, it is obvious that they were naming an individual well known to each of them. What Cranston should have shown, but did not, was that either Wade or Grey knew "Lock the tobacconist." On the other hand, while Everest did know the latter, Cranston never introduced any evidence to show that Everest even knew who John Locke was. Moreover, it is otiose to assume that every reference to Locke—or any other exile—would normally include his first name. Virtually all of these individuals were well known to the English government. *They* knew who John Locke was. He, after all, was identified with Shaftesbury; he had been removed by the king from his place at Oxford a few months before the confessions of Wade and Grey; the latter, along with Ferguson, had been named one of his close companions in Holland; he was known to be staying in the house of the man (Dare) who was the chief financial conduit for Monmouth's Rebellion; and he was one of the eighty fugitives specifically named in a memorial presented to the Dutch authorities by the English government indicating the persons they wanted arrested and extradited to England to stand trial. Indeed, in these circumstances, it is *any other "Lock"* introduced into the discussion whose first name would have to be given in order to distinguish him from the Locke the English government already knew to be a subversive.

The second point relates to the information contained in the manuscripts from which I have cited, whose existence was unknown to Cranston or his predecessors. In them, as we have seen, Locke is associated with Mrs. Smith, Argyll, Sir Patience Ward, and the Scotsmen in Utrecht (especially John Cochrane who managed much of Argyll's affairs). We have, in other words, independent confirmation from other sources of the association of Locke with the individuals named by Grey and Wade. There is no need, therefore, to search for another "Lock" to serve as a substitute for John Locke. And there the issue might be presumed to rest, except for the fact that there was another individual named (Nicholas) Lock involved in the revolutionary movement. He was, as Everest reported, a tobacconist of London. Cranston's error lay in his conclusion

[208] Cranston, pp. 250–251; *CSPD*, 26:222–228 (Everest's deposition).

that the existence of this Lock absolved Locke from the responsibility of having contributed money to the revolutionary cause, when in fact the evidence indicated only that more than one Locke was a supporter of that cause. The real problem, therefore, lies in trying to sort out their respective roles, and in determining which individual is being discussed on which occasion, rather than using the identity of their names as a means of dismissing the evidence against John Locke. This problem could not be resolved in the absence of an examination of the correspondence and intelligence reports submitted by Chudleigh and Skelton, since both Lockes are objects of surveillance by the spies working for the English envoys. From the context, and from the identification of "Lock the tobacconist" or "Locke, Shaftesbury's secretary," it is almost always possible to determine which person is being discussed.[209] And it is worth emphasizing again, the reports submitted by the double agent in Utrecht were from an individual who unequivocally identified his subject as being John Locke, and to whom the latter was well known personally. Nevertheless, there are a few occasions when it is not altogether clear which Locke an informer is reporting on, perhaps because neither individual is known to him by sight, or because he is relaying information that he has only heard from others, and for which he is unable to supply the contextual material necessary to make such a distinction between the two Lockes.

On May 9, 1684, Chudleigh sent a description of the other Lock to Whitehall:

> Mr. Lock who was formerly a tobacco merchant living in St. Bartholomew's Close . . . fled at the first breaking out of the late [Rye House] plot, and was some time at Cleves with Argyle, and has kept company with Ayloffe, Ferguson, and the worst of those villains ever since, residing for the most part at Utrecht.

Lock was residing with Mrs. Smith, and had two sons still living in England. He was reputed to be very rich, and a friend of Mr. Shepherd, the wine merchant. Because Lock was "in his nature very timorous," Chudleigh thought "that if he were apprehended and roundly handled, it's possible he might be brought to make considerable discoveries."[210] In his report, Chudleigh, who did not know this Lock, relied upon the information supplied him by Everest, then working as one of his spies.

Later Skelton was in a similar situation, forwarding some material as enclosures with his letter to Middleton concerning "one Lock who is a

[209] Cranston seems not to know who Nicholas Lock was, but Macaulay knew of him, though he, too, used him to absorb all the political references in order to protect John Locke (1:491n.).

[210] Add. MS 41810, fol. 64.

stranger to me, and so are his circumstances, except what I find in the account" provided by his informer.[211] According to the latter, "Lock is an old Quaker or Anabaptist tobacco trader to the English plantations, formerly dwelling in Bartholomew Close, who . . . first came out of England about three years ago [1683]." To obtain this information, Edmund Everard, who was an old friend and who was not known to Lock to be a spy, got him drunk and pumped him with questions. Lock maintained that although he had associated with Argyll and Mrs. Smith, "he never knew of their designs, for they knew it was against his principles either to fight at all, or to take up arms by way of resistance against Kings or magistrates," and he swore "that he never contributed nor gave a farthing to them directly nor indirectly" to further the rebellion.[212] Lock's testimony does not merit a particularly high rating on the credibility scale, especially when the fact that he was seeking a pardon from the English government is taken into account. Nevertheless, Everard was his friend, and his statements were confirmed in two separate interviews with his son, Joshua Lock. The latter, who was nineteen at the time (1686), did admit that he had been sympathetic to Monmouth's Rebellion, but he also denied that he gave one penny in support of the cause. He was in no position to contribute money, he explained, because, despite his reputed wealth, his father allowed him a small (£8) yearly allowance.[213] Apparently, it was Nicholas Lock, rather than John, who "was not a giving man." On another occasion, he refused Ferguson's request for money.[214] It may be, however, despite his denial, that Nicholas Lock did contribute something toward Argyll's invasion, but even if he did, it would not obviate John Locke's own, and separately identifiable, actions on behalf of the revolutionary movement.[215]

[211] Add. MS 41813, fol. 96.

[212] Add. MS 41819, fols. 13–14.

[213] Add. MS 41818, fol. 291. Joshua Lock was involved with Disney in the printing of Monmouth's Declaration, and even delivered a copy personally to Lord Delamere (*State Trials*, 4:227).

[214] Add. MS 41813, fols. 189–190.

[215] The evidence that Nicholas Lock did contribute to Monmouth's Rebellion comes from James Burton, who, however, got the amounts wrong for Mrs. Smith, and claimed that Lock was in Norway (which he was not). His testimony is not very credible or informed. More important is Richard Goodenough's assertion that Lock was a contributor to Monmouth's Rebellion, though he gives no amount. Both Burton and Goodenough identify the person they are referring to as Lock the tobacconist, on the assumption, I maintain, that the government would not otherwise know who they were talking about, whereas neither Wade nor Grey refer to Lock the tobacconist, but to Locke, a man well known to their interrogators (Landsdowne MS 1152, fol. 227). The most important testimony, of course, would have come from Dare, who was shot by Fletcher of Saltoun at the outset of the rebellion. To which it should be added that a great many papers pertaining to Monmouth's Rebellion

Since both men were closely associated with the same individuals, their paths, figuratively if not literally, crossed on several occasions. If there is a difference, it is that Nicholas emphasized his nonconformity (he is usually described as being an Anabaptist) and religious reasons for leaving England, while John was deeply concerned with the political issues. Both were relevant concerns for the English exiles in general, and for supporters of Monmouth and Argyll in particular. Yet following Monmouth's defeat, Nicholas accepted a pardon from the king and returned to England, while John Locke refused to allow his friends to obtain a pardon for him, and returned home only in the wake of James II's defeat and the Glorious Revolution.

One project both Lockes may have had a hand in is the writing and distribution of Monmouth's Declaration. Ferguson was the chief author of Monmouth's Declaration, but both it and the one drafted for Argyll were discussed at various meetings of the radicals. Since the former had long planned to make an invasion, something may have existed in writing prior to the spring of 1685, but Monmouth's Declaration could only have been written subsequent to his planning meetings with Argyll that took place during March. The meeting in Dare's house in Amsterdam on April 3 is the most probable locus for Ferguson's presentation of the declaration.[216] During the next two weeks, there were several large meetings of the radicals in various cities called to discuss, among other things, the declarations setting forth the aims of the rebellion.

In addition to being written, the declaration had to be printed, and the leading candidate must be Locke's friend and landlord, Vandervelde the bookseller, in whose house Argyll himself often stayed.[217] More to the point, perhaps, in this case are the intelligence reports submitted to Skelton informing him that a "Mr. Churchill, a bookseller" from London

---

were lost or destroyed. From a list of examinations that were at one time in the possession of the government (Landsdowne MS 1152, fol. 229) it is clear, to cite only two pertinent instances, that neither the interrogation of Battiscombe nor that of Nelthorp has survived. In November 1685, Bishop Sprat took some of these papers with him to the country, where he was supposed to write the continuation of his earlier volume on the Rye House conspiracy (fol. 271). After Sprat's death, many of these papers were destroyed by the Reverend William Glover, a curate in Kent (Add. MS 19399, fol. 141).

216 Richard Goodenough testifed in his examination before the Privy Council that Ferguson had written Monmouth's Declaration, and brought it to Dare's house to be approved by a group of radicals which included Goodenough, Grey, Wade, Tiley, Nelthorp, and reading between the lines, a number of others Goodenough does not name, since all of the above were already dead or in the hands of the government (Landsdowne MS 1152, fol. 242; Roberts, *Life of Monmouth*, p. 232).

217 Add. MS 41818, fol. 79. Since the declaration was printed in Flemish, French, and English in Holland prior to Monmouth's departure, it is likely that more than one printer/bookseller was involved (D'Avaux, *Negotiations*, 3:249).

made a secret trip to Holland, and that it was Churchill who supplied the paper for Monmouth's Declaration. Either he or his brother "printed or had a hand in printing Monmouth's Declaration," according to the informant. Moreover, Churchill was lodging with Vandervelde, "a notorious bookseller for the rebels' interest."[218] Locke had come to Amsterdam in the midst of this flurry of meetings, and may have stayed with Vandervelde himself before returning to Utrecht.[219] The double agent in Utrecht reported that "this printer from London" was a friend of Locke, from whom he had learned a great deal about the radicals' plans.[220] The probability that Locke first came to know Churchill, the eventual publisher of his *Two Treatises of Government*, through the latter's association with the radicals in Holland is interesting.

Whether or not Locke was involved in the preparation of Monmouth's Declaration, he appears to have become very concerned at just this time about his manuscript copy of the *Two Treatises* in England. Writing to Clarke two days after the April 3 meeting of Argyll and Monmouth, Locke directed his friend to locate a trunk containing some books—that is, manuscripts—wrapped as parcels. The first parcel discussed "nuts, acorns . . . and such other things of nature's production as she herself offers to human use," which appears to be an allusion to a thin manuscript on property, not yet incorporated into the text of the *Two Treatises*.[221] A second, bigger parcel "relating to the animal kingdom as it is divided in the beginning of Gen[esis]" is surely the draft of at least the *First Treatise*, since Locke's discussion of Filmer is the only time he ever addressed himself to Adam, the creation of the world, and the Book of Genesis. A third parcel, "which is the biggest," was a copy of the manuscript Locke and Tyrrell wrote jointly in 1681 against Stillingfleet's attack on the Dissenters. The reason Locke is so concerned is that Tyrrell either had already taken custody of these manuscripts or wanted to do so, and

[218] Add. MS 41818, fols. 79–80; Add. MS 41812, fol. 226.

[219] MS b.1, fol. 55; MS f.8, fols. 267–268.

[220] Add. MS 41812, fols. 43–46. The syntax in this letter is not altogether clear, but the writer appears to be saying that both Churchill and Locke are staying in his home.

[221] *Correspondence*, 2:708. One reason that this reference cannot be to the *Second Treatise* as a whole is that Locke is indifferent to its fate, whereas he is especially concerned about the *First Treatise* and the Locke-Tyrrell manuscript, and he wants them put somewhere safe or destroyed. Politically, this would make no sense at all, for whatever the subversive ideas contained in the last two manuscripts, they pale alongside those of the *Second Treatise*. Although one cannot proceed too far on the basis of this allusion, it is strange that the notion that the chapter on property was a separately written manuscript has never received any consideration from commentators on the *Two Treatises*. This is not to say, of course, that its argument was not consonant with that of the whole work, as was suggested in Chapter 6.

although "he is a very good man," these works were not, at that moment, safe in his hands. For once Monmouth landed in May, as Locke then knew he would, these manuscripts might very easily fall into the hands of the authorities. Therefore, Locke writes, "I positively insist on it to have the two last mentioned parcels immediately disposed of according as I directed in mine of February 22" (lost). Tyrrell did not know, at least from Locke, of the impending invasion, and his political commitment to the cause had never approached the radicalism of Locke and Clarke, though he had always been a personal friend of Locke. However, it is Clarke's political judgment that Locke trusts, but whether the "disposal" instructions in his missing letter meant that the manuscripts should be destroyed, conveyed to Locke, or simply relocated in a safer place, we do not know. Locke also wrote to Clarke about some manuscripts "at my namesakes" house, apparently transferred there by Mrs. Percival.[222] Locke was particularly concerned about two books "in quarto" he left with her that he wanted Clarke to locate if they were not at Mr. Locke's. This may well be a reference to the other Locke, one of whose sons was still living in London, and who, as we have seen, were participants in the radical movement.[223] In any event, Locke's correspondence with Clarke between early April and the first week in May 1685 demonstrates his insistent concern about matters that cannot be "delayed," relating to the relocation in some safe (politically trustworthy) place of his political writings in anticipation of the forthcoming invasion by Argyll and Monmouth.

Meanwhile, James II was on the throne, and with the help of Skelton's intelligence, was kept informed of the radicals' activities. On April 28, he wrote to William that "some of the fugitive rebels . . . have had a meeting with the Duke of Monmouth there very privately, and have some design in hand on Scotland . . . they have bought arms, and are sending them by the way of Amsterdam, for the West Highlands of Scotland, with an intention of making a rising there." On May 5, James wrote to his son-in-law that Argyll was already on his way to Scotland, "and that the Duke of Monmouth has designed to . . . come over hither into England . . . to make, if he can, some disturbance." But, he added, "I am preparing for him and the other in both kingdoms." What James sought, above all, was to have these rebels arrested, or at the very least, to have them

[222] *Correspondence*, 2:718; cf. p. 698.

[223] Lock-the-tobacconist's house in London was a meeting place for radicals. On one of his trips to England, Cragg had met with an agent of the London radicals at Lock's house in an effort to get a message to Wildman, and Monmouth proposed to use Lock's house as a major communications headquarters once the rebellion began (Landsdowne MS 1152, fol. 266; HMC 12th Report, appendix, pt. 6, p. 399).

"sent away out of the country . . . it being very necessary to have these turbulent traitors driven out of Holland."[224]

On May 1, Skelton was sent a list of fugitives that he was instructed to present to the Dutch authorities along with an official request from the English government that the named individuals be arrested and extradited to England to stand trial for treason. In his communication, Middleton indicated that he could not be sure which individuals were actually residing in Holland, and he left it to Skelton to determine this and also to add names to the list of persons inadvertently omitted by Middleton.[225] Skelton submitted the memorial, which included Locke's name, and on May 17 the list was published and distributed to local authorities throughout Holland with orders to the magistrates to arrest the individuals.[226]

Throughout April and May, Locke was commuting between Utrecht and Amsterdam, the respective headquarters of Argyll and Monmouth. On May 17, he was meeting with Ferguson in Utrecht, but the following day, he went to Amsterdam, where Grey and Monmouth were. On the nineteenth, he returned to Utrecht, but on the twenty-third, he was back in Amsterdam, where he stayed until the Monmouth expedition sailed.[227] On May 22, Locke bought a copy of the *London Gazette*, which carried

[224] Dalrymple, 2:19–20. Skelton had sent a report (April 28) that Argyll had sailed and that "Monmouth is to follow very suddenly" for England. He advised that some frigates be sent to cruise the coasts of Scotland and England to intercept these expeditions (Add. MS 41812, fol. 36).

[225] Add. MS 41823, fol. 13.

[226] Skelton wrote to Middleton on May 8 informing him that he had added Locke's name to the memorial the secretary had sent him (Add. MS 41812, fol. 58). A copy of the May 17 memorial with Locke's name on it is in the British Library (Sloane MS 1983B, fol. 38; Add. MS 17677 (GG), fols. 262–266). Locke owned a copy of this memorial, misleadingly listed in his library catalog as "Schelton [*sic*] Memoirs" (*LL* #2569; cf. MS f. 16, fol. 200). This was not a rash action on Skelton's part. Even after he had submitted the May 17 memorial, he drew up a second list of names that had been omitted; these included Thomas Dare, Wilmore, Starkey, and Harris, all of them radicals, but inadvertently left off the first list (Add. MS 41817, fol. 77). Moreover, Skelton also received from Middleton a second list of names of people the government wanted extradited, and it appears that Locke's name was on this list (Middleton had not seen the May 17 memorial). For, Skelton wrote in reply with reference to "the names you sent me on the second list . . . as for Mr. Lock, that was secretary to my Lord Shaftesbury, he is not mentioned in this last memorial, for before that I had any order for it, I had put him into the first list, which is printed" (Add. MS 41812, fol. 100). In other words, in the context of the other names added to the first government list, and in view of Locke's name on the second government list, Skelton's decision to add Locke's name to the May 17 memorial represented an informed expression of the government's attitude and intelligence concerning the radicals; it was not a slanderous action against an innocent man by a bumbling envoy, as some of Locke's biographers have maintained.

[227] MS f.8, fol. 273.

the first published reports of Argyll's landing in Scotland, and contained excerpts from his declaration.[228] In preparation for his own sailing with Monmouth, Dare transferred almost all the funds in his custody belonging to Locke to Sir John Banks.[229] On May 29, Locke paid for some wine at Mr. Vandervelde's for what may have been a celebratory gathering among the radicals in honor of Monmouth's departure.[230] Locke's last financial transaction with Dare is recorded on May 30, the day before the expedition finally sailed.[231] Clearly, Locke was in close contact right up to the last moment with those "turbulent traitors" who were being sent out of Holland with the Duke of Monmouth to raise some "disturbance" in England, if they could.

[228] MS f.34, fol. 3. Given the disparity between Old and New Style dates and no way of telling to what extent Locke recorded items in his journal after the fact, one cannot be certain which issue of the *London Gazette* this notation refers to. However, having read through all the issues (which are, with few exceptions, extremely uninteresting), I am convinced that this notation, and the one cited in Chapter 10 below containing Argyll's Declaration, give the date of the newspaper. If Locke bought the *Gazette* according to the news it contained, then he purchased the May 22 and June 2 issues for the specifically political news they contained. The alternative is to conclude that he simply made two random purchases of the *Gazette*, breaking a pattern of two years of nonreadership. The May 21–25 issue of the *Gazette* not only printed James II's speech opening the Parliament, but also the news of Argyll's landing in Scotland, and excerpts from his declaration. The spy in Utrecht had indicated in one of his reports in late May that Locke and Cross were anxiously waiting to hear the news concerning Argyll's landing in Scotland (Add. MS 41812, fol. 70).

[229] These funds were transferred to Dr. Peter Guenellon (MS b.1, fol. 55).

[230] MS f.34, fol. 3.

[231] MS f.8, fol. 273; MS b.1, fol. 55.

10

KEEPING THE FAITH

THE story of Monmouth's Rebellion, and the defeat of his spirited but ill-equipped army, has often been told. Because it was, in the words of one contemporary, "a romantic kind of invasion," Monmouth's Rebellion became part of a folkloric tradition that survived, especially in the memories of residents of the west country, long after the executioner's ax brought an end to Monmouth's "misguided" ambitions.[1] From a military standpoint, and with benefit of hindsight, it is easy to criticize this abortive adventure to which so many radicals in Holland had pledged their lives and fortunes. Argyll's failure to stick to the agreed upon plan, according to which his army was supposed to march toward the Lowlands, mobilizing recruits from among the large number of dissidents in that area, got the joint enterprise off to a poor start. Against the advice of his own lieutenants, Argyll set up his standard in the Highlands, near his own estate, hoping to draw all of his own tenants into the cause before advancing into the Lowlands.[2] This decision, along with the fact that he issued, in addition to the official declaration drafted for the rebellion, a private declaration listing the injustices committed by the government against him and his family, had the effect of personalizing the cause. Since Argyll, unlike Monmouth, was not a widely liked individual, his personal concerns and welfare were not the means by which others were likely to be persuaded to take up arms. The intransigence and haughtiness of Argyll's leadership were serious constraints imposed upon any possible success for the Scottish part of Monmouth's Rebellion.

The *London Gazette* provided a cryptic, but not always accurate, account of the progress of the rebellion. It reported Argyll's landing in Scotland, noting that his agents had distributed a "long and canting declaration" justifying the invasion, which was too diffuse—and too libel-

[1] James Welwood, *Memoirs of the Most Material Transactions in England for the Last Hundred Years*, 1700, p. 165; Bryan Little, *The Monmouth Episode*, London: Werner Laurie, 1956, p. ix. It was also, as Ranke said, "an execution of the plans" formulated by Shaftesbury and the Rye House plotters (Leopold von Ranke, *The History of England*, 6 vols., 1875, 4:244). The application of "misguided" to Monmouth is that of William Penn, *A Third Letter from a Gentleman in the Country, to his Friend in London, upon the Subject of the Penal Laws and Tests*, 1687, p. 9. Locke owned all three *Letters* (*LL* #2247–2249).

[2] Macaulay provides a good account of the mistakes and confusions of Argyll's invasion (1:496–512; cf. John Erskine, *Journal of Hon. John Erskine of Carnock, 1683–1687*, 1893, pp. 120ff.).

ous—to be printed. It did, however, report the gist of the shorter declaration, describing the "personal injuries" suffered by Argyll.[3] On June 2, Locke bought the *London Gazette*, obviously in order to follow the progress of the rebellion, and his recorded comment in his journal, "*Vanitas Vanitatum*," may well reflect a certain measure of disgust—shared by other radicals in Holland—at Argyll's attribution of such importance to his own private grievances at the expense of the broader objectives of the rebellion.[4] The exiles, however, did not have to depend upon the *London Gazette* for their information. Messengers, mostly women, shuffled back and forth between England and Holland daily carrying intelligence reports to those who had remained behind in Holland.[5]

The latter continued to hold meetings, though there was little they could do, practically speaking, to advance the cause. On June 10, Locke, John Starkey, and a number of other radicals met in Utrecht to discuss their situation.[6] Only a few days before, warrants had been issued for the arrest of Locke's friend, Edward Clarke, as well as for Wildman, Charlton, Trenchard, and others.[7] At the end of June, the *London Gazette* reported Argyll's defeat and capture. The July 6 issue gave a brief account of his execution.[8] At about the time Argyll's defeat became known to the exiles in Holland, Skelton wrote to Middleton that Mrs. Smith and Starkey had left Utrecht "to return speedily to Amsterdam where Lock that was Shaftesbury's secretary is at this time with divers others, whose names and the places where they are to be found will be sent by me in a few days."[9] And in his next dispatch, Skelton enclosed a lengthy intelligence report from his double agent in Utrecht, disclosing the aliases, hiding places, and political objectives of the radicals. "Dr. John Lock, alias John-

[3] *London Gazette*, May 21–25, 1685. Both declarations are printed in Robert Wodrow, *The History of the Sufferings of the Church of Scotland from the Restoration to the Revolution*, 4 vols., 1830, 4:286–291; John Willcock, *A Scots Earl in Covenanting Times: Being the Life and Times of Archibald the 9th Earl of Argyll*, Edinburgh: Andrew Elliot, 1907, pp. 359–361.

[4] MS f.8, fol. 276. The June 1–4 issue of the *Gazette* contained a fuller account of Argyll's Declaration and the military situation in Scotland. Ferguson had made a special point of asserting in Monmouth's Declaration that it was not for any redress of personal injuries or "private discontents" that they had taken up arms (Landsdowne MS 1152, fol. 259).

[5] Add. MS 41817, fol. 183; Add. MS 41812, fol. 138; Add. MS 41818, fol. 77.

[6] Add. MS 41817, fol. 125

[7] In addition to those named in the text, warrants were issued for John Freke, Walter Yonge, Major Breman, and Captain Matthews. Clarke's warrant was dated June 4; the others, May 19, or in other words (except for Clarke), prior to Argyll's landing in Scotland (*CSPD*, [James II], 1:157, 178).

[8] *London Gazette*, June 22–25, 1685; July 2–6, 1685.

[9] Add. MS 41812, fol. 138. Starkey is mentioned in a letter from Churchill to Locke in 1688 (*Correspondence*, 3:476).

son," was hiding "in great privacy" at Vandervelde's house. Nearby, on the same street, Joseph and Israel Hayes were in hiding. The report goes on to list the activities and whereabouts of Mrs. Smith, Starkey, Wilmore, and other associates of Locke, all of whom were identified as individuals who had acted in one way or another "to assist in Monmouth's rebellion."[10]

That rebellion was, at the moment, in deep trouble. Monmouth's intentions were to establish a camp near Taunton, with the expectation that thousands would rally to his standard. He wanted to defeat James on the battlefield, as a professional soldier commanding a professional army. At a minimum, Monmouth estimated he would need six weeks to train and arm his men, prior to engaging the king's troops in a major battle. He hoped that various county militias, under the leadership of the nobility, would place themselves at his disposal, and this defection—plus a diversionary uprising in London, managed by Wildman, Colonel Danvers, and others—would buy Monmouth the time he needed. The London revolt never materialized. James was not so foolish as to send his troops out of the city, and neither Wildman nor Danvers were prepared to risk an open confrontation with them in the streets of London. A few radicals managed to slip out of the city to join forces with Monmouth, but Wildman, Danvers, Charlton, and Trenchard were not among their number. A quick and shocking victory—Bristol was the obvious target—would have immediately established the credibility and seriousness of the rebellion, but Monmouth was unwilling to take the gamble of staking everything upon the outcome of one battle so early in the campaign.[11] After being allowed "to ramble up and down for several weeks" around the countryside, as Bishop Fell angrily put it, Monmouth's army suffered its decisive defeat at Sedgemoor.[12] Less than a month after his landing at Lyme Regis, the *London Gazette* reported "the entire defeat of the rebels" and the capture of Monmouth and Lord Grey.[13]

Locke was in hiding at Vandervelde's house when the news of Monmouth's execution reached the exiles in Holland.[14] The summer and fall of 1685 must have been a particularly disheartening period for Locke. Between July and October, not only Monmouth and Argyll, but also Nel-

[10] Add. MS 41817, fols. 218–219; Add. MS 41812, fols. 84–85. Locke was, in fact, staying at Vandervelde's house, as his journal shows (MS f.34, fol. 5).

[11] Little, *Monmouth Episode*, pp. 32, 127, 135–137, 142; Peter Earle, *Monmouth's Rebels*, London: Weidenfeld and Nicolson, 1977, p. 61.

[12] Cited in Earle, *Monmouth's Rebels*, p. 65.

[13] *London Gazette*, July 6–9, 1685. The July 13–16 issue reported Monmouth's execution.

[14] MS f.34, fol. 5.

thorp, Ayloffe, Christopher Battiscombe, Thomas Dare, and many others known to him had been killed or executed. Besides Clarke, Freke, Walter Yonge, Grey, Goodenough, Wade, and John Cochrane were only a few of Locke's friends who had been arrested.[15] Locke also knew Mrs. Gaunt—who was executed in October—and Mrs. Nelthorp, both of whom served as messengers for the radicals. They had left on their last trip for England just a few days before Monmouth's defeat.[16] Mrs. Goodenough was staying at Dare's house in Amsterdam at the time the *London Gazette* reported the capture of her husband.[17] There is a pathetic letter from Mrs. Dare to Locke, written in mid-July at the nadir of the radicals' political fortunes, promising to honor her late husband's debt to Locke as soon as she can.[18]

Yet even in their period of shared sorrow and defeat, the exiles continued to meet. Locke records in his journal that on August 4 he spent twelve shillings on a social gathering "with my countrymen." On the fifteenth of that month, Locke records another, more modest, dinner party with his countrymen.[19] The latter are not identified, but some of those who had been with Argyll or Monmouth and had escaped were now beginning to arrive in Holland. Among the recent arrivals was John Atherton, an individual who had been "a sturdy instrument of the late Earl of Shaftesbury," an active Rye House plotter, and more recently (with Goodenough and Nelthorp) a participant in Monmouth's Rebellion. But the most prominent new arrival, who had not, however, participated in the rebellion, was John Trenchard. He and his wife arrived in Amsterdam in early August, and the evening of the fifteenth, which Locke recorded in his journal, was in all likelihood spent with them.[20] Trenchard moved on to Utrecht, and Locke decided on August 18, to change his lodgings and go into deeper hiding. He sent his baggage to the house of his friend, Phillipus Limborch, who had offered to find Locke a safe refuge at the house of a relative, Dr. Veen.[21]

[15] Add. MS 34508, fol. 21; Morrice, 1:462; Narcissus Luttrell, *A Brief Relation of State Affairs*, 6 vols., 1857, 1:342, 346, 355.

[16] Add. MS 41817, fol. 225. Mrs. Gaunt served as a regular messenger for the rebels (Add. MS 41812, fol. 138).

[17] Add. MS 41817, fol. 237. Goodenough was captured near Exeter on July 15 (*London Gazette*, July 16–20, 1685).

[18] *Correspondence*, 2:726 (July 24). Mrs. Dare wrote to Locke again on August 23, 1685, but the letter has not survived (MS f.34, fol. 5).

[19] MS f.34, fols. 4–5.

[20] Add. MS 41817, fol. 274. Trenchard's exact residence is not given by the informer, but he was staying at a house on Calverstraat, which is where Vandervelde, with whom Locke was then staying, lived.

[21] Following the August 15 dinner, Trenchard probably left Amsterdam for Utrecht on

At the end of August, Locke received a letter from the Earl of Pembroke, informing him that he had interceded on Locke's behalf with James II. "I have so satisfied the King," Pembroke boasted,

> that he has assured me he will never believe any ill reports of you; he bid me write to you to come over. I told him I would then bring you to kiss his hand and he was fully satisfied I should. Pray for my sake let me see you before this summer be over. I believe you will not mistrust me; I am sure none can the King's word.[22]

Locke, however, had no intention of kissing James' hand, nor did he ever in the course of his life display any considerable trust in his word. Instead of accepting Pembroke's offer and the chance to return to England, Locke decided upon greater concealment and a withdrawal from Amsterdam altogether. He packed up his goods and set off on September 11 for Cleves, passing through Utrecht.[23] Locke evidently intended to spend the winter at Cleves, staying in the house of Mr. Meyers, secretary to the Elector of Brandenburg. Meyers had done much for the radicals, providing refuge in his house for Goodenough, Nelthorp, and many others.[24]

In any event, Locke did not remain at Cleves, but instead returned to Amsterdam sometime before December. We can only guess at his reasons for doing so, but certain political developments in England and Holland may have had something to do with his decision. Included in the stream of refugees pouring into Holland in the fall of 1685 were Sir John Thompson, a Whig member of Parliament, the dissenting minister Matthew Meade, who had been privy to the Rye House Plot, and Lord Wharton, accompanied by John Howe, another prominent dissenting minister.[25]

August 17 or 18 (Add. MS 41818, fols. 10, 13). Locke paid Vandervelde for his lodgings in July extending to August 17, when it appears he changed his residence. Two undated notes to Limborch relating to this intention were almost certainly written at this time. The note indicating that he is moving that evening was written on a Saturday. August 18, 1685 was a Saturday (*Correspondence*, 2:724–725). In late August and early September, Locke received two letters (lost) from Utrecht, following which he arranged to have his baggage sent there, and he passed through Utrecht sometime between September 11 and 13 on his way to Cleves (MS f.34, fols. 5–6).

[22] *Correspondence*, 2:729.

[23] MS f.34, fol. 6.

[24] The government was keeping Locke under surveillance and knew that he was staying at Meyers' house (Add. MS 41812, fols. 218, 224).

[25] Add. MS 41818, fol. 106. Thompson married the daughter of the Earl of Anglesey, and both she and her mother were members of John Owen's congregation in London. In addition to Owen, Thompson was a close friend of John Howe and Lord Wharton. His father had been a prominent member of Cromwell's government, and during February 1685, Thompson was one of those meeting with Brandon, Macclesfield, Charlton, and others—probably for the purpose of mobilizing support for Argyll and/or Monmouth (Lacey, p.

Major Wildman had also joined the exiles, possibly traveling as a member of Wharton's entourage. Wharton, Howe, and Wildman had gone to reside in Cleves, around the time or shortly after Locke's arrival in that city.[26] On October 6, Thompson, Walter Cross, and Patience Ward went to Cleves to meet with the radicals there. "They sent for Doctor John Locke" and also Mrs. Smith to join in the consultations.[27] Shortly after this meeting, Skelton's double agent in Utrecht reported that the radicals had formulated a new and "deeply laid" plot, which was just at its beginnings and would take a considerable time to put into effect.[28] Following this meeting, the participants dispersed—Thompson, Cross, and Ward returning to Utrecht, while Locke and Wildman left Cleves for Amsterdam.[29]

The radicals in Holland in the winter of 1685–1686 were at a crossroads. In the wake of Monmouth's defeat, many of them wished to return to England or Scotland. They were without a popular or forceful leader; they had lived in exile in a foreign country for three years, and in some instances, longer; many of them had given up their livelihoods, estates, and families to fight for a cause in which they believed. Now they wanted to go home. There was talk in the coffeehouses that the next Parliament would pass an Act of Oblivion, making such a return possible, but no one could be sure that Parliament would meet or what it might do when it

---

448; MS English History C.711, fols. 22–26; Add. MS 41812, fol. 224; Add. MS 41818, fol. 106; Walter Wilson, *The History and Antiquities of Dissenting Churches*, 4 vols., 1808–1814, 3:19–37).

[26] How or when Wildman reached Holland is uncertain, but the earliest mention of his being there is in early October in the company of Wharton and Howe (Add. MS 41812, fols. 209, 224; Add. MS 41818, fol. 106).

[27] Add. MS 41812, fol. 224; Add. MS 41818, fol. 106. Howe is mentioned as Locke's friend in *Correspondence*, 3:58. Locke had known Patience Ward since at least the 1670s. He is referred to in the *Correspondence* as Locke's friend (3:145, 267). For Locke's association with Cross, see Chapter 9, note 113, above.

[28] This letter from the double agent in Utrecht is dated October 22 (Add. MS 41818, fol. 112). Since Thompson and Meade were staying at the author's house, his information is probably very reliable.

[29] Thompson and the others returned to Utrecht around October 19, but it was not until November 20 that Wildman and Charlton were reported to be in Amsterdam (Add. MS 41818, fols. 106, 152). Locke was still in Cleves on October 18, when he received a letter from Limborch. His movements between that date and December 7, when he clearly was in Amsterdam, are difficult to determine. De Beer's speculation that he returned to Amsterdam around October 27 is as good as any guess, but he might just as easily have remained in Cleves until November, which is the date given by Le Clerc, and returned to Amsterdam at the same time as Wildman (*Correspondence*, 2:754–760; Jean LeClerc, *An Account of the Life and Writings of John Locke*, 3d ed., 1714, p. 13).

did.[30] A few individuals, therefore, began to inquire discreetly about the possibility of receiving a pardon from the king. However, since a large proportion of exiles were Dissenters, even a pardon for their political activities would not suffice. For what was the point of returning to England only to suffer the same religious persecution that had been responsible for their leaving or their political involvement in revolution in the first place? Their discussions thus also turned to the issue of toleration and its prospects, given the political climate of England. In early January, one of Skelton's spies reported that "last night at their Club," the rebels were "very hot upon the subject of the pardon and indulgence, some saying they would not accept of the pardon, because that papists must at the same time have the benefit of the indulgence," while others maintained that an act of indulgence was the most prudent thing James could do to secure the peace of England. Still others insisted that the king could not grant a suspension of the penal laws without parliamentary consent.[31]

At the same time, though they were exhausted and discouraged, hundreds of these exiles were dedicated and hardened opponents of James II, Catholicism, and what they believed was an arbitrary and illegal political regime in England. From the early days of the exclusion crisis, they had placed themselves in opposition to the Stuarts, seeking every opportunity to bring about their downfall. They were not about to give up the struggle. And as we have seen, a new conspiracy was rising from the ashes of rebellion. These individuals neither sought nor wanted a pardon from the king; quite simply, they wanted his removal from office. Nothing less than that was likely to induce them to return to England. It is worth insisting upon that Locke, both by his long-held convictions and by his concrete actions between 1685 and 1689, clearly placed himself in the same camp as these radicals. It would have been far easier for him, through several friends with powerful influence with the king, to have obtained a pardon than it was for many of his associates who were nevertheless successful in their endeavors. Moreover, unlike many of his fellow radicals, Locke had never suffered for dissenting religious beliefs, so that fear of persecution did not in his case act as a deterrent from seeking to live a life of quiet desperation in England.

On another level, the radicals in Holland faced the problem of practical survival. Since the summer of 1685, their numbers had greatly increased, and this only intensified the economic hardships shared by members of

[30] Add. MS 41812, fol. 213; Add. MS 41818, fol. 108. On December 24, 1685, Skelton's informant reported that the rebels had high hopes of receiving a general pardon (Add. MS 41813, fol. 19).

[31] Add. MS 41818, fol. 205.

the exile community. Tradesmen, shoemakers, and various types of workers in the clothing trade were now refugees in Rotterdam and Amsterdam, living on the brink of starvation.[32] By the end of the year, Skelton was receiving disturbing reports from his spies that plans were being laid to establish a linen factory—actually, several in different places—to provide employment for the radicals.[33] If these plans were successful, not only would the exiles survive, they might amass enough funds to mount another invasion against James II.

From the winter of 1685 on, therefore, all of these factors were intertwined: the issue of toleration, pardons for the radicals, an English clothing industry established in Holland, and a new conspiracy to overthrow James II. This new plot formed by the radicals eventually merged with the larger and more powerful forces that brought William and Mary to the throne, and will be considered in Chapter 11. Here we shall be concerned with the way in which various participants in the revolutionary movement in Holland responded to the temptations of toleration and a pardon as inducements to abandon those economic and political activities which, from James II's perspective, posed a serious threat to the stability

[32] Though it is a tangential issue, the social composition of Monmouth's army does have a bearing on the status and identification of these refugees from England. Trevelyan followed Macaulay in characterizing Monmouth's supporters as an army of "peasants." Surprisingly, Ogg also adopted this view (G. M. Trevelyan, *England under the Stuarts*, London: Methuen, 1965, pp. 413–414; David Ogg, *England in the Reigns of James II and William III*, Oxford: Clarendon Press, 1955, pp. 147–149). This assertion has been decisively refuted by Earle's study, which demonstrated that most of Monmouth's rebels came from towns and areas where "a large proportion of their population engaged in industry and commerce." The major part of his army consisted of artisans and tradesmen. "The typical rebel was a weaver or a shoemaker, a tailor or a woolcomber" (*Monmouth's Rebels*, pp. 17, 191). See his appendix (pp. 200–204) for an occupational study, showing that 53 percent of the individuals were engaged in the cloth-making industry, 12.5 percent in clothing, 11 percent in building-metal industries, and only 11 percent in agriculture. In a list of 213 rebels whose occupations are specified, 120 were textile workers (G. N. Clark, *The Later Stuarts*, Oxford: Oxford University Press, 1940, p. 115). Contemporaries, including Evelyn, knew this. One informer's report speaks of the shoemakers and weavers leaving London to join up with Monmouth, and other documents list carpenters, brewers, bricklayers, and weavers among the occupations of captured prisoners (John Evelyn, *The Diary of John Evelyn*, ed. E. S. De Beer, 6 vols., Oxford: Clarendon Press, 1955, 4:452; Allan Fea, *King Monmouth*, London: John Lane, 1902, p. 244; Little, *Monmouth Episode*, p. 132; Iris Morley, *A Thousand Lives: An Account of the English Revolutionary Movement, 1660–1685*, London: Andre Deutsch, 1954, p. 189; Add. MS 41818, fol. 125). Hence, it is not surprising that reports of the arrival in Rotterdam and other cities of shoemakers and other tradesmen "who fled after Monmouth's Rebellion" were being forwarded to Middleton by Skelton in the fall of 1685 (Add. MS 41812, fol. 235).

[33] Add. MS 41818, fols. 226, 229. Several hundred refugees arrived in Utrecht in the space of a few weeks during October and November 1685, and many more had arrived in Amsterdam (John Carswell, *The Descent on England*, New York: John Day, 1969, p. 55).

of his regime. Although Locke may not have faced the same economic hardships as many of the political refugees pouring into Holland after Monmouth's defeat, he did, like them, have to think about the issue of toleration and whether he would return to England on the conditions offered by James. The political circumstances under which the question of toleration was posed, therefore, have a bearing upon Locke's intellectual development, as well as upon the relationship between toleration as a specific political problem to be resolved and the revolutionary political objectives set forth in the *Two Treatises of Government*. Though not published until after the Glorious Revolution, Locke's *Letter on Toleration* was written during his exile in Holland—specifically, between 1685 and 1688. Since 1667, Locke had supported a policy of toleration, but the *Letter*, as a particular document and argument reflecting that conviction, arose within a context in which toleration had become, once again, an immediate political issue, both for James' subjects in England and for the exiled radicals in Holland.

Locke had gone to Cleves to continue work on the *Essay Concerning Human Understanding*, but this project was temporarily put aside after the radicals' meeting in Cleves, and Locke's return to Amsterdam.[34] Locke's discussion of philosophical problems, that is, was rather abruptly interrupted in favor of a more pressing political problem: toleration. According to Limborch, Locke wrote the *Epistola de tolerantia* during the winter of 1685–1686. Thus it appears that a draft of the *Epistola* was in existence by the end of January 1686.[35] The work was dedicated and written in the form of a letter to Locke's friend Limborch. Yet, curiously, we have no evidence that the manuscript was actually delivered to Limborch until just prior to its publication, which he arranged, three years later.[36] The explanation for this delay seems to lie with the shifting currents of English politics during this period rather than with anything to do with Locke's relationship to Limborch as such. For there is no reason to suppose that anything occurred between 1686 and 1689 that affected what Locke had to say *to Limborch* on the general subject of toleration, but a great deal happened during those three years that affected the meaning of

[34] See his letter to Limborch (October 6, 1685) from Cleves, *Correspondence*, 2:748.

[35] Limborch's letter to Lady Masham indicating that Locke wrote the *Epistola* during the winter of 1685–1686 is cited by Raymond Klibansky in his preface to *Toleration*, p. ix. On December 7, 1685, Locke bought a quire of paper; on January 12, 1686, another half quire; and on February 4, another quire of paper (MS f.34, fol. 7).

[36] Montuori speculates that Locke gave the manuscript of the *Epistola* to Limborch, but there is no evidence of this, and had Limborch received the work prior to 1688, the fact would surely have been mentioned in his correspondence with Locke (*A Letter Concerning Toleration*, ed. Mario Montuori, The Hague: Martinus Nijhoff, 1963, p. xxiii).

any argument relating to toleration so far as Locke's countrymen were concerned. A draft of the *Epistola*, then, certainly existed in 1686, but the extent to which Locke worked on and revised its arguments prior to his departure from Holland is much more difficult to determine. There are good reasons to assume that Locke did make such revisions—none of his major works, with the possible exception of *The Reasonableness of Christianity*, seems to have escaped the process of extended revising—but we do not have for the *Letter* a record of Locke's reading and notes accompanying its composition, as we do for the *Two Treatises* or the *Essay Concerning Human Understanding*.

Raymond Klibansky, in his recent edition of the original Latin text along with an English translation of the *Letter*, provides some helpful information regarding the context of the debate on toleration as it existed among the French Protestant refugees and Dutch Remonstrants during the 1680s.[37] Since many of these individuals—Pierre Bayle, Pierre Jurieu, Jean Le Clerc, and, of course, Limborch himself—were known to Locke, it is reasonable to assume the importance to him of what they had to say on the issue of toleration. There is, however, another context, I am suggesting, provided by the arguments addressed to an audience of English Dissenters, both those resident in England and the exiles living in Holland, for the position adopted by Locke in the *Letter on Toleration*. These arguments were not only similar in their phraseology and treatment of certain issues to those advanced by Locke, but the English debate on toleration between 1686 and 1689 necessarily assigned to the *Letter* a particular location along a spectrum of political perspectives that emerged during this period. Locke's defense of a natural law/parliamentary sovereignty approach to toleration, and his rejection of the king's use of the prerogative and the toleration of Catholics, is thus not only compatible with, but forms part of the argument of, the *Two Treatises of Government*.[38]

Immediately upon James' ascension to the throne, the debate on toleration was reopened, occasioned by one of the Duke of Buckingham's last sallies into the political arena. Buckingham's plea for toleration restated the standard objections to persecution, but in view of the prominence of the author, the work could hardly be ignored.[39] William Penn's

[37] *Toleration*, preface, pp. x–xv.

[38] Both Tyrrell and William Molyneaux associated the *Letter on Toleration* with the *Two Treatises*, and in their view, this was a commonly held association (*Toleration*, p. xxiv).

[39] Duke of Buckingham, *A Short Discourse upon the Reasonableness of Men's Having a Religion*, 3d ed., 1685. In fact, the work is mostly about the use of reason in religion, and the issues of belief, faith, and demonstration, but he does conclude (pp. 18–20) that every individual must choose for himself, through the use of his reason, what religion to accept.

Considerations Moving to a Toleration and Liberty of Conscience provided a second to Buckingham's pamphlet.[40] Both tracts were answered by the author of *The Vanity of All Pretences for Toleration*, a clever and shrewd reply to some of the arguments for toleration.[41] Yet, the very fact that the Dissenters were pressing their claims for toleration in the wake of the Rye House Plot and Monmouth's Rebellion seems to have caught the spokesmen for the government off guard. John Nalson, one of the staunchest defenders of the king's authority, exclaimed,

> I confess I could scarcely have believed it had been possible to have found a pen so bold, as to demand liberty and toleration to carry on new associations, exclusions, and Rye House assassinations.[42]

Since the association of toleration with faction and rebellion had always constituted one of the strongest and most frequently cited grounds for its denial, it was indeed both a bold and surprising move that its proponents should choose this particular moment to make their case. The "dangers from the growth of a party that has . . . by several conspiracies . . . and a formed project of rebellion" sought to bring the government to ruin, the author of *The Vanity of All Pretences* insisted, are neither imaginary nor groundless objections to toleration.[43] The latter, Nalson argued, was nothing more than "the foundation of all their future designs of subverting the government," and the Archimedean lever for establishing a commonwealth.[44]

This traditional objection to toleration might have weighed convincingly against its defenders, except for one thing: James II had decided to grant an indulgence to Nonconformists, including Catholics. The king's

---

On the numerous replies to Buckingham's tract, see C. E. Whiting, *Studies in English Puritanism from the Restoration to the Revolution, 1660–1688*, London: Society for Promoting Christian Knowledge, 1931, pp. 538–539. Locke does not seem to have owned Buckingham's tract, but Benjamin Furley did, as well as many other tracts on the penal laws and toleration controversy (*Bibliotheca Furleiana*, 1714).

[40] William Penn, *Considerations Moving to a Toleration and Liberty of Conscience*, 1685. This work, according to the author, was "occasioned by the tract published by the Duke of Buckingham."

[41] *The Vanity of All Pretences for Toleration*, 1685, is specifically described as an answer to Buckingham's tract and also to Penn's *Considerations* (*LL* #2953).

[42] John Nalson, *Toleration and Liberty of Conscience Considered*, 1685, p. 6. Repeal of the penal laws and toleration were among the specific demands listed in Monmouth's Declaration (Landsdowne MS fol. 260).

[43] *Vanity of Pretences*, p. 3. That toleration was merely "the nurse" to "faction" and sedition was an argument made by other replies to Buckingham. See Richard E. Boyer, *English Declarations of Indulgence, 1687 and 1688*, The Hague: Mouton, 1968, p. 39. This is not, however, a very helpful book in general.

[44] Nalson, *Toleration Considered*, p. 7

decision to pursue a policy of toleration tended to undermine the force of the security argument, since national security was a determination so largely within the province of the executive's judgment. According to a conversation with James reported by Barrillon in his dispatch to Louis XIV of February 19, 1685, the king "knew well enough he should never be in safety, till a liberty of conscience was established firmly in [the Catholics] favor in England. That it was to this he was wholly to apply himself as soon as he saw a possibility."[45] First, James needed to secure parliamentary approval for his continuation of the practice of receiving the customs revenue, but once these economic "foundations of his reign" had been laid, there was no doubt that he would turn to "the re-establishment of the catholic religion in England."[46] Toleration of dissent and the removal of all penalties and disabilities attached to religious belief was a necessary means, in James' view, to the realization of that end. Monmouth's Rebellion delayed the timing of James' efforts to institute toleration, though it served as a catalyst in prompting Parliament to grant him the money—and a standing army—he needed to pursue his long-range goals. Still, by the end of 1685, James had committed himself to a series of decisions that formed part of his policy of toleration.[47] In January 1686, he granted a dispensation from the Test Act penalties to nearly one hundred Catholic officers in the army.[48] In March, James issued a general pardon to those who had acted against the government during the past five years, though a number of individuals were specifically exempted from this act of clemency.[49] These and other actions will be examined in greater detail in the next chapter insofar as they were perceived as providing the justificatory basis for the Glorious Revolution, but they indicate the direction in which James' thinking was moving; that is, he could simultaneously build positive support for his political authority by placing Catholics in positions of power within the army and the civil administration, while removing the major negative factor, religious persecution of Nonconformists, which supplied the pretense for much of the political hostility to the government. To the degree that this policy was

[45] Dalrymple, 2:3.

[46] Dalrymple, 2:38; cf. ibid., pp. 2, 4.

[47] These plans for a general toleration were known and being discussed in England at the end of 1685 (Macaulay, 2:190–191; Carswell, *Descent*, p. 72).

[48] Carswell, *Descent*, p. 73.

[49] Excepted from the general pardon were all those who accompanied Monmouth into England from Holland. In addition, all fugitives from justice living in exile were given until September 29, 1686 to surrender themselves to a justice of the peace in order to take advantage of the terms of the pardon. The proclamation was printed in the *London Gazette*, March 11–15, 1686. A list of individuals excepted is printed as appendix C to J. G. Muddiman, ed., *The Bloody Assizes*, London: William Hodge, 1929, pp. 232–233.

successful, it would certainly put aside the rebellion issue with respect to toleration. On the other hand, it necessarily pushed other issues, such as the king's use of the prerogative and the toleration of Catholics, to the forefront of the controversy.

A major issue in the discussion of toleration, an anonymous "gentleman at Oxford" observed in *The Judgment and Doctrine of the Clergy of the Church of England . . .*, was whether the king possessed an inherent supreme power enabling him to dispense with the penal laws against Nonconformists. And, he concluded, "our reverend clergy of the Church of England have unanimously concurred in this point of doctrine." In support of this statement, he filled the next twenty-five pages of the tract with citations from various clerical and legal authorities defending this inherent supreme power of the monarch.[50] In *Vox Cleri Pro Rege*, the author places Filmer's definition of the absolute power of the sovereign as his ability to give laws to his subjects without their consent on the title page, indicating the thesis of the argument to be pursued in the pamphlet.[51] The latter contains numerous citations from *Patriarcha*, and after one of them, the author declares that "now the power to make laws is acknowledged by almost all our dignified clergy to be a right inherent in the King." If this is so, he argues, then "the dispensing power [is] but a natural inference from it."[52] It was certainly true that, on the ground of the king's prerogative, the Anglican church had left itself very little room for maneuvering. For, as William Penn noted in one of his many tracts written in defense of James II's action, the church's objection to the *means* of granting toleration was disingenuous in view of all the arguments in favor of the king's prerogative with which its supporters had in the past bombarded those who advocated a reliance upon parliamentary consent as the supreme legislative power of government.[53] In an officially commissioned and widely distributed tract, John Northleigh registered the complaint that "those who ran up the prerogative to the height of its power" (namely, the Anglican clergy), had now turned their backs on Filmer.[54]

With respect to the Dissenters, however, the case was more complicated. They had never been so strongly supportive of the king's prerog-

[50] *The Judgment and Doctrine of the Clergy of the Church of England Concerning One Special Branch of the King's Prerogative, viz., in Dispensing with the Penal Laws*, 1687, pp. 3–4; cf. ibid., pp. 5–30 (*LL* #2250).

[51] *Vox Cleri Pro Rege*, 1687, title page (*LL* #975).

[52] *Vox Cleri*, p. 29. For other citations from *Patriarcha* on the king's prerogative, see pp. 21–22, 24–25, 30, 39.

[53] Penn, *Third Letter*, pp. 4–6.

[54] John Northleigh, *Parliamentum Pacificum*, 1688, p. 19.

ative, even in those circumstances in which, as in 1672, many of them had nevertheless accepted the practical benefits of the Act of Indulgence. The theory of government subscribed to by most Dissenters was designed to circumscribe the exercise of any prerogative power within rather narrowly defined limits, and generally speaking, they rejected altogether any doctrine—as advocated by Filmer—of the king's "inherent supreme power".[55] Yet James' efforts to gain support among the Dissenters through the indulgence were meeting with considerable success. Not only did they accept the concrete benefits of toleration, a number of Dissenters wrote tracts defending James II's use of the prerogative. Henry Care, for example, who had been a prominent Whig pamphleteer during the exclusion crisis, argued both for the right of the Dissenters to accept the indulgence, and for the latter's legality as an exercise of prerogative within the framework of the common law.[56] As with the Anglicans, however, the past record of the Dissenters on this issue was cited against them in the course of this propaganda war. In his *Letter to a Dissenter*, Halifax played at great length on the irony of the situation in forcing a reversal of principles. Suddenly, "the men of Taunton" have become champions of loyalty and the king's power.[57] He caustically chided the Dissenters for having become public advocates of the indulgence. In allowing themselves to become propagandists for James, he wrote, "you become voluntary aggressors, and look like counsel retained by the prerogative against your old friend Magna Charta."[58]

Clearly, if the toleration debate were reducible simply to the issue of the existence and exercise of the king's prerogative, both Anglicans and Dissenters were on slippery ground in their attempts to move from the level of a practical consideration of the merits of indulgence to more principled arguments and the fundamental presuppositions of their respective political theories. But even within the range of practical consequences, the division between James' supporters and his critics was sharply focused on the issue of Catholicism. James' action was not mitigated by wartime considerations, which had formed a significant part of the defense of the 1672 Act of Indulgence. Unlike his brother, he was an open Catholic who

[55] For a general consideration of this issue as a background to the 1685–1688 debate, see E. F. Churchill, "The Dispensing Power of the Crown in Ecclesiastical Affairs," *Law Quarterly Review*, no. 152 (October 1922), pp. 420–434; Paul Birdsall, "*Non Obstante*: A Study of the Dispensing Power of English Kings," in *Essays in History and Political Theory in Honor of Charles Howard McIlwain*, Cambridge: Harvard University Press, 1936, pp. 37–76.

[56] Henry Care, *Animadversions on a Late Paper Entitled a Letter to a Dissenter*, 1687.

[57] Halifax, *A Letter to a Dissenter*, 1687, p. 4.

[58] Halifax, *Letter*, p. 9.

made no secret of his zeal on behalf of that religion. The suspicions that the indulgence was merely an instrumental weapon in the scheme to restore Catholicism to England that had always accompanied Charles' efforts to effect a toleration became, in James' case, direct accusations. Fear of popery once again functioned as a focal point of the political debate. Nevertheless, Ralph Thoresby expressed the views of many of his countrymen on James' suspension of the penal laws when he recorded in his diary that "though we dreaded a snake in the grass, we accepted it with due thankfulness."[59]

Catholics and some Dissenters were therefore supportive of the indulgence, while Anglicans, generally, opposed it. What we have not yet considered, however, is the radical Dissenter's position; that is, someone favoring toleration, but sufficiently a critic of the king's prerogative power or sufficiently anti-Catholic to oppose James II's indulgence. The object of the argument, from this perspective, was to recast the debate so that the king's prerogative—the claim to which virtually no one denied—appeared within the context of a higher legislative authority, while at the same time stressing the great political dangers posed by the threat of popery. This is the position adopted by Locke, and by the diehard radicals in Holland who refused the king's "great clemency" and the opportunity to return to an England ruled by a Catholic monarch. Whatever the practical benefits of toleration to the Dissenters, there was a minority whose political commitments prevented them from setting aside the obligations and experiences of the 1680s that had brought them together as members of a revolutionary organization. For these individuals, Penn's rather tactless reminder in one of his pamphlets that "there [would have] been no rebellion in the West" led by the "misguided" Monmouth if James had made it clear at the outset of his reign that he intended to support a policy of toleration, only served to heighten the sense of betrayal of the cause for which their comrades had sacrificed their lives that was now attached to any political support for James II.[60]

Numerous participants in the 1685–1688 debate on toleration recognized the fundamental character of the political theoretical issues in conflict. Like many others, Roger L'Estrange saw that in the choice between a political system structured around the king's absolute power and a claim on behalf of the priority of a particular religious belief, the long-term consequences of the first commitment were greater and more important

[59] Ralph Thoresby, *Diary*, 2 vols., 1830, 1:186. As Welwood put it, toleration was the bait to gain support for the introduction of popery (*Memoirs*, p. 191). Morrice, on the other hand, was upset that more Dissenters had not expressed their thankfulness to James for the indulgence (Morrice, 2:161).

[60] Penn, *Third Letter*, p. 9.

to the maintenance of the whole social order in England than those attached to the short-term granting of toleration, especially if the latter depended, as it did, upon the exercise of the king's sovereign authority. Thus, despite the fact that he could claim seniority as the most inveterate and prolific opponent of toleration, L'Estrange entered the fray on the side of James II. In his *Answer to a Letter to a Dissenter*, he attacked what he called the author's dangerous doctrines relating to the king's prerogative. "He that would take the just measures of the prerogatives of power," L'Estrange argued, "should properly look back into the original of government." The question of toleration, in other words, could not be resolved independently of an examination of the foundations of government. In the *Answer*, L'Estrange defends the view that "government itself was immediately from God," and hence, political authority is necessarily legitimized through a theory of divine right. Though presented without the citations from Filmer, the *Answer* echoes the position set forth in *Vox Cleri*: that given a divine right theory of government, the king's suspension of the penal laws is merely a particular exercise of a power that is his according to the Law of Nature and "the original of government."[61]

The radicals could hardly refuse this challenge, and they quickly brought their theory of the original of government into the forefront of the attack on James' indulgence. In *A Letter Containing Some Reflections on His Majesty's Declaration for Liberty of Conscience*, Gilbert Burnet argued that "the King's suspending of laws strikes at the root of this whole government, and subverts it." This, he explained, was because "the essence of all governments consists in . . . the legislative authority" established by the members of that society. In England, Burnet maintained, that authority was primarily in the hands of Parliament. "So that the placing this legislative power singly in the king is a subversion of this whole government." For James to claim such a power was "contrary to the trust that is given to the prince" by the people and their representatives, and such action, Burnet warned, would only encourage men with desperate designs to engage in active resistance to the government.[62] This is a relatively mild statement of the position with which Burnet was to become more prominently associated during the next two years.

Robert Ferguson developed the radical position in several tracts he wrote during this period in which he attacked James' indulgence and its defense by William Penn. It was true, as L'Estrange argued, that the orig-

[61] Roger L'Estrange, *An Answer to a Letter to a Dissenter*, 1687, pp. 48–49.

[62] Gilbert Burnet, *A Letter Containing Some Reflections on His Majesty's Declaration for Liberty of Conscience*, 1687, in *A Collection of Eighteen Papers relating to the Affairs of Church and State during the Reign of King James the Second*, 1689, pp. 26–31.

inal of government was bound up with this controversy. It was also clear, to Ferguson, that political authority must derive either from some "Divine Charter" or from the consent of the people.[63] At the same time, he insisted that toleration was "a right settled upon mankind antecedent to all civil government and human laws, having its foundation in the Law of Nature, which no prince or state can legitimately violate and infringe."[64] The question, therefore, was one of reconciling the legitimacy of government by popular consent with the natural right to toleration. This is the problem to which Ferguson—and, it should be obvious, Locke—addresses himself.

Ferguson begins by tracing all the power claimed by the monarch to its original source: "an agreement and concession of the people" setting forth the "rights, liberties and privileges they [have] reserved unto themselves, and what authority and jurisdiction they [have] delegated and made over unto the Sovereign." Such a contractual definition of political power operates as a definite limit upon the exercise of a ruler's prerogative. Moreover, in its positive formulation, the social contract establishes "the sense of the whole society" as "signified by their representatives in Parliament." Yet this government is instituted solely for the safety and good of the members of the body politic.[65] The main ends of political authority, however constituted, are directed toward "things of a civil and inferior nature" and have nothing to do with matters of "conscience" or religious belief. "The empire over conscience," according to Ferguson, remains in God's hands and "antecedent to all civil government."[66] Thus, "it is the natural right of every man to choose in what religion, and in which way of faith and worship" he will place his trust.[67] Toleration is therefore a natural right that individuals, even through consent, cannot cede to any public authority. Ferguson carried the radical argument to its logical limits, defending both the political authority of the people and the Parliament against James' "invasion" upon "all our laws and . . . property" through the use of his prerogative, while providing a defense of toleration as a natural right that, if the legislative authority (Parliament) acts pursuant to the ends of government as dictated by the Law of Nature, must be included within the category of those rights and privileges the

[63] Robert Ferguson, *A Representation of the Threatening Dangers*, 1688, p. 37.

[64] Ferguson, *Representation*, p. 36.

[65] Ferguson, *Representation*, pp. 24–25, 29; cf. idem, *A Brief Justification of the Prince of Orange's Descent into England*, 1689, pp. 5–15.

[66] Ferguson, *Representation*, p. 37.

[67] *Ferguson*, p. 458. Owen had also argued that "liberty of conscience is of natural right" John Owen, *Truth and Innocency Vindicated: In a Survey of a Discourse Concerning Ecclesiastical Polity*, 1669, p. 259).

people have reserved unto themselves. Since Ferguson argues that "we may not only lawfully, but we ought to defend what is reserved to ourselves, if it be invaded and broken in upon," his attack upon James as "the traitor and rebel" who has attempted "to subvert the laws of the society" and "all the rules of the Constitution" is, of course, a call to resistance.[68] Ferguson's tract is particularly addressed to "the dissenting party," with which he associates himself, and it is a plea to his fellow Nonconformists not to sacrifice the basic principles of revolutionary political theory for the "short opportunity afforded them of acquiring gain."[69]

In another tract written by a radical exile in 1687, the author maintains that "exercising a power of dispensing with the laws" is a betrayal of trust by the king, and represents an attempt "to subvert and extirpate the laws and liberties of his people." In this situation, the abuse of power deprives the king of his public authority and he becomes merely a private individual, and the people are returned to the state of nature. Since the king's actions have ceased to be legitimate, the author defends the right of the people to resist him.[70] The radical arguments for toleration, in other words, easily elide into a defense of revolutionary principles. As Penn sneeringly remarks in one of his tracts, the opposition of Dissenters to James' indulgence reflected a "green ribbon" mentality.[71] Even Burnet singled out a radical clique of exiles, whose views on toleration he associated with those of Wildman, who pressed the issue further than he was willing to go.[72]

The debate on toleration during the 1685–1688 period is thus not only rooted in the discussions of toleration that preceded it, but it is also quite consciously linked with the political theory associated with Shaftesbury and the Rye House conspiracy; and finally, as both the dates and the phraseology of the pamphlets suggest, the radicals' response to James' suspension of the penal laws is virtually inseparable from the arguments they employed in the works they wrote in defense of the Glorious Revolution. Although Ferguson's political arguments were closest to those advanced by Locke, the context for the issues discussed in the *Letter on Toleration* was both broader, philosophically speaking, and also directly tied, in practical terms, to the political fate of the radicals in Holland.

In the summer of 1686, James II sent William Penn to Holland in order

[68] Ferguson, *Representation*, p. 30.

[69] Ferguson, *Representation*, p. 33; *Ferguson*, p. 254.

[70] *An Argument for Self-Defense*, reprinted in *Somers Tracts*, 3:528–530.

[71] William Penn, *A Second Letter from a Gentleman in the Country, to His Friends in London, upon the Subject of the Penal Laws and Tests*, 1687, p. 3.

[72] Burnet, 2:495.

to secure the Prince of Orange's approval for his policy of toleration.[73] The latter let it be known that he favored the toleration of Dissenters, especially if this was achieved through parliamentary consent, and that the penal laws against Catholics could also be removed, provided they lived peaceably. He did not, however, support James' intention to repeal the Test Acts, which barred Catholics from public offices, since William of Orange was willing to do nothing to raise the Catholics to a place of prominence in society.[74] This response, which conceded all the objectives of James' policy except those which smacked of arbitrary designs or the greater institutionalization of popery, angered James, and widened the already growing breach that existed between him and his son-in-law.[75] Despite the failure of Penn's mission in this specific respect—other possible objectives of his visit to Holland are considered below—throughout 1686–1687, James sought to provide the foundations for political stability for his regime through a concerted propaganda campaign directed at the radical exiles in Holland. He seems to have believed that these Republicans and Dissenters posed the most serious threat to the peace of England, partly for reasons of their ideological conviction, and partly because of the possible effect upon or support from William their revolutionary plans might have.

One of the leading Scottish radicals, James Stewart, was offered a pardon, in return for which he undertook to persuade his colleagues to return home. Stewart was the author of Argyll's Declaration and had been deeply involved in the revolutionary movement. Precisely how many radicals Stewart maintained a correspondence with we do not know, but his series of letters to his friend William Carstares inadvertently assumed a greater historical importance than James had intended for them. "I assure you," Stewart wrote only a week after his arrival in England, that "equal liberty and ease is his Majesty's design."[76] Subsequent letters to Carstares insisted upon the sincerity of James' intentions, and were frankly designed to neutralize the subversive objectives entertained by

[73] John Miller, *James II: A Study in Kingship*, Hove, Eng.: Wayland Publishers, 1977, p. 175; Catherine Owens Peare, *William Penn*, New York: Lippincott, 1957, p. 297: Ranke, *History*, 4:389–390.

[74] Stephen B. Baxter, *William III*, London: Longmans, Green, 1966, p. 219.

[75] Macaulay, 2:216. According to James Stewart, James II was "no ways satisfied with the distinction made of the Tests from the Penal Laws," and he did not wish to discuss the matter further (Carswell, *Descent*, p. 109).

[76] Carswell, *Descent*, pp. 96–97. Stewart and Carstares had been friends since the 1670s, when they were both part of Du Moulin's spy network. They were arrested in 1674 for distributing a pamphlet attacking the Cabal, and sent as prisoners to Edinburgh Castle (p. 26). Some of the letters exchanged between Stewart and Carstares can be found in *CSPD*, (James II), 3:35–36, 40–42, 68.

the radicals in Holland. As Stewart himself put it, he believed he could "contribute my small endeavors" toward "the removing of some mistakes and jealousies, which I knew to be entertained in those parts [Holland] that I had left." Through his correspondence, he wanted to show how different things in England were "from what I and others had believed them, while I was in Holland."[77]

Carstares showed these letters to Gaspar Fagel, William Bentinck, William's chief adviser and friend, and William himself, as indeed he had virtually been instructed to do by Stewart.[78] In November 1687, Carstares sent Stewart a letter, enclosing one from Fagel, in both Latin and English, which expressed in carefully drawn prose William's position on toleration. Copies of Fagel's letter were distributed to various English and Scottish exiles in Holland, and subsequently, it was printed as a tract, which was widely distributed in both England and Holland.[79]

Fagel's *Letter* provoked numerous replies and defenses, and clearly established the international framework for the debate on toleration. The radical exiles in Holland, who were divided among themselves on the issue of support for or opposition to James' toleration policy, were placed directly in the midst of a propaganda and power struggle between James II and William, and ultimately, between England and Holland. In very concrete and practical terms, the exiles' position on the issue of toleration was tied to their willingness to accept a pardon from James and return to Britain, as an endorsement of Stewart's claim that all was well there, or to remain in Holland and continue the fight against James, counting on the support and encouragement of William. A specific instance of the latter had been provided by William's decision to send his emissary, Dykvelt, to England as a countermove to Penn's visit to Holland. Dykvelt consulted with various opponents of James' indulgence, including a number of Dissenters, whom he urged to stand firm in their opposition.[80] Throughout 1686–1687, therefore, the political campaign over toleration was waged on a level that extended from the personal decisions of indi-

[77] James Stewart, *Answer to a Letter Writ by Mijn Heer Fagel*, 1688, p. 4.

[78] In a letter dated July 29, 1687, and written from Windsor where Stewart was staying, he told Carstares, "I expect you will make all I have written so fully understood at the Hague, specially with the Prince" (Carswell, *Descent*, p. 98). See also, *CSPD*, (James II), 3:68.

[79] By the end of 1687, 50,000 copies of Fagel's *Letter* had been distributed in England (Carswell, *Descent*, p. 109). Awnsham Churchill was arrested for selling and/or printing Fagel's *Letter* (MS PWA 2159, Nottingham Library). It should be noted, however, that Halifax's *Letter to a Dissenter* (as well as some of Penn's tracts) was translated into Dutch, and thus was also part of the international debate on toleration.

[80] James Muilenburg, *The Embassy of Everaard Van Weede, Lord of Dykvelt, to England in 1687*, University Studies, vol. 20, nos. 3,4, Lincoln: University of Nebraska, 1920, pp. 22–23; James Ralph, *The History of England*, 1744, p. 952; S. Baxter, *William III*, p. 218.

vidual Dissenters in England or Holland to one that made the issue a matter of international foreign policy involving the major superpowers—England, Holland, and indirectly, France.[81]

The pamphlet controversy provoked by Fagel's *Letter* not only added a new political dimension to the toleration debate, it also added considerably to the material composition of the debate, through the repetition of phrases and arguments in the numerous published tracts that had to be taken into account by the advocates or opponents of toleration. One of the best of these works was Henry Care's *Animadversions upon Mijn Heer Fagel's Letter*. Care had been a Whig and a Dissenter, and his purpose in writing the *Animadversions* was to urge Dissenters to accept the existing toleration, rather than, as he put it, reject James' indulgence on the presumption that some better settlement of toleration might be enacted by a future generation. This not-so-veiled reference to the expectation that William, as king of England, would establish both Protestantism and toleration in the form the radicals desired, was cloaked under the vague allusion to "the determination of Divine Providence" as to what the future would bring.[82] The political message was by now a very familiar one, but the language and arguments employed by Care in support of this conclusion are quite interesting, and address at length a philosophical aspect of the toleration debate that was only briefly alluded to in my discussion of Ferguson's writings.

He begins by asking "on whose shoulders the weight of government, whether Legislative or Executive, lies." This question directs him, as it had others, to the original of government and its functional purpose, which is to provide "for the good of mankind."[83] From the language used, it may be inferred that Care accepts consent as the means by which governments are established, though he never directly states this. What is of most concern, however, is the sharp distinction he draws between the provinces of civil authority and religion. "Each of these," he insists, "are distinct from the other" and their respective claims upon individuals' actions can be confined within "their distinct spheres . . . without in-

[81] There is a detailed discussion of the considerable interest and concern of the radical exiles in Fagel's *Letter* and the general toleration debate in a letter from Patrick Hume to William's chief adviser, William Bentinck (N. Japiske, ed., *Correspondentie Van Willem III en Van Hans Willem Bentinck*, 5 vols., The Hague: Martinus Nijhoff, 1929, 2:599–603). Locke owned a copy of Fagel's *Letter* (*LL* #1089).

[82] Henry Care, *Animadversions upon Mijn Heer Fagel's Letter*, 1688, p. 26. This dilemma is recorded in a note by Morrice, 1:626. Penn condemned the "unwarrantable use of Providence" by the Dissenters hoping for better terms under William (*The Great and Popular Objection against the Repeal of the Penal Laws and Tests Briefly Stated and Considered*, 1688, p. 17).

[83] Care, *Animadversions upon Fagel*, p. 5.

croaching one upon the other." This dichotomy is central to the argument of the *Animadversions*, and in elaborating upon the sphere of civil authority, Care writes: "[It] is not essentially necessary to, nor under the immediate care or concern of the civil government, that all their subjects should be compelled by any temporal penalties or disabilities to be of one and the same religion."[84] Like Ferguson, Care associates toleration with the Law of Nature and the "common reason of mankind." Hence, there is a "distinct sphere" of juridical authority wherein "a liberty for every man's exercise of his religion, according to the dictates of his conscience, (guided by common reason, and the measure of his understanding of the will of God therein)" cannot be restrained by any "human law." In short, "the Divine Laws which respect the essential parts of the worship of God are in themselves invariable, and not to be changed by any human authority."[85]

From this natural law defense of toleration, however, he draws the opposite inference from that made by Ferguson; namely, that the king may exercise his prerogative "for the good of mankind" even against the existing laws because the latter violate the Law of Nature and are therefore void.[86] Within the logic of the argument employed by the radicals, especially as buttressed by the "distinct spheres" portrayal of social life, it was difficult to fault this conclusion, however distasteful it might appear on other grounds (such as the practical consequences of James' Catholicism). For the whole purpose of the prerogative, as Locke put it, was to employ it on behalf of the common good of society, even in those situations in which the realization of the latter necessitated the suspension or abrogation of an existing statute law, which of course was the point directly at issue in this debate.[87] That such a defense of James' use of the prerogative could be made, not from the standpoint of a divine right argument, but within the framework of a natural law defense of toleration, obviously placed the political opponents of James' indulgence in some difficulty with respect to the development of their own theoretical position.

The *Animadversions* presents the "distinct spheres" dichotomy as part of a theoretical perspective that is elaborated at some length, but others (and most notably, Penn) had employed the distinction in their tracts. "The soul of man," Penn declared, "is out of the reach of the magistrate's sword." Compulsion, therefore, cannot be used in matters of faith, since force cannot substitute itself for those things which do affect a man's understanding. Coercion may produce a kind of outward conformity in the

[84] Care, *Animadversions upon Fagel*, pp. 22, 26.

[85] Care, *Animadversions upon Fagel*, pp. 25–26.

[86] Care, *Animadversions upon Fagel*, p. 6.

[87] *ST*, pars. 160–161, 164.

performance of religious activities, but, Penn insisted, it only creates hypocrites with respect to matters of faith.[88] The human understanding must answer to the evidence supplied by reason and, when that fails, it may appeal to faith; but on no account can it be directed by the application of force.

In *The Reasonableness of Toleration,* Penn places the two-spheres argument within the framework supplied by "common reason" and the Law of Nature, according to which "no particular person has a right to impose a force upon the judgment of his brother."[89] Since the "legislative power" is only ordained by individuals to look after their "worldly interests" and outward actions, it can claim no province over the liberty of individual consciences.[90] Similarly, in the second of his three *Letters* on the subject of the penal laws and Test Act, Penn had circumscribed the province of government within the realm of "the civil interest" of the people.[91] From this standpoint, he was able to proclaim, as Care and Ferguson had, that "liberty of conscience is the natural right of mankind, and the general interest of England."[92] Clearly, in his defense of toleration, Penn relied upon the distinction between the "civil interests" of individuals, for the protection of which political authority was appropriately created, and their spiritual welfare, which he placed above the magistrate's sword. This distinction was tied not only to a natural law/natural rights argument, but also to the force/understanding issue as part of a definition of what constitutes a rational being, with respect to the grounds for an individual's belief.[93]

Locke owned a substantial number of the tracts on toleration from which I have cited, including all of Penn's *Letters* on the penal laws. Though for reasons already suggested, we cannot know for certain the extent to which his views on toleration were influenced by or were direct responses to particular works that were published between 1685 and 1688—including those written by Dutch or French Protestants—it does

[88] William Penn, *Advice to Freeholders and Other Electors of Members to Serve in Parliament in Relation to the Penal Laws and the Tests,* 1687, p. 2. Care's *Animadversions* was dedicated to his friend, William Penn.

[89] William Penn, *The Reasonableness of Toleration and the Unreasonableness of Penal Laws and Tests,* 1687, p. 9.

[90] Penn, *Reasonableness,* pp. 30–31. "Civil interest is the foundation and end of civil government" (William Penn, *One Project for the Good of England,* [1680], p. 2).

[91] Penn, *Second Letter,* p. 5. In fact, "civil interests" is a term used throughout Penn's writings (J. A. W. Gunn, *Politics and the Public Interest in the Seventeenth Century,* London: Routledge and Kegan Paul, 1969, p. 188).

[92] William Penn, *Some Free Reflections upon the Occasion of the Public Discourse about Liberty of Conscience,* 1687, p. 20; cf. ibid., pp. 8, 10.

[93] Penn, *Advice to Freeholders,* p. 4.

seem unreasonable to suppose that he was oblivious to the major political and theoretical components of the toleration debate during that period. Nor could he imagine, certainly not at the point of its publication, that his own argument would not be immediately endowed with a political significance, given the already existing structure of that debate.

Yet, before turning directly to a consideration of the arguments of the *Letter on Toleration*, I want to provide some indication of the kinds of judgments Locke had made on the issue of toleration within the context of his political thinking of the 1680s, even before this particular debate materialized. There are two reasons for this endeavor, apart from the fact that it involves the examination of a manuscript that has been almost totally ignored by Locke scholars. First, since the manuscript was written during 1681, whatever it expresses of Locke's views on toleration is directly coterminous with the writing of the *Two Treatises of Government*, and is, therefore, clearly connected with the radical dimensions of Locke's political thought, which developed during that period. And second, at least one individual, Locke's coauthor of the manuscript, James Tyrrell, recognized the importance of its arguments to the 1685–1688 debate on toleration. There is, in other words, a historical link between Locke's political theory as formulated within the context of Shaftesbury's revolutionary political movement and the toleration debate of 1685–1688 that merits some consideration as part of the explication of the meaning attached to the specific arguments of the *Letter*, or indeed of the *Two Treatises* itself.

The manuscript in question was occasioned by a notorious sermon preached by Edward Stillingfleet in May 1680, entitled "The Mischief of Separation." It was a spirited attack on the Dissenters who were accused, in effect, of committing treason by fomenting the political and spiritual disunity of the nation at a time when the dangers to England posed by popery were most serious.[94] Owen, Baxter, Howe, Humfrey, and many others published replies to Stillingfleet.[95] The latter attempted to answer his critics in a much longer work, *The Unreasonableness of Separation*, published early in 1681. All of Stillingfleet's critics pursued the attack in

[94] The Dissenters merely "serve the design of our enemies," the papists (Edward Stillingfleet, *The Mischief of Separation*, 1680, p. 57).

[95] For a list of some of the replies to Stillingfleet's sermon, see William Orme, *Memoirs of the Life, Writings, and Religious Connections of John Owen*, 1820, pp. 414–417; Whiting, *Studies in Puritanism*, p. 524. Locke owned the replies by John Owen (*LL* #3006) and John Howe (*LL* #2785), but in the Locke-Tyrrell manuscript, there are also references to the replies by others, including Richard Baxter. Stillingfleet's sermon is not listed among the works in Locke's library (nor is *The Unreasonableness of Separation*) unless it is the unidentified sermon by Stillingfleet (*LL* #2786). Locke did own *The Unreasonableness of Separation*, however (see MS f.6, fol. 50).

a veritable flood of replies to this book that were published in 1681.[96] The Locke-Tyrrell manuscript, though it was not published, was also a reply to *The Unreasonableness of Separation*. It was written during May 1681, following the dissolution of the Oxford Parliament, and at a time when a substantial portion of the *Two Treatises* already existed in draft form.[97] Locke's willingness to undertake a joint project is in itself interesting, since it could be used to lend support to the inference that this was not an isolated venture on Locke's part, and that other pamphlets, involving Ferguson or Shaftesbury, might have been composed in the same fashion. Be that as it may, the manuscript in its physical appearance is also unusual in that it is written in three different hands. Besides Locke and Tyrrell, the third handwriting belongs to Locke's amanuensis, Sylvester Brownover. Within the text, the handwriting frequently changes between paragraphs on the same page, sometimes within the same paragraph, less frequently within the same sentence, and once, even within a single word![98] Clearly, by whatever definition can be formulated for the concept of joint authorship, the Locke-Tyrrell manuscript fulfills its criteria. Nevertheless, we shall be concerned primarily with an exposition of Locke's position in this work, so far as that can be determined with the greatest degree of accuracy, given the nature of the manuscript.[99]

[96] Edward Stillingfleet, *The Unreasonableness of Separation*, 1681. This controversy, though it has received virtually no attention, is very interesting, especially for the directness with which Dissenters were beginning to challenge the political authority of Parliament, and because it engaged all the major figures among the Nonconformists. Even in 1685, Stillingfleet could refer to the still-raging storm of criticism provoked by his sermon and its defense (Whiting, *Studies in Puritanism*, p. 529). There is a very brief discussion of the sermon and its critics in Gerald R. Cragg, *Puritanism in the Period of the Great Persecution, 1660–1688*, Cambridge: Cambridge University Press, 1957, pp. 233–236.

[97] Cranston (p. 193) is mistaken in describing the manuscript as a reply to Stillingfleet's sermon. It is a reply to the latter's book, that is, the *Unreasonableness*. Although the second is a defense of the first, the two are distinctly different documents, and it is the arguments Stillingfleet employs in the book that are answered by Locke and Tyrrell. Cranston is also mistaken in dating the manuscript in April 1680, since Stillingfleet's sermon was not preached until May 1680. Locke records in his journal that Stillingfleet's *Unreasonableness* arrived at Oakeley (Tyrrell's house) on April 4, 1681. The two may have begun work on their answer then, but since Locke left Oakeley on April 6, and did not return until May 11, where, except for a day trip to Oxford, he remained until May 19, the manuscript in its present form was probably written during the latter period (MS f.5, fol. 39).

[98] The manuscript, which in typescript runs to more than four hundred pages, is largely in Tyrrell's hand, which is quite distinct from that of Locke. Much closer to the latter's handwriting is that of Brownover, who, since he was Locke's secretary and not an independent author, I have taken to be expressing Locke's views. (I wish to thank Mr. De Beer for allowing me to see his typescript copy of this manuscript.)

[99] Lord King printed some excerpts from the manuscript (2:195–218), but, besides misdating the publication of Stillingfleet's *Unreasonableness* as 1683, he quoted passages in-

In a manner too complicated to be elaborated here, Stillingfleet had joined two explosive issues in the *Unreasonableness*: First, what are the sources of authority for the clergy? And second, On what basis can a minority claim the right to act against the law sanctioning an established church in a political society founded upon "general consent"? On the first question, he maintained that it was "absurd and unreasonable" to suppose that in early Christian times "the government of the church had altogether a democratical form." Christ did not give "the people" the right to choose their pastors, and if *he* did not endorse this democratic procedure, what authority can be claimed for it by the Nonconformists? To this argument, Stillingfleet appended the usual antidemocratic polemics. Who are "the people"? "Must all have equal votes?" Democracy leads to "tumults and disorders," and the worst pastors would be selected by the majority, who are themselves evil and sinful, and so forth.[100] On the second question, Stillingfleet argued that if "a small part of the people may disown the public acts of Parliament" in this case, why cannot the claim authorizing such action against "established laws, passed by general consent in Parliament" be appealed to by other minorities? In his view, there was no ground for such acts of civil disobedience; moreover, if one instance were allowed to stand, the domino theory dictated that other examples would inevitably arise.[101]

As might be imagined, there were some spirited and interesting responses to these questions, of which John Humfrey's tract merits special notice, not only because of his willingness to confront directly, and from a radical perspective, the political issues raised by Stillingfleet, but also because his arguments in this controversy are rather clearly linked with their reappearance in the distinctly political tracts he wrote at the time of the Glorious Revolution.[102] Apart from particular substantive arguments

---

discriminately as belonging to Locke, most of which were actually written by Tyrrell. He seems not to have known that the work was jointly written with Tyrrell. Thus, while I would emphasize the joint character of the work, particularly as to its basic arguments, I have tried to retain some separable identity for Locke's specific contribution.

100 Stillingfleet, *Unreasonableness*, pp. 309, 330–331.

101 Stillingfleet, *Unreasonableness*, pp. 134–135, 328.

102 John Humfrey, *An Answer to Dr. Stillingfleet's Book of the Unreasonableness of Separation*, 1682. Humfrey defends the "consent of every man in particular" as the basis for the organizational authority of both the Church and the State (p. 21). He also links Stillingfleet's attack on the Dissenters with Parker's *Discourse* (p. 38). In his definitions of "community," "political society," and "Constitution," Humfrey is clearly indebted to Lawson's political theory. Both in this work and in his earlier, *An Answer to Dr. Stillingfleet's Sermon by Some Nonconformists*, 1680, Humfrey's approach to the isssues seems very close to that of Locke. On the other replies to the *Unreasonableness*, see Orme, *Life of Owen*, pp. 419–420; Whiting, *Studies in Puritanism*, pp. 525–526.

that they both employed, there is, I believe, a similarity in this respect between Humfrey and Locke. What is interesting about the Locke/Tyrrell manuscript, however, is that there is an attempt by Locke to set aside *any* claims for political authority in matters of religion. In place of the divine-right-versus-consent debate about church authority, Locke adopts a state of nature/natural law approach that views religious issues through the eyes of the individual.[103]

Locke's argument in the manuscript depends, as it does in the *Letter*, upon a natural law framework that limits magisterial authority over matters pertaining to religion. He refers to "that law which God hath placed in the nature of man to preserve the being and welfare of himself and other men in this world" as the standard of all morality. It is discoverable by the same "light of nature" that teaches man that "he is under the government and disposal of an invisible and supreme being . . . [who] overrules all human affairs and sovereignly dispenses good and evil in this world, and on whom depends eternal happiness and misery in another." Now, while "a great part" of the moral obligations individuals are under with respect to natural law have "fallen under the magistrate's care, in whom the government of civil society is committed, as the greatest means of the preservation of mankind," yet this authority, Locke insists, does not extend to the concerns of religion.[104] Like Ferguson, Locke seeks to defend political authority based upon consent of the people, and at the same time, to place the individual's religious beliefs outside that sphere of authority.

"The establishment of the civil power," he writes, can "lay no obligation on me without the consent and agreement of the body of the people . . . and [the] civil magistrate [has] no power to oblige me . . . without the concurrence of the body of the people."[105] But, Locke argues, even if the legal obligations in civil society are rooted in the consent of the people, this cannot affect a structure of obligations established by a higher authority (God). Locke's fundamental premise is that it is "part of my liberty as a Christian and as a man to choose of what church or religious society I will be of, as most conducing to the salvation of my soul, of

[103] Humfrey, Owen, and others intimated that Stillingfleet was invoking a divine-right-of-church-authority argument, while they were defending a consensual notion of church authority, but in the participants' detailed discussion of the issues, the debate was far from being so clear cut. Because Tyrrell enters into this discussion at length, this statement also applies to his treatment of the subject. Locke may have shared his views on every one of the specific topics discussed, but because his interpolations are brief, it is easier to apply the statement in the text to his contribution to the manuscript.

[104] MS c.34, fols. 75–76.

[105] MS c.34, fol. 120. Here and in another instance, "majority" (of the people) is crossed out in the text and replaced with "body."

which I alone am judge, and over which the magistrate has no power at all."[106] In matters of faith and worship, every man must "in his own conscience be judge [of] what he will do."[107] So that the essence of the whole controversy respecting the claims of religion and politics boils down to this: "whether I must choose my own way to salvation or another choose for me."[108] This is the way the question is framed at the outset of the manuscript by Tyrrell. In answering it, Locke writes,

> I affirm that it is out of the power of any man to make another a representative for himself in matters of religion, much less can another make one for him, since nobody can give another man authority to determine in what way he should worship God Almighty.[109]

Given the juridical structure of Lockean natural rights as being derivative from obligations that individuals owe to God that they *cannot* renounce, even through the act of consent, Locke's position is surely expressed by Tyrrell's statement that individuals have a "natural and evangelical right of taking care of their own salvation."[110] Thus, Locke concludes, there may be such a thing as a "national consent" embodied in parliamentary statutes that "is sufficient to make a law that obliges every subject in civil matters." Even so, the same political authority cannot "make a law that shall oblige every subject in matters of religion."[111] There is, for Locke, an absolute difference between the obligatory force of the law individuals are under that pertains to "men in their great eternal concernment of their souls" and the obligations laid upon them respecting "the short and trivial concernments of their estates."[112] In short, "the magistrate . . . can have no power to enjoin any indifferent thing in the worship of God . . . nor require [the people's] obedience" to any such command, "farther than their own consciences approve of it."[113] As in the *Letter,* Locke has relied upon a radical dichotomy between the two spheres of religion and civil interests, buttressed by a radical Protestant appeal to the absoluteness of individual conscience as an essential component of "Christian liberty."

The political implications of this view are that neither the king through

[106] MS c.34, fol. 74.

[107] MS c.34, fol. 121. Locke has written "judge" above "persuaded" in this sentence.

[108] MS c.34, fol. 5a.

[109] MS c.34, fol. 122. This is a direct reply to statements by Stillingfleet on pp. 134–135 of the *Unreasonableness.* Also, see the note, "Toleratio," MS d.1, fol. 125.

[110] MS c.34, fol. 101.

[111] MS c.34, fol. 122; cf. ibid., fol. 130.

[112] MS c.34, fol. 86.

[113] MS c.34, fol. 75; cf. ibid., fol. 119.

the use of his prerogative and dispensing power nor Parliament through the enactment of laws is entitled to interfere with the individual's natural right to worship as he chooses. This is not an argument framed in terms of a constitutional struggle for power between the king and Parliament, nor is it one that justifies religious toleration on pragmatic grounds, however it is granted. Indeed, there is a mild but direct attack on the Dissenters in the Locke-Tyrrell manuscript because, as Tyrrell puts it, the Dissenters have been willing to "admit the magistrate's power when they think they have him on their side."[114] But if, as Locke argues, there is no legitimate power to be exercised "by any human authority," then the favorable or unfavorable consequences of the exercise of such power is irrelevant.[115] Thus, "men may indeed choose representatives to make civil laws for them," Tyrrell observes, "because they have power to submit all their civil rights to them, and to dispose of their temporal concernments . . . but a man has no power to submit his faith to the will, and opinion of another man."[116] Hence, while "it is true, what is done in Parliament in civil things may be truly said to be the consent of the nation, because they are done by their representatives who are empowered to that purpose," does anyone believe, Tyrrell asks, that anyone can "empower another to make religion for him, as he does civil laws[?] I am sure I never did, nor think I can. It is the persuasion of every man's own conscience . . . and his voluntary uniting himself" to a church that makes him a member of it. This right of the individual to give his consent to a particular church, Tyrrell insists, "cannot be disposed of by the majority of a House of Commons, who, with all their representative power cannot by a vote make anyone believe the doctrines of infallibility or transubstantiation."[117]

As the last phrase indicates, the argument for toleration and liberty of conscience was made in the midst of the fears that a Catholic sovereign would use his authority over a national church to enforce the return of popery to England. It was important, therefore, to defend the individual's right of religious belief against *all* forms of political authority, including a representative Parliament, which had steadfastly defended the claims of the Anglican church, in order to guard against the complicity by any political institution in this endeavor. "For I ask," Tyrrell wrote, "what will become of their national church if the magistrate be of another religion or come to differ from them? Supposing now a popish Prince in England, I ask what will become of their Church of England, that great bulwark

[114] MS c.34, fols. 42, 103.

[115] MS c.34, fol. 75.

[116] MS c.34, fols. 113–114; cf. ibid., fol.122.

[117] MS c.34, fol. 118.

against popery!"[118] This question, it will be recalled, had first been posed by Shaftesbury in 1675, as reported by the author of *A Letter from a Person of Quality to His Friend in the Country.*[119] Apart from a false sense of security against the reestablishment of popery created by the reliance upon a national church that is subject to the will of the (popish) prince, Stillingfleet's attack upon the Dissenters was made at the worst possible moment—"at a time when popery so threatens and so nearly surrounds us and is ready by any way it can find open to enter upon us."[120] It was foolhardy, Tyrrell argued, to direct the nation's attention away from its united opposition to a "people that have declared themselves ready by blood, violence, and destruction to ruin our religion and government," and the efforts of the Whigs to save us from "being subjects to a Prince that has declared enmity and war to us" for not being of his (Catholic) faith.[121] As Locke put it, "I see not where it can end . . . for by this way of reasoning," we must, "for unity sake" in religion be brought by compulsion to be members of the national church, which will itself "be brought under one universal monarchy"—papal tyranny.[122]

It is interesting that the prospects of such a future forced the raising of the question of active resistance in a form analogous to the way in which the issue is posed in the *Two Treatises of Government.* "For when it is asked," Tyrrell writes, "whether the people may reform if the magistrate does not?, it in the bottom means this: whether the people may use force against the magistrate to alter either the doctrine or discipline of the church which he by force has established or maintained?"[123] Although this question is raised, it is not answered in the Locke-Tyrrell manuscript. The implications, however, are rather clear in view of the position adopted by the authors that any attempt by the magistrate—however constituted—to exercise authority over the individual's conscience was illegal and an example of the exercise of force without authority, coupled with a specific attack upon "papal tyranny" and the return of Catholicism to England. Both the general and the specific grounds for a theory of armed resistance, as developed in the *Two Treatises,* are presented in the Locke-Tyrrell manuscript.

With respect to toleration, therefore, Locke's political thinking in 1681 was committed to a natural rights defense of liberty of conscience against the claims of all forms of political authority, including representative

[118] MS c.34, fol. 14.
[119] *Works,* 9:207.
[120] MS c.34, fol. 30.
[121] MS c.34, fols. 11, 26.
[122] MS c.34, fol. 92v.
[123] MS c.34, fol. 102.

government. This defense necessitated an absolute separation between the sphere of religion (which was defined by its concernment for the eternal salvation of the individual's soul) and the sphere of politics (whose province extended only to men's estates and civil interests). This argument for toleration was advanced in the context of an attack upon popery and the view that Catholics, but especially a popish prince, existed in a state of war with Protestants and could thus claim no benefits— including, of course, toleration—of natural law, which the practices of popery, ipso facto, violated. And finally, in support of this theoretical perspective, the question of whether "the people may use force against the magistrate" was raised as a response to the persecution of Dissenters by the Anglican church and the prospects of England's being ruled by a popish king.

It is perhaps not so surprising, then, that Tyrrell should write to Locke at the end of December 1686, with the suggestion: "I could wish you would send for your papers in the red trunk which we writ together; and out of them perfect your intended discourse concerning Toleration and Persecution." Certainly, he understood the manuscript's relevance—and so far as we know, Tyrrell was the only person who knew of its existence—to the discussion then going on in England regarding James' general pardon and his intentions to declare an indulgence. He observes that, in his opinion, no one save a few extremists in the various religious "parties" could "be offended at it; and of them, most confess the thing in theory, though they deny it in practice."[124] Tyrrell did not know that Locke had written, or was writing, the *Epistola*, but he was familiar with the kinds of arguments contained in that work that had already been incorporated into their joint manuscript of 1681, and these, he was convinced, could be employed at that particular moment (1686–1687) to further the cause of toleration.

Nor was Tyrrell the only one of Locke's English friends to be sensitive to Locke's particular interest in toleration and James' political policies. On March 1, 1687, John Freke informed Locke that "there is a proclamation of Indulgence in Scotland which we daily expect to see here in print," a copy of which he advised Locke to obtain from their mutual friend, Benjamin Furly, for, Freke adds, "tis worth your reading."[125] After the publication of James II's Declaration of Indulgence for England on April 14, 1687, Tyrrell wrote Locke again urging him to write or perfect his "discourse about Liberty of Conscience." He reported to Locke that James' Indulgence "gives so general a satisfaction that more are displeased at the manner of doing it than at the thing itself." That is, the

124 *Correspondence*, 3:92.
125 *Correspondence*, 3:149.

king's use of prerogative had apparently irritated more people than the mere fact of religious toleration. Because of this, Tyrrell's plea for Locke's revision of the 1681 manuscript is now couched in terms of the political campaign then being mounted to obtain parliamentary approval for toleration. Locke's "discourse" would be most appropriate "now to dispose people's minds to pass it into a law, whenever the Parliament sits."[126]

The problem, however, was not quite so simple as Tyrrell imagined. For one thing, it was not at all clear to the radicals in Holland that anything approaching a freely elected Parliament would be allowed by James to sit. They suspected, rightly, that he would use his executive powers and his revisions of borough and city charters to insure that a packed Parliament would be elected, one that could be counted upon to repeal both the penal laws *and* the Test Act against Catholics. This is an issue to which we shall return later, but suffice it to say that Locke was not prepared to write on behalf of toleration in a situation in which Catholics would prove to be beneficiaries of the policy. And, second, there were international political considerations to be taken into account, to which reference has already been made, but of which Tyrrell appears to have been ignorant. Finally, Locke *had* revised his arguments on the issue of liberty of conscience, in the *Epistola*, but in a manner that preserved the basic natural law framework of a defense of toleration without employing that framework as part of a polemical critique of the actions of Parliament, as he had in the 1681 manuscript.

The *Letter on Toleration* is an interesting document because, as a contribution to the political debate on toleration, it represents an attempt both to occupy the higher ground of principles and at the same time to rake up the most basic antipopery prejudices and fears that shaped the popular response to James' policies. As I shall argue, both aspects of his argument are indicative of the radical Dissenters' perspective. In his presentation of the two-spheres position, Locke writes:

> I esteem it above all things necessary to distinguish exactly the business of civil government from that of religion, and to settle the just bounds that lie between the one and the other.[127]

[126] *Correspondence*, 3:191.

[127] *Works*, 5:9. Though I have consulted Gough's translation, I have used Popple's translation as printed in Locke's *Works*. No one, in my view, has made the case for substituting any other translation for the one that was accepted by Locke himself. Locke's notation, "without my privity," means, as Gough and Klibansky point out, that the translation was carried out without his active participation (*Toleration*, pp. xlii–xliii, 45). It does not mean without his knowledge, since Locke clearly knew of the translation; nor, on the other hand, does it mean without his approval. None of those who have sought to replace Popple's version have any grounds for transforming a factual statement into an evaluative one, sug-

A few pages later, he observes that "the boundaries on both sides are fixed and immovable."[128] Now, in order to demonstrate the absoluteness of this distinction, Locke relies, as he had in the Locke-Tyrrell manuscript, upon placing the liberty of the individual's conscience outside the structure of political authority, however established. In other words, toleration is the expression of a natural rights claim, when the latter is seen as the fulfillment of the individual's natural law obligations, which is the juridical structure of *all* Lockean natural rights.

The fundamental premise of the *Letter*, repeated numerous times in that work, is Locke's insistance that "the care of each man's salvation belongs only to himself." The reason for this, he explains, is that "every man has an immortal soul, capable of eternal happiness or misery, whose happiness depending upon his believing and doing those things in this life which are necessary to the obtaining of God's favor, and are prescribed by God to that end." From which it follows, for Locke, that "the highest obligation that lies upon mankind" is to carry out those "ends" prescribed by God, especially as they relate to salvation.[129] God's law is a directive to mankind, but the responsibility for obedience lies solely and absolutely with the individual. Thus, "those things that every man ought sincerely to inquire into himself, and by meditation, study, search, and his own endeavors attain the knowledge of, cannot be looked upon as the peculiar possession of any sort of men . . . The care, therefore, of every man's soul belongs unto himself, and is to be left unto himself."[130] God, Locke argues, has never "given any such authority to one man over another, as to compel anyone to his religion. Nor," he adds, "can any such power be vested in the magistrate by the consent of the people, because no man can so far abandon the care of his own salvation as blindly to leave to the choice of any other, whether prince or subject, to prescribe to him what

gesting Locke's disapproval of the English version produced by Popple. Gough mentions Locke's meticulous correction of the first edition of the *Letter* (p. 46), but he seems not to appreciate the importance of the fact that, given the opportunity to make any changes in meaning in Popple's translation where the latter had not faithfully reproduced his own intended meaning, Locke chose not to do so. On the contrary, he defended that translation at great length in his replies to Proast. While it is useful to have the Gough translation available, his infelicitous substitutions ("civil goods" for "civil interests"), and his general effort to tone down the *Letter*, making it less "partisan" in character (p. 51), make it, in my judgment, a far less reliable document than Popple's translation. The latter was familiar with the writings of his contemporaries who contributed to the debate on toleration (as was Locke), and understood why the issue *was* a partisan one. On the question of the seventeenth-century meaning of the *Letter*, I believe Popple's translation is superior to any modern version of that work.

[128] *Works*, 5:21.

[129] *Works*, 5:23, 29, 41, 43–44.

[130] *Works*, 5:25.

faith or worship he shall embrace. For no man can, if he would, conform his faith to the dictates of another."[131] In other words, "the just boundaries" between religion and government depend upon the presumption that "every man . . . has the supreme and absolute authority of judging for himself" in matters of religion.[132] This individualism is itself dependent upon there being a direct obligatory tie between the individual and God with respect to the dictates of natural law, since it is this linkage that mitigates against any claim for authority advanced by any other private individual or by the magistrate. From this standpoint, Locke can maintain that toleration is "agreeable to the Gospel and to reason," and that religious persecution is "contrary to the laws of the Gospel and to the precepts of charity."[133]

In the passage cited above, Locke framed his argument in such a way as to deny to either the individual's consent or "the consent of the people" the legitimacy of transferring to another the individual's obligation to secure his own religious salvation. Since Locke has not abandoned his position that political authority depends upon the consent of individuals and is directed toward preserving the public good—which is reaffirmed in the *Letter*—that work is able to defend both the legitimacy of legislative power grounded in consent and a natural rights claim for liberty of conscience that lies outside the sphere of all political authority. Hence, "liberty of conscience is every man's natural right."[134] This, as we have seen,

[131] *Works*, 5:10–11.

[132] *Works*, 5:41.

[133] *Works*, 5:9, 53.

[134] *Works*, 5:47–48. Gough omits this phrase because, he argues, what Locke is defending "is toleration for dissenting sects, not liberty of conscience for individuals, and he does not mention natural right" (*Toleration*, p. 161). This is one of the examples of Gough's misunderstanding of Locke's argument. Not only does Locke repeatedly defend the liberty of conscience of individuals as a prior condition to the formation of *any* church, but he lists this "liberty" among the "natural rights" that individuals have a right to defend with force if necessary (*Works*, 5:53–54). In Gough's translation, "the conscience of each individual and the salvation of his soul, for which he is accountable to God only" is listed as being among "the rights which God and nature have granted them" (individuals) and which they may defend with force if those rights are attacked (*Toleration*, p. 147). Even in this particular passage, aside from the structure of the entire *Letter* in which the general argument for toleration depends upon a natural rights claim to the individual's absolute authority over matters pertaining to his own salvation and religious worship, it is clear that Locke does intend to make precisely the argument Gough chooses to omit. In his defense of this position in the *Third Letter for Toleration*, Locke refers to the "natural liberty" every individual has in the state of nature, which includes the freedom of worship, "and so every man has a right to toleration" (*Works*, 5:212). Moreover, Gough seems to have forgotten that Locke had already committed himself in the *Essay Concerning Toleration* to "an absolute and universal right to toleration" of the individual's religious beliefs (Fox-Bourne, 1:176). And as I have argued above, this position is reaffirmed in the 1681 manuscript he wrote with Tyrrell.

is the position advanced by Ferguson and the radical Dissenters and by Locke and Tyrrell in the 1681 manuscript. As in other instances, the abstractness of the argument is not a retreat from the political debate to philosophy; on the contrary, it represents the most radical political position in that debate. For at one stroke, Locke's *Letter* sets aside entirely the controversy over the exercise of the king's prerogative versus the securing of parliamentary consent for toleration by insisting that *no* political institution has a right to enact laws that pertain to the individual's religious beliefs. At best, parliamentary repeal of the penal laws will merely undo what should never have been done in the first place. This is also the position taken by Locke's friend and fellow radical, John Howe. Since individuals have a natural right to liberty of conscience according to the Law of Nature, no civil law, however enacted, Howe argued, can interfere with this freedom of worship. Thus, the penal laws and Test Acts are, ipso facto, null and void. Hence, by practicing toleration, the Dissenters, Howe insisted, are not endorsing "an illegal dispensing power" exercised by James II, but are merely reaffirming their natural rights.[135]

The second point of interest about the *Letter* is the directness and specificity of its political position. Toleration has so often been viewed as the logical outcome of a rational or enlightened liberal position, that it has been forgotten by commentators what a distinctly political act it was in the period from 1686 to 1688 to offer a defense of the Dissenters.[136] They were, after all, a very small minority of the total religious population; they had repeatedly been perceived as being political subversives; and enough of them had been prominently involved in various conspiracies and rebellions during the previous twenty-five years to make the charge stick. It was not a popular undertaking for one to speak openly in their defense. Even when the climate shifted somewhat after 1687 under James' patronage, any support for dissent that was combined with an attack on Catholicism, as is the case with the *Letter*, staked out a position that was, to an even greater extent, a minority viewpoint.

In pursuing this political perspective, Locke attacks the motives of the Anglican clergy in their fanatical persecution of the Dissenters, as well as the intentions of James in granting an indulgence to the latter. These "ex-

135 John Howe, *The Case of the Protestant Dissenters, Represented and Argued*, 1689, pp. 1–2.

136 See, for example, Fox-Bourne, who maintains that Locke was "far bolder" in his treatment of toleration than were his contemporaries because he approached the subject "from the standpoint of a philosopher" (1:167–169). This view is endorsed by Gunn, who concludes that Locke's writings on toleration "were not political in emphasis" (*Public Interest*, p. 199). These statements are typical of those in the secondary literature, and they reflect the failure of interpreters to investigate what, in fact, contemporaries were saying in the political debate over toleration in 1685–1688.

claimers against schism," Locke observes, "do hardly ever let loose this their zeal for God, with which they are so warmed and inflamed, unless where they have the civil magistrate on their side."[137] By invoking the magistrate's aid on behalf of "their intemperate zeal," the clergy "betray their ambition and show that what they desire is temporal dominion."[138]

> For who does not see that these good men are indeed more ministers of the government than ministers of the Gospel, and that by flattering the ambition and favoring the dominion of princes and men in authority, they endeavor with all their might to promote that tyranny in the commonwealth which otherwise they should not be able to establish in the church?[139]

Thus, for "a participation of the spoil," they have used the magistrate as the means "to increase their own power." Popple's translation refers explicitly to "the predominating faction of a court-church," which certainly describes accurately who Locke has in mind as the focus of his attack.[140] For as he remarks—in both versions of the *Letter*—the established church "is for the most part more apt to be influenced by the court than the court by the church."[141] Locke's anticlericalism in the *Letter* is echoed in the *Two Treatises*, where the "flattery and ambition" of princes, the deception of the people, and their own quest for temporal power are registered as the hallmarks of the clergy, and particularly, of the Anglican church.[142] Locke's position expresses more than a plea for toleration; it is also a political attack on the authority of the Anglican clergy, the main ground of which is constituted by an exposure of their base and self-interested motives.

Nor are James' intentions allowed to stand without criticism. Locke repeats in the *Letter* all the standard allegations against Catholics that were so common in the exclusion-crisis pamphlet literature. These faults not only made them ineligible for toleration, but they also placed Catholics within such a morally disreputable framework that no rational individual could possibly place that trust and power which belongs to the magistrate in the hands of a Catholic ruler. "No opinions contrary to human society,

[137] *Works*, 5:20.

[138] *Works*, 5:23, 53.

[139] *Works*, 5:54.

[140] *Works*, 5:36. It is only "worldy interest" and "the support of a domineering hierarchy" that comprise "the chief motives" of those who support the penal laws (Penn, *Reasonableness*, p. 30). Morrice referred to the established clergy as "the hierarchists" (Morrice, 2:90).

[141] *Works*, 5:27; *Toleration*, p. 99.

[142] *TT*, preface; *FT*, pars. 3, 10.

or to those moral rules which are necessary to the preservation of civil society," Locke argues, "are to be tolerated by the magistrate." As he recognizes, however, since it would be "madness" for any church to teach such precepts openly, the reader must see that we are dealing here with a "secret evil." For these crafty men use "specious words designed to throw dust in people's eyes" to accomplish their ends. This argument—that we may presume to know what the secret and evil intentions of some individuals are even if they do not profess that these are their intentions—would be a truly remarkable claim for Locke to make if his audience did not understand perfectly well that he was only articulating what they believed, and what other writers had said for several generations, about Catholics. Thus, when the latter maintain that "faith is not to be kept with heretics," they mean "that the privilege of breaking faith belongs unto themselves." In addition, Catholics "arrogate unto themselves the power of deposing kings." Most revealing of all, Locke repeats the shibboleth that, because Catholics believe "that dominion is founded in grace," this proposition enables them to "lay claim to the possession of all things." In short, the hoary threat of a Catholic confiscation of Protestant property rights is once more hurled into the battle against popery. These charges, taken together, are sufficient grounds for denying toleration to Catholics. They are summarized by Locke in the language of conspiracy that leaves no doubts as to the consequences and dangers of the repeal of the Test Acts against the Catholics.

> For what do these and the like doctrines signify but that they may and are ready upon any occasion to seize the government and possess themselves of the estates and fortunes of their fellow subjects; and that they only ask leave to be tolerated by the magistrate so long until they find themselves strong enough to effect it?[143]

Locke was not about to let his readers forget that the papists were always planning and were ready "to attack us," as he and Tyrrell had maintained in their joint manuscript.[144] Nor should they forget that they were "subjects to a Prince that has declared enmity and war to us."[145] In the *Letter*, Locke argues that because Catholics owe their primary allegiance to "another prince . . . of a foreign jurisdiction," to permit a member of that church to be magistrate would, in effect, "allow his own people to be

[143] *Works*, 5:45–46. Ferguson also contributed a fiercely anti-Catholic tract to the toleration debate, restating the "savageness and barbarity" of the papists (N.T. [Robert Ferguson], *Animadversions upon a Pretended Answer to Myn Heer Fagel's Letter*, [1688?]).

[144] MS c.34, fol. 8.

[145] MS c.34, fol. 26.

enlisted as soldiers against his own government."[146] This was a charge frequently levelled against James II during this period, for he was busily granting commissions to Catholics as officers in the army, as well as filling many civil offices with his "own people."[147] Moreover, Locke denies that "the frivolous and fallacious distinction between the court and the church afford[s] any remedy to this incovenience; since both are equally subject to the absolute authority of the same person." Using the metaphor of a Mohammedan for James, Locke argues that "it is ridiculous" for someone to profess himself a Mohammedan "only in his religion" while claiming to be a supporter of the established Christian civil and ecclesiastical institutions if, as Locke believes, his religion in fact requires that he "yield blind obedience" to a foreign prince. James' intentions, in other words, are not to be trusted no matter how he "frames the feigned oracles of his religion" to suit his own political purposes.[148] Dissenters, such as Penn, who made the mistake of attributing sincerity to James would discover, to their peril, that no papist ruler is to be trusted. This, too, was the message the radicals wished to convey to their fellow Dissenters, and, more generally, to all those who shared Locke's fear and distrust of Catholics. It is against just such a viewpoint that Penn complained of the "panic fear . . . now animated more than ever against popery" which was being whipped up in order to call into question the king's intentions in establishing toleration.[149]

By taking the high road in the toleration debate, the *Letter* staked out a radical natural law/toleration position that set aside many of the specific political assertions and counterassertions exchanged by other writers; at the same time, by descending to particulars and a lower level of the controversy, the *Letter* embodied a sharp attack on the motives of the Anglican clergy, the dangers of popery, and the untrustworthiness of James II as a ruler. Apart from its justly noted elegance in style, this rather explosive combination, which expresses the two crucial dimensions of the radical Dissenter perspective, makes the *Letter on Toleration* a work of unusual political interest.

Finally, Locke addresses the problem of rebellion, which he insists is

146 *Works*, 5:46.

147 Dalrymple, 2:71; Carswell, *Descent*, p. 73. The changes in the army in Ireland were proceeding at such a rapid pace in July 1686, that the Earl of Clarendon wrote to Sunderland, "I doubt not the whole army will be composed within a month . . . as his Majesty would have it" (*The Correspondence of Henry Hyde, Earl of Clarendon*, 2 vols., 1828, 1:485).

148 *Works*, 5:46–47.

149 Penn, *Free Reflections*, p. 16. More than two hundred pamphlets attacking popery were published between 1685 and 1688 (John Miller, *Popery and Politics in England, 1660–1688*, Cambridge: Cambridge University Press, 1973, p. 252).

the consequence of religious persecution. He begins with the recognition that the dissenting churches are accused of being "nurseries of factions and seditions," and this charge, he notes, is "thought to afford the strongest matter of objection against this doctrine of toleration." In essence, Locke's response is to reverse the point, maintaining that "these accusations would soon cease if the law of toleration were once so settled" that no religious persecution were practiced. Pointing to the similarities between religious and other types of assemblies that are not taken to be subversive, Locke argues that the fundamental difference between the two lies in the fact that individuals are persecuted for their religious beliefs.

> For if men enter into seditious conspiracies, it is not religion inspires them to it in their meetings, but their sufferings and oppressions that make them willing to ease themselves. Just and moderate governments are everywhere quiet, everywhere safe; but oppression raises ferments and makes men struggle to cast off an uneasy and tyrannical yoke.[150]

Hence toleration breeds peace, while oppression is the cause of sedition and rebellion. Since "it is very difficult for men patiently to suffer themselves to be stripped of the goods which they have got by their honest industry and, contrary to all the laws of equity, both human and divine, to be delivered up for a prey to other men's violence . . . what else can be expected," Locke asks, "but that these men . . . should in the end think it lawful for them to resist force with force, and to defend their natural rights (which are not forfeitable upon account of religion) with arms as well as they can?"[151] For Locke, as for Ferguson, the demand for toleration is a rights claim justifiable to the point of armed resistance against the "tyrannical yoke" of religious persecution. It is hardly surprising, therefore, that, as noted earlier, the language and arguments of the 1686–1688 toleration debate merge imperceptibly with the justificatory defenses provided by the radicals of the Glorious Revolution.

Religious persecution, however, is not the only catalyst of rebellion. The misuse of political power by the magistrate may also lead to armed resistance by the people. This problem arises in the *Letter* insofar as the magistrate acts in manner that changes the established property rights of his subjects "for a reason which in no way concerns the civil community, I mean for religion." Nor does the magistrate's "private judgment" about religious matters "give him any new right of imposing laws upon his sub-

[150] *Works*, 5:47–49.
[151] *Works*, 5:53–54.

jects," since, as Locke has shown, this ground for political action "neither was in the constitution of the government granted him nor ever was in the power of the people to grant." These actions of the magistrate have even less a claim to legitimacy, of course, if they are taken in order to "enrich and advance his followers and fellow sectaries with the spoils of others."[152] If it is recalled that James II had removed magistrates, judges, and other civil servants from offices that, in the seventeenth century, had a certain proprietary status, replacing these individuals with Catholics or persons pledged to support his authority, the basis for Locke's charge becomes clearer.[153]

But what if the magistrate believes he is acting for the public good? Locke asks. This was the claim, defended by some Dissenters, that provided James with the strongest case for accepting the legitimacy of his suspension of the penal laws, and his blanket waiver of the Test Acts. More precisely, the question is, What if he believes he is acting for the public good, "and his subjects believe the contrary? Who shall be judge between them? I answer, God alone. For there is no judge upon earth between the supreme magistrate and the people." Here the similarity of the language with that of the *Two Treatises* is unmistakable. As in the latter work, Locke observes in the *Letter* that "there are two sorts of contests amongst men, the one managed by law, the other by force; and . . . where the one ends, the other always begins."[154] Earlier in the *Letter*, Locke had defended the right of individuals to use force "in self-defense against unjust violence."[155] Thus, the proposition that force exercised without authority by the magistrate—which is the case with respect to *all* matters of religion—may be met with force by those who must defend themselves against his actions constitutes the bedrock of political action in the *Letter on Toleration* just as it does in the *Two Treatises of Government*.

As in the past, the toleration debate in the late 1680s drew attention to the connections between toleration and the advancement of trade. None of the general arguments on this issue were new, but there was a very

[152] *Works*, 5:44.

[153] Given the differing views on property rights, this is a gray area, but as an illustration of the point, Clarendon mentions the case of a captain in the army who paid £1,600 for his commission, but was summarily dismissed by James in favor of a Catholic. Several similar cases are discussed in his correspondence. The point is that a number of civil and military offices could be purchased for a sum of money, and although the king retained an absolute right of appointment and dismissal, the fact that an individual could suffer the loss of his property as a consequence of the king's arbitrary action made even Tories like Clarendon uncomfortable (Clarendon, *Correspondence*, 1:436–437).

[154] *Works*, 5:45; *ST*, pars. 202, 204.

[155] *Works*, 5:17.

specific focus in the discussion of trade—namely, the clothing industry. There were two reasons for this. First, many of the Dissenters held occupations that were directly or indirectly tied to textiles and woolen manufacture, especially as it existed in the west country. Second, the establishment by the exiles in Holland of a clothing industry capable of producing English cloth without the normal import and export costs posed a serious economic threat to the woolen industry in England. There was, therefore, a distinctly economic dimension attached to the political battle for the loyalty of the Dissenters. James II's administration was prepared to go to considerable lengths to neutralize the radicals' economic attack on England. Moreover, if the government were successful, the exiles in Holland would find themselves in such financial straits, without any means of livelihood, that they would eventually be forced into accepting a return to England on the conditions provided by James or else face starvation.[156]

In his *Considerations Moving to a Toleration*, Penn described the Dissenters as "being a chief part of the trading people of the nation, considered as merchants, shopkeepers, clothiers" and so forth. To this general—and somewhat exaggerated—assertion, he added an anecdote about a dissenting clothier who, as a consequence of persecution and the confiscation of his property, had left England for Holland, leaving in his wake many unemployed workers who depended upon him for their own existence. This situation, Penn maintained, was typical of what was happening in England, and it would not be reversed until toleration was granted.[157] To this aspect of the argument for toleration, both Nalson and the author of *The Vanity of all Pretenses for Toleration* replied, in effect, So what? There were enough honest artisans and tradesmen in England, they insisted, to fill the jobs of any Dissenters who left the country.[158] Not everyone, however, was prepared to take such a sanguine attitude toward the situation. On March 26, 1686, the woolen manufacturers in Gloucestershire presented a petition to the Committee for Trade and Plantations in which they complained that "the decay of trade in the country is so considerable of late that multitudes are not able to subsist, [and] near a fifth part of the value of some parishes being expended in relieving their poor." A few weeks later, the clothiers of Coventry complained directly to the king, citing "the manifest decay of their trade to the utter ruin of some hundred families." Similar petitions from clothiers in Suffolk, Es-

[156] This policy was suggested by one of Skelton's agents and forwarded by the envoy to Middleton (Add. MS 41813, fol. 114).

[157] Penn, *Considerations*, p. 4.

[158] Nalson, *Toleration Considered*, pp. 30–31; *Vanity of Pretences*, pp. 64–65.

sex, and in fact from areas throughout England poured in during 1686.[159] The woolen manufacturers in Scotland added their voices to the growing complaints about the decay of trade. Whatever opponents might believe concerning the importance of the economic consequences attached to the argument for toleration, the government could not afford to ignore those consequences. And indeed it did not. When the petition from the clothiers in Scotland was passed on to James by the Scottish Privy Council, he immediately granted them a dispensation from taking the oath of supremacy and a toleration for Dissenters in Scotland.[160] Quite apart from his own personal commitment to toleration, in other words, James was prepared to act as king to insure that the economic benefits of trade were not sacrificed on the altar of religious belief.

In Holland, meanwhile, attempts were being made to provide employment for Penn's dissenting clothiers through the establishment of a linen factory in Friesland. Everard, a former radical and now one of Skelton's spies, reported at the end of January 1686 that a number of rebels were coming to Holland from the west of England, around Exeter, to assist in this endeavor. Everard added his own observation that, if successful, the project would prove very prejudicial to the English manufacture of cloth. He also made a recommendation that, as events developed, proved to be quite important. "I do believe," he wrote, "that a pardon if it comes out soon may recall these men before they are settled."[161] James II did issue a general pardon in March of that year, but for various reasons, this dispensation did not reach far enough to affect the individuals concerned in this enterprise. For one thing, the general pardon excepted rebels who had fought with Monmouth, and some of them were directly involved in the linen factory.[162] In April, Skelton wrote to Middleton, again urging the government to accept Everard's suggestion, which he had included in one of his earlier reports. "If any of the rebels be thought fit objects of his Majesty's mercy, I hope it will light upon the trading part of them, who (as I have formerly hinted) will be most injurious to our wool trade at home if they settle at Luxembourg or Leewarden."[163]

159 *CSPD*, (James II), 2:87, 125–126. In 1686, the English woolen industry was in an economic crisis (J. de L. Mann, *The Cloth Industry in the West of England from 1640 to 1880*, Oxford: Clarendon Press, 1971, p. 21; William R. Scott, *The Constitution and Finance of English, Scottish, and Irish Joint-Stock Companies to 1720*, 3 vols., Cambridge: Cambridge University Press, 1912, 1:309).

160 Morrice, 1:626.

161 Add. MS 41818, fol. 226.

162 Tiley and Hilliard, who were captains under Monmouth, as well as Colonel Danvers and Major Manley, were involved with the cloth-manufacturing project (Add. MS 41818, fols. 235, 280).

163 Add. MS 41813, fol. 110.

The exiles in Holland received considerable financial and political assistance from the Dutch authorities and resident merchants, of whom Locke's friend and financial associate, Israel Hayes, was the most prominent.[164] According to the contract for the linen factory in Friesland—a copy of which Skelton obtained and sent to Middleton—the exiles were to be provided with a workhouse rent free for twenty years; a small tooling mill was to be built at state expense, and the looms and machines supplied; an interest-free ten-year loan of 25,000 guilders was granted; three hundred children would be supplied to work in the factory, with the state paying their wages for the first year; employees and owners would be given a twenty-year exemption from paying taxes; and a contract from the militia in the province to purchase all its clothing from the factory was part of the agreement. In addition, the state would pay the salary for an English minister, and his assistant, for the congregation of workers, and there were promises that efforts would be made to hire more English professors at the university.[165] Obviously, the Dutch were extremely interested in furthering this enterprise. They recognized, as clearly as did Skelton, that the manufacture of English cloth on Dutch soil constituted an economic coup for them, viewed in the context of international trade.

A woolen factory set up by William Waller in Luxembourg had already provoked complaints from English merchants in Hamburg who, Skelton wrote, "are in great fear of losing their trade if Waller and other rebels' designs of this nature be not subverted."[166] And, in a report from one of his agents that he passed along to Middleton, the opinion of English merchants was cited to the effect that "nothing is more certain than that if a speedy stop be not put to the design, the woolen manufactory must be ruined at home."[167] One estimate placed the yearly value of the English clothing trade with Holland at £800,000. Since Tiley estimated that the terms of the Dutch contract would allow him to produce cloth 15 percent cheaper than in England, and with no transportation costs, it is hardly surprising that "a state of near panic ensued as the scale of this challenge by the rebels became apparent."[168] The English government recognized the seriousness of the situation, and it accepted the recommendation of

[164] Add. MS 41813, fol. 233.

[165] Add. MS 41819, fol. 121; Add. MS 41818, fols. 201–203.

[166] Add. MS 41813, fol. 96. Waller had attempted to establish a woolen factory at Bremen at the end of 1683, with the intention of providing both employment and a safe haven for radicals and Dissenters. Armstrong and Grey were conducting negotiations with the Elector of Brandenburg's ministers at the time the former was seized by Chudleigh (Add. MS 41824; Oliver H. Richardson, "Religious Toleration under the Great Elector and Its Material Results," *English Historical Review* 25 (January 1910):106–110; *CSPD*, 27:305).

[167] Add. MS 41813, fols. 114, 150.

[168] Earle, *Monmouth's Rebels*, pp. 156–158.

Everard and Skelton to make use of the king's pardoning power to break the back of this "subversive" design. According to one well-placed Dutch source, these orders came directly from James II, in response to the "fatal blow" to the English clothing trade caused by the exiles' enterprise.[169] Certainly, the king was surrounded by a chorus of advisers urging such action, for in addition to the petitions from the English clothiers and merchants themselves and Skelton's diplomatic reports, Penn was churning out pamphlets that all but made the economic prosperity of England wholly dependent upon toleration. In *A Persuasive to Moderation to Church Dissenters*, for example, he argued that toleration would persuade the exiles in Holland who were occupationally tied to the woolen trade to return to England.[170]

Through his intelligence, Skelton learned that Nicholas Lock—the other Locke—was the chief capitalist sponsor of the woolen factory. He and another employer, Christopher Cooke, were promised pardons by James on the condition that, as Cooke was told, he "forwith break off his designs and return himself, with his estate and servants and mechanics into England."[171] Along with Tiley's decision to turn informer on his comrades, and Trenchard's efforts in persuading many of the exiles to sue for pardons, this action was successful in putting an end to all the manufacturing enterprises involving the exiles.[172] By the end of July 1686, Everard could report that the factory at Leewarden had been closed down, and the workers had left.[173] A few weeks later, Everard asked Skelton to intercede on his behalf for a pardon and the chance to return to England as the reward for his having been so instrumental, as indeed he was, in

[169] Cornelius de Witt, *A Letter from Holland touching Liberty of Conscience*, 1688, pp. 2–3. Nor was James alone in his concern: Louis XIV and his ambassador, D'Avaux, were also alarmed by the prospects that the exiles would establish factories in Holland, which they viewed as a serious economic threat to France (Nesca A. Robb, *William of Orange: A Personal Portrait*, vol. 2: *The Later Years, 1674–1702*, New York: St. Martin's Press, 1966, p. 238).

[170] William Penn, *A Persuasive to Moderation to Church Dissenters in Prudence and Conscience*, [1686], in William Penn, *The Select Works of William Penn*, 4th ed., 3 vols., 1825, 2:529–530.

[171] Cited in Earle, *Monmouth's Rebels*, p. 159; Lock's involvement with the linen factory in Lüenburg and his importance (and that of Cooke) as a capitalist financier of the project is described in Add. MS 41819, fol. 13 and Add. MS 41813, fols. 112–113. Skelton received notice from Middleton on April 27, 1686, that Cooke and the two "Locks" would be pardoned (Add. MS 41823, fol. 39). On May 7, Cooke and the two "Locks" were given two months in which to return to England and comply with the conditions of the pardon (Add. MS 41813, fol. 130).

[172] Add. MS 41813, fols. 201–202; Add. MS 41819, fol. 121 (Tiley); Add. MS 41819, fol. 58.

[173] Add. MS 41813, fols. 201–203.

ruining "those two seminaries of rebellion" at Lüneburg and Leewarden.[174]

Meanwhile, a number of radicals applied for individual pardons from James II. Samuel Barnardiston, a wealthy merchant, who may have been one of the financial backers of the woolen factory, Edward Norton, Patience Ward, John Shower, a dissenting minister, as well as John Hampden, Trenchard, Lord Brandon, and others in England, received pardons during 1686, and an even larger number of radicals reconciled themselves to a submission to the king the following year.[175] On the basis of the intelligence received from his spies, Skelton reported to Middleton at the end of April 1686 that some of the rebels, particulary Colonel Danvers, Major Manley, and Captain Matthews were surprised and angry at the fact that some merchants had been offered and had accepted pardons from James. The promise of an indulgence coupled with the willingness of the king to grant pardons to individual exiles had created a serious division within the ranks of the radicals, a fact that Skelton was only too happy to pass along to his superiors. The hard-liners, like Danvers and Manley, might "curse those who seek for pardons," but the fact was that Skelton was receiving requests and inquiries from various exiles as to whether they were eligible recipients of James' clemency, and what actions they would have to perform in order to receive a pardon.

We have seen how Locke sided with the radical Dissenters in their opposition to James II on the issue of toleration. Did he also align himself with the hard-line radicals on the question of applying for and accepting a pardon? As I shall argue that he did, perhaps it is best to begin by disposing of a myth that has cropped up from time to time in the secondary literature concerning the pardon and Locke's relationship to William Penn. It is sometimes alleged that Penn actually obtained a pardon for Locke from James II, a statement for which there is no historical foundation whatsoever.[176]

Since the source of the confusion that underlies this erroneous asser-

[174] Add. MS 41813, fols. 204, 233.

[175] *CSPD* (James II), 2:163; Add. MS 41813, fols. 96, 189; Add. MS 41818, fol. 289; Add. MS 41819, fols. 45, 116, 206, 240; Doreen J. Milne, *The Rye House Plot, with Special Reference to Its Place in the Exclusion Contest and Its Consequences Till 1685*, Ph.D. diss., University of London, 1949, p. 320; HMC 12th Report, appendix, pt. 6, pp. 305–307.

[176] Buranelli not only repeatedly and erroneously insists that Penn obtained a pardon for Locke, and that the latter was in fact pardoned by James II (pp. 84, 174, 185, 204), he also states without evidence of any kind that Locke offered to procure a pardon for Penn following the Glorious Revolution (Vincent Buranelli, *The King and the Quaker*, Philadelphia: University of Pennsylvania Press, 1962, p. 174). See also Hans Fantel, *William Penn: Apostle of Dissent*, New York: William Morrow, 1974, pp. 223–224. Apparently, Fox-Bourne also believed that Locke had been pardoned (2:51).

tion will be considered below, let me turn to the second proposition that constitutes the myth of Locke's pardon. While denying that Locke ever actually accepted a pardon from James, a number of Locke scholars have maintained that he was offered a pardon but refused it because he was innocent of any wrongdoing.[177] Unlike the first allegation, this position can claim a specific historical source: Lady Masham's letter to Jean Le Clerc written more than a year after Locke's death, in which she maintained that a pardon "was actually offered him, but he would not accept of it as not owning that he needed it."[178] If this were an account provided by Edward Clarke, even allowing for the many intervening years after the fact, its accuracy might well be accepted, for Clarke was as fully informed of Locke's political activities and thinking during his period of exile in Holland as any individual in England. Lady Masham, on the other hand, knew virtually nothing of those activities, as their correspondence during the 1680s shows. She was one of the least informed of Locke's friends in England as to his political involvement with the radicals. It is true that because of their close association in the last years of his life, Locke could have discussed with Lady Masham various experiences of his life in exile, and these discussions could have included the subject of his pardon. Yet, all this is supposition for which there exists, so far as I know, no corroborative evidence.

Lady Masham's statement consists of three parts: (1) that a pardon was offered to Locke; (2) that he refused it; and (3) his reason for doing so (his innocence). If a pardon *was offered* Locke and he *refused* it, there ought to be some evidence in the historical record for these actions, since someone would have had to convey the information, officially or unofficially, to Locke in Holland for the offer to exist.[179] But, as Locke's correspondence throughout this period demonstrates, *he* was not aware of any specific offer of a pardon to him. Indeed, as we shall see, what he had heard were vague rumors about a pardon of which he knew nothing. Locke's letters to his friends are therefore written with a view of requesting their assistance in getting to the bottom of these rumors. This, obviously, is

[177] Joseph E. Illick, *William Penn the Politician*, Ithaca: Cornell University Press, 1965, p. 137; Edward Beatty, *William Penn as Social Philosopher*, New York: Columbia University Press, 1939, pp. 5–6, 10; Samuel M. Janney, *The Life of William Penn*, 1852, p. 259; Whiting, *Studies in Puritanism*, p. 181; King, 1:291–292.

[178] Cranston, p. 298.

[179] Most of the pardons granted to the exiles in Holland are reported on in the correspondence between the envoy and the Secretary of State. In addition to this source, there are the *Calendar of State Papers*, the *London Gazette*, and various other lists, both contemporary and in later scholarly works. In none of this material is there even a hint or a discussion of any pardon being considered for Locke. Until some document does turn up, its existence must be regarded as being apocryphal.

not the same thing as seeking their assistance in obtaining a pardon for him, and in fact, constitutes a direct refutation of Lady Masham's assertion that a definite offer of a pardon was made to Locke and that he consciously refused it. As for the reason for Locke's refusal of this phantom pardon, Lady Masham is simply wrong. Locke was not innocent of having committed actions for which he required a pardon. Nor, even when viewed in the context of the actions of Locke's friends and associates, is there any basis for Lady Masham's interpretation of the situation as experienced by the radicals in Holland. Some of them protested their innocence *and* applied for pardons; some confessed their guilt and applied for pardons; and some refused to consider applying for pardons. But no one, among the scores of contemporaries in Locke's situation, ever refused an offered pardon on the grounds that he was innocent. In the context of the political atmosphere prevailing in Holland in the 1680s, such an occurrence is so comically extraordinary that, had it happened, it would immediately have gained notoriety for the individual in question.

On the basis of the historical evidence available, therefore, we must conclude that no pardon was ever offered to Locke, that he did not refuse to accept a pardon, and finally, that he never applied for or requested any of his friends to apply for a pardon from James II. The myth of Locke's "pardon," like the myth of his political innocence, deserves a decent and long-overdue burial. But having disposed of these phantoms and rumors, we are now in a position to take up what is, in fact, the most puzzling aspect of the situation: Why did Locke refuse to apply for a pardon, especially when, as the record makes clear, he had so many encouragements to do so from friends in England who were in a position to obtain a pardon for him?

The first such offer appears to have come from the Earl of Pembroke who wrote to Locke on August 20, 1685, that he had spoken to James on Locke's behalf, and that he had "so satisfied the King that he has assured me he will never believe any ill reports of you. He bid me write to you to come over." To which Pembroke added the plea that, "for his sake," Locke might return to England before the end of the summer.[180] We have already discussed Locke's reaction to this letter, which provided no encouragement to Pembroke that Locke would reappear in England. If he had wished to return, however, Pembroke was certainly in a position to back up his guarantee of Locke's safety, since the earl was, during this period, very much in the king's favor.[181]

[180] *Correspondence*, 2:729.

[181] Pembroke had led part of the army that defeated Monmouth. It was probably as a reward for this service that he received a bounty of £1,000 from James shortly after this letter

The second serious entreaty came from Tyrrell in a letter written shortly after James' 1687 Declaration of Indulgence. Tyrrell wrote that he wished Locke would "come over and see the face of things here . . . he would find a strange alteration in men's humors, and need not doubt a favorable reception."[182] Tyrrell obviously believed that the toleration extended to Dissenters, and James' "strange" turn toward currying their favor and support provided sufficient grounds for Locke to expect "a favorable reception." A few days later, John Freke wrote to Locke, in a canting fashion, referring to James as a Lady who was "changing her family and furniture" and who was "on the brink of matrimony" with the Dissenters. Freke had not only been asked "to be at the wedding, but to . . . assist in drawing the Settlement." Freke was not unwilling to lend his efforts to the cause of toleration, but he doubted that "the present tenant [the Anglican church] will hardly be willing to be so bound up as is necessary" to support the claims of the Nonconformists. Freke conveyed the fact that Locke's friends thought he could be of some assistance in this endeavor. Finally, Freke indicates that if Locke wants his studentship at Oxford returned to him, "I shall use my interest to get you your place again."[183] In a later letter, Freke writes that he is skeptical that the "wedding" or the settlement will ever be celebrated, though his "kinsman," William Penn, is very confident that it will take effect.[184] In another allusion, Freke informs Locke that he might "easily be pardoned" if he desired it.[185] At the end of August 1687, Tyrrell reaffirmed the point, adding that "if you have a mind to be that way inclined, your friend W. P. [Penn] is a great favorite at Court, and can upon recommendation do you any kindness he pleases."[186]

Nor was Tyrrell wrong in his assessment, for Penn was actively seeking pardons for numerous radicals in Holland. It was through his efforts that Aaron Smith and John Trenchard, both deeply involved in the Rye House Plot, obtained their pardons in 1687.[187] Another of Locke's friends, Thomas Papillon, received a pardon through Penn. In his case, we have some information bearing on the conditions of the pardon that supplies, I believe, a clue as to why Locke was never inclined to sue for a pardon.

---

was written (John Y. Akerman, ed., *Moneys Received and Paid for Secret Services of Charles II and James II*, 1851, p. 113). A year later, when the general climate for a pardon was even more favorable, Pembroke was still in great favor with James II, who stayed at his house in August (*London Gazette*, August 30-September 2, 1686).

182 *Correspondence*, 3:193.

183 *Correspondence*, 3:200–201.

184 *Correspondence*, 3:209.

185 *Correspondence*, 3:217.

186 *Correspondence*, 3:257.

187 Add. MS 40621, fols. 252–255. Janney, *Life of Penn*, pp. 292ff.

In exchange for the latter, Papillon was to promise that he "will live peaceably and quietly, and not intermeddle in public affairs, nor obstruct the taking off the penal laws and tests" against the Catholics.[188] These were conditions to which Locke could not consent.

In December 1687, Tyrrell renewed his plea for Locke to return to England, where, "as things stand here you need not doubt of a good reception." This message, it will be recalled, is the one that Stewart in his letters to Carstares and Penn in his numerous tracts, were attempting to sell to the exiles in order to persuade them to make their peace with James. Tyrrell added that Locke could "be restored to your place again if you think it worth while."[189] Considering how piqued Locke was at having been expelled from Christ Church—as Tyrrell knew—we may well wonder why he showed not the slightest interest in regaining his place at Oxford until after William was securely seated on the throne.[190] But Tyrrell was not content to plead with Locke; he had already involved himself, perhaps merely by passing along some gossip, perhaps by a more active intervention on his part, in spreading a rumor that Penn had asked the king for a pardon for Locke. Locke's friend and radical Whig, Dr. Thomas, informed him of Tyrrell's rumor at the end of November 1687. For the next six months, Locke's correspondence is filled with angry outbursts at Tyrrell's "meddling" in affairs about which he understood nothing, coupled with requests to his friends to ascertain what truth, if any, there was in the story that James had agreed to give Locke a pardon. On March 19, 1688, Locke wrote to Clarke:

> I was surprised [to hear] that W. P. had procured your cousin a pardon. I know not how to understand it, since if there be any truth in your cousin's professions he knows nothing of it: you will therefore do well to inform yourself as dexterously as you can from Mr. P. by a third and skillful hand what there is in it.[191]

Almost at the same time as this letter was written, Dr. Thomas arrived in Holland for a visit with Locke, bearing a letter from Tyrrell that explained that the latter had spoken to Penn and discovered that the pardon was not for John Locke, but for "one Mat: Lock excepted in the proclamation," that is, in James II's general pardon of March 1686.[192] Tyrrell got even this piece of information wrong, for the person excepted was Joshua Lock,

[188] A. F. W. Papillon, *Memoirs of Thomas Papillon*, 1887, p. 244. For other individuals pardoned through Penn's efforts, see Morrice, 2:159.

[189] *Correspondence*, 3:311.

[190] Cranston, pp. 313–314.

[191] *Correspondence*, 3:406.

[192] *Correspondence*, 3:384.

son of Nicholas Lock, the capitalist financier of the rebels' clothing industry in Holland.[193] Both Joshua and his father had been pardoned by James in May 1686, as part of the strategy of breaking up that clothing industry.[194] Tyrrell had obviously heard that a "Locke" had been pardoned, and he had assumed that it was his friend rather than the other Locke. On nothing more solid than this erroneous gossip and confusion promulgated by Tyrrell has the assertion of Locke's pardon ever been based. Small wonder that Locke was enraged at Tyrrell's "imprudent meddling" that had produced a situation in which Locke found himself, as he wrote to Clarke, "mightily troubled with this odd business."[195] As late as May 1688, Locke wrote to the latter:

> It is necessary, and that for fresh reasons, that he [Tyrrell] should unsay to W. P. and own to him, that it was without the order or privity of the person concerned [Locke], and so take off the suspicion of slighting or affront, which it cannot but be prejudicial for his friend to lie under with a man of that interest.[196]

Clearly, Locke had not only not requested a pardon, he wanted Tyrrell to make it plain to Penn and as politely as possible under the circumstances, that he did not wish it to *appear* that he had made such a request, even indirectly, through any of his friends. In other words, not even when his friends John Howe, Trenchard, Patience Ward, and Thomas Papillon received their pardons and returned to England at the end of 1687, did Locke consider joining their ranks. Indeed, his reaction was sufficiently similar to that of William Carstares who was placed in the same situation that the latter incident is worth our attention for the light it sheds on the attitude of some radicals toward accepting a pardon from James II. It was rumored in the Dutch papers, Carstares noted, that he was about to be pardoned. Some people have assumed that he was an accessory to this action, and "so they may very justly thereupon imagine me to be a villain." But, Carstares wrote, "I do solemnly declare, that I never demanded it, or contributed in the smallest degree to the obtaining of it"; rather, "some busy people were officiously concerning themselves about me." Carstares in-

[193] Muddiman, *Bloody Assizes*, appendix C, pp. 232–233.

[194] The order to draw up a general pardon for Joshua and Nicholas Lock was given on May 16, 1686 (*CSPD*, [James II], 2:132). Fox-Bourne assumed that Skelton had inadvertently written "Joshua" instead of "John" Locke (2:26).

[195] *Correspondence*, 3:450. Locke was certainly not, as Fox-Bourne believed, "doubtless grateful for the well-meant efforts of his friends" to secure a pardon for him (2:24).

[196] *Correspondence*, 3:455. As Locke's friend, James Johnston, wrote in one of his intelligence reports to Bentinck, Penn was a man who was "feared" because of his influence as a member of James II's court (MS PWA 2163).

sisted that he was firmly resolved never to return to England during James' lifetime, "unless it be in conjunction with others . . . to vindicate the liberty of England, and to rescue religion and laws from under his talons."[197] This response to the prospects of a pardon from James reflected, I believe, Locke's attitude in 1687–1688; in fact, if the author had not mentioned his wife, the document might have been written by Locke.

The last phrase in Locke's letter to Clarke cited above is interesting, for it shows that Locke had no wish to alienate Penn because of the harm "a man of that interest" with James II might do to him. Locke never considered approaching Penn directly, even to clarify the situation regarding the rumored pardon; rather, he acted with utmost secrecy and in a roundabout fashion. It has sometimes been asserted that Locke and Penn were good friends, but there is, I believe, nothing in the record to substantiate this proposition and much that tells against it.[198] Apart from serving as an emissary to William to persuade him to accept James' policy of repealing the penal laws and Test Acts, Penn's journey to Holland in 1686 appears to have had the subsidiary purpose of employing the Quaker's talents to convince individual exiles to return to England.[199] Although, according to Penn's biographers, "little or nothing is known of his activities in Holland" following his conference with William at The Hague, we do know that Penn spent part of August in Amsterdam.[200] It is often assumed that he met with Locke during this period, and while this is possible, since Locke was in Amsterdam at the time, it is much less certain that such a meeting took place than has been commonly supposed.[201] For

[197] *State Papers and Letters Addressed to William Carstares*, 1774, p. 30. It should be noted that Howe returned to England as an agent acting for William in order to persuade the Dissenters in England to stand firm in their opposition to James II. He functioned as part of the intelligence network set up by James Johnston, sent by William to England. These activities are discussed more fully in Chapter 11.

[198] Mabel R. Brailsford, *The Making of William Penn*, Freeport, N.Y.: Books for Libraries Press, 1930, p. 95.

[199] One of those to whom Penn promised a pardon in exchange for his return to England and service to James II was James Stewart (Janney, *Life of Penn*, p. 272; Ralph, *History*, p. 978; Carswell, *Descent*, p. 83).

[200] Peare, *Penn*, p. 297. Indeed, this is something of an understatement. Stephen Baxter (*William III*, p. 217) dates Penn's visit in November, when the evidence shows that he had already returned from Holland to London by or on September 15. William I. Hull says Penn came to Amsterdam before the end of June 1686 (*William Penn and the Dutch Quaker Migration to Pennsylvania*, Baltimore: Genealogical Publishing Co., 1970, p. 106). Both Peare (p. 297) and Hull (p. 121) agree, however, that Penn was in Amsterdam sometime during August. See note 201 below.

[201] One of Skelton's informers who did not know Penn reported on August 22, 1686, that "an Irish Quaker" (Penn) had come to Amsterdam recently, and was associating with Peyton, Bethel, and their "party" (Add. MS 41813, fol. 234). It was said by one of those who

the fact is, Locke and Penn, for reasons having to do with James II's policies, already discussed, were on opposite sides and were working toward different political ends. Penn had become, for the radicals, the stalking-horse leading the Dissenters to accept James' sincerity, while for them the king remained the same embodiment of popery and absolutism he had appeared to be during the exclusion crisis.

On one of his propaganda tours into the West Midlands in 1687 to secure the repeal of penal laws and Tests, Penn was shouted down when he tried to preach.[202] His reputation among the exiles in Holland fared no better. Penn's friend and translator, William Sewel of Amsterdam, found it necessary to undertake a defense of Penn because, as he wrote to the latter, the things said about him "in this part of the world have sometimes struck me with a sad horror."[203] We cannot be certain that Locke shared this negative perception of Penn, but I believe De Beer is correct in detecting a sarcastic undertone in Locke's references to Penn— "your man of Cork"—in his letters to Furley and others during this period.[204] It is of some interest, therefore, to consider Locke's reaction to and comments upon Penn's frame of government drafted for the Pennsylvania colony, of which he was the governor. It is particularly instructive to compare Locke's reading of this draft constitution with the notations made by Furley and Sidney, who really were friends of Penn.

Furley wrote a lengthy article-by-article critique of Penn's draft, but the comments, even when critical, are polite and constructive.[205] Sidney's

attended the Quaker meetings in Amsterdam that "several Englishmen of considerable note, who fled the country," and who were accused of having been involved in the Rye House Plot, were in attendance at these meetings, but no names are mentioned. Also interesting is another firsthand account that Furley acted as translator for his Dutch colleagues for some of the sermons preached by Penn in Holland (Hull, *Penn*, pp. 107–108, 116–117). These circumstances place Penn in close proximity to Locke, and make a meeting between the two men probable.

[202] Miller, *James II*, pp. 172–173.

[203] Peare, *Penn*, p. 306.

[204] *Correspondence*, 3:256–257, 315, 320. In his August 29, 1687, letter to Locke (p. 256), Tyrrell urged the latter to publish some of his manuscripts, which, according to Tyrrell, Locke could do without being "suspected of Quakerism." Gough takes this allusion as implying a hostility on Locke's part toward Quaker beliefs (J. W. Gough, "James Tyrrell, Whig Historian and Friend of John Locke," *Historical Journal* 19, no. 3 [1976]:592). This is unlikely. Locke was, after all, staying with Benjamin Furley, the leading Quaker in Holland. What the reference means, I believe, is that in Tyrrell's view, Locke could publish his manuscripts on natural law and their joint discourse on toleration without being associated with Penn's propaganda efforts on behalf of James II. Locke evidently disagreed with this assessment.

[205] Peare, *Penn*, p. 226; Julius F. Sachse, "Benjamin Furley," *Pennsylvania Magazine of History and Biography* 19, no. 3 (1895):277–306. Furley's comments on Penn's frame of government are included as an appendix to this article.

comments were more critical—Penn's laws for Pennsylvania were "the basest laws in the world, not to be endured or lived under"—but they occur in the context of a solid friendship that existed between the two men. They exchanged many letters, discussed revisions and amendments in Penn's frame of government, and generally engaged in a give-and-take in which a respect for each other's different views was a basic ingredient of the discussion.[206] I believe Locke's comments differ markedly from those of either Furley or Sidney, though like them he is critical of Penn's frame of government. Locke's observations were recorded in his journal under the date of November 6, 1686, or several months after Penn's departure from Holland. In both their sarcastic and their cryptic tone, they are remarkably similar to Locke's marginal notes on Parker's *Discourse of Ecclesiastical Polity* and William Sherlock's *Case of Allegiance*. Since neither Parker nor Sherlock was a friend of Locke, the petulence of the latter's tone in his treatment of Penn's constitution ought to be borne in mind. There is virtually nothing constructive about Locke's remarks, and unlike those of Sidney, they reveal no willingness on Locke's part to engage himself in the effort of revision and improvement.

On Penn's proposed law to punish anyone who "derides or abuses" another individual because of his religious beliefs, Locke remarks that such a law will be a "matter of perpetual prosecution and animosity." On the law to deal with the punishment for adultery, Locke characterizes it as an exercise of "arbitrary power." That all freemen should meet in one place to choose the council, Locke finds "inconvenient." In another law, he detects "a very large and dangerous power thus unlimited." Penn's scheme for a state-supported system of education is for Locke "the surest check upon liberty of conscience, suppressing all displeasing opinions in the bud." Plans for the creation of the judicial system are pithily labeled "dangerous." And so it goes. Interspersed with sarcastic questions as to what Penn can possibly mean are the recurrent observations that Penn's ideas for establishing a government are arbitrary and dangerous. Not surprisingly, Locke's summary comment is that "the whole is so far from a frame of government that it scarce contains a part of the materials."[207] Penn could hardly have wished for a multitude of friends like Locke to remind him that he understood little about government.

[206] M. R. Brailsford, *Making of Penn*, pp. 359–360; Alex Charles Ewald, *The Life and Times of the Hon. Algernon Sidney*, 2 vols., 1873, 2:198–199; Peare, *Penn*, p. 226. There are at least twenty drafts of Penn's "frame of government" in existence (Fantel, *Penn*, p. 156). For a discussion of Penn's political ideas in relation to those of Sidney and Harrington, see Mary Maples, "William Penn, Classical Republican," *Pennsylvania Magazine of History and Biography* 81, no. 2 (April 1957):138–156.

[207] MS f.9, fols. 33–41.

The point I am making, however, is that in November 1686, Locke was inclined to regard Penn as a spokesman for arbitrary and dangerous political power, and that he regarded even the best of his intentions, as in the case of antidefamation laws or education, as reflecting a naïveté that was, in its consequences, harmful. It is not unreasonable to suppose, I suggest, that Locke's attitude toward Penn and his political role as a spokesman for James II is reflected in these notes on Pennsylvania. For certainly Penn could not have fared better in the latter capacity than he is portrayed in these notes, and in all likelihood he fared much worse, since the issues at stake in England concerned Locke much more directly and deeply than did any projected constitution for Pennsylvania.

Neither toleration, James' general pardon, the entreaties of his friends, nor their offers to obtain for Locke a pardon could entice Locke to return to England. He was, however, willing to come home the instant it was clear that the threat of popery and slavery—and "the ruin" of England, as he put it in the preface to the *Two Treatises*—had been brought to an end. Yet in the larger perspective, so far as James' policy was directed toward winning the support of the Dissenters through his calculated use of the pardoning power, the indulgence, and the propaganda efforts of Penn, that policy—at least from 1686 to 1687—must be rated relatively successful. By these and other means, the government hoped to drive the radicals out of Holland completely. What actually happened, however, is that James' policy created a division within the ranks of the radicals, and for those who remained in Holland, that policy had the effect of stiffening the resistance among the ideologically committed radicals. Instead of forcing them out of Holland, James' policy pushed them closer to William, who now appeared to be the only means by which they would see England again.

11

A RADICAL MANIFESTO

IF the radicals drew a positive lesson from Monmouth's defeat, it was that successful rebellions required more planning and secrecy than that which had characterized their two previous efforts to organize popular resistance to the Stuart tyranny. At the end of October 1685, or shortly after the gathering of radicals—including Locke—at Cleves, Skelton's double agent reported that there was a new and "deeply laid" plot against James II being discussed by the exiles. This plot, the informer wrote, was just at its beginnings, and would take a considerable amount of time to be put into effect.[1] The following July, Everard, Skelton's spy in Amsterdam, independently confirmed the existence of this new conspiracy, which involved Major Wildman and some Scottish rebels who were meeting nightly at Major Manley's house. Yet, since Everard was viewed with some suspicion by some of the radicals, he was not able to supply the kind of detailed information concerning this conspiracy that is contained in Skelton's intelligence reports on the plans for Monmouth's Rebellion or the establishment of the clothing industry in Holland.[2] Thus despite the fact that Skelton's spy network was a highly efficient one and his double agent in Utrecht was exceptionally well informed and extremely reliable in his accounts of the rebels' plans, the various dimensions of this new plot were never disclosed in the English envoy's reports to the secretaries of state in England. As a consequence, there was a serious breakdown in the quality of intelligence being supplied to the English government during the two years prior to William's invasion.

There are several contingent factors that contributed to this situation, apart from the redoubled efforts of the radicals to maintain secrecy. In July 1686, Skelton received the news of his appointment to Paris, and although he did not actually depart until several months later, he was so happy to leave Holland that, except for one notorious incident, his preoccupations were no longer directed toward the activities of the radicals in Holland.[3] In addition, Skelton lost the services of his two best spies. In August, Everard asked to return to England; he had effectively undermined the exiles' attempt to establish a clothing industry, and the suspi-

[1] Add. MS 41818, fol. 112; Add. MS 41814, fol. 12.

[2] Add. MS 41819, fol. 185. Everard had been attacked by one of the radicals a few weeks before, and Major Manley had threatened to kill him (fol. 162).

[3] Add. MS 41813, fol. 212.

cion that he was a spy for Skelton was growing, thereby undermining his own efficiency and usefulness as an intelligence source.[4] Also, by means not disclosed in these manuscripts, the identity of the double agent in Utrecht had become known to the radicals. In late August 1686, he was attacked and viciously beaten.[5] Obviously, he, too, had to leave the country. Other exiles who might have supplied intelligence had accepted pardons from James, and had already returned to England. Thus, by the end of 1686, Skelton's intelligence system was virtually dismantled. Moreover, his successor, the Marquis d'Albeville, was never able to rebuild that network, nor did he succeed in establishing one of his own. Strangely enough, this seems to be due in part to the fact that Albeville was himself a spy, in the pay of the French secret service—and probably the Dutch—during the period he served as the English envoy in Holland.[6] So far as providing intelligence goes, however, Albeville was a very poor spy. His reports to Middleton are pitiful collections of the rambling thoughts of a mediocre mind coupled with the kind of society gossip that intrigued a foppish courtier desperately seeking a respect that neither William nor Albeville's diplomatic colleagues at The Hague were ever likely to grant him. And unlike Skelton, he did not prowl the streets of Utrecht or Rotterdam, hoping to capture Ferguson or some other radical. He was, therefore, about as far removed from being privy to William's intentions and thoughts on the one hand, and the subversive activities of James' enemies among the exile community in Holland on the other, as any envoy imaginable could possibly have been.[7]

[4] Add. MS 41813, fols. 203–204.

[5] Add. MS 41813, fols. 247, 249.

[6] Macaulay, 2:223; John Carswell, *The Descent on England*, New York: John Day, 1969, p. 86n.; James Muilenberg, *The Embassy of Everaard Van Weede, Lord of Dykvelt, to England in 1687*, University Studies, vol. 20, nos. 3, 4, Lincoln: University of Nebraska, 1920, p. 12; Dalrymple, vol. 2, pt. 1, bk. 4, pp. 29n., 151. Even Princess Anne wrote to a correspondent that she was "afraid to send a letter by Mr. d'Albeville. . . . He has always been counted a spy" (Dalrymple, vol. 2, pt. 1, bk. 4, p. 168).

[7] There is some disagreement about the quality of Albeville's diplomatic reports. Kenyon, who seems to have read few of Albeville's reports, nevertheless states that he "could be relied on to warn [James II] of any important developments" (J. P. Kenyon, *Robert Spencer, Earl of Sunderland, 1641–1702*, London: Longmans, Green, 1958, p. 136). In view of the fact that Albeville knew virtually nothing of the rebels' preparations for William's invasion, this is an incredible statement. Miller also thinks Albeville more competent and informed than Skelton (John Miller, *James II: A Study in Kingship*, Hove, Eng.: Wayland Publishers, 1957, p. 183; cf. Nesca A. Robb, *William of Orange: A Personal Portrait*, vol. 2, *The Later Years, 1674–1702*, New York: St. Martin's Press, 1966, p. 209). In my opinion, there is no basis for this conclusion. As Carswell put it, Albeville was, in almost every respect, the worst person James could have sent as his envoy to Holland (*Descent*, p. 86). Moreover, I agree with Dalrymple on the poor quality of Albeville's dispatches (vol. 2, pt. 1, bk. 4, p.

As a recent historian has observed, of the various elements that participated in the collective effort to bring William to the English throne, only the radical Whigs—those associated with Wharton, Mordaunt, and Macclesfield—have failed to leave any traces of their lines of communication in Holland. All the other groups who subsequently constituted the political basis for the overthrow of James had their contacts with William III's agents in England or Holland.[8] Locke and Wildman were as close to these individuals as any of the exiles in Holland, but this fact, unfortunately, does little to advance our knowledge of the preparation and organization of the radicals in the absence of the documents and correspondence necessary to fill out the details of this relationship. At the same time, William was sufficiently secretive about his own intentions and his decision to invade England that these have themselves become the subject of an extended debate and controversy.[9] Of the activities in Holland during this period of the person who had served as William's agent inside the radical movement from its inception—namely, William Carstares—we know virtually nothing.[10] At every level of possible contact, therefore,

153). Albeville hung around The Hague, was personally obnoxious to William and not trusted by anyone remotely close to him, and signally failed to accomplish anything. He made no effective protests, captured no rebels, and was unbelievably uninformed about the plans for William's invasion. Compared to Skelton, there is not a single duty of the envoy that Albeville carried out more effectively.

[8] Carswell, *Descent*, p. 131.

[9] At one extreme, Lucile Pinkham maintains that William's invasion of England was the outgrowth of a longstanding personal ambition on his part, and that the plans for this invasion were laid as early as the summer of 1686 (*William III and the Respectable Revolution*, Cambridge: Harvard University Press, 1954, pp. 19–20, 67). For different reasons, Ranke also believed that William's plans for the invasion were developed during the summer of 1686, and that his meeting with the Elector of Brandenburg in July of that year represented the execution of one part of those plans (Carswell, *Descent*, p. 80). At the other extreme is Stephen Baxter, who claims that William was "forced" to agree to an invasion of England in May 1688, in order to forestall the establishment of a republic (Stephen B. Baxter, *William III*, London: Longmans, Green, 1966, pp. 231–232).

[10] Carstares, it should be remembered, had been a member of William's secret service since the 1670s. His chief concern during his torture was not that he might confess a few details concerning the Rye House conspiracy, which he did, but that he might be forced to reveal his connections with William, which he did not (K. H. D. Haley, *William of Orange and the English Opposition, 1672–4*, Oxford: Clarendon Press, 1953, pp. 59, 205–206; Carswell, *Descent*, p. 26). Upon his return to Holland in 1685, Carstares was rewarded by William for having maintained that secret (*State Papers and Letters Addressed to William Carstares*, 1774, pp. 24–25). For the next four years, as his correspondence with James Stewart makes clear, Carstares was free to act as a direct agent of William. His payment of money to the captain of one of Argyll's ships (p. 35) raises the question of how deeply William was involved in Monmouth's Rebellion, and to what ends. (Carstares provided William with an accounting of how he had disbursed the money given him for intelligence services, and the above payment appears as one of these items of disbursement.) If Carstares was an efficient

there are serious breaks in the flow of information among the radicals themselves and between them and other participants in the Glorious Revolution.

These limitations should not be interpreted, however, as evidence that the radicals' resistance to James had waned or collapsed, leaving a vacuum to be filled by the Tories and moderate Whigs who cooperated to bring about a respectable revolution. Some radicals, it is true, were won over by James' propaganda campaign and the institution of toleration, but beneath the politeness and smiles of that approach, there was another set of tactics, marked by violence and deceit, which James employed against the radicals, and they in turn used against him. The nature of this subterranean warfare waged between the king and the exiles must be appreciated in order to grasp the intensity and dimensions of the hostility to James II that characterized the radical theoretical perspective.

In this chapter, I will provide a sketch of the activities of the radicals, including Locke, in the period preceding the Glorious Revolution, in order to lay the groundwork for an understanding of their assessment—positive and negative—of that event as a realization of the objectives of their political movement. We must also consider to what extent the arguments of the *Two Treatises*, in particular, provided the rationale for that revolution, especially when they are viewed in the context of the general political debate that surrounded William's victory.

While James was offering the olive branch of toleration to the exiles on the one hand, he was on the other issuing orders to Skelton to forcibly seize whomever he could among the radicals and have them surreptitiously shipped back to England to meet the fate that had befallen Thomas Armstrong. In polite but firm tones of anger and disappointment, he reminded William that "you know of how great concern it is to me to have those seditious people sent away" from Holland.[11] Even this was an understatement, for James was in fact obsessively angry that the radicals in Holland seemed to live just beyond the reach of his political power.[12]

---

intelligence agent—and everything suggests that he was—then William was at least informed about everything the radicals were doing, including the Rye House conspiracy. (It is difficult to see why Carstares would have been rewarded by William if he had not been acting as his agent during the 1680s.) In 1687, he reminded Bentinck of "the obligations that for many years I have been under to his Highness [William]" (*CSPD*, [James II], 3:44). Nevertheless, very few traces of Carstares' activity remain in his papers or correspondence, and almost nothing from the 1685–1688 period.

[11] Dalrymple, 2:55–56. Earlier, James had told William "how important it is to me, to have those people destroyed" (p. 54).

[12] Add. MS 34512, fols. 3, 17, 40–41. There was also, in some cases, a legal-theoretical point at issue: whether the king, alone, had the authority to declare a person a rebel, simply as an expression of his will (Add. MS 34510, fols. 96–97).

They were living reminders of James' limitations as king of England to control the activities of some of his subjects. These demands to capture the radicals became so insistent that Skelton, in a dispatch that perfectly combined the penchant for orderliness and compliance with the frustration and anxiety of a harassed civil servant, asked Middleton to give him a list of priorities as to which of the radicals were most wanted by the government. The Secretary of State replied, rather cursorily, that Skelton was to get as many of the radicals as he could, since one "can hardly choose amongst such a crew." Ferguson headed the list, but he was closely followed by Captain Matthews, Colonel Danvers, and Major Manley.[13] In the fall of 1685, Sunderland wrote to the English envoy in Brussels about Skelton's having seized one of the participants in Monmouth's Rebellion. Although he was a relatively obscure figure within the radical organization, James sent his personal yacht to collect the prisoner for his return to England.[14] A few months later, Sunderland wrote to Skelton, reminding him that he must insist again to the Dutch authorities that the fugitives not be harbored in Holland, "which his Majesty thinks of so much consequence to the peace of his government that he has commanded you to insist positively upon it, till you have obtained satisfaction therein."[15]

Skelton did his best to comply with these orders. At first, he tried to act within the legal constraints under which he was compelled to operate as a foreign diplomat. He notified the local authorities, obtained arrest warrants, and accompanied the Dutch officers to the fugitive's residence. Time after time, this approach failed, either because the Dutch authorities supplied the suspect with advance information that Skelton was seeking his arrest, or because of the intelligence sources the radicals had within Skelton's own organization. On Christmas Day 1685, Skelton went to arrest James Stewart "and broke open the house, but found nobody there." Stewart and seven or eight others had fled a few hours earlier, having received information that warrants for their arrests had been issued.[16] Skelton's reports to England are filled with similar examples of his frustrated attempts to capture the radicals, including one particularly colorful account of an all-night stakeout of Ferguson's residence. Nevertheless, Ferguson crept out a window at 3 a.m. and escaped across the rooftops of Amsterdam.[17] Skelton's superiors, however, were not interested in ex-

[13] Add. MS 41812, fols. 174, 228; Add. MS 41823, fol. 33.

[14] MS Rawlinson, A 266, fol. 83

[15] MS Rawlinson, A 266, fol. 107.

[16] Add. MS 41813, fol. 46.

[17] Add. MS 41817, fols. 240–241. Ferguson "hath slipped through the net so often that I shall never think him sure until that I have him in my house" (Add. MS 41812, fol. 232).

cuses or failures. Skelton was forced to recognize that since the Dutch magistrates "will not consent to the public seizing of [the exiles], therefore it must be done in some more private way."[18] Skelton directed his primary attention toward the seizing of Ferguson, though he was willing to take almost anyone he could literally get his hands on. For reasons that are not entirely clear, James II became personally obsessed with capturing Gilbert Burnet, who arrived in Holland in May 1686. He put a price on Burnet's head, and as late as 1688, James dispatched his yacht, along with fifteen men, on a secret mission to Holland with the object of seizing Burnet, and in all likelihood arranging for his execution in England.[19]

Although the local authorities generally hindered the efforts of the English government to drive "these seditious people" out of Holland, there was a certain amount of necessary cooperation at the higher levels of authority that could be extracted from England's ally against the French. William's position was that no matter how disaffected toward the English government the exiles in Holland might be, they "will not be molested." If pushed, he was prepared to concede that action could be taken against "such as have been actually in the rebellion"—that is, those who had fought with Monmouth against James.[20] Nevertheless, in general, it is fair to say that William turned a deaf ear toward James' pleas to harass or arrest the radicals. William was not the only object of the English government's diplomatic pleas. The States-General, the legislative body of the Dutch Republic, after much hemming and hawing had, on the eve of Monmouth's Rebellion, finally agreed to issue a proclamation demanding the arrest of the eighty-five fugitives on a list submitted to them by Skelton. This cooperation, it is true, was too little too late, and none of those named in the proclamation was ever arrested by Dutch magistrates. Still, Skelton pursued this tactic in 1686, requesting the States-General to issue an order banishing the rebels from all the provinces of the Netherlands. At the end of June, he wrote to Middleton in discouraging tones about the prospects of securing such a proclamation.[21] But a month later, Middleton was informed that the banishment proclamation had been published and was being distributed throughout the provinces.[22]

[18] Add. MS 41813, fol. 3. Russian agents were sent to Holland to seize Sir James Dalrymple surreptitiously (A. J. G. Mackay, *Memoir of Sir James Dalrymple*, 1873, p. 207).

[19] Dykvelt reported that James "showed himself preoccupied in such a degree on the subject of Burnet," that he refused to accept "any reasons on this subject," declaring that "I will not rest until this rebel shall have been removed from" Holland (Add. MS 34510, fol. 98; cf. Add. MS 34512, fol. 73). Johnston reported to Bentinck the scheme to seize Burnet (MS PWA, 2141, 2143, 2149; see also, Morrice, 2:239).

[20] Add. MS 41813, fol. 84.

[21] Add. MS 41813, fol. 170.

[22] Add. MS 41813, fol. 225.

Everard reported to Skelton that some of the exiles were being "pressed by the last Proclamation" and were in a state of some anxiety concerning their fate.[23] But, again, none of them was arrested by the Dutch magistrates. Even so, they were officially wanted men—from the standpoint of the English and the Dutch governments—and they were forced to live in the shadows and on the edge of respectability. If the winds of politics shifted suddenly, they might find themselves subject to the penalties that hung over their heads. This was not very likely, given the grounds of opposition that existed between William and James, but neither could the situation in which they were placed provide the radicals in Holland with much security. It is hardly surprising, then, that some of them took advantage of James' offer of a pardon, while others began to align their fate with the prospects of William's coming to the throne in England. These were, in fact, the only options available to the radicals who wished to escape from the limbo of illegality in which they found themselves following the defeat of Monmouth's Rebellion.

In addition to coping with their official banishment by the Dutch and their unofficial seizure by the English authorities, the radicals had, by 1686, grown accustomed to living in an atmosphere darkened by the pervasiveness of suspicion and mistrust. Spies and informers were everywhere. Some of the staunchest radicals had abandoned the cause, either to secure their safety or for the payment of money, turning on their former comrades. Much of the idealism and mutual support that had held the political movement together during the early 1680s, despite personality and political differences among the participants, seemed to have evaporated. The constant pressure of being under attack coupled with the failure to achieve their objectives was beginning to take its toll on the radicals. As the accumulated effect of years of struggle, a certain tone of nastiness and urgency had crept into the radicals' opposition to James' government. At the same time, the scope of that opposition was widening, so that from 1686 to 1688, the radicals found themselves surrounded—indeed engulfed—by an ever larger circle of political allies. The result was that the radicals developed greater resources of intelligence within James' government, thus neutralizing the latter's attempts to destroy their own organization, while at the same time adopting a more violent attitude toward those within their ranks who showed any willingness to cooperate with that government.

Skelton's agents were, of course, intercepting and opening mail addressed to the exiles, but toward the end of 1685, the English envoy became convinced that *his* mail was being intercepted and opened by some

[23] Add. MS 41813, fol. 156.

postmasters sympathetic to the radicals.[24] Also, his double agent in Utrecht reported that there was "a lady by the Princess of Orange who gives an account of all things" to Sir John Thompson's wife.[25] It was perhaps because of this access to Court gossip that Skelton found himself in an embarrassing situation in October 1685, when his spy in William's household, Dr. Covel, was discovered, and forced to return to England in disgrace.[26] One of Skelton's tactics had been to recruit as informers some of the officers in the English regiments stationed in Holland who had relatives in the radical movement. This, too, backfired when he discovered that one of his agents, Captain Goodwin, was "a spy for Bethel and the rebels," and had kept them informed of various efforts to seize a particular fugitive.[27] By mid-1686, other English officers known to be assisting Skelton in capturing the radicals were put under extreme pressure from their superiors and fellow officers who showed their displeasure at such activities by threatening and ostracizing the individual.[28]

In addition to the resources available to them in Holland, the exiles appear to have had intelligence sources within the English government. In particular, the information forwarded to the Secretary of State by Skelton was being sent back secretly to the radicals by their informants in London. Precise details from the reports of the double agent in Utrecht were conveyed to individuals in Holland, and this naturally began to draw the net of suspicion closer to Skelton's chief source of information.[29] There was in fact a spy in Middleton's office, one of the clerks, who was acting as a Dutch agent. He was not discovered until February 1688, but whether he supplied information to the English exiles as well as to the Dutch authorities is not known.[30] However, the Dutch diplomat, van Citters, who had his own sources of information at Whitehall, did inform the Amsterdam magistrates that Joseph Tiley, who had fought with Monmouth, had turned informer. The magistrates resolved to proceed against Tiley as a spy and to punish him if they could.[31] Skelton's consul general

[24] Add. MS 41812, fols. 211, 220–221.

[25] Add. MS 41818, fol. 108.

[26] In October 1685, William intercepted a letter that revealed that "Dr. Covel had for a long time been a malicious spy in the household" (Marion E. Grew, *William Bentinck and William III*, London: John Murray, 1924, pp. 94–95).

[27] Add. MS 41812, fol. 208; Add. MS 41818, fol. 50.

[28] Add. MS 41813, fol. 257.

[29] Add. MS 41818, fol. 185. According to Skelton's spies, everything he wrote to the Court "was communicated to the factious party," and "there were considerable persons about his Majesty with whom they had correspondence" (Add. MS 41812, fol. 68).

[30] George Hilton Jones, *Charles Middleton: The Life and Times of a Restoration Politician*, Chicago: University of Chicago Press, 1967, p. 122; Morrice, 2:239.

[31] Add. MS 41814, fol. 1.

in Amsterdam was recalled in early 1686, and one of the reasons given for the action was his propensity to reveal secrets to the radicals when they succeeded in getting him drunk.[32] In other words, by 1686, the radicals had mounted a successful counterattack against Skelton in the espionage war. If they were not so successful in achieving their own aims, they could at least frustrate the objectives English government hoped to realize through the efforts of its envoy in Holland.

At the same time, the radicals showed little tolerance toward defectors within their own ranks. Upon the discovery of the Rye House Plot, one of those privy to its details—John Row of Bristol—gave every indication of turning informer if he were arrested. In the discussions as to what to do with Row, some conspirators were for drowning him, but others decided to provide him with some clothes and money and ship him off to Switzerland, where he could be stashed out of the way, under the protection of those radicals who went to stay with General Ludlow.[33] Now, three years later, prevailing opinion was running in favor of the harsher response. Complaints were made that one of the informers in London had not been murdered by one of the newly arrived fugitives in Holland before he left England.[34] When Everard was discovered to be Skelton's spy, the radicals used their influence with the Dutch authorities in Amsterdam to have his goods seized, to have all the merchants and tradesmen call in Everard's debts, and to cancel all his credit, leaving him in dire financial straits.[35] The Utrecht double agent, as was mentioned, was attacked by a gang of radicals associated with Colonel Danvers and Major Wildman, and suffered serious injuries.[36] The stakes in the political conflict in 1686 were no higher than they had been in the earlier days of the political movement, but the radicals had improved their skills in the battle for intelligence and hardened their attitude toward backsliders from the cause. Both developments made it increasingly difficult to obtain the information necessary to unravel the details of their plans.

Concomitant with the declining availability of information about the

[32] Add. MS 41818, fol. 275.

[33] Add. MS 41818, fols. 159, 214. Now, in January 1686, both Trenchard and Captain Matthews were threatening Row again (fol. 206).

[34] Major Manley was upset that the newly arrived fugitive had not murdered Robert Cragg before leaving London. Cragg was in custody, providing information to the authorities. The radicals were "extremely concerned" because "he knows all and . . . can bring many to the gallows" (Add. MS 41818, fol. 207).

[35] Add. MS 41819, fol. 224.

[36] Add. MS 41813, fol. 247. The Utrecht spy suffered a serious concussion from "the many blows he received upon his head" and the loss of an eye in the attack. Samuel Harris, a friend and associate of Wilmore, Starkey, Wildman, and Colonel Danvers, appears to have been one of the attackers (Add. MS 41814, fol. 32).

radicals' activities in general, there is an increasing scarcity of details concerning Locke's movements and associations recorded in his journals during the last two years of his exile. Considering the impressive level of secrecy Locke was able to maintain regarding his political activities throughout his life, this added caution draws a virtually impenetrable curtain around those activities between 1686 and 1688. As with other radicals, we can steal a glimpse here and there as to what they and Locke are up to, but too many pieces of the picture are missing to provide a continuous narrative of their designs or to fill in the gaps between these glimpses. Interestingly, Locke's secrecy actually *increased*, despite the fact that he was not one of the individuals named as an exception to James II's general pardon of March 1686. If the absence of his name on the government's list of most-wanted fugitives made Locke feel any safer, this reaction is not reflected in his journals.[37] There is, for example, a noticeable, but unexplained, break in the items recorded in one of his notebooks extending from the middle of June 1686 to January 1687.[38]

Following his return to Amsterdam from Cleves at the end of 1685, Locke went into hiding at Dr. Veen's house living under a pseudonym. Apparently, he remained there until May 31, 1686, when he left Amsterdam for Haarlem.[39] Meanwhile, the new plot, which at this stage seems to have been focused upon another effort to stir up the Scots, was moving forward. In February, Skelton's spies reported that several English radicals and Dutch merchants who had acted as purchasing agents of arms and ammunition for Monmouth's Rebellion were again holding meetings about buying weapons.[40] John Nisbet and William Carstares, who had served as the chief liaisons between the English and Scottish radicals during the Rye House Plot, were meeting with various Scottish exiles in Utrecht.[41] James Stewart, who had purchased arms for Argyll's invasion, was also there.[42] On February 19, Skelton's double agent reported that Benjamin Furley had come to Utrecht, along with Locke's friend Sir Patience Ward, and both men had gone to consult with Lord Wharton at Cleves.[43] How long they remained there is not known, but shortly thereafter, Carstares went to Cleves.[44] Simultaneously with these consulta-

[37] Cranston, p. 257.

[38] MS f.34, fol. 9.

[39] MS f.9, fol. 7.

[40] Add. MS 41818, fols. 229, 234, 274; Add. MS 41813, fol. 104.

[41] John Erskine, *Journal of Hon. John Erskine of Carnock, 1683–1687*, 1893, pp. 172, 177.

[42] Erskine, *Journal*, p. 179. This notation, dated March 11, describes a specific conversation between Stewart and Erskine, but it appears that the former had been in Utrecht for some time before this.

[43] Add. MS 41818, fol. 256.

[44] Erskine, *Journal*, p. 179.

tions, one gunsmith in Utrecht shipped four hundred muskets to Scotland, and was preparing three hundred dragoons' pieces to be sent there.[45]

In April, Mrs. Smith, the chief financial backer of Argyll's expedition, went to Amsterdam.[46] John Nisbet and several Scots also went there to meet with Major Manley and the English radicals, a fact duly reported to Skelton by his spies in that city. In his own report to Middleton, the envoy included the warning that a new plot—"a second disturbance"—as he put it, was being hatched by the rebels in Utrecht and Amsterdam, and that some arms had already been purchased by them in Utrecht to further the design.[47] In early May, just at the time of Skelton's letter, Locke recorded another of those unusual financial transactions in his journal, namely, the receipt of £250 from "Muliner & Magnus."[48] Whether Locke was again assisting in the effort to purchase arms on behalf of the Scots and this "second disturbance" being planned in 1686 as he had assisted them earlier is not easily determinable from the available evidence.

Throughout 1686–1687, a number of English radicals made trips to Holland, either to urge William to invade England or to strengthen the connections between the radicals in Holland and the underground resistance to James II in England. One of these visitors was Locke's friend, Sir Walter Yonge, who met with Locke at Amsterdam toward the end of May.[49] Locke and Yonge traveled to Haarlem to meet with their mutual friend, John Freke.[50] Some "business" in which Freke and Yonge appear to have been concerned carried Locke suddenly back to Amsterdam, where he contacted and probably stayed at the house of Vandervelde, the bookseller, whose place only a few weeks earlier had served as a refuge for some of the Scottish radicals from Utrecht.[51] Locke returned to Rotterdam to be with Yonge, where, incidentally, he probably first met Benjamin Furley, who was to become his very close friend. In view of the lat-

[45] Carswell, *Descent*, p. 71. One of the exiles, whose father had been involved with Ferguson and Shaftesbury, reported that he had been asked to be the purchasing agent to buy three or four ships as part of the invasion plan. This report is dated 1687, but the proposal may have been made some considerable time before that (Add. MS 41820, fol. 275).

[46] Erskine accompanied her on this trip, staying at Vandervelde's house, where Locke was receiving his mail during this period (*Journal*, pp. 185–186).

[47] Add. MS 41813, fol. 104; Erskine, *Journal*, p. 190.

[48] MS f.29, fol. 16.

[49] *Correspondence*, 3:5.

[50] MS f.9, fol. 7. Another of Locke's friends, Richard Duke (cf. *Correspondence*, 3:26ff.) was also arrested at the time of Monmouth's Rebellion for "dangerous and seditious practices." Duke was Yonge's brother-in-law, and both men were good friends of Clarke and Freke (Frank H. Ellis, "John Freke and *The History of Insipids*," *Philological Quarterly* 44, no. 4 [October 1965]:478).

[51] MS f.9, fol. 7; *Correspondence*, 3:6. Erskine was one of the many radicals who sometimes stayed at Vandervelde's (*Journal*, p. 186).

ter's association with Ward, Lord Wharton, and other English radicals, it is interesting that Locke came to know Furley through two other radicals, Yonge and Freke, who were like Locke longstanding participants in the resistance movement against James II.[52] At the end of June, just after the arrival of Freke and Yonge, Skelton reported that his informants in Utrecht and Amsterdam told him that the "new design" was going forward.[53]

In early July, Skelton's double agent reported that Patience Ward, John Thompson, and about thirty other radicals came for a meeting in Utrecht, though he could not supply any details as to its agenda.[54] On July 8, Locke went to Utrecht, presumably in order to attend that meeting, staying only a couple of days before returning to Amsterdam.[55] In addition to Freke and Yonge, a number of other English radicals journeyed to Holland during 1686 for reasons that are, to say the least, suspicious. One of them, Lord Macclesfield, was seen in Amsterdam in mid-July. Skelton reported to Middleton that Macclesfield was "passionately" disaffected to James' government, and had threatened Skelton's informant with bodily harm if the latter attempted to follow him through the streets of Amsterdam.[56] Macclesfield was staying at the house of Locke's friend Israel Hayes.[57] Ferguson, who had been in Utrecht prior to the July meeting there, had now come to Amsterdam, but other than further reports of the new plot forming around the Scottish rebels, Major Wildman, Major Manley, and others, little information can be gleaned from Skelton's dispatches to England during this period.

Another radical, Lord Mordaunt—sometimes said to have been the first member of the nobility to urge William's invasion of England—arrived in Holland during the summer of 1686.[58] In his entering book, Roger Morrice records a curious incident involving Mordaunt's visit to Holland, the purpose of which is admitted on all sides to be shrouded in mystery. According to Morrice, Mordaunt learned that accusations of treason had been lodged against him by two individuals—a man and wife living in Utrecht—who were part of Skelton's spy network. Mordaunt went to Utrecht, and using his influence, had the pair examined publicly

[52] MS f.9, fols. 13–14; *Correspondence*, 3:40.

[53] Add. MS 41813, fol. 170.

[54] Add. MS 41813, fol. 179.

[55] Locke accompanied Yonge, Duke, and, probably Freke to Utrecht. They were en route to drink the mineral waters at Spa, but they may very well have spent some time with the radicals in Utrecht (*Correspondence*, 3:13–15).

[56] Add. MS 41813, fol. 190.

[57] Add. MS 41819, fol. 235.

[58] Carswell, *Descent*, p. 126; Dalrymple, vol. 2, pt. 1, bk. 4, p. 20.

by the magistrates, before whom they were forced to repeat the accusations against Mordaunt. The latter was, unknown to them, in the courtroom at the time, and challenged their testimony on the basis that they obviously did not know who he was.[59] Precisely when this incident took place is hard to say, but it may very well be related to the fact that the beating of Skelton's double agent in Utrecht occurred at the end of August 1686.[60] In mid-September, Skelton wrote to Middleton that Mordaunt had been in Holland, very mysteriously, and that he had not learned of his visit until after his departure.[61] Mordaunt himself subsequently wrote to Bentinck, William's adviser, apologizing for his extremely hasty departure from Holland, though without specifying the reasons for that action.[62] We cannot be sure where Locke was during this period. There is a letter from him dated September 5 in which he explains that he is "now and then" away from Amsterdam "on my wanderings," but since these are unrecorded in his diary, Locke's whereabouts cannot be determined.[63] On October 2, however, he wrote to Limborch from Utrecht, and since he appears to have been separated from his friends in Amsterdam for some time, Locke may have resided in Utrecht during much of September, while Mordaunt was still in that city.[64]

On October 12, Captain Slater, one of the English officers in Skelton's organization, happened to meet Sir Robert Peyton in the street, near the Rotterdam docks, where the king's yacht was moored, "and hoping that he might have got him on board without noise, did with the assistance of some other English officers, seize upon him, but he made such an outcry that he was to be transported into England and there murdered, that immediately the rabble flocked about them, so that for fear of a rescue they

[59] Morrice, 1:648–649.

[60] The Utrecht spy was attacked around August 22, 1686 (Add. MS 41813, fol. 247). Mordaunt was certainly in Holland before that date, and appears to have returned to England sometime in September. Despite the fact that he was the victim of a beating, the Utrecht double agent was charged by the magistrates with being a spy, and was fined 300 guilders (Add. MS 41814, fol. 32). This seems to support the theory that he was exposed publicly as a spy prior to the beating, and that the latter was therefore more or less the direct outcome of the incident involving Mordaunt described by Morrice.

[61] Add. MS 41814, fol. 18. On September 17, the date of this report, Skelton believed that Mordaunt had left the country, but a week later, he reported to Middleton that Mordaunt had been in Utrecht for some time but was now residing somewhere in the country (fol. 33).

[62] N. Japiske, ed., *Correspondentie Van Willem III en Van Hans Willem Bentinck*, 5 vols., The Hague: Martinus Nijhoff, 1929, 2:7.

[63] *Correspondence*, 3:29.

[64] Locke simply says that "after many days of almost continuous wanderings . . . many things have drawn me to this city [Utrecht]; whether they will keep me here I do not know." We have no record of his "wanderings," nor any clue as to what "things" required that he be in Utrecht (*Correspondence*, 3:34–35; see note 61 above).

forced [Peyton] into a house, which was forthwith beset with thousands of people." This is the account of the affair—which immediately became an international cause célèbre—provided to Middleton by Skelton, to which the latter adds that all of Peyton's papers were seized, some of which in Skelton's view were quite revealing and were being forwarded to Middleton. At the same time, he indicates that the Dutch magistrates have been to see him to complain about the illegal act of violence committed on their streets, and they haved insisted that Peyton remain in Holland, since his name was not on the recent proclamation.[65] The outcry against this "violation and infringement on the public protection" was tremendous. The Dutch ambassador complained to James II, who denied that he had given Skelton any order or commission for such a seizure, and claimed that he was "extremely displeased" by the action. The Privy Council registered its unanimous disapproval of Skelton's action, and the king ordered all proceedings for the extradition of Peyton dropped, although not until nearly six months after the incident.[66]

Locke was in Rotterdam on October 8, and may have been in that city when the attempt was made on Peyton.[67] In any event, he certainly heard of this last parting blow by Skelton against the radicals in Holland. Locke evidently did not remain long in Rotterdam, returning to Utrecht before the end of October.[68] On November 13, his friend John Freke wrote him there concerning "the design I mentioned to you against [name missing] is talked of everywhere but none can tell what it is and *my author* tells me that the Lord M[ordaunt's] business at your town has spoiled it and either broken or altered their measures *as he is informed by a letter last post*."[69] Since Freke is clearly refering to Mordaunt's exposure of two of Skelton's spies, the "design" that has been "spoiled" must have been some scheme of Skelton, or the English government, directed against the exiles. No specific person is named by Freke, and it is even possible that the design was against or included Locke. For, just at the time of Freke's letter, Morrice recorded in his journal that the government had now become convinced that there was, in fact, a new plot being hatched by the radicals in Holland, perhaps on the basis of the confirming evidence contained in Peyton's papers. Accordingly, it issued some new

[65] Add. MS 41814, fol. 48; Add. MS 41820, fols. 26–27.

[66] Add. MS 34508, fols. 137–139. Captain Slater maintained that James II *had* given his approval to the seizure of Peyton (*The Letterbook of Sir George Etherege*, London: Oxford University Press, 1928, p. 352). On March 16, 1687, James ordered the proceedings against Peyton dropped; two months, earlier, however, he had seized Peyton's property (Add. MS 34510, fols. 5, 10).

[67] *Correspondence*, 3:34.

[68] Locke wrote to Limborch from Utrecht on October 11 (*Correspondence*, 3:43).

[69] *Correspondence*, 3:60.

warrants and some individuals were arrested.[70] At the same time, Skelton complained to William on behalf of James about Locke "and certain others" and "asked to be given power to arrest those whose names he had given and to send them to England." It is not clear that William acceded to this request, but through Bentinck and Dykvelt, the information that Skelton was seeking to arrest certain individuals in Utrecht, including Locke, was conveyed to the magistrates of that city. As one of Locke's correspondents informed him, "when this information was received here," perhaps because of the Peyton incident, "your friends began to fear that if the matter were pressed you might not eventually be able to escape the clutches of the man who had such designs on your safety in this place."[71] Locke had gone to Utrecht to spend the winter there, but at the beginning of December 1686, an order for his expulsion from the city was issued by the magistrates. He wrote to Limborch that "I neither understand the matter . . . nor should I wish a word to be said about it."[72] In light of the information, cited above, which later was supplied to Locke, it seems plausible, as De Beer suggests, to see this "expulsion" as a somewhat drastic but friendly attempt by Locke's friends to get him to leave Utrecht, where he was in some immediate danger of being seized by Skelton or his agents. Locke was sufficiently cognizant of the danger to his person that he "found reason" to alter his will, a new copy of which he sent to Clarke immediately following his expulsion from Utrecht.[73]

In some fashion, therefore, it appears that Mordaunt's exposure of Skelton's spies may have been linked with the attack on the double agent in Utrecht, prompting a counterresponse by Skelton through the seizure of Peyton and the attempt to secure the arrest of Locke and certain other radicals living in Utrecht. Why, exactly, Skelton focused upon or included Locke can only be guessed at, but Locke's association with and friendship for Mordaunt may well have had something to do with it. It is also possible that Locke's involvement with the Scottish radicals in Utrecht, from whence the purchase and shipment of armaments to Scotland had been made, provided the rationale for Skelton's renewed animosity toward Locke.[74] The latter's expulsion can be seen as a forced retreat in the skirmishes between Skelton and the radicals, prior to the

[70] Morrice, 1:656. The date of this entry is November 13, 1686, but Morrice does not give the names or number of those arrested.

[71] *Correspondence*, 3:290–291.

[72] *Correspondence*, 3:76–77.

[73] *Correspondence*, 3:77–78. It should be noted that William personally controlled affairs in Utrecht and the actions of the magistrates in that city (Add. MS 41813, fol. 229; S. Baxter, *William III*, p. 178).

[74] It should not be forgotten that Locke knew the double agent very well, having stayed in his house. He also knew Samuel Harris, one of the assailants.

envoy's own departure for Paris. Notwithstanding the absence of more detailed information, what we can learn about the activities of the radicals in Holland, Locke included, during 1686 indicates that some of them were still wholly dedicated to the cause of overthrowing James' government, that some plan of action was being formulated and, through arms shipments, being implemented, and that they were still receiving protection and assistance from the Dutch authorities, extending to the highest levels, through Bentinck and Dykvelt, to William himself.

Locke retired to Rotterdam, where, for most of the remainder of his stay in Holland, he lived with Benjamin Furley. He also resumed writing, though whether on philosophy, toleration, or politics is not clear.[75] In mid-February 1687, however, Locke asked Clarke to retrieve that half of the *Tractatus "de Morbo Gallico"* which he had left with Mrs. Smithsby in London, adding, "You may easily [perceive] why I would have that tract *De Morbo Gallico*."[76] If we put together the timing of Locke's anxiety concerning the whereabouts of this work (immediately following Shaftesbury's arrest in 1681, at the end of July 1682 when serious plans for an insurrection were being formulated by Shaftesbury, during the trials of the Rye House conspirators and especially Sidney's trial in November 1683, and immediately preceeding Monmouth's Rebellion in 1685), those concerns are distinctly tied to a recognition of that work's relationship to Locke's political activity and more generally to the radicals' plans for making a revolution.[77] It would appear, therefore, that by February 1687 these plans had taken sufficient shape that Locke proposed to revise or expand the *Two Treatises* in preparation for the realization of those revolutionary objectives. Clarke was one of the few people who would "easily perceive why" Locke wanted his manuscript, because Clarke was again acting as an agent in the transferral of funds for the cause, as he had done in the months prior to Monmouth's Rebellion.

Not surprisingly, after a two-year lapse in their interest in such matters, the two men begin to exchange canting letters about "seeds," "abele trees," and gardening, a form of discourse, incidentally, employed by

[75] While it is true that Locke enjoyed the comfort and hospitality of Furley's home, his retirement there was not a peaceful withdrawal from political activity. On the contrary, Furley, who had provided lodgings for Sidney and for a number of English radicals involved in the conspiracies of the 1660s, had the reputation for being a kind of protector of English fugitives. His house was, in effect, a sanctuary for political radicals, and Locke's decision to live there following his expulsion from Utrecht represents an acceptance of this protection. Of course, Furley was his friend, but Locke had many friends in Holland whom he had known for much longer and with whom he could have resided. The point I am making is that none of them could have offered him the political protection that Furley could.

[76] *Correspondence*, 3:131.

[77] Laslett, pp. 62–65.

Mordaunt in his correspondence with Bentinck.[78] Locke's correspondence with Freke becomes extremely allusive, with references to "fairy gold," and his letters to Furley during this period reveal a strange preoccupation with ducks. Freke's commitment to the radical cause (his refusal to participate in James II's attempt to win over the English Dissenters in 1687 was noted in Chapter 10), coupled with the evidence that Furley was one of the Dutch merchants involved in assisting the radicals, place Locke and Clarke, their close associates, near the center of whatever activity was dictated by the "new deeply laid" plot developed by the radicals. In March 1687, Freke wrote Locke several canting letters about various fictitious individuals, including I believe a reference to their mutual friend Robert Ferguson—who, Freke informed Locke, "speaks hearty as he did when he commanded me to give you his service."[79] Later letters with his Dutch friends indicate that Locke is receiving information by way of Dykvelt and Bentinck, though probably not directly from those individuals.[80] Throughout 1687, Locke kept himself informed of political affairs in England buying on a subscription basis the *London Gazette*.[81] Between August and October of that year, Locke made a number of trips to The Hague—unusual for him, since so far as we know he had not visited William's Court during the previous four years of his exile.[82] Whatever basis there is for supposing "a hearty friendship" between Locke and William, as Fox-Bourne put it, must date from this period. On October 24, 1687, Locke paid for two nights lodging at The Hague, and it is very likely that he was a participant in the meeting among William, Mordaunt, Henry Sidney, and other Englishmen reported on to Middleton a few days later by Albeville's assistant.[83]

Having established the persistence of the radical movement, and Locke's participation within it, I want to consider finally the substantive reasons the radicals offered for their opposition to James II. There are, first, the specific charges that constituted a quasi-legal indictment of

[78] *Correspondence*, 3:62, 101, 165–166; Pinkham, *Respectable Revolution*, p. 41.

[79] *Correspondence*, 3:149. Freke refers to a fictitious individual, "Father Richardson," as a mutual friend of him and Locke, and as someone who "seldom goes out of his chamber." This accurately describes the conditions under which Ferguson was then living. The fact that Freke was independently a friend of Ferguson and that he has reversed Ferguson's initials leads me to suspect that Ferguson is "Father Richardson." Ferguson is mentioned in a letter from Lady Masham to Locke in July 1687 (3:238).

[80] *Correspondence*, 3:290–291.

[81] MS f.34, fols. 12–13. Locke paid for the *Gazettes* after every seventeen issues.

[82] MS f.34, fol. 13. The dates of these visits are listed in Cranston, p. 284.

[83] MS f.34, fol. 13; Add. MS 41815, fol. 64; cf. Fox-Bourne, 2:56–57. Mordaunt obtained a pass to leave England at the end of July 1687, and Lord Brandon received his in early September. Both men were frequent visitors to The Hague (*CSPD*, [James II], 3:400).

James' administration, and, second, the general arguments the radicals employed to justify the Glorious Revolution. In delineating these two dimensions of the radical perspective, I will pay special attention to their relationship to the arguments in the *Two Treatises*. In reconstructing the radical critique of James II, I am primarily interested, as was pointed out in the Introduction, in ascertaining the meaning of the radicals' political theory as it was rooted in their *perception* of reality. While I do want to defend the evidential basis for that perception, naturally there were other evaluations of James II's administration that, in part were in conflict and in part overlapped with the views held by the radicals. The latter's case against James was rooted in their assessment of the actions he took between 1685 and 1688, as well as in their longstanding suspicion of his intentions to establish absolute monarchy and Catholicism in England.

In his speech to Parliament in November 1685, James strongly criticized the militia and the role it had played in Monmouth's Rebellion. That event had provided him with a standing army and the funds necessary to maintain it. For the remainder of his reign, reliance upon the militia was virtually abandoned, and between August 1687 and March 1688, the king dismissed from office eighteen lieutenants of the militia in twenty-one counties.[84] Instead, James concentrated his attention upon improving and "regulating" the standing army at his disposal, which in 1686–1687 was encamped on Hounslow Heath, just outside of London. These improvements included James' waiver of the provisions of the Test Act for army officers. Without this barrier to the promotion of Catholics, the king began systematically to increase their numbers within the higher ranks of the army.[85] Some four thousand soldiers, and more than three hundred officers were cashiered in what appeared to many to represent a purge of Protestants. Not all their replacements were Catholics; nevertheless, the fact that many of these cashiered soldiers retired to Holland, where they were provided for by William, tended to reinforce the belief that Protestant soldiers were being forced to choose between their religion and the pursuit of a military career.[86]

In general, those who opposed James' policy of aiding the Catholics were removed from office and replaced by Catholics or by those pledged

[84] J. P. Kenyon, *The Nobility in the Revolution of 1688*, Hull: University of Hull, 1963, pp. 7–8. James told Barrillon that he intended to use Monmouth's Rebellion as a means of gaining a standing army (Dalrymple, 2:102).

[85] Carswell, *Descent*, p. 73. In 1686, the army at Hounslow Heath numbered 13,000. By early 1688, James II had an army of 37,000 infantry (Lois G. Schwoerer, *No Standing Armies: The Antiarmy Ideology in Seventeenth-Century England*, Baltimore: Johns Hopkins University Press, 1974, p. 146).

[86] Dalrymple, 2:74.

to support that policy. Judges, justices of the peace, sheriffs, corporation magistrates, and civil and military offices at all levels of government were filled according to this criterion. The commissions for judges, previously established for life, were altered so that they continued in office solely at the king's pleasure.[87] Between September 1687 and February 1688, 3,500 individuals were removed from the livery companies in London, an action that, in many instances, probably jeopardized their claims to the suffrage as freemen. A committee of the Privy Council was created in October 1687 to draw up a list of the names of those individuals to be removed from various corporations and one containing the names of their replacements.[88] Thus by 1687, "all corporations and offices of every kind, from the highest to the lowest, were thrown open to Roman Catholics, and some branches of government were engrossed almost entirely by them."[89] In that same year, James abolished the charters of the colonies in Massachusetts, Connecticut, Rhode Island, New Hampsire, and Maine. These formerly separate colonies were consolidated into a single dominion of New England, ruled by an omnipotent governor with no local assemblies, and a decreed religious toleration for Nonconformists. Steps had been taken by James to abolish or restructure the charters of Carolina and Pennsylvania, but proceedings against the latter were halted through the intervention of Penn, the king's friend and propagandist.[90]

David Ogg has provided a good summary of James' actions in Scotland, which, given the prominence of the participation of Scots in the radical movement, must have been closely watched by the exiles in Holland. As early as April 1685, the king had sent a list of legislative acts he wanted the Scottish Parliament to pass. These included the death penalty for those attending conventicles and anyone who harbored such individuals; a measure that would have made it a treasonable offense to refuse to give

[87] Dalrymple, 2:71–72; Jennifer Levin, *The Charter Controversy in the City of London, 1660–1688, and Its Consequences*, London: Athlone Press, 1969, pp. 55ff.; John Evelyn, *The Diary of John Evelyn*, ed. E. S. De Beer, 6 vols., Oxford: Clarendon Press, 1955, 4:540.

[88] Miller, *James II*, p. 179; Kenyon, *Sunderland*, p. 139. James also established a secret Catholic council with whom he met for advice (Kenyon, *Sunderland*, pp. 128, 159). At Reading, twenty-four Tory aldermen were dismissed, and twenty-four new aldermen were appointed by the king. When it was discovered that twenty-three of the new appointees were not sympathetic to the Indulgence, they were dismissed. In the course of a few days, Yarmouth was governed by three different sets of magistrates, appointed and fired by James II. Towns all over Britain followed these examples of what "regulating" the corporations meant in practice—carrying out James II's orders (Macaulay, 2:306–307). For another example, see Pat E. Murrell, "Bury St. Edmunds and the Campaign to Pack Parliament, 1687–8," *Bulletin of the Institute of Historical Research* 54, no. 130 (November 1981):188–206.

[89] Dalrymple, 2:74.

[90] Carswell, *Descent*, p. 72.

evidence in treason trials; an act absolving all civil and military officers acting under the king's commission from all suits and complaints against their actions, whatever their nature; and an act placing the lives and fortunes of all his Majesty's subjects in Scotland between the ages of sixteen and sixty at the absolute disposal of the Crown. In August 1686, James sent a letter to the Scottish Privy Council instructing them to annul the existing laws against Catholics. When the council showed some reluctance to comply with this demand, the king removed a number of its Protestant members, replacing them with Catholics. When even this tactic did not prove successful, James used the prerogative to achieve his ends. All of these proposed laws and actions were, in fact, carried out in Scotland, and as Ogg observes, "it is not unfair to regard them as a hint of what James may have ultimately intended for England."[91] That, at least, is the way in which the radicals in Holland would have interpreted the situation.

Other actions, such as James' replacement of Protestant deans and chancellors at the universities with Catholics, or his attempt to use the established church as a propaganda arm for his policies, are sufficiently notorious subjects of historical scholarship as to require no elaboration here.[92] These actions constituted for the radicals a pattern or long-term strategy, the object of which was to restructure the social and political institutions of England in conformity with the precepts of Roman Catholicism and absolute monarchy. The single most important institution whose existence was threatened by this strategy was Parliament. As they had feared during the exclusion crisis, and as they had become convinced following the dissolution of the Oxford Parliament, the radicals believed that the king's attempt to rule the country without Parliament was the vital step in the implementation of this strategy.

In his early discussions with Barrillon, from which I cited in the last chapter, James had determined, upon his ascension to the throne, to make himself financially independent of Parliament. He was shrewd enough to perceive that claiming the income from customs and excise taxes, which by legislative action had been granted to Charles II, was the means by which this end could be accomplished. And he was determined enough not to wait for parliamentary approval of his seizure of this revenue, though he hoped, as Barrillon phrased it, to put the Parliament in a position of being "under a necessity of granting him what he is resolved to

[91] David Ogg, *England in the Reigns of James II and William III*, Oxford: Clarendon Press, 1955, pp. 171–172, 174.

[92] Macaulay, 2:258–279; J. R. Bloxam, ed., *Magdalen College and King James II, 1686–1688*, 1886. Locke owned several tracts relating to the Magdalen College controversy (*LL* #1865–1866).

take, if they do not, that is, the deceased King's revenues."[93] James also told Barrillon that he had rejected Danby's policy of maintaining pensioners in Parliament through bribes as the means of securing approval for the king's policies. This approach was in James' view both wasteful from a business standpoint, and conceded too much to the authority of the Commons from the perspective of his political theory. He was more inclined to attack the problem at its root, by gaining control over who sat in Parliament in the first instance. It was preferable to keep one's enemies out of office rather than to bribe one's friends in office. Moreover, the means for implementing this policy were already available to James when he came to power.

The quo warranto proceedings against corporation and borough charters, begun by Charles II before the Rye House Plot but carried out with greater rigor and urgency following its discovery, had redefined and restructured the requirements and privileges of parliamentary representation. With the assistance of local Tory magnates, the king drafted new charters designed to insure Tory dominance in both municipal affairs and parliamentary elections. In the words of James II's recent biographer, "The King gained greater control than ever before over the internal affairs of very many boroughs, a control which he used in 1685 to influence the composition of the Commons to an unprecedented extent. The crown, in fact, could now pack Parliament." As James prepared in March 1685 to hold the first general election in England in four years, seventy-six redrafted charters were reissued in the space of a few weeks.[94] This action was repeated prior to the scheduled parliamentary elections of 1688.[95] A comparison of the new with the old borough charters indicates the conscious attempt by James to restrict the suffrage and to tighten the links between the king's appointment and removal of local magistrates and the

[93] Dalrymple, 2:40. According to Barrillon, James told him repeatedly that he intended to rule without Parliament. Seizing the customs and excise revenue would make it "much more easy for me either to put off the assembling of Parliament, or to maintain myself by other means." Once he had gained parliamentary approval for this action, he would have "the means to make him independent of Parliament" (Dalrymple, 2:2, 4; cf. ibid., 1:167). This action had been attacked in Monmouth's Declaration as a violent invasion of Englishmen's estates (Landsdowne MS 1152, fol. 259). This appears to be the first recognition by the radicals of the connection between the customs and excise revenue and the threat of absolutism.

[94] Miller, *James II*, p. 113; J. R. Jones, *Country and Court: England, 1658–1714*, Cambridge: Harvard University Press, 1978, p. 243.

[95] Robert H. George, "The Charters Granted to English Parliamentary Corporations in 1688," *English Historical Review* 55, no. 217 (January 1940):47. These elections were not held.

concentration of local political power in their hands.[96] It was obvious to contemporaries, and not merely to radical Whigs, that James' attack on the charters was a means of "determining the results of elections" to Parliament in favor of the king.[97] Indeed, in Scotland, he had ordered all towns not to hold any elections pending the royal nomination of candidates.[98]

Doubtless every English monarch in the seventeenth century would have liked to have had a more subservient Parliament than existed during his reign, but James' efforts to realize this goal naturally assumed more ominous dimensions because of his Catholicism. The remodeling of Parliament was, in the last analysis, purely instrumental to the institutionalization of popery. For, unlike his predecessors, James II did not need Parliament in order to provide the financial support for his government. Indeed, with the threat of economic blackmail removed, James might have ruled without Parliament for his entire reign, following its dismissal in November 1685, except for one thing: The king wanted the Test Acts and penal laws repealed. He had suspended the penalties attached to these laws through the use of his prerogative, but the actual removal of them from the statute books, a legacy to be left to his fellow Catholics, could only be brought about through legislative action. Apart from this, there was no reason for James to take an interest in calling a Parliament or in its composition. It was plain, therefore, that the campaign against Parliament was subservient to this end.[99]

In fact, James, who was far less devious than his brother, did little to disguise his intentions. The removals and replacements of justices of the peace and deputy lieutenants all over the kingdom were publicly justified in the government's official publication, the *London Gazette*, as measures

[96] R. George, "Charters in 1688," p. 55; Macaulay, 2:307.

[97] This was the opinion, for example, of Sir John Reresby, cited in R. George, "Charters in 1688," p. 53; J. R. Jones, *Country and Court*, p. 34.

[98] Richard Lodge, *The Political History of England: From the Restoration to the Death of William III*, London: Longmans, Green, 1923, pp. 317–318.

[99] Evelyn reported James as saying that the reason he wanted Parliament called was so that the Indulgence could be settled by law so "that it should never be altered by his successors" (*Diary*, 4:553). He was also reported as saying that he wanted the law changed so that Catholics would be allowed to sit as members of the House of Commons (Lacey, p. 201). Carstares believed that repeal of the Tests was only the first step toward altering the succession to the throne so as to insure a Catholic successor. A policy memorandum drafted for James by some extremist Catholics recommended the exclusion of Mary from the succession and a war of extermination against Holland (in alliance with France). As Skelton's correspondence shows, a copy of this memorandum was circulating among the exiles in Holland and was widely discussed (*Carstares State Papers*, p. 28; Kenyon, *Sunderland*, pp. 135–136).

taken to secure the approval of James' Declaration of Indulgence.[100] In the February 1687 Declaration of Indulgence for Scotland (published in the *Gazette*), the king declared the penalties against Nonconformists suspended "by our authority and absolute power and prerogative royal."[101] In the English declaration several months later, the reasons for the action are presented at much greater length, and while it is justified on the basis of the king's royal prerogative, James added that he had "no doubt of the concurrence of our two houses of Parliament when we shall think it convenient for them to meet."[102] The radicals were inclined to interpret the meaning of the second statement in light of the first. By 1688, when James undertook the first systematic attempt to secure the opinions of local magistrates and potential parliamentary candidates as to their disposition toward the repeal of the penal laws and Test Acts should they be elected to office, the king's purposes for calling a Parliament into session and the conditions under which he was likely to do so were inescapably clear to even the most loyal Tory or Anglican. In the declaration published upon William's landing, it was maintained that "a regular plan had been carried on, for the establishment of popery in England. . . . The political liberties of the nation had been violated; for the charters of many boroughs had been seized, their protestant magistrates removed, and popish ones put in their places. A parliament had been delayed to be summoned, until the electors all over Britain were sounded, if they would return representatives named by the court; and those electors were removed from their offices who had refused to comply."[103]

One of those in Holland who advised William on the radicals' position was Patrick Hume, who had returned to Holland in 1686, following a period of travel on the Continent in the wake of Argyll's defeat in Scotland. In his memorandum to William (February 1687) commenting on the Scottish Declaration of Indulgence, Hume made a special point of emphasizing that the real battle was being fought over the control of Parliament. Hume linked James' quest for "an absolute and unbounded power" to his "grand design" to reinstitute Catholicism in Britain, and both of these depended upon his ability to remodel the elections for Parliament in order to obtain individuals who would agree with the king. Some of the exiles, Hume advised William, wanted the latter to write a letter to James protesting these actions and warning him that their consequences "may prove dangerous to his government."[104] The analysis underlying these

[100] Dalrymple, 2:87.
[101] *London Gazette*, February 28–March 3, 1687.
[102] *London Gazette*, April 4–7, 1687.
[103] Dalrymple, vol. 2, pt. 1, bk. 4, p. 42.
[104] Japiske, *Correspondentie*, 2:19–20.

diplomatically stated expressions is starkly clear. In April, Hume sent William another memorandum, commenting upon the English Indulgence. Evidently, in the intervening period, the efficacy of employing such polite restraints in the radicals' communication with William was diminishing. Humè now observed that some of the exiles had lost all patience with James, and there are some persons who "would, if possible, make haste" to put an end to his government. Hume remarked that this fiery temperament was especially characteristic of those who were "most advanced in years" (Wildman, Danvers, Manley, Locke, Ferguson?). At the same time, he wrote, "There are in this country of the British some persons of understanding, experience and credit" who "are not of the ranting, talking sort of men," but who maintain important ties to individuals in England who are influential in Parliament, should that body ever be called to meet. In referring to exiles who "correspond with [members of Parliament] and are able to influence them as much as any," it is easy to believe, viewed against the backdrop of Locke's correspondence, that the latter must have been included within the group of sober, experienced, and nontalking individuals Hume had in mind. In one sense, of course, this division was purely an artificial one, of Hume's creation, for as he hastened to inform William with respect to the radicals, "All of them look upon your Highness as the great wheel which under God must give life and motion to any good project."[105] In short, even those hotheads who downplayed the tremendous difficulties standing in the way of making a revolution probably did not, in the last analysis, seriously contemplate taking such an action without the assistance of William.

Hence, when Penn, in his aptly titled pamphlet, *Advice to Freeholders and Other Electors of Members to Serve in Parliament in Relation to the Penal Laws and the Tests*, disclosed his intentions to persuade people "to contribute to the making proper elections" of representatives who accepted "his Majesty's gracious purpose" in suspending the penalties against Nonconformists, he was sharply answered by the exiles in Holland.[106] James' policy, Ferguson declared, was nothing less than "an assault upon the Legislative Authority." Not only his use of the prerogative, but his attempts to exclude those who disagree with his policies from membership in Parliament, was an obvious illustration of this point.[107] In *The Great and Popular Objection against the Repeal of the Penal Laws and Tests Briefly Stated and Considered*, Penn tried to refute the "objec-

[105] Japiske, *Correspondentie*, 2:13, 19. Hume was not the only exile sending William memorandums. Various exiles drew up memorials, or advisory papers, for him (pp. 14–15).

[106] William Penn, *Advice to Freeholders and Other Electors of Members to Serve in Parliament in Relation to the Penal Laws and the Tests*, 1687, p. 2.

[107] N. T. [Robert Ferguson], *Animadversions upon a Pretended Answer to Myn Heer Fagel's Letter*, [1688?], p. 27.

tion" that James was trying to pack the Parliament in order to bring about the repeal of the Test Acts.[108] To the radicals, Penn was either naive or deceitful in his propagandistic efforts to win over the Dissenters to James' side. In fact, there are grounds for endorsing both charges against Penn.[109] To the latter, James' "gracious purposes" were being "frustrated by unreasonable malcontents," individuals with a "green ribbon mentality."[110] From the standpoint of Hume and the radicals, however, "the securing of the Commons' House is the chief point" of constitutional government, and, they were convinced, James "will not call Parliament if he doubt of their taking off the Tests."[111] In somewhat broader language, Ferguson declared that "the sense of the whole society [is] signified by their representatives in Parliament." In this respect, an attack upon that institution was an attack upon the political existence of "the whole community."[112] Quite apart from the separate and cumulative actions taken by James that tended to verify the radicals' belief in a conspiracy against the English Constitution, therefore, the core of their political argument rested squarely upon the importance and role they assigned to free elections and parliamentary government. The radical position had been constructed by Shaftesbury (and Locke) around that central point in the early 1680s, and throughout that decade, it retained its architectonic importance in the radicals' political theory.

In that section of the *Second Treatise* which reproduces these arguments and indictments against James II's actions, Locke begins by echoing Ferguson's characterization of the legislative authority as "the sense

[108] William Penn, *The Great and Popular Objection against the Repeal of the Penal Laws and Tests Briefly Stated and Considered*, 1688, p. 7. He had also cursorily dismissed this claim in his *A Third Letter from a Gentleman in the Country, to His Friend in London, upon the Subject of the Penal Laws and Tests*, 1687, pp. 12–13.

[109] In his 1687 tract, *Some Free Reflections upon the Occasion of the Public Discourse about Liberty of Conscience*, Penn had referred to the existence of the Test Act as "unwarrantable" (p. 10). Yet, in an unpublished essay written at the same time, Penn argued that it was in the interest of all Dissenters to repeal the penal laws but to retain the Test Acts as a defense against Catholics. Penn went so far as to say—a complete reversal of his published views—that "I will rather let the penal laws stand as they are than do anything that may tend towards the repeal of the Test." For the discussion of this manuscript and of Penn's inconsistency on this issue, see Joseph E. Illick, *William Penn the Politician*, Ithaca: Cornell University Press, 1965, pp. 90–95; Lacey, pp. 191–192, 348. In his *One Project for the Good of England*, [1680], (p. 10), a few years earlier, Penn himself had suggested a new Test Act against Catholics. As Johnston wrote in one of his intelligence reports, Penn "does good with one hand, and harm with the other" (Lacey, p. 198).

[110] Penn, *Advice to Freeholders*, p. 2; idem, *A Second Letter from a Gentleman in the Country, to His Friends in London, upon the Subject of the Penal Laws and Tests*, 1687, p. 3.

[111] *CSPD* (James II), 3:128.

[112] Robert Ferguson, *A Representation of the Threatening Dangers*, 1688, p. 25.

of the whole society." It is, he argues, "in their Legislative, that the members of a commonwealth are united, and combined together into one coherent living body. This is the soul that gives form, life, and unity to the commonwealth." Locke goes on to speak of the legislature as "the essence and union of the society," without which the latter cannot, politically speaking, exist, but must suffer "dissolution and death."[113] This proposition lays the foundation for the argument that an attack upon the legislature or its ability to function is an attack upon "the essence" of political society, as Locke understands it. Beginning with paragraph 214, therefore, he presents the specific illustrations of how such an attack has been carried out by James. The first point he mentions is an instance in which the legislature has "put in execution, and required to be obeyed" certain laws in place of which the prince has substituted "his own arbitrary will," so that other policies and rules are "pretended and enforced" than what the legislature intended.[114] This certainly reflects the radicals' judgment with respect to James II's suspension of the Test Acts.

Two paragraphs later, Locke condemns the exercise of arbitrary power by the prince so that "the electors, or ways of election are altered, without the consent, and contrary to the common interest of the people."[115] For, the prince has at his disposal "the force, treasure, and offices of the state" as the means whereby he can "terrify or suppress" those opposed to him. If he is successful in corrupting or changing the legislative authority, then so far as society is concerned, this action "produces effects very little different from foreign conquest."[116] In James' case, because of his submission to popery, this *is* in fact the result. Thus, "the delivery also of the people into the subjection of a foreign power . . . is certainly a change of the legislative, and so a dissolution of the government."[117] As we have seen, such a foreign subjection is, from the radical standpoint, the inevitable consequence of the king's allegiance to the pope and Roman Catholicism. All of these particular charges are summarized by Locke in paragraph 222, which was added to the text in 1688–1689, just prior to its publication.[118] The executive, Locke argues, acts "contrary to his trust, when he either employs the force, treasure, and offices of the society, to corrupt the representatives, and gain them to his purposes: or openly pre-

[113] *ST*, par. 212.

[114] *ST*, par. 214.

[115] *ST*, par. 216.

[116] *ST*, par. 218.

[117] *ST*, par. 217.

[118] Locke's specific references to James II's campaign in 1688 to determine prospective parliamentary candidates and electors who would "give their votes" in a future election and session of Parliament can only have been written in that year (Laslett, p. 431n.).

engages the electors, and prescribes to their choice, such, whom he has by solicitations, threats, promises, or otherwise to his designs; and employs them to bring in such, who have promised beforehand, what to vote, and what to enact." This is a rather specific description of James' 1688 survey of the voters' and candidates' views on the penal laws and Test Acts.[119] For, Locke observes,

> To prepare such an assembly as this, and endeavor to set up the declared abettors of his own will, for the true representatives of the people, and the lawmakers of the society, is certainly as great a breach of trust, and as perfect a declaration of a design to subvert the government, as is possible to be met with.

Moreover, if one considers the various "rewards and punishments visibly employed to the same end" by the prince, " 'twill be past doubt what is doing."[120]

These activities of James are detailed, from the official viewpoint, of course, in the *London Gazette,* which Locke read regularly throughout 1687. Locke's English friends also kept him well informed. In December 1687, Tyrrell wrote to him about the "new regulating the corporations" and the "terms" upon which James was making appointments of justices of the peace or deputy lieutenants.[121] In February 1688, both Clarke and Tyrrell wrote Locke about the many individuals who "are likewise turned out and put in" office on the basis of "complying with that which is called his Majesty's present interest." The rationale for such actions, Tyrrell noted, is that "they say there will be a parliament in May," and in order to guarantee that it suits "his Majesty's designs, it is fit the Corporations should undergo a new alteration," that is, a rewriting of their charters. As Clarke phrased the point, appealing to his solidarity with what he knew to be Locke's political position, "the world is full of change, but I am still the same unalterably."[122]

[119] For a description and discussion of these efforts, see J. P. Kenyon, ed., *The Stuart Constitution, 1603–1688,* Cambridge: Cambridge University Press, 1966, p. 496.

[120] *ST,* par. 222.

[121] *Correspondence,* 3:311–312.

[122] *Correspondence,* 3:378–380. In view of the fact that Clarke was precisely the kind of radical Whig James II was at that moment attempting to win over to his policies, this statement carries a significant resonance. Nathaniel Wade, who had become one of James' Whig collaborators, reported that Taunton would choose Clarke and Trenchard, or if not the latter then Clarke's brother William, in the forthcoming 1688 parliamentary elections. Clarke was also proposed for an appointment as a deputy lieutenant of Somersetshire (MS Rawlinson A 139B, fols. 183, 231, 249; *CSPD* [James II], 3:116). In 1688, Stringer and Yonge were also named to deputy lieutenancies (pp. 136, 199). See also J. R. Jones, "James II's Whig Collaborators," *Historical Journal* 3, no. 1 (1960):65–73.

To summarize the discussion, in Locke's specific indictment of James II, the latter's exercise of arbitrary power, his contravening the legislative intent of particular statutes, and his designs to establish the foreign doctrines of popery are all duly noted as grounds for resistance to the prince; yet, the central allegation, and the one discussed at length in the *Second Treatise* by Locke, is James' direct assault upon a "freely chosen" legislature; that is, an assembly selected without a revocation of the "ways of election" and the definition of "electors" established by the people themselves, and without the employment of threats or rewards to corrupt the representatives, and capable of deciding how to "freely act and advise" the commonwealth as to the public good after "examination, and mature debate" of the issues. If, as Locke maintains in the preface to the *Two Treatises*, "our present King William" has, by his invasion, been the instrument of the preservation of the peoples' "just and natural rights" when the nation "was on the very brink of slavery and ruin," it is chiefly because he has restored to the people their right to have freely elected Parliaments to represent them, without which all other rights are in jeopardy.[123]

In turning, finally, to a more general consideration of the political debate surrounding the Glorious Revolution and the appearance in print of the *Two Treatises of Government*, it can be taken for granted that most of the basic arguments employed in that debate are by now quite familiar. The issues of the origins of government, the derivation of political obligations from the Law of Nature, the concepts of the state of nature, social contract, trusteeship, assertions of equality, claims for natural rights, the right to resistance—in short, the social language of seventeenth-century liberalism—reappeared in the pamphlets and tracts published from 1688 to 1690. In my concluding remarks, therefore, I will try to focus attention on those issues most specific to the circumstances of the Glorious Revolution, or alternatively, upon the way in which those circumstances altered slightly the meaning of familiar general concepts, as the means of elucidating the radicals' assessment of that revolution. This last point is illustrated by the previous chapter's discussion of toleration, which by 1689 had become an important part of any political solution as envisioned by the radicals.

If we begin with the realization that William III provided the umbrella under which several divergent groups found shelter, it is clear that the origins of the political debate regarding the purposes and objectives of the Glorious Revolution is rooted in the exchange of ideas among members of those groups in Holland prior to William's actual departure for Eng-

[123] *Two Treatises*, preface.

land. For they were faced with the immediate practical task of drafting a declaration that would set forth the collective aims of that enterprise. Once in England, the scope of this debate quickly widened, both as a consequence of the influx of new groups of supporters with their own specific objectives, and as a result of the opposition provoked by William's invasion. It is also true that both of these developments, as well as the revelations about the direction in which the revolution was moving produced by the accumulated weight of the practical decisions made by William, had a dissolving effect upon the coherence of the group of exiles who accompanied him to England. Insofar as radicalism retains its identity as a distinguishable perspective on the political spectrum in 1689, therefore, except for one major disagreement prior to William's departure from Holland, it emerges gradually, breaking off from the other positions in the political debate, as the revolution unfolds.

One factor that reinforced the theoretical significance of a commitment to parliamentary government as the primary justificatory axis for the English exiles' conception of the revolution was the practical consensus they shared on the need for a Parliament to be called into session. As in the Rye House conspiracy, everyone, from rabid Republicans to defenders of a constitutional monarchy, could agree that a freely elected House of Commons was essential to political society as they defined it, however much their theories, taken as a whole, tended to proceed down different ideological paths. Hence the central clause of William's declaration—and the only reason for his coming to England that he publicly circulated by other means—was a promise to guarantee a freely elected Parliament that would decide what to do about any other matters of controversy. The questions of how such a Parliament would be called, who would be a member of it, what exactly its status was—problems whose answers reflected divisions within the group and tended to shatter its consensus—lay in the future.

The major disagreement between two identifiable factions within the exile community concerned the extent to which the explanation for William's expedition was limited to a critique and indictment of James II's actions, or whether it would also take into account the arbitrary and tyrannical actions of Charles II. To a significant degree, this split placed the radicals on one side and the moderate Whigs on the other, and it clearly constitutes the opening wedge of that division, which grew increasingly wider as the revolution progressed. With the assistance of Burnet, Fagel had drafted a declaration reflecting William's views. This draft was unacceptable to the radicals, and, on their behalf Wildman produced his version of a revolutionary declaration "in which he had coupled the grievances of the last reign with those of [James II]." In his draft, Wildman also "laid down a scheme of government," and sharply attacked the Anglican clergy. None of these points sat well with Burnet or William. At the same time, Wildman and the radicals were "violently opposed" to Burnet's draft declaration. "The dispute was stiffly maintained on both sides," and reached such public proportions that even Albeville was able to report to Middleton that there were "great disagreements" over William's manifesto and "divers draughts have been penned."[124] Macclesfield and Mordaunt, as well as others around them and Wildman, refused to engage in the expedition if Burnet's version were accepted as the justification for the revolution. Henry Sidney and the Duke of Shrewsbury, on the other hand, were strenuously opposed to Wildman's draft, maintaining that it would only alienate most of the nobility and gentry, and virtually all of the clergy, on whose support, they argued, the success of William's venture ultimately depended.[125]

It is not difficult to see what was at stake in this dispute or why it should have arisen. The most committed radicals had spent ten years of their lives in active resistance to Charles and his brother, losing in the process many of their closest friends as martyrs to the cause. They deeply resented the fact that a few last-minute converts to that cause, and some others who were not even (from their point of view) bona fide members of the resistance movement, should now put themselves in a position of dictating the rationale for the invasion. In terms of the political realities of the situation, however, the radicals did not reflect William's views, nor did they possess the kind of support in England that could be successfully mobilized to defeat James. That the revolution depended upon the support of the nobility and gentry, not to mention that of William, was obvious. A compromise was worked out between the two factions, which papered over this division in the ranks of the exiles.

In light of what has been said, it does not require great acumen to see where Locke stood in this dispute. Except for scattered passages here and there that refer specifically to James II, the *Second Treatise* is a sustained indictment and critique of the actions of Charles II (and incidentally of the Anglican clergy). Its central arguments were thought through and formulated from that standpoint, and it is clearly meant to reflect the posi-

[124] James Ralph, *The History of England*, 1744, p. 1023; Add. MS 41816, fols. 209, 251. The Scottish radicals also drafted an address to William that included a detailed critique of the crimes of Charles II (Robert Wodrow, *The History of the Sufferings of the Church of Scotland from the Restoration to the Revolution*, 4 vols., 1830, 4:477–481). On September 17, 1688, Albeville's assistant wrote Middleton that William's Declaration "is so publicly spoke of, that people from remote places sent hither for copies" (fol. 181). Locke owned a copy of William's Declaration (*LL* #2134).

[125] Ralph, *History*, p. 1023; Dalrymple, vol. 2, pt. 1, bk. 4, p. 40.

tion defended by Wildman and the radicals as it was articulated on the eve of William's departure. The publication of the *Two Treatises* in 1689 represents, therefore, the single most effective statement of the radicals' position to appear in print in the wake of the Glorious Revolution. It is important to remember as part of any explanation of why, after all, Locke should even have decided to publish his manuscript that, in light of the controversy described above, the argument advanced by Locke, endorsed by his friends Wildman, Mordaunt, and Macclesfield was from the outset of the revolution perceptibly to the left of the position adopted by the majority of William's supporters.

Before proceeding to a consideration of those issues which arose during the revolution, perhaps it is useful to say something briefly about Gilbert Burnet's role in that undertaking, as a means of clarifying Locke's relationship to him personally, as well as to those for whom Burnet claimed to be a spokesman. Burnet had never been close to those around Shaftesbury, and especially not to radicals such as Ferguson, Wildman, or Sidney. There is no reason to doubt that this proposition applies to Locke as well, and no evidence to suggest otherwise. One could go even further and say that, from the radicals' standpoint, there was a good deal of hostility toward Burnet, whom they suspected of being a spy.[126] This hostility increased at the time of Russell's execution because of Burnet's role in hectoring Russell to make a statement renouncing the right of resistance (which many suspected was a forgery written by Burnet himself).[127] Bur-

[126] In a letter to the fourth Earl of Shaftesbury written by someone who had been part of the first earl's political family in the 1680s, the author writes of Burnet that you "must remember that the Bishop was generally looked upon to be employed by the Court" during the exclusion crisis (PRO 30/24/17/pt. 2/18). That there was some basis for this suspicion can be seen from a letter from Burnet to Charles II, dated January 29, 1680 (but probably 1681), in which Burnet promises to furnish information to the king through Mr. Chiffinch (MS Add. d.23, fol. 6, Bodleian Library).

[127] There are several documents in the Shaftesbury papers by Thomas Stringer and others that attack "Burnet's wicked, false, and profane history," and his role at the time of Essex's death and Russell's imprisonment (W. D. Christie, *A Life of Anthony Ashley Cooper, First Earl of Shaftesbury*, 2 vols., 1871, vol. 2, appendix 8, pp. cxxv–cxxviii). In the Rawlinson manuscripts, there is a letter from Burnet to Henry Compton, Bishop of London, dated July 30, 1683, on the back of which is written: "For my part I cannot deny but that I have been of [the] opinion, that a free nation like this might defend their religion and liberties when invaded and taken from them, though under pretence and color of law. But some worthy and eminent divines, who have had the charity to be often with me and whom I value and esteem to a very great degree, have offered me weighty reasons to persuade me that faith and patience are the proper ways for the preservation of religion," and that it is better to suffer persecution than to engage in resistance (MS Rawlinson C 983, fol. 67). The controversy over whether this statement was dictated by Russell and written down by Burnet, or whether this is a draft of a statement by Burnet that Russell refused to sign is not, however, resolved by the existence of this document.

net's popularity with the radicals cannot have been increased when, although he had advance information as to Monmouth's projected invasion, he decided to leave England to avoid any suspicion that he was a supporter of that rebellion, despite the fact that, at the time, his wife lay dying and had only a few more weeks to live.[128] When Burnet came to Holland in May 1686, therefore, he was hardly the person whom the radicals would receive openly as a member of their ranks. And for his part, Burnet wanted nothing to do with the radicals. In a letter to a friend, Burnet wrote:

> I have nothing to do neither with the Scots at Rotterdam nor with the English that are believed to be in Amsterdam, for as I have seen none of them, so I am resolved that my soul shall never enter into their secrets . . . [I am so far removed from] the dark men of the last age that I am further than ever from all things that lead to the drawing the sword against those in whose hands God hath put it. So that you may depend upon it that I will never be directly or indirectly so much as in the knowledge of things of that nature.[129]

At the same time, he wrote to Lady Russell that he "liked not their ["the English refugees"] neighborhood," and since the exiles "were up and down in most of the towns of Holland except at the Hague," Burnet decided, "upon that ground," that The Hague was "the fittest place to retire to."[130] Clearly, Burnet had no desire or inclination to associate himself with the radicals in Holland or with their plans for "a second disturbance" in England or Scotland. As late as May 1687, he could boast that he had preached a sermon at The Hague against "the lawfulness of subjects rising in arms against their sovereign." It is the duty of subjects, Burnet argued, "to submit and bear all the ill administration that might be in the government, but never to rise in arms upon that account."[131] If, by 1688, he had drifted into the revolutionary movement, this was certainly not because of any deeply held revolutionary views on his part.

Thus, to the radicals in Holland, Burnet appeared as an ideological interloper, and worse, as something of a fawning and pretentious courtier.

[128] Burnet, 2:151, 157. Burnet also persuaded Lady Russell not to contribute any money to Monmouth's supporters, for which "I was severely railed at . . . by these men." Neither Delamere nor Hampden trusted Burnet (pp. 151–152).

[129] MS Add. d.23, fol. 1.

[130] Newcastle MS, NeC.13 (May 7, 1686). "I settled in the Hague upon my coming into Holland, because I was willing to be under the observation of his majesty's envoy; and I chose this place the rather, because it was known that none of those that lay under sentences come to it" (cited in Wodrow, *Sufferings of the Church*, 4:408).

[131] Cited in Wodrow, *Sufferings of the Church*, 4:409.

His efforts, immediately after his arrival, to ingratiate himself with all the dignitaries at the conference between William and the Elector of Brandenburg is recorded, with some mild disgust at the exhibition, in Erskine's journal. Erskine had sailed and fought with Argyll, and was a close friend of Carstares, Nisbet, and other radicals; he had little tolerance for a man like Burnet.[132] Nevertheless, the very fact that he was physically at The Hague, his own propensity to attach himself to William, and James II's obsessive hatred for Burnet gave the latter a prominence and standing with William that other exiles in Holland were not able to claim. In other words, the clash between Burnet and Wildman in 1688, precipitated by their opposing conceptions of what the revolution was about, was no momentary eruption or merely the confrontation between individuals with very different personalities. It was simply the occasion for bringing out into the open a longstanding simmering hostility between Burnet and the radicals who had formed their commitments under the political leadership of Shaftesbury and Monmouth.

There is no mention of Locke in Burnet's autobiography, and barely more than a grudging recognition paid to Burnet in Locke's manuscripts and correspondence. Certainly, there is no basis for supposing the existence of a reservoir of good feeling or friendship between the two men. While Burnet's silence about Locke is, in its own way, revealing, any reconstruction of the relationship between them must naturally be based upon the few references in Locke's writings. Most of these, as in a letter to Shaftesbury in 1680, are merely passing references to an individual known to Locke and his correspondent.[133] A more interesting comment appears in Locke's letter to Limborch, written from Utrecht in October 1686, or a few months after Burnet's arrival in Holland. Limborch maintained a separate correspondence with Burnet, and held a much more positive attitude toward him than did Locke. Evidently, Limborch had recently had some discussions with Burnet, about which he wrote to Locke in a letter now lost. Locke's comment is contained in his reply to this let-

[132] Erskine, *Journal*, p. 201; Carswell, *Descent*, pp. 78–79.

[133] *Correspondence*, 2:227. As Goldie observes, Burnet consciously omitted any mention of Samuel Johnson from his *History of My Own Time* as a response to Johnson's dislike and criticisms of Burnet (Mark Goldie, "The Roots of True Whiggism, 1688–94," *History of Political Thought* 1, no. 2 [June 1980]:234). In fact, Burnet's *History* has very little to say about any of the radicals (Ferguson, Wildman, et al.), all of whom, with the possible exceptions of Argyll, Monmouth, Essex, and Russell, he appears to have disliked. In his use of silence, therefore, Johnson may not have been an isolated case in Burnet's treatment of them. The omission of Locke from Burnet's *History*, given his claims to be recognized, quite apart from his association with Shaftesbury and his political activities in Holland (e.g., his friendship with Limborch, Boyle, and Newton, and his works on philosophy and toleration), is much easier to explain on these political grounds than on any other.

ter. He writes that "if you have found signs of greater mildness and broad-mindedness in Burnet, I am glad of it."[134] The implication, as I read it, being that Locke has not, heretofore, had much reason for supposing that Burnet had such characteristics. The difference in the two men's assessment of Burnet seems borne out by an exchange of letters early in 1689. Limborch, having been informed by Locke that Burnet has been made Bishop of Salisbury, registers his "assurance" that he will remain as "broad-minded" in England as Limborch found him to be in Holland. "For never can I believe that the high office of bishop will in any way or in any degree change that worthy man's mind, which he has often so frankly and roundly expressed to me."[135] In his reply, Locke gives an account of Burnet's coronation sermon that "won general approval" and that Locke has no doubt "is being published."[136] He adds, "I saw Burnet today; I told him you were preparing to write him a letter of congratulation as soon as you knew for certain that the bishop's crosier had been bestowed on him, and he was grateful for the information." These reportorial comments by Locke are interspersed with an account of the progress toward the establishment of toleration. And it is in that context that Locke observes, "whether *your friend* Burnet is likely, as you feel sure, to be of the same mind at Salisbury as he was at Amsterdam is a thing that some people are beginning to doubt."[137] Locke does not say that he is included among the "some people," but the tone of his remarks—including an anecdotal exchange between William and Burnet about the size of the latter's ego that Locke reports in this letter—do suggest the distance between his feelings and those of Limborch toward Burnet. There is no reason to make too much of Locke's relationship to Burnet, one way or the other, except to show that, like other radicals, Locke retained a certain amount of skepticism with respect to Burnet's sincerity toward the political aims of the radical movement, and that no personal bond existed between the two that might have overridden these political differences.

An interesting sidelight on this situation is provided by the fact that Burnet's nephew, James Johnston, was deeply involved in the radical movement, and he was a very good friend of Locke. Indeed, in both respects, this is an understatement of the facts. A few fleeting glimpses of

[134] *Correspondence*, 3:44.

[135] *Correspondence*, 3:589.

[136] Gilbert Burnet, *A Sermon Preached at the Coronation of William and Mary*, 1689. Locke owned a number of sermons by Burnet, though apparently not this one. However, from his letter to Limborch, it appears that Locke was a member of the audience and heard it preached (*Correspondence*, 3:597–598).

[137] *Correspondence*, 3:598–599.

Johnston are contained in Erskine's journal, but from them it is clear that he, along with Carstares, was circulating among the radical exiles throughout 1686.[138] In the following year, Johnston was sent by William on a secret mission into England, complete with mail drops, false identities, correspondence in cipher, invisible ink, and so forth. Though he kept an eye on and maintained contact with Penn, Johnston's supportive associates in this intelligence-gathering endeavor were Locke's friends John Howe and Lord Mordaunt.[139] Through Bentinck, Johnston kept William informed of affairs in England right up to the time of his arrival. In the words of a recent scholar, Johnston was "the most effective agent William ever sent to England."[140] Following the Glorious Revolution, William rewarded him with the post of Secretary of State for Scotland. Johnston and Locke were friends in Holland and carried on a correspondence following the Glorious Revolution.[141] Locke sent him copies of his published works (though none to his uncle, Burnet), and left a legacy for Johnston in his will.[142] Both Johnston and Locke were closer to each other than either was to Burnet, and one reason for this, I am suggesting, lies in their mutual involvement in, and Burnet's aloofness from, the radical political movement.

The controversy among the exiles over the content of William's declaration might be viewed simply as a debate over nuances and the distribution of emphasis placed upon certain points. Yet in a larger sense, it could be argued that the entire political debate generated by the Glorious Revolution concentrated upon the shades of meaning and nuances contained in the political vocabulary that Englishmen had used since the 1640s. It was, so to speak, a debate of refinement rather than one that produced new concepts or a restructuring of political theories. In part, it is this feature that makes it difficult to appreciate the radical perspective in that debate, for any gross categorization that aligns a social contract theory on one side and a divine right theory on the other will certainly miss or obscure the specific importance attached to particular arguments by the radicals.[143]

[138] Erskine, *Journal*, pp. 209, 214.

[139] Carswell, *Descent*, p. 131. Although Howe had accepted a pardon from James, this appears to have been merely the means to get him back into England. Before he left Holland, he had a conference with William who urged Howe to stand firm, and he did, in fact, become one of the leaders of the resistance to James (Robert F. Horton, *John Howe*, 1895, p. 163; Lacey, pp. 180–181, 189, 344).

[140] Carswell, *Descent*, p. 113.

[141] Cranston, p. 370.

[142] MS c.25, fol. 70 (Locke's legacies). Locke sent Johnston copies of his *Some Thoughts Concerning Education* and *Considerations on the Lowering of Interest* (fol. 53).

[143] See for example, Gerald Straka's confused treatment of a divine right, patriarchal the-

If we begin our discussion of the political ideas of 1689 with the Convention debate, it is possible to see how issues raised but not pursued in that debate were proscribed from the political discussion held by the Whig-Tory coalition that produced the Revolution Settlement. These issues were, however, taken up and defended by radical pamphleteers. And on the other hand, the questions of dominant importance to the members of the Convention—whether James had "abdicated" or "deserted" the throne, whether the latter was "vacant," and so on—were not, for the radicals, the important points at issue. If these topics are treated at all in their writings, it is in passing and peripherally in relation to arguments that they view as being much more significant in terms of their practical and theoretical importance.

In the first place, it must be recognized that the Convention was *not* debating the very point the radicals had insisted upon as a condition of their participation in the revolution: Charles II's contribution to "a long train of abuses" which that event was intended to remedy. The actions of James, and of him alone, provided the focus of their discussion. Even here, however, the first interpretive foreclosure in that discussion was a noticeably important one. From the radicals' standpoint, James was "the worst of traitors," and "an enemy of the people." He was engaged in "a despotical tyranny" against the Constitution, and therefore he, and not those who oppose him, "is the traitor and rebel."[144] In his *A Brief Justification of the Prince of Orange's Descent into England*, written as the title indicates as a summary defense of the radicals' perception of the revolution, Ferguson refers to the "force and fraud" by which James has deprived the nation of its liberties, and according to this general indictment, he has degenerated into a tyrant. Since "the first and highest treason is that which is committed against the Constitution," Ferguson has no reluctance in affirming that James is both a "traitor" and a "rebel."[145] More

---

ory of government, which he merges with a "divine providence" justification for the Glorious Revolution. Not only are these theories distinct, before and after the revolution, and endowed with different political meanings, but Straka incorporates into his providential framework some theorists who are contractarians, thus further obfuscating the nature of the political debate in 1689 ("The Final Phase of Divine Right Theory in England, 1688–1702," *English Historical Review* [October 1962], pp. 638–658).

[144] Ferguson, *Representation*, pp. 30, 53. Edward Stephens, *Important Questions of State, Law, Justice and Prudence*, 1689, p. 9.

[145] Robert Ferguson, *A Brief Justification of the Prince of Orange's Descent into England*, 1689, pp. 9–10; idem, *Representation*, pp. 38, 51. This is also the position taken by the author of *The Letter Which Was Sent to the Author of the Doctrine of Passive Obedience and Jure Divino Disproved Answered*, 1689, p. 11. For the evidence and argument that the author of this radical tract was also the author of the plagiarized Lockean pamphlet, *Political Aphorisms*, see Richard Ashcraft and M. M. Goldsmith, "Locke, Revolution Principles, and the Formation of Whig Ideology," *Historical Journal* 26, no. 4 (1983):773–800.

examples could be cited demonstrating the radicals' propensity to employ this language in their justificatory writings defending the Glorious Revolution, but since we have previously considered the distinctive importance of this language to the radicals' political theory, I will not burden the reader with further quotations. Suffice it to say that the violent terminology the radicals devised and employed against Charles II and James II at the time of Monmouth's Rebellion was retained and used by them in 1689. Considering their insistence upon the continuity of the resistance movement viewed as a whole, discussed above, this is hardly surprising.

According to the notes taken during the Convention debates by various participants, this language did make a brief appearance in the course of that debate, but it quickly receded into the background and was, officially at least, wholly laid aside. One member observed that "he is a tyrant who acts against his own laws . . . [or] in breach of his oath" to the people.[146] This point was taken up and elaborated by Sir Robert Howard, who not only repeated the citation from Bracton relating to the difference between a king and a tyrant, but wanted that term specifically applied by the Convention to James II. He therefore "moves some stronger words to be inserted in the question" before them.[147] Except for one further instance (cited below), this language characterizing James II as a "tyrant," "rebel," or "traitor," or proposing to indict him for "treason" against the Constitution, so far as I can determine, disappeared from the Convention debates. This may not seem surprising, especially if such terms are viewed merely as excessive rhetoric used by the radicals. Yet, there is no doubt that the latter actually believed James to be a traitor, and the Convention's failure to characterize him in those terms demonstrates that the overwhelming majority of its members did not share that belief.[148]

The "stronger words" Howard wanted inserted into the motion maintained that "James II having endeavored to subvert the constitution, by breaking the original contract," had left them free to determine the form of government and James' successor.[149] After much debate, these words were included in the resolution as it was finally passed by the Convention, and it might be argued that since "subverting" and "overthrowing" the Constitution incorporated the essential meaning of the radicals' allegations against James, the absence of a "rebel-traitor" terminology should

[146] These are the notes made by John Somers, printed in *Miscellaneous State Papers, 1501–1726*, ed. Philip Yorke, 2 vols., 1778, 2:402; Grey, 9:9.

[147] *Miscellaneous State Papers*, 2:402–403.

[148] As one radical writer put it, "There is a vast difference between a king . . . that falls into some error . . . and a tyrant who overturns the laws of the state" (Pierre Allix, *Reflections upon the Opinions of Some Modern Divines Concerning the Nature of Government in General, and That of England in Particular*, 1689, p. 35 [*LL* #1297]).

[149] *Miscellaneous State Papers*, 2:402–403.

not be made too much of. But it must be remembered, as John Hampden reminded those at the conference to reconcile the wording of the two motions passed by the Lords and Commons, it is true that the debate is "only about a few words, but the Commons think they are words so significant" and relate to such "weighty matters" that they cannot easily be laid aside.[150] In this case, there was an essential theoretical point underlying these "few words." To assert that James was guilty of "breaking the original contract between king and people," was important to the radicals, but it was not enough. It had to be insisted, as they did in their pamphlets, that by violating the fundamental laws of the kingdom, he "forfeited" his right to be king.

Now something close to this claim was raised in the debate. George Treby maintained that "when the fundamental laws themselves are invaded . . . these are violations which shake off the king."[151] At least one other speaker's remarks on James' violation of the Constitution also seem to imply that he has forfeited his right to be king, but it is hard to tell from the notes. John Howe, however, stated the point unequivocally, and in doing so, made it very clear what from the radical viewpoint the theoretical issue was. James' tyranny, Howe argued, had put an end to his authority as king even before his departure from England. In other words, he had "forfeited the Crown" through his tyrannical actions prior to William's arrival.[152] It is this point—that James had "forfeited" his right to be king "before the Prince of Orange landed"—that the radicals insisted upon and that the Convention refused to accept.[153] Rather, from their standpoint, the issue could not be stated so sharply. Speaking for the Tories, Finch advised his colleagues to stick to the narrow fact that James "is not king," and that the throne must be "filled with the next successor." Others were willing to incorporate the king's subversion of the Constitution as a "part of the question."[154] What they were not willing to do was to adopt the radicals' position that James' forfeiture of his trust was plainly, and by itself, a sufficient ground for the revolution. When Finch put the question to the Convention as to whether the meaning of its res-

[150] Add. MS 5710, fol. 6. This is another journal of the Convention debates kept by one of those in attendence.

[151] *Miscellaneous State Papers*, 2:409.

[152] Lois G. Schwoerer, "A Jornall of the Convention at Westminister begun the 22 of January 1688/9," *Bulletin of the Institute of Historical Research* 49, no. 120 (November 1976):250–251. "It is evident, that James II has forfeited all his rights to the crown, even before his desertion" (Allix, *Reflections upon Opinions*, p. 98).

[153] *Letter to the Author*, p. 24. In Edward Stephens' view, James' departure was merely "the flight of a criminal from justice" (*Authority Abused by the Vindication of the Last Year's Transactions*, 1690, p. 8).

[154] *Miscellaneous State Papers*, 2:405–406.

olution asserting James' "abdication" was tied to his maladministration of the government or to his fleeing the country, many of his colleagues shouted, "Both."[155] If by raising the question, Finch hoped to split the opposition to James into two theoretically distinct camps, he manifestly failed. For the majority of the Convention, it was neither necessary nor helpful to clarify the confusion on this issue. We can put this another way by recognizing that *their* controversy centered upon the question as to whether James had "deserted" or "abdicated" the throne by leaving England. The first term, as Somers pointed out, merely signified that the king had withdrawn from the kingdom and might, if he chose, return again, whereas "abdication" signified that, by breaking the contract, James "thereby renounced to be a king according to the Constitution."[156] The first word, therefore, dealt with the "fact" that James was not now king, while the second pertained to his "maladministration." Not surprisingly, the final wording of the resolution as adopted by the Convention represented a compromise, reflecting both positions:

> King James the Second, having endeavored to subvert the Constitution of the kingdom by breaking the original contract between king and people; and . . . having violated the fundamental laws, and withdrawn himself out of the kingdom, hath abdicated the government, and that the throne is thereby vacant.[157]

As some contemporaries observed, it was rather difficult to extract from this syntax precisely what causal reasoning was being employed as a means of justifying the Convention's actions. But, I am arguing, that was exactly the point: to avoid the radical implications of the "forfeiture" argument. For even the Whig commitment to "abdication" presupposed James' departure from the country as a vital aspect of that term's meaning. The Tories attempted to score a point against their opponents by suggesting that if the king's "departure" was not "voluntary," then it necessarily implied that it was the force of William's invading army that had driven James out of the kingdom. Hence, he could not truly be said to have "abdicated" the crown, for in their view the word necessarily implied a voluntary action. In reply, one Convention member summarily brushed aside this objection, declaring that, "as for his departure out of the kingdom, [it] is not material whether it was voluntary or involun-

155 Schwoerer, "A Jornall," p. 260.

156 White Kennett, *A Complete History of England*, 2d ed., 3 vols., 1719, 3:546. The extended and rather tedious debate concerning the meaning of these two words can be found in Cobbett, 5:61–107.

157 Kennett, *History*, 3:542–544; Dalrymple, vol. 2, pt. 1, bk. 5, p. 272.

tary."[158] But, from the radical perspective, the proper response was that *whether James left England at all* was "not material" to the point at issue. Referring specifically to the "wretched inventions" of words and "hypocrisy" displayed in the resolution passed by the Convention Parliament, one radical criticized the use of "desertion and abdication, instead of plain English forfeiture, which the Scotch parliament honestly called forefaulting."[159]

A second issue, closely connected to the "forfeiture" aspect of the radical argument, represented a specification of the circumstances that followed from such a "forfeiture" of authority by the king: that all political power was returned into the hands of the people, who were then free to employ that power in reconstructing their political institutions howsoever they saw fit. Now this notion is *not* identical with a bland and generally stated commitment to a contract theory of government in some form, although interpreters and historians have frequently confused the two propositions.[160] Contemporaries, however, were more careful in choosing their terms. Put simply, many of them—most Whigs and some Tories—were willing to accept consent of the people as the basis for political authority, and even perhaps the existence of some definite "contract" that could be invoked in a quasi-legal sense as a restraint upon the actions of the king. What they drew back from accepting—with expressions of horror at the idea—was the fact that by the assertion that power was returned into the hands of the people, the radicals really and literally meant *the people*. In order to appreciate what was at stake in this controversy, it is necessary to pay some attention to several secondary disputes. The first concerned the status of the Convention itself, in relation on the one hand to a normal Parliament, and on the other to the people of England at large. And the second relates to a specific use of certain concepts borrowed from Hobbes' political theory with the intention of undermining the reasonableness of the radicals' claim that political power has been placed in the hands of the people. We shall begin, as before, with the formulation of the issues by members of the Convention.

To the general assertion that government is founded in an original con-

[158] Add. MS 5710, fols. 26–27.

[159] Samuel Johnson, cited in J. P. Kenyon, *Revolution Principles: The Politics of Party, 1689–1720*, Cambridge: Cambridge University Press, 1977, p. 39. The Scottish Parliament's resolution is discussed by Wodrow, *Sufferings of the Church*, 4:482–484.

[160] See the general discussion of contract theory as representative of some homogenous Whig position in J. R. Western, *Monarchy and Revolution: The English State in the 1680s*, London: Blandford Press, 1972, pp. 308–322; George L. Cherry, "The Role of the Convention Parliament (1688–89) in Parliamentary Supremacy," *Journal of the History of Ideas* (June 1956), pp. 393–396.

tract, Clarendon replied that this contractual language "hath not long been used or known in any of our law books or public records."[161] Despite Clarendon's objection, a resolution incorporating the notion of a contract was passed by the Lords. That, presumably, should have terminated the debate, on that particular issue at least. However, I shall argue, what it actually did was to expose to clearer view the latent problems attached to a commitment to a contractual position—so much so, in fact, that the very concept of a "contract" quietly disappeared during the course of the debates.[162] We are somewhat nearer to the point when it is recognized that contractual theory existed in several different forms at the end of the seventeenth century. These competing interpretations could have, and were given, different political implications.[163] The most radical version asserted, as the Levellers had, that political society was formed through an agreement of the people, though what precise socioeconomic characteristics qualified one to be included among "the people" was not always clearly stated.

With this in mind, we can begin to appreciate the fact that it is not so much the idea that there is an "original contract between king and people," which is startling in its implications—as several Tories remarked, this only means that monarchy is elective rather than hereditary—as it is Sir Robert Howard's assertion that power has "devolved on the people." What, his colleagues wanted to know, did he mean by that? Howard evidently identified the Convention with the people, at least in the particular argument he was making. "We are the people," he insisted at one point, "and we must form ourselves" into a government to replace the one that has "dissolved."[164] And, another participant asked, in the case of the dissolution of government due to the departure of the king, "who then should have [political power], but the Lords and Commons"?[165] But the

[161] Add. MS 5710, fol. 18.

[162] H. T. Dickinson, "The Eighteenth-Century Debate on the 'Glorious Revolution,' " *History* 61, no. 201 (February 1976):32. This drift was certainly evident in Burnet's writings. In "the most radical piece he ever produced"—namely, the *Enquiry into the Measures of Submission*, 1688, which was written on the eve of the revolution—Burnet defends armed resistance in terms of natural rights, state of nature, and the formation of government through a contract. In the midst of the meeting of the Convention Parliament, Burnet "published by Authority" another tract, *Enquiry into the Present State of Affairs*, 1688, in which none of these concepts appears and which as a whole is much more conservative (Mark Goldie, "The Revolution of 1689 and the Structure of Political Argument;" *Bulletin of Research in the Humanities* 83 [Winter 1980]:473–564; cf. ibid., pp. 510–511).

[163] See on this point, Harro Hopfl and Martyn P. Thompson, "The History of Contract as a Motif in Political Thought," *American Historical Review* 84, no.4 (October 1979):919–944.

[164] *Miscellaneous State Papers*, 2:402, 411; Grey, 9:20.

[165] Add. MS 5710, fol. 66.

Tories ridiculed the notion that any implication could be drawn from contract theory that political power returned into the hands of the people at large, *and* they attacked with equal vigor the proposition that any Parliament or Convention could be simply identified with "the people." "We are not the people collectively nor representatively," Sir Robert Sawyer told his colleagues. Rather, "copyholders, leaseholders, etc., are the people."[166] Clearly, Finch pleaded, you do not want to say that "the constitution is dissolved" and that therefore power is "devolved upon the people." "No wise man" and very few of those present, he maintained, were really prepared to accept the consequences that followed from that proposition.[167] Any serious claim advanced on behalf of the proposition necessarily meant one of two things: either that since "we are not elected by those who have no share in the government by the constitution of it," the franchise ought to be sufficiently extended to include those "people" in a "share in the government," so that we might more plausibly represent ourselves as speaking for "the people" of the nation at large; or, when "the whole Constitution is dissolved," it must follow that "every man has equal right and equal power."[168] But, if that is the case, the Tories argued, then "Lords only represent their own vote as individuals, and ought not to meet as an estate."[169] "*If* we were in the state of nature," Finch observed, "we should have little title to any of our estates."[170] There were, in other words, social and political consequences attached to the radical version of contractual language that effectively undermined the claims for authority exercised by propertied individuals and members of Parliament.

It is important to recognize that, despite the polemical uses to which it was being put in the Convention debate, this was no mere Tory point. The Whigs fully appreciated the resonance of the arguments. It is true that the latter represent a revival of the critique made by the Tories on the claims advanced by the exclusion Whigs, but their opponents who listened to the Convention debates were not so radical as Shaftesbury's fol-

[166] *Miscellaneous State Papers*, 2:403; Grey, 9:21–22.

[167] *Miscellaneous State Papers*, 2:405.

[168] H. Horowitz, "Parliament and the Glorious Revolution," *Bulletin of the Institute of Historical Research* 47, no. 115 (May 1974):51. In reply to Finch's charge, George Treby argued that "we represent . . . those that *deserve* a share in the government" (Grey, 9:13; italics added). This, in my opinion, is a statement of the official Whig viewpoint, which immediately and sharply distanced itself from the radical, populist rhetoric with which Finch was attempting to associate the Convention Whigs.

[169] *Miscellaneous State Papers*, 2:403. This is the implication drawn by Sawyer from Howard's remarks: If power is in the hands of "the people," then what are *we* doing here? (Grey, 9:21).

[170] Grey, 9:18; italics added.

lowers had been, nor were they the direct product of three recent national elections. Moreover, it will be recalled that even at the height of their radical political activity in 1682, many Whigs had disassociated themselves from the "tradesmen" and "rabble" who might be loosely identified as "the people." The tendency to make such a disavowal had grown even stronger among the Whigs as they were constituted in 1689. As recent scholarship has demonstrated, the Glorious Revolution Settlement was a conservative one, reflecting the fact that "the governing classes were reluctant to accept the full-blown Whig case in favor of the contract theory and the right of subjects forcibly to resist their sovereign."[171]

If we turn to the political debate as it existed outside the Convention, the radicals' appeal to the people was directly stated and elaborated upon at length. When the government is dissolved, one radical author declared, all political power returns to the people, and they "may establish whatever form of government they choose."[172] Thus, "the people," another pamphleteer added, "may erect a new [government], either according to the old model, if they like it so well, or any other that they like or approve of better."[173] "Let us remember the state we are in," the author of *Good Advice Before it be Too Late* advised his readers, "a state that puts the supreme power in the hands of the people, to place it as they will and . . . as they see fit for the public utility."[174] Now, when the Levellers employed this argument and language in their tracts in the late 1640s, it was easy to believe that by "the people" they meant the shoemakers, weavers, carpenters, and tradesmen in the army and in London who comprised the overwhelming majority of their supporters. Indeed, as Richard Overton argued, the army was the only truly representative institution capable of governing the country. Hence, "an appeal to the people" was certainly

[171] Dickinson, "Debate on Glorious Revolution," pp. 29, 32. The view that the government was dissolved and that the constituent power of government was returned to the hands of the people was rejected by all of Locke's contempories, except the radicals, precisely because of the association of these ideas with "radical democracy" (Julian Franklin, *John Locke and the Theory of Sovereignty*, Cambridge: Cambridge University Press, 1978, pp. x, 102ff.; see the works cited in note 205 below).

[172] *A Letter to a Friend, Advising in This Extraordinary Juncture, How to Free the Nation from Slavery*, 1689, pp. 14–15; *A Word to the Wise for Settling the Government*, 1689, p. 1; William Denton, *Jus Regiminis: Being a Justification of Defensive Arms in General*, 1689, pp. 21, 88.

[173] [N.T.], *Some Remarks upon Government, and Particularly upon the Establishment of the English Monarchy, relating to this Present Juncture*, 1689, printed in *State Tracts*, 1:162.

[174] John Humfrey, *Good Advice Before it be Too Late*, 1689, p. 24. Power has reverted to the people, who may settle the government however they wish (*Four Questions Debated*, 1689, pp. 5–6; Denton, *Jus Regiminis*, pp. 20–21).

meant to include the lower classes *and* to endow them with a corporative political existence, in relation to which all specific legislative or executive institutions (such as Parliament) were allowed only secondary claims to political power. Theoretically, therefore, these radical intimations were attached to the use of this language, at least by tradition, when it reappeared in 1689.

Whether particular authors, or the radicals viewed as a group, positively intended their words to be interpreted in this way is not so easily determined—in part, because the obviously identifiable audience receptive to such an interpretation (the army) is not part of the political scene in 1689.[175] Nevertheless, I believe there are good reasons for supposing that these radical implications are constitutive of the meaning of their political theory. First, as was demonstrated in Chapter 7, the radical position reemerged in the 1680s in the context of a political movement dominated in its composition by the same socioeconomic groups who had provided the audience for the Levellers. The language, therefore, retained its radical resonance in the 1681–1683 period (and in 1685), and no author could pretend to appeal to that language several years later without being aware that this particular meaning and these social groups would be linked with it. Second, it is reasonable to suppose that some pamphleteers in 1689 were consciously and personally identified with the Levellers. The obvious example of course is Wildman, who was a Leveller and was simply reaffirming what he had said forty years earlier. But there must have been others.[176] Third, the radicals' opponents read them as if they meant to affirm a Leveller position. Naturally, this is not an invariably reliable criterion, but, in the give-and-take of debate, it is usually possible to find a disavowal of some *generally* mistaken interpretation, as for example, the Levellers' repeated rejection of an imputed intent on their part to level all property. The radicals in 1689, however, unlike the Whigs, did not disassociate themselves from the imputation attached to their language suggesting that "the people" were "copyholders" or artisans, that the franchise should be extended, or that the people at large were a corpora-

[175] That there was such an audience, however, has been demonstrated by Goldie ("True Whiggism"). Weston and Greenberg are mistaken in asserting that the radical viewpoint "found no substantial outlet in 1689" (Corinne Comstock Weston and Janelle Renfrow Greenberg, *Subjects and Sovereigns: The Grand Controversy over Legal Sovereignty in Stuart England*, Cambridge: Cambridge University Press, 1981, p. 219). Apart from Locke, the works of Samuel Johnson, Ferguson, and the author of *Political Aphorisms* went through multiple editions during 1688–1690.

[176] I do not mean, of course, that anyone was likely to identify himself as a Leveller. Given the difficulties of demonstrating who, in 1689, read and were influenced by Leveller tracts, the most one can say is that, as in the case of John Humfrey, there was a "Leveller tone" to his writings.

tive body. Finally, later radicals who consciously sought to identify their position with the radicals of 1689 specifically interpreted their ideas from this standpoint.

In *A Brief Justification,* Ferguson links the assertion that the people have "reserved privileges, liberties, and rights" that precede and need not be specifically incorporated into a constitution, remaining as a reservoir in the hands of the people, with an insistence upon "the birthright of every Englishman" to lay claim to these rights regardless of whether they have been "acknowledged" or "distinctly expressed" in particular documents or statutes.[177] Both the argument and the specific phraseology were repeatedly used by Lilburne and other Levellers in their tracts. When Wildman writes in one of his pamphlets of the "customs and privileges" of "the freemen of the cities and towns" of England, and the fact that government is "founded on equal freedom . . . [that is, on] every subject's free consent . . . to be given personally" to the laws enacted "by his deputies" in Parliament, I can see no reason for believing that his views have substantially changed since he presented them at the Putney debates, or in *London's Liberties,* a tract that was reprinted in 1682.[178] Is it surprising, then, that the author of *Reflections upon Our Late and Present Proceedings in England* should, first, link together several radical tracts whose titles he cites, and second, taking their common argument that power has returned to the people, maintain that "if we should appeal to the sense of the people in general," then the logical implication of this proposition is that they "must be allowed to have a right of suffrage."[179] I believe Lacey is correct when, referring to the tracts by John Humfrey, he speaks of "a Leveller coloration to his thinking."[180] There were, in other words, echoes—and in the 1690s, we are not entitled to call them more than that—of the Levellers' language in the radicals' defense of the Glorious Revolution.

Later, in one of the most radical pamphlets he ever wrote, Daniel Defoe specifically addressed himself this question in the context of the principles upon which "the late revolution was made."[181] He repeats the various crimes committed by James II, as well as the general allegation of "tyr-

[177] Ferguson, *Brief Justification,* pp. 3–8, 13; cf. idem, *Representation,* p. 24.

[178] John Wildman, *A Memorial from the English Protestants to Their Highnesses . . . the Prince and Princess of Orange,* 1688, in *A Collection of State Tracts,* 1705, 3 vols., 1:1.

[179] *Reflections upon Our Late and Present Proceedings in England,* 1689, p. 5.

[180] Lacey, p. 227.

[181] Daniel Defoe, *The Original Power of the Collective Body of the People of England Examined and Asserted,* 1701; 3d ed., n.d., p. 6. These principles are distinctly Lockean and radical, but in addition, Defoe views the actions of the revolution and Convention as having taken place in a situation in which all political power had, in fact, reverted into the hands of the people (pp. v–vii, 9).

anny and oppression'' as justificatory reasons for that revolution. But the primary point Defoe wishes to make is that there is always a reservoir of political power in the people, as a distinct collective body, and that if for any reason government is dissolved, ''the people have the right to place the trust of government where they see fit.'' To the questions, Who are ''the people''? and How can they act together? Defoe cites the Glorious Revolution as an instance in which ''the people assembled in an universal mob to take the right of government upon themselves.'' This does not mean that they have to give ''their personal suffrages'' to every single issue, but it also clearly does not mean that the people are to be identified with Parliament or representative government in general. In fact, Defoe is unequivocal in defining ''the people'' as ''the freeholders'' of the country. ''When therefore I am speaking of the right of the people,'' he explains, ''I would be understood of the freeholders.'' Naturally, I am not attempting, ex post facto, to saddle all the 1689 radicals with the burden of Defoe's identification of the people with freeholders. Rather, the point is that the claim that power ''devolved on the people'' clearly seemed to imply, both for its defenders and its critics, that *some* collective entity—''freemen,'' ''freeholders,'' ''copyholders,'' or all Englishmen entitled to claim their ''birthright''—exercised a distinctive political power at a level below that embodied in a corporative institution such as Parliament.[182] Other radicals also defended the 1689 revolution as the outcome of the dissolution of government, a return to the state of nature, and political power reverting into the hands of the people.[183]

One reason the radicals did not have to be more specific in their concrete identification of ''the people'' is that they accepted, unanimously, so far as I can tell, the legitimacy of the Convention as a proper institutional representation of the nation. In this sense, Howard was not mistaken in his identification of the members of the Convention with the people. Nevertheless, judging by what the radicals *expected* that body to do in relation to the issues it actually debated, one can perceive a difference in the meaning of this association. Comparing a convention with a Parliament, one radical explained that the former was not only a more representative institution than the latter, but also, it stood in a ''higher capac-

[182] Defoe, *Original Power*, pp. 15–17. ''The people of England . . . were a people before there was such a thing as a Constitution'' (p. 8).

[183] *The Revolution Vindicated* in *State Tracts*, 1705, 3:695–697. This is the first appearance of this pamphlet, although a note explains that the manuscript was written some years before. I do not accept Kenyon's ascription of this work to Burnet (*Revolution Principles*, pp. 210, 219); nothing he wrote after 1688 uses language so radical as is employed in this tract. Moreover, even in his most radical period, Burnet did not believe that political power reverted to ''the people'' in the state of nature.

ity" because it was able to speak for "the community," an entity that, according to the author, can be identified with the people as they exist in a state of nature.[184] In other words, it was precisely because political power had returned into the hands of the people that the Convention could claim "the supreme power" to act for their interests.[185] Ferguson wrote in similar terms of the Convention as "the great Council and . . . representative of the nation" existing in a state of nature, such as he believed the condition of England to be in 1688.[186] For this reason, he maintained, members of the Lords or Commons "cannot sit in the nature of a formal Parliament," until after the constitutional issues have been resolved by the Convention. Nor could one of the houses of Parliament claim a veto over the actions of the other; rather, both the nature of the Convention and the practical exigencies attendant upon the revolution (and existence in a state of nature) required that these representatives of the people produce some kind of national consensus.[187] This view was endorsed by the radical author of *A Letter to a Friend*, who referred to the gathering as "a national convention made up of the representatives of the community." The latter, in order to be "truly national," he explained, "must be larger than a House of Commons ordinarily is," as indeed the Convention was.[188]

The extreme opposition to this viewpoint characterized the Convention as merely a collection of individuals holding "private and unauthorized opinions."[189] Its members, however, including Tories, could hardly afford to go that far, although various individuals were not reluctant to raise self-critical questions in the Convention debates regarding the source of authority for their actions. Nevertheless, whatever particular members said, the fact is that Convention members acted, in the last analysis, *as if they were members of Parliament*. They tended to ignore the "higher capacity" that the radicals attributed to them, though naturally they could

[184] Humfrey, *Good Advice*, p. 23.

[185] *Four Questions Debated*, p. 9.

[186] Ferguson, *Brief Justification*, p. 32. The "exercise of absolute power . . . dissolves the government, and brings us all into a state of nature, by discharging us from the ties . . . we formerly lay under" (idem, *Representation*, p. 31).

[187] Ferguson, *Brief Justification*, p. 33.

[188] *Letter to a Friend*, p. 15.

[189] Jeremy Collier, *The Desertion Discussed*, 1689, in *State Tracts*, 1:110. No member of the Convention went quite this far, though the Tories insisted that this would be the logical conclusion of any argument that maintained that England in 1688 existed in a state of nature. Edward Seymour, however, in denying that the Convention was a legal Parliament, characterized his colleagues as a "council" of individuals called to give "advice" to the king (Grey, 9:94–96).

not ignore the peculiar circumstances under which they were meeting as a legislative body. To the author of *Some Remarks upon Government*, however, "this great Convention" offered the opportunity to "rebuild" the English political system, or to make "very considerable" alterations in its structure.[190] This pamphlet provides an extremely interesting neo-Harringtonian analysis of the government, leading to the conclusion that the "factious interests and dissensions" that have arisen during the last two centuries are rooted in a constant struggle between property and power. The author contends that this struggle cannot be resolved if the government is "rebuilt upon its old foundations," although he is realistic enough to admit that the traditional form of a "mixed monarchy" is the most likely outcome of the Convention's action.[191] The point is not that he, or a few others, held out hopes for a Commonwealth to emerge from the Convention. Quite apart from this general objective, there are all kinds of "constitutional" grievances and propositions—changes in the suffrage, adoption of the secret ballot, abolition of a standing army, creation of an independent judiciary, and so on—which he expected the Convention at least to discuss before it relinquished its authority into the hands of a "normal Parliament."[192] One might well believe that king, Lords, and Commons represented the happiest constitutional arrangement in the world and still expect that the Convention would not shirk its "higher" responsibilities to the "community" by not taking advantage of the situation to examine the possibilities of making some modifications in the English Constitution. The radicals, I am arguing, did entertain such an expectation, one that, judging from the Convention debates, was not shared by its participants. The progressive dissatisfaction on the part of the radicals with the course the revolution was taking in 1689 is, in part, traceable to their growing consciousness that a unique opportunity for making constitutional revisions had presented itself to the nation, and that the pettiness and triviality of the debates conducted by members of the Convention had allowed this opportunity to slip away without so much as even being noticed by them.

It may seem paradoxical that the radicals could accept the Convention and not show any concern for the fact that it had not actually been elected

[190] *Some Remarks*, pp. 151, 158. The people, Edward Stephens declared, have a "natural and original right" to make "real alterations in the laws, and in the very constitution of the government from what they were before" (*Important Questions*, p. 7).

[191] *Some Remarks*, pp. 157–158; cf. ibid., p. 151. Someone was seized, however, at the end of January 1689 for distributing to members of the Convention a tract advocating a Commonwealth (Morrice, 2:449).

[192] *Some Remarks*, pp. 158–162; cf. Humfrey's recommendations in *Good Advice*, pp. 24–26.

by the people—though neither had the Levellers' army. But what they wanted to defend was the proposition that the "community" retained a reservoir of political power in its hands that could be represented by some nationally constituted entity that was not dependent upon the normal mode of political operations. This view, as Defoe explicitly states at length in his pamphlet, provides the people with a legitimization of political power that they can use as leverage against *any* existing political institution. That was what the radicals sought to defend, and it explains why they attached such creative expectations to the Convention. But if the latter was specifically distinctive in relation to a Parliament, what was the Convention's relationship to the people?

As has been mentioned, the Convention functioned, according to the radicals, within the context of a state of nature. The people, Ferguson declared, have been "restored . . . to their state and condition of primitive freedom."[193] That England in 1688 had been returned to a state of nature was a fundamental premise of the radicals' argument. The author of *Reflections upon Our Late and Present Proceedings* was not wrong in noting that those who put forward "new models" of government in their writings invariably begin with the assumption that we are in "a state of nature wherein the people are at liberty to agree upon any government, or none at all."[194] Yet, as was noted earlier, the concept of the state of nature was not the exclusive property of radicals. As one of the Convention members observed, "it is not we that have brought ourselves into this state of nature"; rather, the king's actions have created this "state of confusion" that the Convention is attempting to resolve.[195] Still another view was expressed by the author of *The Thoughts of a Private Person . . .* who recognized that England had been returned to a state of nature in which individuals now had to look to a defense of their rights as private persons. Together, these individuals constitute "a multitude, but no body corporate."[196]

Tories, however, both within and outside the Convention, were quick to fasten upon the radical implications of this argument, with which they attempted to drive their Whig opponents toward the well-marked shelter of moderation. The particular instrument at their disposal was, as it had

[193] Ferguson, *Brief Justification*, p. 9.

[194] *Reflections upon Proceedings*, p. 4; cf. *Letter to a Friend*, p. 14; *Some Remarks*, pp. 152, 162; Matthew Tindal, *An Essay Concerning Obedience to the Supreme Powers, and the Duty of Subjects in All Revolutions*, 1694, pp. 36–40 (*LL* #2926); Denton, *Jus Regiminis*, pp. 21ff.

[195] Add. MS 5710, fol. 31.

[196] *The Thoughts of a Private Person about the Justice of the Gentlemen's Undertaking at York*, 1689, p. 11.

been in 1682, the Hobbesian identification of the "state of nature" with a "state of war," coupled with the social terror of "the rabble" levelling the property of the wealthy as the particularization of Hobbes' concept. Another Convention member's characterization of England existing in a state of nature must be rejected, Rochester declared, because if it were accepted, the nation would be "in a perpetual state of war."[197] Another speaker warned that "we must not leave ourselves to the rabble," a point with which several of his colleagues registered their agreement.[198] As John Bramston recorded in his *Autobiography*, the primary objective was "to avoid confusion . . . to prevent anarchy, and the rabble from spoiling and robbing the noble and wealthy."[199] The radicals, of course, hardly viewed the people or the state of nature from this perspective. To them, the people were sober, reasonable individuals capable of acting for the public good. They were willing to admit that a certain amount of "confusion" or even crimes were endemic features of a state of nature; what they plainly rejected, however, as the Levellers before them had done, was the equation of their interpretation of the situation with a Hobbesian war of all against all, or a rabble determined to attack existing property relations. Against this imputation, Ferguson confidently appealed to "the rational and ingenious part of mankind" who not only existed in a state of nature, but who would prove to be the means of saving England from the "ignorant and mercenary men" who had encouraged James' efforts to establish a tyranny.[200]

It is not quite accurate to say, as Kenyon does, that "the close association of Hobbes with contract was in itself sufficient to damn the idea in most men's minds."[201] Rather, what is true is that insofar as that identification *could* be made, it was certainly damning so far as the radicals were concerned. But the meanings of concepts such as "the state of nature" or "contract" were embedded in a political struggle and were, as contemporaries recognized, associated with particular socioeconomic groups. The fact that this or that author had given prominence to a specific notion did not, in itself, determine the outcome of this struggle. It is important, therefore, as was argued in Chapter 7, to recognize that Hobbes' theory

[197] Add. MS 5710, fol. 31.

[198] Alan Simpson, "Notes of a Noble Lord, 22 January to 12 February 1688/9," *English Historical Review* 52, no. 205 (January 1937):95.

[199] John Bramston, *Autobiography*, 1845, p. 355.

[200] Ferguson, *Brief Justification*, p. 21. What the radicals' opponents emphasized, one writer remarked, was "the disorderly state of nature," and they did so, he explained, in order to justify a "blind and absolute subjection" to the magistrate (*Revolution Vindicated*, p. 695).

[201] Kenyon, *Revolution Principles*, pp. 16–17.

in particular was, throughout the last half of the seventeenth century, a very useful weapon to be employed *against* the radicals, and that his theory was virtually *never* employed by them as a means of justifying or achieving *their* theoretical goals. One reason the radicals so frequently dragged Hooker into the debate on their side is that he endorsed the rational character of mankind, the origins of political society in the consent of the people, and a state of nature as a prepolitical condition of individuals.[202] These were centrally important propositions within the radicals' armory, advanced by an eminently respectable Anglican churchman, who could not anachronistically be browbeaten with the charge of Hobbism. Hooker, of course, was not the exclusive refuge of respectability of the radicals; he was frequently cited as a "judicious" authority on behalf of more moderate, but non-Hobbesian versions of contract theory.

By the same token, the use of Hobbesian language to fend off radicalism was not a practice uniquely identified with Toryism. Burnet, for example, preached several sermons in 1689 extolling the fact that the nation had been saved by William from "a state of liberty, without any restraint, that leaves all men to a full freedom of acting as they please." Such a condition Burnet equated with "a constant state of war," a "miserable" situation in which individuals are exposed to "the wildness of ungoverned multitudes . . . the madness of lawless men." One cannot help feeling that Burnet has here multiplied his image of Major Wildman a thousandfold. Certainly, the latter must have been included among Burnet's "discontented" and "few ambitious . . . restless spirits," who were not wholly satisfied with the outcome of the revolution.[203] In another sermon, Burnet gave public thanks for the fact that "we are not exposed to the fury of a levelling multitude, nor the confusions of an equality among men," where our "estates and liberties" would be "at the mercy of [the] mere humor and passion" of capricious individuals.[204] To Burnet and to the Tories, in short, the identification of a Hobbesian state of war with a state of nature and "levelling multitudes" effectively placed a roadblock

[202] Morrice reflected that Hooker, "who went far beyond Baxter in placing the original of power in the populacy," had not been burned at Oxford in 1683 (Morrice, 2:80). George Treby cited Hooker in Convention debates to establish that government began from the consent of the people (Add. MS 5710, fol. 23; cf. Pierre Allix, *An Examination of the Scruples of Those Who Refuse to Take the Oath of Allegiance*, 1689, p. 21 [*LL* #62]; Denton, *Jus Regiminis*, p. 23). By the time William Atwood wrote *The Fundamental Constitution of the English Government*, 1690, he could say that so "many have cited the judicious Hooker till it is threadbare" to use him to prove that government is founded in the consent of the people (p. 4 [*LL* #147]; I have used a 1973 reprint of this tract published by Scholarly Resources, Wilmington, Del.).

[203] Burnet, *Sermon at the Coronation*, pp. 9–12.

[204] Gilbert Burnet, *An Exhortation to Peace and Unity*, 1689, p. 7.

in the path of the radicals' claims for liberty or political power. And, more generally, what these Whigs and Tories were responding to was any attempt by those on the left wing of the revolution to direct that event toward more populist or radical channels.

All of the scholars who have surveyed the political literature of 1689–1690 in the last twenty years agree that there was a small but important minority of radical Whig writers, including Locke, whose works expressed a viewpoint that was disavowed by the vast majority of Whigs and Tories who formulated a pragmatically based, if theoretically confused, defense of the established government.[205] Most recently, the author of the most extensive bibliographical discussion of the political writings of this period finds dramatic confirmation of the dominance of this moderate perspective in those writings, and he, too, locates the *Two Treatises* at the far left of the political spectrum as part of a very small and select group of radical tracts.[206] The mainstream of the 1689–1690 debate concerning the meaning of the Glorious Revolution focused upon preserving the hereditary succession of the monarchy, justifying a de facto allegiance to the king (William) in possession of authority, relating obedience of the subject to protection provided by the sovereign, citing historical precedents for the displacement of one monarch by another, justifying the rights of a conqueror to authority, emphasizing the voluntary abdication of James II, and allusions to the providential and exceptional character of the bloodless transference of power that obviously expressed some fulfillment of God's intentions for England. I cannot, for reasons of space, reconstruct the dimensions of that political debate, as was attempted for the exclusion crisis period in Chapters 5 through 7, but even if this were done, it is clear from this summary of the range of arguments advanced in those political tracts that not one of them is of any importance to Locke or to his justification of the Glorious Revolution as presented in the *Second Treatise*. Indeed, as Goldie remarks, "not only did Locke avoid the conventional whiggish device of combining contract with possession, abdication, and conquest, he specifically repudiated these doctrines."[207]

In other words, I believe the evidence demonstrates unequivocally that, within the context of the 1689–1690 debate both within the Convention

[205] Franklin, *Locke and Sovereignty*; Kenyon, *Revolution Principles*; Western, *Monarchy and Revolution*; H. T. Dickinson, *Liberty and Property: Political Ideology in Eighteenth-Century Britain*, London: Methuen, 1979; idem, "Debate on Glorious Revolution"; Martyn P. Thompson, "The Reception of Locke's *Two Treatises of Government*, 1690–1705," *Political Studies* 24, no. 2 (June 1976):184–191; J. H. Plumb, *The Origins of Stability, 1675–1725*, Boston: Houghton Mifflin, 1967.

[206] Goldie, "Revolution of 1689," pp. 479–480.

[207] Goldie, "Revolution of 1689," p. 518.

Parliament and outside of it, Locke's *Two Treatises* expresses a distinctive radical perspective, and that it does so in language that contemporaries clearly perceived to have those qualities. To illustrate this point, I will make use of one particular detailed commentary on the basic characteristics of the radical postion, and then turn to Locke's argument in order to show how he reproduces precisely these distinctive positions in the *Second Treatise*. Finally, I will try to show how Locke's contemporaries recognized this associative relationship between the *Two Treatises* and the radical political perspective as it existed in 1689–1690.

Of the many tracts published in the wake of the Glorious Revolution, there is an extremely impressive though little-known response to the radicals' position, a brief examination of which can usefully serve as a summary of the points I have been making, as well as provide a transition to the introduction of Locke's *Two Treatises* into the discussion.[208] What makes this pamphlet impressive is the fact that it is a careful, point-by-point consideration of the major themes of the radicals' political theory, "a very popular one, and therefore in great reputation with too many amongst us."[209] Not only is the work cogently written, but the author is faithful in reproducing the radicals' arguments and does not try for cheap victories by misrepresenting them. The theory he is attacking is one grounded upon the proposition that there is a "Fundamental Contract" according to which, if the king transgresses the limitations of his authority, the latter "is forfeitable and revocable."[210] In this situation, individuals are returned to "a state of mere nature," and political power reverts to the community, which is authorized to protect its reservoir of "rights, immunities and privileges as unalienable properties," with armed resistance if necessary.[211]

"By a community," he writes, "these men understand not a society of men, actually consenting and formed into a public government, but only a society of families . . . voluntarily, rationally, and justly assembling and associating themselves from mutual benevolence in order to the common good and safety."[212] This argument implies that since "all men being equal by nature, every man is born free," and "all authority and power is radically and originally in every single person." Government is

[208] Lewes Sharp, *The Church of England Doctrine of Non-Resistance Justified and Vindicated*, 1691. This tract is not mentioned in Goldie's bibliography of the political debate on the Glorious Revolution.

[209] Sharp, *Church*, p. 33.

[210] Sharp, *Church*, epistle dedicatory; pp. 4, 37.

[211] Sharp, *Church*, pp. 33, 36. Sharp argues that all "rights" are in fact acts of grace or condescensions on the part of the Sovereign.

[212] Sharp, *Church*, p. 37.

established through the "mutual consent" given by these individuals.[213] In attacking this theory, the author relies upon a watered-down version of Filmer's patriarchalism, which is only casually and not very convincingly introduced into the discussion at certain points.[214] His primary object, however, is not to present and defend his own view of government, but to undermine the popular appeal of the radical perspective. He therefore marshals those objections against radicalism which he feels are most effective and are generally convincing to his contemporary readers. And it is this clearly delineated strategy that is of most interest to us as a commentary on the political debate surrounding the Glorious Revolution.

The radicals' conception of the state of nature, he argues, is simply a "hopeful condition," a mere "Platonical idea" that they have projected onto mankind. It cannot be accepted, he suggests, because if we accept the radicals' contention that political power has devolved into the hands of the people, this can only mean, in practice, that "the major part" of the community will decide the issues. But, "the major part of every community being ordinarily the worser part," it would be foolish to assign such political power to "the multitude."[215] In his view, if a state of nature were to be taken literally, it could only be "a state of war" in which every individual stands as an "enemy" to every other individual, "and then no man hath anything he can call his own."[216] Thus, "the dissolution of the government" would lead necessarily "to the destruction of the whole community."[217]

The author is straightforwardly clear about identifying this Hobbesian condition with the fact that it would mean that people would "leave their proper rank and station" and attempt to "go up higher and take the place of our betters." To endorse the arguments for equality advanced by the radicals is to subvert "the moral order of things," and to allow individuals "to break out of their ranks" in the effort to redistribute political and social power.[218] He denies that individuals are "free-born," or that there is a "moral power" or "natural right" attached to the multitude, because such a viewpoint destroys the assumption that "the relative duties of su-

[213] Sharp, *Church*, pp. 32, 35.

[214] Sharp argues that "no man ever was or can be so free-born" as the radicals claim because we are born into the dependency of families, and government represents the outgrowth of a natural tendency inherent in paternal dominion. At the same time, he endorses Filmer's claim that Adam was given both political and economical power "by divine prescription." Following the Flood, however, the genealogy of this prescriptive power could not be so easily traced, and on God's allowance, various forms of government came into existence (Sharp, *Church*, pp. 33–34).

[215] Sharp, *Church*, pp. 37, 39.

[216] Sharp, *Church*, pp. 5, 60.

[217] Sharp, *Church*, p. 40.

[218] Sharp, *Church*, p. 10; cf. ibid., p. 2.

periors and inferiors" has its "foundation in Nature." Instead, the radicals' theory imagines that these relationships derive only from "contracts and agreements," and on that basis, it might well be argued that "every nation, city, town, [or] parish" is free to "choose what government seems best to them."[219] Clearly, from his standpoint, if the radicals' arguments were to "make a deep impression on men's minds," the status of the existing social and political order would be in serious trouble.

In light of the kinds of arguments the radicals were making in 1689, their intentions in making them, and their readers' and critics' understanding of those arguments, let us turn to a consideration of Locke's *Two Treatises of Government* as a contribution to this political debate. His specific condemnation of James II's actions, already discussed, appears in the final chapter of the *Second Treatise*, "Of the Dissolution of Government." Those actions are cited as examples of the kind of maladministration on the part of the executive that brings about the dissolution of government. That Locke believes the government of England in 1688–1689 has been "dissolved" is quite clear. In a paragraph obviously added to the text in 1689, Locke argues that when the executive "neglects and abandons" his responsibility, "this is demonstratively to reduce all to anarchy, and so effectually to dissolve the government . . . and the people become a confused multitude, without order or connection."[220] In short, the people are returned to the state of nature.

> In these and the like cases, when the government is dissolved, the people are at liberty to provide for themselves, by erecting a new Legislative, differing from the other, by the change of persons, or form, or both as they shall find it most for their safety and good. For the society can never, by the fault of another, lose the native and original right it has to preserve itself, which can only be done by a settled Legislative, and a fair and impartial execution of the laws made by it.[221]

Some commentators have denied that Locke means to equate these conditions of the dissolution of government with the state of nature, but this is a mistake.[222] For it is precisely the existence of a Legislative and the

[219] Sharp, *Church*, pp. 36–37, 39.

[220] *ST*, par. 219.

[221] *ST*, par. 220; cf. ibid., par. 185.

[222] See for example, Franklin, *Locke and Sovereignty*, p. 107; Martin Seliger, *The Liberal Politics of John Locke*, London: George Allen and Unwin, 1968, pp. 105ff.; John Dunn, *The Political Thought of John Locke*, Cambridge: Cambridge University Press, 1969, p. 181. Despite the fact that he recognizes that Locke "often seems to talk as if the dissolution of government brings about a state of nature," Laslett concludes that the dissolution of government "does not itself bring back the state of nature," and that Locke is confused about what he means to say (pp. 114–115).

"fair and impartial execution of the laws" that describes the difference between life in civil society and life in the state of nature.[223] As Locke explains in his chapter, "Of Political or Civil Society,"

> Wherever therefore any number of men are so united into one society, as to quit every one his executive power of the Law of Nature, and . . . he authorizes . . . the Legislative . . . to make laws for him as the public good of the society shall require . . . this puts men out of a state of nature into that of a commonwealth, by setting up a judge on earth, with authority to determine all the controversies, and redress the injuries, that may happen to any member of the commonwealth; which judge is the Legislative, or magistrates appointed by it. And wherever there are any number of men, *however associated*, that have no such decisive power to appeal to, there they are still in the state of nature.[224]

This point is repeated several times throughout the *Second Treatise*.[225] Thus, Locke observes, an individual "can never be again in the liberty of the state of nature, unless by any calamity, the government he was under comes to be dissolved."[226] Certainly Englishmen in 1689, whatever their political views, would have recognized the applicability of this proposition to their situation.

If, however, the government is dissolved, and men are returned to the state of nature, what becomes of the political power that formerly existed? For, as Locke observes, one must "distinguish between the dissolution of the society, and the dissolution of the government," as many of the radicals' critics, employing Hobbesian notions, did not.[227] Society,

[223] *ST*, par. 220; cf. ibid., pars. 22, 87, 89, 91, 94, 131, 136, 137. Tindal, who not only read the *Two Treatises* closely but incorporated many plagiarized passages from Locke into his own work, observed that it is by referring "their differences to a standing impartial judge" that people remove themselves from the state of nature (*Essay Concerning Obedience*, p. 52; cf. ibid., p. 2). Whenever "the legislative is altered" the government is dissolved, and the people are returned to the state of nature because, although they exist as a "community," the establishment of a form of government "by the consent and appointment of the people" is, for Locke, a definite action. Hence, until the people "constitute to themselves a new Legislative," through which "the members of a commonwealth are united, and combined together into one coherent living body," they have not removed themselves from the state of nature (*ST*, par. 212). It is precisely because Locke is *not* engaged in constructing a formal logical theory, but addressing himself to the commission of a specific political act, that he can view England in 1688 as existing in a state of nature, as his radical associates did.

[224] *ST*, par. 89 (italics added).

[225] *ST*, pars. 87, 90, 94.

[226] *ST*, par. 121.

[227] *ST*, par. 211.

that is, continues to exist after the dissolution of government even in the state of nature. This is because political power returns to "the Community," which is the creation of the original social contract among individuals. Thus "the power that every individual gave the society, when he entered into it, can never revert to the individuals again, so long as the society lasts, but will always remain in the Community." Political power and "the Legislative can never revert to the people, whilst that government lasts," because once specific political institutions with lawmaking authority are established, the people "have given up their political power . . . and cannot resume it." But, Locke argues, "when by the miscarriages of those in authority, it is forfeited," then, through "the forfeiture of their rulers," political power "reverts to the society, and the people have a right to act as supreme, and continue the legislative in themselves, or erect a new form, or under the old form place it in new hands, as they think good."[228] The argument he is making presumes, therefore, that the dissolution of government returns men to the state of nature, but not as separate individuals; rather, the people, acting as "the community" retain a corporative political power.

> And thus the Community may be said in this respect to be always the supreme power, but not as considered under any form of government, because this power of the people can never take place till the government be dissolved.[229]

In other words, Locke's assessment of the Glorious Revolution and the condition of England in 1689 exactly expresses the radicals' position.

To rephrase the point as an interrogatory, we might ask, Given what was being said by the radicals in 1689, how would Locke's contemporaries have interpreted the meaning of these statements? Following a brief attempt to answer this question through an exploration of the text of the *Second Treatise*, as a further illustration of this argument, I will discuss a few examples of the actual reactions evoked by the appearance of the *Two Treatises*. Finally, in the postscript that follows this chapter, I will conclude with an examination of the little evidence available to us that sheds some light on Locke's intentions in publishing his major work on political theory.

If Locke is addressing himself to an audience whose members are, or recently were, in a state of nature, what are the characteristics of that audience, and to what degree would they be likely to find it an acceptable description of themselves? The commonly accepted answer is that Locke

[228] *ST*, par. 243.
[229] *ST*, par. 149.

was obviously addressing himself to the aristocracy, the propertied classes. Indeed, even when there is no supporting evidence to offer on behalf of this interpretation, it has been steadfastly maintained, and all alternative readings of the *Two Treatises* have been summarily dismissed.[230] This is not surprising when we take into account two other assumptions that provide the context for this interpretation. First, the Glorious Revolution itself "was almost entirely a movement of the aristocracy," or at least the propertied classes.[231] And second, the *Two Treatises* provided the more or less officially accepted justification for this revolution.[232] Thus, as a triad, there is a symmetrical and reinforcing quality to these propositions. The last proposition, however, is manifestly untrue. The *Two Treatises* was not accepted as official Whig doctrine; on the contrary, "the radical implications of Locke's political theory" were attacked and rejected.[233] But if, as recent historical scholarship has demonstrated, the traditional argument breaks down, we are left without any clear understanding of *why* this "movement of the aristocracy" found Lockean political theory unacceptable. This point is especially difficult to explain if we retain the first assumption: that Locke is addressing his argument primarily to the landed class. Was he so ignorant of their political predilections as to misjudge what kinds of arguments would have an appeal to them? Or were they, as his readers, so obtuse as not to perceive that beneath all the populist rhetoric, Locke was really a source of great assurance of political stability and aristocratic conservatism? It is time, I suggest, to take the language of the *Two Treatises* seriously, and to recognize in so doing that the work was primarily addressed not to the aristocracy and the landed class, but rather to the urban merchants, tradesmen, artisans, and independent small gentry who constituted the social

[230] John Dunn, *Political Obligation in Its Historical Context*, Cambridge: Cambridge University Press, 1980, pp. 60–61; Christopher Hill, *The Century of Revolution, 1603–1714*, New York: W. W. Norton, 1966, p. 298; Dickinson, *Liberty and Property*, p. 78.

[231] Harold Laski, *Political Thought in England from Locke to Bentham*, London: Oxford University Press, 1920, p. 24; Western, *Monarchy and Revolution*, p. 1; Plumb, *Origins of Stability*, pp. 30, 69, 140, 152, 187.

[232] Sabine speaks of "a crass form of class government" whose justification was supplied by Locke's political theory (George Sabine, *A History of Political Theory*, 3d ed., New York: Holt, Rinehart and Winston, 1961, p. 517. For Leslie Stephen, Locke's political theory represented "the formal apology of Whiggism," a view echoed more recently by Gough in his assertion that "Whig opinion welcomed [Locke's] work as a philosophical exposition and justification of the principles by which they were proud to have been guided" in making the Glorious Revolution (Leslie Stephen, *History of English Thought in the Eighteenth Century*, 2 vols., New York: Harcourt, Brace and World, 1962, 2:114; John W. Gough, *The Social Contract*, 2d ed., Oxford: Clarendon Press, 1957, p. 135; cf. G. N. Clark, *The Later Stuarts*, Oxford: Clarendon Press, 1940, pp. 78, 141–142).

[233] Dickinson, *Liberty and Property*, p. 71.

foundations for any radical political theory—including Locke's—in seventeenth-century England.

The *Two Treatises of Government* reflects the language of Shaftesbury and the Rye House Plot and of Monmouth's Rebellion, and not the language of the Whig and Tory magnates who managed the Glorious Revolution. The individuals most deeply involved in marshaling the social, economic, and political forces necessary to settle the crown on William and Mary were, with a few exceptions, the very men who had prosecuted the Rye House conspirators and who led the army and militia against Monmouth's troops. It is hardly surprising that they preferred not to be reminded of the events and ideas associated with the radicals' activities in the 1680s.[234] It is from this standpoint, I shall argue, that we can understand the reception given to the *Two Treatises*, and the gulf that stands between the arguments of that work and the posture adopted by the defenders of William III's government and by those who tried to create an official Whig ideology in the 1690s.

In the *Second Treatise*, Locke argues that individuals in the state of nature are "all equal and independent" and no one has more "power and jurisdiction" than any other, there being no "subordination or subjection" among them. They are independent, he insists, because they exist without "depending upon the will of any other man."[235] Not only is the language of Locke's general description of man's natural condition reminiscent of that employed in the Leveller tracts, but the last statement cited is the specific criterion upon which the Levellers relied for their determination as to who was or was not eligible to exercise his natural rights through the suffrage. When later Locke takes up the discussion of various social relations among individuals, he allows that various sorts of factors—age, merit, birth—may place some men "above the common level," but all this, he argues, is perfectly consistent with the principle of equality "in respect of jurisdiction or dominion one over another." This is so because "every man" has an "equal right . . . to his natural freedom," which consists in his not being subjected to the will or authority of any other man.[236]

In a direct answer to Filmer's contention that men are "born under the dominion of another," Locke reinstates the Levellers' claims that "all

[234] J. P. Kenyon, "The Revolution of 1688: Resistance and Contract," in *Historical Perspectives: Studies in English Thought and Society in Honor of J. H. Plumb*, ed. Neil McKendrick, London: Europa Publications, 1974, p. 58; Peter Earle, *Monmouth's Rebels*, London: Weidenfeld and Nicolson, 1977, pp. 190–193; Kenyon, *Revolution Principles*, pp. 2, 62.

[235] *ST*, par. 4.

[236] *ST*, par. 54.

men . . . born are free."[237] This confrontation occurs at the end of a discussion of the historical development of various kinds of social relations in the state of nature in which families, tribes, and cities are mentioned.[238] Moreover, in terms of these social relations, Locke is willing to make a number of concessions to patriarchalism.[239] On the point cited above, however, the discussion is specifically about the form of government, and here, if being under the "dominion of another" were permitted to be a general category descriptive of the political condition of individuals, then no "lawful" government would be possible.[240] Later, in the context of considering whether a "government can have a right to obedience from a people who have not freely consented to it," Locke maintains that until the people "are put in a full state of liberty to choose their government and governors," by giving "their free consent," with the status of "being all free-men," it cannot claim such a right.[241] He then reiterates what he takes to be the political status of these "freemen," reminding the reader that, "their persons are free by a native right, and their properties, *be they more or less,* are their own, and at their own dispose" and not under the "dominion" of anyone else.[242] The conclusion being, I am arguing—as did the Levellers—that individuals retain their "free-born" status so long as they do not lose it through particular social or historical developments, and the *amount* of property they possess is not, by itself, a sufficient criterion as to whether they have retained their status as freemen, though of course it is a very important factor affecting this determination.

We can say, therefore, as Locke does, that only an individual's consent can place him under a political authority, but it is also true that, for Locke, an individual retains his status as a freeman so long as he does not make himself dependent "upon the will of any other man," *whatever the spe-*

237 *ST*, pars. 113, 119.

238 *ST*, pars. 101–112.

239 *ST*, pars. 105–107, 110, 112.

240 It is precisely because the criteria for political dependency and social dependency are *not* identical, I am arguing, that the former cannot simply be deduced from the latter in such a way as to make political freedom merely a dependent consequence of social class relationships, as most commentators on Locke would have it. Indeed, it is the failure to appreciate the radicals' willingness to break with this medieval assumption and their substitution of reason for property that accounts for the historical neglect of certain radical tendencies within the tradition of liberal political thought as they manifested themselves in the seventeenth century. Yet Marx perceived that it was this disjuncture between social and political power that was theoretically distinctive of liberalism as a social theory and that, practically speaking, lay at the heart of the problematic attitude adopted by liberals toward the actions of the state.

241 *ST*, par. 192.

242 *ST*, par. 194 (italics added).

cific social relations that arise in the course of time. For as paragraph 28 and other passages in the *Second Treatise* make clear, "servants" dependent upon the will of another man may certainly be envisioned as a category included within the social relations of the state of nature.[243] In other words, "civil society" and "the state of nature" are for Locke correlative terms defined with respect to "jurisdiction or dominion" in a strictly *political* sense. Either existential condition is compatible with various kinds of social relations. It is true, of course, as was argued in chapters 5 and 6, that the historical development of these social relations may affect or determine which individuals retain their "native rights" as "free-born" men through their ability to act as "equal and independent" persons, but insofar as they do retain this status, there is nothing in the *Second Treatise* that justifies the action of someone else in taking from them this natural right as a claim for political power.

When the question was put to the Levellers by their opponents as to what their claim to political power was based upon, if not a certain amount of property or a "fixed share" in the kingdom, they replied that this political power was a "native right" grounded in the reason that all men were presumed to possess. When Locke raises the issue of what determines whether an individual is a "free," "equal," "independent" person under the law, natural or civil, he gives the same reply. It is his "reason and ability to govern himself" that he is presumed to have that supplies the standard. This means that his understanding is able "to direct his will," and his status as "a freeman" under "the law of England," resides in the fact that he has "the liberty to dispose of his actions and possessions according to his own will."

It might be asked, How, in more concrete terms, can it be determined when an individual has arrived at such a stage where he is presumed to be rational in a distinctly political sense? To this question, Locke supplies two answers, neither of which could have been too comforting to his propertied readers. The first is a natural criterion of age and is independent of particular political institutions. That is, when a person arrives at the "age of discretion" (taken by Locke as being twenty-one), "then he is a freeman," politically speaking, whether he exists under an already established government or in the state of nature. This, Locke makes clear, is only a presumptive criterion of "reason" and political rights; the real test is whether he retains the liberty to act "according to his own will" or is dependent upon the will of another.[244] The second concretization of this claim for political rights is one established by commonwealths them-

[243] *ST*, par. 28.
[244] *ST*, par. 59; cf. ibid., pars. 54, 61.

selves: the requirement that individuals subscribe to "oaths of fealty, or allegiance" or make some other "public owning of" their acceptance of its legitimacy. For no government would make such a requirement or derive much security from its existence unless it presumed that individuals subscribing to such oaths were able "to act like free men"—rational, independent persons directing their own wills.[245] Considering how far down into seventeenth-century English society this practice reached, including not only all the higher military and civil officers, but also the lowest levels of civil servants and magistrates, schoolteachers, members of corporations, livery companies, and so forth, this criterion for the political status of a freeman certainly included members of socioeconomic groups below the statutory requirement of a forty-shilling freehold.[246]

When Locke turns to a consideration of "the beginning of political societies," he summarizes all the above criteria constitutive of a freeman, and postulates that this political power is exercised "to make one Community," which is to say "one body," to act for them, "wherein the majority have right to act and conclude the rest."[247] The majority of whom? The majority of the "freemen" who constituted the community—the consent of "every man" capable of exercising political power. For if the majority cannot act for the whole, political society would be "immediately dissolved" and individuals would be returned to the state of nature. It is interesting that Locke states that individuals can constitute a political society in which "any number greater than the majority" can act for the whole, but not one in which the number is less than "the majority of the Community."

> And thus that which begins and actually constitutes any political society, is nothing but the consent of any number of freemen capable of a majority to unite and incorporate into such a society.[248]

It is worth pausing at this point to remind ourselves that every one of these Lockean assumptions was subjected to violent criticism in 1689 by contemporaries who had no hesitation in associating them with claims to a "natural right of the multitude," a suffrage based upon "the majority,"

[245] *ST*, par. 62.

[246] For a general discussion of the role of oaths in seventeenth-century English society, see the chapter, "From Oaths to Interest," in *Society and Puritanism in Pre-Revolutionary England*, by Christopher Hill, 2d ed., New York: Schocken Books, 1967, pp. 382–419. In the early months of 1689, Parliament was debating a bill requiring all clergy, governors, professors, college fellows, and schoolmasters to take an oath of allegiance to the government (Grey, 9:216–217). Locke's library shows that he bought more than a dozen tracts in 1689 discussing the oath-of-allegiance controversy.

[247] *ST*, pars. 95–97.

[248] *ST*, par. 99.

or the "levelling" rabble. And conversely, no one except the radicals in 1689 was making such arguments. And even most of their tracts were not so unequivocally committed to this radical language as was the *Second Treatise*.

I am not suggesting that Locke's text is, in itself, unequivocally clear as to who qualifies for membership in his political society with respect to the socioeconomic status of these individuals. Indeed, as I noted earlier, there were sound political reasons for maintaining an ambiguous posture on this and several related issues. What this means, however, is that in a situation in which various interpretations of the text are possible, it is legitimate to ask, What kind of evidence can be presented relating to the author's intentions or the nature of the audience to whom his remarks are directed that might increase the plausibility of one interpretation relative to the others? And in that context, I am arguing that there are serious deficiencies with respect to the standard assumption that Locke intended to direct his argument chiefly toward those substantial property holders who also constitute the members of his political society as defined in the *Second Treatise*. No such conservative audience can be shown to exist in 1689 who derived *that* meaning from their reading of the text; no conservative authors, directing their arguments toward the audience of large property owners, can be shown to exist who were advancing the same arguments Locke puts forward in his work; nor, given Locke's political activities, associates, and objectives in the 1680s, does such a reading of the text make sense in terms of his intentions as a political actor. In all these respects, however, it can be shown that there is a historical context for the radical interpretation of the text, and I believe, therefore, that at least a prima facie case must be conceded for the plausibility of reading the arguments of the *Second Treatise* from this standpoint.

Since political power in 1688 had reverted into the hands of the community, the notion that the fate of the country, dependent upon the decision to erect whatever form of government they desired, rested with "the majority of the community," not only would have, but as we have seen, *did* terrify people. It is not difficult to see why this was so. When Locke describes how "the majority having . . . the whole power of the community naturally in them, may employ all that power in making laws for the community from time to time, and executing those laws by officers of their own appointing," he calls this form of government "a perfect democracy." Now, I am not suggesting that Locke is advocating a democratic commonwealth. Rather, there are two points worth noting about this statement that commentators have ignored. The first is that without some very explicit restrictions to the contrary, all men, upon entering into political society, are assumed by Locke to be able to exercise their natural right of suffrage "in making laws for the Community." Of course, various practices concerning the right to vote, as we saw in Chapter 4, were in force in seventeenth-century England, but the "common right" to the suffrage, both as a principle of adjudicating controversies employed by Parliament, and as a claim contained in the Levellers' political writings, placed the burden of proof upon those seeking to restrict this "natural right" of freemen. In beginning with democracy as the first and broadest "form of government," Locke is employing the same reasoning with respect to the exercise of political power.

The second point, which rests upon all that has been said about the first, is that, in 1688–1689, *political power has reverted back to the community, and therefore, into the hands of the majority.* All those restrictions placed upon the exercise of the suffrage which are purely consequent upon the specific characteristics of a specific form of government have now "lapsed," along with the government itself. Obviously, and simply as a matter of logic, such restrictions as are tied to the form of government cannot retain their validity when the form of government itself has dissolved, as it had through the actions of James II and the occurrence of the revolution. No wonder that, according to the radicals' reasoning, proposals were made for rewriting the Constitution that involved a restructuring of the suffrage, or that they looked to some "national" representative of "the community" with a more extensive base of political power than that attributable to a normal House of Commons. That Locke applies the reasoning in this paragraph to the situation in 1689 seems evident from his reaffirmation of the argument that political power has reverted to the people, and "when it is so reverted, the Community may dispose of it again anew into what hands they please, and so constitute a new form of government."[249] That this new form of government included the possibility of "a perfect democracy" as an outcome (though a very unlikely one) of the Convention was, in itself, a frightening prospect for Englishmen to contemplate. Leaving this extreme aside, however, it certainly followed, again as a logical implication from Locke's reasoning, that any "compounded and mixed form" of government might emerge from the exercise of constitutional power by "the majority of the community." Even if the latter were not so unwise as to keep this power in their hands (as a democracy), the very fact that they *had* it was the realistic point in controversy, and the precept that marked off the radicals from all other political positions current in 1689.

I have offered a radical reading of the text of the *Second Treatise* as, I believe I have shown, the radicals themselves formulated their argument

[249] *ST*, par. 132.

and their critics perceived it in 1689. Even if it were granted for the moment that this was not the way Locke intended that his argument should be read, there is no doubt that, given what his contemporaries were saying, his audience had more than a plausible ground for reading the *Second Treatise* from this perspective. To strengthen this point further, and to separate it, methodologically speaking, from the way in which eighteenth- or nineteenth-century readers interpreted the work, over which Locke had no control, it must be noted that Locke did not exist in a state of innocence with respect to his knowledge of the kinds of arguments being made or how they were being interpreted by his contemporaries, as his pamphlet buying and his interest in the activities of the Convention Parliament demonstrate.[250] As an author, therefore, he must be assumed to have a certain amount of responsibility for employing a language and particular arguments that have been generally identified with a specific political viewpoint, positively and negatively, by the audience to whom his own work is addressed.

Having established a plausible context in terms of which Locke's readers could have read the *Two Treatises*, let us ask, Is this the way in which, in fact, they *did* read that work? If Locke's book had provoked numerous replies or widespread comment in 1689–1690, it might be easier (though not necessarily) to answer this question. As several scholars have noted, however, this was not the case. Relatively speaking, the *Two Treatises of Government* did not attract a significant amount of attention, and explicit references to it by other authors are few, though the total is slightly larger than has been generally assumed.[251] Since these references have been discussed elsewhere, I do not propose a general review of them here; rather, I shall look at one of these references from a Whig, another from a radical, and, indirectly, a third from a Tory, in order to determine from their remarks the degree to which the perception of Locke's argument as an expression of the radical political perspective is the consensual bedrock of their responses, positive and negative, to his work.

William Atwood was a Whig lawyer who had involved himself in the Brady-Petyt debate over legal history during the exclusion crisis. He may

[250] Locke became a regular subscriber to Mr. Fox's newsletters in 1689 (MS f.10, fol. 20). He bought several acts of Parliament, including the Toleration Act (MS f.34, fols. 21–22; *LL* #11). As a period in which Locke purchased political pamphlets, 1689–1690 represents a peak surpassed only by 1680–1682. In addition to numerous individual titles, Locke also bought the collection issued as *State Tracts* in 1689 (*LL* #2759; MS b.2, fols. 115–116; MS f.16, passim).

[251] In addition to the works cited in note 254 below, see Jeffrey M. Nelson, "Unlocking Locke's Legacy: A Comment," *Political Studies* 26, no. 1 (1978):101–108; Dickinson, *Liberty and Property*, pp. 57–90; Franklin, *Locke and Sovereignty*, pp. 87–126.

have known Locke personally from that period since he was very close to their mutual friend, James Tyrrell. Following the Glorious Revolution, Atwood wrote several tracts defending that event and William's claim to the throne, the most famous of which was *The Fundamental Constitution of the English Government*. It is in this work that Atwood refers several times to the *Two Treatises of Government*. Indeed, he calls the latter the best work on "civil polity" in English.[252] Atwood, then, is generally positive in his attitude toward Locke's book. The primary reason for this response appears to be the fact that they share a common enemy in Filmer, and as was noted earlier, Whig political theory, whether framed from a historical-legalistic standpoint or as a natural rights/natural law position, was united in its opposition to Filmer and divine right in any of its several guises. Atwood praises the author of the *Two Treatises* for his demolition—assisted by the work of his "learned friend," Tyrrell's *Patriarcha non Monarcha*—of the Filmerian theory.[253] On this ground, Whigs of all persuasions could agree. Nevertheless, Atwood has an important criticism to make of Locke's argument.

Interpreters and historians who have referred to Atwood's comments on Locke have argued that the difficulty of linking the *Two Treatises of Government* with orthodox Whig political thought in 1689 (as represented by Atwood) arose from the fact that Locke was "too philosophical" in his treatment of politics. This specific interpretation of Atwood's response to Locke is then generalized as a characterization of the contemporaneous reaction to the *Two Treatises*, and in this form, the argument has become a shibboleth in the secondary literature on Locke. His ideas, it is alleged, were too abstract, couched in the language of concepts such as the state of nature, natural law, and so on, to be appreciated by his contemporaries. Thus, as Kenyon puts it, Locke's "austerely unhistorical approach" to politics made his political theory "seem irrelevant to the problems of current politics."[254] This position is itself without historical foundation, and entirely too abstract in relation to the political debate as it actually existed in 1689. Kenyon and others are entitled to their own views as to whether the *Two Treatises* is "too philosophical" or politically "irrelevant," but as a presumptively historically grounded reading of Locke's contemporaries' reaction to the book, there is not the slightest shred of evidence in its favor. Not one of those who referred to Locke or his book said anything whatsoever about its being too philosophical or

[252] Atwood, *Fundamental Constitution*, p. 101.

[253] Atwood, *Fundamental Constitution*, p. 4.

[254] Kenyon, *Revolution Principles*, pp. 17–18. For the charge that Locke was "too philosophical," see Martyn P. Thompson, "Reception of Locke's *Two Treatises*," pp. 187–188; and idem, "Reception and Influence: A Reply to Nelson on Locke's *Two Treatises of Government*," *Political Studies* 28, no. 1 (March 1980):104.

politically irrelevant to the issues as a reason for either liking or disliking the work. Rather, as we shall see, Atwood's criticism is both more specific and more politically focused upon the events of 1689 than this canonical reading of Locke suggests.

Most of the *Fundamental Constitution* is a historical commentary on the relations between kings and Parliaments in the English past, but toward the end of the work, Atwood takes up a discussion of "our" recent Convention and its legal and political status. It is at this point that he criticizes some writers who "are too loose in their notions," because they "suppose the consequence of a dissolution of this contract to be a mere commonwealth, or absolute anarchy, wherein everybody has an equal share in the government." Atwood clearly has Locke in mind, for he cites the passage from the *Second Treatise* on the dissolution of government, with power returning into the hands of the people, as an illustration of his point. It is precisely this point he refuses to accept; that is, power does not return to "the people." Rather, he insists, it is "evident the government may still continue," even in the circumstances of James II's flight and the Glorious Revolution, to which this discussion is being applied. For in Atwood's view, the notion that the people could "new mold the government, or set up the like, as they thought fit," is exactly the kind of "anarchy and confusion" he wishes to prevent. To argue for this proposition, he maintains, is to bring "government back to its first principles sooner than our Constitution allows." In other words, the abdication of the king reverts political power no further than into the hands of Parliament; it certainly does not place that power in the hands of the people, nor has the government been "dissolved," nor can any new constitutional order be erected by the people, "as they think fit." These propositions are far too radical, politically speaking, for Atwood to accept. He affirms this point by citing from the radical tract, *A Letter to a Friend*, the very arguments quoted earlier, and repeated by Locke. These arguments, he notes, were employed to justify a view of the Convention as a "truly national" and "larger representative of the people" than a normal Parliament, and as a means of endorsing the people's right to make constitutional changes in the English government, a claim that is anathema to Atwood, but one that, as we have seen, Locke himself supported. There can be no doubt that Atwood's criticism of Locke is focused precisely upon the latter's willingness to endorse these "loose" and "anarchical" ideas of radical writers like the author of the tract he names, and that in his opinion, the ideas of both men are meant to apply to the political situation of 1688–1689.

But why does Atwood object so strenuously to this part of Locke's argument? When he refers to the "anarchy" of a dissolution of government, power reverting to the people, and the state of nature as a prepolitical condition, Atwood spells out the social implications of the argument very clearly. By insisting upon the "equality" of this condition, and the absence of "subordination or subjection" in the state of nature, this position endorses the claim that "not only landed men . . . but copyholders, servants," and "every individual plebian" would be entitled to have a "share" in the government.[255] Atwood echoes the warning of speakers in the Convention about not allowing "the rabble" to gain political power. Anarchy, to him, means that political power "escheats to every man within the kingdom, freeman and servants" and that is a truly frightening proposition.[256] As Burnet, another Whig, articulated these fears, he thought the claim that the government was dissolved might be "carried so far, as to infer from it, that all men's properties, honors, rights, and franchises were dissolved."[257]

In order to defeat these implications, Atwood insists that any "state of nature," should it exist, must be identified with Hobbes' state of war.[258] In short, Atwood criticizes Locke for incorporating into the *Two Treatises* certain specific arguments that he explicitly identifies with the radicals, which he links to the political events of 1688–1689 and the Convention, and which he reads as a defense of the rights of "plebians" below the level of those "landed men" who constitute the membership of Parliament. Though a Whig, Atwood is not above using the Tories' tactic of citing Hobbes as a means of undermining the appeal of this political argument. This distinctly political reaction, and not some disaffection with philosophy, provides the ground for and significance of Atwood's criticism of the *Two Treatises of Government*.

The radical reference to that work is contained in a popular tract, *Political Aphorisms*, published in 1690. It is an unusual reference in that this pamphlet, in the space of thirty-one pages, manages to cite approximately

[255] Atwood, *Fundamental Constitution*, p. 100; appendix, p. 19.

[256] Atwood, *Fundamental Constitution*, p. 10; appendix, p. 14.

[257] Cited in Dickinson, *Liberty and Property*, p. 327. This was also the view of Tyrrell, whose Whig principles were consistently to the right of those of Locke. Later, Blackstone defended the actions of the Whig and Tory magnates at the time of the Glorious Revolution against "the wild extremes into which the visionary theories of some zealous republicans" would have led them had they accepted the view of the "total dissolution of the government, according to the principles of Mr. Locke which would have reduced the society almost to a state of nature." To Blackstone, as to Burnet, Atwood, and Tyrrell, that meant that "all distinctions of honor, rank, offices, and property" were "levelled," and "the people" were at liberty to erect "a new system of state" (Franklin, *Locke and Sovereignty*, pp. 110–112). Allowing for the polemical exaggeration of the levelling effect of Locke's political theory, nevertheless it is clear that these spokesmen for the offical Whig position did perceive a definite extremist tendency in that theory from which they wished to disassociate themselves.

[258] Atwood, *Fundamental Constitution*, pp. 100–101.

twenty-five sentences or paragraphs from the *Two Treatises*, all of them plagiarized in the sense that their origins are never identified or acknowledged. *Political Aphorisms* is a statement of the radical viewpoint, and the core of its argument is provided by these passages from Locke—his conception of the state of nature, the right to resistance, forfeiture of the trust, dissolution of the government, power reverting to the people, and many more points are incorporated into the author's argument. I have discussed the importance, composition, and history of this pamphlet at length elsewhere.[259] Suffice it to say here that the radical author of *Political Aphorisms* had no difficulty in perceiving the affinity between his position and that of Locke, and he, unlike Atwood, endorses the very arguments in the *Two Treatises* which the latter rejects, and, I am arguing, on the same grounds—their relation to his political perspective in 1689–1690.

The third, Tory, reference can be treated even more briefly because it is the same pamphlet, *The Church of England Doctrine of Non-Resistance Justified and Vindicated*, from which I cited earlier as part of the delineation of the contextual parameters of the political debate in 1689. It is an indirect reference to Locke because it is a reply to *Political Aphorisms*, the argument of which is literally taken from the *Two Treatises of Government*. I will not repeat the criticisms advanced by this Tory author against the radical arguments of these two works that, as we can now see, were quite clearly directed—especially since he proceeds carefully, point by point, in his critique—against the views expressed in Locke's *Two Treatises*. Across the political spectrum, therefore, from Tory to Whig to the radicals in 1689, that work was perceived as a radical political statement, clearly relevant and popular in the context of the political events of the Glorious Revolution. Whether this was a good or bad feature of the book depended upon the political perspective of the interpreter, but there is absolutely no ambiguity in the minds of Locke's readers as to *his* political position.

[259] Ashcraft and Goldsmith, "Formation of Whig Ideology." Tindal in his *Essay Concerning Obedience* also borrows from Locke's *Two Treatises* to support his radical position. A few of these citations specifically direct the reader to Locke's work, but a number of other passages are simply plagiarized or paraphrased.

POSTSCRIPT

WHAT happened to the *Two Treatises of Government* after it appeared in print, how its arguments were viewed through the eyes of Paine, Jefferson, Adam Smith, Rousseau, Bentham, and Marx, is another story. I have tried to explain how and why the work came to be written and what meaning its ideas had for Locke and for those associated with him in the political movement organized to defeat the forces of popery and tyranny. Yet, with the exception of the concluding section of the last chapter, all that has been said regarding the *Two Treatises* could be defended in relation to the process of *writing* that work, even if it had never been published. Nearly ten years elapsed between the time Locke began work on the *Two Treatises* and his delivery of the completed manuscript to the printer. Given that a number of Locke's other works went through a similar gestation period, and considering the special political circumstances of the 1680s that inhibited the publication of a work like the *Two Treatises*, the fact of this time lapse is not, in itself, especially problematic.

Still, the decision to publish a written work is a separately identifiable action, and we may well ask, Why did Locke make his manuscript available to the public? Strangely enough, this question has never been asked. It has always been assumed that Locke published the *Two Treatises* in order to justify the Glorious Revolution. When Peter Laslett challenged the previously accepted orthodoxy in order to place the writing of the work within the exclusion-crisis period, he left this part of the orthodoxy in place. Locke himself says in the preface that he hopes his "discourse concerning government" will prove "sufficient to establish the throne of our great restorer, our present King William; and to make good his title in the consent of the people . . . and to justify to the world, the people of England, whose love of their just and natural rights, with their resolution to preserve them, saved the nation when it was on the very brink of slavery and ruin."[1] It would appear, therefore, that the proposition is solidly confirmed by Locke's own words.

On further reflection, however, it must be evident that the claim that Locke wished to justify the Glorious Revolution, while it says something, does not say very much. For, except for the Jacobites (an active and vocal minority who rejected the revolution) *everybody* who published works

[1] *Two Treatises*, preface.

during this period did so in order to justify that event.[2] As a characterization of the appearance in print of the *Two Treatises*, this proposition, though true, is hardly discriminating in its application to that work in the context of the publication of hundreds of others. Is it possible to be more specific as to Locke's reasons for publishing the *Two Treatises*? I believe it is. Even Locke's decision to publish his work, I shall argue, was an act of solidarity on his part with the radical cause as it existed in 1689–1690. At a time when the radicals' interpretation of the significance of the Glorious Revolution was under direct attack from the Tories and was treated with complicitous silence by the Court Whigs, and at a moment when their disappointments and dashed expectations at the course the revolution was taking were mounting, the radicals launched an ideological counterattack. Suddenly, critical evaluations of the revolution from the left appeared in print. These were coupled with pamphlets asserting its justification in the most radical terms.[3] Locke's *Two Treatises of Government*, I am arguing, was in fact one of the opening shots fired in this defense of radicalism.

That the *Two Treatises* expressed a radical viewpoint, I think I have demonstrated in terms of both the text and the context, but in order to connect the radicals' ideological battle against other justifications offered on behalf of King William with Locke's intentions in publishing his work, we need to have a clearer view of his personal conception of the Glorious Revolution. Unfortunately, Locke's direct comments on that event are scarce. Nevertheless, from Locke's correspondence and an important manuscript that has only recently come to light, I think it is possible to reconstruct the basic dimensions of that conception. At the end of December 1688, Locke's friend, Dr. Charles Goodall, wrote to him of "the wonderful success" that God had given to the Prince of Orange in his undertaking "to deliver our miserable and distressed kingdoms from popery and slavery," a characterization of that event shared by Locke, as his friends knew very well. Goodall went on to report James II's flight, and the composition and assembly of members of the Convention. Goodall hoped his news "will encourage you to return to London as soon as you can settle your affairs in Holland."[4]

On January 31, 1689, Lady Mordaunt, who, it should be noted was active (independently of her husband, Lord Mordaunt) in the radical cause

[2] For a critical discussion of nearly two hundred post-Revolution pamphlets, see Mark Goldie, "The Revolution of 1689 and the Structure of Political Argument," *Bulletin of Research in the Humanities* 83 (Winter 1980):473–564.

[3] Mark Goldie, "The Roots of True Whiggism, 1688–94," *History of Political Thought* 1, no. 2 (June 1980):220–224. My indebtedness to this very important article is evident in the discussion below.

[4] *Correspondence*, 3:530–531.

as one of James Johnston's intelligence sources, wrote to Locke that King James' departure and the establishment of "this convention" have "given us . . . an occasion not of amending the government, but of melting it down and mak[ing] all new, which makes me wish you there to give them a right scheme of government, having been infected by that great man, Lord Shaftesbury."[5] Clearly, she had reason to believe that this "melting down" role assigned to the Convention was a viewpoint shared by Locke, as indeed it was. In a very important letter to Clarke on the eve of his departure from Holland, Locke wrote:

> Men very much wonder here to hear of Committees of Privileges, of Grievances, etc., as if this were a formal parliament and were not something of an other nature and had not business to do of greater moment and consequence. . . . People are astonished here to see them meddle with any small matters . . . for that now they have an opportunity offered to find remedies and set up a constitution that may be lasting for the security of civil rights and the liberty and property of all the subjects of the nation. These are thoughts worthy [of] such a convention as this, which if (as men suspect here) they think of themselves as a parliament and put themselves into the slow methods of proceeding usual therein, and think of mending some faults piecemeal or anything less than the great frame of the government, they will let slip an opportunity which cannot even from things within last long.[6]

That Locke believed the Convention to be a constitutional-remedying body offered a unique opportunity "to find remedies and set up a constitution" for England rather than "a formal parliament" whose limited and "piecemeal" approach to reform was unsatisfactory is abundantly clear from this letter. This view he shared with other radicals. John Humfrey, for example, in his *Good Advice Before it be Too Late*, written simultaneously with the date of Locke's letter, pleaded with the Convention to rewrite the Constitution, warning them that "if they do it not now, the ages to come will have occasion to blame them forever."[7]

The radicals were not committed to a Commonwealth, their opponents' accusations to the contrary notwithstanding, but they did think in "larger" and more "national" terms about the events of the revolution,

[5] *Correspondence*, 3:538. James Johnston wrote to Bentinck that both Lord and Lady Mordaunt were enthusiastic supporters of William's invasion, and Lady Mordaunt was included in his group of spies or informants (N. Japiske, ed., *Correspondentie Van Willem III en Van Hans Willem Bentinck*, 5 vols., The Hague: Martinus Nijhoff, 1929, 2:597–598).

[6] *Correspondence*, 3:545–546.

[7] John Humfrey, *Good Advice Before it be Too Late*, 1689, p. 25.

and they displayed a marked impatience with those whose minds were wholly preoccupied with meddling with small matters and who could not recognize that issues "of greater moment and consequence" were at stake in determining the outcome of the revolution. As Locke noted, if "the great frame of the government" (the Constitution itself) "has not been invaded" by James II's actions, then "men have done very ill to complain." But if it has, then it is the obligation of this Convention to see "where the frame has been put out of order" and repair the "original constitution." The constitutional role of the Convention, in other words, is directly tied to the radicals' assertion that James' invasion of the Constitution—and not William's landing in England—is the basis for his forfeiture of authority and the dissolution of the government. As we have seen, this represented a keystone of the radicals' political theory and their interpretation of the meaning of the Glorious Revolution. And it is precisely this assertion of James' forfeiture that, by the end of 1689, is under concerted attack in the sermons and pamphlets being published.

Following his return to England, Locke continued to complain with "indignation" of "the dilatory methods and slow proceedings" of the Convention, at a time when "the urgency of affairs" in "this crisis" demanded a firmer and swifter defense of "the Protestant and English interest" against its enemies, domestic and foreign. Indeed, so angry was Locke at this "delay" in the progress of the completion of the revolution that he regarded it as nothing less than a "criminal" action on the part of those responsible.[8] In April, he wrote to Clarke that the refusal of the House of Lords to consent to the Commons' bill requiring bishops to take an oath of allegiance to William and Mary had "put a stop" to "the settlement of the country," adding that, "I grow more and more sick of this world."[9] This is not, I suggest, a reflection of any suicidal inclinations on Locke's part; rather, he, like a growing number of others on the left, have become "sick" with the way events were unfolding, the individuals restored to power and prominence, the active propaganda efforts of the Anglican clergy, and in general, those tendencies which were undermining the force of the revolution and "the settlement of the country." Locke had, after all, written to Mordaunt a few weeks before that "I wish for no other happiness in this world but to see [the revolution] completed and shall never be sparing of my mite where it may contribute any way to it."[10] If Locke felt that his health would not permit him to accept an ambassadorial post abroad, he could, nevertheless, contribute something to-

8 *Correspondence*, 3:575–576. This letter is addressed to Lord Mordaunt.

9 *Correspondence*, 3:604.

10 *Correspondence*, 3:576.

ward the effort to get the revolution and the redemption of England back on the right track. That contribution, I am arguing, was nothing less than a radical manifesto, embodying the true principles of government.

By August, just two weeks before he delivered the *Two Treatises* to the printer, Locke is writing to Limborch of "the machinations of some people" who are responsible for the divisions within the country, and the fact that "it is certainly a mistake that no bishops have taken the oath of allegiance." Even worse, "some of them are persisting in their opinion," by which I believe Locke means not only that they are refusing to accept the necessity for such an oath, but also that this action is supported by their opinion concerning the legitimacy of the existing government and, in a larger sense, by various watered down versions of the political theory to which they have always subscribed.[11]

In April 1689, some radicals proposed that the new oath of allegiance be subscribed to by all adult males as an expression of universal popular consent to the government, and as a tactic designed to put extreme pressure on the Tories. Samuel Johnson even suggested that those who refused the oath should be treated as outlaws.[12] In a radical tract published just before the *Two Treatises* went to press, the author expressed amazement that so soon after the revolution there should be "so many discontented persons among us," a "considerable body of malcontents," who refused to acknowledge the legitimacy of the government on de jure grounds.[13] He presents the Lockean resistance argument, emphasizing that, "it is evident, that James II has forfeited all rights to the crown, even before his desertion," and hence, he was justly and rightly opposed by the people who were entitled to take up arms against him. Nevertheless, the author is disturbed by the fact that six months after the revolution this principle still has not been accepted by many, including some persons holding government positions. The clergy are particularly responsible for teaching erroneous political doctrines, and must repent for having betrayed "the natural rights of the society." However, all "those who oppose themselves" to the doctrine of forfeiture and resistance "are de-

[11] *Correspondence*, 3:673–674.

[12] Goldie, "True Whiggism," p. 221. Howe argued in the Commons that those who refused to take the oath were prima facie enemies to William's government and secret supporters of James II (Cobbett, 5:226).

[13] Peter Allix, *Reflections upon the Opinions of Some Modern Divines Concerning the Nature of Government in General, and That of England in Particular*, 1689, preface. This work was licensed on June 29, and was therefore probably available in early August. For the inclusion of Allix in the small group of radical pamphleteers, see Goldie, "Revolution of 1689," p. 508.

clared enemies of the state, and . . . the authors and abettors of tyranny and popery."[14]

The radicals were outraged by the return of their old enemies—Danby, Nottingham, and Halifax—to power.[15] Indeed, Morrice wrote of Nottingham that "the whole kingdom . . . [was] alarmed" that he would be privy to the secret counsels of state.[16] In June, John Howe declared in the Commons that "I cannot believe that those who have sat in Council with King James, to the last, are fit now to be in Council."[17] Howe made such a fierce attack on Danby that the king sent Dykvelt as a personal emissary to plead with him to moderate his remarks, but to no avail. Howe replied that he was doing the king a service by "rescuing him from false friends."[18] Other radicals took up this theme, the effect of which was to increase the level of William's hostility toward them. By the beginning of August, the king was openly angry with Mordaunt, Howe, and Delamere, and he wanted to send John Hampden as ambassador to Spain just to be rid of him.[19] In October, Francis Charlton made known his dissatisfaction with William for employing Halifax.[20] On Christmas Day 1689, Thomas Wharton wrote a vehemently insolent letter to William railing against the "knaves" he employed as ministers.[21] Robert Ferguson objected to William's continuing "to employ those that were the instruments of the former tyranny," and he believed that "posterity will lose most of the benefit of this Revolution."[22] At the end of 1689, one of the radicals, in effect, spoke for them all when, reflecting upon the year's events, he remarked upon the "happy progress of the late Revolution, and the unhappy progress of affairs since."[23] This point is elaborated in

[14] Allix, *Reflections*, pp. 98–99. Wildman reaffirmed this point in a parliamentary speech in July (Grey, 9:381).

[15] Henry Horowitz, *Parliament, Policy and Politics in the Reign of William III*, Manchester: Manchester University Press, 1977, p. 40; E. L. Ellis, "William III and the Politicians," in *Britain after the Glorious Revolution*, ed. Geoffrey Holmes, London: Macmillan, 1969, pp. 115–134. It was around August, Halifax noted in his diary, that Danby and Nottingham had become "very great again" in the government (H. C. Foxcroft, *The Life and Letters of George Savile*, 2 vols., 1898, 2:232).

[16] Lacey, p. 232.

[17] Grey, 9:281.

[18] Macaulay, 3:366–367; Cobbett, 5:283–284.

[19] Foxcroft, *Savile*, 2:228–229, 231. According to Halifax, William appeared to be slightly paranoid about the prospects of republicanism and was inclined to see "a design for a commonwealth" everywhere (2:225–227; cf. ibid., 2:203).

[20] Foxcroft, *Savile*, 2:247.

[21] Goldie, "True Whiggism," p. 221. For the parliamentary criticism of these ministers in December, see Grey, 9:480–490.

[22] *Ferguson*, pp. 275–276.

[23] Goldie, "True Whiggism," p. 224.

Authority Abused, a tract sharply critical of the course of the revolution from the standpoint of the left. In the preface directed to William, the author warns the king in no uncertain terms to keep faith with the revolution, and not to permit it to become bogged down in a morass of petty concerns of "some prudential politicians," because such a development "will be dangerous to you, and may produce as great disappointments as those of the last year." More ominously, he observes that the consequences "may be as destructive" as those precipitated by James' similar actions. He is especially angry that "propagators of false notions concerning the constitution of this government" have not only been allowed to disseminate their dangerous views, but they have actually published them "by authority" under the imprimatur of a chief Secretary of State. This is too much, and it is a clear sign (to him) that "we are again relapsing into the same unhappy circumstances" of the past. Hence, the combination of evil counselors of state and their "mercenary" spokesmen represent "the evil practices of those persons who were the authors of our disappointments the last year."[24] The radicals pursued this counterattack in *Plain English*, another left-wing denunciation of "the unhappy progress of affairs" during 1689. The author contrasts the actions and beliefs of those he calls the "betrayers of their country" with the actions and beliefs of those committed to "that cause for which the noble Lord Russell fell."[25] This dichotomy was expressed concretely through a series of parliamentary investigations into the death of Essex, and the trials of Russell, Sidney, and others, in which Wildman, Mordaunt, and Samuel Johnson were the guiding spirits and active participants. Although this was, as one scholar has aptly termed it, a rear-guard action by the radicals, it did contribute to the further embarrassment of those government ministers who had played a role in the Rye House prosecutions. A political ballad published simultaneously with these proceedings resurrected the "ghosts" of Russell and Sidney who condemned the "monstrous villains" employed by William.[26]

The messages, warnings, and reflections are bitter and unmistakable in their meaning. By the end of 1689, the radicals, increasingly isolated

[24] Edward Stephens, *Authority Abused by the Vindication of the Last Year's Transactions*, 1690, preface, pp. 1–2. In *The True English Government, and Mis-Government of the Four Last Kings, with the Ill Consequences Thereof, Briefly Noted in Two Little Tracts*, 1689, Stephens had observed that recalling to mind the examples illustrated by "these fatal mischiefs" would serve as "examples of caution" to the present king and his ministers (pp. 1, 4).

[25] *Plain English: Humbly Offered to the Consideration of His Majesty, and His Great Council, the Lords and Commons in Parliament Assembled*, 1690, p. 1 (*LL* #2325).

[26] Goldie, "True Whiggism," pp. 222–223; Macaulay, 3:345–346.

from access to political power, ignored and somewhat resented by William, and subjected to the proliferating abuse in the pamphlets and sermons being churned out by a self-assertive clergy returned to power, were, to say the least, disappointed with the outcome of the revolution. Later, looking back in 1696 upon that event, one of them summarized these feelings, already present in the period we are considering:

> The late happy Revolution (which came on too soon, and was cut off too short) was not so highly beneficial to us, as was by some expected.[27]

It is regrettable that there are no letters from Locke to Clarke for the remainder of 1689 following the one of April 13 in which he complains about the halt in the progress of the revolution settlement, for Clarke is the one person to whom Locke confided his deepest political feelings and beliefs. If there were expressions of political dissatisfaction running through Locke's thoughts during this period, they would surely find an outlet in his correspondence with his friend. There is, however, a short and very important memorandum, drafted by Locke and sent to Clarke, setting down the former's thoughts about the political circumstances as they existed at the end of 1689.[28] This recently discovered manuscript was written shortly after the *Two Treatises of Government* had gone to press—or in other words, just at the time the radicals were launching their critique of the government.[29] It reflects, I believe, the general tone of their disappointment, and it identifies Locke as someone who shares their position in 1689–1690.

The manuscript opens with the observation that "complaints are everywhere so loud and the apprehensions that people droop are so visible, that they cannot but be taken notice of." It is not, Locke explains, external events or the dangers posed by James' forces in Ireland "which

[27] Goldie, "True Whiggism," p. 235. Even Evelyn, no sympathizer with republicanism, could not avoid recording the fact in his diary that by the end of 1689, there was "as universal a discontent against [King] William . . . as was before against [King] James" (John Evelyn, *The Diary of John Evelyn*, ed. E. S. De Beer, 6 vols., Oxford: Clarendon Press, 1955, 5:4).

[28] MS e.18. This manuscript was sold with some other papers belonging to Edward Clarke in the 1920s, but was lost sight of until it was again offered for sale by Sotheby's in 1982. It was purchased by the Bodleian Library and is being prepared for publication with an introduction by Clayton Roberts and James Farr ("John Locke on the Glorious Revolution: A Rediscovered Document," forthcoming). I wish to express my appreciation to Professors Roberts and Farr for sending me a copy of the manuscript prior to its publication.

[29] Locke's reference to a "year" following William's landing dates the manuscript sometime between November 1689 (when the *Two Treatises* appeared in print) and February 1690 (Roberts and Farr, "A Rediscovered Document," p. 3).

throw a dread amongst us"; rather, the complaints and disappointments spring from "our divisions" within the country relating to politics. Any discussion of latter must begin, of course, from "our delivery from popery and slavery" through the revolution. Anyone who has a concern for the security of England must protect it from the threat of James' return, a French invasion, and the consequent rule by "Jesuits." Hence, those "who would not betray England and expose it to a popish rage and revenge" must obviously "join in a sincere loyalty to his present Majesty and a support of his government."

Several obstacles stand in the path of this "union" grounded upon a defense of national security and feelings of "mutual charity." First, there must be a general act of oblivion, so that "passionate heats" exchanged between enemies can be set aside. Second, the doctrine of the divine right of kings must altogether be given up, because, according to Locke, it represents "an irreconcilable opposition to . . . our present constitution." Whoever subscribes to this political theory "must be an avowed enemy to King William and the present government." It is therefore necessary, Locke insists, that there be "a solemn and public renunciation of a doctrine that annuls his title." Failure to make such a declaration can only mean, Locke argues, that the individual is under a merely "pretended loyalty" to William, but actually "believes himself still King James's subject," and is thus one of "the secret enemies of the government." This false doctrine of *jure divino* can have no other purpose than to "overturn our present settlement."[30] This theme was subsequently taken up by Matthew Tindal, a radical, and one of the few individuals to refer publicly and favorably in his own writings to the *Two Treatises*, from which he sometimes quotes (not always with acknowledgment). Tindal is angry at those who have not yet acknowledged the de jure legitimacy of the government, including some individuals who "have thrust themselves into places of the greatest trust." To refuse this acknowledgment is to place themselves in "a state of war" with the government and other members of society.[31] De facto recognition, Tindal insists, is not really owning allegiance to the king, but it is simply to accept him as a usurper.[32] And like Locke, Tindal lays much of the blame for this state of affairs upon the clergy and their teaching of false notions about government.

In his manuscript, Locke observes that some people have begun to speak as if William's position on the throne is due simply to the *fact* of his coming to England and to the fact of James' departure. This interpretation is totally unacceptable to Locke. It is, he insists, "the miscarriages

[30] MS e.18, fols. 1–2.

[31] Matthew Tindal, *An Essay Concerning Obedience to the Supreme Powers, and the Duty of Subjects in All Revolutions*, 1694, pp. 45–46, 53.

[32] Tindal, *Essay Concerning Obedience*, p. 54.

of the former reigns'' which ''gave a rise and right'' to the making of the Glorious Revolution, not James' ''desertion'' of the throne. That these miscarriages were, in themselves, ''a sufficient cause of the change we have seen and the deliverance we have received'' is a point which those who refuse ''to disown and condemn those miscarriages'' cannot understand. If James' ''miscarriages'' were not the justificatory basis for his forfeiture of authority, then ''our complaints were mutiny'' and we who accompanied William to power are guilty of rebellion, ''and we ought to return as fast as we can to our old obedience'' (to James). Those of us who think otherwise, however, and cite James' miscarriages as a train of events having ''no other end but an abdication,'' now insist upon ''a public condemnation and abhorrence of them'' as a guarantee of loyalty and support for the existing government. Silence, Locke argues, is not a sufficiently positive response. Either William is publicly accepted as a king ''by right'' on the grounds indicated by Locke, or individuals must ''plainly call him usurper,'' as the French king does.[33]

Locke then launches an attack against those who, like Nottingham, had advocated a regency for William, while maintaining James' title to the throne. ''I do not hear that these men have ever disowned or recanted what they were then so publicly for . . . and if they are still of their old opinion, tis fit that too should be known and they thereby distinguished from those who heartily unite in the support of the present government.'' How can such men—some of whom filled the highest offices in the land—be ''friends'' of the government, Locke asks? If ''the great men at court who have place and pay declare not openly and zealously for it,'' how can anyone expect the rest of the nation to display ''a steady resolution of fidelity and obedience'' to the government? To all these facts must be added a recognition that ''the press openly scatters doubts'' concerning the legitimacy of the revolution, and the ''private casuists'' and ''zealous partisans'' among us who have darker aims are able to take advantage of this ''disorder and confusion.''[34]

All in all, it is not an encouraging picture. The legitimacy of the revolution, as viewed by the radicals, is under attack from within the government itself and at the highest levels of power, from the clergy who have

[33] MS e.18, fols. 3–4. This was also Stephens' point. There are some persons, he notes, who make ''King James' abdication to consist only in his departure . . . without any regard to his precedent actions.'' From Stephens' standpoint, however, James' departure was merely ''the flight of a criminal from justice,'' and it was precisely his ''precedent actions'' that justified the Convention's actions, not his departure as such (*Authority Abused*, p. 8). This argument was pursued at greater length in his *Important Questions of State, Law, Justice and Prudence*, 1689.

[34] MS e.18, fols. 4–6. Stephens also attacks those counselors who were responsible for the ''miscarriages'' of the reigns of Charles II and James II who are now ''to be received into favor'' in William's government (*Authority Abused*, p. 9).

resuscitated their theories of divine right, and more indirectly, from those whose silence or confusion only contributes to the worsening of the situation. Nothing less than a solemn and public pledge of loyalty, premised upon an equally public renunciation of the miscarriages of the last two reigns, will serve to clear the air (along with an act of general oblivion). These were the views of a hard-line radical, views Locke shared with those who had remained true to the "noble cause" of Lord Russell as they were being expressed at the end of 1689 when this manuscript was written. They help to explain, I suggest, Locke's decision to make his own public and solemn statement on the revolution. The radicals, as much as anyone else, had an obligation to make their position clear as to the rightness of the revolution and the legitimacy of the present government.

In fact, two years later, every one of the points made by Locke in his manuscript were echoed by John Hampden in his *Some Short Considerations Concerning the State of the Nation* (1692).[35] The government, Hampden argues, is "entirely unsettled" because some people "openly renounce and impugn the principles" that justify the revolution of 1689, and hence the establishment of William's reign. These individuals "will suffer no mention to be made of the original contract broken by King James," but instead they write books and tracts that are "destructive . . . to all the ends proposed to be compassed in the revolution." These works are actually licensed by a Secretary of State, and, Hampden reflects, "it is astonishing to think, that the officers in the chiefest trusts of the nation are not obliged to own this a lawful government." For, as Locke had noted, many of them have never abjured the authority of James, and they only accepted William as their king de facto. It was incomprehensible to the radicals that either James' tyranny or the principles of the revolution could be so "publicly disputed" and covertly or overtly denounced by the very people who, in the wake of that revolution, had been brought back into power.[36]

Finally, I think it is possible from this standpoint to appreciate the reason Locke published the *Two Treatises of Government* anonymously, and sought to keep his authorship of the work a secret, even from friends. It was not the penchant of an obsessive personality, as some biographers seem determined to insist.[37] Rather, Locke had many personal friends

[35] This tract is printed as appendix 7 in Cobbett, 5:lxv–lxxxii. Some of Hampden's phraseology is so close to that used by Locke in his memorandum to Clarke that it is almost possible to believe that Hampden had seen a copy. This is merely speculation, but the fact that Hampden was a close friend of Walter Yonge and was well known to both Clarke and Freke places it within the realm of possiblity.

[36] Hampden, *Some Considerations*, in Cobbett, 5:lxxii–lxxiv.

[37] Laslett refers to the "abnormal, obsessive . . . peculiarity in Locke's personality" for secrecy (Laslett, pp. 5–6; Cranston, p. xi, and passim).

who were members of William's government, and others who were members of Parliament. He might very well have stood to lose their friendship, or their personal confidences, if the *Two Treatises* were read, as we know it was, as a distinctly radical document, especially given the timing of its appearance in print, in conjunction with the explicitly critical attacks on the government then being formulated by the radicals.[38] Locke was true enough to his beliefs not to shrink from publishing the work, but why should he in addition make himself offensive to his friends among the Court Whigs, not to mention powerful Tories like Halifax, Danby, and Nottingham, who were already looking for ways to remove Wildman from office and to have Ferguson arrested.[39] And if a summary observation be permitted, perhaps it is not too much to say that the publication of the *Two Treatises of Government* was, after all, the payment by Locke of a debt he owed to the Earl of Shaftesbury and to the "noble cause" for which he and thousands of others had fought.

[38] When Locke was preparing his early *Two Tracts on Government* for publication in 1661, he indicated that he wished the work to appear anonymously because "I should be sure to incur the censure of many of my acquaintance" if it were known that he was the author of the work (*FTG*, p. 118). I believe Locke applied the same reasoning to the publication of the *Two Treatises*. Locke's friend, the Earl of Pembroke—to cite only one illustration—was one of those who had, along with Nottingham, voted for William's regency.

[39] Nottingham had ordered Ferguson and his papers seized in 1689, but he was ordered by the Court to release him. Nevertheless, even after William had told him to leave Ferguson alone, Nottingham pressed the issue. Ferguson was again arrested, at Nottingham's urging in June 1690. Meanwhile, Danby was attempting to have Wildman removed from the Post Office (Morrice, 3:156–159; *Ferguson*, p. 284; Andrew Browning, *Thomas Osborne, Earl of Danby*, 3 vols., Glasgow: Jackson, 1951, 2:164–166).

INDEX

Library of Congress Cataloging-in-Publication Data

Ashcraft, Richard.
Revolutionary politics & Locke's two treatises of government.

Includes index.
1. Locke, John, 1632–1704—Contributions in political science.
2. Locke, John, 1632–1704. Two treatises of government.
3. Dissenters—Great Britain—History—17th century. I. Title. II. Title:
Revolutionary politics and Locke's two treatises of government.
JC153.L87A84 1986 320'.092'4 85–43269
ISBN 0-691-07703-7 (alk. paper)
ISBN 0-691-10205-8 (pbk.)